JUST AND UNJUST WARS

Fifth Edition

JUST
AND
UNJUST
WARS

A MORAL ARGUMENT
WITH HISTORICAL ILLUSTRATIONS

Fifth Edition

MICHAEL WALZER

BASIC BOOKS
A MEMBER OF THE PERSEUS BOOKS GROUP
NEW YORK

Books published by Basic Books are available at special discounts for bulk pur-
chases in the United States by corporations, institutions, and other organizations.
For more information, please contact the Special Markets Department at the Perseus Books Group, 2300 Chestnut Street, Suite 200, Philadelphia, PA 19103, or call
(800) 810-4145, ext. 5000, or e-mail special.markets@perseusbooks.com.

Designed by Jack Lenzo

Library of Congress Cataloging-in-Publication Data
Walzer, Michael.
  Just and unjust wars : a moral argument with historical illustrations / Michael
Walzer. — Fifth edition.
    pages cm
  Includes bibliographical references and index.
  ISBN 978-0-465-05271-4 (hardcover : alk. paper) — ISBN 978-0-465-05270-7
(e-book) 1. War. 2. War—Moral and ethical aspects. 3. Just war doctrine. I. Title.
  U21.2.W345 2015
  172'.42—dc23
                                    2015010999
  LSC-C

Printing 8, 2022

Aux martyrs de l'Holocauste
Aux révoltés des Ghettos
Aux partisans de forêts
Aux insurgés des camps
Aux combatants de la résistance
Aux soldats des forces alliées
Aux sauveteurs de frères en peril
Aux vaillants de l'immigration clandestine
A l'éternité

—Inscription at *Yad Vashem* Memorial, Jerusalem

CONTENTS

PREFACE TO THE FIFTH EDITION

THE BOOK OF ECCLESIASTES ENDS WITH A COMPLAINT: "OF MAKING MANY books, there is no end." On the occasion of the fifth edition of *Just and Unjust Wars*, I can't complain about that; I am grateful for the re-making of this book. But it is also true that "Of making many wars, there is no end," and this should be a universal human complaint. I am writing just as the United States is ending two of the longest wars in its history (in Afghanistan and Iraq)—and beginning another (to degrade and defeat the Islamic State in Syria and, again, Iraq). Each new edition of *Just and Unjust Wars* has coincided with new wars and new questions about war. I wrote about humanitarian intervention in the preface to the third edition and about wars for regime change in the preface to the fourth.

As this latest edition is being prepared for publication, intense arguments are under way about asymmetric warfare—arguments that overlap a great deal with central issues in this book. But asymmetric warfare has its own set of moral difficulties and immoral cruelties that require specific, detailed consideration and judgment. For reasons I will come to, judgment is especially important—hence this newly prepared preface.

Most of the wars of the past several decades have been asymmetric; notably, for American citizens, the war against the Taliban in Afghanistan and the second Iraq war (after the first few weeks, when the success of the invasion produced an unexpected insurgency)—also the Israeli wars in Lebanon and Gaza, the Sri Lankan war against the Tamil rebels, and the Russian war in Chechnya. Asymmetric warfare isn't new; the guerrilla wars discussed in chapter 11, especially the Vietnam War, are earlier examples. Some writers believe that traditional just war theory, with its long-established rules about when to fight and how to fight, cannot deal with asymmetry. But if the theory "worked," as I think it did, in helping Americans understand what was wrong in Vietnam, there is no reason why it can't work in other times and places. It is a good theory; we remain indebted to the Catholic theologians who invented it centuries ago.

But the theory was invented to deal with what we now call "conventional" warfare—where two armies are engaged and each one is pretty much like the other in organization and armaments. If there are any rules that govern the fighting, it is easy to imagine that they will be the same for the two armies and for all their soldiers. Wars of that sort are—we should be thankful—rare these days. Iran and Iraq fought an old-fashioned war in the 1980s, and the 1991 Iraq war, against the conquest of Kuwait, was roughly conventional. We can all think of possible wars like those, but they are not likely to happen anytime soon.

In the more immediate conditions of asymmetry, by contrast, there is only one army, organized, armed, and disciplined by a modern state; its opponents are insurgents, less well-organized, less well-armed, and often without a coordinated system of military discipline or of military justice. Do the same rules apply to armies and insurgents? I want to say that they do, but that requires an argument.

The insurgents claim the prerogatives of weakness—which follow, they say, from the conventional doctrines of military necessity and last resort applied to their special circumstances. So the old rules do apply, but given the circumstances, not in the same way to the two sides. The insurgents have to be able to hide from the army's overwhelming firepower, so they can't wear uniforms. They can't fight along a "front"; they have to be able to strike anytime, anywhere, so they can't always distinguish combatants from civilians. In any case, military targets are often too dangerous for them to attack; killing civilians, they argue, is often the only thing they can do, so it is their "last resort" even if they don't actually try anything else. And they can't build fortresses or military bases, for if they don't have a "front," they also don't have a "rear" where they can assemble or regroup in safety. The only protection they have is the cover of their own people's homes and neighborhoods.

For the conventional army, insurgents claiming these prerogatives are a big problem. The army gets no circumstantial exemption from the old rules; it is expected above all to maintain the distinction between combatants and civilians, even if the insurgents deliberately blur the distinction.

But how can its soldiers fight against enemies who hide among the civilian population without killing civilians?

The proportionality rule (see "The Argument of Henry Sidgwick" in chapter 8) is supposed to provide criteria for judging those deaths, but proportionality in warfare is not an exact science. Historically, in conventional wars, the rule has most often been read permissively: the value of the military target is so great that a fairly high number of civilian casualties (collateral damage, as it is called) is "not disproportionate." Think about an Allied decision to bomb a German tank factory in World War II. The factory is located in a working-class neighborhood—not for the sake of civilian cover but because that is where factories were built before workers had cars. Given the aiming devices available in 1943, any attack on the factory would kill many civilians. But the death of many civilians, indeed, of almost any number of civilians, is "not disproportionate" to the value of stopping the production of tanks for the German war effort. This same argument can be made, and was regularly made, in defense of attacks on considerably less valuable targets—which is the reason for my skepticism about the proportionality rule in this book.

In recent asymmetric conflicts, by contrast, the rule has been read restrictively. Asymmetry makes for micro-battles, small-scale engagements, and in these engagements, given the overwhelming power of the army and the weakness of the insurgents, even a very small number of civilian casualties seems disproportionate to the military value of the target. For the target may be nothing more than a couple of insurgents firing from the roof of a small apartment building (in Afghanistan) or a single rocket launching crew in the parking lot of a hospital (in Gaza).

The army argues that it has to respond to the gunfire from the roof and to the rockets from the parking lot, and the civilians it kills, even if their number looks disproportionate, are the moral responsibility of the insurgents who have chosen to fight from civilian cover. The insurgents blame the army's soldiers, who are indeed the actual killers; at the same time the insurgents commonly benefit from the civilian deaths in the court of public opinion. The weak are even more attractive when they are also victims, and it is probably true that insurgent fighters don't only hide behind civilians; they also deliberately expose civilians to attack. But the other side may also benefit from civilian deaths. The army aims, it says, only at military targets, but the collateral damage from its attacks may serve to deter future insurgent war making or discourage civilian support for the insurgents. So perhaps the army isn't as careful as it might be to avoid collateral damage.

Sorting all this out doesn't require us to abandon or significantly revise just war theory. It does require that the theory be applied, as the insurgents say, with close attention to the circumstances of asymmetry. Close attention is also critical attention: it doesn't necessarily support the insurgents' claims, nor does it allow just any military response from the army. But before addressing these battlefield issues, I need to consider, briefly, how the battles begin.

The army is, as it were, already in power, serving a sovereign state whose political policies and moral authority are contested, rightly or wrongly. So it's the insurgents who usually start the war. Claiming the prerogatives that I have just described, they often attack civilian targets, inviting a military response, the more savage the better. But how was the decision to attack reached? The insurgents are militarily weak, but they are not always or everywhere politically weak. They might have launched a political campaign against the policies and authority of the state—through repeated demonstrations, civil disobedience, a mass march, a general strike—and there probably were people in the insurgent organization who argued for this policy: politics before war. If war is the *continuation* of politics by other means, as Clausewitz said, then politics should come first; military force is supposed to be a "last resort," but even if that's not right, the use of force shouldn't come before or instead of political action (see my *Arguing about War*, chapters 6–7, for an argument about the metaphysical character of "lastness"). We should look for a political struggle in advance of any decision to go to war. It seems to me that the justice of the war, assuming for now the justice of the cause, hangs on this previous struggle. When war is not the continuation but the replacement of politics, we should probably call it unjust.

I am not going to say anything more about the causes for which insurgents fight; the recent history of asymmetric war includes a range of violent struggles—from national liberation to religious crusade. Most just war theorists would call the first of these just and the second unjust; that is my own view. But what is critically at issue in asymmetric warfare is less the cause than the conduct of the war. The focus on conduct derives from the extreme danger to which civilians are subjected, first by the insurgents and then by the army. How civilians are treated is a matter of *jus in bello*, justice in war, but it certainly reflects on the character of the insurgents and of the army (and of the state for which the army fights). A just cause can be undone if it is pursued in unjust ways. Or, better, when we condemn the conduct of an asymmetric war, we are also arguing that the cause, if it is just, must be pursued differently—by a different kind of war or by a return to politics.

Now, let's say, the fighting has begun, and the first attacks are aimed indiscriminately at civilians—with an argument attached: we can't do anything else. This is the standard argument in defense of terrorism, and it is hard to sustain, even if we set aside the political struggle that has just been pre-empted. Not every military target is impregnable to the insurgents. There are always vulnerable targets that can be attacked, if there is a will to attack them—as anyone knows who has toured the sprawling facilities of a modern army. Further evidence for this claim comes from inside the insurgent organization itself, where there are always dissidents who oppose attacks on civilians and argue for the possibility of a purely military campaign. They testify both to the strength of the conventional rules of war and to the weakness of the argument from necessity. I see no reason to give up on those rules; they apply also, as we will see, to the other side.

The insurgents can in fact distinguish soldiers and civilians among their enemies, and we should condemn every refusal or failure to do that. Their stronger argument is that they can't help their enemies make the same distinction—they can't separate themselves from their own civilians. Theirs, they say, is a popular insurgency; they fight from among the people because they are the people and the people are the insurgents. They aren't going to march off to some distant battlefield where they are certain to be overwhelmed. They will fight from where they live, or from where their people live, with whom they are one. Their human shields are volunteers, and if the insurgents benefit from the death of those shields, that is, from civilian deaths, they are not responsible for them. If the enemy army can't separate the insurgents from the people, it should give up, for there is no way that it can fight justly.

That is the primary argument of the insurgents, and it is much better than a common secondary argument: that they are fighting from such densely populated areas that they can't distance their fighters from residential neighborhoods. In the Gaza war of 2014, Israel claimed that some 15 percent of the rockets fired by Hamas were fired from residential neighborhoods and from schools, mosques, and hospitals within those neighborhoods. But if 85 percent of the rockets were fired from uninhabited areas, we have to conclude that the other firings were deliberately sited to provoke counterfire that would kill and injure civilians. Clearly the provocation worked. Population density is a problem for the army; I don't think it is an excuse for the insurgents. If the excuse isn't persuasive in Gaza, with one of the highest ratios of people to space in the world, then it must be far less persuasive in places like Vietnam, Afghanistan, and Iraq.

But the insurgents' claim that they are fighting from where they live, that they are at one with their people, is more plausible—though the claim obviously has different truth value in different countries, at different times. The closer the insurgents are to their people, the stronger the argument for oneness, the more likely it is that they won't be blamed for not wearing uniforms (think of the Minutemen in the American War of Independence) or for fighting from homes and neighborhoods. But when they fight that way, they cannot blame the army for the civilians it kills in response—so long as the soldiers live by the rules that still apply to them.

Many conventional wars have been fought in crowded urban neighborhoods; we shouldn't expect insurgents to miss the opportunities offered by cities and also by towns and villages. There is, however, a difference here: a conventional army, fighting its way through a city, will probably kill civilians, but these killings do not benefit the opposing army. In asymmetric warfare, the army's killings definitely benefit the insurgents, who are therefore liable to the charge, which I have already made, that they deliberately expose civilians to enemy fire. But suppose they have the support of many of the men and women they expose, from whose homes and neighborhoods they choose to fight. Then, indeed, the army responding to insurgent attacks will face a difficult and highly charged moral and political decision: how to deal with "the people," that is, with unarmed but possibly hostile civilians, who are indistinguishable from the insurgents.

Here is what I take to be the central issue in asymmetric warfare (it's also an issue in conventional wars, but asymmetry gives it special significance): How should the army fight when its fighting puts "enemy" civilians at risk? "Enemy" is in scare quotes because, while some of these civilians may well sympathize with or actively support the insurgents (as the insurgents claim), some of them do not; some of them just wish they were somewhere else. And there are always the children, one-third or more of the population, who aren't anyone's enemies. So the insurgents are fighting from among a mixed group of civilians; the army's soldiers are attacking.

How should the soldiers plan, organize, and carry out their attack? The key moral issue can be specified more clearly: What risks should the army ask its soldiers to take in order to reduce the risks they impose on "enemy" civilians?

In a sense, the question is unfair. It isn't the soldiers' fault that they aren't fighting on a conventional battlefield against a uniformed enemy. The moral difficulties of asymmetric warfare are imposed on the soldiers, not chosen by them. Nonetheless, they are well-armed and well-trained, and they are backed up by all the resources of a high-tech military force; the civilians they encounter are unarmed and untrained, highly vulnerable, with no backup at all. And it is the soldiers who, whatever their own intentions, put those civilians at risk. I argue in this book, with examples from World War II, Korea, and Vietnam, that soldiers have to accept some risk (I don't attempt to say how much) in order to protect civilians from their own deadly fire. The revised version of the double effect doctrine that I describe in chapter 9, which sets up this question, has been widely discussed and adopted by many just war theorists. But the specific issue of risk taking didn't get much attention until the wars in Afghanistan and Gaza.

The moral burden I place on soldiers is unfair in another way. The insurgents don't take any risks to avoid putting civilians at risk; instead, they often take risks or, in the case of suicide bombers, they choose death precisely in order to kill and injure civilians. Soldiers are supposedly fighting to protect those civilians, so why make their fight harder and more dangerous? Why ask them to take risks to avoid killing "enemy" civilians whom their enemies are deliberately putting at risk? There is a pragmatic answer to this question: asymmetric war is also a political struggle—a battle for civilian support, that is, for "hearts and minds." The U.S. Army's revised rules of engagement for soldiers in Afghanistan, announced in 2010, were aimed above all at reducing civilian casualties. The rationale was very simple, and it fits many other asymmetric wars: you don't win hearts and minds by destroying bodies. But in Israel's Gaza wars, winning the hearts and minds of the inhabitants of the Gaza Strip was probably not a plausible war aim (though Israel certainly would have benefited if Gazans came to believe that the Israeli army was more committed to civilian well-being than the Hamas militants were). In any case, a similar pragmatic argument applies: it is global rather than local hearts and minds that are at issue now, but in international society as it is today the loss is equally damaging—or even more damaging.

Pragmatic arguments, however, only hold if they work—in this case if a significant reduction of collateral damage brings with it local support or global sympathy. The moral argument holds whether or not this happens: *these people should not be killed, and these soldiers have an obligation to do everything they can to avoid killing them.* It is possible, as some critics claim, that the effective meaning of this obligation is that the soldiers won't be able to win asymmetric wars. Asymmetry describes a struggle between a very strong and a very weak military force: a high-tech army against a low-tech insurgency. The difference in firepower is huge. And yet, throughout history, the army rarely defeats the insurgents; even when it doesn't lose the war, it doesn't actually win. The U.S. Army could not defeat the Vietcong in Vietnam; nor could the United States along with its NATO allies defeat the Taliban in Afghanistan; nor were we able to defeat either the Sunni or the Shiite militias in Iraq. The Israelis did not lose the wars in Lebanon and Gaza, but they can't be said to have won. It is indeed possible to win—by giving up on hearts and minds and on any semblance of moral decency and simply killing and killing until the insurgents' civilian cover is literally gone. The Russians in Chechnya and the government of Sri Lanka in its war against the Tamil rebels demonstrate that these wars can be won by a modern army. But can they be won by an army committed to just rules of engagement?

The answer to this question depends not only on the commitment and competence of the army but also on the moral/political judgments of everyone else, locally and globally. So it is important to condemn military actions that break the rules, even if these actions don't reach to massive attacks on the civilian population. The army must not look to benefit from the collateral damage it inflicts in the course of legitimate attacks on military targets; it must take positive measures to limit civilian injury. And these positive measures include soldiers accepting risk, to some degree, in order to minimize the risks they impose on civilians. One form of risk taking has been fairly common in both America's and Israel's wars: warning of attacks to come, so that civilians can flee—and insurgents can prepare, if that is possible, for the attack. It is a good thing to warn civilians of impending danger, but warnings are not sufficient. As American soldiers learned in Vietnam, many people don't leave: they are caring for elderly parents or sick children; they are afraid that their homes will be looted; they have no safe place to go.

There are, then, other things that must be done—and not done. Consider my earlier example of Taliban insurgents firing at American soldiers from the roof of a small apartment building in an Afghan town. The soldiers don't know who is in the building. They could simply pull back and call in an air strike—taking no risks themselves but radically endangering any civilians in the building. The 2010 rules of engagement rightly rule this out, so the soldiers have (in this simplified example) only three options: they can try to get someone into the building to see if civilians are living there, or they can try to get soldiers onto an adjacent roof, so that they can fire directly at the insurgents. Both these actions require the soldiers to accept (some degree of) risk. Or they can withdraw and wait for another encounter with the Taliban insurgents. No army likes to leave the battlefield to the enemy, but if the officer in the field thinks that the risks of the other options are too great, that is the right thing to do.

But what if there are civilians on the roof, dragged up there by force or willingly standing with the insurgents? And what if the army unit's withdrawal would leave other units, fighting nearby, at risk? Then, even if soldiers succeed in getting onto adjacent roofs, civilians will be killed or injured. Who is responsible for those deaths? If the numbers seem disproportionate to the military value of the building, as they probably will, given the restrictive understanding of proportionality, the army will be blamed. I believe, by contrast, that whenever soldiers have accepted risks in order to minimize the injuries they inflict on civilians, the blame should fall elsewhere. Calling in an air strike would probably be a war crime; killing civilians in a firefight in the circumstances I have just described is not.

Since attacks from the air, from planes or drones, involve no risk for the attacking forces, it might be argued that our judgments is these cases can only be shaped by calculations of proportionality. That may be true, and then we will need to find our way to calculations that are neither too permissive nor too restrictive. But successful air attacks, aimed at legitimate targets, depend heavily on information from the ground, and the collection of information is a dangerous business. Too often, attacks have been launched without sufficient knowledge about the targets or with knowledge provided by unreliable informants, who are often pursuing private vendettas. Many civilians die in attacks of that sort, which should always be condemned. But when the intelligence work is seriously undertaken and its risks accepted, and when civilians are killed because they are being used as cover or deliberately exposed, the army can rightly claim that it has done the best it could in the circumstances of asymmetry.

It is important to get these judgments right because, as I've already said, asymmetric wars are also political struggles. The insurgents, the soldiers, and the endangered civilians are not the only people involved; all the rest of us are involved. In a sense, this is true also in conventional wars. The point of writing a book like *Just and Unjust Wars* is to facilitate the judgments that citizens have to make about the wars their countries fight. But in asymmetric warfare, the responsibility to judge the war, to join the arguments about how it is being fought, extends more widely. The world's judgments are important, and if the "world" gets things right, the war will probably end with justice done.

The insurgents should be condemned when they attack civilians and when they deliberately put civilians at risk; they should be praised and supported when they struggle, in the circumstances of asymmetry, to fight justly. The army should be condemned when it fails to do everything it can do, in the circumstances of asymmetry, to avoid killing civilians, and it should be praised and supported when it lives by the moral rules of engagement. Strong judgments of this sort will promote good endings, and I suspect that in the long run the anticipation of strong judgments will make asymmetric wars less likely.

Michael Walzer
Princeton, New Jersey
May 2015

PREFACE TO THE FIRST EDITION

I DID NOT BEGIN BY THINKING ABOUT WAR IN GENERAL, BUT ABOUT particular wars, above all about the American intervention in Vietnam. Nor did I begin as a philosopher, but as a political activist and a partisan. Certainly, political and moral philosophy ought to help us at those difficult times when we choose sides and make commitments. But it does so only indirectly. We are not usually philosophical in moments of crisis; most often, there is no time. War especially imposes an urgency that is probably incompatible with philosophy as a serious enterprise. The philosopher is like Wordsworth's poet who reflects in tranquility upon past experience (or other people's experience), thinking about political and moral choices already made. And yet these choices are made in philosophical terms, available because of previous reflection. It was, for example a matter of great importance to all of us in the American anti-war movement of the late 1960s and early 1970s that we found a moral doctrine ready at hand, a connected set of names and concepts that we all knew—and that everyone else knew. Our anger and indignation were shaped by the words available to express them, and the words were at the tips of our tongues even though we had never before explored their meanings and connections. When we talked about aggression and neutrality, the rights of prisoners of war and civilians, atrocities and war crimes, we were drawing upon the work of many generations of men and women, most of whom we had never heard of. We would be better off if we did not need a vocabulary like that, but given that we need it, we must be grateful that we have it. Without this vocabulary, we could not have thought about the Vietnam War as we did, let alone have communicated our thoughts to other people.

No doubt we used the available words freely and often carelessly. Sometimes this was due to the excitement of the moment and the pressures of partisanship, but it also had a more serious cause. We suffered from an education which taught us that these words had no proper descriptive use and no objective meaning. Moral discourse was excluded from the world of science, even of social science. It expressed feelings, not perceptions, and there was no reason for the expression of feelings to be precise. Or rather, any precision it achieved had an entirely subjective reference: it was the domain of the poet and the literary critic. I don't need to rehearse this point of view (I shall criticize it in detail later on), though it's less prevalent now than it once was. What is crucial is that we disputed it, knowingly or unknowingly, every time we criticized American conduct in Vietnam. For our criticisms had the form at least of reports on the real world, not merely on the state of our own tempers. They required evidence; they pressed us, however trained we were in the loose use of moral language, toward analysis and investigation. Even the most skeptical among us came to see that these criticisms *could* be true (or false).

In those years of angry controversy, I promised myself that one day I would try to set out the moral argument about war in a quiet and reflective way. I still want to defend (most of) the particular arguments that underlay our opposition to the American war in Vietnam, but also and more importantly I want to defend the business of arguing, as we did and as most people do, in moral terms. Hence this book, which may be taken as an apology for our occasional carelessness and a vindication of our fundamental enterprise.

NOW, THE LANGUAGE WITH WHICH WE ARGUE ABOUT WAR AND JUSTICE IS similar to the language of international law. But this is not a book about the positive laws of war. There are many such books, and I have often drawn upon them. Legal treatises do not, however, provide a fully plausible or coherent account of our moral arguments, and the two most common approaches to the law reflected in the treatises are both in need of extra-legal supplement. First of all, legal positivism, which generated major scholarly works in the late nineteenth and early twentieth centuries, has become in the age of the United Nations increasingly uninteresting. The UN Charter was supposed to be the constitution of a new world, but, for reasons that have often been discussed, things have turned out differently.[1] To dwell at length upon the precise meaning of the Charter is today a kind of utopian quibbling. And because the UN sometimes pretends that it already is what it has barely begun to be, its decrees do not command intellectual or moral respect—except among the positivist lawyers whose business it is to interpret them. The lawyers have constructed a paper world, which fails at crucial points to correspond to the world the rest of us still live in.

The second approach to the law is oriented in terms of policy goals. Its advocates respond to the poverty of the contemporary international regime by imputing purposes to that regime—the achievement of some sort of "world order"—and then reinterpreting the law to fit those purposes.[2] In effect, they substitute utilitarian argument for legal analysis. That substitution is certainly not uninteresting, but it requires a philosophical defense. For the customs and conventions, the treaties and charters that constitute the laws of international society do not invite interpretation in terms of a single purpose or set of purposes. Nor are the judgments they require always explicable from a utilitarian standpoint. Policy-oriented lawyers are in fact moral and political philosophers, and it would be best if they presented themselves that way. Or, alternatively, they are would-be legislators, not jurists or students of the law. They are committed, or most of them are committed, to restructuring international society—a worthwhile task—but they are not committed to expounding its present structure.

My own task is different. I want to account for the ways in which men and women who are not lawyers but simple citizens (and sometimes soldiers) argue about war, and to expound the terms we commonly use. I am concerned precisely with the present structure of the moral world. My starting point is the fact that we do argue, often to different purposes, to be sure, but in mutually comprehensible fashion: else there would be no point in *arguing*. We justify our conduct; we judge the conduct of others. Though these justifications and judgments cannot be studied like the records of a criminal court, they are nevertheless a legitimate subject of study. Upon examination they reveal, I believe, a comprehensive view of war as a human activity and a more or less systematic moral doctrine, which sometimes, but not always, overlaps with established legal doctrine.

In fact, the vocabulary overlaps more than the arguments do. Hence I must say something about my own use of language. I shall always refer to laws of international society (as these appear in legal handbooks and

military manuals) as *positive* laws. For the rest, when I talk of law, I am
referring to the moral law, to those general principles that we commonly
acknowledge, even when we can't or won't live up to them. When I talk of
the rules of war, I am referring to the more particular code that governs
our judgments of combat behavior, and that is only partially articulated
in the Hague and Geneva conventions. And when I talk of crimes, I am
describing violations of the general principles or of the particular code:
so men and women can be called criminals even when they cannot be
charged before a legal tribunal. Since positive international law is radically
incomplete, it is always possible to interpret it in the light of moral principles and to refer to the results as "positive law." Perhaps that is what has to
be done in order to flesh out the legal system and render it more attractive
than it presently is. But it is not what I have done here. Throughout the
book, I treat words like aggression, neutrality, surrender, civilian, reprisal,
and so on, as if they were terms in a moral vocabulary—which they are,
and always have been, though most recently their analysis and refinement
have been almost entirely the work of lawyers.

I want to recapture the just war for political and moral theory. My
own work, then, looks back to that religious tradition within which Western politics and morality were first given shape, to the books of writers
like Maimonides, Aquinas, Vitoria, and Suarez—and then to the books
of writers like Hugo Grotius, who took over the tradition and began to
work it into secular form. But I have not attempted a history of just war
theory, and I quote the classical texts only occasionally, for the sake of
some particularly illuminating or forceful argument.[3] I refer more often to
contemporary philosophers and theologians (and soldiers and statesmen),
for my main concern is not with the making of the moral world but with
its present character.

Perhaps the most problematic feature of my exposition is the use of
the plural pronouns: we, our, ourselves, us. I have already demonstrated
the ambiguity of those words by using them in two ways: to describe that
group of Americans who condemned the Vietnam War, and to describe
that much larger group who understood the condemnation (whether or
not they agreed with it). I shall limit myself henceforth to the larger group.
That its members share a common morality is the critical assumption of
this book. In my first chapter I try to make a case for that assumption.
But it's only a case, it's not conclusive. Someone can always ask, "What is
this morality *of yours?*" That is a more radical question, however, than the

questioner may realize, for it excludes him not only from the comfortable world of moral agreement, but also from the wider world of agreement and disagreement, justification and criticism. The moral world of war is shared not because we arrive at the same conclusions as to whose fight is just and whose unjust, but because we acknowledge the same difficulties on the way to our conclusions, face the same problems, talk the same language. It's not easy to opt out, and only the wicked and the simple make the attempt.

I am not going to expound morality from the ground up. Were I to begin with the foundations, I would probably never get beyond them; in any case, I am by no means sure what the foundations are. The substructure of the ethical world is a matter of deep and apparently unending controversy. Meanwhile, however, we are living in the superstructure. The building is large, its construction elaborate and confusing. But here I can offer some guidance: a tour of the rooms, so to speak, a discussion of architectural principles. This is a book of practical morality. The study of judgments and justifications in the real world moves us closer, perhaps, to the most profound questions of moral philosophy, but it does not require a direct engagement with those questions. Indeed, philosophers who seek such an engagement often miss the immediacies of political and moral controversy and provide little help to men and women faced with hard choices. For the moment, at least, practical morality is detached from its foundations, and we must act as if that separation were a possible (since it is an actual) condition of moral life.

But that's not to suggest that we can do nothing more than describe the judgments and justifications that people commonly put forward. We can analyze these moral claims, seek out their coherence, lay bare the principles that they exemplify. We can reveal commitments that go deeper than partisan allegiance and the urgencies of battle; for it is a matter of evidence, not a pious wish, that there are such commitments. And then we can expose the hypocrisy of soldiers and statesmen who publicly acknowledge these commitments while seeking in fact only their own advantage. The exposure of hypocrisy is certainly the most ordinary, and it may also be the most important, form of moral criticism. We are rarely called upon to invent new ethical principles; if we did that, our criticism would not be comprehensible to the people whose behavior we wanted to condemn. Rather, we hold such people to their own principles, though we may draw these out and arrange them in ways they had not thought of before.

There is a particular arrangement, a particular view of the moral world, that seems to me the best one. I want to suggest that the arguments we make about war are most fully understood (though other understandings are possible) as efforts to recognize and respect the rights of individual and associated men and women. The morality I shall expound is in its philosophical form a doctrine of human rights, though I shall say nothing here of the ideas of personality, action, and intention that this doctrine probably presupposes. Considerations of utility play into the structure at many points, but they cannot account for it as a whole. Their part is subsidiary to that of rights; it is constrained by rights. That is above all true of the classical forms of military maximization: the religious crusade, the proletarian revolution, the "war to end war." But it's true also, as I will try to show, of the more immediate pressures of "military necessity." At every point, the judgments we make (the lies we tell) are best accounted for if we regard life and liberty as something like absolute values and then try to understand the moral and political processes through which these values are challenged and defended.

The proper method of practical morality is casuistic in character. Since I am concerned with actual judgments and justifications, I shall turn regularly to historical cases. My argument moves through the cases, and I have often foregone a systematic presentation for the sake of the nuances and details of historical reality. At the same time, the cases are necessarily sketched in outline form. In order to make them exemplary, I have had to abridge their ambiguities. In doing that, I have tried to be accurate and fair, but the cases are often controversial and no doubt I have sometimes failed. Readers upset by my failures might usefully treat the cases as if they were hypothetical—invented rather than researched—though it is important to my own sense of my enterprise that I am reporting on experiences that men and women have really had and on arguments that they have really made. In choosing experiences and arguments for discussion, I have relied heavily on World War II in Europe, the first war of which I have memories and the paradigm, for me, of a justified struggle. For the rest, I have tried to pick out the obvious cases: those that have figured largely in the literature of war and those that play a part in contemporary controversies.

The structure of the book is explained in the second and third chapters, which introduce the main argument. Here I only want to say that my presentation of the moral theory of war is focused on the tensions within the theory that make it problematic and that make choice in wartime difficult and painful. The tensions are summed up in the dilemma of winning and fighting well. This is the military form of the means/ends problem, the central issue in political ethics. I address it directly, and resolve or fail to resolve it, in Part Four; and the resolution, if it works, must be relevant also to the choices faced in politics generally. For war is the hardest place: if comprehensive and consistent moral judgments are possible there, they are possible everywhere.

Cambridge, Massachusetts, 1977

ACKNOWLEDGMENTS

IN WRITING ABOUT WAR, I HAVE HAD THE SUPPORT OF MANY ALLIES, institutional and personal. I began my research during the academic year 1971–72, while working at the Center for Advanced Study in the Behavioral Sciences in Stanford, California. I wrote a version of the preface and of chapter 1 at Mishkenot Sha'ananim (Peaceful Habitations) in Jerusalem, Israel, in the summer of 1974—a visit made possible by the Jerusalem Foundation; the bulk of the book was completed in 1975–76, while I was a Guggenheim Fellow.

For almost a decade, I went to school with the members of the Society for Ethical and Legal Philosophy, and while none of them are responsible for any of the arguments in this book, they have collectively had a great deal to do with the writing of it. I am especially grateful to Judith Jarvis Thompson, who read the entire manuscript and made many valuable suggestions. With Robert Nozick I have quarreled amicably about some of the hardest issues in the theory of war and his arguments, hypothetical cases, queries, and proposals helped me shape my own presentation.

My friend and colleague Robert Amdur read most of the chapters and he often forced me to think about them again. Marvin Kohl and Judith Walzer read portions of the manuscript; their comments on matters of style and substance have often been incorporated into my pages. I am grateful also to Philip Green, Yehuda Melzer, Miles Morgan, and John Schrecker.

During a quarter at Stanford University and for several years at Harvard, I taught a course on the just war, and learned while I was teaching—from colleagues and students alike. I will always be glad of the cooling skepticism of Stanley Hoffmann and Judith Shklar. I also benefited from the comments and criticisms of Charles Bahmueller, Donald Goldstein, Miles Kahler, Sanford Levinson, Dan Little, Gerald McElroy, and David Pollack.

Martin Kessler of Basic Books conceived this book almost before I did, and assisted and encouraged me at every stage of the writing of it.

When I was almost finished, Betty Butterfield undertook to type the final draft and set an astonishing pace, both for herself and for me; without her, the completion of the book would have taken much longer than it did.

An early version of chapter 12, on terrorism, appeared in *The New Republic* in 1975. In chapters 4 and 16 I have drawn upon arguments first developed in *Philosophy and Public Affairs* in 1972. In chapters 14 and 15, I have used portions of an article published in 1974 in the Israeli philosophical quarterly *Iyyun*. I am grateful to the editors of the three journals for permission to reprint these materials.

I AM GRATEFUL TO THE VARIOUS PUBLISHERS WHO HAVE KINDLY PERMITted me to reprint material which first appeared under their auspices:

Rolf Hochhuth, "Little London Theater of the World/Garden," lines 38–40, in *Soldiers: An Obituary for Geneva*. Copyright © 1968 by Grove Press, Inc. Reprinted by permission of Grove Press, Inc.

Randall Jarrell, "The Death of the Ball Turret Gunner," line 1, copyright © 1945 by Randall Jarrell. Renewed copyright © 1972 by Mrs. Randall Jarrell; and "The Range in the Desert," lines 21–24, copyright © 1947 by Randall Jarrell. Renewed copyright © 1974 by Mrs. Randall Jarrell. Both appeared in *The Complete Poems*. Reprinted by permission of Farrar, Straus & Giroux, Inc.

Stanley Kunitz, "Foreign Affairs," lines 10–17, in *Selected Poems*. 1928–1958. Copyright © 1958 by Stanley Kunitz. This poem originally appeared in *The New Yorker*. Reprinted by permission of Little, Brown and Company in association with the Atlantic Monthly Press.

Wilfred Owen, "Anthem for Doomed Youth," line 1, and "A Terre," line 6, in *The Collected Poems of Wilfred Owen*, edited by C. Day Lewis. Reprinted by permission of the Owen Estate and Chatto and Windus Ltd. and New Directions Publishing Corporation.

Gillo Pontecoro, *The Battle of Algiers*, edited and with an introduction by PierNico Solinas. Scene 68, pages 79–80. Reprinted by permission of Charles Scribner's Sons.

Louis Simpson, "The Ash and the Oak" in *Good News of Death and Other Poems. Poets of Today II.* Copyright © 1955 by Louis Simpson. Reprinted by permission of Charles Scribner's Sons.

PART ONE

THE MORAL REALITY OF WAR

AGAINST "REALISM"

FOR AS LONG AS MEN AND WOMEN HAVE TALKED ABOUT WAR, THEY HAVE talked about it in terms of right and wrong. And for almost as long, some among them have derided such talk, called it a charade, insisted that war lies beyond (or beneath) moral judgment. War is a world apart, where life itself is at stake, where human nature is reduced to its elemental forms, where self-interest and necessity prevail. Here men and women do what they must to save themselves and their communities, and morality and law have no place. *Inter arma silent leges*: in time of war the law is silent.

Sometimes this silence is extended to other forms of competitive activity, as in the popular proverb, "All's fair in love and war." That means that anything goes—any kind of deceit in love, any kind of violence in war. We can neither praise nor blame; there is nothing to say. And yet we are rarely silent. The language we use to talk about love and war is so rich with moral meaning that it could hardly have been developed except through centuries of argument. Faithfulness, devotion, chastity, shame, adultery, seduction, betrayal; aggression, self-defense, appeasement, cruelty, ruthlessness, atrocity, massacre—all these words are judgments, and judging is as common a human activity as loving or fighting.

It is true, however, that we often lack the courage of our judgments, and especially so in the case of military conflict. The moral posture of mankind is not well represented by that popular proverb about love and war. We would do better to mark a contrast rather than a similarity: before Venus, censorious; before Mars, timid. Not that we don't justify or condemn particular attacks, but we do so hesitantly and uncertainly (or loudly and recklessly), as if we were not sure that our judgments reach to the reality of war.

THE REALIST ARGUMENT

Realism is the issue. The defenders of *silent leges* claim to have discovered an awful truth: what we conventionally call inhumanity is simply humanity under pressure. War strips away our civilized adornments and reveals our nakedness. They describe that nakedness for us, not without a certain relish: fearful, self-concerned, driven, murderous. They aren't wrong in any simple sense. The words are sometimes descriptive. Paradoxically, the description is often a kind of apology: yes, our soldiers committed atrocities in the course of the battle, but that's what war does to people, that's what war is like. The proverb, all's fair, is invoked in defense of conduct that appears to be unfair. And one urges silence on the law when one is engaged in activities that would otherwise be called unlawful. So there are arguments here that will enter into my own argument: justifications and excuses, references to necessity and duress, that we can recognize as forms of moral discourse and that have or don't have force in particular cases. But there is also a general account of war as a realm of necessity and duress, the purpose of which is to make discourse about particular cases appear to be idle chatter, a mask of noise with which we conceal, even from ourselves, the awful truth. It is that general account that I have to challenge before I can begin my own work, and I want to challenge it at its source and in its most compelling form, as it is put forward by the historian Thucydides and the philosopher Thomas Hobbes. These two men, separated by 2,000 years, are collaborators of a kind, for Hobbes translated Thucydides' *History of the Peloponnesian War* and then generalized its argument in his own *Leviathan*. It is not my purpose here to write a full philosophical response to Thucydides and Hobbes. I wish only to suggest, first by argument and then by example, that the judgment of war and of wartime conduct is a serious enterprise.

The Melian Dialogue

The dialogue between the Athenian generals Cleomedes and Tisias and the magistrates of the island state of Melos is one of the high points of

Thucydides' *History* and the climax of his realism. Melos was a Spartan colony, and its people had "therefore refused to be subject, as the rest of the islands were, unto the Athenians; but rested at first neutral; and afterwards, when the Athenians put them to it by wasting of their lands, they entered into open war."[1] This is a classic account of aggression, for to commit aggression is simply to "put people to it" as Thucydides describes. But such a description, he seems to say, is merely external; he wants to show us the inner meaning of war. His spokesmen are the two Athenian generals, who demand a parley and then speak as generals have rarely done in military history. Let us have no fine words about justice, they say. We for our part will not pretend that, having defeated the Persians, our empire is deserved; you must not claim that having done no injury to the Athenian people, you have a right to be let alone. We will talk instead of what is feasible and what is necessary. For this is what war is really like: "they that have odds of power exact as much as they can, and the weak yield to such conditions as they can get."

It is not only the Melians here who bear the burdens of necessity. The Athenians are driven, too; they must expand their empire, Cleomedes and Tisias believe, or lose what they already have. The neutrality of Melos "will be an argument of our weakness, and your hatred of our power, among those we have rule over." It will inspire rebellion throughout the islands, wherever men and women are "offended with the necessity of subjection"— and what subject is not offended, eager for freedom, resentful of his conquerors? When the Athenian generals say that men "will everywhere reign over such as they be too strong for," they are not only describing the desire for glory and command, but also the more narrow necessity of inter-state politics: reign or be subject. If they do not conquer when they can, they only reveal weakness and invite attack; and so, "by a necessity of nature" (a phrase Hobbes later made his own), they conquer when they can.

The Melians, on the other hand, are too weak to conquer. They face a harsher necessity: yield or be destroyed. "For you have not in hand a match of valor upon equal terms . . . but rather a consultation upon your safety. . . ." The rulers of Melos, however, value freedom above safety: "If you then to retain your command, and your vassals to get loose from you, will undergo the utmost danger: would it not in us, that be already free, be great baseness and cowardice, if we should not encounter anything whatsoever rather than suffer ourselves to be brought into bondage?" Though they know that it will be a "hard matter" to stand against the power and fortune of Athens, "nevertheless we believe that, for fortune, we shall be nothing inferior, as having the gods on our side, because we stand innocent against men unjust." And as for power, they hope for assistance from the Spartans, "who are of necessity obliged, if for no other cause, yet for consanguinity's sake and for their own honor to defend us." But the gods, too, reign where they can, reply the Athenian generals, and consanguinity and honor have nothing to do with necessity. The Spartans will (necessarily) think only of themselves: "most apparently of all men, they hold for honorable that which pleaseth and for just that which profiteth."

So the argument ended. The magistrates refused to surrender; the Athenians laid siege to their city; the Spartans sent no help. Finally, after some months of fighting, in the winter of 416 B.C., Melos was betrayed by several of its citizens. When further resistance seemed impossible, the Melians "yielded themselves to the discretion of the Athenians: who slew all the men of military age, made slaves of the women and children; and inhabited the place with a colony sent thither afterwards of 500 men of their own."

The dialogue between the generals and the magistrates is a literary and philosophical construction of Thucydides. The magistrates speak as they well might have done, but their conventional piety and heroism is only a foil to what the classical critic Dionysius calls the "depraved shrewdness" of the Athenian generals.[2] It is the generals who have often seemed unbelievable. Their words, writes Dionysius, "were appropriate to oriental monarchs . . . but unfit to be spoken by Athenians. . . ."* Perhaps Thucydides means us to notice the unfitness, not so much of the words but of the policies they were used to defend, and thinks we might have missed it had he permitted the generals to speak as they probably in fact spoke,

---

*Even oriental monarchs are not quite so toughminded as the Athenian generals. According to Herodotus, when Xerxes first disclosed his plans for an invasion of Greece, he spoke in more conventional terms: "I will bridge the Hellespont and march an army through Europe into Greece, and punish the Athenians for the outrage they committed upon my father and upon us." (*The Histories*, Book 7, trans. Aubrey de Selincourt.) The reference is to the burning of Sardis, which we may take as the pretext for the Persian invasion. The example bears out Francis Bacon's assertion that "there is that justice imprinted in the nature of men that they enter not upon wars (whereof so many calamities do ensue) but upon some, at least specious, grounds and quarrels." (Essay 29, "Of the True Greatness of Kingdoms and Estates.")

weaving "fair pretenses" over their vile actions. We are to understand that Athens is no longer itself. Cleomedes and Tisias do not represent that noble people who fought the Persians in the name of freedom and whose politics and culture, as Dionysius says, "exercised such a humanizing influence on everyday life." They represent instead the imperial decadence of the city state. It is not that they are war criminals in the modern sense; that idea is alien to Thucydides. But they embody a certain loss of ethical balance, of restraint and moderation. Their statesmanship is flawed, and their "realistic" speeches provide an ironic contrast to the blindness and arrogance with which the Athenians only a few months later launched the disastrous expedition to Sicily. The *History*, on this view, is a tragedy and Athens itself the tragic hero.[3] Thucydides has given us a morality play in the Greek style. We can glimpse his meaning in Euripides' *The Trojan Women*, written in the immediate aftermath of the conquest of Melos and undoubtedly intended to suggest the human significance of slaughter and slavery—and to predict a divine retribution:[4]

> *How ye are blind*
> *Ye treaders down of cities, ye that cast*
> *Temples to desolation, and lay waste*
> *Tombs, the untrodden sanctuaries where lie*
> *The ancient dead; yourselves so soon to die!*

But Thucydides seems in fact to be making a rather different, and a more secular, statement than this quotation suggests, and not about Athens so much as about war itself. He probably did not mean the harshness of the Athenian generals to be taken as a sign of depravity, but rather as a sign of impatience, toughmindedness, honesty—qualities of mind not inappropriate in military commanders. He is arguing, as Werner Jaeger has said, that "the principle of force forms a realm of its own, with laws of its own," distinct and separate from the laws of moral life.[5] This is certainly the way Hobbes read Thucydides, and it is the reading with which we must come to grips. For if the realm of force is indeed distinct and if this is an accurate account of its laws, then one could no more criticize the Athenians for their wartime policies than one could criticize a stone for falling downwards. The slaughter of the Melians is explained by reference to the circumstances of war and the necessities of nature; and again, there is nothing to say. Or rather, one can *say* anything, call necessity cruel and war hellish; but while these statements may be true in their own terms, they do not touch the political realities of the case or help us understand the Athenian decision.

It is important to stress, however, that Thucydides has told us nothing at all about the Athenian decision. And if we place ourselves, not in the council room at Melos where a cruel policy was being expounded, but in the assembly at Athens where that policy was first adopted, the argument of the generals has a very different ring. In the Greek as in the English language, the word *necessity* "doubles the parts of indispensable and inevitable."[6] At Melos, Cleomedes and Tisias mixed the two of these, stressing the last. In the assembly they could have argued only about the first, claiming, I suppose, that the destruction of Melos was necessary (indispensable) for the preservation of the empire. But this claim is rhetorical in two senses. First, it evades the moral question of whether the preservation of the empire was itself necessary. There were some Athenians, at least, who had doubts about that, and more who doubted that the empire had to be a uniform system of domination and subjection (as the policy adopted for Melos suggested). Secondly, it exaggerates the knowledge and foresight of the generals. They are not saying with certainty that Athens will fall unless Melos is destroyed; their argument has to do with probabilities and risks. And such arguments are always arguable. Would the destruction of Melos really reduce Athenian risks? Are there alternative policies? What are the likely costs of this one? Would it be right? What would other people think of Athens if it were carried out?

Once the debate begins, all sorts of moral and strategic questions are likely to come up. And for the participants in the debate, the outcome is not going to be determined "by a necessity of nature," but by the opinions they hold or come to hold as a result of the arguments they hear and then by the decisions they freely make, individually and collectively. Afterwards, the generals claim that a certain decision was inevitable; and that, presumably, is what Thucydides wants us to believe. But the claim can only be made afterwards, for inevitability here is mediated by a process of political deliberation, and Thucydides could not know what was inevitable until that process had been completed. Judgments of necessity in this sense are always retrospective in character—the work of historians, not historical actors.

Now, the moral point of view derives its legitimacy from the perspective of the actor. When we make moral judgments, we try to recapture that perspective. We reiterate the decision-making process, or we rehearse our own future decisions, asking what we would have done (or what we would do) in similar circumstances. The Athenian generals recognize the importance of such questions, for they defend their policy certain "that you likewise, and others that should have the same power which we have, would do the same." But that is a dubious knowledge, especially so once we realize that the "Melian decree" was sharply opposed in the Athenian assembly. Our standpoint is that of citizens debating the decree. What *should* we do?

We have no account of the Athenian decision to attack Melos or of the decision (which may have been taken at the same time) to kill and enslave its people. Plutarch claims that it was Alcibiades, chief architect of the Sicilian expedition, who was "the principal cause of the slaughter . . . having spoken in favor of the decree."[7] He played the part of Cleon in the debate that Thucydides does record, that occurred some years earlier, over the fate of Mytilene. It is worth glancing back at that earlier argument. Mytilene had been an ally of Athens from the time of the Persian War; it was never a subject city in any formal way, but bound by treaty to the Athenian cause. In 428, it rebelled and formed an alliance with the Spartans. After considerable fighting, the city was captured by Athenian forces, and the assembly determined "to put to death . . . all the men of Mytilene that were of age, and to make slaves of the women and children: laying to their charge the revolt itself, in that they revolted not being in subjection as others were. . . ."[8] But the following day the citizens "felt a kind of repentance . . . and began to consider what a great and cruel decree it was, that not the authors only, but that the whole city should be destroyed." It is this second debate that Thucydides has recorded, or some part of it, giving us two speeches, that of Cleon upholding the original decree and that of Diodotus urging its revocation. Cleon argues largely in terms of collective guilt and retributive justice; Diodotus offers a critique of the deterrent effects of capital punishment. The assembly accepts Diodotus' position, convinced apparently that the destruction of Mytilene would not uphold the force of treaties or ensure the stability of the empire. It is the appeal to interest that triumphs—as has often been pointed out—though it should be remembered that the occasion for the appeal was the repentance of the citizens. Moral anxiety, not political calculation, leads them to worry about the effectiveness of their decree.

In the debate over Melos, the positions must have been reversed. Now there was no retributivist argument to make, for the Melians had done

Athens no injury. Alcibiades probably talked like Thucydides' generals, though with the all-important difference I have already noted. When he told his fellow citizens that the decree was necessary, he didn't mean that it was ordained by the laws that govern the realm of force; he meant merely that it was needed (in his view) to reduce the risks of rebellion among the subject cities of the Athenian empire. And his opponents probably argued, like the Melians, that the decree was dishonorable and unjust and would more likely excite resentment than fear throughout the islands, that Melos did not threaten Athens in any way, and that other policies would serve Athenian interests and Athenian self-esteem. Perhaps they also reminded the citizens of their repentance in the case of Mytilene and urged them once again to avoid the cruelty of massacre and enslavement. How Alcibiades won out, and how close the vote was, we don't know. But there is no reason to think that the decision was predetermined and debate of no avail: no more with Melos than with Mytilene. Stand in imagination in the Athenian assembly, and one can still feel a sense of freedom.

But the realism of the Athenian generals has a further thrust. It is not only a denial of the freedom that makes moral decision possible; it is a denial also of the meaningfulness of moral argument. The second claim is closely related to the first. If we must act in accordance with our interests, driven by our fears of one another, then talk about justice cannot possibly be anything more than talk. It refers to no purposes that we can make our own and to no goals that we can share with others. That is why the Athenian generals could have woven "fair pretenses" as easily as the Melian magistrates; in discourse of this sort anything can be said. The words have no clear references, no certain definitions, no logical entailments. They are, as Hobbes writes in *Leviathan*, "ever used with relation to the person that useth them," and they express that person's appetites and fears and nothing else. It is only "most apparent" in the Spartans, but true for everyone, that "they hold for honorable that which pleaseth them and for just that which profiteth." Or, as Hobbes later explained, the names of the virtues and vices are of "uncertain signification."[9]

> For one calleth wisdom, what another calleth fear; and one cruelty what another justice; one prodigality, what another magnanimity . . . etc. And therefore such names can never be true grounds of any ratiocination.

"Never"—until the sovereign, who is also the supreme linguistic authority, fixes the meaning of the moral vocabulary; but in the state of war, *"never"* without qualification, because in that state, by definition, no sovereign rules. In fact, even in civil society, the sovereign does not entirely succeed in bringing certainty into the world of virtue and vice. Hence moral discourse is always suspect, and war is only an extreme case of the anarchy of moral meanings. It is generally true, but especially so in time of violent conflict, that we can understand what other people are saying only if we see through their "fair pretenses" and translate moral talk into the harder currency of interest talk. When the Melians insist that their cause is just, they are saying only that they don't want to be subject; and had the generals claimed that Athens deserved its empire, they would simply have been expressing the lust for conquest or the fear of overthrow.

This is a powerful argument because it plays upon the common experience of moral disagreement—painful, sustained, exasperating, and endless. For all its realism, however, it fails to get at the realities of that experience or to explain its character. We can see this clearly, I think, if we look again at the argument over the Mytilene decree. Hobbes may well have had this debate in mind when he wrote, "and one [calleth] cruelty what another justice. . . ." The Athenians repented of their cruelty, writes Thucydides, while Cleon told them that they had not been cruel at all but justly severe. Yet this was in no sense a disagreement over the meaning of words. Had there been no common meanings, there could have been no debate at all. The cruelty of the Athenians consisted in seeking to punish not only the authors of the rebellion but others as well, and Cleon agreed that that would indeed be cruel. He then went on to argue, as he had to do given his position, that in Mytilene there were no "others." "Let not the fault be laid upon a few, and the people absolved. For they have all alike taken arms against us. . . ."

I cannot pursue the argument further, since Thucydides doesn't, but there is an obvious rejoinder to Cleon, having to do with the status of the women and children of Mytilene. This might involve the deployment of additional moral terms (innocence, for example); but it would not hang—any more than the argument about cruelty and justice hangs—on idiosyncratic definitions. In fact, definitions are not at issue here, but descriptions and interpretations. The Athenians shared a moral vocabulary, shared it with the people of Mytilene and Melos; and allowing for cultural differences, they share it with us too. They had no difficulty, and we have none, in understanding the claim of the Melian magistrates that the invasion of their island was unjust. It is in applying the agreed-upon words to actual cases that we come to disagree. These disagreements are in part generated and always compounded by antagonistic interests and mutual fears. But they have other causes, too, which help to explain the complex and disparate ways in which men and women (even when they have similar interests and no reason to fear one another) position themselves in the moral world. There are, first of all, serious difficulties of perception and information (in war and politics generally), and so controversies arise over "the facts of the case." There are sharp disparities in the weight we attach even to values we share, as there are in the actions we are ready to condone when these values are threatened. There are conflicting commitments and obligations that force us into violent antagonism even when we see the point of one another's positions. All this is real enough, and common enough: it makes morality into a world of good-faith quarrels as well as a world of ideology and verbal manipulation.

In any case, the possibilities for manipulation are limited. Whether or not people speak in good faith, they cannot say just anything they please. Moral talk is coercive; one thing leads to another. Perhaps that's why the Athenian generals did not want to begin. A war called unjust is not, to paraphrase Hobbes, a war misliked; it is a war misliked for particular reasons, and anyone making the charge is required to provide particular sorts of evidence. Similarly, if I claim that I am fighting justly, I must also claim that I was attacked ("put to it," as the Melians were), or threatened with attack, or that I am coming to the aid of a victim of someone else's attack. And each of these claims has its own entailments, leading me deeper and deeper into a world of discourse where, though I can go on talking indefinitely, I am severely constrained in what I can say. I must say this or that, and at many points in a long argument this or that will be true or false. We don't have to translate moral talk into interest talk in order to understand it; morality refers in its own way to the real world.

Let us consider a Hobbist example. In chapter XXI of *Leviathan*, Hobbes urges that we make allowance for the "natural timorousness" of mankind. "When armies fight, there is on one side, or both, a running away; yet when they do it not out of treachery, but fear, they are not esteemed to do it unjustly, but dishonorably." Now, judgments are called for here: we are to distinguish cowards from traitors. If these are words of "inconstant signification," the task is impossible and absurd. Every traitor would plead natural timorousness, and we would accept the plea or not depending on whether the soldier was a friend or an enemy, an obstacle to our advancement or an ally and supporter. I suppose we sometimes do behave that way, but it is not the case (nor does Hobbes, when it comes to cases, suppose that it is) that the judgments we make can only be understood in these terms. When we charge a man with treason, we have to tell a very special kind of story about him, and we have to provide concrete evidence that the story is true. If we call him a traitor when we cannot tell that story, we are not using words inconstantly, we are simply lying.

STRATEGY AND MORALITY

Morality and justice are talked about in much the same way as military strategy. Strategy is the other language of war, and while it is commonly said to be free from the difficulties of moral discourse, its use is equally problematic. Though generals agree on the meaning of strategic terms— entrapment, retreat, flanking maneuver, concentration of forces, and so on—they nevertheless disagree about strategically appropriate courses of action. They argue about what ought to be done. After the battle, they disagree about what happened, and if they were defeated, they argue about who was to blame. Strategy, like morality, is a language of justification.* Every confused and cowardly commander describes his hesitations and panics as part of an elaborate plan; the strategic vocabulary is as available to him as it is to a competent commander. But that is not to say that its terms are meaningless. It would be a great triumph for the incompetent if they were, for we would then have no way to talk about incompetence. No doubt, "one calleth retreat what another calleth strategic deployment. . . ."

---

*Hence we can "unmask" strategic discourse just as Thucydides did with moral discourse. Imagine that the two Athenian generals, after their dialogue with the Melians, return to their camp to plan the coming battle. The senior in command speaks first: "Don't give me any fine talk about the need to concentrate our forces or the importance of strategic surprise. We'll simply call for a frontal assault; the men will organize themselves as best they can; things are going to be confused anyway. I need a quick victory here, so that I can return to Athens covered with glory before the debate on the Sicilian campaign begins. We'll have to accept some risks; but that doesn't matter since the risks will be yours, not mine. If we are beaten, I'll contrive to blame you. That's what war is like." Why is strategy the language of hard-headed men? One sees through it so easily. . . .

But we do know the difference between these two, and though the facts of the case may be difficult to collect and interpret, we are nevertheless able to make critical judgments.

Similarly, we can make moral judgments: moral concepts and strategic concepts reflect the real world in the same way. They are not merely normative terms, telling soldiers (who often don't listen) what to do. They are descriptive terms, and without them we would have no coherent way of talking about war. Here are soldiers moving away from the scene of a battle, marching over the same ground they marched over yesterday, but fewer now, less eager, many without weapons, many wounded: we call this a retreat. Here are soldiers lining up the inhabitants of a peasant village, men, women, and children, and shooting them down: we call this a massacre.

It is only when their substantive content is fairly clear that moral and strategic terms can be used imperatively, and the wisdom they embody expressed in the form of rules. Never refuse quarter to a soldier trying to surrender. Never advance with your flanks unprotected. One might construct out of such commands a moral or a strategic war plan, and then it would be important to notice whether or not the actual conduct of the war conformed to the plan. We can assume that it would not. War is recalcitrant to this sort of theoretical control—a quality it shares with every other human activity, but which it seems to possess to an especially intense degree. In *The Charterhouse of Parma*, Stendhal provides a description of the battle of Waterloo that is intended to mock the very idea of a strategic plan. It is an account of combat as chaos, therefore not an account at all but a denial, so to speak, that combat is accountable. It should be read alongside some strategic analysis of Waterloo like that of Major General Fuller, who views the battle as an organized series of maneuvers and countermaneuvers.[10] The strategist is not unaware of confusion and disorder in the field; nor is he entirely unwilling to see these as aspects of war itself, the natural effects of the stress of battle. But he sees them also as matters of command responsibility, failures of discipline or control. He suggests that strategic imperatives have been ignored; he looks for lessons to be learned.

The moral theorist is in the same position. He too must come to grips with the fact that his rules are often violated or ignored—and with the deeper realization that, to men at war, the rules often don't seem relevant to the extremity of their situation. But however he does this, he does not surrender his sense of war as a human action, purposive and premeditated, for whose effects someone is responsible. Confronted with the many crimes committed in the course of a war, or with the crime of aggressive war itself, he searches for human agents. Nor is he alone in this search. It is one of the most important features of war, distinguishing it from the other scourges of mankind, that the men and women caught up in it are not only victims, they are also participants. All of us are inclined to hold them responsible for what they do (though we may recognize the plea of duress in particular cases). Reiterated over time, our arguments and judgments shape what I want to call *the moral reality of war*—that is, all those experiences of which moral language is descriptive or within which it is necessarily employed.

It is important to stress that the moral reality of war is not fixed by the actual activities of soldiers but by the opinions of mankind. That means, in part, that it is fixed by the activity of philosophers, lawyers, and publicists of all sorts. But these people don't work in isolation from the experience of combat, and their views have value only insofar as they give shape and structure to that experience in ways that are plausible to the rest of us. We often say, for example, that in time of war soldiers and statesmen must make agonizing decisions. The pain is real enough, but it is not one of the natural effects of combat. Agony is not like Hobbist fear; it is entirely the product of our moral views, and it is common in war only insofar as those views are common. It was not some unusual Athenian who "repented" of the decision to kill the men of Mytilene, but the citizens generally. They repented, and they were able to understand one another's repentance, because they shared a sense of what cruelty meant. It is by the assignment of such meanings that we make war what it is—which is to say that it could be (and it probably has been) something different.

What of a soldier or statesman who does not feel the agony? We say of him that he is morally ignorant or morally insensitive, much as we might say of a general who experienced no difficulty making a (really) difficult decision that he did not understand the strategic realities of his own position or that he was reckless and insensible of danger. And we might go on to argue, in the case of the general, that such a man has no business fighting or leading others in battle, that he ought to know that his army's right flank, say, is vulnerable, and ought to worry about the danger and take steps to avoid it. Once again, the case is the same with moral decisions:

soldiers and statesmen ought to know the dangers of cruelty and injustice and worry about them and take steps to avoid them.

HISTORICAL RELATIVISM

Against this view, however, Hobbist relativism is often given a social or historical form: moral and strategic knowledge, it is said, changes over time or varies among political communities, and so what appears to me as ignorance may look like understanding to someone else. Now, change and variation are certainly real enough, and they make for a tale that is complex in the telling. But the importance of that tale for ordinary moral life and, above all, for the judgment of moral conduct is easily exaggerated. Between radically separate and dissimilar cultures, one can expect to find radical dichotomies in perception and understanding. No doubt the moral reality of war is not the same for us as it was for Genghis Khan; nor is the strategic reality. But even fundamental social and political transformations within a particular culture may well leave the moral world intact or at least sufficiently whole so that we can still be said to share it with our ancestors. It is rare indeed that we do not share it with our contemporaries, and by and large we learn how to act among our contemporaries by studying the actions of those who have preceded us. The assumption of that study is that they saw the world much as we do. That is not always true, but it is true enough of the time to give stability and coherence to our moral lives (and to our military lives). Even when world views and high ideals have been abandoned—as the glorification of aristocratic chivalry was abandoned in early modern times—notions about right conduct are remarkably persistent: the military code survives the death of warrior idealism. I shall say more about this survival later on, but I can demonstrate it now in a general way by looking at an example from feudal Europe, an age in some ways more distant from us than Greece of the city states, but with which we nevertheless share moral and strategic perceptions.

Three Accounts of Agincourt

Actually, the sharing of strategic perceptions is in this case the more dubious of the two. Those French knights, so many of whom died at Agincourt, had notions about combat very different from our own. Modern critics have still felt able to criticize their "fanatical adherence to the old method of fighting" (King Henry, after all, fought differently) and even to offer practical suggestions: the French attack, writes Oman, "should have been accompanied by a turning movement around the woods . . ."[11] Had he not been "overconfident," the French commander would have seen the advantages of the move. We can talk in a similar way about the crucial moral decision that Henry made toward the end of the battle, when the English thought their victory secure. They had taken many prisoners, who were loosely assembled behind the lines. Suddenly, a French attack aimed at the supply tents far in the rear seemed to threaten a renewal of the fighting. Here is Holinshed's sixteenth-century account of the incident (virtually copied from an earlier chronicle):[12]

> . . . certain Frenchmen on horseback . . . to the number of six hundred horsemen, which were the first that fled, hearing that the English tents and pavilions were a good way distant from the army, without any sufficient guard to defend the same . . . entered upon the king's camp and there . . . robbed the tents, broke up chests, and carried away caskets and slew such servants as they found to make any resistance. . . . But when the outcry of the lackeys and boys which ran away for fear of the Frenchmen . . . came to the king's ears, he doubting lest his enemies should gather together again, and begin a new field; and mistrusting further that the prisoners would be an aid to his enemies . . . contrary to his accustomed gentleness, commanded by sound of trumpet that every man . . . should incontinently slay his prisoner.

The moral character of the command is suggested by the words "accustomed gentleness" and "incontinently." It involved a shattering of personal and conventional restraints (the latter well-established by 1415), and Holinshed goes to some lengths to explain and excuse it, stressing the king's fear that the prisoners his forces held were about to rejoin the fighting. Shakespeare, whose *Henry V* closely follows Holinshed, goes further, emphasizing the slaying of the English servants by the French and omitting the chronicler's assertion that only those who resisted were killed:[13]

> *Fluellen.* Kill the [b]oys and the baggage! 'Tis expressly against the law of arms. 'Tis as arrant a piece of knavery, mark you now, as can be offert.

At the same time, however, he cannot resist an ironical comment:

> *Gower* . . . they have burned and carried away all that was in the king's tent, wherefore the king most worthily hath caused every soldier to cut his prisoner's throat. O, 'tis a gallant king!

A century and a half later, David Hume gives a similar account, without the irony, stressing instead the king's eventual cancellation of his order:[14]

> . . . some gentlemen of Picardy . . . had fallen upon the English baggage, and were doing execution on the unarmed followers of the camp, who fled before them. Henry, seeing the enemy on all sides of him, began to entertain apprehensions from his prisoners; and he thought it necessary to issue a general order for putting them to death; but on discovering the truth, he stopped the slaughter, and was still able to save a great number.

Here the moral meaning is caught in the tension between "necessary" and "slaughter." Since slaughter is the killing of men as if they were animals—it "makes a massacre," wrote the poet Dryden, "what was a war"—it cannot often be called necessary. If the prisoners were so easy to kill, they were probably not dangerous enough to warrant the killing. When he grasped the actual situation, Henry, who was (so Hume wants us to believe) a moral man, called off the executions.

French chroniclers and historians write of the event in much the same way. It is from them that we learn that many of the English knights refused to kill their prisoners—not, chiefly, out of humanity, rather for the sake of the ransom they expected; but also "thinking of the dishonor that the horrible executions would reflect on themselves."[15] English writers have focused more, and more worriedly, on the command of the king; he was, after all, their king. In the later nineteenth century, at about the same time as the rules of war with respect to prisoners were being codified, their criticism grew increasingly sharp: "a brutal butchery," "cold-blooded wholesale murder."[16] Hume would not have said that, but the difference between that and what he did say is marginal, not a matter of moral or linguistic transformation.

To judge Henry ourselves we would need a more circumstantial account of the battle than I can provide here.[17] Even given that account, our opinions might differ, depending on the allowance we were willing to make for the stress and excitement of battle. But this is a clear example, of a situation common in both strategy and morality, where our sharpest disagreements are structured and organized by our underlying agreements, by the meanings we share. For Holinshed, Shakespeare, and Hume—traditional chronicler, Renaissance playwright, and Enlightenment historian—and for us too, Henry's command belongs to a category of military acts that requires scrutiny and judgment. It is *as a matter of fact* morally problematic, because it accepts the risks of cruelty and injustice. In exactly the same way, we might regard the battle plan of the French commander as strategically problematic, because it accepted the risks of a frontal assault on a prepared position. And, again, a general who did not recognize these risks is properly said to be ignorant of morality or strategy.

In moral life, ignorance isn't all that common; dishonesty is far more so. Even those soldiers and statesmen who don't feel the agony of a problematic decision generally know that they should feel it. Harry Truman's flat statement that he never lost a night's sleep over his decision to drop the atomic bomb on Hiroshima is not the sort of thing political leaders often say. They usually find it preferable to stress the painfulness of decision-making; it is one of the burdens of office, and it is best if the burdens appear to be borne. I suspect that many officeholders even experience pain simply because they are expected to. If they don't, they lie about it. The clearest evidence for the stability of our values over time is the unchanging character of the lies soldiers and statesmen tell. They lie in order to justify themselves, and so they describe for us the lineaments of justice. Wherever we find hypocrisy, we also find moral knowledge. The hypocrite is like that Russian general in Solzhenitsyn's *August 1914*, whose elaborate battle reports barely concealed his total inability to control or direct the battle. He knew at least that there was a story to tell, a set of names to attach to things and happenings, so he tried to tell the story and attach the names. His effort was not mere mimicry; it was, so to speak, the tribute that incompetence pays to understanding. The case is the same in moral life: there really is a story to tell, a way of talking about wars and battles that the rest of us recognize as morally appropriate. I don't mean that particular decisions are necessarily right or wrong, or simply right or wrong, only that there is a way of seeing the world so that moral decision-making makes sense. The hypocrite knows that this is true, though he may actually see the world differently.

Hypocrisy is rife in wartime discourse, because it is especially important at such a time to appear to be in the right. It is not only that the moral stakes are high; the hypocrite may not understand that; more crucially, his actions will be judged by other people, who are not hypocrites, and whose judgments will affect their policies toward him. There would be no point to hypocrisy if this were not so, just as there would be no point to lying in a world where no one told the truth. The hypocrite presumes on the moral understanding of the rest of us, and we have no choice, I think, except to take his assertions seriously and put them to the test of moral realism. He pretends to think and act as the rest of us expect him to do. He tells us that he is fighting according to the moral war plan: he does not aim at civilians, he grants quarter to soldiers trying to surrender, he never tortures prisoners, and so on. These claims are true or false, and though it is not easy to judge them (nor is the war plan really so simple), it is important to make the effort. Indeed, if we call ourselves moral men and women, we must make the effort, and the evidence is that we regularly do so. If we had all become realists like the Athenian generals or like Hobbists in a state of war, there would be an end alike to both morality and hypocrisy. We would simply tell one another, brutally and directly, what we wanted to do or have done. But the truth is that one of the things most of us want, even in war, is to act or to seem to act morally. And we want that, most simply, because we know what morality means (at least, we know what it is generally thought to mean).

It is that meaning that I want to explore in this book—not so much its general character, but its detailed application to the conduct of war. I am going to assume throughout that we really do act within a moral world; that particular decisions really are difficult, problematic, agonizing, and that this has to do with the structure of that world; that language reflects the moral world and gives us access to it; and finally that our understanding of the moral vocabulary is sufficiently common and stable so that shared judgments are possible. Perhaps there are other worlds to whose inhabitants the arguments I am going to make would seem incomprehensible and bizarre. But no such people are likely to read this book. And if my own readers find my arguments incomprehensible and bizarre, that will not be because of the impossibility of moral discourse or the inconstant signification of the words I use, but because of my own failure to grasp and expound our common morality.

2

THE CRIME OF WAR

THE MORAL REALITY OF WAR IS DIVIDED INTO TWO PARTS. WAR IS ALWAYS judged twice, first with reference to the reasons states have for fighting, secondly with reference to the means they adopt. The first kind of judgment is adjectival in character: we say that a particular war is just or unjust. The second is adverbial: we say that the war is being fought justly or unjustly. Medieval writers made the difference a matter of prepositions, distinguishing *jus ad bellum*, the justice of war, from *jus in bello*, justice in war. These grammatical distinctions point to deep issues. *Jus ad bellum* requires us to make judgments about aggression and self-defense; *jus in bello* about the observance or violation of the customary and positive rules of engagement. The two sorts of judgment are logically independent. It is perfectly possible for a just war to be fought unjustly and for an unjust war to be fought in strict accordance with the rules. But this independence, though our views of particular wars often conform to its terms, is nevertheless puzzling. It is a crime to commit aggression, but aggressive war is a rule-governed activity. It is right to resist aggression, but the resistance is subject to moral (and legal) restraint. The dualism of *jus ad bellum* and *jus in bello* is at the heart of all that is most problematic in the moral reality of war.

It is my purpose to see war whole, but since its dualism is the essential feature of its wholeness, I must begin by accounting for the parts. In this chapter, I want to suggest what we mean when we say that it is a crime to begin a war, and in the next I will try to explain why it is that there are rules of engagement that apply even to soldiers whose wars are criminal. This chapter introduces Part Two, where I will examine in detail the nature of the crime, describe the appropriate forms of resistance, and consider the ends that soldiers and statesmen may legitimately seek in fighting just wars. The next chapter introduces Part Three, where I will discuss the legitimate means of warfare, the substantive rules, and show how these rules apply in combat conditions and how they are modified by "military necessity." Only then will it be possible to confront the tension between ends and means, *jus ad bellum* and *jus in bello*.

I am not sure whether the moral reality of war is wholly coherent, but for the moment I need not say anything about that. It's enough that it has a recognizable and relatively stable shape, that its parts are connected and disconnected in recognizable and relatively stable ways. We have made it so, not arbitrarily, but for good reasons. It reflects our understanding of states and soldiers, the protagonists of war, and of combat, its central experience. The terms of that understanding are my immediate subject matter. They are simultaneously the historical product of and the necessary condition for the critical judgments that we make every day; they fix the nature of war as a moral (and an immoral) enterprise.

THE LOGIC OF WAR

Why is it wrong to begin a war? We know the answer all too well. People get killed, and often in large numbers. *War is hell.* But it is necessary to say more than that, for our ideas about war in general and about the conduct of soldiers depend very much on how people get killed and on who those people are. Then, perhaps, the best way to describe the crime of war is simply to say that there are no limits at either of these points: people are killed with every conceivable brutality, and all sorts of people, without distinction of age or sex or moral condition, are killed. This view of war is brilliantly summed up in the first chapter of Karl von Clausewitz's *On War*, and though there is no evidence that Clausewitz thought war a crime, he has certainly led other people to think so. It is his early definitions (rather than his later qualifications) that have shaped the ideas of his successors, and so it is worth considering them in some detail.

The Argument of Karl von Clausewitz

"War is an act of force," Clausewitz writes, ". . . which theoretically can have no limits."[1] The idea of war carries with it for him the idea of limitlessness, whatever actual restraints are observed in this or that society. If we imagine a war fought, as it were, in a social vacuum, unaffected by "accidental" factors, it would be fought with no restraint at all in the weapons used, the tactics adopted, the people attacked, or anywhere else. For military conduct knows no intrinsic limits; nor is it possible to refine our notions of war so as to incorporate those extrinsic moral codes that Clausewitz sometimes calls "philanthropic." "We can never introduce a modifying principle into the philosophy of war without committing an absurdity." The more extreme the battle is, then, the more general and intense the violence employed on one side and the other, the closer to war in the conceptual sense ("absolute war") it is. And there can be no imaginable act of violence, however treacherous or cruel, that falls outside of war, that is not-war, for the logic of war simply is a steady thrust toward moral extremity. That is why it is so awful (though Clausewitz does not tell us this) to set the process going: the aggressor is responsible for all the consequences of the fighting he begins. In particular cases, it may not be possible to know these consequences in advance, but they are always potentially terrible. "When you resorted to force," General Eisenhower once said, ". . . you didn't know where you were going. . . . If you got deeper and deeper, there was just no limit except . . . the limitations of force itself."[2]

The logic of war, according to Clausewitz, works in this way: "each of the adversaries forces the hand of the other." What results is a "reciprocal action," a continuous escalation, in which neither side is guilty even if it acts first, since every act can be called and almost certainly is pre-emptive. "War tends toward the utmost exertion of forces," and that means toward increasing ruthlessness, since "the ruthless user of force who shrinks from no amount of bloodshed must gain an advantage if his opponent does not do the same."[3] And so his opponent, driven by what Thucydides and Hobbes call "a necessity of nature," does the same, matching the ruthlessness of the other side whenever he can. But this description, though it is a useful account of how escalation works, is open to the criticism that I have already made. As soon as we focus on some concrete case of military and moral decision-making, we enter a world that is governed not by abstract tendencies but by human choice. The actual pressures toward escalation are greater here, less there, rarely so overwhelming as to leave no room for maneuver. Wars no doubt are often escalated, but they are also (sometimes) fought at fairly steady levels of violence and brutality, and these levels are (sometimes) fairly low.

Clausewitz grants this, though without surrendering his commitment to the absolute. War, he writes, "may be a thing which is sometimes war in a greater, sometimes in a lesser degree." And again, "There can be wars of all degrees of importance and energy, from a war of extermination down to a mere state of armed observation."⁴ Somewhere between these two, I suppose, we begin to say, all's fair, anything goes, and so on. When we talk that way, we are not referring to the general limitlessness of war, but to particular escalations, particular acts of force. No one has ever experienced "absolute war." In this or that struggle, we endure (or commit) this or that brutality, which can always be described in concrete terms. It is the same with hell: I cannot conceptualize infinite pain without thinking of whips and scorpions, hot irons, other people. Now, what is it that we think about when we say, war is hell? What aspects of warfare lead us to regard its initiation as a criminal act?

The same questions can be introduced in another way. War is not usefully described as an act of force without some specification of the context in which the act takes place and from which it derives its meaning. Here the case is the same as with other human activities (politics and commerce, for example): it's not what people do, the physical motions they go through, that are crucial, but the institutions, practices, conventions that they make. Hence the social and historical conditions that "modify" war are not to be considered as accidental or external to war itself, for war is a social creation. At particular points in time, it takes shape in particular ways, and sometimes at least in ways that resist the "utmost exertion of forces." What is war and what is not-war are in fact something that people decide (I don't mean by taking a vote). As both anthropological and historical accounts suggest, they can decide, and in a considerable variety of cultural settings they have decided, that war is limited war—that is, they have built certain notions about who can fight, what tactics are acceptable, when battle has to be broken off, and what prerogatives go with victory into the idea of war itself.* Limited war is always specific to a time and

---

*This, of course, is exactly what Clausewitz wants to deny. In technical terms, he is arguing that war is never an activity constituted by its rules. War is never like

place, but so is every escalation, including the escalation beyond which war is hell.

THE LIMIT OF CONSENT

Some wars are not hell, and it will be best to begin with them. The first and most obvious example is the competitive struggle of aristocratic young men, a tournament on a larger scale and with no presiding officer in the stands. Examples can be found in Africa, ancient Greece, Japan, and feudal Europe. Here is a "contention by arms" that has often captured the imagination, not only of children, but also of romantic adults. John Ruskin made it his own ideal: "creative or foundational war is that in which the natural restlessness and love of contest are disciplined, by consent, into modes of beautiful—though it may be fatal—play. . . ."[5] Creative war may not be terribly bloody, but that is not the crucial thing about it. I have read accounts of tournaments that make them sound brutal enough, but no such account would lead anyone to say that it was a crime to organize a tournament. What rules out such a claim, I think, is Ruskin's phrase "by consent." His beautiful aristocrats do what they choose to do, and that is why no poet ever described their deaths in terms comparable to those of Wilfred Owen writing of infantrymen in World War I:[6]

What passing-bells for these who die as cattle?

"To the youths who voluntarily adopt it as their profession," writes Ruskin, "[war] has always been a grand pastime. . . ." We take their choice as a sign

---

a duel. The social practise of duelling includes and accounts for only those acts of violence specified in the rulebook or the customary code. If I wound my opponent, shoot his second, and then beat him to death with a stick, I am not duelling with him; I am murdering him. But similar brutalities in war, though they violate the rules, are still regarded as acts of war (war crimes). Hence there is a formal or linguistic sense in which military action is limitless, and this has undoubtedly influenced our understanding of such action. At the same time, however, "war" and related words are at least sometimes used in a more restrictive sense, as in the famous speech of Sir Henry Campbell-Bannerman, one of the leaders of the Liberal Party in Britain during the Boer War: "When is war not war? When it is fought by methods of barbarism. . . ." We do still refer to the Boer War, but the argument is not idiosyncratic. I will provide other examples later on.

that what they are choosing cannot be awful, even if it looks that way to us. Perhaps they ennoble the brutal melee; perhaps not; but if this kind of war were hellish, these well-born young men would be doing something else.*

A similar argument can be made whenever fighting is voluntary. Nor does it matter a great deal if the men involved don't choose to fight, so long as they can choose to break off fighting without dire consequences. In certain primitive societies, whole age cohorts of young males go off to battle; individuals cannot avoid combat without exposing themselves to dishonor and ostracism. But there is no effective social pressure or military discipline on the battlefield itself. And then there takes place, as Hobbes says, "on both sides a running away."[7] When running away is acceptable, as it often is in primitive warfare, battles will obviously be short and casualties few. There is nothing that resembles "the utmost exertion of forces." Those men who don't run away, but stand and fight, do so not because of the necessities of their case, but freely, as a matter of choice. They seek out the excitement of battle, perhaps because they enjoy it, and their subsequent fate, even if it is very painful, can't be called unjust.

The case of mercenaries and professional soldiers is more complex and needs to be examined with some care. In Renaissance Italy, wars were fought by mercenary soldiers recruited by the great *condottieri*, partly as a business venture, partly as a political speculation. City-states and principalities had to rely on such men because the political culture of the time did not allow for effective coercion. There were no conscript armies. The result was warfare of a very limited sort, since recruits were expensive and each army represented a considerable capital investment. Battle became a matter largely of tactical maneuver; physical confrontation was rare; relatively few soldiers were killed. Wars had to be won, as two of the *condottieri* wrote, "rather by industry and cunning than by actual clash of arms."[8] Thus the great defeat of the Florentines at Zagonara: "no deaths occurred [in the battle]," Machiavelli tells us, "except those of Lodovico degli Obizi and two of his men, who, having fallen from their horses, were drowned in the mud."[9] But, once again, I don't want to stress the limited character

---

*We can glimpse the mood of the happy warrior in a letter that Rupert Brooke wrote to a friend at the very beginning of World War I, before he knew what it would be like: "Come and die. It'll be great fun." (Quoted in Malcolm Cowley, *A Second Flowering*, New York, 1974, p. 6.)

of the fighting but something prior to that, from which the limits follow: a certain sort of freedom in choosing war. Mercenary soldiers signed up on terms, and if they could not actually choose their campaigns and tactics, they could to some degree fix the cost of their services and so condition the choices of their leaders. Given that freedom, they might have fought very bloody battles and the spectacle would not lead us to say that war was a crime. A fight between mercenary armies is undoubtedly a bad way of settling political disputes, but we judge it bad for the sake of the people whose fate is being settled, not for the sake of the soldiers themselves.

Our judgments are very different, however, if the mercenary armies are recruited (as they most often are) from among desperately impoverished men, who can find no other way of feeding themselves and their families except by signing up. Ruskin makes this point well when he tells his aristocratic warriors: "Remember, whatever virtue and goodliness there may be in this game of war, rightly played, there is none when you . . . play it with a multitude of small human pawns . . . [when you] urge your peasant millions into gladiatorial war. . . ."[10] Then battle becomes a "circus of slaughter" in the midst of which no consensual discipline is possible, and those who die do so without ever having had a chance to live in another way. Hell is the right name for the risks they never chose and the agony and death they endure; the men responsible for that agony are rightly called criminals.

Mercenaries are professional soldiers who sell their services on the open market, but there are other professionals who serve only their own prince or people and, though they may earn their bread by soldiering, disdain the name of mercenary. "We're either officers who serve their Tsar and country," says Prince Andrey in *War and Peace*, "and rejoice in the success and grieve at the defeat of the common cause, or we're hirelings who have no interest in our master's business."[11] The distinction is too gross; in fact there are intermediate positions; but the more a soldier fights because he is committed to a "common cause," the more likely we are to regard it as a crime to force him to fight. We assume that his commitment is to the safety of his country, that he fights only when it is threatened, and that then he has to fight (he has been "put to it"): it is his duty and not a free choice. He is like a doctor who risks his life during an epidemic, using professional skills he chose to acquire but whose acquisition is not a sign that he hopes for epidemics. On the other hand, professional soldiers are sometimes exactly like those aristocratic warriors who relish battle, driven more by a lust for victory than by patriotic conviction, and then we may well be unmoved by their deaths. At least we will not say, they would not want us to say, what Owen says of his comrades in the trenches, that "one dies of war like any old disease."[12] They died instead of their own free will.

War is hell whenever men are forced to fight, whenever the limit of consent is breached. That means, of course, that it is hell most of the time; throughout most of recorded history, there have been political organizations capable of marshalling armies and driving soldiers into battle. It is the absence of political discipline or its ineffectiveness in detail that opens the way for "creative war." The examples I have given are best understood as limiting cases, establishing the boundaries of hell. We ourselves are old inhabitants—even if we live in democratic states where the government that decides to fight or not to fight is popularly elected. For I am not considering now the legitimacy of that government. Nor am I immediately interested in the willingness of a potential soldier to vote for a war he has been led to believe is necessary or to volunteer for it. What is important here is the extent to which war (as a profession) or combat (at this or that moment in time) is a personal choice that the soldier makes on his own and for essentially private reasons. That kind of choosing effectively disappears as soon as fighting becomes a legal obligation and a patriotic duty. Then "the waste of the life of the combatants is one which," as the philosopher T. H. Green has written, "the power of the state compels. This is equally true whether the army is raised by voluntary enlistment or by conscription."* For the state decrees that an army of a certain size be raised, and it sets out to find the necessary men, using all the techniques of coercion and persuasion at its disposal. And the men it finds, precisely because they go to war under constraint or as a matter of conscience, can

---

*Green is arguing against the proposition I have hitherto maintained: that no wrong is done in war if "the persons killed are voluntary combatants." He denies this on the grounds that a soldier's life is not merely his own. "The individual's right to life is but the other side of the right which society has in his living." But that, it seems to me, is only true in certain sorts of societies; it is hardly an argument that could have been made to a feudal warrior. Green goes on to argue, more plausibly, that in his own society it makes little sense to talk of soldiers fighting voluntarily: war is now a state action. The chapter on "The Right of the State over the Individual in War" in Green's *Principles of Political Obligation*, provides an especially clear description of the ways in which moral responsibility is mediated in the modern state; I have relied on it often in this and later chapters.

no longer moderate their battles; the battles are no longer theirs. They are political instruments, they obey orders, and the practice of war is shaped at a higher level. Perhaps they really are obligated to obey orders in this or that case, but war is radically changed by the fact that they do so generally. The change is best represented for the modern period (though there are historical analogues) by the effects of conscription. "Hitherto soldiers had been costly, now they were cheap; battles had been avoided, now they were sought, and however heavy were the losses, they could rapidly be made good by the muster-roll."[13]

Napoleon is said to have boasted to Metternich that he could afford to lose 30,000 men a month. Perhaps he could have lost that many and still have maintained political support at home. But he could not have done so, I think, had he had to ask the men he was about to "lose." Soldiers might agree to such losses in a war forced upon them by the enemy, a war of national defense, but not in the sorts of wars that Napoleon fought. The need to seek their consent (whatever the form in which it was sought and given or not given) would surely limit the occasions of war, and if there were any chance at all of reciprocity from the other side, it would limit its means too. This is the sort of consent I have in mind. Political self-determination is not, judging from twentieth-century history, an adequate substitute, though it isn't easy to think of one that would be better. In any case, it is when individual consent fails that "acts of force" lose whatever appeal they previously had and become the constant object of moral condemnation. And after that, war also tends to escalate in its means, not necessarily beyond all limits, but certainly beyond those limits that ordinary humanity, as free of political loyalty as of political constraint, would establish if it could.

THE TYRANNY OF WAR

War is most often a form of tyranny. It is best described by paraphrasing Trotsky's aphorism about the dialectic: "You may not be interested in war, but war is interested in you." The stakes are high, and the interest that military organizations take in an individual who would prefer to be somewhere else, doing something else, is frightening indeed. Hence the peculiar horror of war: it is a social practice in which force is used by and against men as loyal or constrained members of states and not as individuals who choose their own enterprises and activities. When we say, war is hell, it is the victims of the fighting that we have in mind. In fact, then, war is the very opposite of hell in the theological sense, and is hellish only when the opposition is strict. For in hell, presumably, only those people suffer who deserve to suffer, who have chosen activities for which punishment is the appropriate divine response, knowing that this is so. But the greater number by far of those who suffer in war have made no comparable choice.

I do not mean to call them "innocent." That word has come to have a special meaning in our moral discourse. It doesn't refer there to the participants but to the bystanders of battle, and so the class of innocent men and women is only a subset (though it is often a frighteningly large subset) of all those in whom war takes an interest without asking their consent. The rules of war by and large protect only the subset, for reasons I will have to consider later on. But war is hell even when the rules are observed, even when only soldiers are killed and civilians are consistently spared. Surely no experience of modern warfare has etched its horror so deeply in our minds as the fighting in the trenches of World War I—and in the trenches civilian lives were rarely at risk. The distinction of combatants and bystanders is enormously important in the theory of war, but our first and most fundamental moral judgment does not depend upon it. For in one sense at least, soldiers in battle and nonparticipating civilians are not so different: the soldiers would almost certainly be nonparticipants if they could.

The tyranny of war is often described as if war itself were the tyrant, a natural force like flood or famine or, personified, a brutal giant stalking his human prey, as in these lines from a poem by Thomas Sackville:[14]

> Lastly stood War, in glittering arms y-clad,
> With visage grim, stern looks, and blackly hued;
> In his right hand a naked sword he had
> That to the hilts was all with blood embrued,
> And in his left (that kings and kingdoms rued)
>   Famine and fire he held, and therewithal
>   He razed towns, and threw down towers and all.

Here is the Grim Reaper in uniform, armed with a sword instead of a scythe. The poetic image enters also into moral and political thought, but only, I think, as a kind of ideology, obscuring our critical judgment. For it is a piece of mystification to represent tyrannical power as an abstract force. In battle as in politics, tyranny is always a relation among persons or groups of persons. The tyranny of war is a peculiarly complex relation because coercion is common on both sides. Sometimes, however, it is possible to distinguish the sides and to identify the statesmen and soldiers who first took the naked sword to hand. Wars are not self-starting. They may "break out," like an accidental fire, under conditions difficult to analyze and where the attribution of responsibility seems impossible. But usually they are more like arson than accident: war has human agents as well as human victims.

Those agents, when we can identify them, are properly called criminals. Their moral character is determined by the moral reality of the activity they force others to engage in (whether or not they engage in it themselves). They are responsible for the pain and death that follow from their decisions, or at least for the pain and death of all those persons who do not choose war as a personal enterprise. In contemporary international law, their crime is called aggression, and I will consider it later on under that name. But we can understand it initially as the exercise of tyrannical power, first over their own people and then, through the mediation of the opposing state's recruitment and conscription offices, over the people they have attacked. Now, tyranny of this sort rarely encounters domestic resistance. Sometimes the war is opposed by local political forces, but the opposition almost never extends to the actual exercise of military power. Though mutinies are common in the long history of war, they are more like peasant *jacqueries,* quickly and bloodily suppressed, than revolutionary struggles. Most often, real opposition comes only from the enemy. It is the men and women on the other side who are most likely to recognize and resent the tyranny of war; and whenever they do that, the contest takes on a new significance.

When soldiers believe themselves to be fighting against aggression, war is no longer a condition to be endured. It is a crime they can resist—though they must suffer its effects in order to resist it—and they can hope for a victory that is something more than an escape from the immediate brutality of battle. The experience of war as hell generates what might be called a higher ambition: one doesn't aim to settle with the enemy but to defeat and punish him and, if not to abolish the tyranny of war, at least to reduce the probability of future oppression. And once one is fighting for purposes of this sort, it becomes terribly important to win. The conviction that victory is morally critical plays an important part in the so-called "logic of war." We don't call war hell because it is fought without restraint. It is more nearly right to say that, when certain restraints are passed, the hellishness of war drives us to break with every remaining restraint in order to win. Here is the ultimate tyranny: those who resist aggression are forced to imitate, and perhaps even to exceed, the brutality of the aggressor.

General Sherman and the Burning of Atlanta

We are now in a position to understand what Sherman had in mind when he first announced that war is hell. He wasn't merely describing the awfulness of the experience, nor was he denying the possibility of moral judgment. He made such judgments freely, and he surely thought of himself as a righteous soldier. His maxim sums up, with admirable brevity, a whole way of thinking about war—a one-sided and partial way of thinking, I shall argue, but powerful nonetheless. In his view, war is entirely and singularly the crime of those who begin it, and soldiers resisting aggression (or rebellion) can never be blamed for anything they do that brings victory closer. The sentence *War is hell* is doctrine, not description: it is a moral argument, an attempt at self-justification. Sherman was claiming to be innocent of all those actions (though they were his own actions) for which he was so severely attacked: the bombardment of Atlanta, the forced evacuation of its inhabitants and the burning of the city, the march through Georgia. When he issued the order for the evacuation and burning of Atlanta, the city's aldermen and the Confederate commander, General Hood, protested his plans: "And now, sir," wrote Hood, "permit me to say that the unprecedented measure you propose transcends, in studied and ingenious cruelty, all acts ever before brought to my attention in the dark history of war." Sherman replied that war is indeed dark. "War is cruelty and you cannot refine it."[15] And therefore, he went on, "those who brought war into our country deserve all the curses and maledictions a people can pour out." But he himself deserves no curses at all. "I know I had no hand in making this war." He is only fighting it, not by choice but because he has to. He has been forced to use force, and the burning of Atlanta (so that the city could not again serve as a military depot for Confederate forces) is simply one more example of that use, one of the entailments of war. It is cruel, no doubt, but the cruelty isn't his own; it belongs, so to speak, to the men of the Confederacy: "You who, in the midst of peace and prosperity, have plunged a nation into war. . . . " The Confederate leaders can easily restore peace by yielding obedience to federal law, but he can do so only by military action.

Sherman's argument expresses the anger that is commonly directed against those who begin a war and inflict its tyrannies on the rest of us. We disagree, of course, when it comes to giving the tyrants a proper name. But that disagreement is intense and heated only because we agree on the moral stakes. What is at issue is responsibility for death and destruction, and Sherman is by no means the only general to take a lively interest in such matters. Nor is he the only general to think that if his cause is just he cannot be blamed for the death and destruction he spreads around him— for war is hell.

It is the Clausewitzian idea of limitlessness that is at work here, and if that idea is right, there would indeed be no response to Sherman's argument. But the tyranny of war is no more limitless than is political tyranny. Just as we can charge a tyrant with particular crimes over and above the crime of ruling without consent, so we can recognize and condemn particular criminal acts within the hell of war. When we answer the question, "Who started this war?" we have not finished distributing responsibility for the suffering that soldiers inflict. There are further arguments to make. That's why General Sherman, though he insisted that the cruelty of war could not be refined, claimed nevertheless to be refining it. "God will judge . . . ," he wrote, "whether it be more humane to fight with a town full of women [and children] at our back or to remove them in time to places of safety among their own friends and people." This is another kind of justification; and whether or not it is made in good faith, it suggests (what is certainly true) that Sherman had some responsibility for the people of Atlanta, even though he did not begin the war of which they were victims. When we focus exclusively on the fact of aggression, we are likely to lose sight of that responsibility and to talk as if there were only one morally relevant decision to be made in the course of a war: to attack or not to attack (to resist or not to resist). Sherman wants to judge war only at its outermost boundaries. But there is a great deal to be said about its interior regions, as he himself admits. Even in hell, it is possible to be more or less humane, to fight with or without restraint. We must try to understand how this can be so.

3

THE RULES OF WAR

THE MORAL EQUALITY OF SOLDIERS

Among soldiers who choose to fight, restraints of various sorts arise easily and, one might say, naturally, the product of mutual respect and recognition. The stories of chivalric knights are for the most part stories, but there can be no doubt that a military code was widely shared in the later Middle Ages and sometimes honored. The code was designed for the convenience of the aristocratic warriors, but it also reflected their sense of themselves as persons of a certain sort, engaged in activities that were freely chosen. Chivalry marked off knights from mere ruffians and bandits and also from peasant soldiers who bore arms as a necessity. I suppose that it survives today: some sense of military honor is still the creed of the professional soldier, the sociological if not the lineal descendent of the feudal knight. But notions of honor and chivalry seem to play only a small part in contemporary combat. In the literature of war, the contrast between "then and now" is commonly made—not very accurately, but with a certain truth, as in this poem by Louis Simpson:[1]

At Malplaquet and Waterloo
They were polite and proud,
They primed their guns with billets-doux
And, as they fired, bowed.
At Appomattox too, it seems

Some things were understood...
But at Verdun and at Bastogne
There was a great recoil,
The blood was bitter to the bone
The trigger to the soul....

Chivalry, it is often said, was the victim of democratic revolution and of revolutionary war: popular passion overcame aristocratic honor.[2] That draws the line before Waterloo and Appomattox, though still not quite correctly. It is the success of coercion that makes war ugly. Democracy is a factor only insofar as it increases the legitimacy of the state and then the effectiveness of its coercive power, not because the people in arms are a bloodthirsty mob fired by political zeal and committed to total war (in contrast to their officers, who would fight with decorum if they could). It is not what the people do when they enter the arena of battle that turns war into a "circus of slaughter," but, as I have already argued, the mere fact that they are there. Soldiers died by the thousands at Verdun and the Somme simply because they were available, their lives nationalized, as it were, by the modern state. They didn't choose to throw themselves at barbed wire and machine guns in fits of patriotic enthusiasm. The blood is bitter to their bones, too; they, too, would fight with decorum if they could. Their patriotism is, of course, a partial explanation of their availability. The discipline of the state is not merely imposed on them; it is also a discipline they accept, thinking that they have to for the sake of their families and their country. But the common features of contemporary combat: hatred for the enemy, impatience with all restraint, zeal for victory—these are the products of war itself whenever masses of men have to be mobilized for battle. They are as much the contribution of modern warfare to democratic politics as of democracy to war.

In any case, the death of chivalry is not the end of moral judgment. We still hold soldiers to certain standards, even though they fight unwillingly—in fact, precisely because we assume that they all fight unwillingly. The military code is reconstructed under the conditions of modern warfare so that it comes to rest not on aristocratic freedom but on military servitude. Sometimes freedom and servitude co-exist, and then we can study the difference between them in clinical detail. Whenever the game of war is revived, the elaborate courtesies of the chivalric age are revived with it— as among aviators in World War I, for example, who imagined themselves (and who have survived in the popular imagination) as airborne knights. Compared to the serfs on the ground, these were aristocrats indeed: they fought in accordance with a strict code of conduct that they invented themselves.[3] There was thralldom in the trenches, however, and mutual recognition took a very different form. Briefly, on Christmas Day 1914, German and French troops came together, drank and sang together, in the no-man's land between their lines. But such moments are rare in recent history, and they are not occasions for moral invention. The modern rules of war depend upon an abstract rather than a practical fellowship.

Soldiers cannot endure modern warfare for long without blaming someone for their pain and suffering. While it may be an example of what Marxists call "false consciousness" that they do not blame the ruling class of their own or of the enemy country, the fact is that their condemnation focuses most immediately on the men with whom they are engaged. The level of hatred is high in the trenches. That is why enemy wounded are often left to die and prisoners are killed—like murderers lynched by vigilantes—as if the soldiers on the other side were personally responsible for the war. At the same time, however, we know that they are not responsible. Hatred is interrupted or overridden by a more reflective understanding, which one finds expressed again and again in letters and war memoirs. It is the sense that the enemy soldier, though his war may well be criminal, is nevertheless as blameless as oneself. Armed, he is an enemy; but he isn't *my* enemy in any specific sense; the war itself isn't a relation between persons but between political entities and their human instruments. These human instruments are not comrades-in-arms in the old style, members of the fellowship of warriors; they are "poor sods, just like me," trapped in a war they didn't make. I find in them my moral equals. That is not to say simply that I acknowledge their humanity, for it is not the recognition of fellow men that explains the rules of war; criminals are men too. It is precisely the recognition of men who are not criminals.

They can try to kill me, and I can try to kill them. But it is wrong to cut the throats of their wounded or to shoot them down when they are trying to surrender. These judgments are clear enough, I think, and they suggest that war is still, somehow, a rule-governed activity, a world of permissions and prohibitions—a moral world, therefore, in the midst of hell. Though there is no license for war-makers, there is a license for soldiers, and they hold it without regard to which side they are on; it is the first and most important of their war rights. They are entitled to kill, *not anyone*, but men whom we know to be victims. We could hardly understand such a title if we did not recognize that they are victims too. Hence the moral reality of war can be summed up in this way: when soldiers fight freely, choosing one another as enemies and designing their own battles, their war is not a crime; when they fight without freedom, their war is not their crime. In both cases, military conduct is governed by rules; but in the first the rules rest on mutuality and consent, in the second on a shared servitude. The first case raises no difficulties; the second is more problematic. We can best explore its problems, I think, if we turn from the trenches and the front lines to the general staff at the rear, and from the war against the Kaiser to the war against Hitler—for at that level and in that struggle, the recognition of "men who are not criminals" is hard indeed.

The Case of Hitler's Generals

In 1942, General von Arnim was captured in North Africa, and it was proposed by members of Dwight Eisenhower's staff that the American commander "should observe the custom of by-gone days" and permit von Arnim to visit him before he was sent into captivity. Historically, such visits were not merely matters of courtesy; they were occasions for the reaffirmation of the military code. Thus General von Ravenstein, captured by the British that same year, reports: "I was taken to see . . . Auchinleck himself in his office. He shook hands with me and said: 'I know you well by name. You and your division have fought with chivalry.'"[4] Eisenhower, however, refused to allow the visit. In his memoirs, he explained his reasons:[5]

> The custom had its origin in the fact that the mercenary soldiers of old had no real enmity toward their opponents. Both sides fought for love of a fight, out of a sense of duty or, more probably, for money. . . . The tradition that all professional soldiers are comrades in arms has . . . persisted to this day. For me, World War II was far too personal a thing to entertain such feelings. Daily as it progressed there grew within me the conviction that, as never before . . . the forces that stood for human good and men's rights were . . . confronted by a completely evil conspiracy with which no compromise could be tolerated.

On this view, it doesn't matter whether or not von Arnim had fought well; his crime was to have fought at all. And similarly, it may not matter how

General Eisenhower fights. Against an evil conspiracy, what is crucial is to win. Chivalry loses its rationale, and there are no limits left except "the limitations of force itself."

That was Sherman's view too, but it does not account for the judgments that we make of his conduct, or of Eisenhower's, or even of von Arnim's and von Ravenstein's. Consider now the better-known case of Erwin Rommel: he, too, was one of Hitler's generals, and it is hard to imagine that he could have escaped the moral infamy of the war he fought. Yet he was, so we are told by one biographer after another, an honorable man. "While many of his colleagues and peers in the German army surrendered their honor by collusion with the iniquities of Nazism, Rommel was never defiled." He concentrated, like the professional he was, on "the soldier's task of fighting." And when he fought, he maintained the rules of war. He fought a bad war well, not only militarily but also morally. "It was Rommel who burned the Commando Order issued by Hitler on 28 October 1942, which laid down that all enemy soldiers encountered behind the German line were to be killed at once. . . ."[6] He was one of Hitler's generals, but he did not shoot prisoners. Is such a man a comrade? Can one treat him with courtesy, can one shake his hand? These are the fine points of moral conduct; I do not know how they might be resolved, though I am sympathetic with Eisenhower's resolution. But I am sure, nevertheless, that Rommel should be praised for burning the Commando Order, and everyone who writes about these matters seems equally sure, and that implies something very important about the nature of war.

It would be very odd to praise Rommel for not killing prisoners unless we simultaneously refused to blame him for Hitler's aggressive wars. For otherwise he is simply a criminal, and all the fighting he does is murder or attempted murder, whether he aims at soldiers in battle or at prisoners or at civilians. The chief British prosecutor at Nuremberg put this argument into the language of international law when he said, "The killing of combatants is justifiable . . . only where the war itself is legal. But where the war is illegal . . . there is nothing to justify the killing and these murders are not to be distinguished from those of any other lawless robber bands."[7] And then Rommel's case would be exactly like that of a man who invades someone else's home and kills only some of the inhabitants, sparing the children, say, or an aged grandmother: a murderer, no doubt, though not one without a drop of human kindness. But we don't view Rommel that way: why not? The reason has to do with the distinction of *jus ad bellum* and *jus in bello*. We draw a line between the war itself, for which soldiers are not responsible, and the conduct of the war, for which they are responsible, at least within their own sphere of activity. Generals may well straddle the line, but that only suggests that we know pretty well where it should be drawn. We draw it by recognizing the nature of political obedience. Rommel was a servant, not a ruler, of the German state; he did not choose the wars he fought but, like Prince Andrey, served his "Tsar and country." We still have misgivings in his case, and will continue to have them, for he was more than just unlucky in his "Tsar and country." But by and large we don't blame a soldier, even a general, who fights for his own government. He is not a member of a robber band, a willful wrongdoer, but a loyal and obedient subject and citizen, acting sometimes at great personal risk in a way he thinks is right. We allow him to say what an English soldier says in Shakespeare's *Henry V*: "We know enough if we know we are the king's men. Our obedience to the king wipes the crime of it out of us."[8] Not that his obedience can never be criminal; for when he violates the rules of war, superior orders are no defense. The atrocities that he commits are his own; the war is not. It is conceived, both in international law and in ordinary moral judgment, as the king's business—a matter of state policy, not of individual volition, except when the individual is the king.

It might, however, be thought a matter of individual volition whether particular men join the army and participate in the war. Catholic writers have long argued that they ought not to volunteer, ought not to serve at all, if they know the war to be unjust. But the knowledge required by Catholic doctrine is hard to come by; and in case of doubt, argues the best of the Schoolmen, Francisco de Vitoria, subjects must fight—the guilt falling, as in *Henry V*, on their leaders. Vitoria's argument suggests how firmly political life is set, even in the pre-modern state, against the very idea of volition in time of war. "A prince is not able," he writes, "and ought not always to render reasons for the war to his subjects, and if the subjects cannot serve in the war except they are first satisfied of its justice, the state would fall into grave peril. . . ."[9] Today, of course, most princes work hard to satisfy their subjects of the justice of their wars; they "render reasons," though not always honest ones. It takes courage to doubt these reasons, or to doubt them in public; and so long as they are only doubted, most men will be persuaded (by arguments something like Vitoria's) to fight. Their routine habits of law-abidingness, their fear, their patriotism, their moral investment in the state, all favor that course. Or, alternatively, they are so terribly young when the disciplinary system of the state catches them up and sends them into war that they can hardly be said to make a moral decision at all:[10]

> From my mother's sleep I fell into the State.

And then how can we blame them for (what we perceive to be) the wrongful character of their war?*

Soldiers are not, however, entirely without volition. Their will is independent and effective only within a limited sphere, and for most of them that sphere is narrow. But except in extreme cases, it never completely disappears. And at those moments in the course of the fighting when they must choose, like Rommel, to kill prisoners or let them live, they are not mere victims or servants bound to obedience; they are responsible for what they do. We shall have to qualify that responsibility when we come to consider it in detail, for war is still hell, and hell is a tyranny where soldiers are subject to all sorts of duress. But the judgments we actually make of their conduct demonstrate, I think, that within that tyranny we have carved out a constitutional regime: even the pawns of war have rights and obligations.

During the past hundred years, these rights and obligations have been specified in treaties and agreements, written into international law. The very states that enlist the pawns of war have stipulated the moral character of their mutual slaughter. Initially, this stipulation was not based upon any notion of the equality of soldiers but upon the equality of sovereign states, which claimed for themselves the same right to fight (right to make war) that individual soldiers more obviously possess. The argument that I have

---

*But these young men, Robert Nozick argues, "are certainly not encouraged to think for themselves by the practice of absolving them of all responsibility for their actions within the rules of war." That is right; they are not. But we cannot blame them in order to encourage the others unless they are actually blameworthy. Nozick insists that they are: "It is a soldier's responsibility to determine if his side's cause is just. . . . " The conventional refusal to impose that responsibility flatly and across the board is "morally elitist." (*Anarchy, State, and Utopia*, New York, 1974, p. 100.) But it isn't elitist merely to recognize the existence of authority structures and socialization processes in the political community, and it may be morally insensitive not to. I do agree with Nozick that "some bucks stop with each of us." A great deal of this book is concerned with trying to say which ones those are.

made on behalf of soldiers was first made on behalf of states—or rather on behalf of their leaders, who, we were told, are never willful criminals, whatever the character of the wars they begin, but statesmen serving the national interest as best they can. When I discuss the theory of aggression and of responsibility for aggression, I will have to explain why that is an inadequate description of what statesmen do.[11] For now, it is enough to say that this view of sovereignty and political leadership, which was never in accord with ordinary moral judgment, has also lost its legal standing, replaced in the years since World War I by the formal designation of war-making as a criminal activity. However, the rules of engagement have not been replaced but expanded and elaborated, so that we now have both a ban on war and a code of military conduct. The dualism of our moral perceptions is established in the law.

War is a "legal condition which equally permits two or more groups to carry on a conflict by armed force."[12] It is also, and for our purposes more importantly, a moral condition, involving the same permissiveness, not in fact at the level of sovereign states, but at the level of armies and individual soldiers. Without the equal right to kill, war as a rule-governed activity would disappear and be replaced by crime and punishment, by evil conspiracies and military law enforcement. That disappearance seems to be heralded by the United Nations Charter, where the word "war" does not appear but only "aggression," "self-defense," "international enforcement," and so on. But even the UN's "police action" in Korea was still a war, since the soldiers who fought in it were moral equals even if the states were not. The rules of war were as relevant there as in any other "conflict by armed force," and they were equally relevant to the aggressor, the victim, and the police.

Two Sorts of Rules

The rules of war consist of two clusters of prohibitions attached to the central principle that soldiers have an equal right to kill. The first cluster specifies when and how they can kill, the second whom they can kill. My chief concern is with the second, for there the formulation and reformulation of the rules reach to one of the hardest questions in the theory of war—that is, how those victims of war who can be attacked and killed are to be distinguished from those who cannot. I don't believe that this question must be answered in this or that specific way if war is to be a moral condition. It is necessary, however, that at any particular moment there be an answer.

War is distinguishable from murder and massacre only when restrictions are established on the reach of battle.

The first set of rules does not involve any such fundamental issue. Rules specifying how and when soldiers can be killed are by no means unimportant, and yet the morality of war would not be radically transformed were they to be abolished altogether. Consider, for example, those battles described by anthropologists in which warriors fight with bows and unfeathered arrows. The arrows fly less accurately than they would if they were feathered; they can be dodged; few men are killed.[13] It is clearly a good rule, then, that arrows not be feathered, and we may fairly condemn the warrior who first arms himself with the superior and forbidden weapon and hits his enemy. Yet the man he kills was liable to be killed in any case, and a collective (intertribal) decision to fight with feathered arrows would not violate any basic moral principle. The case is the same with all other rules of this kind: that soldiers be preceded into battle by a herald carrying a red flag, that fighting always be broken off at sunset, that ambushes and surprise attacks be prohibited, and so on. Any rule that limits the intensity and duration of combat or the suffering of soldiers is to be welcomed, but none of these restraints seem crucial to the idea of war as a moral condition. They are circumstantial in the literal sense of that word, highly particularized and local to a specific time and place. Even if in practice they endure for many years, they are always susceptible to the transformations brought about by social change, technological innovation, and foreign conquest.*

The second set of rules does not seem similarly susceptible. At least, the general structure of its provisions seems to persist without reference to social systems and technologies—as if the rules involved were (as I think they are) more closely connected to universal notions of right and wrong. Their tendency is to set certain classes of people outside the permissible range of warfare, so that killing any of their members is not a legitimate act of war but a crime. Though their details vary from place to place, these rules point toward the general conception of war as a *combat between combatants*, a conception that turns up again and again in anthropological

---

*They are also susceptible to the kind of reciprocal violation legitimized by the doctrine of reprisal: violated by one side, they can be violated by the other. But this does not seem to be true of the other sort of rules, described below. See the discussion of reprisals in chapter 13.

and historical accounts. It is most dramatically exemplified when war is actually a combat between military champions, as among many primitive peoples, or in the Greek epics, or in the biblical tale of David and Goliath. "Let no man's heart fail within him," says David, "thy servant will go and fight this Philistine."[14] Once such a contest has been agreed upon, soldiers themselves are protected from the hell of war. In the Middle Ages, single combat was advocated for precisely this reason: "Better for one to fall than the whole army."[15] More often, however, protection has been offered only to those people who are not trained and prepared for war, who do not fight or cannot: women and children, priests, old men, the members of neutral tribes, cities, or states, wounded or captured soldiers.* What all these groups have in common is that they are not currently engaged in the business of war. Depending on one's social or cultural perspective, killing them may appear wanton, unchivalrous, dishonorable, brutal, or murderous. But it is very likely that some general principle is at work in all these judgments, connecting immunity from attack with military disengagement. Any satisfactory account of the moral reality of war must specify that principle and say something about its force. I shall attempt to do both these things later on.

The historical specifications of the principle are, however, conventional in character, and the war rights and obligations of soldiers follow from the conventions and not (directly) from the principle, whatever its force. Once again, war is a social creation. The rules actually observed or violated in this or that time and place are necessarily a complex product, mediated by cultural and religious norms, social structures, formal and informal bargaining between belligerent powers, and so on. Hence, the details of noncombatant immunity are likely to seem as arbitrary as the rules that determine when battles should start and stop or what weapons may be used. They are more important by far, but similarly subject to social revision. Exactly like law in domestic society, they will often represent an incomplete or distorted embodiment of the relevant moral

---

*The lists are often more specific and more picturesque than this, reflecting the character of a particular culture. Here is an example from an ancient Indian text, according to which the following groups of people are not to be subjected to the exigencies of battle: "Those who look on without taking part, those afflicted with grief . . . those who are asleep, thirsty, or fatigued or are walking along the road, or have a task on hand unfinished, or who are proficient in fine art." (S. V. Viswanatha, *International Law in Ancient India*, Bombay, 1925, p. 156.)

principle. They are subject, then, to philosophical criticism. Indeed, criticism is a crucial part of the historical process through which the rules are made. We might say that war is a philosophical creation. Long before philosophers are satisfied with it, however, soldiers are bound by its canons. And they are equally bound, because of their own equality, and without reference to the content or the incompleteness of the canons.

THE WAR CONVENTION

I propose to call the set of articulated norms, customs, professional codes, legal precepts, religious and philosophical principles, and reciprocal arrangements that shape our judgments of military conduct *the war convention*. It is important to stress that it is our judgments that are at issue here, not conduct itself. We cannot get at the substance of the convention by studying combat behavior, any more than we can understand the norms of friendship by studying the way friends actually treat one another. The norms are apparent, instead, in the expectations friends have, the complaints they make, the hypocrisies they adopt. So it is with war: relations between combatants have a normative structure that is revealed in what they say (and what the rest of us say) rather than in what they do—though no doubt what they do, as with friends, is affected by what they say. Harsh words are the immediate sanctions of the war convention, sometimes accompanied or followed by military attacks, economic blockades, reprisals, war crimes trials, and so on. But neither the words nor the actions have any single authoritative source; and, finally, it is the words that are decisive—the "judgment of history," as it is called, which means the judgment of men and women arguing until some rough consensus is reached.

The terms of our judgments are most explicitly set forth in positive international law: the work of politicians and lawyers acting as representatives of sovereign states, and then of jurists codifying their agreements and searching out the rationale that underlies them. But international law arises out of a radically decentralized legislative system, cumbrous, unresponsive, and without a parallel judicial system to establish the specific details of the legal code. For that reason, the legal handbooks are not the only place to find the war convention, and its actual existence is demonstrated not by the existence of the handbooks but by the moral arguments that everywhere accompany the practice of war. The common law of combat is developed through a kind of practical casuistry. Hence the method of this book: we look to the lawyers for general formulas, but to historical cases and actual debates for those particular judgments that both reflect the war convention and constitute its vital force. I don't mean to suggest that our judgments, even over time, have an unambiguous collective form. Nor, however, are they idiosyncratic and private in character. They are socially patterned, and the patterning is religious, cultural, and political, as well as legal. The task of the moral theorist is to study the pattern as a whole, reaching for its deepest reasons.

Among professional soldiers, the war convention often finds advocates of a special kind. Though chivalry is dead and fighting unfree, professional soldiers remain sensitive (or some of them do) to those limits and restraints that distinguish their life's work from mere butchery. No doubt, they know with General Sherman that war is butchery, but they are likely to believe that it is also, simultaneously, something else. That is why army and navy officers, defending a long tradition, will often protest commands of their civilian superiors that would require them to violate the rules of war and turn them into mere instruments for killing. The protests are mostly unavailing—for instruments, after all, they are—but within their own sphere of decision, they often find ways to defend the rules. And even when they don't do that, their doubts at the time and justifications after the fact are an important guide to the substance of the rules. Sometimes, at least, it matters to soldiers just whom they kill.

The war convention as we know it today has been expounded, debated, criticized, and revised over a period of many centuries. Yet it remains one of the more imperfect of human artifacts: recognizably something that men have made, but not something that they have made freely or well. It is necessarily imperfect, I think, quite aside from the frailties of humankind, because it is adapted to the practice of modern war. It sets the terms of a moral condition that comes into existence only when armies of victims meet (just as the chivalric code sets the terms of a moral condition that comes into existence only when there are armies of free men). The convention accepts that victimization or at least assumes it, and starts from there. That is why it is often described as a program for the toleration of war, when what is needed is a program for its abolition. One does not abolish war by fighting it well; nor does fighting it well make it tolerable. War is hell, as I have already said, even when the rules are strictly observed. Just for that reason, we are sometimes made angry by the very idea of rules or cynical about their meaning. They only serve as Prince Andrey says in that impassioned outburst that evidently also expresses Tolstoy's conviction to make us forget that war is "the vilest thing in life. . . ."[16]

> And what is war, what is needed for success in war, what are the morals of the military world? The object of warfare is murder; the means employed in warfare—spying, treachery, and the encouragement of it, the ruin of a country, the plunder of its inhabitants . . . trickery and lying, which are called military strategy; the morals of the military class—absence of all independence, that is, discipline, idleness, ignorance, cruelty, debauchery, and drunkenness.

And yet, even people who believe all this are capable of being outraged by particular acts of cruelty and barbarism. War is so awful that it makes us cynical about the possibility of restraint, and then it is so much worse that it makes us indignant at the absence of restraint. Our cynicism testifies to the defectiveness of the war convention, and our indignation to its reality and strength.

The Example of Surrender

Anomalous the convention often is, but binding nonetheless. Consider for a moment the common practice of surrendering, the detailed features of which are conventionally (and in our own time, legally) established. A soldier who surrenders enters into an agreement with his captors: he will stop fighting if they will accord him what the legal handbooks call "benevolent quarantine."[17] Since it is usually made under extreme duress, this is an agreement that would have no moral consequences at all in time of peace. In war it does have consequences. The captured soldier acquires rights and obligations specified by the convention, and these are binding without regard to the possible criminality of his captors or to the justice or urgency of the cause for which he has been fighting. Prisoners of war have a right to try to escape—they cannot be punished for the attempt—but if they kill a guard in order to escape, the killing is not an act of war; it is murder. For they committed themselves to stop fighting, gave up their right to kill, when they surrendered.

It is not easy to see all this as the simple assertion of a moral principle. It is the work of men and women (with moral principles in mind) adapting to the realities of war, making arrangements, striking bargains. No doubt, the bargain is generally useful to captives and captors alike, but it is not necessarily useful in every case to either of them or to mankind as a whole. If our purpose in this particular war is to win as soon as possible, the spectacle of a prison camp must seem strange indeed. Here are soldiers making themselves at home, settling in for the duration, dropping out of the war before it is over, and bound not to renew the fighting, even if they can (through sabotage, harassment, or whatever), because they promised at the point of a gun not to do so. Surely these are promises that can sometimes be broken. Yet prisoners are not invited to calculate the relative utilities of keeping or of breaking them. The war convention is written in absolutist terms: one violates its provisions at one's moral, as at one's physical peril. But what is the force of these provisions? They derive ultimately from principles that I will take up later on, which explain the meaning of quarter, disengagement, and immunity. They derive immediately and specifically from the consensual process itself. The rules of war, alien as they often are to our sense of what is best, are made obligatory by the general consent of mankind.

Now that, too, is a consent given under a kind of duress. Only because there is no escape from hell, it might be said, have we labored to create a world of rules within it. But let us imagine an escape attempt, a liberation struggle, a "war to end war." Surely it would be foolish then to fight according to the rules. The all-important task would be to win. But it is always important to win, for victory can always be described as an escape from hell. Even the victory of an aggressor, after all, ends the war. Hence the long history of impatience with the war convention. That history is nicely summed up in a letter written in 1880 by the Prussian chief of staff, General von Moltke, to protest the Declaration of St. Petersburg (an early effort to codify the rules of war): "The greatest kindness in war," wrote von Moltke, "is to bring it to a speedy conclusion. It should be allowable, with that view, to employ all means save those that are absolutely objectionable."[18] Von Moltke stops short of a total denial of the war convention; he recognizes absolute prohibitions of some unspecified sort. Almost everyone does. But why stop short if that means falling short of the "greatest kindness"? This is the form of the most common argument in the theory of war and of the most common moral dilemma in its practice. The war convention is found to stand in the way of victory and, it is usually said, a lasting peace. Must its provisions, must this particular provision be obeyed? When victory means the defeat of aggression, the question is not only important; it is painfully difficult. We want to have it both ways: moral decency in battle and victory in war; constitutionalism in hell and ourselves outside.

PART TWO

THE THEORY OF AGGRESSION

4

LAW AND ORDER IN
INTERNATIONAL SOCIETY

AGGRESSION

Aggression is the name we give to the crime of war. We know the crime because of our knowledge of the peace it interrupts—not the mere absence of fighting, but peace-with-rights, a condition of liberty and security that can exist only in the absence of aggression itself. The wrong the aggressor commits is to force men and women to risk their lives for the sake of their rights. It is to confront them with the choice: your rights or (some of) your lives! Groups of citizens respond in different ways to that choice, sometimes surrendering, sometimes fighting, depending on the moral and material condition of their state and army. But they are always justified in fighting; and in most cases, given that harsh choice, fighting is the morally preferred response. The justification and the preference are very important: they account for the most remarkable features of the concept of aggression and for the special place it has in the theory of war.

Aggression is remarkable because it is the only crime that states can commit against other states: everything else is, as it were, a misdemeanor. There is a strange poverty in the language of international law. The equivalents of domestic assault, armed robbery, extortion, assault with intent to kill, murder in all its degrees, have but one name. Every violation of the territorial integrity or political sovereignty of an independent state is called aggression. It is as if we were to brand as murder all attacks on a man's person, all attempts to coerce him, all invasions of his home. This refusal of differentiation makes it difficult to mark off the relative seriousness of aggressive acts—to distinguish, for example, the seizure of a piece of land or the imposition of a satellite regime from conquest itself, the destruction of a state's independence (a crime for which Abba Eban, Israel's foreign minister in 1967, suggested the name "policide"). But there is a reason for the refusal. All aggressive acts have one thing in common: they justify forceful resistance, and force cannot be used between nations, as it often can between persons, without putting life itself at risk. Whatever limits we place on the means and range of warfare, fighting a limited war is not like hitting somebody. Aggression opens the gates of hell. Shakespeare's *Henry V* makes the point exactly:[1]

> *For never two such kingdoms did contend*
> *Without much fall of blood, whose guiltless drops*
> *Are every one a woe, a sore complaint*
> *'Gainst him whose wrongs gives edge unto the swords*
> *That makes such waste in brief mortality.*

At the same time, aggression unresisted is aggression still, though there is no "fall of blood" at all. In domestic society, a robber who gets what he wants without killing anyone is obviously less guilty, that is, guilty of a lesser crime, than if he commits murder. Assuming that the robber is prepared to kill, we allow the behavior of his victim to determine his guilt. We don't do this in the case of aggression. Consider, for example, the German seizures of Czechoslovakia and Poland in 1939. The Czechs did not resist; they lost their independence through extortion rather than war; no Czech citizens died fighting the German invaders. The Poles chose to fight, and many were killed in the war that followed. But if the conquest of Czechoslovakia was a lesser crime, we have no name for it. At Nuremberg, the Nazi leadership was charged with aggression in both cases and found guilty in both.[2] Once again, there is a reason for this identity of treatment. We judge the Germans guilty of aggression in Czechoslovakia, I think, because of our profound conviction that they ought to have been resisted— though not necessarily by their abandoned victim, standing alone.

The state that does resist, whose soldiers risk their lives and die, does so because its leaders and people think that they should or that they have to fight back. Aggression is morally as well as physically coercive, and that is one of the most important things about it. "A conqueror," writes Clausewitz, "is always a lover of peace (as Bonaparte always asserted of himself); he would like to make his entry into our state unopposed; in order to prevent this, we must choose war. . . . "[3] If ordinary men and women did not ordinarily accept that imperative, aggression would not seem to us so serious a crime. If they accepted it in certain sorts of cases, but not in others, the single concept would begin to break down, and we would eventually have a list of crimes more or less like the domestic list. The challenge of the streets, "Your money or your life!" is easy to answer: I surrender my money and so I save myself from being murdered and the thief from being a murderer. But we apparently don't want the challenge of aggression answered in the same way; even when it is, we don't diminish the guilt of the aggressor. He has violated rights to which we attach enormous importance. Indeed, we are inclined to think that the failure to defend those rights is never due to a sense of their unimportance, nor even to a belief (as in the street-challenge case) that they are, after all, worth less than life itself, but only to a stark conviction that the defense is hopeless. Aggression is a singular and undifferentiated crime because, in all its forms, it challenges rights that are worth dying for.

THE RIGHTS OF POLITICAL COMMUNITIES

The rights in question are summed up in the lawbooks as territorial integrity and political sovereignty. The two belong to states, but they derive ultimately from the rights of individuals, and from them they take their force. "The duties and rights of states are nothing more than the duties and rights of the men who compose them."[4] That is the view of a conventional British lawyer, for whom states are neither organic wholes nor mystical unions. And it is the correct view. When states are attacked, it is their members who are challenged, not only in their lives, but also in the sum of things they value most, including the political association they have made. We recognize and explain this challenge by referring to their rights. If they were not morally entitled to choose their form of government and shape the policies that shape their lives, external coercion would not be a crime; nor could it so easily be said that they had been forced to resist in self-defense. Individual rights (to life and liberty) underlie the most important judgments that we make about war. How these rights are themselves founded I cannot try to explain here. It is enough to say that they are somehow entailed by our sense of what it means to be a human being. If they are not natural, then we have invented them, but natural or invented, they are a palpable feature of our moral world. States' rights are simply their collective form. The process of collectivization is a complex one. No doubt, some of the immediate force of individuality is lost in its course; it is best understood, nevertheless, as it has commonly been understood since the seventeenth century, in terms of social contract theory. Hence it is a moral process, which justifies some claims to territory and sovereignty and invalidates others.

The rights of states rest on the consent of their members. But this is consent of a special sort. State rights are not constituted through a series of transfers from individual men and women to the sovereign or through a series of exchanges among individuals. What actually happens is harder to describe. Over a long period of time, shared experiences and cooperative activity of many different kinds shape a common life. "Contract" is a metaphor for a process of association and mutuality, the ongoing character of which the state claims to protect against external encroachment. The protection extends not only to the lives and liberties of individuals but also to their shared life and liberty, the independent community they have made, for which individuals are sometimes sacrificed. The moral standing of any particular state depends upon the reality of the common life it protects and the extent to which the sacrifices required by that protection are willingly accepted and thought worthwhile. If no common life exists, or if the state doesn't defend the common life that does exist, its own defense may have no moral justification. But most states do stand guard over the community of their citizens, at least to some degree: that is why we assume the justice of their defensive wars. And given a genuine "contract," it makes sense to say that territorial integrity and political sovereignty can be defended in exactly the same way as individual life and liberty.*

---

* The question of when territory and sovereignty can rightly be defended is closely connected to the question of when individual citizens have an obligation to join the defense. Both hang on issues in social contract theory. I have discussed the second question at length in my book *Obligations: Essays on Disobedience, War, and Citizenship* (Cambridge, Mass., 1970). See especially "The Obligation to Die for the State" and "Political Alienation and Military Service." But neither in that book nor in this one do I deal in any detail with the problem of national minorities—groups of people who do not fully join (or do not join at all) in the contract

It might also be said that a people can defend its country in the same way as men and women can defend their homes, for the country is collectively as the homes are privately owned. The right to territory might be derived, that is, from the individual right to property. But the ownership of vast reaches of land is highly problematic, I think, unless it can be tied in some plausible way to the requirements of national survival and political independence. And these two seem by themselves to generate territorial rights that have little to do with ownership in the strict sense. The case is probably the same with the smaller properties of domestic society. A man has certain rights in his home, for example, even if he does not own it, because neither his life nor his liberty is secure unless there exists some physical space within which he is safe from intrusion. Similarly again, the right of a nation or people not to be invaded derives from the common life its members have made on their piece of land—it had to be made somewhere—and not from the legal title they hold or don't hold. But these matters will become clearer if we look at an example of disputed territory.

The Case of Alsace-Lorraine

In 1870, both France and the new Germany claimed these two provinces. Both claims were, as such things go, well founded. The Germans based themselves on ancient precedents (the lands had been part of the Holy Roman Empire before their conquest by Louis XIV) and on cultural and linguistic kinship; the French on two centuries of possession and effective government.[5] How does one establish ownership in such a case? There is, I think, a prior question having to do with political allegiance, not with legal titles at all. What do the inhabitants want? The land follows the people. The decision as to whose sovereignty was legitimate (and therefore as to whose military presence constituted aggression) belonged by right to the men and women who lived on the land in dispute. Not simply to those who owned the land: the decision belonged to the landless, to town dwellers and factory workers as well, by virtue of the common life they had made. The great majority of these people were apparently loyal to France,

---

that constitutes the nation. The radical mistreatment of such people may justify military intervention (see chapter 6). Short of that, however, the presence of national minorities within the borders of a nation-state does not affect the argument about aggression and self-defense.

and that should have settled the matter. Even if we imagine all the inhabitants of Alsace-Lorraine to be tenants of the Prussian king, the king's seizure of his own land would still have been a violation of their territorial integrity and, through the mediation of their loyalty, of France's too. For tenantry determines only where rents should go; the people themselves must decide where their taxes and conscripts should go.

But the issue was not settled in this way. After the Franco-Prussian war, the two provinces (actually, all of Alsace and a portion of Lorraine) were annexed by Germany, the French conceding German rights in the peace treaty of 1871. During the next several decades, the question was frequently asked, whether a French attack aimed at regaining the lost lands would be justified. One of the issues here is that of the moral standing of a peace treaty signed, as most peace treaties are signed, under duress, but I shall not focus on that. The more important issue relates to the endurance of rights over time. Here the appropriate argument was put forward by the English philosopher Henry Sidgwick in 1891. Sidgwick's sympathies were with the French, and he was inclined to regard the peace as a "temporary suspension of hostilities, terminable at any time by the wronged state. . . ." But he added a crucial qualification:[6]

> We must . . . recognize that by this temporary submission of the vanquished . . . a new political order is initiated, which, though originally without a moral basis, may in time acquire such a basis, from a change in the sentiments of the inhabitants of the territory transferred; since it is always possible that through the effects of time and habit and mild government—and perhaps through the voluntary exile of those who feel the old patriotism most keenly—the majority of the transferred population may cease to desire reunion. . . . When this change has taken place, the moral effect of the unjust transfer must be regarded as obliterated; so that any attempt to recover the transferred territory becomes itself an aggression. . . .

Legal titles may endure forever, periodically revived and reasserted as in the dynastic politics of the Middle Ages. But moral rights are subject to the vicissitudes of the common life.

Territorial integrity, then, does not derive from property; it is simply something different. The two are joined, perhaps, in socialist states where the land is nationalized and the people are said to own it. Then if their country is attacked, it is not merely their homeland that is in danger but their collective property—though I suspect that the first danger is more deeply felt than the second. Nationalization is a secondary process; it assumes the prior existence of a nation. And territorial integrity is a function of national existence, not of nationalization (any more than of private ownership). It is the coming together of a people that establishes the integrity of a territory. Only then can a boundary be drawn, the crossing of which is plausibly called aggression. It hardly matters if the territory belongs to someone else, unless that ownership is expressed in residence and common use.

This argument suggests a way of thinking about the great difficulties posed by forcible settlement and colonization. When barbarian tribes crossed the borders of the Roman Empire, driven by conquerors from the east or north, they asked for land to settle on and threatened war if they didn't get it. Was this aggression? Given the character of the Roman Empire, the question may sound foolish, but it has arisen many times since, and often in imperial settings. When land is in fact empty and available, the answer must be that it is not aggression. But what if the land is not actually empty but, as Thomas Hobbes says in *Leviathan*, "not sufficiently inhabited"? Hobbes goes on to argue that in such a case, the would-be settlers must "not exterminate those they find there but constrain them to inhabit closer together."[7] That constraint is not aggression, so long as the lives of the original settlers are not threatened. For the settlers are doing what they must do to preserve their own lives, and "he that shall oppose himself against [that], for things superfluous, is guilty of the war that thereupon is to follow."[8] It is not the settlers who are guilty of aggression, according to Hobbes, but those natives who won't move over and make room. There are clearly serious problems here. But I would suggest that Hobbes is right to set aside any consideration of territorial integrity-as-ownership and to focus instead on life. It must be added, however, that what is at stake is not only the lives of individuals but also the common life that they have made. It is for the sake of this common life that we assign a certain presumptive value to the boundaries that mark off a people's territory and to the state that defends it.

Now, the boundaries that exist at any moment in time are likely to be arbitrary, poorly drawn, the products of ancient wars. The mapmakers are likely to have been ignorant, drunken, or corrupt. Nevertheless, these lines establish a habitable world. Within that world, men and women (let us assume) are safe from attack; once the lines are crossed, safety is gone.

I don't want to suggest that every boundary dispute is a reason for war. Sometimes adjustments should be accepted and territories shaped so far as possible to the actual needs of nations. Good borders make good neighbors. But once an invasion has been threatened or has actually begun, it may be necessary to defend a bad border simply because there is no other. We shall see this reason at work in the minds of the leaders of Finland in 1939: they might have accepted Russian demands had they felt certain that there would be an end to them. But there is no certainty this side of the border, any more than there is safety this side of the threshold, once a criminal has entered the house. It is only common sense, then, to attach great importance to boundaries. Rights in the world have value only if they also have dimension.

THE LEGALIST PARADIGM

If states actually do possess rights more or less as individuals do, then it is possible to imagine a society among them more or less like the society of individuals. The comparison of international to civil order is crucial to the theory of aggression. I have already been making it regularly. Every reference to aggression as the international equivalent of armed robbery or murder, and every comparison of home and country or of personal liberty and political independence, relies upon what is called the *domestic analogy*.[9] Our primary perceptions and judgments of aggression are the products of analogical reasoning. When the analogy is made explicit, as it often is among the lawyers, the world of states takes on the shape of a political society the character of which is entirely accessible through such notions as crime and punishment, self-defense, law enforcement, and so on.

These notions, I should stress, are not incompatible with the fact that international society as it exists today is a radically imperfect structure. As we experience it, that society might be likened to a defective building, founded on rights; its superstructure raised, like that of the state itself, through political conflict, cooperative activity, and commercial exchange; the whole thing shaky and unstable because it lacks the rivets of authority. It is like domestic society in that men and women live at peace within it (sometimes), determining the conditions of their own existence, negotiating and bargaining with their neighbors. It is unlike domestic society in that every conflict threatens the structure as a whole with collapse. Aggression challenges it directly and is much more dangerous than domestic crime, because there are no policemen. But that only means that the "citizens" of international society must rely on themselves and on one another. Police powers are distributed among all the members. And these members have not done enough in the exercise of their powers if they merely contain the aggression or bring it to a speedy end—as if the police should stop a murderer after he has killed only one or two people and send him on his way. The rights of the member states must be vindicated, for it is only by virtue of those rights that there is a society at all. If they cannot be upheld (at least sometimes), international society collapses into a state of war or is transformed into a universal tyranny.

From this picture, two presumptions follow. The first, which I have already pointed out, is the presumption in favor of military resistance once aggression has begun. Resistance is important so that rights can be maintained and future aggressors deterred. The theory of aggression restates the old doctrine of the just war: it explains when fighting is a crime and when it is permissible, perhaps even morally desirable.* The victim of aggression fights in self-defense, but he isn't only defending himself, for aggression is a crime against society as a whole. He fights in its name and not only in his own. Other states can rightfully join the victim's resistance; their war has the same character as his own, which is to say, they are entitled not only to repel the attack but also to punish it. All resistance is also law enforcement. Hence the second presumption: when fighting breaks out, there must always be some state against which the law can and should be enforced. Someone must be responsible, for someone decided to break the peace of the society of states. No war, as medieval theologians explained, can be just on both sides.[10]

There are, however, wars that are just on neither side, because the idea of justice doesn't pertain to them or because the antagonists are both aggressors, fighting for territory or power where they have no right. The first case I have already alluded to in discussing the voluntary combat of aristocratic warriors. It is sufficiently rare in human history that nothing

---

*I shall say nothing here of the argument for nonviolent resistance to aggression, according to which fighting is neither desirable nor necessary. This argument has not figured much in the development of the conventional view. Indeed, it poses a radical challenge to the conventions: if aggression can be resisted, and at least sometimes successfully resisted, without war, it may be a less serious crime than has commonly been supposed. I will take up this possibility and its moral implications in the Afterword.

more need be said about it here. The second case is illustrated by those wars that Marxists call "imperialist," which are not fought between conquerors and victims but between conquerors and conquerors, each side seeking dominion over the other or the two of them competing to dominate some third party. Thus Lenin's description of the struggles between "have" and "have-not" nations in early twentieth-century Europe: ". . . picture to yourselves a slave-owner who owned 100 slaves warring against a slave-owner who owned 200 slaves for a more 'just' distribution of slaves. Clearly, the application of the term 'defensive' war in such a case . . . would be sheer deception. . . . "[11] But it is important to stress that we can penetrate the deception only insofar as we can ourselves distinguish justice and injustice: the theory of imperialist war presupposes the theory of aggression. If one insists that all wars on all sides are acts of conquest or attempted conquest, or that all states at all times would conquer if they could, then the argument for justice is defeated before it begins and the moral judgments we actually make are derided as fantasies. Consider the following passage from Edmund Wilson's book on the American Civil War:[12]

I think that it is a serious deficiency on the part of historians . . . that they so rarely interest themselves in biological and zoological phenomena. In a recent . . . film showing life at the bottom of the sea, a primitive organism called a sea slug is seen gobbling up small organisms through a large orifice at one end of its body; confronted with another sea slug of an only slightly lesser size, it ingurgitates that, too. Now the wars fought by human beings are stimulated as a rule . . . by the same instincts as the voracity of the sea slug.

There are no doubt wars to which that image might be fit, though it is not a terribly useful image with which to approach the Civil War. Nor does it account for our ordinary experience of international society. Not all states are sea-slug states, gobbling up their neighbors. They are always groups of men and women who would live if they could in peaceful enjoyment of their rights and who have chosen political leaders who represent that desire. The deepest purpose of the state is not ingestion but defense, and the least that can be said is that many actual states serve that purpose. When their territory is attacked or their sovereignty challenged, it makes sense to look for an aggressor and not merely for a natural predator. Hence we need a theory of aggression rather than a zoological account.

The theory of aggression first takes shape under the aegis of the domestic analogy. I am going to call that primary form of the theory the *legalist paradigm*, since it consistently reflects the conventions of law and order. It does not necessarily reflect the arguments of the lawyers, though legal as well as moral debate has its starting point here.[13] Later on, I will suggest that our judgments about the justice and injustice of particular wars are not entirely determined by the paradigm. The complex realities of international society drive us toward a revisionist perspective, and the revisions will be significant ones. But the paradigm must first be viewed in its unrevised form; it is our baseline, our model, the fundamental structure for the moral comprehension of war. We begin with the familiar world of individuals and rights, or crimes and punishments. The theory of aggression can then be summed up in six propositions.

1. *There exists an international society of independent states.* States are the members of this society, not private men and women. In the absence of an universal state, men and women are protected and their interests represented only by their own governments. Though states are founded for the sake of life and liberty, they cannot be challenged in the name of life and liberty by any other states. Hence the principle of non-intervention, which I will analyze later on. The rights of private persons can be recognized in international society, as in the UN Charter of Human Rights, but they cannot be enforced without calling into question the dominant values of that society: the survival and independence of the separate political communities.

2. *This international society has a law that establishes the rights of its members—above all, the rights of territorial integrity and political sovereignty.* Once again, these two rest ultimately on the right of men and women to build a common life and to risk their individual lives only when they freely choose to do so. But the relevant law refers only to states, and its details are fixed by the intercourse of states, through complex processes of conflict and consent. Since these processes are continuous, international society has no natural shape; nor are rights within it ever finally or exactly determined. At any given moment, however, one can distinguish the territory of one people from that of another and say something about the scope and limits of sovereignty.

3. *Any use of force or imminent threat of force by one state against the political sovereignty or territorial integrity of another constitutes aggression and is a criminal act.* As with domestic crime, the argument here focuses narrowly on actual or imminent boundary crossings: invasions and physical assaults. Otherwise, it is feared, the notion of resistance to aggression would have no determinate meaning. A state cannot be said to be forced to fight unless the necessity is both obvious and urgent.

4. *Aggression justifies two kinds of violent response: a war of self-defense by the victim and a war of law enforcement by the victim and any other member of international society.* Anyone can come to the aid of a victim, use necessary force against an aggressor, and even make whatever is the international equivalent of a "citizen's arrest." As in domestic society, the obligations of bystanders are not easy to make out, but it is the tendency of the theory to undermine the right of neutrality and to require widespread participation in the business of law enforcement. In the Korean War, this participation was authorized by the United Nations, but even in such cases the actual decision to join the fighting remains a unilateral one, best understood by analogy to the decision of a private citizen who rushes to help a man or woman attacked on the street.

5. *Nothing but aggression can justify war.* The central purpose of the theory is to limit the occasions for war. "There is a single and only just cause for commencing a war," wrote Vitoria, "namely, a wrong received."[14] There must actually have been a wrong, and it must actually have been received (or its receipt must be, as it were, only minutes away). Nothing else warrants the use of force in international society—above all, not any difference of religion or politics. Domestic heresy and injustice are never actionable in the world of states: hence, again, the principle of nonintervention.

6. *Once the aggressor state has been militarily repulsed, it can also be punished.* The conception of just war as an act of punishment is very old, though neither the procedures nor the forms of punishment have ever been firmly established in customary or positive international law. Nor are its purposes entirely clear: to exact retribution, to deter other states, to restrain or reform this one? All three figure largely in the literature, though it is probably fair to say that deterrence and restraint are most commonly accepted. When people talk of fighting a war against war, this is usually what they have in mind. The domestic maxim is, punish crime

to prevent violence; its international analogue is, punish aggression to prevent war. Whether the state as a whole or only particular persons are the proper objects of punishment is a harder question, for reasons I will consider later on. But the implication of the paradigm is clear: if states are members of international society, the subjects of rights, they must also be (somehow) the objects of punishment.

UNAVOIDABLE CATEGORIES

These propositions shape the judgments we make when wars break out. They constitute a powerful theory, coherent and economic, and they have dominated our moral consciousness for a long time. I am not concerned to trace their history here, but it is worth emphasizing that they remained dominant even during the eighteenth and nineteenth centuries, when lawyers and statesmen regularly argued that war-making was the natural prerogative of sovereign states, not subject to legal or moral judgment. States went to war for "reasons of state," and these reasons were said to have a privileged character, such that they needed only to be alluded to, not even expounded, in order to terminate all argument. The common assumption in the legal literature of the time (roughly from the age of Vattel to that of Oppenheim) is that states always have, like Hobbist individuals, a right to fight.[15] The analogy is not from domestic to international society, but from the state of nature to international anarchy. But this view never seized the popular imagination. "The idea of war and the launching of it," writes the foremost historian of the theory of aggression, "were for the ordinary man and for public opinion always loaded with moral significance, demanding full approval if waged with right and condemnation and punishment if without. . . ."[16] The significance ordinary men attached was exactly of the sort I have been describing: they drew the terrifying experience of war, as Otto von Bismarck once complained, back to the familiar ground of everyday life. "Public opinion," Bismarck wrote, "is only too ready to consider political relations and events in the light of those of civil law and private persons generally. . . . [This] shows a complete lack of understanding of political matters."[17]

I am inclined to think that it shows a deep understanding of political matters, though not always in its applications a knowledgeable or sophisticated understanding. Public opinion tends to focus on the concrete reality of war and on the moral meaning of killing and being killed. It addresses the questions that ordinary men cannot avoid: should we support this war? should we fight in it? Bismarck works from a more distant perspective, turning the people who ask such questions into pawns in the high game of *real-politik*. But ultimately the questions are insistent and the distant perspective untenable. Until wars are really fought with pawns, inanimate objects and not human beings, warfare cannot be isolated from moral life. We can get a clear view of the necessary links by reflecting on the work of one of Bismarck's contemporaries and on one of the wars at which the German chancellor connived.

Karl Marx and the Franco-Prussian War

Like Bismarck, Marx had a different way of understanding political matters. He regarded war not merely as the continuation but as the necessary and inevitable continuation of politics, and he described particular wars in terms of a world historical scheme. He had no commitment to the existing political order, nor to the territorial integrity or political sovereignty of established states. The violation of these "rights" raised no moral problem for him; he did not seek the punishment of aggressors; he sought only those outcomes that, without reference to the theory of aggression, advanced the cause of proletarian revolution. It is entirely characteristic of Marx's general views that he should have hoped for a Prussian victory in 1870 because it would lead to German unification and ease the course of socialist organization in the new Reich and because it would establish the dominance of the German over the French working class.[18]

> The French need a drubbing [he wrote in a letter to Engels]. If the Prussians are victorious, then the centralization of state power will be favorable to the centralization of the working class. German preponderance will shift the center of the working class movement in Western Europe from France to Germany and . . . the German working class is theoretically and organizationally superior to that of France. The superiority of the Germans over the French . . . would mean at the same time the superiority of our theory over Proudhon's, etc.

But this was not a view that Marx could defend in public, not only because its publication would embarrass him among his French comrades, but for reasons that go directly to the nature of our moral life. Even the most advanced members of the German working class would not be willing to kill French workers for the sake of German unity or to risk their own lives merely in order to enhance the power of their party (or of Marx's theory!) within the ranks of international socialism. Marx's argument was not, in the most literal sense of the word, a *possible* account of the decision to fight or of the judgment that the war the Germans fought was, at least initially, a just war. If we are to understand that judgment, we would do better to begin with the simplistic assertion of a British member of the General Council of the International: "The French," said John Weston, "had invaded first."[19]

We know now that Bismarck worked hard and with all his usual ruthlessness to bring about that invasion. The diplomatic crisis that preceded the war was largely of his contrivance. Nothing that he did, however, can plausibly be said to have threatened the territorial integrity or political sovereignty of France; nothing that he did forced the French to fight. He merely exploited the arrogance and stupidity of Napoleon III and his entourage and succeeded in putting the French in the wrong; it was the tribute he paid to the public opinion he deplored. Hence it has never been necessary to correct the argument of John Weston or of those members of the German Social Democratic Workers' Party who declared in July 1870 that it was Napoleon who had "frivolously" destroyed the peace of Europe: "The German nation . . . is the victim of aggression. Therefore . . . with great regret, [we] must accept the defensive war as a necessary evil."[20] The "First Address" of the International on the Franco-Prussian War, drafted by Marx on behalf of the General Council, took the same view: "On the German side, the war is a war of defense" (though Marx went on to ask, "Who put Germany to the necessity of defending herself?" and to hint at the true character of Bismarckian politics).[21] French workers were called upon to oppose the war and to drive the Bonapartists from power; German workers were urged to join the war, but in such a manner as to maintain "its strictly defensive character."

Some six weeks later, the war of defense was over, Germany was triumphant at Sedan, Bonaparte a prisoner, his empire overthrown. But the fighting continued, for the chief war aim of the German government was not resistance but expansion: the annexation of Alsace-Lorraine. In the "Second Address" of the International, Marx accurately described the war after Sedan as an act of aggression against the people of the two provinces and against the territorial integrity of France. He did not believe that either the German workers or the new French republic would be capable of punishing that aggression in the near future, but he looked for punishment nonetheless: "History will measure its retribution, not by the extent of the square miles conquered from France, but by the intensity of the crime of reviving, in the second half of the nineteen century, *the policy of conquest.*"[22] What is striking here is that Marx has enlisted history not in the service of the proletarian revolution but in the service of conventional morality. Indeed, he invokes the example of the Prussian struggle against the first Napoleon after Tilset and so suggests that the retribution he has in mind will take the form of a future French attack on the German Reich, a war of exactly the sort that Henry Sidgwick also thought justified by the German "policy of conquest." But whatever Marx's program, it is clear that he is working within the terms set by the theory of aggression. When he is forced to confront the actualities of war and to describe in public the possible shape of a socialist foreign policy, he falls back upon the domestic analogy and the legalist paradigm in their most literal forms. Indeed, he argued in the "First Address" that it was the task of socialists "to vindicate the simple laws of morals and justice, which ought to govern the relations of private individuals, as the rules paramount of the intercourse of nations."[23]

Is this Marxist doctrine? I am not sure. It has little in common with Marx's philosophic pronouncements on morality and little in common with the reflections on international politics that fill his letters. But Marx was not only a philosopher and a letter-writer; he was also a political leader and the spokesman of a mass movement. In these latter roles, his world-historical view of the significance of war was less important than the particular judgments he was called upon to make. And once he was committed to judgment, there was a certain inevitability to the categories of the theory of aggression. It was not a question of adjusting himself to what is sometimes condescendingly called the "level of consciousness" of his audience, but of speaking directly to the moral experience of its members. Sometimes, perhaps, a new philosophy or religion can reshape that experience, but this was not the effect of Marxism, at least not with regard to international warfare. Marx simply took the theory of aggression seriously, and so he placed himself in the front ranks of those ordinary men and women about whom Bismarck complained, who judged political events in the light of domestic morality.

THE ARGUMENT FOR APPEASEMENT

The war of 1870 is a hard case because, with the exception of those French liberals and socialists who challenged Bonaparte and those German social-democrats who condemned the annexation of Alsace-Lorraine, none of its participants are very attractive. The moral issues are muddy, and it would not be difficult to argue that the struggle was in fact an aggressive war on both sides, rather than on each in succession. But the issues are not always muddy; history provides wonderfully clear examples of aggression. The historical study of war virtually begins with such an example (with which I also began): the Athenian attack on Melos. But the easy cases raise problems of their own, or rather, one characteristic problem. Aggression most often takes the form of an attack by a powerful state upon a weak one (that is why it is so readily recognizable). Resistance seems imprudent, even hopeless. Many lives will be lost, and to what end? Even here, however, our moral preference holds. We not only justify resistance; we call it heroic; we do not measure the value of justice, apparently, in terms of lives lost. And yet such measurements can never be entirely irrelevant: who would want to be ruled by political leaders who paid them no mind? So justice and prudence stand in an uneasy relation to one another. Later on, I will describe various ways in which the argument for justice incorporates prudential considerations. But now it is important to stress that the legalist paradigm tends in a radical way to exclude them.

The paradigm as a whole is commonly defended in utilitarian terms: resistance to aggression is necessary to deter future aggressors. But in the context of international politics, an alternative utilitarian argument is almost always available. This is the argument for appeasement, which suggests that giving in to aggressors is the only way of avoiding war. In domestic society, too, we sometimes choose appeasement, negotiating with kidnappers or extortionists, for example, when the costs of refusal or resistance are greater than we can bear. But we feel badly in such cases, not only because we have failed to serve the larger communal purpose of deterrence, but also and more immediately because we have yielded to coercion and injustice. We feel badly even though all that we have yielded is money, whereas in international society appeasement is hardly possible unless we are willing to surrender values far more important. And yet the costs of war are such that the argument for surrender can often be put very strongly. Appeasement is a bad word in our moral vocabulary, but the argument is not morally obtuse. It represents the most significant challenge to what I have been calling the presumption in favor of resistance, and I want now to examine it in some detail.

Czechoslovakia and the Munich Principle

The defense of appeasement in 1938 sometimes involved the claim that the Sudeten Germans were, after all, entitled to self-determination. But that is a claim that might have been met through some sort of autonomy within the Czech state or through boundary changes considerably less drastic than those that Hitler demanded at Munich. In fact, Hitler's goals reached far beyond the vindication of a right, and Chamberlain and Daladier knew this, or should have known it, and surrendered anyway.[24] It was the fear of war rather than any view of justice that explains their actions. This fear was given theoretical expression in a very intelligent little book, published in 1939 by the English Catholic writer Gerald Vann. Vann's argument is the only attempt that I have come across to apply just war theory directly to the problem of appeasement, and for that reason I shall look at it closely. He defends what might be called the "Munich principle":[25]

> If a nation finds itself called upon to defend another nation which is unjustly attacked and to which it is bound by treaty, then it is bound to fulfill its obligations. . . . It may, however, be its right, and even its duty, to try to persuade the victim of aggression to avoid the ultimate evil of a general conflict by agreeing to terms less favorable than those which it can claim in justice . . . provided always that such a surrender of rights would not mean in fact a surrender once and for all to the rule of violence.

The "duty" here is simply "seek peace"—Hobbes' first law of nature and presumably near the top of Catholic lists as well, though Vann's phrase "the ultimate evil of a general conflict" suggests that it is nearer to the top than in fact it is. In just-war doctrine, as in the legalist paradigm, the triumph of aggression is a greater evil. But it is certainly a duty to avoid violence if one possibly can; this is a duty that the rulers of states owe to their own people and to others as well, and it may override obligations established by international treaties and conventions. But the argument requires the limiting clause at the end, which I would have thought applicable in September 1938. That clause is worth examining, since its purpose is obviously to tell us when to appease and when not.

Imagine a state whose government strives to press its boundaries or its sphere of influence outward, a little bit here, a little bit there, continually over a period of time—not quite Edmund Wilson's sea-slug state, something nearer to a conventional "great power." Certainly the people against whom the pressure is being brought have a right to resist; Allied states and possibly other states as well ought to support their resistance. But appeasement, by the victim or the others, would not necessarily be immoral—this is Vann's argument—and there might even be a duty to seek peace at the expense of justice. Appeasement would involve a surrender to violence, but given a conventional power, it would not or might not involve absolute subjection to the "rule of violence." I take it that absolute subjection is what Vann means by "once and for all." He cannot mean "forever," for governments fall, states decay, people rebel; we know nothing about forever. "Rule of violence" is a more difficult term. Vann can hardly set the limit of appeasement at the point where it means yielding to greater physical force; that is always what it means. As a moral limit, the phrase must point to something more unusual and more frightening: the rule of men committed to the continual use of violence, to a policy of genocide, terrorism, and enslavement. Then appeasement would be, quite simply, a failure to resist evil in the world.

Now that is exactly what the Munich agreement was. Vann's argument, once we have understood its terms, undermines his own case. For there can be no doubt that Nazism represented the rule of violence, and that its true character was sufficiently known at the time. And there can be no doubt that Czechoslovakia was surrendered to Nazism in 1938; the remnants of its territory and sovereignty could not be defended—at least not by the Czechs—and that, too, was known at the time. But it remains a question whether Vann's argument might not apply to other cases. I will skip the Polish war, for the Poles were confronted again by Nazi aggression and had, no doubt, learned from the Czech experience. But the situation of Finland a few months later was different. There the "Munich principle" was urged by all of Finland's friends and by many Finns as well. It did not seem to them, despite the Czech experience, that an acceptance of Russian terms in the late fall of 1939 would have been "a surrender once and for all to the rule of violence."

Finland

Stalin's Russia was not a conventional great power, but its behavior in the months before the Finnish war was very much in the style of traditionalist power politics. It sought to expand at the expense of the Finns, but the demands it made were moderate, closely linked to questions of military security, without revolutionary implications. What was at issue, Stalin insisted, was nothing more than the defense of Leningrad, which was then within artillery range of the Finnish border (he did not fear a Finnish attack but a German attack from Finnish territory). "Since we cannot move Leningrad," he said, "we must move the border."[26] The Russians offered to yield more land (though less valuable land) than they sought to take over, and that offer gave the negotiations at least something of the character of an exchange between sovereign states. At an early point in the talks, Marshal Mannerheim, who had no illusions about Soviet policy, strongly recommended making the deal. It was more dangerous for Finland than for Russia for the Finns to be so close to Leningrad. Stalin may well have intended an eventual annexation of Finland, or its transformation into a communist state, but that was not apparent at the time. Most Finns thought the danger, though serious enough, was something less than that. They feared further encroachments and pressures of a more ordinary kind. Hence the Finnish case offers a useful test of the "Munich principle." Should Finland have agreed to terms less favorable than it could justly claim in order to avoid the carnage of war? Should its allies have pressed such terms upon it?

The first question cannot be answered flatly either way; the choice belongs to the Finns. But the rest of us have an interest, and it is important to try to understand the moral satisfaction with which their decision to fight was greeted throughout the world. I am not referring here to the excitement that always attends the beginnings of a war and that rarely lasts for long, but rather to the sense that the Finnish decision was exemplary (as the British, French, and Czech decision to surrender, greeted with an uneasy combination of relief and shame, was not). There is, of course, a natural sympathy for the underdog in any competition, including war, and a hope that he can pull off an unexpected victory. But in the case of war, this is specifically a moral sympathy and a moral hope. It has to do with the perception that underdogs are also (usually) victims or potential victims: their struggle is right. Even if national survival is not at stake—as in fact it was, for the Finns, once the war began—we hope for the defeat of the aggressor in much the same way as we hope for the defeat of a neighborhood bully, even if he is not a murderer. Our common values are confirmed and enhanced by the struggle; whereas appeasement, even when it is the better part of wisdom, diminishes those values and leaves us all impoverished.

Our values would also have been diminished, however, had Stalin quickly overwhelmed the Finns and then treated them as the Athenians did the Melians. But that suggests less the desirability of surrender than the critical importance of collective security and resistance. Had Sweden, for example, been publicly committed to send troops to fight with the Finns, there would probably never have been a Russian attack.[27] And the British and French plans to come to Finland's aid, inept and self-serving as these were, probably played a decisive part, along with the early and unexpected victories of the Finnish army, in persuading the Russians to seek a negotiated settlement. The new borders established in March 1940 were far worse than those that had been offered to Finland four months earlier; thousands of Finnish soldiers (and a greater number of Russians) were dead; hundreds of thousands of Finnish civilians were driven from their homes. But against all this must be set the vindication of Finnish independence. I don't know how one strikes the balance, still less how one might have done so in 1939 when vindication seemed an unlikely or at best a chancy prospect. Nor can its value be measured even now; it involves national pride and self-respect as much as freedom in policy-making (which no state possesses absolutely and Finland, since 1940, to a lesser degree than many). If the Finnish war is commonly thought to have been worthwhile, it is because independence is not a value that can easily be traded off.*

---

*It is probably less important, then, that these calculations be rightly made (since we cannot be sure what that would mean) than that they be made by the right people. One might usefully compare the decisions of the Melians and the Finns in this regard. Melos was an oligarchy, and its leaders, who wanted to fight, refused to allow the Athenian generals to address a popular assembly. Presumably they feared that the people would refuse to risk their lives and their city for the oligarchs. Finland was a democracy; its people knew the exact nature of the Russian demands; and the government's decision to fight apparently had overwhelming popular support. It would fit well with the rest of the theory of aggression if the Finns were again taken as exemplary: the decision to reject appeasement is best made by the men and women who will have to endure the war that follows (or by their representatives). This says nothing, of course, about the arguments one

The "Munich principle" would concede the loss or erosion of independence for the sake of the survival of individual men and women. It points toward a certain sort of international society, founded not on the defense of rights but on the adjustment to power. No doubt there is realism in this view. But the Finnish example suggests that there is also realism in the alternative view, and in a twofold sense. First, the rights are real, even to the people who must die to defend them; and second, the defense is (sometimes) possible. I don't want to argue that appeasement can never be justified, only to point to the great importance we collectively attach to the values the aggressor attacks. These values are summed up in the existence of states like Finland—indeed, of many such states. The theory of aggression presupposes our commitment to a pluralist world, and that commitment is also the inner meaning of the presumption in favor of resistance. We want to live in an international society where communities of men and women freely shape their separate destinies. But that society is never fully realized; it is never safe; it must always be defended. The Finnish war is a paradigmatic example of the necessary defense. That is why, for all the complexity of the diplomatic maneuvering that preceded the war, the actual fighting has about it a great moral simplicity.

The defense of rights is a reason for fighting. I want now to stress again, and finally, that it is the only reason. The legalist paradigm rules out every other sort of war. Preventive wars, commercial wars, wars of expansion and conquest, religious crusades, revolutionary wars, military interventions—all these are barred and barred absolutely, in much the same way as their domestic equivalents are ruled out in municipal law. Or, to turn the argument around once more, all these constitute aggressive acts on the part of whoever begins them and justify forceful resistance, as their equivalents would in the homes and streets of domestic society.

But this is not yet a complete characterization of the morality of war. Though the domestic analogy is an intellectual tool of critical importance, it doesn't offer an entirely accurate picture of international society. States are not in fact like individuals (because they are collections of individuals), and the relations among states are not like the private dealings of men and women (because they are not framed in the same way by authoritative law). These differences are not unknown or obscure. I have been ignoring

---

might want to make in the popular assembly: these might well be prudential and cautionary rather than defiant and heroic.

them only for the sake of analytical clarity. I have wanted to argue that as an account of our moral judgments, the domestic analogy and the legalist paradigm possess great explanatory power. The account is still incomplete, however, and I must look now at a series of issues and historical cases that suggest the need for revision. I cannot exhaust the range of possible revision, for our moral judgments are enormously subtle and complex. But the major points at which the argument for justice requires the amendment of the paradigm are clear enough; they have long been the focus of legal and moral debate.

5

ANTICIPATIONS

THE FIRST QUESTIONS ASKED WHEN STATES GO TO WAR ARE ALSO THE easiest to answer: who started the shooting? who sent troops across the border? These are questions of fact, not of judgment, and if the answers are disputed, it is only because of the lies that governments tell. The lies don't, in any case, detain us long; the truth comes out soon enough. Governments lie so as to absolve themselves from the charge of aggression. But it is not on the answers to questions such as these that our final judgments about aggression depend. There are further arguments to make, justifications to offer, lies to tell, before the moral issue is directly confronted. For aggression often begins without shots being fired or borders crossed.

Both individuals and states can rightfully defend themselves against violence that is imminent but not actual; they can fire the first shots if they know themselves about to be attacked. This is a right recognized in domestic law and also in the legalist paradigm for international society. In most legal accounts, however, it is severely restricted. Indeed, once one has stated the restrictions, it is no longer clear whether the right has any substance at all. Thus the argument of Secretary of State Daniel Webster in the *Caroline* case of 1842 (the details of which need not concern us here): in order to justify pre-emptive violence, Webster wrote, there must be shown "a necessity of self-defense . . . instant, overwhelming, leaving no choice of means, and no moment for deliberation."[1] That would permit us to do little more than respond to an attack *once we had seen it coming* but before we had felt its impact. Pre-emption on this view is like a reflex action, a throwing up of one's arms at the very last minute. But it hardly requires much of a "showing" to justify a movement of that sort. Even the most presumptuous aggressor is not likely to insist, as a matter of right, that his victims stand still until he lands the first blow. Webster's formula seems to be the favored one among students of international law, but I don't believe that it addresses itself usefully to the experience of imminent war. There is often plenty of time for deliberation, agonizing hours, days, even weeks of deliberation, when one doubts that war can be avoided and wonders whether or not to strike first. The debate is couched, I suppose, in strategic more than in moral terms. But the decision is judged morally, and the expectation of that judgment, of the effects it will have in allied and neutral states and among one's own people, is itself a strategic factor. So it is important to get the terms of the judgment right, and that requires some revision of the legalist paradigm. For the paradigm is more restrictive than the judgments we actually make. We are disposed to sympathize with potential victims even before they confront an instant and overwhelming necessity.

Imagine a spectrum of anticipation: at one end is Webster's reflex, necessary and determined; at the other end is preventive war, an attack that responds to a distant danger, a matter of foresight and free choice. I want to begin at the far end of the spectrum, where danger is a matter of judgment and political decision is unconstrained, and then edge my way along to the point where we currently draw the line between justified and unjustified attacks. What is involved at that point is something very different from Webster's reflex; it is still possible to make choices, to begin the fighting or to arm oneself and wait. Hence the decision to begin at least resembles the decision to fight a preventive war, and it is important to distinguish the criteria by which it is defended from those that were once thought to justify prevention. Why not draw the line at the far end of the spectrum? The reasons are central to an understanding of the position we now hold.

PREVENTIVE WAR AND THE BALANCE OF POWER

Preventive war presupposes some standard against which danger is to be measured. That standard does not exist, as it were, on the ground; it has nothing to do with the immediate security of boundaries. It exists in the mind's eye, in the idea of a balance of power, probably the dominant idea in international politics from the seventeenth century to the present day. A preventive war is a war fought to maintain the balance, to stop what is thought to be an even distribution of power from shifting into a relation of dominance and inferiority. The balance is often talked about as if it were the key to peace among states. But it cannot be that, else it would not need to be defended so often by force of arms. "The balance of power, the pride of modern policy . . . invented to preserve the general peace as well as the freedom of Europe," wrote Edmund Burke in 1760, "has only preserved its liberty. It has been the origin of innumerable and fruitless wars."[2] In fact, of course, the wars to which Burke is referring are easily numbered. Whether or not they were fruitless depends upon how one views the connection between preventive war and the preservation of liberty. Eighteenth-century British statesmen and their intellectual supporters obviously thought the connection very close. A radically unbalanced system, they recognized, would more likely make for peace, but they were "alarmed by the danger of universal monarchy."* When they went to war on behalf of the balance, they thought they were defending, not national interest alone, but an international order that made liberty possible throughout Europe.

That is the classic argument for prevention. It requires of the rulers of states, as Francis Bacon had argued a century earlier, that they "keep due sentinel, that none of their neighbors do overgrow so (by increase of territory, by embracing of trade, by approaches, or the like) as they become more able to annoy them, than they were."[3] And if their neighbors do "overgrow," then they must be fought, sooner rather than later, and

---

*The line is from David Hume's essay "Of the Balance of Power," where Hume describes three British wars on behalf of the balance as having been "begun with justice, and even, perhaps, from necessity." I would have considered his argument at length had I found it possible to place it within his philosophy. But in his *Enquiry Concerning the Principles of Morals* (Section III, Part I), Hume writes: "The rage and violence of public war: what is it but a suspension of justice among the warring parties, who perceive that this virtue is now no longer of any *use* or advantage to them?" Nor is it possible, according to Hume, that this suspension itself be just or unjust; it is entirely a matter of necessity, as in the (Hobbist) state of nature where individuals "consult the dictates of self-preservation alone." That standards of justice exist alongside the pressures of necessity is a discovery of the *Essays*. This is another example, perhaps, of the impossibility of carrying over certain philosophical positions into ordinary moral discourse. In any case, the three wars Hume discusses were none of them necessary to the preservation of Britain. He may have thought them just because he thought the balance generally useful.

without waiting for the first blow. "Neither is the opinion of some of the Schoolmen to be received: that a war cannot justly be made, but upon a precedent injury or provocation. For there is no question, but a just fear of an imminent danger, though no blow be given, is a lawful cause of war." Imminence here is not a matter of hours or days. The sentinels stare into temporal as well as geographic distance as they watch the growth of their neighbor's power. They will fear that growth as soon as it tips or seems likely to tip the balance. War is justified (as in Hobbes' philosophy) by fear alone and not by anything other states actually do or any signs they give of their malign intentions. Prudent rulers assume malign intentions.

The argument is utilitarian in form; it can be summed up in two propositions: (1) that the balance of power actually does preserve the liberties of Europe (perhaps also the happiness of Europeans) and is therefore worth defending even at some cost, and (2) that to fight early, before the balance tips in any decisive way, greatly reduces the cost of the defense, while waiting doesn't mean avoiding war (unless one also gives up liberty) but only fighting on a larger scale and at worse odds. The argument is plausible enough, but it is possible to imagine a second-level utilitarian response: (3) that the acceptance of propositions (1) and (2) is dangerous (not useful) and certain to lead to "innumerable and fruitless wars" whenever shifts in power relations occur; but increments and losses of power are a constant feature of international politics, and perfect equilibrium, like perfect security, is a utopian dream; therefore it is best to fall back upon the legalist paradigm or some similar rule and wait until the overgrowth of power is put to some overbearing use. This is also plausible enough, but it is important to stress that the position to which we are asked to fall back is not a prepared position, that is, it does not itself rest on any utilitarian calculation. Given the radical uncertainties of power politics, there probably is no practical way of making out that position—deciding when to fight and when not—on utilitarian principles. Think of what one would have to know to perform the calculations, of the experiments one would have to conduct, the wars one would have to fight—and leave unfought! In any case, we mark off moral lines on the anticipation spectrum in an entirely different way.

It isn't really prudent to assume the malign intent of one's neighbors; it is merely cynical, an example of the worldly wisdom which no one lives by or could live by. We need to make judgments about our neighbor's intentions, and if such judgments are to be possible we must stipulate certain acts or sets of acts that will count as evidence of malignity. These stipulations are not arbitrary; they are generated, I think, when we reflect upon what it means *to be threatened*. Not merely *to be afraid*, though rational men and women may well respond fearfully to a genuine threat, and their subjective experience is not an unimportant part of the argument for anticipation. But we also need an objective standard, as Bacon's phrase "just fear" suggests. That standard must refer to the threatening acts of some neighboring state, for (leaving aside the dangers of natural disaster) I can only be threatened by someone who is threatening me, where "threaten" means what the dictionary says it means: "to hold out or offer (some injury) by way of a threat, to declare one's intention of inflicting injury."[4] It is with some such notion as this that we must judge the wars fought for the sake of the balance of power. Consider, then, the Spanish Succession, regarded in the eighteenth century as a paradigmatic case for preventive war, and yet, I think, a negative example of threatening behavior.

The War of the Spanish Succession

Writing in the 1750s, the Swiss jurist Vattel suggested the following criteria for legitimate prevention: "Whenever a state has given signs of injustice, rapacity, pride, ambition, or of an imperious thirst of rule, it becomes a suspicious neighbor to be guarded against: and at a juncture when it is on the point of receiving a formidable augmentation of power, securities may be asked, and on its making any difficulty to give them, its designs may be prevented by force of arms."[5] These criteria were formulated with explicit reference to the events of 1700 and 1701, when the King of Spain, last of his line, lay ill and dying. Long before those years, Louis XIV had given Europe evident signs of injustice, rapacity, pride, and so on. His foreign policy was openly expansionist and aggressive (which is not to say that justifications were not offered, ancient claims and titles uncovered, for every intended territorial acquisition). In 1700, he seemed about to receive a "formidable augmentation of power"—his grandson, the Duke of Anjou, was offered the Spanish throne. With his usual arrogance, Louis refused to provide any assurances or guarantees to his fellow monarchs. Most importantly, he refused to bar Anjou from the French succession, thus holding open the possibility of a unified and powerful Franco-Spanish state. And then, an alliance of European powers, led by Great Britain, went to war against what they assumed was Louis' "design" to dominate Europe. Having drawn his criteria so closely to his case, however, Vattel concludes on a sobering note: "it has since appeared that the policy [of the Allies] was too suspicious." That is wisdom after the fact, of course, but still wisdom, and one would expect some effort to restate the criteria in its light.

The mere augmentation of power, it seems to me, cannot be a warrant for war or even the beginning of warrant, and for much the same reason that Bacon's commercial expansion ("embracing of trade") is also and even more obviously insufficient. For both of these suggest developments that may not be politically designed at all and hence cannot be taken as evidence of intent. As Vattel says, Anjou had been invited to his throne "by the [Spanish] nation, conformably to the will of its last sovereign"—that is, though there can be no question here of democratic decision-making, he had been invited for Spanish and not for French reasons. "Have not these two Realms," asked Jonathan Swift in a pamphlet opposing the British war, "their separate maxims of Policy? . . ."[6] Nor is Louis' refusal to make promises relating to some future time to be taken as evidence of design—only, perhaps, of hope. If Anjou's succession made immediately for a closer alliance between Spain and France, the appropriate answer would seem to have been a closer alliance between Britain and Austria. Then one could wait and judge anew the intentions of Louis.

But there is a deeper issue here. When we stipulate threatening acts, we are looking not only for indications of intent, but also for rights of response. To characterize certain acts as threats is to characterize them in a moral way, and in a way that makes a military response morally comprehensible. The utilitarian arguments for prevention don't do that, not because the ways they generate are too frequent, but because they are too common in another sense: *too ordinary.* Like Clausewitz's description of war as the continuation of policy by other means, they radically underestimate the importance of the shift from diplomacy to force. They don't recognize the problem that killing and being killed poses. Perhaps the recognition depends upon a certain way of valuing human life, which was not the way of eighteenth-century statesmen. (How many of the British soldiers who shipped to the continent with Marlborough ever returned? Did anyone bother to count?) But the point is an important one anyway, for it suggests why people have come to feel uneasy about preventive war. We don't want to fight until we are threatened, because only then can we rightly fight. It is a question of moral security. That is why Vattel's concluding remark about the War of the Spanish Succession, and Burke's general argument about the fruitlessness of such wars, is so worrying. It is inevitable, of course, that political calculations will sometimes go wrong; so will moral choices; there is no such thing as perfect security. But there is a great difference, nonetheless, between killing and being killed by soldiers who can plausibly be described as the present instruments of an aggressive intention, and killing and being killed by soldiers who may or may not represent a distant danger to our country. In the first case, we confront an army recognizably hostile, ready for war, fixed in a posture of attack. In the second, the hostility is prospective and imaginary, and it will always be a charge against us that we have made war upon soldiers who were themselves engaged in entirely legitimate (non-threatening) activities. Hence the moral necessity of rejecting any attack that is merely preventive in character, that does not wait upon and respond to the willful acts of an adversary.

PRE-EMPTIVE STRIKES

Now, what acts are to count, what acts do count as threats sufficiently serious to justify war? It is not possible to put together a list, because state action, like human action generally, takes on significance from its context. But there are some negative points worth making. The boastful ranting to which political leaders are often prone isn't in itself threatening; injury must be "offered" in some material sense as well. Nor does the kind of military preparation that is a feature of the classic arms race count as a threat, unless it violates some formally or tacitly agreed-upon limit. What the lawyers call "hostile acts short of war," even if these involve violence, are not too quickly to be taken as signs of an intent to make war; they may represent an essay in restraint, an offer to quarrel within limits. Finally, provocations are not the same as threats. "Injury and provocation" are commonly linked by Scholastic writers as the two causes of just war. But the Schoolmen were too accepting of contemporary notions about the honor of states and, more importantly, of sovereigns.[7] The moral significance of such ideas is dubious at best. Insults are not occasions for wars, any more than they are (these days) occasions for duels.

For the rest, military alliances, mobilizations, troop movements, border incursions, naval blockades—all these, with or without verbal menace, sometimes count and sometimes do not count as sufficient indications of hostile intent. But it is, at least, these sorts of actions with which we are concerned. We move along the anticipation spectrum in search, as it were, of enemies: not possible or potential enemies, not merely present ill-wishers, but states and nations that are already, to use a phrase I shall use again with reference to the distinction of combatants and noncombatants, *engaged in harming us* (and who have already harmed us, by their threats, even if they have not yet inflicted any physical injury). And this search, though it carries us beyond preventive war, clearly brings us up short of Webster's pre-emption. The line between legitimate and illegitimate first strikes is not going to be drawn at the point of imminent attack but at the point of sufficient threat. That phrase is necessarily vague. I mean it to cover three things: a manifest intent to injure, a degree of active preparation that makes that intent a positive danger, and a general situation in which waiting, or doing anything other than fighting, greatly magnifies the risk. The argument may be made more clear if I compare these criteria to Vattel's. Instead of previous signs of rapacity and ambition, current and particular signs are required; instead of an "augmentation of power," actual preparation for war; instead of the refusal of future securities, the intensification of present dangers. Preventive war looks to the past and future, Webster's reflex action to the immediate moment, while the idea of being under a threat focuses on what we had best call simply *the present*. I cannot specify a time span; it is a span within which one can still make choices, and within which it is possible to feel straitened.[8]

What such a time is like is best revealed concretely. We can study it in the three weeks that preceded the Six Day War of 1967. Here is a case as crucial for an understanding of anticipation in the twentieth century as the War of the Spanish Succession was for the eighteenth, and one suggesting that the shift from dynastic to national politics, the costs of which have so often been stressed, has also brought some moral gains. For nations, especially democratic nations, are less likely to fight preventive wars than dynasties are.

The Six Day War

Actual fighting between Israel and Egypt began on June 5, 1967, with an Israeli first strike. In the early hours of the war, the Israelis did not acknowledge that they had sought the advantages of surprise, but the deception was not maintained. In fact, they believed themselves justified in attacking first by the dramatic events of the previous weeks. So we must focus on those events and their moral significance. It would be possible, of course, to look further back still, to the whole course of the Arab-Jewish conflict in the Middle East. Wars undoubtedly have long political and moral pre-histories. But anticipation needs to be understood within a narrower frame. The Egyptians believed that the founding of Israel in 1948 had been unjust, that the state had no rightful existence, and hence that it could be attacked at any time. It follows from this that Israel had no right of anticipation since it had no right of self-defense. But self-defense seems the primary and indisputable right of any political community, merely because it is *there* and whatever the circumstances under which it achieved statehood.* Perhaps this is why the Egyptians fell back in their more formal arguments upon the claim that a state of war already existed between Egypt and Israel and that this condition justified the military moves they undertook in May 1967.[9] But the same condition would justify Israel's first strike. It is best to assume, I think, that the existing cease-fire between the two countries was at least a near-peace and that the outbreak of the war requires a moral explanation—the burden falling on the Israelis, who began the fighting.

The crisis apparently had its origins in reports, circulated by Soviet officials in mid-May, that Israel was massing its forces on the Syrian border. The falsity of these reports was almost immediately vouched for by United Nations observers on the scene. Nevertheless, on May 14, the Egyptian government put its armed forces on "maximum alert" and began a major buildup of its troops in the Sinai. Four days later, Egypt expelled the United Nations Emergency Force from the Sinai and the Gaza Strip; its withdrawal began immediately, though I do not think that its title had been intended to suggest that it would depart so quickly in event of emergency. The Egyptian military buildup continued, and on May 22, President Nasser announced that the Straits of Tiran would henceforth be closed to Israeli shipping.

In the aftermath of the Suez War of 1956, the Straits had been recognized by the world community as an international waterway. That meant

---

* The only limitation on this right has to do with internal, not external legitimacy: a state (or government) established against the will of its own people, ruling violently, may well forfeit its right to defend itself even against a foreign invasion. I will take up some of the issues raised by this possibility in the next chapter.

that their closing would constitute a *casus belli*, and the Israelis had stated at that time, and on many occasions since, that they would so regard it. The war might then be dated from May 22, and the Israeli attack of June 5 described simply as its first military incident: wars often begin before the fighting of them does. But the fact is that after May 22, the Israeli cabinet was still debating whether or not to go to war. And, in any case, the actual initiation of violence is a crucial moral event. If it can sometimes be justified by reference to previous events, it nevertheless has to be justified. In a major speech on May 29, Nasser made that justification much easier by announcing that if war came, the Egyptian goal would be nothing less than the destruction of Israel. On May 30, King Hussein of Jordan flew to Cairo to sign a treaty placing the Jordanian army under Egyptian command in event of war, thus associating himself with the Egyptian purpose. Syria already had agreed to such an arrangement, and several days later Iraq joined the alliance. The Israelis struck on the day after the Iraqi announcement.

For all the excitement and fear that their actions generated, it is unlikely that the Egyptians intended to begin the war themselves. After the fighting was over, Israel published documents, captured in its course, that included plans for an invasion of the Negev; but these were probably plans for a counter-attack, once an Israeli offensive had spent itself in the Sinai, or for a first strike at some later time. Nasser would almost certainly have regarded it as a great victory if he could have closed the Straits and maintained his army on Israel's borders without war. Indeed, it would have been a great victory, not only because of the economic blockade it would have established, but also because of the strain it would have placed on the Israeli defense system. "There was a basic asymmetry in the structure of forces: the Egyptians could deploy . . . their large army of long-term regulars on the Israeli border and keep it there indefinitely; the Israelis could only counter their deployment by mobilizing reserve formations, and reservists could not be kept in uniform for very long. . . . Egypt could therefore stay on the defensive while Israel would have to attack unless the crisis was defused diplomatically."[10] *Would have to attack*: the necessity cannot be called instant and overwhelming; nor, however, would an Israeli decision to allow Nasser his victory have meant nothing more than a shift in the balance of power posing possible dangers at some future time. It would have opened Israel to attack at any time. It would have represented a drastic erosion of Israeli security such as only a determined enemy would hope to bring about.

The initial Israeli response was not similarly determined but, for domestic political reasons having to do in part with the democratic character of the state, hesitant and confused. Israel's leaders sought a political resolution of the crisis—the opening of the Straits and a demobilization of forces on both sides—which they did not have the political strength or support to effect. A flurry of diplomatic activity ensued, serving only to reveal what might have been predicted in advance: the unwillingness of the Western powers to pressure or coerce the Egyptians. One always wants to see diplomacy tried before the resort to war, so that we are sure that war is the last resort. But it would be difficult in this case to make an argument for its necessity. Day by day, diplomatic efforts seemed only to intensify Israel's isolation.

Meanwhile, "an intense fear spread in the country." The extraordinary Israeli triumph, once fighting began, makes it difficult to recall the preceding weeks of anxiety. Egypt was in the grip of a war fever, familiar enough from European history, a celebration in advance of expected victories. The Israeli mood was very different, suggesting what it means to live under threat: rumors of coming disasters were endlessly repeated; frightened men and women raided food shops, buying up their entire stock, despite government announcements that there were ample reserves; thousands of graves were dug in the military cemeteries; Israel's political and military leaders lived on the edge of nervous exhaustion.[11] I have already argued that fear by itself establishes no right of anticipation. But Israeli anxiety during those weeks seems an almost classical example of "just fear"—first, because Israel really was in danger (as foreign observers readily agreed), and second, because it was Nasser's intention to put it in danger. He said this often enough, but it is also and more importantly true that his military moves served no other, more limited goal.

The Israeli first strike is, I think, a clear case of legitimate anticipation. To say that, however, is to suggest a major revision of the legalist paradigm. For it means that aggression can be made out not only in the absence of a military attack or invasion but in the (probable) absence of any immediate intention to launch such an attack or invasion. The general formula must go something like this: states may use military force in the face of threats of war, whenever the failure to do so would seriously risk their territorial integrity or political independence. Under such circumstances it can fairly be said that they have been forced to fight and that they are the victims of aggression. Since there are no police upon whom they can call, the moment at which states are forced to fight probably comes sooner than it would for individuals in a settled domestic society. But if we imagine an unstable society, like the "wild west" of American fiction, the analogy can be restated: a state under threat is like an individual hunted by an enemy who has announced his intention of killing or injuring him. Surely such a person may surprise his hunter, if he is able to do so.

The formula is permissive, but it implies restrictions that can usefully be unpacked only with reference to particular cases. It is obvious, for example, that measures short of war are preferable to war itself whenever they hold out the hope of similar or nearly similar effectiveness. But what those measures might be, or how long they must be tried, cannot be a matter of *a priori* stipulation. In the case of the Six Day War, the "asymmetry in the structure of forces" set a time limit on diplomatic efforts that would have no relevance to conflicts involving other sorts of states and armies. A general rule containing words like "seriously" opens a broad path for human judgment—which it is, no doubt, the purpose of the legalist paradigm to narrow or block altogether. But it is a fact of our moral life that political leaders make such judgments, and that once they are made the rest of us do not uniformly condemn them. Rather, we weigh and evaluate their actions on the basis of criteria like those I have tried to describe. When we do that we are acknowledging that there are threats with which no nation can be expected to live. And that acknowledgment is an important part of our understanding of aggression.

6

INTERVENTIONS

affairs of other states follows readily from the legalist paradigm and, less readily and more ambiguously, from those conceptions of life and liberty that underlie the paradigm and make it plausible. But these same conceptions seem also to require that we sometimes disregard the principle; and what might be called the rules of disregard, rather than the principle itself, have been the focus of moral interest and argument. No state can admit to fighting an aggressive war and then defend its actions. But intervention is differently understood. The word is not defined as a criminal activity, and though the practice of intervening often threatens the territorial integrity and political independence of invaded states, it can sometimes be justified. It is more important to stress at the outset, however, that it always has to be justified. The burden of proof falls on any political leader who tries to shape the domestic arrangements or alter the conditions of life in a foreign country. And when the attempt is made with armed force, the burden is especially heavy—not only because of the coercion and ravages that military intervention inevitably brings, but also because it is thought that the citizens of a sovereign state have a right, insofar as they are to be coerced and ravaged at all, to suffer only at one another's hands.

SELF-DETERMINATION AND SELF-HELP

The Argument of John Stuart Mill

These citizens are the members, it is presumed, of a single political community, entitled collectively to determine their own affairs. The precise nature of this right is nicely worked out by John Stuart Mill in a short article published in the same year as the treatise *On Liberty* (1859) and especially useful to us because the individual/community analogy was very much in Mill's mind as he wrote.[1] We are to treat states as self-determining communities, he argues, whether or not their internal political arrangements are free, whether or not the citizens choose their government and openly debate the policies carried out in their name. For self-determination and political freedom are not equivalent terms. The first is the more inclusive idea; it describes not only a particular institutional arrangement but also the process by which a community arrives at that arrangement—or does not. A state is self-determining even if its citizens struggle and fail to establish free institutions, but it has been deprived of self-determination if such institutions are established by an intrusive neighbor. The members of a political community must seek their own freedom, just as the individual must cultivate his own virtue. They cannot be set free, as he cannot be made virtuous, by any external force. Indeed, political freedom depends upon the existence of individual virtue, and this the armies of another state are most unlikely to produce—unless, perhaps, they inspire an active resistance and set in motion a self-determining politics. Self-determination is the school in which virtue is learned (or not) and liberty is won (or not). Mill recognizes that a people who have had the "misfortune" to be ruled by a tyrannical government are peculiarly disadvantaged: they have never had a chance to develop "the virtues needful for maintaining freedom." But he insists nevertheless on the stern doctrine of self-help. "It is during an arduous struggle to become free by their own efforts that these virtues have the best chance of springing up."

Though Mill's argument can be cast in utilitarian terms, the harshness of his conclusions suggests that this is not its most appropriate form. The Millian view of self-determination seems to make utilitarian calculation unnecessary, or at least subsidiary to an understanding of communal liberty. He doesn't believe that intervention fails more often than not to serve the purposes of liberty; he believes that, given what liberty is, it *necessarily* fails. The (internal) freedom of a political community can be won only by the members of that community. The argument is similar to that implied in the well-known Marxist maxim, "The liberation of the working class can come only through the workers themselves."[2] As that maxim, one would think, rules out any substitution of vanguard elitism for working class democracy, so Mill's argument rules out any substitution of foreign intervention for internal struggle.

Self-determination, then, is the right of a people "to become free by their own efforts" if they can, and nonintervention is the principle guaranteeing that their success will not be impeded or their failure prevented by the intrusions of an alien power. It has to be stressed that there is no right to be protected against the consequences of domestic failure, even against a bloody repression. Mill generally writes as if he believes that citizens get the government they deserve, or, at least, the government for which they are "fit." And "the only test . . . of a people's having become fit for popular institutions is that they, or a sufficient portion of them to prevail in the contest, are willing to brave labor and danger for their liberation." No one can, and no one should, do it for them. Mill takes a very cool view of political conflict, and if many rebellious citizens, proud and full of hope in their own efforts, have endorsed that view, many others have not. There is no shortage of revolutionaries who have sought, pleaded for, even demanded outside help. A recent American commentator, eager to be helpful, has argued that Mill's position involves "a kind of Darwinian definition [*The Origin of the Species* was also published in 1859] of self-determination as survival of the fittest within the national boundaries, even if fittest means most adept in the use of force."[3] That last phrase is unfair, for it was precisely Mill's point that force could not prevail, unless it were reinforced from the outside, over a people ready "to brave labor and danger." For the rest, the charge is probably true, but it is difficult to see what conclusions follow from it. It is possible to intervene domestically in the "Darwinian" struggle because the intervention is continuous and sustained over time. But foreign intervention, if it is a brief affair, cannot shirt the domestic balance of power in any decisive way toward the forces of freedom, while if it is prolonged or intermittently resumed, it will itself pose the greatest possible threat to the success of those forces.

The case may be different when what is at issue is not intervention at all but conquest. Military defeat and governmental collapse may so shock a social system as to open the way for a radical renovation of its political arrangements. This seems to be what happened in Germany and Japan after

World War II, and these examples are so important that I will have to consider later on how it is that rights of conquest and renovation might arise. But they clearly don't arise in every case of domestic tyranny. It is not true, then, that intervention is justified whenever revolution is; for revolutionary activity is an exercise in self-determination, while foreign interference denies to a people those political capacities that only such exercise can bring.

These are the truths expressed by the legal doctrine of sovereignty, which defines the liberty of states as their independence from foreign control and coercion. In fact, of course, not every independent state is free, but the recognition of sovereignty is the only way we have of establishing an arena within which freedom can be fought for and (sometimes) won. It is this arena and the activities that go on within it that we want to protect, and we protect them, much as we protect individual integrity, by marking out boundaries that cannot be crossed, rights that cannot be violated. As with individuals, so with sovereign states: there are things that we cannot do to them, even for their own ostensible good.

And yet the ban on boundary crossings is not absolute—in part because of the arbitrary and accidental character of state boundaries, in part because of the ambiguous relation of the political community or communities within those boundaries to the government that defends them. Despite Mill's very general account of self-determination, it isn't always clear when a community is in fact self-determining, when it qualifies, so to speak, for nonintervention. No doubt there are similar problems with individual persons, but these are, I think, less severe and, in any case, they are handled within the structures of domestic law.* In international

---

*The domestic analogy suggests that the most obvious way of not qualifying for nonintervention is to be incompetent (childish, imbecilic, and so on). Mill believed that there were incompetent peoples, barbarians, in whose interest it was to be conquered and held in subjection by foreigners. "Barbarians have no rights as a *nation* [i.e., as a political community]. . . ." Hence utilitarian principles apply to them, and imperial bureaucrats legitimately work for their moral improvement. It is interesting to note a similar view among the Marxists, who also justified conquest and imperial rule at certain stages of historical development. (See Shlomo Avineri, ed., *Karl Marx on Colonialism and Modernization*, New York, 1969.) Whatever plausibility such arguments had in the nineteenth century, they have none today. International society can no longer be divided into civilized and barbarian halves; any line drawn on developmental principles leaves barbarians on both sides. I shall therefore assume that the self-help test applies equally to all peoples.

society, the law provides no authoritative verdicts. Hence, the ban on boundary crossings is subject to unilateral suspension, specifically with reference to three sorts of cases where it does not seem to serve the purposes for which it was established:

- when a particular set of boundaries clearly contains two or more political communities, one of which is already engaged in a large-scale military struggle for independence, that is, when what is at issue is secession or "national liberation";
- when the boundaries have already been crossed by the armies of a foreign power, even if the crossing has been called for by one of the parties in a civil war, that is, when what is at issue is counter-intervention; and
- when the violation of human rights within a set of boundaries is so terrible that it makes talk of community or self-determination or "arduous struggle" seem cynical and irrelevant, that is, in cases of enslavement or massacre.

The arguments that are made on behalf of intervention in each of these cases constitute the second, third, and fourth revisions of the legalist paradigm. They open the way for just wars that are not fought in self-defense or against aggression in the strict sense. But they need to be worked out with great care. Given the readiness of states to invade one another, revisionism is a risky business.

Mill discusses only the first two of these cases, secession and counter-intervention, though the last was not unknown even in 1859. It is worth pointing out that he does not regard them as exceptions to the nonintervention principle, but rather as negative demonstrations of its reasons. Where these reasons don't apply, the principle loses its force. It would be more exact, from Mill's standpoint, to formulate the relevant principle in this way: *always act so as to recognize and uphold communal autonomy.* Nonintervention is most often entailed by that recognition, but not always, and then we must prove our commitment to autonomy in some other way, perhaps even by sending troops across an international frontier. But the morally exact principle is also very dangerous, and Mill's account of the argument is not at this point an account of what is actually said in everyday moral discourse. We need to establish a kind of *a priori* respect for state boundaries; they are, as I have argued before, the only boundaries communities ever have. And that is why intervention is always justified as if it were an exception to a general rule, made necessary by the urgency or extremity of a particular case. The second, third, and fourth revisions have something of the form of stereotyped excuses. Interventions are so often undertaken for "reasons of state" that have nothing to do with self-determination that we have become skeptical of every claim to defend the autonomy of alien communities. Hence the special burden of proof with which I began, more onerous than any we impose on individuals or governments pleading self-defense: intervening states must demonstrate that their own case is radically different from what we take to be the general run of cases, where the liberty or prospective liberty of citizens is best served if foreigners offer them only moral support. And that is how I shall characterize Mill's argument (though he characterizes it differently) that Great Britain ought to have intervened in defense of the Hungarian Revolution of 1848 and 1849.

SECESSION

The Hungarian Revolution

For many years before 1848, Hungary had been a part of the Hapsburg Empire. Formally an independent kingdom, with a Diet of its own, it was effectively ruled by the German authorities in Vienna. The sudden collapse of those authorities during the March Days—symbolized by the fall of Metternich—opened the way for liberal nationalists in Budapest. They formed a government and demanded home rule within the Empire; they were not yet secessionists. Their demand was initially accepted, but controversy developed over the issues that have always plagued federalist schemes: the control of tax revenue, the command of the army. As soon as "order" was restored in Vienna, efforts began to reassert the centralist character of the regime, and these soon took the familiar form of military repression. An imperial army invaded Hungary, and the nationalists fought back. The Hungarians were now rebels or insurgents; they quickly established what international lawyers call their belligerent rights by defeating the Austrians and taking control of much of old Hungary. In the course of the war, the new government shifted leftwards; in April 1849, a republic was proclaimed under the presidency of Lajos Kossuth.[4]

The revolution might be described, in contemporary terms, as a war of national liberation, except that the boundaries of old Hungary included a very large Slavic population, and the Hungarian revolutionaries seem to have been as hostile to Croat and Slovene nationalism as the Austrians were to their own claims for communal autonomy. But this is a difficulty that I am going to set aside, for it did not appear as such at the time; it did not enter into the moral reflections of liberal observers like Mill. The Hungarian Revolution was greeted with enthusiasm by such men, especially in France, Britain, and the United States, and its emissaries were eagerly received. Governmental response was different, in part because nonintervention was the general rule to which all three governments subscribed, in part because the first two were also committed to the European balance of power and therefore to the integrity of Austria. In London, Palmerston was formal and cold: "The British government has no knowledge of Hungary except as one of the component parts of the Austrian Empire."[5] The Hungarians sought only diplomatic recognition, not military intervention, but any British dealings with the new government would have been regarded by the Austrian regime as an interference in its internal affairs. Recognition, moreover, had commercial consequences that might have engaged the British more closely on the side of Hungary, for the revolutionaries hoped to purchase military supplies on the London market. Despite this, the establishment of formal ties, once the Hungarians had demonstrated that "a sufficient portion of them" were committed to independence and willing to fight for it, would not have been difficult to justify in Millian terms. There can be no doubt of the existence (though there was a reason to doubt the extent) of the Hungarian political community; it was one of the oldest nations in Europe, and its recognition as a sovereign state would not have violated the moral rights of the Austrian people. Military supply to insurgent armies is indeed a complex issue, and I will come back to it with reference to another case, but none of the complexities are apparent here. Soon enough, however, the Hungarians needed far more than guns and ammunition.

In the summer of 1849, the Austrian emperor asked for the help of Tsar Nicholas I, and Hungary was invaded by a Russian army. Writing ten years later, Mill argued that the British should have responded to this intervention with an intervention of their own.[6]

It might not have been right for England (even apart from the question of prudence) to have taken part with Hungary in its noble struggle against Austria; although the Austrian government in Hungary was in some sense a foreign yoke. But when, the Hungarians having shown themselves likely to prevail in this struggle, the Russian despot interposed, and joining his force to that of Austria, delivered back the Hungarians, bound hand and foot, to their exasperated oppressors, it would have been an honorable and virtuous act on the part of England to have declared that this should not be, and that if Russia gave assistance to the wrong side, England would aid the right.

The qualification "in some sense a foreign yoke" with regard to Austrian rule in Hungary is curious, for whatever its meaning, it must also qualify the nobility and rightness of the Hungarian struggle for independence. Since Mill does not intend the latter qualification, we need not take the former seriously. The clear tendency of his argument is to justify assistance to a secessionist movement at the same time as it justifies counterintervention—indeed, to assimilate the one to the other. In both cases, the rule against interference is suspended because a foreign power, morally if not legally alien, is already interfering in the "domestic" affairs, that is, in the self-determinations of a political community.

Mill is right, however, to suggest that the issue is easier when the initial interference involves the crossing of a recognized frontier. The problem with a secessionist movement is that one cannot be sure that it in fact represents a distinct community until it has rallied its own people and made some headway in the "arduous struggle" for freedom. The mere appeal to the principle of self-determination isn't enough; evidence must be provided that a community actually exists whose members are committed to independence and ready and able to determine the conditions of their own existence.[7]* Hence the need for political or military struggle sustained over

---

*There is a further issue here, having to do with the natural resources that are sometimes at stake in secessionist struggles. I have argued that "the land follows the people" (chapter 4). But the will and capacity of the people for self-determination may not establish a right to secede if the secession would remove not only land but also vitally needed fuel and mineral resources from some larger political community. The Katangan controversy of the early 1960s suggests the possible difficulties of such cases—and invites us to worry also about the motives of intervening states. But what was missing in Katanga was a genuine national movement capable, on its own, of "arduous struggle." (See Conor C. O'Brien, *To Katanga and Back*, New York, 1962.) Given the existence of such a movement, I would be inclined to support secession. It would then be necessary, however, to raise more general questions about distributive justice in international society.

time. Mill's argument doesn't cover inarticulate and unrepresented peoples, or fledgling movements, or risings quickly suppressed. But imagine a small nation successfully mobilized to resist a colonial power but slowly being ground down in the unequal struggle: Mill would not insist, I think, that neighboring states stand by and watch its inevitable defeat. His argument justifies military action against imperial or colonial repression as well as against foreign intervention. Only domestic tyrants are safe, for it is not our purpose in international society (nor, Mill argues, is it possible) to establish liberal or democratic communities, but only independent ones. When it is required for the sake of independence, military action is "honorable and virtuous," though not always "prudent." I should add that the argument also applies to satellite regimes and great powers: designed for the first Russian intervention in Hungary (1849), it precisely fits the second (1956).

But the relation between virtue and prudence in such cases is not easy to make out. Mill's meaning is clear enough: to threaten war with Russia might have been dangerous to Britain and hence inconsistent "with the regard which every nation is bound to pay to its own safety." Now, whether or not it actually was dangerous was surely for the British to decide, and we would judge them harshly only if the risks they declined to run were very slight indeed. Even if counter-intervention is "honorable and virtuous," it is not morally required, precisely because of the dangers it involves. But one can make much more of prudence than this. Palmerston was concerned with the safety of Europe, not only of England, when he decided to stand by the Austrian empire. It is perfectly possible to concede the justice of the Millian position, and yet opt for nonintervention on what are currently called "world order" principles.[8] So justice and prudence are (with a certain worldly relish) set in opposition to one another in a way that Mill never imagined they could be. He thought, naively perhaps, that the world would be more orderly if none of its political communities were oppressed by foreign rule. He even hoped that Britain would one day be powerful enough, and have the necessary "spirit and courage," to insist "that not a gun [should] be fired in Europe by the soldiers of one Power against the revolted subjects of another," and to put itself "at the head of an alliance of free peoples. . . ." Today, I suppose, the United States has succeeded to those old-fashioned liberal pretensions, though in 1956 its leaders, like Palmerston in 1849, thought it imprudent to enforce them.

It might also be said that the United States had (and has) no right to enforce them, given the self-serving ways in which its government defines freedom and intervention in other parts of the world. Mill's England was hardly in a better position. Had Palmerston contemplated a military move on behalf of the Hungarians, Count Schwarzenberg, Metternich's successor, was prepared to remind him of "unhappy Ireland." "Wherever revolt breaks out within the vast limits of the British Empire," Schwarzenberg wrote to the Austrian ambassador in London, "the English government always knows how to maintain the authority of the law . . . even at the price of torrents of blood. It is not for us," he went on, "to blame her."[9] He sought only reciprocity, and that kind of reciprocity among great powers is undoubtedly the very essence of prudence.

To set prudence and justice so radically at odds, however, is to misconstrue the argument for justice. A state contemplating intervention or counter-intervention will for prudential reasons weigh the dangers to itself, but it must also, *and for moral reasons*, weigh the dangers its action will impose on the people it is designed to benefit and on all other people who may be affected. An intervention is not just if it subjects third parties to terrible risks: the subjection cancels the justice. If Palmerston was right in believing that the defeat of Austria would shatter the peace of Europe, a British intervention ensuring that defeat would not have been "honorable and virtuous" (however noble the Hungarian struggle). And clearly, an American threat of atomic war in 1956 would have been morally as well as politically irresponsible. Thus far prudence can be, and has to be, accommodated within the argument for justice. But it should be said that this deference to third party rights is not at the same time a deference to the local political interests of the great powers. Nor does it involve the acceptance of a Schwarzenbergian reciprocity. Britain's recognition of Austria's imperial claims does not entitle it to a similar recognition. The prudential acceptance of a Russian sphere of influence in Eastern Europe does not entitle the United States to a free hand in its own sphere. Against national liberation and counter-intervention, there are no prescriptive rights.

Civil War

If we describe the Hungarian Revolution as Mill did, assuming that Palmerston was wrong, ignoring the claims of Croats and Slovenes, it is virtually a paradigm case for intervention. It is also, so described, a historically exceptional, indeed, it is now a hypothetical case. For these circumstances don't often arise in history: a national liberation movement unambiguously embodying the claims of a single, unified political community; capable at least initially of sustaining itself on the battlefield; challenged by an unambiguously foreign power; whose intervention can however be deterred or defeated without risking a general war. More often history presents a tangle of parties and factions, each claiming to speak for an entire community, fighting with one another, drawing outside powers into the struggle in secret, or at least unacknowledged, ways. Civil war poses hard problems, not because the Millian standard is unclear—it would require a strict standoffishness—but because it can be and routinely is violated by degrees. Then it becomes very difficult to fix the point at which a direct and open use of force can plausibly be called a counter-intervention. And it is difficult also to calculate the effects of such a use of force on the already distressed inhabitants of the divided state and on the whole range of possible third parties.

In such cases, the lawyers commonly apply a qualified version of the self-help test.[10] They permit assistance to the established government—it is after all, the official representative of communal autonomy in international society—so long as it faces nothing more than internal dissension, rebellion, and insurgency. But as soon as the insurgents establish control over some substantial portion of the territory and population of the state, they acquire belligerent rights and an equality of status with the government. Then the lawyers enjoin a strict neutrality. Now, neutrality is conventionally regarded as an optative condition, a matter of choice, not of duty. So it is with regard to wars between states, but in civil wars there seem to be very good (Millian) reasons for making it obligatory. For once a community is effectively divided, foreign powers can hardly serve the cause of self-determination by acting militarily within its borders. The argument has been succinctly put by Montague Bernard, whose Oxford lecture "On the Principle of Non-intervention" ranks in importance with Mill's essay: "Of two things, one: the interference in the case supposed either turns the balance, or it does not. In the latter event, it misses its aim; in the former, it gives the superiority to the side which would not have been uppermost without it and establishes a sovereign, or a form of government, which the nation, if left to itself, would not have chosen."[11]

As soon as one outside power violates the norms of neutrality and non-intervention, however, the way is open for other powers to do so. Indeed, it may seem shameful not to repeat the violation—as in the case of the Spanish Civil War, where the noninterventionist policies of Britain, France, and the

United States did not open the way for a local decision, but simply allowed the Germans and Italians to "turn the balance."[12] Some military response is probably required at such moments if the values of independence and community are to be sustained. But though that response upholds values shared throughout international society, it cannot accurately be described as law enforcement. Its character is not readily explicable within the terms of the legalist paradigm. For counter-intervention in civil wars does not aim at punishing or even, necessarily, at restraining the intervening states. It aims instead at holding the circle, preserving the balance, restoring some degree of integrity to the local struggle. It is as if a policeman, instead of breaking up a fight between two people, should stop anyone else from interfering or, if he cannot do that, should give proportional assistance to the disadvantaged party. He would have to have some notions about the value of the fight, and given the ordinary conditions of domestic society, those would be strange notions for him to have. But in the world of states they are entirely appropriate; they set the standards by which we judge between actual and pretended counter-interventions.

The American War in Vietnam

I doubt that it is possible to tell the story of Vietnam in a way that will command general agreement. The official American version—that the struggle began with a North Vietnamese invasion of the South, to which the United States responded in accordance with its treaty obligations— follows the legalist paradigm closely, but is on its surface unbelievable. Fortunately, it seems to be accepted by virtually no one and need not detain us here. I want to pursue a more sophisticated version of the American defense, which concedes the existence of a civil war and describes the U.S. role, first, as assistance to a legitimate government, and secondly, as counter-intervention, a response to covert military moves by the North Vietnamese regime.[13] The crucial terms here are "legitimate" and "response." The first suggests that the government on behalf of which our counter-intervention was undertaken had a local status, a political presence independent of ourselves, and hence that it could conceivably win the civil war if no external force was brought to bear. The second suggests that our own military operations followed upon and balanced those of another power, in accordance with the argument I have put forward. Both these suggestions are false, but they point to the peculiarly confined character of counter-intervention and indicate what one has to say (at least) when one joins in the civil wars of other states.

The Geneva Agreement of 1954, ending the first Vietnamese war, established a temporary frontier between the North and the South, and two temporary governments on either side of the line, pending elections scheduled for 1956.[14] When the South Vietnamese government refused to permit these elections, it clearly lost whatever legitimacy was conferred by the agreements. But I shall not dwell on this loss, nor on the fact that some sixty states nevertheless recognized the sovereignty of the new regime in the South and opened embassies in Saigon. I doubt that foreign states, whether they act independently or collectively, sign treaties or send ambassadors, can establish or disestablish the legitimacy of a government. What is crucial is the standing of that government with its own people. Had the new regime been able to rally support at home, Vietnam today would have joined the divided states of Germany (until 1990) and Korea, and Geneva 1954 would be remembered only as the setting for another cold war partition. But what is the test of popular support in a country where democracy is unknown and elections are routinely managed? The test, for governments as for insurgents, is self-help. That doesn't mean that foreign states cannot provide assistance. One assumes the legitimacy of new regimes; there is, so to speak, a period of grace, a time to build support. But that time was ill-used in South Vietnam, and the continuing dependence of the new regime on the United States is damning evidence against it. Its urgent call for military intervention in the early 1960s is more damning evidence still. One must ask of President Diem a question first posed by Montague Bernard: "How can he impersonate [represent] his people who is begging the assistance of a foreign power in order to reduce them to obedience?"[15] Indeed, it was never a successful impersonation.

The argument might be put more narrowly: a government that receives economic and technical aid, military supply, strategic and tactical advice, and is still unable to reduce its subjects to obedience, is clearly an illegitimate government. Whether legitimacy is defined sociologically or morally, such a government fails to meet the most minimal standards. One wonders how it survives at all. It must be the case that it survives because of the outside help it receives and for no other, no local reasons. The Saigon regime was so much an American creature that the U.S. government's claim to be committed to it and obligated to ensure its survival is hard to understand. It is as if our right hand were committed to our left. There is no independent moral or political agent on the other side of the bond and hence no genuine bond at all. Obligations to one's creatures (except insofar as they pertain to the personal safety of individuals) are as insignificant politically as obligations to oneself are insignificant morally. When the U.S. did intervene militarily in Vietnam, then, it acted not to fulfill commitments to another state, but to pursue policies of its own contrivance.

Against all this, it is argued that the popular base of the South Vietnamese government was undermined by a systematic campaign of subversion, terrorism, and guerrilla war, largely directed and supplied from the North. That there was such a campaign, and that the North was involved in it, is clearly true, though the extent and timing of the involvement are very much in dispute. If one were writing a legal brief, these matters would be critically important, for the American claim is that the North Vietnamese were illegally supporting a local insurgency, with both men and material, at a time when the U.S. was still providing only economic assistance and military supply to a legitimate government. But that claim, whatever its legal force, somehow misses the moral reality of the Vietnamese case. It would be better to say that the U.S. was literally propping up a government—and shortly a series of governments—without a local political base, while the North Vietnamese were assisting an insurgent movement with deep roots in the countryside. We were far more vital to the government than they were to the insurgents. Indeed, it was the weakness of the government, its inability to help itself even against its internal enemies, that forced the steady escalation of American involvement. And that fact must raise the most serious questions about the American defense: for counter-intervention is morally possible only on behalf of a government (or a movement, party, or whatever) that has already passed the self-help test.

I can say very little here about the reasons for insurgent strength in the countryside. Why were the communists able, and the government unable, to "impersonate" Vietnamese nationalism? The character and scope of the American presence probably had a great deal to do with this. Nationalism is not easily represented by a regime as dependent as Saigon was on foreign support. It is also important that North Vietnamese moves did not similarly brand those they benefited as foreign agents. In nations divided as Vietnam was, infiltration across the dividing line is not necessarily regarded as outside interference by the men and women on the other side. The Korean War might look very different than it does if the Northerners had not marched in strength across the 38th parallel, but had made covert contact, instead, with a Southern rebellion. In contrast to Vietnam, however, there was no rebellion—and there was considerable support for the government—in South Korea.[16] These cold war dividing lines have the usual significance of an international border only insofar as they mark off, or come in time to mark off, two political communities within each of which individual citizens feel some local loyalty. Had South Vietnam taken shape in this way, American military activity, in the face of large-scale Northern connivance at terrorism and guerrilla war, might have qualified as counter-intervention. At least, the name would have been an arguable one. As it is, it is not.

It remains an issue whether the American counter-intervention, had it been such, could rightly have assumed the size and scope of the war we eventually fought. Some notion of symmetry is relevant here, though it cannot be fixed absolutely in arithmetic terms. When a state sets out to maintain or restore the integrity of a local struggle, its military activity should be roughly equivalent to that of the other intervening states. Counter-intervention is a balancing act. I have made this point before, but it is worth emphasizing, for it reflects a deep truth about the meaning of responsiveness: *the goal of counter-intervention is not to win the war.* That this is not an esoteric or obscure truth is suggested by President Kennedy's well-known description of the Vietnam War. "In the final analysis," Kennedy said, "it is their war. They are the ones who have to win it or lose it. We can help them, we can give them equipment, we can send our men out there as advisors, but they have to win it—the people of Vietnam against the Communists. . . ."[17] Though this view was reiterated by later American leaders, it is not, unhappily, a definitive exposition of American policy. In fact, the United States failed in the most dramatic way to respect the character and dimensions of the Vietnamese civil war, and we failed because we could not win the war as long as it retained that character and was fought within those dimensions. Searching for a level of conflict at which our technological superiority could be brought to bear, we steadily escalated the struggle, until finally it was an American war, fought for American purposes, in someone else's country.

HUMANITARIAN INTERVENTION

A legitimate government is one that can fight its own internal wars. And external assistance in those wars is rightly called counter-intervention only when it balances, and does no more than balance, the prior intervention of another power, making it possible once again for the local forces to win or lose on their own. The outcome of civil wars should reflect not the relative strength of the intervening states, but the local alignment of forces. There is another sort of case, however, where we don't look for outcomes of that sort, where we don't want the local balance to prevail. If the dominant forces within a state are engaged in massive violations of human rights, the appeal to self-determination in the Millian sense of self-help is not very attractive. That appeal has to do with the freedom of the community taken as a whole; it has no force when what is at stake is the bare survival or the minimal liberty of (some substantial number of) its members. Against the enslavement or massacre of political opponents, national minorities, and religious sects, there may well be no help unless help comes from outside. And when a government turns savagely upon its own people, we must doubt the very existence of a political community to which the idea of self-determination might apply.

Examples are not hard to find; it is their plenitude that is embarrassing. The list of oppressive governments, the list of massacred peoples, is frighteningly long. Though an event like the Nazi holocaust is without precedent in human history, murder on a smaller scale is so common as to be almost ordinary. On the other hand—or perhaps for this very reason—clear examples of what is called "humanitarian intervention" are very rare.[18] Indeed, I have not found any, but only mixed cases where the humanitarian motive is one among several. States don't send their soldiers into other states, it seems, only in order to save lives. The lives of foreigners don't weigh that heavily in the scales of domestic decision-making. So we shall have to consider the moral significance of mixed motives.* It is not necessarily an argument against humanitarian intervention that it is, at best, partially humanitarian, but it is a reason to be skeptical and to look closely at the other parts.

---

* The case is different, obviously, when the lives at stake are those of fellow nationals. Interventions designed to rescue citizens threatened with death in a foreign country have conventionally been called humanitarian, and there is no reason to deny them that name when life and death are really at issue. The Israeli raid on Entebbe airport in Uganda (July 4, 1976) seems likely to become a classic case. Here there is, or ought to be, no question of mixed motives: the only purpose is to rescue *these* people toward whom the intervening power has a special commitment.

Cuba, 1898, and Bangladesh, 1971

Both these cases might be taken up under the headings of national liberation and counter-intervention. But they each have a further significance because of the atrocities committed by the Spanish and the Pakistani governments. The brutal work of the Spaniards is easier to talk about, for it fell short of systematic massacre. Fighting against a Cuban insurgent army that lived off the land and apparently had large-scale peasant support, the Spaniards first worked out the policy of forced resettlement. They called it, without euphemism, *la reconcentración*. General Weyler's proclamation required that:[19]

> All inhabitants of rural areas or areas outside the lines of fortified towns will be concentrated within the towns occupied by troops at the end of eight days. All individuals who disobey or who are found outside the prescribed areas will be considered as rebels and judged as such.

I will ask later on whether "concentration" in itself is a criminal policy. The immediate crime of the Spaniards was to enforce the policy with so little regard for the health of the people involved that thousands of them suffered and died. Their lives and deaths were widely publicized in the United States, not only in the yellow press, and undoubtedly figured in the minds of many Americans as the major justification for the war against Spain. Thus the Congressional resolution of April 20, 1898: "Whereas the abhorrent conditions which have existed for more than three years in the island of Cuba, so near our own borders, have shocked the moral sense of the people of the United States. . . ."[20] But there were other reasons for going to war.

The chief of these were economic and strategic in character, having to do, first, with American investment in Cuban sugar, a matter of interest to a section of the financial community; and second, with the sea approaches to the Panamanian Isthmus where the canal would one day be, a matter of interest to the intellectuals and politicians who championed the cause of American expansion. Cuba was a minor element in the plans of men like Mahan and Adams, Roosevelt and Lodge, who were more concerned with the Pacific Ocean than the Caribbean Sea. But the canal that would connect the two gave it a certain strategic value, and the war to win it was worthwhile insofar as it accustomed Americans to imperialist adventures (and led also to the conquest of the Phillipines). By and large, the historical debate over the causes of the war has focused on the different forms of economic and political imperialism, the search for markets and investment opportunities, the pursuit of "national power for its own sake."[21] It's worth remembering, however, that the war was also supported by anti-imperialist politicians—or rather, that Cuban freedom was supported and then, in consequence of Spanish brutality, the humanitarian intervention of American military forces. The war we actually fought, however, and the intervention urged by populists and radical Democrats were two rather different things.

The Cuban insurgents made three requests of the United States: that we recognize their provisional government as the legitimate government of Cuba, that we provide their army with military supplies, and that American warships blockade the Cuban coast and cut off the supplies of the Spanish army. Given such help, it was said, the insurgent forces would grow, the Spaniards could not long hold out, and the Cubans would be left to reconstruct their country (with American help) and manage their own affairs.[22] This was also the program of American radicals. But President McKinley and his advisors did not believe the Cubans capable of managing their own affairs, or they feared a radical reconstruction. In any case, the U.S. intervened without recognizing the insurgents, invaded the island, and quickly defeated and replaced the Spanish forces. The victory undoubtedly had humane effects. Though the American military effort was remarkably inefficient, the war was short and added little to the miseries of the civilian population. Relief operations, also remarkably inefficient at first, began as soon as the battles were won. In his standard account of the war, Admiral Chadwick boasts of its relative bloodlessness: "War of itself," he writes, "cannot be the great evil; the evil is in the horrors, many of which are not necessarily concomitant. . . . The war now beginning between the United States and Spain was one in which these greater horrors were largely to be absent."[23] The horrors were indeed absent; far more so, at least, than in the long years of the Cuban Insurrection. But the invasion of Cuba, the three years of military occupation, the eventual granting of a drastically limited independence (under the provisions of the Platt Amendment) go a long way toward explaining the skepticism with which America's professions of humane concern have conventionally been regarded. The entire course of action, from 1898 to 1902, might be taken as an example of benevolent imperialism, given the "piratical times," but it is not an example of humanitarian intervention.[24]

The judgments we make in cases such as this don't hang on the fact that considerations other than humanity figured in the government's plans, or even on the fact that humanity was not the chief consideration. I don't know if it ever is, and measurement is especially difficult in a liberal democracy where the mixed motives of the government reflect the pluralism of the society. Nor is it a question of benevolent outcomes. As a result of the American victory, the *reconcentrados* were able to return to their homes. But they would have been able to do that had the United States entered the war on the side of the Spaniards and, together with them, decisively defeated the Cuban insurgents. "Concentration" was a war policy and would have ended with the war, whatever the war's end. The crucial question is a different one. Humanitarian intervention involves military action on behalf of oppressed people, and it requires that the intervening state enter, to some degree, into the purposes of those people. It need not set itself to achieve those purposes, but it also cannot stand in the way of their achievement. The people are oppressed, presumably, because they sought some end—religious toleration, national freedom, or whatever—unacceptable to their oppressors. One cannot intervene on their behalf and against their ends. I don't want to argue that the purposes of the oppressed are necessarily just or that one need accept them in their entirety. But it does seem that a greater attention is due them than the United States was prepared to pay in 1898.

This regard for the purposes of the oppressed directly parallels the respect for local autonomy that is a necessary feature of counter-intervention. The two revisionist principles reflect a common commitment: that intervention be as much like nonintervention as possible. In the one case, the goal is balance; in the other, it is rescue. In neither case, and certainly not in secessions and national liberation struggles, can the intervening state rightly claim any political prerogatives for itself. And whenever it makes such claims (as the United States did when it occupied Cuba and again when it imposed the Platt Amendment), we suspect that political power was its purpose from the start.

The Indian invasion of East Pakistan (Bangladesh) in 1971 is a better example of humanitarian intervention—not because of the singularity or purity of the government's motives, but because its various motives converged on a single course of action that was also the course of action called for by the Bengalis. This convergence explains why the Indians were in and out of the country so quickly, defeating the Pakistani army but not replacing it, and imposing no political controls on the emergent state of Bangladesh. No doubt, strategic as well as moral interests underlay this policy: Pakistan, India's old enemy, was significantly weakened, while India itself avoided becoming responsible for a desperately poor nation whose internal politics was likely to be unstable and volatile for a long time to come. But the intervention qualifies as humanitarian because it was a *rescue*, strictly and narrowly defined. So circumstances sometimes make saints of us all.

I shall not say very much about Pakistani oppression in Bengal. The tale is a terrible one and by now fairly well documented.[25] Faced with a movement for autonomy in what was then its eastern province, the government of Pakistan, in March 1971, literally turned an army loose on its own people—or rather, a Punjabi army loose on the Bengali people, for the unity of east and west was already a broken thing. The resulting massacre only completed the break and made it irreparable. The army was not entirely without direction; its officers carried "death lists" on which appeared the names of the political, cultural, and intellectual leaders of Bengal. There was also a systematic effort to slaughter the followers of these people: university students, political activists, and so on. Beyond these groups, the soldiers ranged freely, burning, raping, killing. Millions of Bengalis fled into India, and their arrival, destitute, hungry, and with incredible stories to tell, established the moral foundation of the later Indian attack. "It is idle to argue in such cases that the duty of the neighboring people is to look on quietly."[26] Months of diplomatic maneuvering followed, but during that time, the Indians were already assisting Bengali guerrillas and offering sanctuary not only to refugees but also to fighting men and women. The two-week war of December 1971 apparently began with a Pakistani air strike, but the Indian invasion required no such prior attack; it was justified on other grounds.

The strength of the Bengali guerrillas and their achievements between March and December are matters of some dispute; so is their role in the two-week war. Clearly, however, it was not the purpose of the Indian invasion to open the way for the Bengali struggle; nor does the strength or weakness of the guerrillas affect our view of the invasion. When a people are being massacred, we don't require that they pass the test of self-help before coming to their aid. It is their very incapacity that brings us in. The purpose of the Indian army, then, was to defeat the Pakistani forces and drive them out of Bangladesh, that is, to win the war. The purpose was different from that of a counter-intervention, and for an important moral reason. People who initiate massacres lose their right to participate in the normal (even in the normally violent) processes of domestic self-determination. Their military defeat is morally necessary.

Governments and armies engaged in massacres are readily identified as criminal governments and armies (they are guilty, under the Nuremberg code of "crimes against humanity"). Hence humanitarian intervention comes much closer than any other kind of intervention to what we commonly regard, in domestic society, as law enforcement and police work. At the same time, however, it requires the crossing of an international frontier, and such crossings are ruled out by the legalist paradigm—unless they are authorized, I suppose, by the society of nations. In the cases I have considered, the law is unilaterally enforced; the police are self-appointed. Now, unilateralism has always prevailed in the international arena, but we worry about it more when what is involved is a response to domestic violence rather than to foreign aggression. We worry that, under the cover of humanitarianism, states will come to coerce and dominate their neighbors; once again, it is not hard to find examples. Hence many lawyers prefer to stick to the paradigm. That doesn't require them, on their view, to deny the (occasional) need for intervention. They merely deny legal recognition to that need. Humanitarian intervention "belongs in the realm not of law but of moral choice, which nations, like individuals must sometimes make. . . ."[27] But that is only a plausible formulation if one doesn't stop with it, as lawyers are likely to do. For moral choices are not simply *made*; they are also judged, and so there must be criteria for judgment. If these are not provided by the law, or if legal provision runs out at some point, they are nevertheless contained in our common morality, which doesn't run out, and which still needs to be explicated after the lawyers have finished.

Morality, at least, is not a bar to unilateral action, so long as there is no immediate alternative available. There was none in the Bengali case. No doubt, the massacres were a matter of universal interest, but only India interested itself in them. The case was formally carried to the United Nations, but no action followed. Nor is it clear to me that action undertaken by the UN, or by a coalition of powers, would necessarily have had a moral quality superior to that of the Indian attack. What one looks for in numbers is detachment from particularist views and consensus on moral rules. And for that, there is at present no institutional appeal; one appeals to humanity as a whole. States don't lose their particularist character merely by acting together. If governments have mixed motives, so do coalitions of governments. Some goals, perhaps, are cancelled out by the political bargaining that constitutes the coalition, but others are superadded; and the resulting mix is as accidental with reference to the moral issue as are the political interests and ideologies of a single state.

Humanitarian intervention is justified when it is a response (with reasonable expectations of success) to acts "that shock the moral conscience of mankind." The old-fashioned language seems to me exactly right. It is not the conscience of political leaders that one refers to in such cases. They have other things to worry about and may well be required to repress their normal feelings of indignation and outrage. The reference is to the moral convictions of ordinary men and women, acquired in the course of their everyday activities. And given that one can make a persuasive argument in terms of those convictions, I don't think that there is any moral reason to adopt that posture of passivity that might be called waiting for the UN (waiting for the universal state, waiting for the messiah . . .).

> Suppose . . . that a great power decided that the only way it could continue to control a satellite state was to wipe out the satellite's entire population and recolonize the area with "reliable" people. Suppose the satellite government agreed to this measure and established the necessary mass extermination apparatus. . . . Would the rest of the members of the U.N. be compelled to stand by and watch this operation merely because [the] requisite decision of U.N. organs was blocked and the operation did not involve an "armed attack" on any [member state]? . . .[28]

The question is rhetorical. Any state capable of stopping the slaughter has a right, at least, to try to do so. The legalist paradigm indeed rules out such efforts, but that only suggests that the paradigm, unrevised, cannot account for the moral realities of military intervention.

The second, third, and fourth revisions of the paradigm have this form: states can be invaded and wars justly begun to assist secessionist movements (once they have demonstrated their representative character), to balance the prior interventions of other powers, and to rescue peoples threatened with massacre. In each of these cases we permit or, after the fact, we praise or don't condemn these violations of the formal rules of sovereignty, because they uphold the values of individual life and communal liberty of which sovereignty itself is merely an expression. The formula is, once again, permissive, but I have tried in my discussion of particular cases to indicate that the actual requirements of just interventions are constraining indeed. And the revisions must be understood to include the constraints. Since the constraints are often ignored, it is sometimes argued that it would be best to insist on an absolute rule of nonintervention (as it would be best to insist on an absolute rule of a nonanticipation). But the absolute rule will also be ignored, and we will then have no standards by which to judge what happens next. In fact, we do have standards, which I have tried to map out. They reflect deep and valuable, though in their applications difficult and problematic, commitments to human rights.

7

WAR'S ENDS, AND THE
IMPORTANCE OF WINNING

WHAT MAY BE CALLED THE MODERNIST VIEW OF WAR IS GRIMLY SUMMED
up in a poem by Randall Jarrell:[1]

> *Profits and death grow marginal:*
> *Only the mourning and the mourned recall*
> *The wars we lose, the wars we win;*
> *And the world is—what it has been.*

War kills; that is all it does; even its economic causes are not reflected in its outcomes; and the soldiers who die are, in the contemporary phrase, wasted. Jarrell speaks in the name of those wasted men, of comrades already dead and of others who know they will soon be killed. And theirs is an authoritative perspective: there have been so many of them. When soldiers die in small numbers, in encompassable battles, they can attribute some meaning to their deaths. Sacrifice and heroism are conceivable notions. But the slaughter of modern warfare overwhelms their capacity for moral understanding; cynicism is their last resort. It is not, however, our last resort, or the most important form of our perceptions of the war in which Jarrell fought. Indeed, most of his fellow survivors would still want to affirm that the world is different, and better, for the Allied victory and the defeat of the Nazi regime. And theirs, too, is an authoritative perspective: there are so many of them. In an age when human sensibility is finely tuned to all the nuances of despair, it still seems important to say of those who die in war *that they did not die in vain*. And when we can't say that, or think we can't, we mix our mourning with anger. We search for guilty men. We are still committed to a moral world.

What does it mean *not to have died in vain*? There must be purposes that are worth dying for, outcomes for which soldiers' lives are not too high a price. The idea of a just war requires the same assumption. A just war is one that it is morally urgent to win, and a soldier who dies in a just war does not die in vain. Critical values are at stake: political independence, communal liberty, human life. Other means failing (an important qualification), wars to defend these values are justified. The deaths that occur in their course, on both sides, are morally comprehensible—which is not to say that they are not also the products of military stupidity and bureaucratic snafu: soldiers die senselessly even in wars that are not senseless.

But if it is sometimes urgent to win, it is not always clear what winning is. On the conventional military view, the only true aim in war is "the destruction of the enemy's main forces on the battlefield."[2] Clausewitz speaks of "the overthrow of the enemy."[3] But many wars end without any such dramatic ending, and many war aims can be achieved well short of destruction and overthrow. We need to seek the legitimate ends of war, the goals that can rightly be aimed at. These will also be the limits of a just war. Once they are won, or once they are within political reach, the fighting should stop. Soldiers killed beyond that point die needlessly, and to force them to fight and possibly to die is a crime akin to that of aggression itself. It is commonly said of just war theory, however, that it does not in fact draw this line at any point short of destruction and overthrow, that the most extreme military argument and the "moralist" argument coincide in requiring that war be fought to its ultimate end. In the aftermath of World War II, a group of writers appeared who insisted that the pursuit of justice was deeply implicated in the horrors of twentieth-century war.[4] They called themselves "realists," and I shall use that name, though these were not in fact followers of Thucydides and Hobbes. Their argument was less general and ultimately less subversive of conventional morality. Just wars turn into crusades, they claimed, and then the statesmen and soldiers who fight them seek the only victory appropriate to their cause: total victory, unconditional surrender. They fight too brutally and too long. They sow justice and reap death. It is a powerful argument, though I shall want to suggest with reference both to the conduct of war and to the purposes for which it is fought that it makes no sense except as a moral argument. The remedy the realists proposed was to give up justice and aim at more modest outcomes. The remedy I want to propose instead is to understand better the justice at which we cannot help aiming.

UNCONDITIONAL SURRENDER

Allied Policy in World War II

The realist position might be summed up in this way. It is a feature of democratic or liberal culture that peace is conceived as a normative condition. Wars can only be fought, then, if some "universal moral principle" requires it: the preservation of peace, the survival of democracy, and so on. And once war begins, this principle must be vindicated absolutely; nothing less than total victory will justify the resort to the "evil instrument" of military force. The threat to peace or democracy must be completely destroyed.[5] "Democratic cultures," as Kecskemeti has written in his well-known book on surrender, "are profoundly unwarlike: to them, war can be justified only if it is waged to eliminate war. . . . This crusading ideology . . . is reflected in the conviction that hostilities cannot be brought to an end before the evil enemy system has been eradicated."[6] The *locus classicus* of this ideology is the thought of Woodrow Wilson, and its most important material expression is the Allied demand for unconditional surrender in World War II.

What is objectionable about democratic idealism, as the realists describe it, is that it sets goals that cannot possibly be reached, for which soldiers can only die in vain. This is a moral objection, and an important one if soldiers have in fact been asked to die for such purposes as "the eradication of evil." Their most heroic efforts, after all, can only bring a particular war to an end; they cannot end war. They can save democracy from a particular threat, but they cannot make the world safe for democracy. But I am inclined to think that the significance of these Wilsonian slogans has been much overestimated in the realist literature. By the time Wilson brought the United States into World War I, the fighting had already been carried well beyond the limits of justice and reason. The worst of those "injuries . . . to the structure of human society which a century will not efface" had already been inflicted, and the men responsible were not innocent Americans but the tough-minded statesmen and soldiers of Britain, France, and Germany. Wilson's Fourteen Points made possible a German surrender on terms that fell far short of the war aims of Lloyd George and Clemenceau.[7] Indeed, it was the German charge that these terms had not been honored in the actual peace settlement (which was true) that led the Allies to insist on unconditional surrender the second time around. "No such arguments will be admitted by us as were used by Germany after the last war," Churchill told the House of Commons in February 1944.[8] "The policy of unconditional surrender," writes Kecskemeti, "represents a studied contrast with President Wilson's political conduct of the war in 1918." But if that is true, it isn't easy to see how both Wilsonian and anti-Wilsonian policies, surrender on terms and unconditional surrender, can be attributed to "the traditional moralistic all-or-nothing American approach to the problem of war and peace."[9]

For all his idealism, Wilson fought a limited war; his ideals set the limits. (Whether these were the right limits or not is another question.) Nor was World War II an unlimited war, despite the refusal of the Allies to offer terms. The demand for unconditional surrender, Churchill assured the Commons, "does not mean that [we] are entitled to behave in a barbarous manner, nor that [we] wish to blot out Germany from among the nations of Europe." What it does mean, he went on, is that "if we are bound, we are bound by our own consciences to civilization. We are not bound to the Germans as the result of a bargain struck."[10] It would have been more precise had he said that the Allies were not bound to the German *government*, for the German people, the greater number of them, at any rate, must be included under the rubric of "civilization." They were entitled to the protection of civilized norms and could never have been entirely at the mercy of their conquerors. There is really no such thing (in the moral world) as the unconditional surrender of a nation, for conditions inhere in the very idea of international relations, as they do in the idea of human relations—and they are roughly the same in each. Even domestic criminals, with whom the authorities don't usually negotiate, never surrender unconditionally. If they cannot stipulate conditions above those established in the law, it is nevertheless true that the law recognizes rights—the right not to be tortured, for example—which are theirs as human beings and as citizens, whatever their crimes. Nations have similar rights in international society, above all the right not to be "blotted out," deprived forever of sovereignty and freedom.*

Concretely, the policy of unconditional surrender involved two commitments: first, that the Allies would not negotiate with Nazi leaders, would have no dealings with them of any sort, "except to instruct them about the details of orderly capitulation"; secondly, that no German government would be recognized as legitimate and authoritative until the Allies had won the war, occupied Germany, and established a new regime. Given the character of the existing German government, these commitments do not seem to me to represent an excessive idealism. But they do suggest the outer limit of what can legitimately be sought in war. The outer limit is the conquest and political reconstruction of the enemy state, and only against an enemy like Nazism can it possibly be right to reach that far. In his lectures on American diplomacy, George Kennan suggests that unconditional surrender should not have been talked about, but he nevertheless agrees "that Hitler was a man with whom a compromise peace was impracticable and unthinkable. . . ."[11] That is, one might say, a realistic moral judgment. It recognizes, without explicitly affirming, the evil of the Nazi regime, and it rightly places Nazism outside the (moral) world of bargaining and accommodation. We can understand the right of conquest and reconstruction only with such an example. The right does not arise in every war; it did not arise, I think, in the war against Japan. It exists only in cases where the criminality of the aggressor state threatens those deep

---

*It was once argued by jurists and philosophers that conquerors had a right to kill or enslave the citizens of a conquered state. Against this view, in the name of natural law or human rights, Montesquieu and Rousseau claimed that the conqueror's prerogatives extended only to the state, not to the individual men and women who composed it. "The state is the association of men, not the men themselves; the citizen may perish and the man remain." (*The Spirit of the Laws*, X.3.) "Sometimes it is possible to kill the State without killing a single one of its members; and war gives no right which is not necessary to the gaining of its object." (*The Social Contract*, I.4.) But this is still too permissive a view, for the rights of individuals include the right of political association, and if the citizen is killed or the state destroyed, something of the man dies too. Even the destruction of a particular regime is only defensible, as I will argue, in exceptional circumstances.

values that political independence and territorial integrity merely stand for in the international order, and when the threat is in no sense accidental or transitory but is inherent in the very nature of the regime.

One must be careful here; it is at this point that just wars come nearest to crusades. A crusade is a war fought for religious or ideological purposes. It aims not at defense or law enforcement, but at the creation of new political orders and at mass conversions. It is the international equivalent of religious persecution and political repression, and it is obviously ruled out by the argument for justice. Yet the very existence of Nazism tempts us, as it tempted General Eisenhower, to imagine World War II as a "crusade in Europe." So we must draw the line between just wars and crusades as clearly as we can. Consider the following argument of a nineteenth-century English jurist:[12]

> The first limitation of the general right, incident to every state, of adopting whatever form of government . . . [it] may please is this:
> No state has a right to establish a form of government which is built upon professed principles of hostility to the government of other nations.

This is to draw the line very dangerously, for it suggests that we might make war against governments whose "professions" we have some reason to dislike or fear. But professions are not to the point. We have no clear knowledge as to when these are likely to be acted out and when they are not. No single form of government seems particularly prone to aggression. It is certainly not the case, as many nineteenth-century liberals imagined, that authoritarian states are more likely to make war than democracies are: the history of democratic regimes, beginning with Athens, offers no evidence of this. Nor is hostility to governments relevant here, except insofar as these represent the self-determining activities of nations. The Nazis were at war with nations, not governments alone; they were not merely professedly but actively hostile to the very existence of entire peoples. And it is only in response to hostility of this sort that the rights of conquest and political reconstruction come into existence.

But suppose the German people had risen against Nazism, as they rose against the Kaiser in 1918, and themselves created a new regime. The Allies were apparently committed not to deal even with a revolutionary German government. "To the morally oriented Allies," writes Kecskemeti, "any abatement from the strict rules of unconditionality meant that some element of the evil past would survive after the loser's surrender and make their victory meaningless."[13] In fact, there was another, and a more realistic, motive for strictness: mutual distrust among Hitler's enemies, the needs of coalition politics. The Western powers and the Russians could agree on nothing except an absolute rule.[14] Justice points the other way, for reasons closely akin to those that mark out and drastically limit the practice of intervention. Had the Germans themselves undertaken to destroy Nazism, there would have been every reason to help them and no need for an external reconstruction of their polity. A German revolution would have made the conquest of Germany morally unnecessary. But there was no revolution and painfully little resistance to Nazi rule. Politically significant opposition developed only within the ruling cadre itself, and only in the latter days of a losing war: thus the *coup d'etat* attempted by the German generals in July 1944. In peacetime, such an attempt would count as an act of self-determination, and if it were successful, other states would have no choice but to deal with the new government. Given a war such as the Nazis fought, and in which the generals were deeply implicated, the case is harder. I am inclined to think that by 1944 the Allies had a right to expect, and to impose, a more thoroughgoing renovation of German political life. Even the generals would have had to surrender unconditionally (as some of them, at least, were ready to do).

Unconditional surrender is rightly regarded as a punitive policy. It is important to see exactly in what sense this is so. The policy would have penalized the German people only insofar as it declared their political liberty temporarily forfeit and subjected them to a military occupation. Pending the establishment of a post-Nazi and an anti-Nazi regime, the Germans were to be placed in political tutelage: it is a consequence of their failure to overthrow Hitler themselves, the chief of the ways in which they were collectively held responsible for the injuries he and his followers caused to other nations. The forfeiture of independence, however, entails no further loss of rights; the punishment was limited and temporary; it assumed, as Churchill said, the continued existence of a German nation. But the Allies also aimed at more particular and far-reaching punishments. They refused to compromise with the Nazi regime because they planned to put its leading members on trial for their lives. To wage war with such a goal in mind, Kecskemeti argues, is to succumb to "the pedagogic fallacy," that is, to try to build a peaceful post-war world "on the undying memory of a just chastisement." But that cannot be done because deterrence doesn't work in international as it does in domestic society: the number of actors is far smaller; their deeds are not stereotyped and reiterated; the lessons of punishment are interpreted very differently by those who administer and by those who receive them; and in any case, they soon become irrelevant as circumstances change.[15] Now, "just chastisement" is exactly what the legalist paradigm would require, and Kecskemeti's criticism points toward the need for further revision. But he argues only that deterrence is ineffective, and his argument, while it is plausible enough, is by no means certainly true. I want to suggest instead that the special character of international society makes the full measure of domestic law enforcement *morally* infeasible, and at the same time that the special character of Nazism in fact required the "chastisement" of the leading Nazis.

What is special about international society is the collective character of its members. Each decision-maker stands for an entire community of men and women; the impact of his aggressive and defensive wars is felt over a wide geographic and political range. War affects more people than domestic crime and punishment, and it is the rights of those people that force us to limit its purposes. We might consider a new version of the domestic analogy, oriented toward collective rather than individual action: the attack of one state upon another is more like a feudal raid than a criminal assault (even when it is, literally, a criminal assault). It resembles a feud more than a mugging, not only because there are no commonly accepted police, but also because the rituals of punishment will more probably extend than cut off the violence. Short of the most severe and extraordinary measures—extermination, exile, political dismemberment—an enemy state, like an aristocratic clan, and unlike a common criminal, cannot be entirely deprived of the power of renewed activity. But such measures can never be defended, and so enemy states must be treated, morally as well as strategically, as future partners in some sort of international order.

Stability among states, as among aristocratic factions and families, rests upon certain patterns of accommodation and restraint, which statesmen and soldiers would do well not to disrupt. But these patterns are not simply diplomatic artifacts; they have a moral dimension. They depend upon mutual understandings; they are comprehensible only within a world of shared values. Nazism was a conscious and willful challenge to the very existence of such a world: a program of extermination, exile, and political dismemberment. In a sense, aggression was the least of Hitler's crimes. It is not quite right, then, to describe the conquest and occupation of Germany and the trial of Nazi leaders as so many (unavailing) efforts to deter future aggressors. They are better understood as the expressions of a collective abhorrence, a reaffirmation of our own deepest values.[16] And it is right to say, as many people said at the time, that the war against Nazism had to end with such a reaffirmation if it was to end meaningfully at all.

JUSTICE IN SETTLEMENTS

The policy of unconditional surrender, directed at the government but not the people of Germany, was an appropriate response to Nazism. But it isn't always appropriate. Doing justice, in the legalist sense, isn't always the right thing to do. (I have already argued that it cannot be the goal of counter-interventions.) The cardinal mistake of the realists is to suppose that if one fights for "universal moral principles," one must always fight in the same way, as if universal principles did not have concrete and diverse applications. We need, then, to look at a case where limited aims were set, not by the requirements of a realistic analysis—for realism imposes no moral requirements; aggressors can be realists, too—but by the argument for justice.

The Korean War

The American war in Korea was officially described as a "police action." We had come to the aid of a state defending itself against a fullscale invasion, committed ourselves to the hard work of international law enforcement. The United Nations' authorization enhanced our commitment, but its terms were in fact shaped unilaterally. Once again, we were at war with aggression itself as well as with a particular foe. Now, what were the war aims of the U.S. government? One would expect that American democracy, slow to anger but terrible in its righteous wrath, should have aimed at the total eradication of the North Korean regime. In fact, our initial aims were limited in character. In the Senate debate over President Truman's decision to rush American troops into battle, it was stated repeatedly that our sole purpose was to drive the North Koreans back to the partition line and to restore the *status quo ante bellum*. Senator Flanders insisted that the President "would not be within his rights in pursuing the Korean forces . . . north of the 38th parallel." Senator Lucas, a spokesman for the administration, "wholeheartedly agreed."[17] The debate focused on constitutional issues; there had been no declaration of war and so the President's "rights" were limited. At the same time, the Senate did not want to declare war and enlarge those rights; its members were satisfied with what might be called a conservative war. "The acquisitive state," writes Liddell Hart, "inherently unsatisfied, needs to gain victory in order to gain its object. . . . The conservative state can attain its object . . . by foiling the other side's bid for victory."[18]

That was the American goal until we ourselves, in the immediate aftermath of MacArthur's triumph at Inchon, crossed the 38th parallel. The decision to cross is not at all easy to figure out, but it seems to be an example of military *hubris* far more than of democratic idealism. Its larger political and moral implications do not seem to have been thought about much at the time; the move was defended mostly in tactical terms. To halt at the old line, it was said, would have surrendered the military initiative to the enemy and allowed him to rebuild his army for a new offensive. "The aggressor's forces should not be permitted to take refuge behind an imaginary line," Ambassador Austin told the UN, "because that would recreate the threat to the peace. . . ."[19] I will leave aside the odd notion that the 38th parallel was an imaginary line (how then did we recognize the initial aggression?). It is not implausible to suggest that the North Koreans had no right to a military sanctuary and that attacks across the 38th parallel with the limited purpose of preventing their regroupment might be justified. In responding to an armed invasion, one can legitimately aim not merely at a successful resistance but also at some reasonable security against future attack. But when we crossed the old line, we also took on a more radical purpose. Now it was the American goal, sanctioned, again, by the UN, to unify Korea by force of arms and create a new (democratic) government. And that required not limited attacks within the borders of North Korea, but the conquest of the entire country. The question is whether wars against aggression necessarily generate such far-reaching and exalted goals. Is this what justice requires?

If it is, we would have done well to settle for something less. But it would be strange for Americans to answer that question in the affirmative, since we had formally branded the North Korean attempt to unify the country by force a criminal aggression. Secretary of State Acheson seems to have felt the difficulty when he told the Senate (during the MacArthur hearings) that unification had never been our *military* objective. We aimed only "to round up the people that were putting on the aggression." That would have created a political vacuum in the North, he went on, and Korea would then have been unified, not through force, but "through elections and that sort of thing. . . ."[20] Disingenuous as this is, it nevertheless is indicative of what the argument for justice requires. Defending the morality of American policy, Acheson is forced to insist on the limited character of our military effort and to deny that it ever was a crusade against communism. He did believe, however, that the success of our police action required something very like the conquest of North Korea.

Clearly, the analogy in his mind was with domestic law enforcement, where one doesn't simply stop the criminal activity and restore the *status quo ante*; one also "rounds up" the criminals and holds them for trial and punishment. But this feature of the domestic model (and hence of the legalist paradigm) is not easily carried over into the international arena. For the roundup of the aggressors will most often require a military conquest, and conquest has effects that reach far beyond the people who are rounded up. It prolongs a war in which large numbers of innocent men and women are virtually certain to die, and it puts a whole nation, as we have seen, under political tutelage. It does this even if its methods are democratic ("free elections and that sort of thing"), because it replaces a regime which the people of the conquered nation had not themselves sought to replace—indeed, for which they had recently fought and died. Unless the activities of that regime are a standing affront to the conscience of mankind, its destruction is not a legitimate military goal. And however grim a picture one paints, the North Korean regime was not such an affront; its policies were more like those of Bismarck's than of Hitler's Germany. Its leaders may well have been guilty of criminal aggression, but their physical capture and punishment seem at most the marginal benefit of a certain sort of military victory, not a reason for seeking such a victory.

The argument at this point might be put in terms of proportionality, a doctrine often said to fix firm limits to the length of wars and the shape of settlements. In this instance, we would have to balance the costs of continued fighting against the value of punishing the aggressors. Given our present knowledge of the Chinese invasion and its consequences, we can say that the costs were disproportionate (and the aggressors never punished). But even without such knowledge, a strong case might have been made that Acheson's "round-up" did not warrant its likely price. On the other hand, it is characteristic of arguments of this sort that an equally strong case could have been made on the other side, simply by enlarging our conception of the purposes of the war. Proportionality is a matter of adjusting means to ends, but as the Israeli philosopher Yehuda Melzer has pointed out, there is an overwhelming tendency in wartime to adjust ends to means instead, that is, to redefine initially narrow goals in order to fit the available military forces and technologies.[21] Perhaps the conquest of North Korea could not be defended as a means of punishing aggressors; it might nonetheless have been defended as a means of doing that and simultaneously abolishing a border that could only be (in fact has been) the focus of future tension—hence, avoiding wars to come. It is necessary in such arguments to *hold ends constant*, but how does one do that? In practice, the inflation of ends is probably inevitable unless it is barred by considerations of justice itself.

Now justice in settlements is a complex notion, but it has a certain minimal content which seems to have been understood well enough by America's leaders at the beginning of the struggle. Once that minimal content has been realized, it is the rights of the people of the enemy country that rule out further fighting, whatever its added value.* These rights

---

* Or it is the rights of one's own people. Consider the classic discussion of proportionality in war in Shakespeare's *Troilus and Cressida* (II.2). Hector and Troilus are debating the surrender of Helen:

Hector. Brother, she is not worth what she doth cost
The keeping.
Troilus. What's aught but as 'tis valued?
Hector. But value dwells not in particular will.
It holds his estimate and dignity
As well wherein 'tis precious of itself
As in the prizer. 'Tis mad idolatry
To make the service greater than the god.

Troilus quickly switches the argument from Helen herself to the honor of the Trojan warriors, and so wins the debate, for the value of honor seems indeed to dwell in particular wills. The move is typical, and it can be countered only with a moral claim: that the Trojan warriors have no right to put a whole city at risk for the sake of their own honor. It is not that the sacrifice is greater than the god, but that the men, women, and children likely to be sacrificed are not necessarily believers in the god and don't share in the worship.

were no doubt badly represented by the North Korean regime, but that in itself is not, as we have seen, a sufficient reason for a war of conquest and reconstruction. It was the crime of the aggressor to challenge individual and communal rights, and states responding to aggression must not repeat the challenge once basic values have been upheld.

I can now restate the fifth revision of the legalist paradigm. Because of the collective character of states, the domestic conventions of capture and punishment do not readily fit the requirements of international society. They are unlikely to have significant deterrent effects; they are very likely to extend rather than restrict the number of people exposed to coercion and risk; and they require acts of conquest that can only be aimed at entire political communities. Except when they are directed against Nazi-like states, just wars are conservative in character; it cannot be their purpose, as it is the purpose of domestic police work, to stamp out illegal violence, but only to cope with particular violent acts. Hence the rights and limits fixed by the argument for justice: resistance, restoration, reasonable prevention. I am afraid that these are not as constraining as they may sound. It will often require a fairly decisive military defeat to persuade aggressor states that they cannot succeed in their conquests. They would not have begun the fighting, obviously, unless their leaders had high hopes. And further military action may be necessary before a peace settlement can be worked out that provides even minimal security for the victim: disengagement, demilitarization, arms control, external arbitration, and so on.* Some combination of these, appropriate to the circumstances of a particular case, constitutes a legitimate war aim. If this falls short of the

---

*The list can be extended to include the temporary occupation of enemy territory, pending a peace settlement or for some period of time stipulated in the settlement. It does not include annexation, even as a measure of security against further attack. This is so partly for reasons that Marx suggests in his "Second Address" (with reference to Alsace-Lorraine): "If limits are to be fixed by military interests, there will be no end to claims, because every military line is necessarily faulty, and may be improved by annexing some outlying territory; and moreover, they can never be fixed finally and fairly because they always must be imposed by the conqueror upon the conquered and consequently carry within them the seeds of fresh wars." It is true, however, that some lines are more "faulty" than others and that one can make out both plausible and implausible versions of the argument Marx is opposing. A stronger case against annexation, I should think, rests on the rights of the inhabitants of the annexed land.

"punishment of aggression," it has to be said that military defeat is always punishing and that the preventive measures I have listed are also penalties, indeed, collective penalties, insofar as they involve a certain derogation of state sovereignty.

"The object in war is a better state of peace."[22] And *better*, within the confines of the argument for justice, means more secure than the *status quo ante bellum*, less vulnerable to territorial expansion, safer for ordinary men and women and for their domestic self-determinations. The key words are all relative in character: not invulnerable, but less vulnerable; not safe, but safer. Just wars are limited wars; there are moral reasons for the statesmen and soldiers who fight them to be prudent and realistic. Overreaching is common in war, however, and has many causes; I do not want to deny that a certain characteristic distortion of the argument for justice is one among them. Democratic idealism in the debased forms of self-righteousness and zeal sometimes prolongs wars, but so does aristocratic pride, military *hubris*, religious and political intolerance. A few sentences from David Hume's essay "On the Balance of Power" suggest that we should add to the list the "obstinacy and passion" with which even sophisticated statesmen, like those of eighteenth-century Britain, defend the balance:[23]

> The same peace which was afterwards made at Ryswick in 1697 was offered so early as the year ninety-two; that concluded at Utrecht in 1712 might have been finished on as good conditions . . . in the year eight; and we might have given at Frankfurt in 1743 the same terms which we were glad to receive at Aix-la-Chappelle in the year forty-eight. Above half of our wars with France . . . are owing more to our own imprudent vehemence than to the ambition of our neighbor.

The realists have (unrealistically) looked for a single enemy; in fact, they have more than they can handle without the support of a fully developed moral doctrine.

In the heated debates over America's Korean war, those political and military figures favoring the expansion of the conflict frequently cited the maxim: *in war there is no substitute for victory*. The idea, it should be said, is more readily traceable to Clausewitz than to Woodrow Wilson; it is anyway a silly idea, since it offers no definition of victory. In the case at hand, that word was presumably meant to describe a condition in which the enemy was utterly broken, without further resources. Given that meaning, it can safely be said that the maxim is historically as well as morally false. Nor is its falsehood an esoteric doctrine; it was widely accepted among American leaders in the early 1950s, and the government was able to sustain, through a difficult time, its search for a substitute. But the maxim is right in another sense. In a just war, its goals properly limited, there is indeed nothing like winning. There are alternative outcomes, of course, but these are accepted only at some cost to basic human values. And that means that there are sometimes moral reasons for prolonging a war. Consider those long months when the Korean negotiations were stalemated over the issue of the forcible repatriation of prisoners. The American negotiators insisted on the principle of free choice, lest the peace be as coercive as war itself, and accepted the continuation of the fighting rather than yield on that point. They were probably right, though it is difficult at this distance to weigh the values involved—and here the doctrine of proportionality is surely relevant. In any case, it follows from the argument for justice that wars can end too soon. There is always a humanitarian impulse to stop the fighting, and attempts are often made by the great powers (or the United Nations) to impose a cease-fire. But it isn't always true that such cease-fires serve the purposes of humanity. Unless they create a "better state of peace," they may simply fix the conditions under which the fighting will be resumed, at a later time and with a new intensity. Or they may confirm a loss of values the avoidance of which was worth a war.

The theory of ends in war is shaped by the same rights that justify the fighting in the first place—most importantly, by the right of nations, even of enemy nations, to continued national existence and, except in extreme circumstances, to the political prerogatives of nationality. The theory incorporates arguments for prudence and realism; it is an effective bar to total war; and it is, I think, harmonious with other features of *jus ad bellum*. But the case is different with the theory of means, to which I now must turn. Here there appear to be tensions and even contradictions that are internal to the argument for justice. It is with reference to the conduct of war and not to the end for which it is fought that the urgent need to do justice seems sometimes to lead statesmen and soldiers to act unjustly, that is, to fight without restraint and with a crusading zeal.

Once we have agreed upon the character of aggression, and of those threats of war that constitute aggression, and of those acts of colonial oppression and foreign interference that justify interventions and counter-interventions, we have also made it possible to identify enemies in the world: governments and armies that can rightly be (and perhaps should be) resisted. The wars that result from this resistance are the responsibility of those governments and armies; the hell of war is their crime. And if it isn't always true that their leaders ought to be punished for their crimes, it is vitally important that they not be allowed to benefit from them. If they can rightly be resisted, they should also be successfully resisted. Hence the temptation to fight by any means—which brings us up against what I have described in Part One as the fundamental dualism of our conception of war. For the rules of encounter take no cognizance whatever of the relative guilt of governments and armies. The theory of *jus in bello*, though it, too, is founded on the rights of life and liberty, stands independently of and apart from the theory of aggression. The limits it imposes are imposed equally and indifferently on aggressors and their adversaries. And the acceptance of these limits—moderation in battle—may well make it difficult to achieve the ends of war, even if these are moderate ends. Can the rules, then, be set aside for the sake of a just cause? I shall try to answer that question, or to suggest some ways in which it might be answered, but only after examining in detail the nature and practical workings of the rules themselves.

PART THREE

THE WAR CONVENTION

8

War's Means and the Importance of Fighting Well

THE PURPOSE OF THE WAR CONVENTION IS TO ESTABLISH THE DUTIES OF belligerent states, of army commanders, and of individual soldiers with reference to the conduct of hostilities. I have already argued that these duties are precisely the same for states and soldiers fighting wars of aggression and wars of defense. In our judgments of the fighting, we abstract from all consideration of the justice of the cause. We do this because the moral status of individual soldiers on both sides is very much the same: they are led to fight by their loyalty to their own states and by their lawful obedience. They are most likely to believe that their wars are just, and while the basis of that belief is not necessarily rational inquiry but, more often, a kind of unquestioning acceptance of official propaganda, nevertheless they are not criminals; they face one another as moral equals.

The domestic analogy is of little help here. War as an activity (the conduct rather than the initiation of the fighting) has no equivalent in a settled civil society. It is not like an armed robbery, for example, even when its ends are similar in kind. Indeed, it is the contrast rather than the correspondence that illuminates the war convention. The contrast is readily explicated; we have only to think about the following sorts of cases. (1) In the course of a bank robbery, a thief shoots a guard reaching for his gun. The thief is guilty of murder, even if he claims that he acted in self-defense.

Since he had no right to rob the bank, he also had no right to defend himself against the bank's defenders. He is no less guilty for killing the guard than he would be for killing an unarmed bystander—a customer, say, depositing his money. The thief's associates might praise him for the first killing, which was in their terms necessary, and condemn him for the second, which was wanton and dangerous. But we won't judge him in that way, because the idea of necessity doesn't apply to criminal activity: it was not necessary to rob the bank in the first place.

Now, aggression is also a criminal activity, but our view of its participants is very different: (2) In the course of an aggressive war, a soldier shoots another soldier, a member of the enemy army defending his homeland. Assuming a conventional firefight, this is not called murder; nor is the soldier regarded after the war as a murderer, even by his former enemies. The case is in fact no different from what it would be if the second soldier shot the first. Neither man is a criminal, and so both can be said to act in self-defense. We call them murderers only when they take aim at noncombatants, innocent bystanders (civilians), wounded or disarmed soldiers. If they shoot men trying to surrender or join in the massacre of the inhabitants of a captured town, we have (or ought to have) no hesitation in condemning them. But so long as they fight in accordance with the rules of war, no condemnation is possible.

The crucial point is that there are *rules* of war, though there are no rules of robbery (or of rape or murder). The moral equality of the battlefield distinguishes combat from domestic crime. If we are to judge what goes on in the course of a battle, then, "we must treat both combatants," as Henry Sidgwick has written, "on the assumption that each believes himself in the right." And we must ask "how the duties of a belligerent, fighting in the name of justice, and under the restraints of morality, are to be determined."[1] Or, more directly: without reference to the justice of their cause, how can soldiers fight justly?

UTILITY AND PROPORTIONALITY

The Argument of Henry Sidgwick

Sidgwick answers this question with a twofold rule that neatly sums up the most common utilitarian view of the war convention. In the conduct of hostilities, it is not permissible to do "any mischief which does not tend materially to the end [of victory], nor any mischief of which the conduciveness to the end is slight in comparison with the amount of the mischief."[2] What is being prohibited here is excessive harm. Two criteria are proposed for the determination of excess. The first is that of victory itself, or what is usually called military necessity. The second depends upon some notion of proportionality: we are to weigh "the mischief done," which presumably means not only the immediate harm to individuals but also any injury to the permanent interest of mankind, against the contribution that mischief makes to the end of victory.

The argument as stated, however, sets the interests of individuals and of mankind at a lesser value than the victory that is being sought. Any act of force that contributes in a significant way to winning the war is likely to be called permissible; any officer who asserts the "conduciveness" of the attack he is planning is likely to have his way. Once again, proportionality turns out to be a hard criterion to apply, for there is no ready way to establish an independent or stable view of the values against which the destruction of war is to be measured. Our moral judgments (if Sidgwick is right) wait upon purely military considerations and will rarely be sustained in the face of an analysis of battle conditions or campaign strategy by a qualified professional. It would be difficult to condemn soldiers for anything they did in the course of a battle or a war that they honestly believed, and had good reason to believe, was necessary, or important, or simply useful in determining the outcome. Sidgwick apparently thought this conclusion inescapable, once we agree to make no judgment as to the relative utility of different outcomes. For then we must grant that soldiers are entitled to try to win the wars they are entitled to fight. That means that they can do what they must to win; they can do their utmost, so long as what they do is actually related to winning. Indeed, they should do their utmost, so as to end the fighting as quickly as possible. The rules of war rule out only purposeless or wanton violence.

That is not, however, a small achievement. If it were made effective in practice, it would eliminate a great deal of the cruelty of war. For it has to be said of many of the people who die in the course of a war, soldiers as well as civilians, that their deaths do not "tend materially to the end [of victory]" or that the contribution they make to that end is "slight" indeed. These deaths are nothing more than the inevitable consequence of putting deadly weapons into the hands of undisciplined soldiers, and armed men into the hands of stupid or fanatical generals. Every military history is a tale of violence and destruction out of all relation to the requirements of combat: massacres on the one hand and, on the other, ill-planned and wasteful battles that are little better than massacres.

Sidgwick's twofold rule seeks to impose an economy of force. It requires discipline and calculation. Any intelligent military strategy, of course, imposes the same requirements. On Sidgwick's view, a good general is a moral man. He keeps his soldiers in check, keyed for battle, so that they don't run amuck among civilians; he sends them to fight only after having thought through a battle plan, and his plan is aimed at winning as quickly and as cheaply as possible. He is like General Roberts at the battle of Paardeberg (in the Boer War), who called off the frontal assaults on the Boer trenches ordered by Kitchener, his second in command, saying that the loss of life "did not appear . . . to be warranted by the exigencies of the situation."[3] A simple decision, though not as common in war as one might expect. I don't know if it was made out of any deep concern for human life; perhaps Roberts was thinking only of his honor as a general (who does not send his men to be slaughtered), or perhaps he was worried about the capacity of the troops to renew the fighting on the following day. It was in any case exactly the sort of decision that Sidgwick would require.

But though the limits of utility and proportionality are very important, they do not exhaust the war convention; indeed, they don't explain the most critical of the judgments we make of soldiers and their generals. If they did, moral life in wartime would be a great deal easier than it is. The war convention invites soldiers to calculate costs and benefits only up to a point, and at that point it establishes a series of clearcut rules—moral fortifications, so to speak, that can be stormed only at great moral cost. Nor can a soldier justify his violation of the rules by referring to the necessities of his combat situation or by arguing that nothing else but what he did would have contributed significantly to victory. Soldiers who reason in that way can never violate Sidgwick's limits, since all that Sidgwick requires is that soldiers . . . reason in that way. But justifications of this kind are not acceptable, or not always acceptable, either in law or morality. They have been "generally rejected," according to the U.S. Army's handbook of military law, " . . . for acts forbidden by the customary and conventional laws of war, inasmuch as [these laws] have been developed and framed with consideration for the concept of military necessity."[4] Now, what sorts of acts are these, and what are the grounds for forbidding them, if Sidgwick's criteria don't apply? I will have to explain later on how "military necessity" is taken into account in framing the prohibitions; I am concerned now with their general character.

Belligerent armies are entitled to try to win their wars, but they are not entitled to do anything that is or seems to them necessary to win. They are subject to a set of restrictions that rest in part on the agreements of states but that also have an independent foundation in moral principle. I don't think that these restrictions have ever been expounded in utilitarian fashion, though it is no doubt a good thing that they be expounded and that military conduct be shaped to their requirements. When we abstract from the utility of particular outcomes, focus exclusively on *jus in bello*, utilitarian calculations are radically constrained. It might be said that if every war in a series extending indefinitely into the future were to be fought with no other limits than those proposed by Sidgwick, the consequences for mankind would be worse than if every war in that same series were fought within limits fixed by some additional set of prohibitions.* But saying that does not suggest which prohibitions are the right ones. And any effort to figure out the right ones by calculating the likely effects over time of fighting wars in certain ways (an enormously difficult task) is sure to run up against unconstrained utilitarian arguments: that victory here and now will end the series of wars, or reduce the probability of future fighting, or avoid immediate and horrifying consequences. Hence anything should be permitted that is useful and proportionate to the victory being sought. Utilitarianism is obviously most effective when it points to outcomes about which we have (relatively) clear ideas. For that reason, it is more likely to tell us that the rules of war should be overridden in this or that case than it is to tell us what the rules are—beyond Sidgwick's minimum injunctions which can't and don't ever have to be overridden.

---

*The alternative utilitarian argument is that of General von Moltke: additional prohibitions merely drag out the fighting, while "the greatest kindness in war is to bring it to a speedy conclusion." But if we imagine a series of wars, this argument probably won't work. At any given level of restraint, let's say, a war will take so many months. If one of the belligerents breaks the rules, it might end more quickly, but only if the other side fails or is unable to reciprocate. If both sides fight at a lower level of restraint, the way may be shorter or longer; there isn't going to be any general rule. And if restraints have broken down in one war, they are unlikely to be maintained in the next, so any immediate benefits probably won't show up in the balance over time.

Until the constraints are lifted and the substantial effects of victory and defeat are weighed in the balance, utilitarianism provides only a general endorsement of the war convention (the twofold rule and any others commonly accepted); after that, it is unlikely to specify rules at all but only particular courses of action. When to lift the constraints is one of the hardest questions in the theory of war. I will try to answer it in Part Four, and I will describe at that time the positive role of utilitarian calculation: to mark out those special cases where victory is so important or defeat so frightening that it is morally, as well as militarily, necessary to override the rules of war. But such an argument is not possible until we have recognized rules beyond Sidgwick's and understood their moral force.

Meanwhile, it is worth dwelling for a moment on the precise nature of the general endorsement. The utility of fighting limited wars is of two sorts. It has to do not only with reducing the total amount of suffering, but also with holding open the possibility of peace and the resumption of pre-war activities. For if we are (at least formally) indifferent as to which side wins, we must assume that these activities will in fact be resumed and with the same or similar actors. It is important, then, to make sure that victory is also in some sense and for some period of time a settlement among the belligerents. And if that is to be possible, the war must be fought, as Sidgwick says, so as to avoid "the danger of provoking reprisals and of causing bitterness that will long outlast" the fighting.[5] The bitterness that Sidgwick has in mind might, of course, be the consequence of an outcome thought to be unjust (like the annexation of Alsace-Lorraine in 1871), but it may also result from military conduct thought to be unnecessary, brutal or unfair, or simply "against the rules." So long as defeat follows from what are widely regarded as legitimate acts of war, it is at least possible that it will leave behind no festering resentment, no sense of scores unsettled, no deeply felt need for individual or collective revenge. (The government or officers' corps of the defeated state may have reasons of its own to encourage such feelings, but that is another matter.) An analogy might be drawn, once again, with a family feud, its origin long forgotten, its justice no longer at issue. A feud of this sort may be carried on for many years, marked by the occasional killing of a father or a grown-up son, an uncle or a nephew, first of one family, then of the other. So long as nothing more happens, the possibility of reconciliation remains open. But if someone in a fit of anger or passion, or even by accident or mistake, kills a woman or a child, the result may well be a massacre or a series of massacres, not stopping until one of the families is wiped out or driven away.[6] The case is at least similar to intermittent war among states. Some limits must be commonly accepted, and more or less consistently maintained, if there is ever to be a peace short of the complete submission of one of the belligerents.

It is probably true that any limits will be useful here, so long as they are in fact commonly accepted. But no limit is accepted simply because it is thought that it will be useful. The war convention must first be morally plausible to large numbers of men and women; it must correspond to our sense of what is right. Only then will we recognize it as a serious obstacle to this or that military decision, and only then can we debate its utility in this or that particular case. For otherwise we would not know which obstacle out of the infinite number that are conceivable, and the very large number that are historically recorded, is to be the subject of our debates. With regard to the rules of war, utilitarianism lacks creative power. Beyond the minimal limits of "conduciveness" and proportionality, it simply confirms our customs and conventions, whatever they are, or it suggests that they be overridden; but it does not provide us with customs and conventions. For that, we must turn again to a theory of rights.

HUMAN RIGHTS

The Rape of the Italian Women

The importance of rights may best be suggested if we look at a historical example placed, as it were, on the margin of Sidgwick's argument. Consider, then, the case of the Moroccan soldiers fighting with Free French forces in Italy in 1943. These were mercenary troops who fought on terms, and the terms included license to rape and plunder in enemy territory. (Italy was enemy territory until the Badoglio regime joined the war against Germany in October, 1943; I don't know if the license was then withdrawn; if so, the withdrawal seems to have been ineffective.) A large number of women were raped; we know the number, roughly, because the Italian government later offered them a modest pension.[7] Now, the argument for giving soldiers privileges of this sort is a utilitarian one. It was made long ago by Vitoria in the course of a discussion of the right of sack: it is not unlawful to put a city to sack, he says, if it is "necessary for the conduct of the war . . . as a spur to the courage of the troops."[8] If this argument were applied to the case at hand, Sidgwick might respond that "necessary" is probably the wrong word here and that the contribution of rape and plunder to military victory is "slight" in comparison with the harm caused to the women involved. That is not an unpersuasive response, but it is not entirely convincing either, and it hardly gets at the root of our condemnation of rape.

What is it we object to in the license given those Moroccan soldiers? Surely our judgment does not hang on the fact that rape is only a trivial or inefficient "spur" to masculine courage (if it is a spur at all: I doubt that brave men are the most likely rapists). Rape is a crime, in war as in peace, because it violates the rights of the woman who is attacked. To offer her as bait to a mercenary soldier is to treat her as if she were not a person at all but a mere object, a prize or trophy of war. It is the recognition of her personality that shapes our judgment.* And this is true even in the absence of a philosophical conception of human rights, as the following passage from the Book of Deuteronomy—the first attempt that I have found to regulate the wartime treatment of women—clearly indicates:[9]

> When thou goest forth to battle against thine enemies, and the Lord thy God deliverest them into thy hands, and thou carriest them away captive, and seest among the captives a woman of goodly form, and thou hast a desire unto her, and wouldst take her to thee to wife; then thou shalt bring her home to thy house . . . and she shall . . . bewail her father and mother a full month; and after that thou mayest go in unto her, and be her husband, and she shall be thy wife. And . . . if thou have no delight in her, then thou shalt let her go whither she will; but thou shalt not sell her . . . for money, thou shalt not deal with her as a slave . . .

---

*In a powerful essay entitled "Human Personality," Simone Weil has attacked this way of talking about what we can and cannot do to other people. Rights talk, she claims, turns "what should have been a cry of protest from the depth of the heart . . . into a shrill nagging of claims and counter-claims. . . ." And she applies her argument to a case very much like ours: "if a young girl is being forced into a brothel she will not talk about her rights. In such a situation, the word would sound ludicrously inadequate." (*Selected Essays: 1934–1943*, ed. Richard Rees, London, 1962, p. 21.) Weil would have us refer ourselves instead to some notion of the sacred, of the image of God in man. Perhaps some such ultimate reference is necessary, but I think she is wrong in her claim about the "sound" of rights talk. In fact, arguments about human rights have played a significant part in the struggle against oppression, including the sexual oppression of women.

This falls far short of contemporary views, though I expect it would be as difficult to enforce today as it was in the time of the Judean kings. Whatever theological or sociological account of the rule is appropriate, it is clear that what is at work here is a conception of the captive woman as a person who must be respected, despite her capture; hence the month of mourning before she is sexually used, the requirement of marriage, the ban on slavery. She has lost some of her rights, we might say, but not all of them. Our own war convention requires a similar understanding. Both the prohibitions that are covered by Sidgwick's twofold rule and those that lie beyond it are properly conceptualized in terms of rights. The rules of "fighting well" are simply a series of recognitions of men and women who have a moral standing independent of and resistant to the exigencies of war.

A legitimate act of war is one that does not violate the rights of the people against whom it is directed. It is, once again, life and liberty that are at issue, though we are now concerned with these two as they are individually rather than collectively possessed. I can sum up their substance in terms I have used before: no one can be forced to fight or to risk his life, no one can be threatened with war or warred against, unless through some act of his own he has surrendered or lost his rights. This fundamental principle underlies and shapes the judgments we make of wartime conduct. It is only inadequately expressed in positive international law, but the prohibitions established there have this principle as their source. Lawyers sometimes talk as if the legal rules were simply humanitarian in character, as if the ban on rape or on the deliberate killing of civilians were nothing more than a piece of kindness.[10] But when soldiers respect these bans, they are not acting kindly or gently or magnanimously; they are acting justly. If they are humanitarian soldiers, they may indeed do more than is required of them—sharing their food with civilians, for example, rather than merely not raping or killing them. But the ban on rape and murder is a matter of right. The law recognizes this right, specifies, limits, and sometimes distorts it, but doesn't establish it. And we can recognize it ourselves, and sometimes do, even in the absence of legal recognition.

States exist to defend the rights of their members, but it is a difficulty in the theory of war that the collective defense of rights renders them individually problematic. The immediate problem is that the soldiers who do the fighting, though they can rarely be said to have chosen to fight, lose the rights they are supposedly defending. They gain war rights as combatants and potential prisoners, but they can now be attacked and killed at will by their enemies. Simply by fighting, whatever their private hopes and intentions, they have lost their title to life and liberty, and they have lost it even though, unlike aggressor states, they have committed no crime. "Soldiers are made to be killed," as Napoleon once said; that is why war is hell.* But even if we take our standpoint in hell, we can still say that *no one else is made to be killed.* This distinction is the basis of the rules of war.

Everyone else retains his rights, and states remain committed, and entitled, to defend these rights whether their wars are aggressive or not. But now they do this not by fighting but by entering into agreements among themselves (which fix the details of noncombatant immunity), by observing these agreements and expecting reciprocal observance, and by threatening to punish military leaders or individual soldiers who violate them. This last point is crucial for an understanding of the war convention. Even an aggressor state can rightly punish war criminals—enemy soldiers, for example, who rape or kill civilians. The rules of war apply with equal force to aggressors and their adversaries. And we can now see that it is not merely the moral equality of soldiers that requires this mutual submission; it is also the rights of civilians. Soldiers fighting for an aggressor state are not themselves criminals: hence their war rights are the same as those of their opponents. Soldiers fighting against an aggressor state have no license to become criminals: hence they are subject to the same restraints as their opponents. The enforcement of these restraints is one of the forms of law enforcement in international society, and the law can be enforced even by criminal states against "policemen" who deliberately kill innocent bystanders. For these bystanders do not forfeit their rights when their states wrongly go to war. An army warring against aggression can violate the territorial integrity and political sovereignty of the aggressor state, but its soldiers cannot violate the life and liberty of enemy civilians.

The war convention rests first on a certain view of combatants, which stipulates their battlefield equality. But it rests more deeply on a certain view of noncombatants, which holds that they are men and women with

---

*In quoting this sentence I do not mean to endorse the military nihilism it represents. Napoleon, especially in his later years, was given to statements of this sort, and they are not uncommon in the literature on war. One writer claims that they illustrate a quality of leadership that he calls "robustness." Napoleon's exclamation, "I do not care a fig for the lives of a million men," is, he says, an extreme example of robustness. One could think of better names. (Alfred H. Burne, *The Art of War on Land*, London, 1944, p. 8.)

rights and that they cannot be used for some military purpose, even if it is a legitimate purpose. At this point, the argument is not entirely dissimilar from that which obtains in domestic society, where a man fighting in self-defense, for example, is barred from attacking or injuring innocent bystanders or third parties. He can attack only his attackers. In domestic society, however, it is relatively easy to distinguish bystanders and third parties, whereas in international society, because of the collectivist character of states and armies, the distinction is harder to make. Indeed, it is often said that it cannot be made at all, for soldiers are only coerced civilians, and civilians are willing supporters of their armies in the field. And then it cannot be what is due to the victims but only what is necessary for the battle that determines our judgments of wartime conduct. Here is the critical test, then, for anyone who argues that the rules of war are grounded in a theory of rights: to make the combatant/noncombatant distinction plausible in terms of the theory, that is, to provide a detailed account of the history of individual rights under the conditions of war and battle—how they are retained, lost, exchanged (for war rights) and recovered. That is my purpose in the chapters that follow.

9

NONCOMBATANT IMMUNITY
AND MILITARY NECESSITY

THE STATUS OF INDIVIDUALS

The first principle of the war convention is that, once war has begun, soldiers are subject to attack at any time (unless they are wounded or captured). And the first criticism of the convention is that this principle is unfair; it is an example of class legislation. It does not take into account that few soldiers are wholeheartedly committed to the business of fighting. Most of them do not identify themselves as warriors; at least, that is not their only or their chief identity; nor is fighting their chosen occupation. Nor, again, do they spend most of their time fighting; they neglect war whenever they can. I want to turn now to a recurrent incident in military history in which soldiers, simply by not fighting, appear to regain their right to life. In fact, they do not regain it, but the appearance will help us understand the grounds on which the right is held, and the facts of the case will clarify the meaning of its forfeiture.

Naked Soldiers

The same tale appears again and again in war memoirs and in letters from the front. It has this general form: a soldier on patrol or on sniper duty catches an enemy soldier unaware, holds him in his gunsight, easy to kill, and then must decide whether to shoot him or let the opportunity pass. There is at such moments a great reluctance to shoot—not always for moral reasons, but for reasons that are relevant nonetheless to the moral argument I want to make. No doubt, a deep psychological uneasiness about killing plays a part in these cases. This uneasiness, in fact, has been offered as a general explanation of the reluctance of soldiers to fight at all. In the course of a study of combat behavior in World War II, S. L. A. Marshall discovered that the great majority of men on the front line never fired their guns.[1] He thought this the result above all of their civilian upbringing, of the powerful inhibitions acquired in its course against deliberately injuring another human being. But in the cases I shall list, this inhibition does not seem a critical factor. None of the five soldiers who wrote the accounts was a "non-firer," nor, so far as I can tell, were the other men who figure importantly in their stories. Moreover, they give reasons for not killing or for hesitating to kill, and this the soldiers interviewed by Marshall were rarely able to do.

1) I have taken the first case from a letter written by the poet Wilfred Owen to his brother in England on May 14, 1917.[2]

> When we were marching along a sunken road, we got the wind up once. We knew we must have passed the German outposts somewhere on our left rear. All at once, the cry rang down, "Line the bank." There was a tremendous scurry of fixing bayonets, tugging of breech covers, and opening pouches, but when we peeped over, behold a solitary German, haring along toward us, with his head down and his arms stretched in front of him, as if he were going to take a high dive through the earth (which I have no doubt he would like to have done). Nobody offered to shoot him, he looked too funny. . . .

Perhaps everyone was waiting for an order to shoot, but Owen's meaning is undoubtedly that no one wanted to shoot. A soldier who looks funny is not at that moment a military threat; he is not a fighting man but simply a man, and one does not kill men. In this case, indeed, it would have been superfluous to do so: the comical German was soon taken prisoner. But that is not always possible, as the remaining cases suggest, and the reluctance or refusal to kill has nothing to do with the existence of a military alternative. There is always a nonmilitary alternative.

2) In his autobiography *Good-bye to All That*, Robert Graves recalls the only time that he "refrained from shooting a German" who was neither wounded nor a prisoner.[3]

> While sniping from a knoll in the support line, where we had a concealed loop-hole, I saw a German, about seven hundred yards away, through my telescopic sights. He was taking a bath in the German third line. I disliked the idea of shooting a naked man, so I handed the rifle to the sergeant with me. "Here, take this. You're a better shot than I am." He got him; but I had not stayed to watch.

I hesitate to say that what is involved here is a moral feeling, certainly not a moral feeling that is conceived to extend across class lines. But even if we describe it as the disdain of an officer and a gentleman for conduct that appears to be unmanly or unheroic, Graves' "dislike" still depends upon a morally important recognition. A naked man, like a funny man, is not a soldier. And what if the obedient and presumably unfeeling sergeant had not been with him?

3) During the Spanish Civil War, George Orwell had a similar experience as a sniper working from a forward position in the republican lines. It would probably never have occurred to Orwell to hand his gun down the hierarchy of ranks; in any case, his was an anarchist battalion, and there was no hierarchy.[4]

> At this moment a man, presumably carrying a message to an officer, jumped out of the trench and ran along the top of the parapet in full view. He was half-dressed and was holding up his trousers with both hands as he ran. I refrained from shooting at him. It is true that I am a poor shot and unlikely to hit a running man at a hundred yards. . . . Still, I did not shoot partly because of that detail about the trousers. I had come here to shoot at "Fascists;" but a man who is holding up his trousers isn't a "Fascist," he is visibly a fellow-creature, similar to yourself, and you don't feel like shooting at him.

Orwell says, "you don't feel like" rather than "you should not," and the difference between these two is important. But the fundamental recognition is the same as in the other cases and more fully articulated. Moreover, Orwell tells us that this "is the kind of thing that happens all the time in wars," though with what evidence he says that, and whether he means that one doesn't feel like shooting or that one doesn't shoot "all the time," I don't know.

4) Raleigh Trevelyan, a British soldier in World War II, has published a "diary of Anzio" in which he recounts the following episode.[5]

> There was a wonderfully vulgar sunrise. Everything was the color of pink geraniums, and birds were singing. We felt like Noah must have done when he saw his rainbow. Suddenly Viner pointed across the stretch of scrubby heath. An individual, dressed in German uniform, was wandering like a sleep-walker across our line of fire. It was clear that for the moment he had forgotten war and—as we had been doing—was reveling in the promise of warmth and spring. "Shall I bump him off?" asked Viner, without a note of expression in his voice. I had to decide quickly. "No," I replied, "just scare him away."

Here, as in the Orwell passage, the crucial feature is the discovery of a man "similar to yourself," doing "as we had been doing." Of course, two soldiers shooting at one another are quite precisely similar; one is doing what the other is doing, and both are engaged in what can be called a peculiarly human activity. But the sense of being a "fellow-creature" depends for obvious reasons upon a different sort of identity, one that is entirely dissociated from anything threatening. The fellowship of spring (reveling in the sun) is a good example, though even that is not untouched by the pressures of "military necessity."

> Only Sergeant Chesteron didn't laugh. He said that we should have killed the fellow, since his friends would now be told precisely where our trenches were.

Sergeants seem to bear much of the burden of war.

5) The most reflective of the accounts I have found is by an Italian soldier who fought the Austrians in World War I: Emilio Lussu, later a socialist leader and anti-fascist exile. Lussu, then a lieutenant, together with a corporal, had moved during the night into a position overlooking the Austrian trenches. He watched the Austrians having morning coffee and felt a kind of amazement, as if he had not expected to find anything human in the enemy lines.[6]

Those strongly defended trenches, which we had attacked so many times without success had ended by seeming to us inanimate, like desolate buildings uninhabited by men, the refuge only of mysterious and terrible beings of whom we knew nothing. Now they were showing themselves to us as they really were, men and soldiers like us, in uniform like us, moving about, talking, and drinking coffee, just as our own comrades behind us were doing at that moment.

A young officer appears and Lussu takes aim at him; then the Austrian lights a cigarette and Lussu pauses. "This cigarette formed an invisible link between us. No sooner did I see its smoke than I wanted a cigarette myself. . . ." Behind perfect cover, he has time to think about his decision. He felt the war justified, "a hard necessity." He recognized that he had obligations to the men under his command. "I knew it was my duty to fire." And yet he did not. He hesitated, he writes, because the Austrian officer was so entirely oblivious to the danger that threatened him.

I reasoned like this: To lead a hundred, even a thousand, men against another hundred, or thousand, was one thing; but to detach one man from the rest and say to him, as it were: "Don't move, I'm going to shoot you. I'm going to kill you"—that was different. . . . To fight is one thing, but to kill a man is another. And to kill him like that is to murder him.

Lussu, like Graves, turned to his corporal but (perhaps because he was a socialist) with a question, not an order. "Look here—I'm not going to fire on a man alone, like that. Will you?" . . . "No, I won't either." Here the line has been clearly drawn between the member of an army who makes war together with his comrades and the individual who stands alone. Lussu objected to stalking a human prey. What else, however, does a sniper do?

It is not against the rules of war as we currently understand them to kill soldiers who look funny, who are taking a bath, holding up their pants, reveling in the sun, smoking a cigarette. The refusal of these five men, nevertheless, seems to go to the heart of the war convention. For what does it mean to say that someone has a right to life? To say that is to recognize a fellow creature, who is not threatening me, whose activities have the savor of peace and camaraderie, whose person is as valuable as my own. An enemy has to be described differently, and though the stereotypes through which he is seen are often grotesque, they have a certain truth. He alienates himself from me when he tries to kill me, and from our common humanity. But the alienation is temporary, the humanity imminent. It is restored, as it were, by the prosaic acts that break down the stereotypes in each of the five stories. Because he is funny, naked, and so on, my enemy is changed, as Lussu says, into a man. "A man!"

The case might be different if we imagine this man to be a whole-hearted soldier. In his bath, smoking his morning cigarette, he is thinking only of the coming battle and of how many of his enemies he will kill. He is engaged in war-making just as I am engaged in writing this book; he thinks about it all the time or at the oddest moments. But this is an unlikely picture of an ordinary soldier. War is not in fact his enterprise, but rather surviving this battle, avoiding the next. Mostly, he hides, is frightened, doesn't fire, prays for a minor wound, a voyage home, a long rest. And when we see him at rest, we assume that he is thinking of home and peace, as we would be. If that is so, how can it be justified to kill him? Yet it is justified, as most of the soldiers in the five stories understand. Their refusals seem, even to them, to fly in the face of military duty. Rooted in a moral recognition, they are nevertheless more passionate than principled decisions. They are acts of kindness, and insofar as they entail any danger at all or lower minutely the odds for victory later, they may be likened to superogatory acts. Not that they involve doing more than is morally required; they involve doing less than is permitted.

The standards of permissibility rest on the rights of individuals, but they are not precisely defined by those rights. For definition is a complex process, historical as well as theoretical in character, and conditioned in a significant way by the pressure of military necessity. It is time now to try to see what that pressure can and cannot do, and the "naked soldier" cases provide a useful instance. In the nineteenth century, an effort was made to protect one type of "naked soldier": the man on guard duty outside his post or at the edge of his lines. The reasons given for singling out this lone fig-ure are similar to those expressed in the five stories. "No other term than murder," wrote an English student of war, "expresses the killing of a lone sentry by a pot shot at long range. It [is] like shooting a partridge sitting."[7] The same idea is obviously at work in the code of military conduct that Francis Lieber drafted for the Union Army in the American Civil War: "Outposts, sentinels, pickets are not to be fired upon, except to drive them in. . . ."[8] Now, a war is easily imaginable in which this idea was extended, so that only soldiers actually fighting, hundreds against hundreds, thousands against thousands, as Lussu says, could be attacked. Such a war would be constituted as a series of set battles, formally or informally announced in advance, and broken off in some clear fashion. The pursuit of a defeated army could be allowed, so neither side need be denied the possibility of a decisive victory. But perpetual harassment, sniping, ambush, surprise attack—all these would be ruled out. Wars have indeed been fought in this way, but the arrangements have never been stable, because they give a systematic advantage to the army that is larger and better equipped. It is the weaker side that persistently refuses to fix any limits on the vulnerability of enemy soldiers (the extreme form of this refusal is guerrilla war), pleading military necessity. What does this mean?

THE NATURE OF NECESSITY (1)

The plea takes a standard form. This or that course of action, it is said, "is necessary to compel the submission of the enemy with the least possible expenditure of time, life, and money."[9] That is the core of what the Germans call *kriegsraison*, reason of war. The doctrine justifies not only whatever is necessary to win the war, but also whatever is necessary to reduce the risks of losing, or simply to reduce losses or the likelihood of losses in the course of the war. In fact, it is not about necessity at all; it is a way of speaking in code, or a hyperbolical way of speaking, about probability and risk. Even if one grants the right of states and armies and individual soldiers to reduce their risks, a particular course of action would be *necessary* to that end only if no other course improved the odds of battle at all. But there will always be a range of tactical and strategic options that conceivably could improve the odds. There will be choices to make, and these are moral as well as military choices. Some of them are permitted and some ruled out by the war convention. If the convention did not discriminate in this way, it would have little impact upon the actual fighting of wars and battles; it would simply be a code of expediency—which is what Sidgwick's twofold rule is likely to come to, under the pressure of actual warfare.

"Reason of war" can only justify the killing of people we already have reason to think are liable to be killed. What is involved here is not so much a calculation of probability and risk as a reflection on the status of the men and women whose lives are at stake. The case of the "naked soldier" is resolved in this way: soldiers as a class are set apart from the world of peaceful activity; they are trained to fight, provided with weapons, required to fight on command. No doubt, they do not always fight; nor is war their personal enterprise. But it is the enterprise of their class, and this fact radically distinguishes the individual soldier from the civilians he leaves behind.* If he is warned that he is always in danger, it is not so great a disruption of his life as it would be in the case of the civilian. Indeed, to warn the civilian is in effect to force him to fight, *but the soldier has already been forced to fight.* That is, he has joined the army because he thinks his country must be defended, or he has been conscripted. It is important to stress, however, that he has not been forced to fight by a direct attack upon his person; that would repeat the crime of aggression at the level of the individual. He can be personally attacked only because he already is a fighter. He has been made into a dangerous man, and though his options may have been few, it is nevertheless accurate to say that he has allowed himself to be made into a dangerous man. For that reason, he finds himself endangered. The actual risks he lives with may be reduced or heightened: here notions of military necessity, and also of kindness and magnanimity, have free play. But the risks can be raised to their highest pitch without violating his rights.

It is harder to understand the extension of combatant status beyond the class of soldiers, though in modern war this has been common enough. The development of military technology, it might be said, has dictated it, for war today is as much an economic as a military activity. Vast numbers of workers must be mobilized before an army can even appear in the field; and once they are engaged, soldiers are radically dependent on a continuing stream of equipment, fuel, ammunition, food, and so on. It is

---

*In his moving account of the French defeat in 1940, Marc Bloch has criticized this distinction: "Confronted by the nation's peril and by the duties that it lays on every citizen, all adults are equal and only a curiously warped mind would claim for any of them the privilege of immunity. What, after all, is a 'civilian' in time of war? He is nothing more than a man whose weight of years, whose health, whose profession . . . prevents him from bearing arms effectively. . . . Why should [these factors] confer on him the right to escape from the common danger?" (*Strange Defeat*, trans. Gerard Hopkins, New York, 1968, p. 130.) But the theoretical problem is not to describe how immunity is gained, but how it is lost. We are all immune to start with; our right not to be attacked is a feature of normal human relationships. That right is lost by those who bear arms "effectively" because they pose a danger to other people. It is retained by those who don't bear arms at all.

a great temptation, then, to attack the enemy army behind its own lines, especially if the battle itself is not going well. But to attack behind the lines is to make war against people who are at least nominally civilians. How can this be justified? Here again, the judgments we make depend upon our understanding of the men and women involved. We try to draw a line between those who have lost their rights because of their warlike activities and those who have not. On the one side are a class of people, loosely called "munitions workers," who make weapons for the army or whose work directly contributes to the business of war. On the other side are all those people who, in the words of the British philosopher G. E. M. Anscombe, "are not fighting and are not engaged in supplying those who are with the means of fighting."[10]

The relevant distinction is not between those who work for the war effort and those who do not, but between those who make what soldiers need to fight and those who make what they need to live, like all the rest of us. When it is militarily necessary, workers in a tank factory can be attacked and killed, but not workers in a food processing plant. The former are assimilated to the class of soldiers—partially assimilated, I should say, because these are not armed men, ready to fight, and so they can be attacked only in their factory (not in their homes), when they are actually engaged in activities threatening and harmful to their enemies. The latter, even if they process nothing but army rations, are not similarly engaged. They are like workers manufacturing medical supplies, or clothing, or anything else that would be needed, in one form or another, in peacetime as well as war. An army, to be sure, has an enormous belly, and it must be fed if it is to fight. But it is not its belly but its arms that make it an army. Those men and women who supply its belly are doing nothing peculiarly warlike. Hence their immunity from attack: they are assimilated to the rest of the civilian population. We call them *innocent* people, a term of art which means that they have done nothing, and are doing nothing, that entails the loss of their rights.

This is a plausible line, I think, though it may be too finely drawn. What is more important is that it is drawn under pressure. We begin with the distinction between soldiers engaged in combat and soldiers at rest; then we shift to the distinction between soldiers as a class and civilians; and then we concede this or that group of civilians as the processes of economic mobilization establish its direct contribution to the business of fighting. Once the contribution has been plainly established, only "military necessity" can determine whether the civilians involved are attacked or not. They ought not to be attacked if their activities can be stopped, or their products seized or destroyed, in some other way and without significant risk. The laws of war have regularly recognized this obligation. Under the naval code, for example, merchant seamen on ships carrying military supplies were once regarded as civilians who had, despite the work they were doing, a right not to be attacked, for it was possible (and it sometimes still is) to seize their ships without shooting at them. But whenever seizure without shooting ceases to be possible, the obligation ceases also and the right lapses. It is not a retained but a war right, and rests only on the agreement of states and on the doctrine of military necessity. The history of submarine warfare nicely illustrates this process, through which groups of civilians are, as it were, incorporated into hell. It will also enable me to suggest the point at which it becomes morally necessary to resist the incorporation.

Submarine Warfare: The Laconia *Affair*

Naval warfare has traditionally been the most gentlemanly form of fighting, possibly because so many gentlemen went into the navy, but also and more importantly because of the nature of the sea as a battlefield. The only comparable land environment is the desert; these two have in common the absence or relative absence of civilian inhabitants. Hence battle is especially pure, a combat between combatants, with no one else involved— just what we intuitively want war to be. The purity is marred, however, by the fact that the sea is extensively used for transport. Warships encounter merchant ships. The rules governing this encounter are, or were, fairly elaborate.[11] Worked out before the invention of the submarine, they bear the marks of their technological as well as their moral assumptions. A merchant ship carrying military supplies could lawfully be stopped on the high seas, boarded, seized, and brought into port by a prize crew. If the merchant seamen resisted this process at any stage, whatever force was necessary to overcome the resistance was also lawful. If they submitted peacefully, no force could be used against them. If it was impossible to bring the ship into port, it could be sunk, "subject to the absolute duty of providing for the safety of the crew, passengers, and papers." Most often, this was done by taking all three on board the warship. The crew and passengers were then to be regarded not as prisoners of war, for their encounter with the warship was not a battle, but as civilian internees.

Now, in World War I, submarine commanders (and the state officials who commanded them) openly refused to act in accordance with this "absolute duty," pleading military necessity. They could not surface before firing their torpedoes, for their ships were lightly armed above decks and highly vulnerable to ramming; they could not provide prize crews from their own small number, unless they, too, were to return to port; nor could they take merchant seamen on board, for there was no room. Hence their policy was to "sink on sight," though they did accept some responsibility to assist survivors after the ship was down. "Sink on sight" was especially the policy of the German government. The only alternative, its defenders have argued, was not to use submarines at all, or to use them ineffectively, which would have conceded control of the sea to the British navy. After the war was over, perhaps because the Germans lost it, the traditional rules were reaffirmed. The London Naval Protocol of 1936, ratified by all the major participants in the last and the next great war (by the Germans in 1939), explicitly provided that "in their action with regard to merchant ships, submarines must conform to the rules of international law to which surface ships are subject." This is still the "binding rule," according to respected authorities on naval law, though anyone who defends the rule must do so "notwithstanding the experience of the Second World War."[12]

We can best gain access to this experience by turning immediately to the famous "*Laconia* order" issued by Admiral Doenitz of the German U-boat command in 1942. Doenitz required not only that submarines strike without warning, but also that they do nothing whatsoever to help the crew members of a sunken ship: "All attempts to rescue the crews of sunken ships should cease, including picking up men from the sea, righting capsized lifeboats, and supplying food and water."[13] This order provoked great indignation at the time, and after the war its promulgation was among the crimes with which Doenitz was charged at Nuremberg. But the judges refused to convict on this charge. I want to look closely at the reasons for their decision. Since their language is obscure, however, I shall also ask what their reasons might have been and what reasons we might have for requiring or not requiring rescue at sea.

The issue clearly was rescue and nothing else; despite the "binding rule" of international law, the policy of "sink on sight" was not challenged by the court. The judges apparently decided that the distinction between merchant ships and warships no longer made much sense.[14]

Shortly after the outbreak of the war, the British Admiralty . . . armed its merchant vessels, in many cases convoyed them with armed escort, gave orders to send position reports upon sighting submarines, thus integrating merchant vessels into the warning system of naval intelligence. On October 1, 1939, the Admiralty announced [that] British merchant ships had been ordered to ram U-boats if possible.

At this point, the court seemed to reason, merchant seamen had been conscripted for military service; hence it was permissible to attack them by surprise exactly as if they were soldiers. But this argument, by itself, is not a very good one. For if the conscription of merchant seamen was a response to illegitimate submarine attacks (or even to the strong probability of such attacks), it cannot be invoked to justify those same attacks. It must be the case that the "sink on sight" policy was justified in the first place. The invention of the submarine had made it "necessary." The old rules were morally if not legally suspended because supply by sea—a military enterprise whose participants had always been liable to attack—had ceased now to be subject to nonviolent interdiction.

The "*Laconia* order" reached much further than this, however, for it suggested that seamen helpless in the sea, unlike wounded soldiers on land, need not be helped once the battle was over. Doenitz's argument was that the battle, in fact, was never over until the submarine was safe in its home port. The sinking of a merchant vessel was only the first blow of a long and tense struggle. Radar and the airplane had turned the wide seas into a single battlefield, and unless the submarine immediately began evasive maneuvers, it was or might be in great trouble.[15] Seamen had once been better off than soldiers, a privileged class of near-combatants treated as if they were civilians; now, suddenly, they were worse off.

Here again is the argument from military necessity, and again we can see that it is above all an argument about risk. The lives of the submarine crew would be endangered, Doenitz claimed, and the probability of detection and attack increased by this or that extent, if they attempted to rescue their victims. Now, this is clearly not always the case: in his account of the destruction of an Allied convoy in the Arctic Sea, David Irving describes a number of incidents in which German submarines surfaced and offered assistance to merchant seamen in lifeboats without increasing their own risks.[16]

Lieutenant-Commander Teichert's U-456 . . . had fired the striking torpedoes. Teichert took his submarine alongside the lifeboats and ordered the Master, Captain Strand, to come aboard; he was taken prisoner. The seamen were asked whether they had sufficient water and they were handed tinned meat and bread by the submarine officers. They were told that they would be picked up by destroyers a few days later.

This occurred only a few months before Doenitz's order prohibited such assistance, and under conditions which made it perfectly safe. Convoy PQ 17 had dispersed, abandoned by its escorts; it was no longer in any sense a fighting force; the Germans controlled the air as well as the sea. The battle was clearly over, and military necessity could hardly have justified a refusal to help. I should think that if such a refusal, under similar circumstances, could be attributed to the "*Laconia* order," Doenitz would indeed be guilty of a war crime. But nothing like this was demonstrated at Nuremberg.

Nor, however, did the court openly adopt the argument from military necessity: that under different circumstances the refusal to help was justified by the risks it entailed. Instead, the judges reaffirmed the binding rule. "If the Commander cannot rescue," they argued, "then . . . he cannot sink a merchant vessel. . . ." But they did not enforce the rule and punish Doenitz. Admiral Nimitz of the U.S. Navy, called to testify by Doenitz's attorney, had told them that "U.S. submarines [generally] did not rescue enemy survivors if by so doing the vessels were exposed to unnecessary or additional risk." British policy had been similar. In view of this, the judges declared that "the sentence of Doenitz is not assessed on the ground of his breaches of the international law of submarine warfare."[17] They did not accept the argument of the defense attorneys that the law had effectively been rewritten by informal collusion among the belligerents. But they apparently felt that this collusion did make the law unenforceable (or at least unenforceable against only one of the parties to its violation)—a proper judicial decision, but one that leaves open the moral question.

In fact, Doenitz and his Allied counterparts had reasons for the policy they adopted, and these reasons fit roughly into the framework of the war convention. Wounded or helpless combatants are no longer subject to attack; in that sense they have regained their right to life. But they are not entitled to assistance so long as the battle continues and the victory of their enemies is uncertain. What is decisive here is not military necessity but the assimilation of merchant seamen to the class of combatants. Soldiers need not risk their lives for the sake of their enemies, for both they and their enemies have exposed themselves to the coerciveness of war. There are some people, however, who are safe against that coerciveness, or who ought to be safeguarded against it, and these people also have a part in the *Laconia* affair.

The *Laconia* was a liner carrying 268 British servicemen and their families, returning home from pre-war stations in the Middle East, and 1,800 Italian prisoners of war. It was torpedoed and sunk off the west coast of Africa by a U-boat whose commander did not know who its passengers were (liners were used extensively by the Allies as troopships). When Doenitz learned of the sinking, and of the identity of the people in the water, he ordered a massive rescue effort involving, initially, a number of other submarines.[18] Italian warships were also asked to hurry to the scene, and the U-boat commander responsible for the sinking radioed in English a general call for help. But the submarines were instead attacked by several Allied planes whose pilots presumably did not know what was going on in the seas below or did not believe what they were told. The confusion is typical enough in time of war: ignorance on all sides, compounded by mutual fear and suspicion.

In fact, the planes did little damage, but Doenitz's response was harsh. He directed the German commanders to confine their rescue efforts to the Italian prisoners; the British soldiers and their families were to be set adrift. It was this spectacle of women and children abandoned at sea, and the subsequent order that seemed to require its repetition, that was widely thought to be outrageous—and rightly so, it seems to me, even though "unrestricted" submarine warfare was by then commonly accepted. For we draw a circle of rights around civilians, and soldiers are supposed to accept (some) risks in order to save civilian lives. It is not a question of going out of their way or of being, or not being, good Samaritans. They are the ones who endanger civilian lives in the first place, and even if they do this in the course of legitimate military operations, they must still make some positive effort to restrict the range of the damage they do. This indeed was Doenitz's own position before the Allied attack, a position he maintained despite criticism from other members of the German High Command: "I cannot put these people into the water. I shall carry on [the rescue effort]." It is not kindness that is involved here, but duty, and it is in terms of that duty that we judge the *"Laconia* order." A rescue effort undertaken for the sake of noncombatants can be broken off temporarily because of an attack, but it cannot be called off in advance of any attack merely because an attack may occur (or recur). For one attack at least has already occurred and put innocent people in danger of death. Now they must be helped.

DOUBLE EFFECT

The second principle of the war convention is that noncombatants cannot be attacked at any time. They can never be the objects or the targets of military activity. But as the *Laconia* affair suggests, noncombatants are often endangered not because anyone sets out to attack them, but only because of their proximity to a battle that is being fought against someone else. I have tried to argue that what is then required is not that the battle be stopped, but that some degree of care be taken not to harm civilians— which means, very simply, that we recognize their rights as best we can within the context of war. But what degree of care should be taken? And at what cost to the individual soldiers who are involved? The laws of war say nothing about such matters; they leave the cruelest decisions to be made by the men on the spot with reference only to their ordinary moral notions or the military traditions of the army in which they serve. Occasionally one of these soldiers will write about his own decisions, and that can be like a light going on in a dark place. Here is an incident from Frank Richards' memoir of the First World War, one of the few accounts by a man from the ranks.[19]

> When bombing dug-outs or cellars, it was always wise to throw the bombs into them first and have a look around them after. But we had to be very careful in this village as there were civilians in some of the cellars. We shouted down to them to make sure. Another man and I shouted down one cellar twice and receiving no reply were just about to pull the pins out of our bombs when we heard a woman's voice and a young lady came up the cellar steps. . . . She and the members of her family . . . had not left [the cellar] for some days. They guessed an attack was being made and when we first shouted down had been too frightened to answer. If the young lady had not cried out when she did, we would have innocently murdered them all.

Innocently murdered, because they had shouted first; but if they had not shouted, and then killed the French family, it would have been, Richards believed, murder simply. And yet he was accepting a certain risk in shouting, for had there been German soldiers in the cellar, they might have scrambled out, firing as they came. It would have been more prudent to throw the bombs without warning, which means that military necessity would have justified him in doing so. Indeed, he would have been justified on other grounds, too, as we shall see. And yet he shouted.

The moral doctrine most often invoked in such cases is the principle of double effect. First worked out by Catholic casuists in the Middle Ages, double effect is a complex notion, but it is at the same time closely related to our ordinary ways of thinking about moral life. I have often found it being used in military and political debates. Officers will tend to speak in its terms, knowingly or unknowingly, whenever the activity they are planning is likely to injure noncombatants. Catholic writers themselves frequently use military examples; it is one of their purposes to suggest what we ought to think when "a soldier in firing at the enemy foresees that he will shoot some civilians who are nearby."[20] Such foresight is common enough in war; soldiers could probably not fight at all, except in the desert and at sea, without endangering nearby civilians. And yet it is not proximity but only some contribution to the fighting that makes a civilian liable to attack. Double effect is a way of reconciling the absolute prohibition against attacking noncombatants with the legitimate conduct of military activity. I shall want to argue, following the example of Frank Richards, that the reconciliation comes too easily, but first we must see exactly how it is worked out.

The argument goes this way: it is permitted to perform an act likely to have evil consequences (the killing of noncombatants) provided the following four conditions hold.[21]

1. The act is good in itself or at least indifferent, which means, for our purposes, that it is a legitimate act of war.
2. The direct effect is morally acceptable—the destruction of military supplies, for example, or the killing of enemy soldiers.
3. The intention of the actor is good, that is, he aims only at the acceptable effect; the evil is not one of his ends, nor is it a means to his ends.
4. The good effect is sufficiently good to compensate for allowing the evil effect; it must be justifiable under Sidgwick's proportionality rule.

The burden of the argument is carried by the third clause. The "good" and evil effects that come together, the killing of soldiers and nearby civilians, are to be defended only insofar as they are the product of a single intention, directed at the first and not the second. The argument suggests the great importance of taking aim in wartime, and it correctly restricts the targets at which one can aim. But we have to worry, I think, about all those unintended but foreseeable deaths, for their number can be large; and subject only to the proportionality rule—a weak constraint—double effect provides a blanket justification. The principle for that reason invites an angry or a cynical response: what different does it make whether civilian deaths are a direct or an indirect effect of my actions? It can hardly matter to the dead civilians, and if I know in advance that I am likely to kill so many innocent people and go ahead anyway, how can I be blameless?[22]

We can ask the question in a more concrete way. Would Frank Richards have been blameless if he had thrown his bombs without warning? The principle of double effect would have permitted him to do so. He was engaged in a legitimate military activity, for many cellars were in fact being used by enemy soldiers. The effects of making "bomb without warning" his general policy would have been to reduce the risks of his being killed or disabled and to speed up the capture of the village, and these are "good" effects. Moreover, they were clearly the only ones he intended; civilian deaths would have served no purpose of his own. And finally, over an extended period of time, the proportions would probably have worked out favorably or at least not unfavorably; the mischief done would, let us assume, be balanced by the contribution to victory. And yet Richards was surely doing the right thing when he shouted his warning. He was acting as a moral man ought to act; he is not an example of fighting heroically, above and beyond the call of duty, but simply of fighting well. It is what we expect of soldiers. Before trying to state that expectation more precisely, however, I want to see how it works in more complex combat situations.

Bombardment in Korea

I am going to follow here a British journalist's account of the way the American army waged war in Korea. Whether it is an entirely just account I do not know, but I am more interested in the moral issues it raises than in its historical accuracy. This, then, was a "typical" encounter on the road to Pyongyang. A battalion of American troops advanced slowly, without opposition, under the shadow of low hills. "We were well into the valley now, half-way down the straight . . . strung out along the open road, when it came, the harsh stutter of automatic fire sputtering the dust around us."[23] The troops stopped and dove for cover. Three tanks moved up, "pounding their shells into the . . . hillside and shattering the air with their machine guns. It was impossible in this remarkable inferno of sound to detect the enemy, or to assess his fire." Within fifteen minutes, several fighter planes arrived, "diving down upon the hillside with their rockets." This is the new technique of warfare, writes the British journalist, "born of immense productive and material might": "the cautious advance, the enemy small arms fire, the halt, the close support air strike, artillery, the cautious advance, and so on." It is designed to save the lives of soldiers, and it may or may not have that effect. "It is certain that it kills civilian men, women, and children, indiscriminately and in great numbers, and destroys all that they have."

Now there is another way to fight, though it is only open to soldiers who have had a "soldierly" training and who are not "roadbound" in their habits. A patrol can be sent forward to outflank the enemy position. In the end, it often comes to that anyway, as it did in this case, for the tanks and planes failed to hit the North Korean machine gunners. "At last, after more than an hour . . . a platoon from Baker Company began working their way through the scrub just under the ridge of the hill." But the first reliance was always on bombardment. "Every enemy shot released a deluge of destruction." And the bombardment had, or sometimes had, its characteristic double effect: enemy soldiers were killed, and so were any civilians who happened to be nearby. It was not the intention of the officers who called in the artillery and planes to kill civilians; they were acting out of a concern for their own men. And that is a legitimate concern. No one would want to be commanded in wartime by an officer who did not value the lives of his soldiers. But he must also value civilian lives, and so must his soldiers. He cannot save them, because they cannot save themselves, by killing innocent people. It is not just that they can't kill a lot of innocent people. Even if the proportions work out favorably, in particular cases or over a period of time, we would still want to say, I think, that the patrol must be sent out, the risk accepted, before the big guns are brought to bear. The soldiers sent on patrol can plausibly argue that they never chose to make war in Korea; they are soldiers nevertheless; there are obligations that go with their war rights, and the first of these is the obligation to attend to the rights of civilians—more precisely, of those civilians whose lives they themselves endanger.

The principle of double effect, then, stands in need of correction. Double effect is defensible, I want to argue, only when the two outcomes are the product of a *double intention*: first, that the "good" be achieved; second, that the foreseeable evil be reduced as far as possible. So the third of the conditions listed above can be restated:

3. The intention of the actor is good, that is, he aims narrowly at the acceptable effect; the evil effect is not one of his ends, nor is it a means to his ends, and, aware of the evil involved, he seeks to minimize it, accepting costs to himself.

Simply not to intend the death of civilians is too easy; most often, under battle conditions, the intentions of soldiers are focused narrowly on the enemy. What we look for in such cases is some sign of a positive commitment to save civilian lives. Not merely to apply the proportionality rule and kill no more civilians than is militarily necessary—that rule applies to soldiers as well; no one can be killed for trivial purposes. Civilians have a right to something more. And if saving civilian lives means risking soldier's lives, the risk must be accepted. But there is a limit to the risks that we require. These are, after all, unintended deaths and legitimate military operations, and the absolute rule against attacking civilians does not apply. War necessarily places civilians in danger; that is another aspect of its hellishness. We can only ask soldiers to minimize the dangers they impose.

Exactly how far they must go in doing that is hard to say, and for that reason it may seem odd to claim that civilians have rights in such matters. What can this mean? Do civilians have a right not only not to be attacked but also not to be put at risk to such and such a degree, so that imposing a one-in-ten chance of death on them is justified, while imposing a three-in-ten chance is unjustified? In fact, the degree of risk that is permissible is going to vary with the nature of the target, the urgency of the moment, the available technology, and so on. It is best, I think, to say simply that civilians have a right that "due care" be taken.[24]* The case is the same in

---

* Since judgments of "due care" involve calculations of relative value, urgency, and so on, it has to be said that utilitarian arguments and rights arguments (relative at least to indirect effects) are not wholly distinct. Nevertheless, the calculations

domestic society: when the gas company works on the lines that run under my street, I have a right that its workmen observe very strict safety standards. But if the work is urgently required by the imminent danger of an explosion on a neighboring street, the standards may be relaxed and my rights not violated. Now, military necessity works exactly like civil emergency, except that in war the standards with which we are familiar in domestic society are always relaxed. That is not to say, however, that there are no standards at all, and no rights involved. Whenever there is likely to be a second effect, a second intention is morally required. We can move some way toward defining the limits of that second intention if we consider two more wartime examples.

The Bombing of Occupied France and the Vemork Raid

During World War II, the Free French air force carried out bombing raids against military targets in occupied France. Inevitably, their bombs killed Frenchmen working (under coercion) for the German war effort; inevitably too, they killed Frenchmen who simply happened to live in the vicinity of the factories under attack. This posed a cruel dilemma for the pilots, which they resolved not by giving up the raids or asking someone else to carry them out, but by accepting greater risks for themselves. "It was . . . this persistent question of bombing France itself," says Pierre Mendes-France, who served in the air force after his escape from a German prison, "which led us to specialize more and more in precision bombing—that is, flying at a very low altitude. It was more risky, but it also permitted greater precision. . . ."[25] The same factories, of course, could have been (perhaps should have been) attacked by squads of partisans or commandos carrying explosives; their aim would have been perfect, not merely more precise, and no civilians except those working in the factories would have been endangered. But such raids would have been extremely dangerous and the chances of success, and especially of reiterated success, very slim.

---

required by the proportionality principle and those required by "due care" are not the same. Even after the highest possible standards of care have been accepted, the probable civilian losses may still be disproportionate to the value of the target; then the attack must be called off. Or, more often, military planners may decide that the losses entailed by the attack, even if it is carried out at minimal risk to the attackers, are not disproportionate to the value of the target: then "due care" is an additional requirement.

Risks of that sort were more than the French expected, even of their own soldiers. The limits of risk are fixed, then, roughly at that point where any further risk-taking would almost certainly doom the military venture or make it so costly that it could not be repeated.

There is obviously leeway for military judgment here: strategists and planners will for reasons of their own weigh the importance of their target against the importance of their soldiers' lives. But even if the target is very important, and the number of innocent people threatened relatively small, they must risk soldiers before they kill civilians. Consider, for example, the one case I have found from the Second World War where a commando raid was tried instead of an air attack. In 1943, the heavy water plant at Vemork in occupied Norway was destroyed by Norwegian commandos operating on behalf of the British S.O.E. (Special Operations Executive). It was vitally important to stop the production of heavy water so as to delay the development of an atomic bomb by German scientists. British and Norwegian officials debated whether to make the attempt from the air or on the ground and chose the latter approach because it was less likely to injure civilians.[26] But it was very dangerous for the commandos. The first attempt failed, and thirty-four men were killed in its course; the second attempt, by a smaller number of men, succeeded without casualties— to the surprise of everyone involved, including the commandos. It was possible to accept such risks for a single operation that would not, it was thought, have to be repeated. For a "battle" that extended over time, consisting of many separate incidents, it would not have been possible.

Later in the war, after production was resumed at Vemork and security considerably tightened, the plant was bombed from the air by American planes. The bombing was successful, but it resulted in the deaths of twenty-two Norwegian civilians. At this point, double effect seems to work, justifying the air attack. Indeed, in its unrevised form it would have worked sooner. The importance of the military aim and the actual casualty figures (foreseeable in advance, let us assume) would have justified a bombing raid in the first place. But the special value we attach to civilian lives precluded it.

Now, the same value attaches to the lives of German as to those of French or Norwegian civilians. There are, of course, additional moral as well as emotional reasons for paying that respect and accepting its costs in the case of one's own people or one's allies (and it is no accident that my two examples involve attacks on occupied territory). Soldiers have direct obligations to the civilians they leave behind, which have to do with the very purpose of soldiering and with their own political allegiance. But the structure of rights stands independently of political allegiance; it establishes obligations that are owed, so to speak, to humanity itself and to particular human beings and not merely to one's fellow citizens. The rights of German civilians—who did no fighting and were not engaged in supplying the armed forces with the means of fighting—were no different from those of their French counterparts, just as the war rights of German soldiers were no different from those of French soldiers, whatever we think of their war.

The case of occupied France (or Norway) is, however, complex in another way. Even if the French pilots had reduced their risks and flown at high altitudes, we would not hold them solely responsible for the additional civilian deaths they caused. They would have shared that responsibility with the Germans—in part because the Germans had attacked and conquered France, but also (and more importantly for our immediate purposes) because they had mobilized the French economy for their own strategic ends, forcing French workers to serve the German war machine, turning French factories into legitimate military targets, and putting the adjacent residential areas in danger. The question of direct and indirect effect is complicated by the question of coercion. When we judge the unintended killing of civilians, we need to know how those civilians came to be in a battle zone in the first place. This is, perhaps, only another way of asking who put them at risk and what positive efforts were made to save them. But it raises issues that I have not yet addressed and that are most dramatically visible when we turn to another, and a much older, kind of warfare.

10

WAR AGAINST CIVILIANS: SIEGES AND BLOCKADES

SIEGE IS THE OLDEST FORM OF TOTAL WAR. ITS LONG HISTORY SUGGESTS that neither technological advance nor democratic revolution are the crucial factors pushing warfare beyond the combatant population. Civilians have been attacked along with soldiers, or in order to get at soldiers, as often in ancient as in modern times. Such attacks are likely whenever an army seeks what might be called civilian shelter and fights from behind the battlements or from within the buildings of a city, or whenever the inhabitants of a threatened city seek the most immediate form of military protection and agree to be garrisoned. Then, locked into the narrow circle of the walls, civilians and soldiers are exposed to the same risks. Proximity and scarcity make them equally vulnerable. Or perhaps not equally so: in this kind of war, once combat begins, noncombatants are more likely to be killed. The soldiers fight from protected positions, and the civilians, who don't fight at all, are quickly made over (in a phrase I have taken from the military literature) into "useless mouths." Fed last, and only with the army's surplus, they die first. More civilians died in the siege of Leningrad than in the modernist infernos of Hamburg, Dresden, Tokyo, Hiroshima, and Nagasaki, taken together. They probably died more painfully, too, even if in old-fashioned ways. Diaries and memoirs of twentieth-century sieges are entirely familiar to anyone who has read, for example,

Josephus' harrowing history of the Roman siege of Jerusalem. And the moral issues raised by Josephus are familiar to anyone who has thought about twentieth-century war.

COERCION AND RESPONSIBILITY

The Siege of Jerusalem 72 A.D.

Collective starvation is a bitter fate: parents and children, friends and lovers must watch one another die, and the dying is terribly drawn out, physically and morally destructive long before it is over. Though it sounds like the end of the world, the following passage from Josephus refers to a time relatively early in the Roman siege.[1]

> The restraint of liberty to pass in and out of the city took from the Jews all hope of safety, and the famine now increasing consumed whole households and families; and the houses were full of dead women and infants; and the streets filled with the dead bodies of old men. And the young men, swollen like dead men's shadows, walked in the market place and fell down dead where it happened. And now the multitude of dead bodies was so great that they that were alive could not bury them; nor cared they for burying them, being now uncertain what should betide themselves. And many endeavoring to bury others fell down themselves dead upon them. . . . And many being yet alive went unto their graves and there died. Yet for all this calamity was there no weeping nor lamentation, for famine overcame all affections. And they who were yet living, without tears beheld those who being dead were now at rest before them. There was no noise heard within the city. . . .

This is not a firsthand account; Josephus was outside the walls, with the Roman army. According to other writers, it is the women who last longest in sieges, the young men who soonest fall into that deadly lethargy that precedes actual death.[2] But the account is accurate enough: that is what a siege is like. Moreover, *that is what it is meant to be like*. When a city is encircled and deprived of food, it is not the expectation of the attackers that the garrison will hold out until individual soldiers, like Josephus' old men, drop dead in the streets. The death of the ordinary inhabitants of the city is expected to force the hand of the civilian or military leadership. The goal is surrender; the means is not the defeat of the enemy army, but the fearful spectacle of the civilian dead.

The principle of double effect, however it is expounded, provides no justification here. These are intentional deaths. And yet siege warfare is not ruled out by the laws of war. "The propriety of attempting to reduce [a city] by starvation is not questioned."[3] If there is a general rule that civilian deaths must not be aimed at, the siege is a great exception—and the sort of exception that seems, if it is morally warranted, to shatter the rule itself. We must consider why it has been made. How can it be thought right to lock civilians up in the death trap of an encircled city?

The obvious answer is simply that the capture of cities is often an important military objective—in the age of the city-state, it was the ultimate objective—and, frontal assault failing, the siege is the only remaining means to success. In fact, however, it is not even necessary that a frontal assault fail before a siege is thought justifiable. Sitting and waiting is far less costly to the besieging army than attacking, and such calculations are permitted (as we have seen) by the principle of military necessity. But this argument is not the most interesting defense of siege warfare and not the one, I think, with which commanders themselves have assuaged their consciences. Josephus suggests the alternative. Titus, he tells us, lamented the deaths of so many Jerusalemites, "and, lifting up his hands to heaven . . . called God to witness, that it was not his doing."[4] Whose doing was it?

After Titus himself, there are only two candidates: the political or military leaders of the city, who have refused to surrender on terms and forced the inhabitants to fight; or the inhabitants themselves, who have acquiesced in that refusal and agreed, as it were, to run the risks of war. Titus implicitly, and Josephus explicitly, opts for the first of these possibilities. Jerusalem, they argue, has been seized by the fanatical Zealots, who have imposed the war upon the mass of moderate Jews, ready otherwise to surrender. There is perhaps a measure of truth in this view, but it is not a satisfactory argument. It makes Titus himself into an impersonal agent of destruction, set off by the obstinacy of others, without plans and purposes of his own. And it suggests that cities (and why not countries?) that do not surrender are justly exposed to total war. Neither of these is a plausible proposition. Even if we reject them both, however, the attribution of responsibility in siege warfare is a complex business. This complexity helps explain though I shall argue that it does not justify the peculiar status of sieges in the laws of war. It also leads us to see that there are moral questions that must be answered before the principle of double effect comes into play. How did those civilians come to be so near the battlefield, where they are now (intentionally or incidentally) killed? Are they there by choice? Or have they been forced into their encounter with war and death?

A city can indeed be defended against the will of its citizens—by an army, beaten in the field, that retreats within its walls; by an alien garrison, serving the strategic interests of a distant commander; by militant, politically powerful minorities of one or another sort. If they were competent casuists, the leaders of any of these groups might reason in the following way: "We know that civilians will die as a result of our decision to fight here rather than somewhere else. But we will not do the killing, and the deaths will not in any way benefit us. They are not our purpose, nor a part of our purpose, nor a means to our purpose. By collecting and rationing food, we will do all we can to save civilian lives. Those who die are not our responsibility." Clearly, such leaders cannot be condemned under the principle of double effect. But they can be condemned nevertheless—so long as the inhabitants of the city decline to be defended. There are many examples of this sort of thing in medieval history: burghers eager to surrender, aristocratic warriors committed (not to the burghers) to continue the fight.[5] In such cases, the warriors surely bear some responsibility for burgher deaths. They are agents of coercion within the city, as the besieging army is without, and the civilians are trapped between the two. But such cases are rare today, as they were in classical times. Political integration and civic discipline make for cities whose inhabitants expect to be defended and are prepared, morally if not always materially, to endure the burdens of a siege. Consent clears the defenders, and only consent can do so.

What of the attackers? I assume that they offer surrender on terms; that is simply the collective equivalent of quarter and should always be available. But surrender is refused. There are then two military options. First, the strongholds of the city can be bombarded and the walls stormed. No doubt, civilians will die, but for these deaths the attacking soldiers can rightly say that they are not to blame. Though they do the killing, these deaths are, in an important sense, not their "doing." The attackers are cleared by the refusal of surrender, which is an acceptance of the risks of war (or, moral responsibility is shifted onto the defending army, which has made surrender impossible). But this argument applies only to those deaths that are in fact incidental to legitimate military operations. The refusal of surrender does not turn the civilians into direct objects of attack. They have not thereby joined the war, though some of them may subsequently be mobilized for warlike activities within the city. They are simply in their "proper and permanent abode," and their status as citizens of a besieged city is no different from their status as citizens of a country at war. If they can be killed, who cannot be? But then it would appear that the second military option is ruled out: the city cannot be surrounded, cut off, its people systematically starved.

The lawyers have drawn the line differently, though they, too, acknowledge that questions of coercion and consent precede questions of direct and indirect effect. Consider the following case from Machiavelli's *Art of War*:[6]

> Alexander the Great, anxious to conquer Leucadia, first made himself master of the neighboring towns and turned all the inhabitants into Leucadia; at last the town was so full of people that he immediately reduced it by famine.

Machiavelli was enthusiastic about this strategy, but it never became accepted military practice. Moreover, it is not accepted even if the purpose of the forced evacuation is more benign than Alexander's: simply to clear the suburbs for military operations, say, or to drive away people whom the besieging army cannot afford to feed. Had Alexander acted from such motives, and then taken Leucadia by storm, the incidental death of any of the evacuees would still be his special responsibility, since he had forcibly exposed them to the risks of war.

The legal norm is the *status quo*.[7] The commander of the besieging army is not conceived to be, and does not think himself to be, responsible for those people who have always lived in the city—who are there, so to speak, naturally—nor for those who are there voluntarily, who sought the protection of city walls, driven only by the general fear of war. He is in the clear with regard to these people, however horribly they die, however much to his purpose it is that they die horribly, because he did not force them into their death place. He did not push them through the gates of the city before he locked them in. This is, I suppose, an understandable way of drawing the line, but it does not seem to me the right way. The hard question is whether the line can be drawn differently without ruling out sieges altogether. In the long history of siege warfare, this question has a specific form: should civilians be allowed to leave the city, saving themselves from starvation and relieving pressure on the collective food supply, after it has been invested? More generally, isn't locking them into the besieged city morally the same as driving them in? And if it is, shouldn't they be let out, so that those that remain, to fight and starve, can really be said to have chosen to remain? During the siege of Jerusalem, Titus ordered that any Jews who fled the city were to be crucified. It is the one point in his narrative where Josephus feels the need to apologize for his new master.[8] But I want to turn now to a modern example, for these questions were directly addressed by the Nuremberg courts after World War II.

THE RIGHT TO LEAVE

The Siege of Leningrad

When its last road and rail links to the east were cut by advancing German forces, on September 8, 1941, Leningrad held over three million people, of whom about 200,000 were soldiers.[9] This was roughly the peacetime population of the city. About half a million people had been evacuated before the siege began, but the number had been made up by refugees from the Baltic states, the Karelian Isthmus, and Leningrad's western and southern suburbs. These people ought to have been moved on, and the evacuation of the city itself speeded up; the Soviet authorities were frighteningly inefficient. But evacuation is always a difficult political issue. To organize it early and on a large scale seems defeatist; it is a way of acknowledging that the army won't be able to hold a line in front of the city. Moreover, it requires a massive effort at a time, it is usually said, when resources and manpower should be concentrated on military defense. And even when the danger is imminent, it is likely to encounter civilian resistance. Politics makes for two sorts of resistance: from those who hope to welcome the enemy and profit from his victory, and from those who are unwilling to "desert" the patriotic struggle. Inevitably, the very authorities organizing the evacuation are also conducting a propaganda campaign that makes desertion seem dishonorable. But the greater resistance is nonpolitical in character, deeply rooted in feelings of place and kin: the unwillingness to leave one's home, to separate from friends and family, to become a refugee.

For all these reasons, the large proportion of Leningraders trapped in the city after September 8 is not unusual in the history of sieges. Nor were they trapped absolutely. The Germans were never able to link up with

Finnish forces either on the western or eastern shores of Lake Lagoda, and so there remained an evacuation route to the interior of Russia, at first by boat across the lake, and then as the waters froze, progressively by foot, sled, and truck. Until large-scale convoys could be organized (in January 1942), however, only a slow trickle of people were able to escape. A more immediate escape route was available—through the German lines. For the siege was maintained along a wide arc south of the city, many miles long and in places thinly held. It was possible for civilians on foot to filter through the lines and, as desperation grew within the city, thousands attempted to do so. The German command responded to these attempts with an order, first announced on September 18, and then repeated two months later, to stop the escapes at all costs. Artillery was to be used "to prevent any such attempt at the greatest possible distance from our own lines by opening fire as early as possible, so that the infantry is spared . . . shooting at civilians."[10] I have not been able to find any account of how many civilians died as a direct or indirect result of this order; nor do I know whether or not infantrymen actually opened fire. But if we assume that the German effort was at least partially successful, many would-be escapees, hearing of the shelling or the shooting, must have remained in the city. And there many of them died. Before the siege ended in 1943, more than a million civilians were dead of starvation and disease.

At Nuremberg, Field Marshal von Leeb, who commanded Army Group North from June to December 1941, and who was therefore responsible for the first months of siege operations, was formally charged with war crimes because of the order of September 18. Von Leeb claimed in defense that what he had done was customary practice in wartime, and the judges, after consulting the legal handbooks, were led to agree. They cited Professor Hyde, an American authority on international law: "It is said that if the commander of a besieged place expels the noncombatants, in order to lessen the number of those who consume his stock of provisions, it is lawful, though an extreme measure, to drive them back so as to hasten the surrender."[11] No effort was made to distinguish "expelled" civilians from those leaving voluntarily, and probably the distinction is not relevant to the guilt or innocence of von Leeb. The benefit to the besieged army would be the same in either case. The laws of war permit the attackers to bar the benefit if they can. "We might wish the law were otherwise," said the judges, "but we must administer it as we find it." Von Leeb was acquitted.

The judges could have found cases in which civilians were allowed to leave besieged cities. During the Franco-Prussian War, the Swiss managed to arrange for a limited evacuation of civilians from Strasbourg. The American commander permitted civilians to leave Santiago before ordering the bombardment of that city in 1898. The Japanese offered free exit for noncombatants trapped in Port Arthur in 1905, but the offer was declined by the Russian authorities.[12] These were all cases, however, in which the attacking army expected to carry the city by storm, and its commanders were willing to make a humanitarian gesture—they would not have said that they were recognizing noncombatant rights—that would cost them nothing. But when the defenders are to be waited out, subjected to slow starvation, the precedents are different. The siege of Plevna in the Russo-Turkish war of 1877 is more typical.[13]

> When Osman Pasha's food supplies began to fail, he turned out the old men and women who were in the town and demanded free passage for them to Sofia or Rakhovo. General Gourko [the Russian commander] refused and sent them back.

And the student of international law who cites this case, then comments: "He could not do otherwise without detriment to his plans." Field Marshal von Leeb might have recalled the shining example of General Gourko.

The argument that needs to be made against both Gourko and von Leeb is suggested by the terms of the German order of September 18. Suppose that large numbers of Russian civilians, convinced that they would die if they returned to Leningrad, had persisted in the face of artillery fire and advanced on the German lines. Would the infantry have shot them down? Its officers were apparently uncertain. That sort of thing was the work of special "death squads," not of ordinary soldiers, even in Hitler's army. Surely there would have been some reluctance, and even some refusals; and surely it would have been right to refuse. Or, suppose that these same refugees were not killed, but rounded up and imprisoned. Would it have been acceptable under the laws of war to inform the commander of the besieged city that they would be held without food, systematically starved, until he surrendered? No doubt, the judges would have found this unacceptable (even though they sometimes recognized the right to kill hostages). They would not have questioned the responsibility of von Leeb for these people whom he had, in my alternative case, actually locked up. But how is the siege of a city different?

The inhabitants of a city, though they have freely chosen to live within its walls, have not chosen to live under siege. The siege itself is an act of coercion, a violation of the *status quo*, and I cannot see how the commander of the besieging army can escape responsibility for its effects. He has no right to wage total war, even if civilians and soldiers within the city are politically united in refusing surrender. The systematic starvation of civilians under siege is one of those military acts which "though permissible by custom, is a glaring violation of the principle by which custom professes to be governed."[14]

The only justifiable practice, I think, is indicated in the Talmudic law of sieges, summed up by the philosopher Maimonides in the twelfth century (whose version is cited by Grotius in the seventeenth): "When siege is laid to a city for the purpose of capture, it may not be surrounded on all four sides, but only on three, in order to give an opportunity for escape to those who would flee to save their lives. . . ."[15] But this seems hopelessly naïve. How is it possible to "surround" a city on three sides? Such a sentence, it might be said, could only appear in the literature of a people who had neither a state nor an army of their own. It is an argument offered not from any military perspective, but from a refugee perspective. It makes, however, the crucial point: that in the direness of a siege, people have a right to be refugees. And then it has to be said that the besieging army has a responsibility to open, if it possibly can, a path for their flight.

In practice, many men and women will refuse to leave. Though I have described civilians under siege as people in a trap, hostage-like, life in the city is not like life in a prison camp; it is both much worse and much better. There is, for one thing, important work to do, and there are shared reasons for doing it. Besieged cities are arenas for a collective heroism, and even after ordinary love of place gives out, the emotional life of the threatened city makes departure difficult, at least for some of the citizens.[16] Civilians performing essential services for the army will not, of course, be permitted to leave; they are in effect conscripted. Along with the civilian heroes of the siege, they are henceforth legitimate objects of military attack. The offer of free exit turns all those people who choose to remain in the city, or who are forced to remain, even if they are still in their "proper and permanent abode," into something like a garrison: they have yielded their civilian rights. It is another example of the coerciveness of war that men and women must, in this case, leave their homes to maintain their immunity. But that is not a judgment on the siege commander. When he opens his lines to civilian refugees, he is reducing the immediate coerciveness of his own activity, and having done that he probably has a right to carry on that activity (assuming that it has some significant military purpose). The offer of free exit clears him of responsibility for civilian deaths.

At this point, the argument needs to be made more general. I have been suggesting that when we judge those forms of warfare that closely involve the civilian population, like sieges (and, as we shall see, guerrilla war), the issue of coercion and consent takes precedence over the issue of direction and indirection. We want to know how civilians came to be in militarily exposed positions: what force was used against them, what choices they freely made. There are a wide range of possibilities:

1. that they are coerced by their ostensible defenders, who must then share responsibility for the resulting deaths, even though they do no killing themselves;
2. that they consent to be defended, and so clear the military commander of the defending army;
3. that they are coerced by their attackers, driven into an exposed position and killed, in which case it doesn't matter whether the killing is a direct effect or a side effect of the attack, for it is a crime either way;
4. that they are attacked but not coerced, attacked in their "natural" place, and then the principle of double effect comes into play and siege by starvation is morally unacceptable; and
5. that they are offered free exit by their attackers, after which those that remain can justifiably be killed, directly or indirectly.

The last two of these are the most important, though I will want to qualify them later on. They require a clearcut reversal of contemporary law as stated or restated at Nuremberg, so as to establish and give substance to a principle that is, I think, commonly accepted: that soldiers are under an obligation to help civilians leave the scene of a battle. In the case of a siege, I want to say, it is only when they fulfill this obligation that the battle itself is morally possible.

But is it still militarily possible? Once free exit has been offered, and been accepted by significant numbers of people, the besieging army is placed under a certain handicap. The city's food supply will now last so much longer. It is precisely this handicap that siege commanders have in the past refused to accept. I don't see, however, that it is different in kind from other handicaps imposed by the war convention. It doesn't make siege operations entirely impractical, only somewhat more difficult—given the ruthlessness of the modern state, one has to say, marginally more difficult; for the presence of large numbers of civilians in a besieged city is unlikely to be allowed to interfere with the provisioning of the army; and, as the Leningrad example suggests, the death of large numbers of civilians is unlikely to be allowed to interfere with the defense of the city. In Leningrad, soldiers did not starve, though civilians died of hunger. On the other hand, civilians were evacuated from Leningrad, once Lake Lagoda had frozen solid, and food supplies were brought in. In different circumstances, free exit might make a greater military difference, forcing a frontal assault on the city (because the besieging army may also have supply problems) or a major prolongation of the siege. But these are acceptable consequences, and they are only "detrimental" to the plans of the siege commander if he has not planned for them in advance. In any case, if he wants (as he probably will want) to lift his hands to heaven and say of the civilians he kills, "It's not my doing," he has no choice but to offer them the chance to leave.

TAKING AIM AND THE DOCTRINE OF DOUBLE EFFECT

The issue is more difficult, however, when a whole country is subjected to siege conditions, when an invading army sets about systematically to destroy crops and food supplies, for example, or when a naval blockade cuts off vitally needed imports. Here free exit is not a plausible possibility (mass migration would be necessary), and the question of responsibility takes on a somewhat different form. Once again, it should be stressed that the struggle to secure and deny supplies is a common feature of ancient as well as modern warfare. It was the subject of legislation long before the modern laws of war were worked out. The Deuteronomic code, for example, explicitly bans the cutting down of fruit trees: "Only the trees of which thou knowest that they are not trees for food, them thou mayest destroy and cut down, that thou mayest build bulwarks against the city. . . ."[17] But few armies seem ever to have respected the ban. It was apparently unknown in Greece; during the Peloponnesian War, the destruction of olive groves was virtually the first act of an invading army; judging from Caesar's *Gallic Wars*, the Romans fought in the same way.[18] In early modern times, long before the scientific destruction of crops became possible, the doctrine of strategic devastation was a kind of conventional wisdom among military commanders. "The Palatinate was wasted [in the Thirty Years War] in order that the imperial armies should be denied the military produce of the country; Marlborough destroyed the farms and crops of Bavaria for a similar purpose [in The War of the Spanish Succession]. . . ."[19] The Shenandoah Valley was laid waste in the American Civil War; and the burning of farms on Sherman's march through Georgia had, among other purposes, the strategic goal of starving the Confederate army. In our own time, and with a more advanced technology, vast sections of Vietnam were subjected to a similar destruction.

The contemporary laws of war require that such efforts be directed, whatever their indirect effects, only against the armed forces of the enemy. Civilians in a city have been thought a legitimate target, civilians at large not so: they are, though in vast numbers, only the incidental victims of strategic devastation. The allowable military purpose here is to make the provisioning of the enemy army impossible, and when generals have exceeded that purpose—attempting, like General Sherman, to end the war by "punishing" the civilian population—they have been commonly condemned. Why this is so I am not sure, though why it should be so is easier to make out. The impossibility of free exit rules out any direct attack on the civilian population.

This is not, however, much protection for civilians, since military supplies cannot be destroyed without first destroying civilian supplies. The morally desirable rule is stated by Spaight: "If under such peculiar conditions as existed in the Confederate States and in South Africa [during the Boer War] . . . the enemy depends for his supplies on the surplus of cereals, etc., held by the noncombatant population, then a commander is justified by the necessity of war in destroying or seizing that *surplus.*"[20] But it is not the case that the army lives off the civilian surplus; more likely, civilians are forced to make do with what is left after the army has been fed. Hence, strategic devastation is not aimed, and cannot be, at "military produce," but at food supplies generally. And civilians suffer long before soldiers feel the pinch. But who is it who inflicts this suffering, the army that destroys food stocks or the army that seizes what remains for itself? This question is taken up in the British government's official history of World War I.

The British Blockade of Germany

In its origins, a blockade was simply a naval siege, an "investment by sea," barring all ships from entering or leaving the blockaded area (usually a major port) and cutting off, so far as possible, all supplies. It was not thought legally or morally justifiable, however, to extend this interdiction to the trade of an entire country. Most nineteenth-century commentators shared the view that the economic life of an enemy country could never be a legitimate military objective. The denial of military supplies was, of course, permissible, and given the possibility of stopping and searching ships on the high seas, elaborate rules were developed for the regulation of wartime trade. Lists of goods qualified as "contraband" and liable to confiscation were regularly published by belligerent powers. Though these lists tended to get longer and more inclusive, the laws of naval warfare stipulated the existence of a category of "conditional contraband" (commonly thought to include foodstuffs and medical supplies) that could not be seized unless it was known to be destined for military use. The relevant principle here was an extension of the combatant/noncombatant distinction. "The seizure of articles of commerce becomes illegitimate so soon as it ceases to aim at enfeebling the naval and military resources of the [enemy] country and puts immediate pressure on the civilian population."[21]

In the course of the First World War, these rules were undermined in two ways; first, by extending the notion of blockade, and then by assuming the military utility of all conditional contraband. The result was full-scale economic warfare, a struggle over supply analogous in its purposes and effects to strategic devastation. The Germans fought this war with the submarine; the British, who controlled at least the surface of the sea, used conventional naval forces, blockading the entire German coast. In this case, conventional forces won the day. The convoy system eventually overcame the submarine threat, whereas the blockade, according to Liddell Hart, was a decisive factor in Germany's defeat. "The spectre of slow enfeeblement ending in eventual collapse," he argues, drove the High Command to undertake its disastrous offensive of 1918.[22] More immediate, and less military consequences can also be traced to the blockade. The "slow enfeeblement" of a country unhappily entails the actual deaths of individual citizens. Though civilians did not starve to death in Germany during the last years of the war, mass malnutrition greatly heightened the normal effects of disease. Statistical studies carried out after the war indicate that some half million civilian deaths, directly attributable to diseases such as influenza and typhus, in fact resulted from the deprivations imposed by the British blockade.[23]

British officials defended the blockade in legal terms by calling it a reprisal for German submarine warfare. More important for our purposes, however, is their consistent denial that the interdiction of supply was aimed at German civilians. The Cabinet had planned only a "limited economic war," directed, as the official history has it, "against the armed forces of the enemy." But the German government maintained its resistance "by interposing the German people between the armies and the economic weapons that had been leveled against them and by making the civil populace bear the suffering inflicted."[24] The sentence invites ridicule, and yet it is hard to imagine any other defense of the naval blockade (or of strategic devastation in land warfare). The passive form of the verb "inflicted" carries the argument. Who did the inflicting? Not the British, though they stopped ships and confiscated cargoes; they took aim at the German army and sought only military ends. And then, the official historian suggests, the Germans themselves pushed civilians into the front line of the economic war—it is as if they had driven them into the forward trenches at the Battle of the Somme—where the British could not help but kill them in the course of legitimate military operations.

If we are to pursue this argument, we will have to assume what seems unlikely: that the British did not in fact aim at the benefits they won from the slow starvation of German civilians. Given that fortunate blindness, the claim that Britain be acquitted of those civilian deaths is at least interesting, though finally unacceptable. It is interesting, first of all, that the official British historian makes the claim in this complex form rather than simply asserting a war right (as in the siege cases) to starve civilians. And it is interesting, secondly, because the acquittal of the British depends so radically on the indictment of the Germans. Without "interposition," the British have no case, for the revised principle of double effect bars the strategy they adopted.

It is, of course, false to say that the German government "interposed" the civilian population between the blockade and the army. The civilians were where they had always been. If they stood behind the army in the national food line, that is where they had always stood. The army's prior claim to resources was not invented in order to cope with the exigencies of the blockade. Moreover, that claim was probably accepted by the great majority of the German people, at least until the very last months of the war. When the British took aim at the enemy army, therefore, they were aiming *through* the civilian population, knowing that the civilians were there and that they were in their normal place, "their proper and permanent abode." In relation to the German army, they were placed in exactly the same way as British civilians in relation to their own army. It may be that the British did not intend to kill them; killing them wasn't (if we take the official history seriously) a means to the end set by the Cabinet. But if the success of the British strategy did not depend upon civilian deaths, it nevertheless required that nothing at all be done to avoid those deaths. Civilians had to be hit before soldiers could be hit, and this kind of attack is morally unacceptable. A soldier must take careful aim *at* his military target and *away from* nonmilitary targets. He can only shoot if he has a reasonably clear shot; he can only attack if a direct attack is possible. He can risk incidental deaths, but he cannot kill civilians simply because he finds them between himself and his enemies.*

This principle rules out the extended form of the naval blockade and every sort of strategic devastation, except in cases where adequate provision can be made, and is made, for noncombatants. It is not a principle that has been commonly accepted in war, at least not by the combatants. But it is consistent, I think, with other parts of the war convention, and it has gradually won acceptance, for political as much as moral reasons, with reference to a very important form of contemporary warfare. The systematic destruction of crops and food supplies is a frequent strategy in anti-guerrilla struggles, and since the governments engaged in such struggles generally claim sovereignty over the territory and population involved, they have been inclined to accept responsibility for feeding

---

*It remains true, however, that the issue of "interposition" (or coercion) has to be resolved first. Consider an example from the Franco-Prussian War of 1870: during the siege of Paris, the French used irregular forces behind enemy lines to attack trains carrying military supplies to the German army. The Germans responded by placing civilian hostages on the trains. Now it was no longer possible to get a "clear shot" at what was still a legitimate military target. But the civilians on the trains were not in their normal place; they had been radically coerced; and responsibility for their deaths, even if these deaths were actually inflicted by the French, lay with the German commanders. On this point, see Robert Nozick's discussion of "innocent shields of threats" in *Anarchy, State and Utopia*, p. 35.

civilians (which is not to say that civilians have always been fed). Just what this involves I will consider in the next chapter. I have been arguing here that even enemy civilians, over whom sovereignty is not claimed, are the responsibility of attacking armies, whenever those armies adopt strategies that put civilians at risk.

11

GUERRILLA WAR

RESISTANCE TO MILITARY OCCUPATION

A Partisan Attack

Surprise is the essential feature of guerrilla war; thus the ambush is the classic guerrilla tactic. It is also, of course, a tactic in conventional war; the concealment and camouflage that it involves, though they were once repugnant to officers and gentlemen, have long been regarded as legitimate forms of combat. But there is one kind of ambush that is not legitimate in conventional war and that places in sharp focus the moral difficulties guerrillas and their enemies regularly encounter. This is the ambush prepared behind political or moral rather than natural cover. An example is provided by Captain Helmut Tausend, of the German Army, in Marcel Ophuls' documentary film *The Sorrow and the Pity*. Tausend tells of a platoon of soldiers on a march through the French countryside during the years of the German occupation. They passed a group of young men, French peasants, or so it seemed, digging potatoes. But these were not in fact peasants; they were members of the Resistance. As the Germans marched by, the "peasants" dropped their shovels, picked up guns hidden in the field, and opened fire. Fourteen of the soldiers were hit. Years later, their captain was still indignant. "You call that 'partisan' resistance? I don't. Partisans for me are men that can be identified, men who wear a special armband or a cap, something with which to recognize them. What happened in that potato field was murder."[1]

The captain's argument about armbands and caps is simply a citation from the international law of war, from the Hague and Geneva conventions, and I shall have more to say about it later on. It is important to stress first that the partisans had here taken on a double disguise. They were disguised as peaceful peasants and also as Frenchmen, that is, citizens of a state that had surrendered, for whom the war was over (just as guerrillas in a revolutionary struggle disguise themselves as unarmed civilians and also as loyal citizens of a state that is not at war at all). It was because of this second disguise that the ambush was so perfect. The Germans thought they were in a rear area, not at the front, and so they were not battle-ready; they were not preceded by a scouting party; they were not suspicious of the young men in the field. The surprise achieved by the partisans was of a kind virtually impossible in actual combat. It derived from what might be called the protective coloration of national surrender, and its effect was obviously to erode the moral and legal understandings upon which surrender rests.

Surrender is an explicit agreement and exchange: the individual soldier promises to stop fighting in exchange for benevolent quarantine for the duration of the war; a government promises that its citizens will stop fighting in exchange for the restoration of ordinary public life. The precise conditions of "benevolent quarantine" and "public life" are specified in the law books; I need not go into them here.[2] The obligations of individuals are also specified: they may try to escape from the prison camp or to flee occupied territory, and if they succeed in their escape or flight, they are free to fight again; they have regained their war rights. But they may not resist their quarantine or occupation. If a prisoner kills a guard in the course of his escape, the act is murder; if the citizens of a defeated country attack the occupation authorities, the act has, or once had, an even grimmer name: it is, or was, "war treason" (or "war rebellion"), a breaking of political faith, punishable, like the ordinary treason of rebels and spies, by death.

But "traitor" does not seem the right name for those French partisans. Indeed, it is precisely their experience, and that of other guerrilla fighters in World War II, that has led to the virtual disappearance of "war treason" from the law books and of the idea of breaking faith from our moral discussions of wartime resistance (and of peacetime rebellion also, when it is directed against alien or colonial rule). We tend to deny, today, that individuals are automatically subsumed by the decisions of their government or the fate of its armies. We have come to understand the moral commitment they may feel to defend their homeland and their political community, even after the war is officially over.[3] A prisoner of war, after all, knows that the fighting will go on despite his own capture; his government is in place, his country is still being defended. But after national surrender the case is different, and if there are still values worth defending, no one can defend them except ordinary men and women, citizens with no political or legal standing. I suppose it is some general sense that there are such values, or often are, that leads us to grant these men and women a kind of moral authority.

But though this grant reflects new and valuable democratic sensibilities, it also raises serious questions. For if citizens of a defeated state still have a right to fight, what is the meaning of surrender? And what obligations can be imposed on conquering armies? There can be no ordinary public life in occupied territory if the occupation authorities are subject to attack at any time and at the hands of any citizen. And ordinary life is a value, too. It is what most of the citizens of a defeated country most ardently hope for. The heroes of the resistance put it in jeopardy, and we must weigh the risks they impose on others in order to understand the risks they must accept themselves. Moreover, if the authorities actually do aim at the restoration of everyday peacefulness, they seem entitled to enjoy the security they provide; and then they must also be entitled to regard armed resistance as a criminal activity. So the story with which I began might end this way (in the film it has no end): the surviving soldiers rally and fight back; some of the partisans are captured, tried as murderers, condemned, and executed. We would not, I think, add those executions to the list of Nazi war crimes. At the same time, we would not join in the condemnation.

So the situation can be summed up: resistance is legitimate, and the punishment of resistance is legitimate. That may seem like a simple standoff and an abdication of ethical judgment. It is actually a precise reflection of the moral realities of military defeat. I want to stress again that our understanding of these realities has nothing to do with our view of the two sides. We can deplore the resistance, without calling the partisans traitors; we can hate the occupation, without calling the execution of the partisans a crime. If we alter the story or add to it, of course, the case is changed. If the occupation authorities do not live up to their obligations under the surrender agreement, they lose their entitlements. And once the guerrilla struggle has reached a certain point of seriousness and intensity, we may decide that the war has effectively been renewed, notice has been given, the front has been re-established (even if it is not a *line*), and soldiers no longer have a right to be surprised even by a surprise attack. Then guerrillas captured by the authorities must be treated as prisoners of war—provided, that is, they have themselves fought in accordance with the war convention.

But guerrillas don't fight that way. Their struggle is subversive not merely with reference to the occupation or to their own government, but with reference to the war convention itself. Wearing peasant clothes and hiding among the civilian population, they challenge the most fundamental principle of the rules of war. For it is the purpose of those rules to specify for each individual a single identity; he must be either a soldier or a civilian. The British *Manual of Military Law* makes the point with special clarity: "Both these classes have distinct privileges, duties, and disabilities. . . . An individual must definitely choose to belong to one class or the other, and shall not be permitted to enjoy the privileges of both; in particular . . . an individual [shall] not be allowed to kill or wound members of the army of the opposed nation and subsequently, if captured or in danger of life, pretend to be a peaceful citizen."[4] That is what guerrillas do, however, or sometimes do. So we can imagine another conclusion to the story of the partisan attack. The partisans successfully disengage, disperse to their homes, and go about their ordinary business. When German troops come to the village that night, they cannot distinguish the guerrilla fighters from any other of the villagers. What do they do then? If, through searches and interrogations—police, not soldier's, work—they seize one of the partisans, should they treat him as a captured criminal or a prisoner of war (leaving aside now the problems of surrender and resistance)? And if they seize no one, can they punish the whole village? If the partisans don't maintain the distinction of soldiers and civilians, why should they?

THE RIGHTS OF GUERRILLA FIGHTERS

As this example suggests, the guerrillas don't subvert the war convention by themselves attacking civilians; at least, it is not a necessary feature of their struggle that they do that. Instead, they invite their enemies to do it. By refusing to accept a single identity, they seek to make it impossible for their enemies to accord to combatants and noncombatants their "distinct privileges . . . and disabilities." The political creed of the guerrillas is essentially a defense of this refusal. The people, they say, are no longer being defended by an army; the only army in the field is the army of the oppressors; the people are defending themselves. Guerrilla war is "people's war," a special form of the *levée en masse*, authorized from below. "The war of liberation," according to a pamphlet of the Vietnamese National Liberation Front, "is fought by the people themselves; the entire people . . . are the driving force. . . . Not only the peasants in their rural areas, but the workers and laborers in the city, along with intellectuals, students, and businessmen have gone to fight the enemy."[5] And the NLF drove the point home by naming its paramilitary forces *Dan Quan*, literally, civilian soldiers. The guerrilla's self-image is not of a solitary fighter hiding among the people, but of a whole people mobilized for war, himself a loyal member, one among many. If you want to fight against us, the guerrillas say, you are going to have to fight civilians, for you are not at war with an army but with a nation. Therefore, you should not fight at all, and if you do, you are the barbarians, killing women and children.

In fact, the guerrillas mobilize only a small part of the nation—a very small part, when they first begin their attacks. They depend upon the counter-attacks of their enemies to mobilize the rest. Their strategy is framed in terms of the war convention: they seek to place the onus of indiscriminate warfare on the opposing army. The guerrillas themselves have to discriminate, if only to prove that they are really soldiers (and not enemies) of the people. It is also and perhaps more importantly true that it is relatively easy for them to make the relevant discriminations. I don't mean that guerrillas never engage in terrorist campaigns (even against their fellow countrymen) or that they never take hostages or burn villages. They do all those things, though they generally do less of them than the anti-guerrilla forces. For the guerrillas know who their enemies are, and they know where they are. They fight in small groups, with small arms, at close quarters—and the soldiers they fight against wear uniforms. Even when they kill civilians, they are able to make distinctions: they aim at well-known officials, notorious collaborators, and so on. If the "entire people" are not really the "driving force," they are also not the objects of guerrilla attack.

For this reason, guerrilla leaders and publicists are able to stress the moral quality not only of the goals they seek but also of the means they employ. Consider for a moment Mao Tse-tung's famous "Eight Points for Attention." Mao is by no means committed to the notion of noncombatant immunity (as we shall see), but he writes as if, in the China of the warlords and the Kuomintang, only the communists respect the lives and property of the people. The "Eight Points" are meant to mark off the guerrillas first of all from their predecessors, the bandits of traditional China, and then from their present enemies, who ravage the countryside. They suggest how the military virtues can be radically simplified for a democratic age.[6]

1. Speak politely.
2. Pay fairly for what you buy.
3. Return everything you borrow.
4. Pay for anything you damage.
5. Do not hit or swear at people.
6. Do not damage crops.
7. Do not take liberties with women.
8. Do not ill-treat captives.

The last of these is particularly problematic, for in the conditions of guerrilla war it must often involve releasing prisoners, something most guerrillas are no doubt loath to do. Yet it is at least sometimes done, as an account of the Cuban revolution, originally published in the *Marine Corps Gazette*, suggests:[7]

> That same evening, I watched the surrender of hundreds of *Batistianos* from a small-town garrison. They were gathered within a hollow square of rebel Tommy-gunners and harangued by Raul Castro:
> "We hope that you will stay with us and fight against the master who so ill-used you. If you decide to refuse this invitation—and I am not going to repeat it—you will be delivered to the custody of the Cuban Red Cross tomorrow. Once you are under Batista's orders again, we hope that you will not take arms against us. But, if you do, remember this:
> "We took you this time. We can take you again. And when we do, we will not frighten or torture or kill you. . . . If you are captured a second time or even a third . . . we will again return you exactly as we are doing now."

Even when guerrillas behave this way, however, it is not clear that they are themselves entitled to prisoner of war status when captured, or that they have any war rights at all. For if they don't make war on noncombatants, it also appears that they don't make *war* on soldiers: "What happened in that potato field was murder." They attack stealthily, deviously, without warning, and in disguise. They violate the implicit trust upon which the war convention rests: soldiers must feel safe among civilians if civilians are ever to be safe from soldiers. It is not the case, as Mao once suggested, that guerrillas are to civilians as fish to the ocean. The actual relation is rather of fish to other fish, and the guerrillas are as likely to appear among the minnows as among the sharks.

That, at least, is the paradigmatic form of guerrilla war. I should add that it is not the form such war always or necessarily takes. The discipline and mobility required of guerrilla fighters often preclude a domestic retreat. Their main forces commonly operate out of base camps located in remote areas of the country. And, curiously enough, as the guerrilla units grow larger and more stable, their members are likely to put on uniforms. Tito's partisans in Yugoslavia, for example, wore distinctive dress, and this was apparently no disadvantage in the kind of war they fought.[8] All the evidence suggests that quite apart from the rules of war, guerrillas, like other soldiers, prefer to wear uniforms; it enhances their sense of membership and solidarity. In any case, soldiers attacked by a guerrilla main force know who their enemies are as soon as the attack begins; ambushed by uniformed men, they would know no sooner. When the guerrillas "melt away" after such an attack, they more often disappear into jungles or mountains than into villages, a retreat that raises no moral problems. Battles of this sort can readily be assimilated to the irregular combat of army units like Wingate's "Chindits" or "Merrill's Marauders" in World War II.[9] But this is not what most people have in mind when they talk about guerrilla war. The paradigm worked out by guerrilla publicists (together with their enemies) focuses precisely on what is morally difficult about guerrilla war—and also, as we shall see, about anti-guerrilla war. In order to deal with these difficulties, I shall simply accept the paradigm and treat guerrillas as they ask to be treated, as fish among the ocean's fish. What then are their war rights?

The legal rules are simple and clearcut, though not without their own problems. To be eligible for the war rights of soldiers, guerrilla fighters must wear "a fixed distinctive sign visible at a distance" and must "carry their arms openly."[10] It is possible to worry at length about the precise meaning of distinctiveness, fixity, and openness, but I do not think we would learn a great deal by doing so. In fact, these requirements are often suspended, particularly in the interesting case of a popular rising to repel invasion or resist foreign tyranny. When the people rise *en masse*, they are not required to put on uniforms. Nor will they carry arms openly, if they fight, as they usually do, from ambush: hiding themselves, they can hardly be expected to display their weapons. Francis Lieber, in one of the earliest legal studies of guerrilla war, cites the case of the Greek rebellion against Turkey, where the Turkish government killed or enslaved all prisoners: "But I take it," he writes, "that a civilized government would not have allowed the fact that the Greeks . . . carried on mountain guerrilla [war] to influence its conduct toward prisoners."[11]

The key moral issue, which the law gets at only imperfectly, does not have to do with distinctive dress or visible weapons, but with the use of civilian clothing as a ruse and a disguise.* The French partisan attack perfectly illustrates this, and it has to be said, I think, that the killing of those German soldiers was more like assassination than war. That is not because of the surprise, simply, but because of the kind and degree of deceit involved: the same sort of deceit that is involved when a public official or party leader is shot down by some political enemy who has taken on the appearance of a friend and supporter or of a harmless passer-by. Now it may be the case—I am more than open to this suggestion—that the German army in France had attacked civilians in ways that justified the assassination of individual soldiers, just as it may be the case that the public official or party leader is a brutal tyrant who deserves to die. But

---

* The case is the same with the wearing of civilian clothing as with the wearing of enemy uniforms. In his memoir of the Boer War, Deneys Reitz reports that Boer guerrillas sometimes wore uniforms taken from British soldiers. Lord Kitchener, the British commander, warned that anyone captured in khaki would be shot, and a considerable number of prisoners were later executed. While he insists that "none of us ever wore captured uniforms with the deliberate intention of decoying the enemy, but only out of sheer necessity," Reitz nevertheless justified Kitchener's order by telling of an incident in which two British soldiers were killed when they hesitated to shoot at guerrillas dressed in khaki. (*Commando*, London, 1932, p. 247.)

assassins cannot claim the protection of the rules of war; they are engaged in a different activity. Most of the other enterprises for which guerrillas require civilian disguise are also "different." These include all the possible varieties of espionage and sabotage; they can best be understood by comparing them to acts carried out behind enemy lines by the secret agents of conventional armies. It is widely agreed that such agents possess no war rights, even if their cause is just. They know the risks their efforts entail, and I see no reason to describe the risks of guerrillas engaged in similar projects any differently. Guerrilla leaders claim war rights for all their followers, but it makes sense to distinguish, if this is possible, between those guerrillas who use civilian dress as a ruse and those who depend upon camouflage, the cover of darkness, tactical surprise, and so on.

The issues posed by the guerrilla war paradigm, however, are not resolved by this distinction. For guerrillas don't merely fight *as* civilians; they fight *among* civilians, and this in two senses. First, their day-to-day existence is much more closely connected with the day-to-day existence of the people around them than is ever the case with conventional armies. They live with the people they claim to defend, whereas conventional troops are usually billeted with civilians only after the war or the battle is over. And second, they fight where they live; their military positions are not bases, posts, camps, forts, or strongholds, but villages. Hence they are radically dependent on the villagers, even when they don't succeed in mobilizing them for "people's war." Now, every army depends upon the civilian population of its home country for supplies, recruits, and political support. But this dependence is usually indirect, mediated by the bureaucratic apparatus of the state or the exchange system of the economy. So food is passed from the farmer to the marketing co-op, to the food processing plant, to the trucking company, to the army commissary. But in guerrilla war, the dependence is immediate: the farmer hands the food to the guerrilla, and whether it is received as a tax or paid for in accordance with Mao's Second Point for Attention, the relation between the two men is face-to-face. Similarly, an ordinary citizen may vote for a political party that in turn supports the war effort and whose leaders are called in for military briefings. But in guerrilla war, the support a civilian provides is far more direct. He doesn't need to be briefed; he already knows the most important military secret; he knows who the guerrillas are. If he doesn't keep this information to himself, the guerrillas are lost.

Their enemies say that the guerrillas rely on terror to win the support or at least the silence of the villagers. But it seems more likely that when they have significant popular support (which they don't always have), they have it for other reasons. "Violence may explain the cooperation of a few individuals," writes an American student of the Vietnamese war, "but it cannot explain the cooperation of a whole social class [the peasantry]."[12] If the killing of civilians were sufficient to win civilian support, the guerrillas would always be at a disadvantage, for their enemies possess far more fire power than they do. But killing will work against the killer "unless he has already pre-empted a large part of the population and then limits his acts of violence to a sharply defined minority." When the guerrillas succeed, then, in fighting among the people, it is best to assume that they have some serious political support among the people. The people, or some of them, are complicitous in guerrilla war, and the war would be impossible without their complicity. That doesn't mean that they seek out opportunities to help. Even when he sympathizes with the goal of the guerrillas, we can assume that the average civilian would rather vote for them than hide them in his house. But guerrilla war makes for enforced intimacies, and the people are drawn into it in a new way even though the services they provide are nothing more than functional equivalents of the services civilians have always provided for soldiers. For the intimacy is itself an additional service, which has no functional equivalent. Whereas soldiers are supposed to protect the civilians who stand behind them, guerrillas are protected by the civilians among whom they stand.

But the fact that they accept this protection, and depend upon it, doesn't seem to me to deprive the guerrillas of their war rights. Indeed, it is more plausible to make exactly the opposite argument: that the war rights the people would have were they to rise *en masse* are passed on to the irregular fighters they support and protect—assuming that the support, at least, is voluntary. For soldiers acquire war rights not as individual warriors but as political instruments, servants of a community that in turn provides services for its soldiers. Guerrillas take on a similar identity whenever they stand in a similar or equivalent relationship, that is, whenever the people are helpful and complicitous in the ways I have described. When the people do not provide this recognition and support, guerrillas acquire no war rights, and their enemies may rightly treat them when captured as "bandits" or criminals. But any significant degree of popular support entitles the guerrillas to the benevolent quarantine customarily offered prisoners of war (unless they are guilty of specific acts of assassination or sabotage, for which soldiers, too, can be punished).*

This argument clearly establishes the rights of the guerrillas; it raises the most serious questions, however, about the rights of the people; and these are the crucial questions of guerrilla war. The intimacies of the struggle expose the people in a new way to the risks of combat. In practice, the nature of this exposure, and its degree, are going to be determined by the government and its allies. So the burdens of decision are shifted by the guerrillas onto their enemies. It is their enemies who must weigh (as we must) the moral significance of the popular support the guerrillas both enjoy and exploit. One can hardly fight against men and women who themselves fight among civilians without endangering civilian lives. Have these civilians forfeited their immunity? Or do they, despite their wartime complicity, still have rights vis-à-vis the anti-guerrilla forces?

THE RIGHTS OF CIVILIAN SUPPORTERS

If civilians had no rights at all, or were thought to have none, it would be a small benefit to hide among them. In a sense, then, the advantages the guerrillas seek depend upon the scruples of their enemies—though there are other advantages to be had if their enemies are unscrupulous: that is why anti-guerrilla warfare is so difficult. I shall want to argue that these scruples in fact have a moral basis, but it is worth suggesting first that they also have a strategic basis. It is always in the interest of the anti-guerrilla forces to insist upon the soldier/civilian distinction, even when the guerrillas act (as they always will if they can) so as to blur the line. All the

---

* The argument I am making here parallels that made by lawyers with reference to "belligerent recognition." At what point, they have asked, should a group of rebels (or secessionists) be recognized as a belligerent power and granted those war rights which customarily belong only to established governments? The answer has usually been that the recognition follows upon the establishment of a secure territorial base by the rebels. For then they actually function like a government, taking on responsibility for the people who live on the land they control. But this assumes a conventional or near-conventional war. In the case of a guerrilla struggle, we may have to describe the appropriate relation between the rebels and the people differently: it is not when the guerrillas look after the people that they acquire war rights, but when the people "look after" the guerrillas.

handbooks on "counter-insurgency" make the same argument: what is necessary is to isolate the guerrillas from the civilian population, to cut them off from their protection and at the same time to shield civilians from the fighting.[13] The last point is more important in guerrilla than in conventional war, for in conventional war one assumes the hostility of "enemy civilians," while in a guerrilla struggle one must seek their sympathy and support. Guerrilla war is a political, even an ideological conflict. "Our kingdoms lay in each man's mind," wrote T. E. Lawrence of the Arab guerrillas he led in World War I. "A province would be won when we had taught the civilians in it to die for our ideal of freedom."[14] And it can be won back only if those same civilians are taught to live for some counter-ideal (or in the case of a military occupation, to acquiesce in the re-establishment of order and ordinary life). That is what is meant when it is said that the battle is for the "hearts and minds" of the people. And one cannot triumph in such a battle by treating the people as so many enemies to be attacked and killed along with the guerrillas who live among them.

But what if the guerrillas cannot be isolated from the people? What if the *levée en masse* is a reality and not merely a piece of propaganda? Characteristically, the military handbooks neither pose nor answer such questions. There is, however, a moral argument to be made if this point is reached: the anti-guerrilla war can then no longer be fought—and not just because, from a strategic point of view, it can no longer be won. It cannot be fought because it is no longer an anti-guerrilla but an anti-social war, a war against an entire people, in which no distinctions would be possible in the actual fighting. But this is the limiting case of guerrilla war. In fact, the rights of the people come into play earlier on, and I must try now to give them some plausible definition.

Consider again the case of the partisan attack in occupied France. If, after the ambush, the partisans hide in a nearby peasant village, what are the rights of the peasants among whom they hide? German soldiers arrive that night, let's say, seeking the men and women directly involved or implicated in the ambush and looking also for some way of preventing future attacks. The civilians they encounter are hostile, but that doesn't make them *enemies* in the sense of the war convention, for they don't actually resist the efforts of the soldiers. They behave exactly as citizens sometimes do in the face of police interrogations: they are passive, blank, evasive. We must imagine a domestic state of emergency and ask how the police might legitimately respond to such hostility. Soldiers can do no more when what they are doing is police work; for the status of the hostile civilians is no different. Interrogations, searches, seizures of property, curfews—all these seem to be commonly accepted (I will not try to explain why); but not the torture of suspects or the taking of hostages or the internment of men and women who are or might be innocent.[15] Civilians still have rights in such circumstances. If their liberty can be temporarily abridged in a variety of ways, it is not entirely forfeit; nor are their lives at risk. The argument would be much harder, however, had the troops been ambushed as they marched through the village itself, shot at from the cover of peasant homes and barns. To understand what happens then, we must look at another historical example.

The American "Rules of Engagement" in Vietnam

Here is a typical incident of the Vietnam War. "An American unit moving along Route 18 [in Long An province] received small arms fire from a village, and in reply the tactical commander called for artillery and air strikes on the village itself, resulting in heavy civilian casualties and extensive physical destruction."[16] Something like this must have happened hundreds, even thousands of times. The bombing and strafing of peasant villages was a common tactic of the American forces. It is a matter of special interest to us that it was permitted by the U.S. Army's "rules of engagement," worked out, so it was said, to isolate the guerrillas and minimize civilian casualties.

The attack on the village near Route 18 looks as if it was intended to minimize only army casualties. It looks like another instance of a practice I have already examined: the indiscriminate use of modern fire power to save soldiers from trouble and risk. But in this case, the trouble and risk are of a sort very different from anything encountered on the front line of a conventional war. It is most unlikely that an army patrol moving into the village would have been able to locate and destroy an enemy position. The soldiers would have found . . . a village, its population sullen and silent, the guerrilla fighters hiding, the guerrilla "fortifications" indistinguishable from the homes and shelters of the villagers. They might have drawn hostile fire; more likely, they would have lost men to mines and booby traps, the exact location of which everyone in the village knew and no one would reveal. Under such circumstances, it was not difficult for soldiers to convince themselves that the village was a military stronghold and a legitimate target. And if it was known to be a stronghold, surely it could be attacked, like any other enemy position, even before hostile fire was encountered. In fact, this became American policy quite early in the war: villages from which hostile fire might reasonably be expected were shelled and bombed before soldiers moved in and even if no movement was planned. But then how does one minimize civilian casualties, let alone win over the civilian population? It was to answer this question that the rules of engagement were developed.

The crucial point of the rules, as they are described by the journalist Jonathan Schell, was that civilians were to be given warning in advance of the destruction of their villages, so that they could break with the guerrillas, expel them, or leave themselves.[17] The goal was to force the separation of combatants and noncombatants, and the means was terror. Enormous risk was attached to complicity in guerrilla war, but this was a risk that could only be imposed on whole villages; no further differentiation was possible. It is not the case that civilians were held hostage for the activities of the guerrillas. Rather, they were held responsible for their own activity, even when this activity was not overtly military. The fact that the activity sometimes was overtly military, that ten-year-old children threw hand grenades at American soldiers (the incidence of such attacks was probably exaggerated by the soldiers, in part to justify their own conduct toward civilians) blurs the nature of this responsibility. But it has to be stressed that a village was regarded as hostile not because its women and children were prepared to fight, but because they were not prepared to deny material support to the guerrillas or to reveal their whereabouts or the location of their mines and booby traps.

These were the rules of engagement: (1) A village could be bombed or shelled without warning if American troops had received fire from within it. The villagers were presumed able to prevent the use of their village as a fire base, and whether or not they actually were able, they certainly knew in advance whether it would be so used. In any case, the shooting itself was a warning, since return fire was to be expected—though it is unlikely that the villagers expected the response to be as disproportionate as it usually was, until the pattern had become familiar. (2) Any village known to be hostile could be bombed or shelled if its inhabitants were warned in advance, either by the dropping of leaflets or by helicopter loudspeaker. These warnings were of two sorts: sometimes they were specific in character, delivered immediately before an attack, so that the villagers only just had time to leave (and then the guerrillas could leave with them), or they were general, describing the attack that might come if the villagers did not expel the guerrillas.

> The U.S. Marines will not hesitate to destroy immediately any village or hamlet harboring the Vietcong. . . . The choice is yours. If you refuse to let the Vietcong use your villages and hamlets as their battlefield, your homes and your lives will be saved.

And if not, not. Despite the emphasis on choice, this is not quite a liberal pronouncement, for the choice in question is very much a collective one. Exodus, of course, remained an individual option: people could move out of villages where the Vietcong had established itself, taking refuge with relatives in other villages, or in the cities, or in government-run camps. Most often, however, they did this only after the bombing had begun, either because they did not understand the warnings, or did not believe them, or simply hoped desperately that their own homes would some- how be spared. Hence it was sometimes thought humane to dispense with choice altogether and forcibly to deport villagers from areas that were con- sidered under enemy control. Then the third rule of engagement went into effect. (3) Once the civilian population had been moved out, the village and surrounding country might be declared a "free fire zone" that could be bombed and shelled at will. It was assumed that anyone still living in the area was a guerrilla or a "hardened" guerrilla supporter. Deporta- tion had stripped away civilian cover as defoliation stripped away natural cover, and left the enemy exposed.[18]

In considering these rules, the first thing to note is that they were rad- ically ineffective. "My investigation disclosed," writes Schell, "that the pro- cedures for applying these restraints were modified or twisted or ignored to such an extent that in practice the restraints evaporated entirely. . . ."[19] Often, in fact, no warning was given, or the leaflets were of little help to villagers who could not read, or the forcible evacuation left large numbers of civilians behind, or no adequate provision was made for the deported families and they drifted back to their homes and farms. None of this, of course, would reflect on the value of the rules themselves, unless the inef- fectiveness were somehow intrinsic to them or to the situation in which they were applied. This was clearly the case in Vietnam. For where the guerrillas have significant popular support and have established a political apparatus in the villages, it is unrealistic to think that the villagers will or can expel them. This has nothing to do with the virtues of guerrilla rule: it would have been equally unrealistic to think that German workers, though their homes were bombed and their families killed, would overthrow the Nazis. Hence the only protection the rules provide is in advising or enforcing the departure not of guerrillas from peaceful villages but of civilians from what is likely to become a battlefield.

Now, in a conventional war, removing civilians from a battlefield is clearly a good thing to do; positive international law requires it wherever possible. Similarly in the case of a besieged city: civilians must be allowed to leave; and if they refuse (so I have argued), they can be attacked along with the defending soldiers. But a battlefield and a city are determinate areas, and a battle and a siege are, usually, of limited duration. Civilians move out; then they move back. Guerrilla war is likely to be very different. The battlefield extends over much of the country and the struggle is, as Mao has written, "protracted." Here the proper analogy is not to the siege of a city but to the blockade or strategic devastation of a much wider area. The policy underlying the American rules of engagement actually envisaged the uprooting and resettlement of a very substantial part of the rural population of Vietnam: millions of men, women, and children. But that is an incredible task, and, leaving aside for the moment the likely criminality of the project, there was never more than a pretense that sufficient resources would be made available to accomplish it. It was inevitable then, and it was known to be inevitable, that civilians would be living in the villages that were shelled and bombed.

What happened is quickly described:[20]

> In August 1967, during Operation Benton, the "pacification" camps became so full that Army units were ordered not to "generate" any more refugees. The Army complied. But search and destroy operations continued. Only now the peasants were not warned before an air-strike was called on their village. They were killed in their villages because there was no room for them in the swamped pacification camps.

I should add that this sort of thing doesn't always happen, even in antiguerrilla war—though the policy of forced resettlement or "concentration," from its origins in the Cuban Insurgency and the Boer War, has rarely been carried out in a humane manner or with adequate resources.[21]

But one can find counter-examples. In Malaya, in the early 1950s, where the guerrillas had the support of only a relatively small part of the rural population, a limited resettlement (to new villages, not concentration camps) seems to have worked. At any rate, it has been said that after the fighting was over, few of the resettled villagers wanted to return to their former homes.[22] That is not a sufficient criterion of moral success, but it is one sign of a permissible program. Since governments are generally thought to be entitled to resettle (relatively small numbers of) their own citizens for the sake of some commonly accepted social purpose, the policy cannot be ruled out altogether in time of guerrilla war. But unless the numbers are restricted, it will be difficult to make the case for common acceptance. And here, as in peacetime, there is some requirement to provide adequate economic support and comparable living space. In Vietnam, that was never possible. The scope of the war was too wide; new villages could not be built; the camps were dismal; and hundreds of thousands of displaced peasants crowded into the cities, forming there a new *lumpen* proletariat, miserable, sick, jobless, or quickly exploited in ill-paid and menial jobs or as servants, prostitutes, and so on.

Even had all this worked, in the limited sense that civilian deaths had been avoided, the rules of engagement and the policy they embodied could hardly be defended. It seems to violate even the principle of proportionality—which is by no means easy to do, as we have seen again and again, since the values against which destruction and suffering are to be measured are so readily inflated. But in this case, the argument is clear, for the defense of resettlement comes down finally to a claim something like that made by an American officer with reference to the town of Ben Tre: we had to destroy the town in order to save it.[23] In order to save Vietnam, we had to destroy the rural culture and the village society of the Vietnamese. Surely the equation does not work and the policy cannot be approved, at least in the context of the Vietnamese struggle itself. (One can always shift, I suppose, to the higher mathematics of international statecraft.)

But the rules of engagement raise a more interesting question. Suppose that civilians, duly warned, not only refuse to expel the guerrillas but also refuse to leave themselves. Can they be attacked and killed, as the rules imply? What are their rights? They can certainly be exposed to risks, for battles are likely to be fought in their villages. And the risks they must live with will be considerably greater than those of conventional combat. The increased risk results from the intimacies I have already described; I would suggest now that it is the only result of those intimacies, at least in the moral realm. It is serious enough. Anti-guerrilla war is a terrible strain on conventional troops, and even if they are both disciplined and careful, as they should be, civilians are certain to die at their hands. A soldier who, once he is engaged, simply fires at every male villager between the ages of fifteen and fifty (say) is probably justified in doing so, as he would not be in an ordinary firefight. The innocent deaths that result from this kind of fighting are the responsibility of the guerrillas and their civilian supporters; the soldiers are cleared by the doctrine of double effect. It has to be stressed, however, that the supporters themselves, so long as they give only political support, are not legitimate targets, either as a group or as distinguishable individuals. Conceivably, some of them can be charged with complicity (not in guerrilla war generally but) in particular acts of assassination and sabotage. But charges of that sort must be proved before some sort of judicial tribunal. So far as combat goes, these people cannot be shot on sight, when no firefight is in progress; nor can their villages be attacked merely because they might be used as firebases or because it is expected that they will be used; nor can they be randomly bombed and shelled, even after warning has been given.

The American rules have only the appearance of recognizing and attending to the combatant/noncombatant distinction. In fact, they set up a new distinction: between loyal and disloyal, or friendly and hostile noncombatants. The same dichotomy can be seen at work in the claims American soldiers made about the villages they attacked: "This place is almost entire V.C. controlled, or pro-V.C." "We consider just about everyone here to be a hard-core V.C., or at least some kind of supporter."[24] It is not the military activities of the villagers that are being stressed in statements of this sort, but their political allegiance. Even with reference to that, the statements are palpably false, since at least some of the villagers are children who cannot be said to have any allegiance at all. In any case, as I have already argued in the example of the villagers of occupied France, political hostility does not make people enemies in the sense of the war convention. (If it did, there would be no civilian immunity at all, except when wars were fought in neutral countries.) They have done nothing to forfeit their right to life, and that right must be respected as best it can be in the course of attacks against the irregular fighters the villagers both resemble and harbor.

It is important to say something now about the possible shape of those attacks, though I cannot talk about them like a military strategist; I can only report on some of the things that strategists say. Bombing and shelling from a distance have undoubtedly been defended in terms of military necessity. But that is as bad an argument strategically as it is morally. For there are other and more effective ways of fighting. Thus a British expert on counter-insurgency writes that the use of "heavily armed helicopters" against peasant villages "can only be justified if the campaign has deteriorated to the extent where it is virtually indistinguishable from conventional war."[25] I doubt that it can be justified even then, but I want to stress again what this expert has grasped: that counter-insurgency requires a strategy and tactics of discrimination. Guerrillas can be defeated (and, similarly, they can win) only at close quarters. With regard to peasant villages, this suggests two different sorts of campaigns, both of which have been extensively discussed in the literature. In areas of "low intensity operations," the villages must be occupied by small units specially trained for the political and police work necessary to seek out guerrilla supporters and informants. In areas where the guerrillas are effectively in control and the fighting intense, the villages must be encircled and entered in force. Bernard Fall has reported in some detail on a French attack of this sort in Vietnam in the 1950s.[26] What is involved here is an effort to bring numbers, expertise, and technology directly to bear, forcing the guerrillas to give battle in a situation where fire can be relatively precise, or driving them into a surrounding net of soldiers. If the soldiers are properly prepared and equipped, they need not accept unbearable risks in fighting of this sort, and they need not inflict indiscriminate destruction. As Fall points out, a very considerable number of men are required for this strategy: "No sealing off of an enemy force could be successful unless the proportion of attackers to defenders was 15 to 1 or even 20 to 1, for the enemy had in its favor an intimate knowledge of the terrain, the advantages of defensive organization, and the sympathy of the population." But these proportions are frequently achieved in guerrilla war, and the "surround and storm" strategy would be eminently feasible were it not for a second and more serious difficulty.

Since the villages are not (or should not be) destroyed when they are stormed, and since the villagers are not resettled, it is always possible for the guerrillas to return once the specially assembled task force has moved on. Success requires that the military operation be followed by a political campaign—and this neither the French in Vietnam nor the Americans who followed them were able to mount in any serious fashion. The decision to destroy villages from a distance was a consequence of this failure, which is not at all the same thing as the "deterioration" of guerrilla into conventional war.

At some point in the military progress of the rebellion, or in the decline of the political capacity of the government that opposes it, it may well become impossible to fight the guerrillas at close quarters. There aren't enough men or, more likely, the government, though it can win particular battles, has no staying power. As soon as the fighting is over, the villagers welcome back the insurgent forces. Now the government (and its foreign allies) face what is in effect, or rather what has become, a people's war. This honorific name can be applied, however, only after the guerrilla movement has won very substantial popular support. It is by no means true all the time. One need only study Che Guevara's abortive campaign in the jungles of Bolivia to realize how easy it is to destroy a guerrilla band that has no popular support at all.[27] From there, one might trace a continuum of increasing difficulty: at some point along that continuum, guerrilla fighters acquire war rights, and at some further point, the right of the government to continue the struggle must be called into question.

This last is not a point which soldiers are likely to recognize or acknowledge. For it is an axiom of the war convention (and a qualification on the rules of war) that if attack is morally possible, counter-attack cannot be ruled out. It cannot be the case that guerrillas can hug the civilian population and make themselves invulnerable. But if it is always morally possible to fight, it is not always possible to do whatever is required to win. In any struggle, conventional or unconventional, the rules of war may at some point become a hindrance to the victory of one side or another. If they could then be set aside, however, they would have no value at all. It is precisely then that the restraints they impose are most important. We can see this clearly in the Vietnam case. The alternative strategies I have briefly outlined were conceivably a way of winning (as the British won in Malaya) until the guerrillas consolidated their political base in the villages. That victory effectively ended the war. It is not, I suppose, a victory that can be distinguished in any definitive fashion from the political and military struggle that preceded it. But one can say with some assurance that it has occurred whenever ordinary soldiers (who are not moral monsters and would fight by the rules if they could) become convinced that old men and women and children are their enemies. For after that, it is unlikely that the war can be fought except by setting out systematically to kill civilians or to destroy their society and culture.

I am inclined to say more than this. In the theory of war, as we have seen, considerations of *jus ad bellum* and *jus in bello* are logically independent, and the judgments we make in terms of one and the other are not necessarily the same. But here they come together. The war cannot be won, and it should not be won. It cannot be won, because the only available strategy involves a war against civilians; and it should not be won, because the degree of civilian support that rules out alternative strategies also makes the guerrillas the legitimate rulers of the country. The struggle against them is an unjust struggle as well as one that can only be carried on unjustly. Fought by foreigners, it is a war of aggression; if by a local regime alone, it is an act of tyranny. The position of the anti-guerrilla forces has become doubly untenable.

12

TERRORISM

THE POLITICAL CODE

The word "terrorism" is used most often to describe revolutionary violence. That is a small victory for the champions of order, among whom the uses of terror are by no means unknown. The systematic terrorizing of whole populations is a strategy of both conventional and guerrilla war, and of established governments as well as radical movements. Its purpose is to destroy the morale of a nation or a class, to undercut its solidarity; its method is the random murder of innocent people. Randomness is the crucial feature of terrorist activity. If one wishes fear to spread and intensify over time, it is not desirable to kill specific people identified in some particular way with a regime, a party, or a policy. Death must come by chance to individual Frenchmen, or Germans, to Irish Protestants, or Jews, simply because they are Frenchmen or Germans, Protestants or Jews, until they feel themselves fatally exposed and demand that their governments negotiate for their safety.

In war, terrorism is a way of avoiding engagement with the enemy army. It represents an extreme form of the strategy of the "indirect approach."[1] It is so indirect that many soldiers have refused to call it war at all. This is a matter as much of professional pride as of moral judgment. Consider the statement of a British admiral in World War II, protesting the terror bombing of German cities: "We are a hopelessly unmilitary nation to imagine that we [can] win the war by bombing German women and children instead of defeating their army and navy."[2] The key word here is unmilitary. The admiral rightly sees terrorism as a civilian strategy. One might say that it represents the continuation of war by political means. Terrorizing ordinary men and women is first of all the work of domestic tyranny, as Aristotle wrote: "The first aim and end [of tyrants] is to break the spirit of their subjects."[3] The British described the "aim and end" of terror bombing in the same way: what they sought was the destruction of civilian morale.

Tyrants taught the method to soldiers, and soldiers to modern revolutionaries. That is a crude history; I offer it only in order to make a more precise historical point: that terrorism in the strict sense, the random murder of innocent people, emerged as a strategy of revolutionary struggle only in the period after World War II, that is, only after it had become a feature of conventional war. In both cases, in war and revolution, a kind of warrior honor stood in the way of this development, especially among professional officers and "professional revolutionaries." The increasing use of terror by far left and ultranationalist movements represents the breakdown of a political code first worked out in the second half of the nineteenth century and roughly analogous to the laws of war worked out at the same time. Adherence to this code did not prevent revolutionary militants from being called terrorists, but in fact the violence they committed bore little resemblance to contemporary terrorism. It was not random murder but assassination, and it involved the drawing of a line that we will have little difficulty recognizing as the political parallel of the line that marks off combatants from noncombatants.

The Russian Populists, the IRA, and the Stern Gang

I can best describe the revolutionary "code of honor" by giving some examples of so-called terrorists who acted or tried to act in accordance with its norms. I have chosen three historical cases. The first will be readily recognizable, for Albert Camus made it the basis of his play *The Just Assassins.*

1) In the early twentieth century, a group of Russian revolutionaries decided to kill a Tsarist official, the Grand Duke Sergei, a man personally involved in the repression of radical activity. They planned to blow him up in his carriage, and on the appointed day one of their number was in place along the Grand Duke's usual route. As the carriage drew near, the young revolutionary, a bomb hidden under his coat, noticed that his

victim was not alone; on his lap he held two small children. The would-be assassin looked, hesitated, then walked quickly away. He would wait for another occasion. Camus has one of his comrades say, accepting this decision: "Even in destruction, there's a right way and a wrong way—and there are limits."[4]

2) During the years 1938–39, the Irish Republican Army waged a bombing campaign in Britain. In the course of this campaign, a republican militant was ordered to carry a pre-set time bomb to a Coventry power station. He traveled by bicycle, the bomb in his basket, took a wrong turn, and got lost in a maze of streets. As the time for the explosion drew near, he panicked, dropped his bike, and ran off. The bomb exploded, killing five passers-by. No one in the IRA (as it was then) thought this a victory for the cause; the men immediately involved were horrified. The campaign had been carefully planned, according to a recent historian, so as to avoid the killing of innocent bystanders.[5]

3) In November 1944, Lord Moyne, British Minister of State in the Middle East, was assassinated in Cairo by two members of the Stern Gang, a right-wing Zionist group. The two assassins were caught, minutes later, by an Egyptian policeman. One of them described the capture at his trial: "We were being followed by the constable on his motorcycle. My comrade was behind me. I saw the constable approach him. . . . I would have been able to kill the constable easily, but I contented myself with . . . shooting several times into the air. I saw my comrade fall off his bicycle. The constable was almost upon him. Again, I could have eliminated the constable with a single bullet, but I did not. Then I was caught."[6]

What is common to these cases is a moral distinction, drawn by the "terrorists," between people who can and people who cannot be killed. The first category is not composed of men and women bearing arms, immediately threatening by virtue of their military training and commitment. It is composed instead of officials, the political agents of regimes thought to be oppressive. Such people, of course, are protected by the war convention and by positive international law. Characteristically (and not foolishly), lawyers have frowned on assassination, and political officials have been assigned to the class of nonmilitary persons, who are never the legitimate objects of attack.[7] But this assignment only partially represents our common moral judgments. For we judge the assassin by his victim, and when the victim is Hitler-like in character, we are likely to praise the assassin's work, though we still do not call him a soldier. The second category is less problematic: ordinary citizens, not engaged in political harming—that is, in administering or enforcing laws thought to be unjust—are immune from attack whether or not they support those laws. Thus the aristocratic children, the Coventry pedestrians, even the Egyptian policeman (who had nothing to do with British imperialism in Palestine)—these people are like civilians in wartime. They are innocent politically as civilians are innocent militarily. It is precisely these people, however, that contemporary terrorists try to kill.

The war convention and the political code are structurally similar, and the distinction between officials and citizens parallels that between soldiers and civilians (though the two are not the same). What lies behind them both, I think, and lends them plausibility, is the moral difference between aiming and not aiming—or, more accurately, between aiming at particular people because of things they have done or are doing, and aiming at whole groups of people, indiscriminately, because of who they are. The first kind of aiming is appropriate to a limited struggle directed against regimes and policies. The second reaches beyond all limits; it is infinitely threatening to whole peoples, whose individual members are systematically exposed to violent death at any and every moment in the course of their (largely innocuous) lives. A bomb planted on a street-corner, hidden in a bus station, thrown into a café or pub—this is aimless killing, except that the victims are likely to share what they cannot avoid, a collective identity. Since some of these victims must be immune from attack (unless liability follows from original sin), any code that directs and controls the fire of political militants is going to be at least minimally appealing. It is so much of an advance over the willful randomness of terrorist attacks. One might even feel easier about killing officials than about killing soldiers, since the state rarely conscripts its political, as it does its military, agents; they have chosen officialdom as a career.

Soldiers and officials are, however, different in another respect. The threatening character of the soldier's activities is a matter of fact; the unjust or oppressive character of the official's activities is a matter of political judgment. For this reason, the political code has never attained to the same status as the war convention. Nor can assassins claim any rights, even on the basis of the strictest adherence to its principles. In the eyes of those of us whose judgments of oppression and injustice differ from their own, political assassins are simply murderers, exactly like the killers of ordinary citizens. The case is not the same with soldiers, who are not judged politically at all and who are called murderers only when they kill noncombatants. Political killing imposes risks quite unlike those of combat, risks whose character is best revealed by the fact that there is no such thing as benevolent quarantine for the duration of the political struggle. Thus the young Russian revolutionary, who eventually killed the Grand Duke, was tried and executed for murder, as were the Stern Gang assassins of Lord Moyne. All three were treated exactly like the IRA militants, also captured, who were held responsible for the deaths of ordinary citizens. That treatment seems to me appropriate, even if we share the political judgments of the men involved and defend their resort to violence. On the other hand, even if we do not share their judgments, these men are entitled to a kind of moral respect not due to terrorists, because they set limits to their actions.

The Vietcong Assassination Campaign

The precise limits are hard to define, as in the case of noncombatant immunity. But we can perhaps move toward a definition by looking at a guerrilla war in which officials were attacked on a large scale. Beginning at some point in the late 1950s, the NLF waged a campaign aimed at destroying the governmental structure of the South Vietnamese countryside. Between 1960 and 1965, some 7,500 village and district officials were assassinated by Vietcong militants. An American student of the Vietcong, describing these officials as the "natural leaders" of Vietnamese society, argues that "by any definition this NLF action . . . amounts to genocide."[8] This assumes that all Vietnam's natural leaders were government officials (but then, who was leading the NLF?) and hence that government officials were literally indispensable to national existence. Since these assumptions are not remotely plausible, it has to be said that "by any definition" the killing of leaders is not the same as the destruction of entire peoples. Terrorism may foreshadow genocide, but assassination does not.

On the other hand, the NLF campaign did press against the limits of the notion of officialdom as I have been using it. The Front tended to include among officials anyone who was paid by the government, even if the work he was doing—as a public health officer, for example—had nothing to do with the particular policies the NLF opposed.[9] And it tended to assimilate into officialdom people like priests and landowners who used their nongovernmental authority in specific ways on behalf of the government. They did not kill anyone, apparently, just because he was a priest or a landowner; the assassination campaign was planned with considerable attention to the details of individual action, and a concerted effort was made "to ensure that there were no unexplained killings."[10] Still, the range of vulnerability was widened in disturbing ways.

One might argue, I suppose, that any official is by definition engaged in the political efforts of the (putatively) unjust regime, just as any soldier, whether he is actually fighting or not, is engaged in the war effort. But the variety of activities sponsored and paid for by the modern state is extraordinary, and it seems intemperate and extravagant to make all such activities into occasions for assassination. Assuming that the regime is in fact oppressive, one should look for agents of oppression and not simply for government agents. As for private persons, they seem to me immune entirely. They are subject, of course, to the conventional forms of social and political pressure (which are conventionally intensified in guerrilla wars) but not to political violence. Here the case is the same with citizens as with civilians: if their support for the government or the war were allowable as a reason for killing them, the line that marks off immune from vulnerable persons would quickly disappear. It is worth stressing that political assassins generally don't want that line to disappear; they have reasons for taking careful aim and avoiding indiscriminate murder. "We were told," a Vietcong guerrilla reported to his American captors, "that in Singapore the rebels on certain days would dynamite every 67th streetcar . . . the next day it might be every 30th, and so on; but that this hardened the hearts of the people against the rebels because so many people died needlessly."[11]

I have avoided noticing until now that most political militants don't regard themselves as assassins at all but rather as executioners. They are engaged, or so they regularly claim, in a revolutionary version of vigilante justice. This suggests another reason for killing only some officials and not others, but it is entirely a self-description. Vigilantes in the usual sense apply conventional conceptions of criminality, though in a rough and ready way. Revolutionaries champion a new conception, about which there is unlikely to be wide agreement. They hold that officials are vulnerable because or insofar as they are actually guilty of "crimes against the people." The more impersonal truth is that they are vulnerable, or more vulnerable than ordinary citizens, simply because their activities are open to such descriptions. The exercise of political power is a dangerous business. Saying this, I do not mean to defend assassination. It is most often a vile politics, as vigilante justice is most often a bad kind of law enforcement; its agents are usually gangsters, and sometimes madmen, in political dress. And yet "just assassinations" are at least possible, and men and women who aim at that kind of killing and renounce every other kind need to be marked off from those who kill at random—not as doers of justice, necessarily, for one can disagree about that, but as revolutionaries with honor. They do not want the revolution, as one of Camus' characters says, "to be loathed by the whole human race."

However the political code is specified, terrorism is the deliberate violation of its norms. For ordinary citizens are killed and no defense is offered—none could be offered—in terms of their individual activities. The names and occupations of the dead are not known in advance; they are killed simply to deliver a message of fear to others like themselves. What is the content of the message? I suppose it could be anything at all; but in practice terrorism, because it is directed against entire peoples or classes, tends to communicate the most extreme and brutal intentions— above all, the tyrannical repression, removal, or mass murder of the population under attack. Hence contemporary terrorist campaigns are most often focused on people whose national existence has been radically devalued: the Protestants of Northern Ireland, the Jews of Israel, and so on. The campaign announces the devaluation. That is why the people under attack are so unlikely to believe that compromise is possible with their enemies. In war, terrorism is associated with the demand for unconditional surrender and, in similar fashion, tends to rule out any sort of compromise settlement.

In its modern manifestations, terror is the totalitarian form of war and politics. It shatters the war convention and the political code. It breaks across moral limits beyond which no further limitation seems possible, for within the categories of civilian and citizen, there isn't any smaller group for which immunity might be claimed (except children; but I don't think children can be called "immune" if their parents are attacked and killed). Terrorists anyway make no such claim; they kill anybody. Despite this, terrorism has been defended, not only by the terrorists themselves, but also by philosophical apologists writing on their behalf. The political defenses mostly parallel those that are offered whenever soldiers attack civilians. They represent one or another version of the argument from military necessity.* It is said, for example, that there is no alternative to terrorist activity if oppressed peoples are to be liberated. And it is said, further, that this has always been so: terrorism is the only means and so it is the ordinary means of destroying oppressive regimes and founding new nations.[12] The cases I have already worked through suggest the falsity of these assertions. Those who make them, I think, have lost their grip on the historical past; they suffer from a malign forgetfulness, erasing all moral distinctions along with the men and women who painfully worked them out.

VIOLENCE AND LIBERATION

Jean-Paul Sartre and the Battle of Algiers

But there is another argument which, because of the currency it has gained, must be taken up here, even though it has no immediate analogue in wartime debates. It has been put forward in its starkest form by Sartre in a justification of FLN terrorism in Algeria, published as a preface to Franz Fanon's *The Wretched of the Earth*. The summary lines of Sartre's argument are these:[13]

> To shoot down a European is to kill two birds with one stone, to destroy an oppressor and the man he oppresses at the same time: there remains a dead man and a free man.

In his usual fashion, with a certain zest for Hegelian melodrama, Sartre is here describing what he takes to be an act of psychological liberation. Only when the slave turns on his master, physically confronts him and

---

* Among revolutionaries as among government officials, this argument often slides from an analysis of particular cases of duress and necessity (which are rarely convincing) to the general claim that war is hell and anything goes. General Sherman's view is upheld, for example, by the Italian leftist Franco Solinas, who wrote the screenplay for Pontecorvo's *The Battle of Algiers* and defended the terrorism of the Algerian FLN: "For centuries they've tried to prove that war is fair play, like duels, but war isn't and therefore any method used to fight it is good. . . . It's not a question of ethics or fair play. What we must attack is war itself and the situations that lead to it." (*The Battle of Algiers*, edited and translated by PierNico Solinas, New York, 1973, pp. 195–96.) Compare the same argument made by American officials in defense of the bombing of Hiroshima, chapter 16.

kills him, does he create himself as a free human being. The master dies; the slave is reborn. Even if this were a believable picture of the terrorist act, the argument is not persuasive; it is open to two obvious and crippling questions. First, is the one-to-one relation necessary? Did it take one dead European to make one free Algerian? If so, there were not enough Europeans living in Algeria; more would have had to be brought over if the Algerian people were to free themselves by Sartrean means. If not, it must follow that someone else besides the man-who-kills can be liberated. . . . How? By watching? By reading about the murder in the newspaper? It is hard to see how vicarious experience can play an important part in a process of personal liberation (as described by an existentialist philosopher).

The second question raises more familiar issues: will any European do? Unless Sartre thinks all Europeans, including children, are oppressors, he cannot believe that. But if it is only liberating to attack and kill an agent of oppression, we are back with the political code. From Sartre's perspective, that cannot be right, since the men and women he is defending had explicitly rejected that code. They killed Europeans at random, as in the well-known scene from the (historically accurate) film *The Battle of Algiers*, in which a bomb is set off in a milk bar where French teenagers are drinking and dancing.[14]

> MILK BAR. EXPLOSION. OUTSIDE. DAY.
> The jukebox is flung into the middle of the street. There is blood, strips of flesh, material . . . the white smoke and shouts, weeping, hysterical girls' screams. One of them no longer has an arm and runs around howling despairingly; it is impossible to control her. . . . The sound of sirens is heard. . . . The ambulances arrive . . .

Such an event is not easily reconstructed as an existentialist encounter between masters and slaves.

Certainly, there are historical moments when armed struggle is necessary for the sake of human freedom. But if dignity and self-respect are to be the outcomes of that struggle, it cannot consist of terrorist attacks upon children. One can argue that such attacks are the inevitable products of oppression, and in a sense, I suppose, that is right. Hatred, fear, and the lust for domination are the psychological marks of oppressed and oppressor alike, and their acting out, on either side, can be said to be radically determined. The mark of a revolutionary struggle against oppression, however, is not this incapacitating rage and random violence, but restraint and self-control. The revolutionary reveals his freedom in the same way as he earns it, by directly confronting his enemies and refraining from attacks on anyone else. It was not only to save the innocent that revolutionary militants worked out the distinction between officials and ordinary citizens, but also to save themselves from killing the innocent. Whatever its strategic value, the political code is intrinsically connected to psychological liberation. Among men and women trapped in a bloody struggle, it is the key to self-respect. The same thing can be said of the war convention: in the context of a terrible coerciveness, soldiers most clearly assert their freedom when they obey the moral law.

13

REPRISALS

DETERRENCE WITHOUT RETRIBUTION

When the British imposed their blockade of Germany in 1916, they called it a reprisal; when the Germans began the systematic bombing of London in 1940, they defended themselves in the same way. No part of the war convention is so open to abuse, is so openly abused, as the doctrine of reprisals. For the doctrine is, or once was thought to be, permissive with regard to all the rest of the convention. It legitimates actions otherwise criminal, if these actions are undertaken in response to crimes previously committed by the enemy. "Reprisals," writes a pacifist critic of the rules of war, "mean doing what you think wrong on the plea that someone else did it first."[1] And, he goes on, someone else will always do it first. Hence reprisals create a chain of wrongdoing at the end of which every responsible actor can point to some other actor and say *"tu quoque."*

It is the explicit purpose of reprisals, however, to break off the chain, to stop the wrongdoing *here*, with this final act. Sometimes—though it has to be said, not often—that purpose is realized. I want to begin with a case in which it was realized, so that we can at least make sense of what was for many years the conventional opinion—as stated, for example, by a nineteenth-century French lawyer: "Reprisals are a means of preventing war from becoming entirely barbarous."[2]

The FFI Prisoners at Annecy

In the summer of 1944, much of France was a battleground. Allied armies were fighting in Normandy; partisan groups, organized now into the French Forces of the Interior and in touch with both the Allies and the Gaullist Provisional Government in Algeria, operated on a large scale in many parts of the country. They wore insignias of battle; they bore their arms openly. It is clear that the 1940 armistice had effectively been voided, and the military struggle resumed. Nevertheless, the German authorities continued to treat captured partisans as war traitors or war rebels, subject to summary execution. On the day after the Allied landings, for example, fifteen partisans captured at Caen were immediately shot.[3] And the executions continued, as the pace of the fighting increased, during the next months. The FFI complained of these executions to the Provisional Government, which in turn sent a formal protest to the Germans. Since they did not recognize the Government, the Germans refused to accept the protest. In their note, the French had threatened reprisals against German prisoners. The continued killing did not, however, elicit any such response—perhaps because troops directly subject to the Provisional Government, recruited outside occupied France, were regularly accorded prisoner-of-war status by the Germans.

In August 1944, large numbers of German soldiers in Southern France began surrendering to partisan groups, and the FFI leadership was suddenly in a position to carry out the Government's threat. "When . . . it became known that the Germans . . . had executed 80 French prisoners, and that further executions were imminent, the FFI command at Annecy decided that 80 of the prisoners in [its] hands would in turn be shot."[4] At this point, the Red Cross intervened, won a postponement of the executions, and sought from the Germans an agreement henceforth to treat captured partisans as prisoners of war. The partisans waited six days and then, the Germans not replying, the 80 prisoners were shot.* The effects of the reprisal are not easy to make out, for the German army was

---

*I have never understood why, in cases like this one, the men are not simply hidden away when their deaths are announced. Why must they actually be killed? Since deceit of various sorts is accepted under the war convention, it certainly should not be ruled out here. But I have been unable to find any case in which such a ruse was tried.

hard-pressed, and many other factors must have figured in its decisions. It is apparently true, however, that no partisans were executed after the Annecy shootings.

Now in one sense, this case is easy to judge: the Geneva Convention of 1929, which the French had signed and the FFI itself reaffirmed, explicitly barred reprisals against prisoners of war.[5] No other group of innocent men and women was granted a similar immunity; prisoners were singled out because of the contract implied by surrender, in which they are promised life and benevolent quarantine. Killing them would be a breach of faith as well as a violation of the positive laws of war. But I shall not focus on this exception to the general rule of reprisals, for it does not open up the larger question, whether the deliberate killing of innocent men and women should ever be declared lawful or morally justified. And I doubt very much that we will want to say, in answer to that question, that some innocent people can be killed and others not. The case of the FFI prisoners is useful because it provides a classic example of reprisal, and one in which our sympathies are likely to be engaged, at least initially, on the side of the "reprisers."

Reprisals of this sort have as their purpose the enforcement of the war convention. In international society, as in Locke's state of nature, every individual member (every belligerent power) claims the right to enforce the law. The content of this right is the same as it is in domestic society: it is first of all a right of retribution, to punish guilty men and women; it is secondly a right of deterrence, to protect oneself and others against criminal activity. In domestic society, these two most often go together. Criminal activity is deterred by punishing or threatening to punish guilty individuals. That, at least, is the commonly accepted doctrine. In international society, however, and especially in wartime, the two rights are not equally enforceable. It is often impossible to get at guilty individuals, but it's always possible to prevent or try to prevent further criminal activity by responding in kind as the French partisans did, that is, by "punishing" innocent people. The result might be described as a one-sided sort of law enforcement: deterrence without retribution.

It might also be described as a prime example of radical utilitarianism—indeed, of a utilitarianism so radical that utilitarian philosophers have been concerned to deny its existence. Yet it is common enough in the theory as well as in the practice of war. One of the criticisms most frequently leveled against utilitarianism is that its calculations would under certain circumstances require the authorities to "punish" an innocent person (to kill or imprison him, under cover of punishment). The usual response has been to adjust the calculations so that they yield different and more conventionally acceptable results.[6] But in the history of international law and in debates over wartime behavior, the effort at adjustment has mostly been foregone. Reprisals have been defended, with admirable directness, on strictly utilitarian grounds. Under the special conditions of combat, at least, utilitarian calculations have indeed required the "punishing" of innocent people. The political or military leaders of belligerent powers have commonly invoked the requirement, claiming that no other means were available to check the criminal excesses of their opponents. And detached observers, students of the law, and venerable doctors have generally accepted this as a possible argument "in extreme cases" (the cases, of course, are often disputed). Hence it is a "principle of war law," according to a leading authority: "For every offense punish someone; the guilty, if possible, but someone."[7]

This is not an attractive principle, and it would not be accurate to explain the traditional acceptance of reprisals by reference to it alone. In wartime, after all, innocent people are often attacked and killed in the name of utility, in order, it is said, to shorten the war, save lives, and so on. But such attacks don't have the same status as reprisals. It is not their utility, assuming now that they are in fact useful, that makes reprisals different, but some other quality. This quality is misunderstood, I think, by those writers who describe reprisal as the most primitive feature of the war convention, a survival of the ancient *lex talionis*.[8] For the talion is a return of evil for evil, and what is crucial about reprisal is precisely that evil, though it may be repeated, is not returned. The new crime has a new victim, who is not the original criminal though he probably has the same nationality. The particular choice is (so far as utility goes) quite impersonal; in this sense, reprisal is chillingly modern. Something, however, of the talion survives: not the idea of return, but the idea of response. Reprisal is characterized by a certain posture of looking back, acting after, which implies a willingness not to act at all, to abide by some set of restraints. "They did it first." This sentence carries a moral argument. I do not believe that it is a very strong argument or one that will take us far. But it serves to mark off reprisal from other, equally useful violations of the war convention. There is no right to commit crimes in order to shorten a war, but there is a right, so it was once thought, to commit crimes (or rather, acts that would otherwise be called crimes) in order to cope with the previous criminal activity of one's enemies.

The backward-looking character of reprisals is confirmed by the rule of proportionality that restrains them. The rule is quite different and far more precise than that which figures, for example, in the doctrine of double effect. The partisan commanders at Annecy acted in strict accordance with its provisions when they decided to kill 80 Germans in response to the killing of 80 Frenchmen. Reprisals are limited with reference to previous crimes, not with reference to the crimes they are designed to deter (not with reference to their effects or their hoped-for effects). This point has sometimes been disputed by writers committed to utilitarian modes of thought. Thus McDougal and Feliciano argue, in characteristic style, "that the kind and amount of permissible . . . violence is that which is reasonably designed so to affect the enemy's expectations about the costs and gains of reiteration or continuation of his initial criminal act as to induce the termination of and future abstention from such act."[9] They admit that the amount of violence, so determined, may be greater than that originally inflicted by the enemy. In the Annecy case, it might well have been less: the shooting of 40 Germans, or 20, or 10, might have had the same effect as the shooting of 80. But however the calculations work out, this kind of forward-looking proportionality has never been accepted either by the general run of theorists writing about war or by ordinary practitioners. During World War II, to be sure, the Germans often responded to partisan activity in the occupied states of Europe by shooting ten hostages for every German killed.[10] This proportion may have reflected a peculiar notion about the relative value of German lives, or it may have been "reasonably designed so to affect the enemy's expectations, etc." In any case, the practice was universally condemned.

It was condemned, of course, not only because of the actual disproportion involved, but also because the previous partisan activity was in many cases not thought to violate the war convention. Hence the German response was simply utilitarian deterrence, not law enforcement. It is another feature of the backward-looking character of reprisals that the acts to which they respond must be crimes, violations of the recognized rules of war. Moreover, the rules must be commonly recognized, on both sides of the battleline, if the special character of reprisals is to be maintained. When the British army resorted to reprisals during the War of 1812, an opposition member of the House of Commons, who thought such conduct barbarous, asked why His Majesty's soldiers didn't scalp their captives when they fought with the American Indians or enslave them in their wars with the Barbary corsairs.[11] I suppose the answer is that scalping and enslavement were not thought illegitimate by the Indians and the corsairs. And so the imitation of these practices by the British would not have been understood as law enforcement (nor would it have had any deterrent effect); it would only have confirmed their enemies' notions of appropriate wartime behavior. Reprisals may involve deterrence without retribution, but this must nevertheless be a reactive deterrence, and what it reacts to is a violation of the war *convention*. If there is no convention, there can be no reprisal.

At the same time, we are uneasy about reprisals precisely because there is a convention, and one that categorically rules out the acts that reprisal usually requires. If it is wrong, and for the deepest reasons, to kill innocent people, how can it be right to kill them? In treatises on international law, the defense of reprisal is always qualified, first by a great show of reluctance and anxiety, and secondly by some words about the extremity of the case.[12] It is not easy to know what this last qualification means, however, and it appears in fact that any violation of the rules is sufficiently "extreme" to justify a proportionate response. Backward-looking proportionality is a genuine limit: it would have barred, for example, the two so-called reprisals with which I began this chapter. But extremity is not a limit at all. It is certainly not true that reprisals are undertaken only when the enemy's crimes pose a drastic danger to the war effort as a whole or to the cause for which the war is being fought. For the purpose of reprisal is not to win the war or prevent the defeat of the cause, but simply to enforce the rules. Perhaps the meaning of the appeal to extremity is like that of the show of reluctance: both suggest a view of reprisal as a last resort. In practice, again, the only action required before one reaches this last resort is a formal protest, such as the French delivered to the Germans in 1944, and a threat to respond in kind if this or that criminal activity is continued. But one might require much more than that, both in the way of law enforcement and in the way of military action. The FFI might, for example, have announced that they would treat German soldiers involved in the execution of captured partisans as war criminals; they might even have begun to publish the names of those who would be accused. Given the military situation of the German army in 1944, such an announcement could well have had a significant effect. Or the partisans might have attempted to raid the prisons or camps where their comrades were being held. Such raids were not impossible, though they would have involved risks entirely absent when one shoots down captured soldiers.

If the notion of last resort were taken seriously, it would limit reprisal in a radical way. But suppose that the partisans had issued the announcement and undertaken the raids without stopping the German executions. Would they then have been justified in shooting their prisoners? "A reckless enemy often leaves his opponent *no other means* of securing himself against the repetition of barbarous outrage."[13] But the truth is that there are always other means, more or less dangerous, more or less effective. To argue against the executions isn't to deny the partisans a last resort. It is only to say, for example, that military raids are their last resort. If the raids fail, they can only be tried again; there is nothing more to be done. (Reprisals might fail, too—they usually do—and what comes after that?) This is the conclusion that I want to defend, and I will defend it, once again, by reflecting on the status and character of the German prisoners.

Who are these men? Once they were soldiers; now they are disarmed and helpless. Perhaps some of them are war criminals; perhaps some of them were involved in the murder of captured partisans. Then, surely, they should be put on trial, not shot out of hand. We will want to hear the evidence against them and make sure that we punish the right ones. Only a trial can signal our own commitment to the rules of war. But here, let us assume, are ordinary prisoners who neither made nor carried out criminal decisions. Their day-to-day activities were very much like those of their enemies. How can they be shot out of hand, treated more cruelly than we would treat suspected criminals? It seems incredible that some number of them should be arbitrarily separated from the rest and then killed, simply so that we can announce their deaths, and all this for the sake of justice! Killing them would be murder: the name is exact, no matter what crimes we hope to avoid by becoming murderers. For these men are not mere material out of whose lives we can fashion a deterrent strategy. Even as prisoners, or precisely as prisoners, they have rights against us.

The current thrust of international law is to condemn reprisals against innocent people, and for essentially the reasons that I have suggested: the helplessness of the victims rules them out as objects of military attack, and their noninvolvement in criminal activity rules them out as objects of retributive violence. The Geneva Convention of 1929, as we have seen, declared prisoners immune; the 1949 Conventions did the same for wounded, sick, and shipwrecked members of the armed forces and for civilian persons in occupied territory.[14] This last provision effectively bars the killing of hostages, the paradigm case of using innocent people for one's own military purposes. The only class of disengaged men and women against whom reprisals are still legally defensible is the civilian population of the enemy country. Its members can still be held hostage, though only at a distance, for the good behavior of their government and army. It has been argued that this way of judging reprisals is a logical extension of the general principle "that persons whose usefulness as bases of enemy power is precluded . . . by belligerent control or capture cease to be legitimate objects of violence."[15] But this is to misstate the general principle. It would allow not only reprisals but also first strikes against enemy civilians. However peaceful their pursuits, after all, these civilians remain a "significant base of enemy power," providing political and economic support to the armed forces. Even children are not "precluded" from serving that power: they will grow up to be soldiers, munitions workers, and so on. Yet such people are protected by the war convention; they are admitted, along with prisoners and wounded soldiers, to the class of the innocent. The underlying purpose of recent developments in the law is not to extend a general principle, which is already (in principle) fully extended, but to prohibit its violation in the special circumstances once thought to justify reprisals. And if there are good reasons for doing that, there would seem to be no good reasons for drawing the line as it has currently been drawn.*

So the necessary judgment is readily summed up: we must condemn all reprisals against innocent people, whether these people are "subject to

---

* It is not difficult, however, to account for the present legal situation. The threat to take reprisals against enemy civilians is a crucial feature of the contemporary system of nuclear deterrence, and statesmen and soldiers are not prepared solemnly to denounce that system. Moreover, though nuclear deterrence rests only on threats, and the acts threatened are of such a nature that moral men and women might well refuse at the final moment to carry them out, no one is prepared in advance to admit to inhibitions. "Any act of cruelty to the innocent," wrote an American jurist of the pre-atomic age, "any act, especially, by which noncombatants are made to feel the stress of war, is what brave men shrink from, although they may feel obliged to threaten it." (T. D. Woolsey, *Introduction to the Study of International Law*, New York, 1908, p. 211.) But can they threaten it effectively if it is known in advance that they will shrink from acting? I will take up the problems of nuclear deterrence in chapter 17.

belligerent control" or not. This is to set radical limits to a practice that once was commonly defended, and not with casual or inconsequential arguments. But I don't want to claim that those old arguments have no force at all. They correctly point to a certain moral difference between the initial crime and the reprisal-response. From a position of great detachment, these two may seem to constitute a vicious circle—and a circle fully accounted for by the pious maxim that "violence breeds violence." The maxim, however, is sometimes wrong and, what is more important, it fails to distinguish violence that is responsive and restrained from violence that is neither. Stand beside the French commanders at Annecy and the circle looks different. German guilt in this case is greater than that of the French, because the Germans acted first, breaking the conventional rules for some military advantage; the French reacted, repeating the violations for the declared purpose of re-establishing the rules. I don't know how to measure the difference between them; perhaps it isn't great; but it is worth stressing that there is a difference, even as we give their crimes a common name.

With regard to the most important of the rules of war, the violation of the rules for the sake of law enforcement is ruled out. The doctrine of reprisal, then, refers only to the lesser parts of the war convention, where the rights of the innocent are not at stake. Consider, for example, the ban on the use of poison gas. Winston Churchill was entirely justified when he warned the German government, early in World War II, that the use of gas by its armies would bring an immediate Allied reprisal.[16] For soldiers have only a war right, and no more basic right, to be attacked with certain weapons and not with others. The rule about poison gas is legally established, but it is not morally required. Hence, when it is violated, parallel and proportionate violations, narrowly aimed at re-establishing the rule and at no larger military purpose, are morally permissible. They are permissible because the people against whom they are directed are already the legitimate objects of military attack. The case is the same with all those informal agreements and reciprocal arrangements that limit the extent and intensity of warfare. Here the threat of reprisal is the major means of enforcement, and there is no reason to hesitate about making the threat or carrying it out. It might be argued that when restraints of this sort are violated, they simply disappear, and then there is no reason to limit one's own violations by attending to the proportionality rule. But that is true only if reprisal fails to restore the old limits. One must aim first at restoration: in that sense, we still use reprisals as a bar to the barbarism of war.

THE PROBLEM OF PEACETIME REPRISALS

But all this assumes that warfare of the ordinary sort is already in progress. What is at issue is the mode or means of attack. In the case of peacetime reprisals, what is at issue is the attack itself. It has come from across the border: a raid of one sort or another. The victim state responds with a second raid, which isn't aimed at re-affirming the rules of war but at re-establishing the broken peace. The crime that is repeated is the act of force, the violation of sovereignty. It will be called aggression and justified as self-defense—talked about, that is, in the language of *jus ad bellum*—but it remains a "military measure short of war" as long as the restraints appropriate to reprisals, established by the theory of *jus in bello*, are maintained. And so it is best discussed here, with reference to those restraints.[17]

The Attack on Khibye and the Beirut Raid

The term "peacetime reprisals" is not entirely accurate. The legal handbooks divide their subject into "war" and "peace," but much of history is a *demi-monde* that neither word adequately describes. It is to this *demi-monde* that reprisals most commonly pertain; they are a form of action appropriate to periods of insurgency, border strife, cease-fire, and armistice. Now it is a feature of such periods that acts of force are not always acts of state in any simple sense. They are not the work of recognized officials and of soldiers acting on official orders, but (often) of guerrilla bands and terrorist organizations—tolerated, perhaps patronized by the officials, but not directly subject to their control. Thus Israel, since its founding in 1948, has repeatedly been attacked by Palestinian guerrillas and terrorists operating out of the neighboring Arab states but not formally affiliated with their armies. In response to these attacks, the Israeli authorities have tried over the years virtually every conceivable form of counter-attack—testing out, as it were, the politics and morality of reprisal. It is a grim and unusual history, providing the theorist with all the examples he could want (and more). And if it doesn't suggest that peacetime reprisals make for peace, it also doesn't point to any alternative response to illegitimate attacks.

Most of the Palestinian raids have been the work of terrorists, not guerrillas; that is, following the argument of the last two chapters, they have been directed randomly against civilian targets: against farmers working near the border, buses on country roads, village schools and houses, and so on. Hence there is no question about their illegitimacy, whatever one thinks of the larger Arab-Israeli conflict. Nor can there be any question that the Israelis have a right to respond in some way. The right exists in the case of any across-the-border raid, but it is especially clear when the raid is aimed at civilians, who can offer no immediate resistance. Nevertheless, particular Israeli responses have indeed been questionable, for it is a hard matter to know what to do in such cases. Terrorists harbored by neighboring states with which one is not openly at war do not provide an easy target. Any military response will be marked by a kind of asymmetry characteristic of peacetime reprisal: the initial foray is unofficial; the counter-attack is the act of a sovereign state, challenging the sovereignty of another state. How do we judge such challenges? What are the rules that govern peacetime reprisals?

The first rule is a familiar one. Though the terrorist raid is aimed at civilians, the reprisal must not be so aimed. Moreover, the "reprisers" must take care that civilians are not the incidental victims of their attack. With regard to its conduct, peacetime reprisal is exactly like war itself, and so certain of our judgments are obvious enough. Consider, for example, the Israeli raid on Khibye:[18]

> Following the killing of a woman and her two children in a village near Lod Airport, the Israelis launched a night attack against the Jordanian village of Khibye on 14 October 1953. . . . [They] fought their way into the village, rounded up the inhabitants, and blew up forty-five houses. Not all the houses were cleared beforehand, and more than forty villagers were buried under the rubble. . . . The brutality of the raid led to sharp protests in Israel and abroad. . . .

These killings probably cannot be called "unintended," and it certainly cannot be said that due care was taken to avoid them; so the protests were justified; the killings were criminal. But what if no civilians had died, or, as in most on-the-ground Israeli reprisals, only a small number, killed in the course of a firefight with Jordanian regulars? What are we to say of the raid itself, of the Jordanian soldiers killed in its course (who had no part in the murder of Israeli civilians), of the houses destroyed? This is not a standard military operation, though it is the most common form of peacetime reprisal. Its purpose is coercive: to force the officials of a neighboring state to keep the peace and to repress guerrillas and terrorists on their own side of the border. But it is not directly or continuously coercive; otherwise it would require a full-scale invasion. Reprisals have the form of a warning: if our villages are attacked, yours will also be attacked. Hence they must always respond to previous raids. And they are governed, after the rule of noncombatant immunity, by the rule of backward-looking proportionality. Though life cannot be balanced against life, the second raid must be similar in character and scope to the first.

I am inclined to defend counter-attacks of this sort, when these two restraints are accepted. The defense, I should stress, doesn't depend in any way upon the notions of extremity or last resort. In peacetime, war is the last resort (and a long series of terrorist raids might justify a war, if no other means seemed likely to end the series). Reprisal is a first resort to force, once diplomacy has proven ineffective. It is, again, a "military measure short of war," an alternative to war, and that description is an important argument in its favor. But the general argument remains a difficult one, as we can see if we turn to another historical example, where (in contrast to Khibye) the rules of immunity and proportionality were scrupulously respected.

In 1968, the focus of Palestinian terrorism shifted from Israel itself to the Israeli national airline and its passengers. On December 26 of that year, two terrorists attacked an Israeli plane preparing for takeoff at Athens Airport.[19] Some 50 people were aboard at the time and, although only one was killed, it was clearly the purpose of the terrorists to kill as many as possible. They aimed their guns at the windows of the plane, at seat level. The two men were captured by Athenian police, and it was discovered that they were members of the Popular Front for the Liberation of Palestine, an organization with headquarters in Beirut. They were traveling on Lebanese documents. Repeatedly over the previous months, Israel had warned the Lebanese government that it could not "escape responsibility" for its support of groups like the PFLP. Now the Israelis undertook a dramatic reprisal.

Two days after the Athens attack, Israeli commandos landed by helicopter at Beirut Airport and destroyed 13 planes belonging to civilian airlines licensed in Lebanon. According to an Israeli news release, the commandos "at great risk to themselves . . . exercised the strictest precautions to prevent civilian casualties. The planes were emptied of passengers and ground crews, and people in the vicinity were led away to safety." Whatever the extent of the risks involved, no one was killed; Lebanese authorities later claimed that two Israeli soldiers were wounded during the attack. From a military point of view, the raid was a spectacular success—and, I think, from a moral point of view too. It was clearly responsive to the incident at Athens; it was parallel and proportionate in its means (for one can destroy a great deal of property in answer to the destruction of human life); and it was carried out so as to avoid civilian deaths.

Despite all this, the Beirut raid was much criticized at the time (and condemned at the UN)—above all, because of the seriousness of the attack upon Lebanese sovereignty. It is the attack upon Jordanian sovereignty that would stand out in the Khibye case, too, had civilian lives been spared. The killing of civilians is an affront to humanity, but attacks on military installations and the destruction of civilian property pose a more narrow and direct challenge to the state. Indeed, that is the purpose of the attacks; and the vulnerability of soldiers, on the one hand, and of airplanes, boats, buildings, and so on, on the other, hangs on the vulnerability of the sovereign state. Soldiers are vulnerable, if the state is, because they are the visible symbols and the active agents of its authority. And civilian property is vulnerable because the innocence of its owners extends only to their persons, not (or not necessarily) to their possessions. The value we attach to human life is such that rights to life are forfeit only when particular men and women are actually engaged in war-making or national defense. But the lesser value of property is such that property rights are forfeit whenever the state that protects property, and taxes it, is itself subject to attack. Individuals can be taxed without becoming legitimate targets, but property, or certain sorts of property, may be a legitimate target even if its owners are not.* But this argument hangs on the liability of the state, and that remains a matter of dispute.

The Israeli argument followed the pattern of positive law (or at least of positive law before the era of the UN). Israel insisted that the Lebanese government had an obligation to prevent the use of its territory as a base for terrorist raids. No one seems to deny the reality of the obligation, but it was argued on behalf of the Lebanese (though not by them) that the government in Beirut was in fact incapable of honoring it. Events since 1968 may seem to have borne out that claim, and if it is right, the Israeli attack would be difficult to defend. It is surely wrong to destroy the property of

---

* This is probably what the lawyers have in mind when they argue that, in cases of reprisal, the private citizen "is held to be identified with his state." The identification is by no means total; it does not obliterate personal rights. Nor, I think, does the effect extend to private homes, which seem to share in the innocence of their inhabitants (unless they have been used as terrorist bases).

innocent people so as to bring pressure on other people who are in any case unable to act differently from the way they are acting. But one should never be too quick to deny the competence of an established government, for a certain loss of sovereignty is the legal and moral result of political powerlessness. If a government literally cannot control the inhabitants of the territory over which it supposedly presides, or police its borders, and if other countries suffer because of this incapacity, then surrogate controlling and policing are clearly permissible. And these may well go beyond the limits commonly accepted for reprisal raids. At this point, reprisal is like retributive punishment in domestic society: as punishment assumes moral agency, so reprisal assumes political responsibility. Both assumptions are worth holding onto, for as long as possible.

The critical question is whether one sovereign state can be forced by another to fulfill its obligations. It is the official position of the UN that this kind of law enforcement, even when it is restrained by the rules of war, is illegal.[20] This position rests not only on the general claim of the UN to declare the (positive) law, but also on its readiness and ability, at least some of the time, to enforce the law itself. But the world organization was clearly not ready or able to enforce the law in 1968; nor has it been ready or able to do so at any time since. Nor is there any evidence that individual members of the UN, however they vote on ritual occasions, are prepared to renounce reprisals when the lives of their own citizens are at stake. Reprisals are clearly sanctioned by the practice of nations, and the (moral) reason behind the practice seems as strong as ever. Nothing the UN has actually done, no effects it can presently have, suggests a centralization of legal or moral authority in international life.*

---

*With regard to the routine UN condemnations of Israeli reprisals, Richard Falk has written: "One may argue against the fairness of such constraints upon Israel's discretion in these circumstances, but it is essentially an extra-legal appeal as the organs of the UN have the procedural capacity to authorize or prohibit specific uses of force, and it is the exercise of this capacity that most clearly distinguishes what is 'legal' from what is 'illegal' . . . in international society." I am not sure that any legislative body, domestic or international, can abolish self-help unless it provides alternative means of help, but I will leave such matters to the lawyers. Assuming Falk is right, it must be said that the extra-legal appeal is a moral appeal the success of which probably will and certainly should undermine the newly enacted "law." See "International Law and the US Role in Vietnam: A Response," in Falk, ed., *The Vietnam War and International Law*, Princeton, 1968, p. 493.

But the sheer unreality of the UN position doesn't by itself establish the legitimacy of peacetime reprisals. In his edition of Kelsen's *Principles of International Law*, Robert Tucker has insisted that anyone defending reprisals must show "that more often than not the independent use of force by states has served the purposes of law. . . ."[21] This is to shift the ground from the effectiveness of the UN to the utility of reprisal itself and to invite a historical examination the results of which are not likely to favor the "reprisers" in any decisive way. But the ground of reprisal is not its overall effectiveness. It is the right, in the difficult conditions of the *demi-monde*, to seek certain effects. So long as the conditions exist, the right must also exist, even if those same conditions (as in Locke's state of nature) make it unlikely that rightful action will have entirely satisfactory consequences. If, in a particular case, reprisal is certain to fail, then obviously it should not be tried. But whenever there is some substantial chance of success, it is the legitimate resort of a victim state; for no state can be required passively to endure attacks upon its citizens.

Reprisal is a practice carried over from the war convention to the world of "peacetime," because it provides an appropriately limited form of military action. It is better, I think, to defend the limits than to try to abolish the practice. Soldiers engaged in a reprisal raid will cross over an international boundary, but they will quickly cross back; they will act destructively, but only up to a point; they will violate sovereignty, but they will also respect it. And finally, they will attend to the rights of innocent people. Reprisals are always limited responses to particular transgressions: crimes against the rules of war, small-scale breaches of the peace. Though they have often been used, they cannot rightly be used, as a cover for invasions or interventions or assaults upon innocent life. It may be that there are moments of extremity and crisis when state's rights and human rights have to be violated; but such moments are not generated by the particular crimes of our enemies, and the violations are not usefully called reprisals. None of the cases of reprisal that I have come across in the lawbooks and the military histories are extreme cases in any meaningful sense of that term. Nor does the war convention provide for extreme cases. Extremity lies, so to speak, beyond the reach of conventional provision. I will consider its character and provenance in Part Four of this book. The analysis of reprisals concludes the discussion of the ordinary means of war. I must turn now to those extraordinary means that the moral urgency of our ends seems sometimes to require.

DILEMMAS OF WAR

14

Winning and Fighting Well

"Asinine Ethics"

Chairman Mao and the Battle of the River Hung

In the year 638 B.C., during the period of China's history known as the Spring and Autumn Era, the two feudal states of Sung and Ch'u fought a battle at the Hung River in central China.[1] The army of Sung, led by its ruler Duke Hsiang, was drawn up in battle formation on the river's northern bank; the Ch'u army had to ford the stream. When its soldiers were halfway across, one of Hsiang's ministers came to him and said, "They are many, and we are few. Pray let us attack them before they are all crossed over." The Duke refused. When the enemy army had reached the northern bank but had not yet re-formed its lines, the minister again asked leave to begin the fight; again the Duke refused. Only after the Ch'u soldiers were properly marshaled did he signal the attack. And then, in the ensuing battle, the Duke himself was wounded and his army put to flight. According to the chronicles, the people of Sung blamed their ruler for the defeat, but he said, "The superior man does not inflict a second wound, and does not take prisoner anyone of grey hairs. When the ancients had their armies in the field, they would not attack an enemy when he was in a defile; and though I am but the poor representative of a fallen dynasty, I will not sound my drums to attack an unformed host."

This is the code of a feudal warrior, an obscure warrior in this case until Mao Tse-tung drew his story out of the chronicles in order to make a modern point. "We are not the Duke of Sung," he declared in one of his lectures *On Protracted War* (1938), "and we have no use for his asinine ethics."[2] Mao's lecture was an innovative discussion of guerrilla tactics. His argument against the Duke of Sung, however, was familiar enough, and to Chinese as well as Western readers. It is an argument common among practical men, like Hsiang's minister, to whom winning is always more important than aristocratic honor. But it enters significantly into the theory of war only when winning is seen to be *morally* important, that is, only when the outcome of the struggle is conceived in terms of justice. Some 200 years after the battle at the River Hung, more than two millennia before the communist revolution, the philosopher Mo Tzu perfectly described Mao's case, as he himself must understand it.[3]

> Suppose there is a country which is being persecuted and oppressed by its rulers, and a Sage . . . in order to rid the world of this pest raises an army and sets out to punish the evil-doers. If, when he has won a victory, he conforms to the doctrine of the Confucians, he will issue an order to his troops saying, "Fugitives are not to be pursued, an enemy who has lost his helmet is not to be shot at; if a chariot overturns, you are to help the occupants to right it"—if this is done, the violent and the disorderly will escape with their lives and the world will not be rid of its pest.

Mo Tzu believed in the doctrine of Righteous War. Mao Tse-tung has introduced into China the western theory of the just war. No doubt, there are fine points of difference between these two ideas, which I cannot pursue here. But they are not different in any major way. They set up the tension between winning and fighting well in similar fashion, and for Mo Tzu and Chairman Mao they point to the same resolution: the feudal rules for fighting well are simply cast aside. The tension is overcome as soon as it is recognized. That doesn't mean that there are no rules of engagement at all; I have already cited Mao's "Eight Points for Attention," which recapitulate in democratic style the old chivalric code. But for Mao himself the "Eight Points" apparently reflect only the utilitarian requirements of guerrilla war, and they cannot stand against the higher utility of winning—which he is likely to describe in extravagant terms, a combination of Wilsonian idealism and Marxist apocalypse: "The aim of war is to eliminate war. . . . Mankind's era of wars will be brought to an end by our own efforts, and beyond doubt the war we wage is part of the final battle."[4] And in the final battle, no one will insist upon the "Eight Points." Exceptions will readily be made whenever the conflict seems critical. Consider, for example, the last of the Eight: "Do not ill-treat captives." Mao has also argued that guerrilla bands on the move cannot take prisoners. "It is best first to require the prisoners to hand over their weapons and then to disperse them or execute them."[5] Since prisoners are not conceived as men-with-rights, the choice between dispersal and execution is purely tactical, and to insist in all cases upon the rule against ill treatment would presumably be an example of "asinine ethics."

Nor were rights thought to be at stake in the old warrior codes. Duke Hsiang believed it unworthy and demeaning to strike a wounded soldier or attack an unformed host. Combat was only possible between peers; otherwise war would not be an occasion for the display of aristocratic virtue. It is not hard to understand why anyone convinced of the moral urgency of victory would be impatient with such notions. Of what use is the (undoubted) virtue of the Duke of Sung if the world is ruled by violence and aggression? Indeed, a war in which the Duke's virtue was more important than a military triumph would seem to be a very unimportant war. Thus the argument of Hsiang's minister after the defeat of the Sung army: "If we grudge a second wound, it would be better not to wound at all. If we would spare the grey-haired, we had better submit to the enemy."[6] Either fight all-out or not at all. This argument is often said to be typical of American thought, but in fact it is universal in the history of war. Once soldiers are actually engaged, and especially if they are engaged in a Righteous War or a just war, a steady pressure builds up against the war convention and in favor of particular violations of its rules. And then, more often than the belligerent powers are prepared to admit—itself a matter of interest—the rules are broken. They are not broken for the sake of military necessity alone. That argument justifies too much, and it does so without reference to the cause for which the war is being fought. The rules are broken for the sake of the cause. It is with some version of the argument for justice that the violations are defended.

On this view, the rules have no standing in any war that is worth fighting. They are at most "rules of thumb," general precepts of honor (or utility) to be observed only until observing them comes into conflict with the requirements of victory. But this is to misunderstand the status of the war convention. If we consider noncombatant immunity rather than warrior honor, and the protection of human rights rather than the expediencies of guerrilla war—that is, if we attend to what is really fundamental in the rules of war—the conflict between winning and fighting well is not so easily resolved. If we recognize, for example, that the protection afforded by the "Eight Points" is morally required, and that men and women are rightly indignant if they are robbed and ravaged by guerrilla bands, then Mao's rules take on a greater significance than their author attributes to them. They cannot simply be set aside; nor can they be balanced, in utilitarian fashion, against this or that desirable outcome. For the rights of innocent people have the same moral effectiveness in the face of just as in the face of unjust soldiers.

And yet the case for breaking the rules and violating those rights is made sufficiently often, and by soldiers and statesmen who cannot always be called wicked, so that we have to assume that it isn't pointless. Anyway, we know its point all too well. We know how high the stakes sometimes are in war and how urgent victory can be. "For there are peoples," as Simone Weil has written, "[who] have never recovered after having once been conquered."[7] The very existence of a community may be at stake, and then how can we fail to consider possible outcomes in judging the course of the fighting? At this point if at no other, the restraint on utilitarian calculation must be lifted. Even if we are inclined to lift it, however, we cannot forget that the rights violated for the sake of victory are genuine rights, deeply founded and in principle inviolable. And there is nothing asinine about this principle: the very lives of men and women are at stake. So the theory of war, when it is fully understood, poses a dilemma, which every theorist (though not, fortunately, every soldier) must resolve as best he can. And no resolution is serious unless it recognizes the force of both *jus ad bellum* and *jus in bello*.

THE SLIDING SCALE AND THE ARGUMENT FROM EXTREMITY

The immediate issue is whether we should discriminate between soldiers fighting a just war and soldiers fighting an unjust war. It is, of course, those who claim membership in the first group who raise the issue, making what might be called an appeal against combatant equality. Though such appeals are particular in character, they have a general form. They all involve the claim that the equality I have been defending is merely conventional and that the truth about war rights is best expressed in terms of a sliding scale: *the more justice, the more right.* Something like this appears to be what the philosopher John Rawls has in mind when he says, "Even in a just war, certain forms of violence are strictly inadmissible; and when a country's right to war is questionable and uncertain, the constraints on the means it can use are all the more severe. Acts permissible in a war of legitimate self-defense, when these are necessary, may be flatly excluded in a more doubtful situation."[8] The greater the justice of my cause, the more rules I can violate for the sake of the cause—though some rules are always inviolable. The same argument can be put in terms of outcomes: the greater the injustice likely to result from my defeat, the more rules I can violate in order to avoid defeat—though some rules, and so on. The value of this position is that it grants the existence of rights (of some sort) while still opening the way for soldiers resisting aggression to do (some of) the things they believe necessary for victory. It allows the justice of one's cause to make a difference in the way one fights. Exactly how much of a difference is allowed, however, is radically unclear, and so is the status of the men and women who are now drawn into the hell of war so that justice can triumph. The practical effects of the argument are probably more far-reaching than its proponents would like, but I will say nothing about these effects until I can look at a number of historical cases. First, however, something more must be said about the structure of the argument.

According to the war convention as I have described it, there is no range of actions, over which the sliding scale might move, between legitimate combat and inadmissible violence. There is only a line, not entirely distinct but meant simply to mark off the one from the other. Given this view, the argument quoted from Rawls might be taken to mean that borderline cases should be decided systematically against that country whose "right to war is questionable" or even that the military and political leaders of that country should keep some distance away from the border, never doubling the doubtfulness of their cause with the doubtfulness of their methods. This last would simply be a plea for scrupulousness, which is always a good thing. But there is another meaning that can be drawn out of Rawls' argument (though I don't think it is his own meaning): that the class of "strictly inadmissible" acts should be kept very small, and space should be opened up within the rules of war where the sliding scale might be applied. The effect of sliding the scale to point x within this space, it should be said, is not to remove all restraints on military action up to that point, but rather to leave only the restraints of usefulness and proportionality. The sliding scale makes way for those utilitarian calculations that rules and rights are intended to bar. It creates a new class of generally inadmissible acts and of quasi-rights, subject to piecemeal erosion by soldiers whose cause is just—or by soldiers who believe that their cause is just. And so it enables those soldiers to do terrible things and to defend in their own consciences and among their associates and followers the terrible things they do.

Now, the extreme form of the sliding-scale argument is the claim that soldiers fighting a just war can do anything at all that is useful in the fighting. This effectively annuls the war convention and denies or suspends the rights that the convention was designed to protect. The war rights of the just are total, and any blame their actions entail falls upon the leaders of the other side. General Sherman took this view of war, as we have seen, and I have called it the "war is hell" doctrine. It is not so much a resolution of the tension between winning and fighting well as a denial of its moral significance. The only kind of justice that matters is *jus ad bellum*. Beyond that there are only such considerations as rational men will always attend to: they will not waste their substance in useless killing of the innocent, though they will kill them readily enough if victory seems to require it. It may be that this is what the sliding scale comes to in any case, but its advocates at least claim to recognize the existence of rules and rights, and so their argument requires a separate analysis.

The only alternative to the sliding scale, it is often said, is a position of moral absolutism. To resist the slide, one must hold that the rules of war are a series of categorical and unqualified prohibitions, and that they can never rightly be violated even in order to defeat aggression.[9] But that is a hard line to take, and especially so in the modern age, when aggression has assumed such frightening forms. Perhaps the Duke of Sung was right not to break the warrior code for the sake of his dynasty. But if what is being defended is the state itself and the political community it protects and the lives and liberties of the members of that community. . . . *Fiat justicia ruat coelum*, do justice even if the heavens fall, is not for most people a plausible moral doctrine.

There is an alternative doctrine that stops just short of absolutism and that I shall try to defend in the chapters that follow. It might be summed up in the maxim: do justice unless the heavens are (really) about to fall.

This is the utilitarianism of extremity, for it concedes that in certain very special cases, though never as a matter of course even in just wars, the only restraints upon military action are those of usefulness and proportionality. Throughout my discussion of the rules of war, I have been resisting this view and denying its force. I have argued, for example, against the notion that civilians can be locked into a besieged city or reprisals taken against innocent people "in extreme cases." For the idea of extremity has no place in the making of the war convention—or if it is said that combat is always extreme, then the idea is naturalized within the convention. The rules are adjusted to the everyday extremities of war; no further adjustment is possible if we are to have any rules at all, and if we are to attend to the rights of the innocent. But now the question is not one of rule-making, but of rule-breaking. We know the form and substance of the moral code; we must decide, at a moment of desperation and looming disaster, whether to live (and perhaps to die) by its rules.

The sliding scale erodes the convention bit by bit, and so it eases the way for the decision-maker who believes himself "forced" to violate human rights. The argument from extremity permits (or requires) a more sudden breach of the convention, but only after holding out for a long time against the process of erosion. The reasons for holding out have to do with the nature of the rights at issue and the status of the men and women who hold them. These rights, I shall argue, cannot be eroded or undercut; nothing diminishes them; they are still standing at the very moment they are overridden: that is why they have to be *overridden*.[10] Hence breaking the rules is always a hard matter, and the soldier or statesman who does so must be prepared to accept the moral consequences and the burden of guilt that his action entails. At the same time, it may well be that he has no choice but to break the rules: he confronts at last what can meaningfully be called necessity.

The tension between the rules of war and the theory of aggression, between *jus in bello* and *jus ad bellum*, can be dealt with in four different ways:

1. the war convention is simply set aside (derided as "asinine ethics") under the pressure of utilitarian argument;
2. the convention yields slowly to the moral urgency of the cause: the rights of the righteous are enhanced, and those of their enemies devalued;

3. the convention holds and rights are strictly respected, whatever the consequences; and
4. the convention is overridden, but only in the face of an imminent catastrophe.

The second and fourth of these are the most interesting and the most important. They explain how it is that morally serious men and women, who have some sense of what rights are, come nevertheless to violate the rules of war, escalate its brutality and extend its tyranny. The fourth seems to me the right argument. It provides the best account of the two kinds of justice and most fully recognizes the force of each. I shall focus on it in the chapters that follow, but try at the same time to suggest the inadequacies and dangers of the sliding scale. I will look first at a number of cases involving the practice of neutrality, perhaps the most disputed feature of the war convention. Since neutral rights constitute a kind of noncombatant immunity, they might have been taken up earlier on. The disputes they have generated, however, raise questions less about the content than about the force and endurance of rights in war. How long must one wait before breaking the rules? The answer I want to defend is best expressed by reversing Chairman Mao's dictum: with reference to our own conventions, and until the very last minute, *we are all the Duke of Sung.*

15

AGGRESSION AND NEUTRALITY

THE DOCTRINE OF NEUTRALITY HAS A TWOFOLD FORM, WHICH IS BEST expressed (and which is conventionally expressed) in the language of rights. States possess, first, a *right to be neutral*, which is simply an aspect of their sovereignty. In any prospective or on-going conflict between two other states, they are free to opt for what might be called the condition of "thirdness." And if they do that, they then possess *neutral rights*, specified at great length in positive international law. As with the war convention generally, the initial right and the subsequent rights exist without reference to the moral character of the belligerent powers or to the probable outcome of the war. The more convinced we are, however, that one of the belligerents is an aggressor or that the outcome is going to be disastrous, the more likely we are to deny the very possibility of noninvolvement. How can the rest of us respect its right to stand and watch if, by violating that right, we might avert the destruction?

These questions have been posed with a special insistence in the years since World War II, but in fact the argument implicit in them is an old one. Consider, for example, a British proclamation issued in 1793: the political and military policies of the revolutionary government of France, it was said, involved "all the surrounding powers in one common danger . . . giving them the right . . . *imposing on them the duty*, to stop the progress of an evil which exists only by the successive violation of all law and property. . . ."[1] The practical consequence of this sort of thing is obvious.

If states don't do their duty, they can be forced to do it. One asserts the urgency of the struggle, and one erodes or denies the right to be neutral, in order to pave the way for the violation of neutral rights. The history of neutrality provides many examples of such violations, defended with some version of the argument from extremity or with the sliding scale, and I shall refer to that history in order to analyze those defenses. But first I must say something about the nature of neutrality itself and its place in the war convention.

The Right to Be Neutral

Neutrality is a collective and voluntary form of noncombatancy. It is collective in that its benefits obtain for all the members of a political community without reference to the status of individuals. Soldiers and civilians are alike protected, so long as their state is "not engaged in war-making." The rights of disengagement distribute equally to all citizens. Neutrality is voluntaristic in that it can be assumed at will by any state with regard to a war or a prospective war between any other states. Individuals can be conscripted, but states cannot. They may ask that other powers formally acknowledge their neutrality, but the condition is unilaterally assumed and the acknowledgment unnecessary. The "scrap of paper" that Germany brushed aside when it invaded Belgium in 1914 did not establish Belgian neutrality; the Belgians themselves did that. And had the Germans formally renounced their guarantee or waited for its expiration, their invasion would still have been the crime it was said to be at the time. It would have been a crime, that is, as long as the Belgians not only claimed the rights but also observed the duties of a neutral state.

These duties can be summed up very simply, although international law on this subject is elaborate and detailed: they require a strict impartiality toward the belligerents, without reference to the justice of their cause or to any sentiments of neighborliness, cultural affinity, or ideological agreement.[2] It is not only fighting on one or another side that is prohibited, but every sort of official discrimination. This rule is very strict; if it is violated, neutral rights are forfeit, and the neutral state is subject to reprisals from whichever belligerent is injured by the violations. The rule applies, however, only to state action. Private citizens remain free to choose sides in a variety of ways, to campaign politically, raise money, even raise volunteers (though they cannot launch forays across the border).

What is more important, normal patterns of trade may be maintained with both belligerents. Hence the neutrality of any given state is likely to be more helpful to one side than to the other. So far as the warring powers are concerned, neutrality is rarely a matter of equal benefit, for neither the balance of private sympathy and effort nor the balance of trade is likely to be even between them.* But neither can complain of the unofficial help the other receives. This is a help that cannot be helped; it derives from the very existence of the neutral state, its geography, economy, language, religion, and so on, and could only be interdicted by the most rigorous coercion of its citizens. But the neutral state is not required to coerce its own citizens. So long as it takes no positive action to help one side or the other, it has fulfilled its duty not to get involved, and then it is automatically entitled to the full enjoyment of its right not to get involved.

The moral basis of the right is not entirely clear, however, in large part because its domestic analogue is so unappealing. In both political and moral life, the "neuter" is not a person one instinctively likes. Perhaps he has a right to avoid if he can the quarrels of his neighbors, but what about their troubles? We have to ask again: can he stand and watch a neighbor being assaulted on the street? Might not the neighbor say at such a time, "You're either for me or against me"? As a revolutionary slogan, that sentence suggests, perhaps, an unwarranted pressure and a threat of retaliations to come. But in the case at hand, its message is simpler and less objectionable. Surely a strict neutrality here, a refusal to discriminate in any way in favor of the victim, would be disquieting and strange. Neighbors are not mere spectators, studying one another's misfortunes from some great distance. The social life they share entails a degree of mutual concern. On the other hand, if I am obligated to be "for" my neighbor, I am not obligated to rush to his rescue—first, because that may not be an effective way of being for him; and second, because it may be disastrous for me. I have a right to weigh the risks of joining the battle. But let's assume that the risks are minor: there are a large number of us watching, and I can count on the support of the others if I take the lead; or there is a policeman

---

*Neutral states have sometimes sought a more perfect neutrality by embargoing all trade with belligerent powers. But this does not seem a plausible course. For if the normal balance of trade favors one belligerent, a total embargo is likely to favor the other. There is no zero point; the *status quo ante bellum* seems the only reasonable norm.

around the corner, and I can count on him to take the lead. Then I have no right to be neutral, and any efforts on my part to escape, make excuses, bury my head in the sand, are sure to be thought reprehensible.

But the right of a state is different, and not only because there is no policeman around the corner. For there may well be a majority of states and an overwhelming predominance of force at least potentially available on behalf of a state under attack, thought to be the victim of aggression. All that stands in the way of mobilizing this force, it may be, is the war convention and the right of neutrality. Even in such a case, the right holds, because risk in war is very different from what it is in domestic fighting. Years ago, John Westlake argued that "neutrality is not morally justifiable unless intervention in the war is unlikely to promote justice or could do so only at a ruinous cost to the neutral."[3] Ruination is to be avoided, but is this only the ruination of states? When a state joins a war, it risks its survival to this or that degree, depending on the nature of the conflict, the power of its allies, and the readiness and fighting capacity of its army; and these risks may be acceptable or not. But at the same time, it condemns an indefinite number of its citizens to certain death. It does this, to be sure, without knowing which citizens those are. But the decision itself is irrevocable: once fighting begins, it is certain that soldiers (and probably civilians, too) will die. The right of neutrality follows from this fact. Like other provisions of the war convention, it represents a limit on the coerciveness of war. At least this group of men and women, citizens of the neutral state, who do not choose to risk their lives, will be protected from having to do so.

But why should these men and women be immune and free when so many others are driven into battle? In what possible way are they entitled to their neutrality? The question is especially important if we imagine a situation where a particular state's decision to be neutral means that more people will be killed than would be killed if it joined the war, for the participation of its armies might turn the tide and shorten the fighting by so many weeks or months. But the leaders of such a state are not required to calculate as if every human life carried the same moral weight for every decision-maker at every moment in time. Their people's lives are not international resources to be distributed in war so as to balance the risks or reduce the losses of other people. These are innocent lives. With reference to the soldiers of the neutral state, that means only that they have not yet been attacked and forced to fight. Still, they are disengaged, and no one has a right to challenge their disengagement. Perhaps that disengagement is a matter of luck; it is often, in cases of successful neutrality, a matter of geography. But people are entitled to their good fortune in such matters, as states are, or are presumed to be, entitled to their geographic locations.*

So neutral citizens are immune from attack; the coerciveness of war can never willfully be extended beyond the limits fixed by the material causes of the conflict and the military organization of the states involved. The leaders of a neutral state are entitled to maintain that immunity; indeed, they may be bound to do so, given the consequences of its loss for their fellow citizens. The same solidarity that makes noninvolvement at home morally questionable may well make it obligatory in the international arena: this group of men and women must save one another's lives first. They cannot do this by killing other people, unless those others are attacking them. The rules of neutrality suggest, however, that they can do it by allowing other people to die rather than dying themselves. If they have incurred obligations toward some of those people—for the sake, perhaps, of collective security—then, of course, they cannot allow them to die; otherwise, the right holds, even if its assertion seems ignoble.

But there is one sort of case in which this right might be denied. Imagine (what is easily imaginable) that some great power launches a campaign of conquest, aimed not merely at this or that state but at some larger ideological or imperial goal. Why should such a campaign be resisted only by its first victims, when in fact many other states will be threatened if the initial resistance fails? Or consider the common argument that aggression anywhere threatens everyone. Aggression is like crime: if one does not stamp it out, it will spread. Then again, there is no reason for the immediate victims to fight alone. They are fighting on behalf of future victims,

---

* But this argument doesn't seem to work with reference to the property and prosperity (rather than the lives) of the citizens. If a state can discriminate economically against an aggressor, even if the costs to itself are considerable, it seems bound to do so, unless the discrimination is likely to involve it in the fighting. Aggressor states, of course, have a right to respond to discriminatory measures, by force if necessary. But they won't always be in a position to respond, and if they are not, the measures may be morally required. When the League of Nations invoked economic sanctions against Italy in the Ethiopian War of 1936, it made the requirement legal as well. But I should think that the moral obligation would have held had there been only an Ethiopian appeal and no League resolution. In any case, the example suggests the relative status of property rights in the theory of war.

that is, of all other states, and the others will reap the benefits of their fighting and dying. How can they stand aside? President Wilson took this position in his war message of April 2, 1917: "Neutrality is no longer feasible or desirable when the peace of the world is involved and the freedom of its peoples."[4] He presumably meant *morally* feasible, since a practical alternative to war, namely continued neutrality, clearly existed. The argument against that alternative must go something like this. If one imagines a particular aggressor moving on from one triumph to another, or if one imagines a radical increase in the incidence of aggression as a result of this particular triumph, then it has to be said that peace and freedom are in general danger. And then continued neutrality is not morally feasible; for while a neutral state has or may have a right to let others die in quarrels of their own, it cannot let them die on its behalf. Any danger that is shared by all the members of international society is morally coercive, even if it is not yet materially present, for all of them.

This argument, however, rests uneasily on "imaginings" about which there is no general agreement and which often look painfully implausible after the fact. It seems very strange today, for example, that any conceivable outcome of World War I could have been thought to pose a universal threat to peace and freedom (or a greater threat than was posed by the actual outcome). And this is so even if one grants that the war began with an act or a series of acts of aggression. The mere recognition of a criminal attack, without some profoundly pessimistic or, as in this case, highly extravagant view of its likely consequences, does not require the leaders of a neutral state to draw President Wilson's conclusions. They can always refuse to do so, imagining in their turn that their own country and the whole world are in no real danger. That is a unilateral view of the situation, to be sure, and one can argue (as I would often be inclined to do) with the leaders who put it forward. But they and their people are entitled to act on it. That is the real right of neutrality.

THE NATURE OF NECESSITY (2)

At this point, however, the crucial moral decision may not lie with the neutral state. The belligerents also have a choice: to respect neutral rights or not. Violations of those rights are usually thought to be an especially bad kind of aggression—on the principle, I suppose, that it is worse to strike out at uninvolved states than at states with which one has been quarreling.

Unless we take a rather permissive view of the initial resort to violence, this seems a dubious principle. On the other hand, attacks on neutrals are usually an especially clear kind of aggression, whereas responsibility for the war itself may be difficult to assess. When armies move across the frontier of a state that has maintained a strict impartiality, we have little difficulty in recognizing the move as a criminal act. Violations short of armed attack are harder to recognize but almost equally reprehensible, for they invite and justify military responses from the other side. If neutrality collapses and the war is extended to new territory and people, the crime is that of the first violator (assuming a proportionate response from the second).

But what if neutrality is violated for a good cause: for the sake of national survival and the defeat of aggression; or, more largely, for the sake of "civilization as we know it" or the "peace and freedom" of the whole world? Here is the paradigmatic form of the collision between *jus ad bellum* and *jus in bello.* The belligerent power believes itself pressed by the exigencies of a just war. The neutral state is firm in its rights: its citizens are not bound to sacrifice themselves to someone else's exigencies. The belligerent power talks of the vital importance of the ends for which it is fighting; the neutral state invokes the rules of war. Neither side is entirely convincing, though in particular cases we must choose between them. I have tried to make the strongest possible case for neutral rights. Their violation almost certainly entails the killing (or the causing to be killed) of innocent people, and so it is not a casual matter even when the end in view is very important. Indeed, we are likely to recognize good men fighting for important ends by their reluctance to invade neutral states and force their citizens to fight. The value of that reluctance will be apparent if we look at two cases in which neutral rights were wrongly violated: first, on the plea of necessity, and second, with the argument *more justice, more right.* The first is the most famous violation of neutrality since the Athenian attack on Melos, and I have given it the name originally assigned in wartime propaganda.

The Rape of Belgium

The German attack on Belgium in August 1914 is unusual in that it was openly and honestly described by the Germans themselves as a violation of neutral rights. The speech of Chancellor von Bethmann Hollweg to the Reichstag on August 4 deserves to be remembered.[5]

Gentlemen, we are now in a state of necessity, and necessity knows no law. Our troops have already entered Belgian territory.

Gentlemen, that is a breach of international law. It is true that the French government declared at Brussels that France would respect Belgian neutrality as long as her adversary respected it. We know, however, that France stood ready for an invasion. France could wait, we could not. A French attack on our flank on the lower Rhine might have been disastrous. Thus we were forced to ignore the rightful protests of the Government of Belgium. The wrong—I speak openly—the wrong we thereby commit we will try to make good as soon as our military aims have been attained.

He who is menaced as we are and is fighting for his highest possession can only consider how he is to hack his way through (*durch-haven*).

This is frank talk, though it is not quite like the "frankness" of the Athenian generals at Melos. For the chancellor does not step outside the moral world when he defends the German invasion. He grants that a wrong has been done, and he promises to make it good after the fighting is over. That promise was not taken seriously by the Belgians. Their neutrality having been violated and their borders crossed, they had no reason to expect anything good from the invaders; nor did they believe that their independence would be respected. They chose to resist the invasion, and once their soldiers were fighting and dying, it is hard to see how the wrong the Germans had done could ever be made good.

The force of von Bethmann Hollweg's argument lies not in the promise of reparation, but in the plea of necessity. This will be a useful occasion to consider again what the plea might mean—and to suggest that here, as in military history generally, it means a great deal less than it appears to do. We can see clearly in the chancellor's speech the two levels at which the concept works. First, there is the instrumental or strategic level: the attack on Belgium was necessary, it is being argued, if German defeat was to be avoided. But that is an improbable argument. The attack had long seemed to the General Staff the most expedient way of striking a hard blow against the French and winning a quick victory in the west (before Germany was fully engaged with the Russians on the eastern front).[6] By no means, however, was it the only way of defending German territory. A French invasion along the lower Rhine, after all, could only outflank the German army if the Germans were mobilized for action further north (along the Belgium frontier). The chancellor's actual claim was that the odds of victory would be improved and German lives saved if the Belgians were sacrificed. But that expectation, which turned out to be wrong, had nothing to do with necessity.

The second level of the argument is moral: not only is the attack necessary to win, but winning itself is necessary, since Germany is fighting for its "highest possession." I don't know what von Bethmann Hollweg thought Germany's highest possession was. Perhaps he had in mind some notion of honor or military glory, which could only be upheld by victory over the nation's enemies. But honor and glory belong to the realm of freedom, not necessity. We are likely to think that Germany's victory was morally necessary (essential, required) only of its survival as an independent nation or the very lives of its people were at stake. And on the best construction of the German cause, that was certainly not the case; what was at stake was Alsace-Lorraine, Germany's African colonies, and so on. So the argument fails on both levels. It would have to succeed on both, I think, before the violation of Belgian neutrality could be defended.

The German chancellor puts forward exactly the sort of argument that would be appropriate at a time of genuine extremity. He rejects every kind of deceitfulness. He does not pretend that the Belgians have failed in their duty of impartiality. He does not claim that the French have already violated Belgian neutrality or even that they are threatening to do so. He does not argue that Belgium cannot rightly stand aside in the presence of (French) aggression. He recognizes the force of the war convention and hence of the right of neutrality, and he makes the case for overriding that right. He wants to override it, however, not at the last minute but at the very first, and not when Germany's survival is in danger but when the dangers are of a more ordinary kind. So his is not a plausible case; its structure is right, but not its content. Nor was it thought plausible at the time. The German invasion was almost universally condemned (by many Germans, too). It was an important reason for the determination and high morale with which Britain entered the war and for the sympathy with which the Allied cause was viewed in other neutral countries—the United States, above all.[7] Even Lenin, who led the leftist opposition to the war, thought the defense of Belgium a reason to fight: "Let us suppose that all the states interested in the observation of international treaties declared war on Germany, with the demand for the liberation and indemnification of Belgium. In such a case, the sympathies of Socialists would, of course, be on the side of Germany's enemies."[8] But, he went on, that is not what the war is really about. He was right; the war as a whole does not lend itself to an easy description in terms of justice and injustice. But the attack on Belgium does. We must turn now, and at much greater length, to a harder case.

THE SLIDING SCALE

Winston Churchill and Norwegian Neutrality

The day after Britain and France declared war on Germany in 1939, King Haakon VII formally proclaimed Norway's neutrality. The policy of the king and his government was not founded on political or ideological indifference. "We never had neutrality of thought in Norway," the Foreign Minister wrote, "and I never wanted it." Norway's political and cultural ties were with the Allies, and there seems no reason to doubt what historians of the period tell us: "The Norwegians firmly believed in the high ideals of democracy, individual freedom, and international justice."[9] They were not, however, prepared to fight for those ideals. The war was a struggle among the great powers of Europe, and Norway was very much a small power, traditionally disengaged from European *machtpolitik*, and now virtually disarmed. Whatever the moral importance of the issues over which the war was being fought, the Norwegian government could hardly intervene in any decisive way. Nor could it intervene at all without accepting great risks. Its first task was to make sure that Norway was still intact and its citizens alive at the end.

With this purpose in mind, the government adopted a strict policy of "neutrality in deed." On balance, this policy favored the Germans, even though most of Norway's normal trade was with the Allied powers, especially Britain. For the Germans depended on Norway for a very large part of their iron ore supply. The ore was mined at Gallivare in northern Sweden, and during the summer months it was shipped out of the Swedish town of Lulea on the Baltic Sea. But in the winter, the Baltic froze; then the ore was moved by rail to Narvik on the Norwegian coast, the nearest warm-water port. There German ships picked it up and carried it down the coast, keeping within Norwegian territorial waters so as to avoid the British navy. The German ore supply was thus protected by Norwegian (and Swedish) neutrality, and for this reason the invasion of Norway was no part of Hitler's original strategic plan. Instead, "[he] emphasized repeatedly that in his opinion the most desirable attitude for Norway as well as for the rest of Scandinavia would be one of complete neutrality."[10]

The British view was very different. During the long months of the "phony war," Scandinavian neutrality was a constant topic of Cabinet discussion. Winston Churchill, then First Lord of the Admiralty, proposed one plan after another to interdict the shipments of iron ore. Here was a chance, he argued, here was the only chance, to strike a quick blow against Germany. Instead of waiting for a German attack in France and the Low Countries, the Allies could force Hitler to disperse his armies and to fight—Churchill never doubted that the Germans would fight for their ore supply—in a part of the world where the strength of the British navy could most effectively be brought to bear.[11] The French were also disinclined to wait for an attack on their own soil. Sir Edward Spears writes of Prime Minister Daladier that "his views on military matters were confined to keeping warlike operations as remote from France as possible."[12] The Norwegian prime minister no doubt had a parallel idea in mind. But there is this difference: the war which the Norwegians wished to see fought in France, and which the French were ready to fight in Norway, was France's and not Norway's war. Churchill confronted the same difficulty; Norwegian neutrality was a bar to each of his plans. It was only a moral and legal bar, perhaps, for he did not expect the Norwegians to fight very hard for their neutrality, but it was an important bar nonetheless, since the British were inclined to distinguish themselves from their enemies by their respect for international law and justice. "All the cards are against us in playing with these neutrals," General Ironside, Chief of the Imperial General Staff, confided to his diary. "Germany does not mean to respect them if it so suits her and we must respect them."[13] The case was especially difficult because it did in fact suit the Germans, but not the British, to respect Norway's neutral rights.

The Russo-Finnish war opened a new possibility for Allied strategists (and moralists). The League of Nations, which had said nothing about the German attack on Poland, now condemned the Russians for waging an aggressive war. Churchill, who "sympathized ardently with the Finns," proposed to send troops to Finland in fulfillment of Britain's obligations under the Covenant—and to send them via Narvik, Gallivare, and Lulea. Under the plan drawn up by the General Staff, only a battalion of soldiers would actually have reached Finland, while three divisions would have guarded the "lines of communication" across Norway and Sweden, not

only stopping the shipments of iron ore, but seizing it at its source and digging in for an expected German response in the spring.[14] It was a bold plan
which would almost certainly have led to a German invasion of Sweden
and Norway and to large-scale military operations in the two countries.
"We have more to gain than to lose," Churchill argued, "by a German
attack on Norway." One immediately wants to ask whether the Norwegians had more to gain than to lose. Apparently they did not think so, for
they rejected repeated requests that they permit the free passage of British
troops. The Cabinet decided in favor of the expedition anyway, but the
instructions prepared for its commander would have allowed him to proceed only in the face of "token opposition." General Ironside worried that
the political will necessary for success did not exist. "We must . . . remain
quite cynical about anything except stopping the iron ore."[15] The Cabinet
seems to have been cynical enough about its Finnish cover. As it turned
out, however, the members were unwilling to do without it, and when the
Finns sued for peace in March 1940, the plan was shelved.

Churchill now pressed a more modest proposal. He urged the mining of Norwegian territorial waters, so as to force German merchant ships
out into the Atlantic where the British navy could capture or sink them.
It was a proposal he had made immediately after the war began and that
he brought forward whenever his larger plans seemed in danger. Even
this "genteel little act of bellicosity," however, encountered opposition.
Though the Cabinet seemed favorable to Churchill's original presentation
(in September 1939), "the Foreign Office arguments about neutrality were
weighty, and I could not prevail. I continued . . . to press my point by every
means and on all occasions." It is interesting to note, as Liddell Hart does,
that a similar project had been brought forward in 1918 and rejected by
the Commander-in-Chief, Lord Beatty. "[He] said it would be most repugnant to the officers and men in the Grand Fleet to steam in overwhelming
strength into the waters of a small but high-spirited people and coerce
them. If the Norwegians resisted, as they probably would, blood would
be shed; this, said the Commander-in-Chief, 'would constitute a crime
as bad as any that the Germans had committed elsewhere.'"[16] The words
have a somewhat archaic ring (and it should be said that Beatty's last line,
repeated in 1939–40, would not have been true), but many Englishmen
still felt a similar repugnance. These were more likely to be professional
diplomats and soldiers than civilian politicians. General Ironside, for
example, not always the cynic he pretended to be, wrote in his diary that

the mining of Norwegian waters, though it could be described as "a reprisal for the way Germany had treated neutral ships . . . may well start off some form of totalitarian war."[17]

Churchill presumably believed that Britain was in for that kind of war anyway, given the political character of its enemy. He defended his proposal with a moral argument focusing on the nature and long-term goals of the Nazi regime. It is not merely that he did not sympathize with Beatty's repugnance; he told the Cabinet that such feelings courted disaster, not for Britain alone but for all Europe.[18]

> We are fighting to re-establish the reign of law and to protect the liberties of small countries. Our defeat would mean an age of barbaric violence, and would be fatal, not only to ourselves, but to the independent life of every small country in Europe. Acting in the name of the Covenant, and as virtual mandatories of the League and all it stands for, we have a right, indeed are bound in duty, to abrogate for a space some of the conventions of the very laws we seek to consolidate and reaffirm. Small nations must not tie our hands when we are fighting for their rights and freedom. The letter of the law must not in supreme emergency obstruct those who are charged with its protection and enforcement. It would not be right or rational that the aggressive Power should gain one set of advantages by tearing up all laws, and another set by sheltering behind the innate respect for law of its opponents. Humanity, rather than legality, must be our guide.

This is a powerful argument, though its rhetoric is sometimes misleading; it requires close examination. I want to begin by accepting Churchill's description of the British as defenders of the rule of law. (Indeed, they vindicated their claim to that title by refusing for months to adopt his proposals.) It may even be accurate to talk of Britain as the "virtual mandatory" of the League of Nations, so long as one understands that phrase to mean that it was not the actual mandatory; the British decision to invade Norwegian waters was as unilateral as was Norway's decision to stay out of the war. The problem lies in the consequences Churchill believes to follow from the justice of Britain's cause.

He puts forward a version of what I have called the sliding scale argument: the greater the justice of one's cause, the more rights one has in battle.* But Churchill pretends that these are rights against the Germans. The British, he says, are entitled to violate those legal conventions behind which Germany is sheltering. Legal conventions, however, have (or sometimes have) their moral reasons. The purpose of the laws of neutrality is not primarily to protect belligerent powers but to save the lives of neutral citizens. It was in fact the Norwegians who were sheltered by the "letter of the law"; the Germans were only its secondary beneficiaries. This ordering suggests the crucial difficulty with the sliding scale. However much the rights of the British are enhanced by the justice of their cause, they can hardly acquire a title to kill *Norwegians* or to put their lives at risk unless Norwegian rights are somehow simultaneously diminished. The sliding scale argument presupposes and requires some such symmetry, but I do not see how it can be generated. It is not enough to argue that the just side can do more. Something must be said about the objects as well as the subjects of this military doing. Who is being done to? In this case, the objects are Norwegian citizens, who are in no sense responsible for the war into which they are to be dragged. They have not challenged the rule of law or the peace of Europe. How have they become liable to attack?

There is an implicit answer to this question in Churchill's Cabinet memorandum. He obviously believes that the Norwegians ought to be involved in the struggle against Germany, not only because their involvement would be good for Britain, but also because, if Britain and France were forced into a "shameful peace," they would certainly be among the "next victims." Neutral rights fade away, he argues, when brought up against aggression and illegal violence on the one hand and legitimate resistance on the other. Or at least, they fade away whenever the aggressor poses a general threat: to the rule of law, the independence of small nations, and so on. Britain is fighting on behalf of Germany's future victims, and they must sacrifice their rights rather than hinder the struggle. Taken as moral exhortation, this seems to me, in the circumstances of

---

* Hugo Grotius, who generally favors the sliding scale, is particularly clear on the question of neutrality: "From what has been said we can understand how it is permissible for one who is waging a just war to take possession of a place situated in a country free from hostilities." He sets three conditions, the first of which does not quite fit the Norwegian case: "that there is not an imaginary but a real danger that the enemy will seize the place and cause irreparable damage." But Churchill might have argued that the Germans enjoyed all the benefits of seizure without the effort. See *Of the Law of War and Peace*, Book II, Chapter ii, Section x.

1939–40, entirely justified. But it remains a question whether the sacrifice is to be required because the Norwegians recognize the German threat or because the British do. Churchill is repeating Wilson's argument of 1917: neutrality is not morally feasible. But this is a dangerous argument when made not by the leader of a neutral state but by a leader of one of the belligerents. It is not a question now of the voluntary surrender of neutral rights, but of their "abrogation for a time." And even that phrase is a euphemism. Since human life is at stake, the abrogation is not temporary, unless Churchill plans to raise the dead after the war is over.

In most wars, it can plausibly be said that one side fights justly, or probably does, or fights with greater justice than the other, and in all these cases the enemy against which it fights may well pose a general threat. The right of third parties to be neutral is a moral entitlement to ignore those distinctions and to recognize or not to recognize that threat. It may well be that they have to fight if they do recognize a danger to themselves, but they cannot rightly be forced to fight if they do not. They may be morally blind, or obtuse, or selfish, but these faults do not turn them into the resources of the righteous. This is, however, exactly the effect of Churchill's argument: the sliding scale is a way of transferring the rights of third parties to the citizens and soldiers of a state whose war is, or is said to be, just.

But there is another argument in Churchill's memorandum which does not require the application of the sliding scale; it is most clearly suggested by the phrase "supreme emergency." In an emergency, neutral rights can be overridden, and when we override them we make no claim that they have been diminished, weakened, or lost. They have to be overridden, as I have already said, precisely because they are still there, in full force, obstacles to some great (necessary) triumph for mankind. To British strategists, Norwegian neutrality was an obstacle of just this sort. It appears now that they greatly exaggerated the effects they could have had on Germany's war effort by cutting off the ore shipments. But their estimates were honestly made, and they were shared by Hitler himself. "We can under no circumstances afford to lose the Swedish ore," he told General Falkenhurst in February 1940. "If we do, we will soon have to wage war with wooden sticks."[19] That attractive prospect must have weighed heavily with the British Cabinet. They had available to them a simple utilitarian argument, backed up by a theory of justice, for violating Norway's neutral rights: the violations were militarily necessary to defeat Nazism, and it was morally essential that Nazism be defeated.

Here again is the two-level argument, and in this case the argument works on the second level: the moral necessity is clear (I will try to explain why this is so in the next chapter). That is why we are likely to be far more sympathetic to Churchill's than to von Bethmann Hollweg's position. But the instrumental or strategic claim is as questionable in the Norwegian as in the Belgian example. The Allied armies had not yet fought a single battle; the force of the German *blitzkrieg* had not yet been felt in the West; the military significance of the airplane was not yet understood. The British still had full confidence in the Royal Navy. The First Lord of the Admiralty certainly had such confidence: all his Norwegian plans depended upon naval power. Only a Churchill, having called the situation at the beginning of 1940 a "supreme emergency," could still find words to describe Britain's danger six months later. The truth is that when the British finally decided "to sail in overwhelming strength into the waters of a small but high-spirited people and coerce them," they were not thinking of avoiding defeat but (like the Germans in 1914) of winning a quick victory.

So the British move is another example of overriding at the first minute rather than the last. We judge it less harshly than the German attack on Belgium, not only because of what we know of the character of the Nazi regime, but also because we look back on the events of the next months which so quickly brought Britain to the brink of national disaster. But it has to be stressed again that Churchill had no foresight of that disaster. To understand and weigh the actions he advocated, we must stand beside him in those early months of the war and try to think as he did. Then the question is simply this: can one do *anything*, violating the rights of the innocent, in order to defeat Nazism? I am going to argue that one can indeed do what is necessary, but the violation of Norwegian neutrality was not necessary in April 1940; it was only a piece of expediency. Can one then reduce the risks of fighting Nazism, at the expense of the innocent? Surely one cannot do that, however just the struggle. Churchill's argument hangs on the reality and the extremity of the crisis, but here (in his own view) there was no crisis. The "phony war" was not yet a supreme emergency. The emergency came on unexpectedly, as emergencies are likely to do, its dangers first revealed by the fighting in Norway.

The final British decision was made late in March, and the Leads were mined on April 8. The next day, the Germans invaded Norway. Eluding the British navy, they landed troops all along the coast, even as far north as Narvik. It was a response not so much to the actual laying of the mines as to the months of plans, arguments, and hesitations, none of which were concealed from Hitler's agents and strategic analysts. It was also the response Churchill had expected and hoped for, though it came too soon and with complete surprise. The Norwegians fought bravely and briefly; the British were tragically unready to defend the country they had made vulnerable to attack. There were a number of counter-landings by British troops; Narvik was captured and held for a short time; but the navy was ineffective against the German airforce, and Churchill, still First Lord of the Admiralty, presided over a series of humiliating evacuations.[20] Germany's ore supply was safe for the duration of the war, as it would have been had Norway's neutrality been respected. Norway was an occupied country, with a fascist government; many of its soldiers were dead; the "phony war" was over.

At Nuremberg in 1945, German leaders were charged with having planned and carried out an aggressive war against Norway. Liddell Hart finds it "hard to understand how the British and French governments had the face to approve . . . this charge."[21] His indignation derives from his belief that neutral rights are equally invulnerable to the claims of just and unjust belligerents. So they are, and it would have been better if after the war the British had acknowledged that the mining of the Leads had been a breach of international law and that the Germans were entitled, if not to invade and conquer Norway, at least to respond in some military way. I do not want to deny the anomaly of the argument that Hitler's Germany could have any rights at all in its wars of conquest. German entitlements, however, came by way of Norwegian rights, and so long as one recognizes the practice of neutrality, there is no way around them. In a supreme emergency, indeed, it may be necessary "to hack one's way through," but it is no virtue to be too eager to do that or to do it too soon, for it is not the opposing army that is hacked through in such a case, but innocent men and women, whose rights are intact, whose lives are at stake.

16

SUPREME EMERGENCY

THE NATURE OF NECESSITY (3)

Everyone's troubles make a crisis. "Emergency" and "crisis" are cant words, used to prepare our minds for acts of brutality. And yet there are such things as critical moments in the lives of men and women and in the history of states. Certainly, war is such a time: every war is an emergency, every battle a possible turning point. Fear and hysteria are always latent in combat, often real, and they press us toward fearful measures and criminal behavior. The war convention is a bar to such measures, not always effective, but there nevertheless. In principle at least, as we have seen, it resists the ordinary crises of military life. Churchill's description of Britain's predicament in 1939 as a "supreme emergency" was a piece of rhetorical heightening designed to overcome that resistance. But the phrase also contains an argument: that there is a fear beyond the ordinary fearfulness (and the frantic opportunism) of war, and a danger to which that fear corresponds, and that this fear and danger may well require exactly those measures that the war convention bars. Now, a great deal is at stake here, both for the men and women driven to adopt such measures and for their victims, so we must attend carefully to the implicit argument of "supreme emergency."

Though its use is often ideological, the meaning of the phrase is a matter of common sense. It is defined by two criteria, which correspond to the two levels on which the concept of necessity works: the first has to do with the imminence of the danger and the second with its nature. The two criteria must both be applied. Neither one by itself is sufficient as an account of extremity or as a defense of the extraordinary measures extremity is thought to require. Close but not serious, serious but not close—neither one makes for a supreme emergency. But since people at war can rarely agree on the seriousness of the dangers they face (or pose for one another), the idea of closeness is sometimes made to do the job alone. Then we are offered what might best be called the back-to-the-wall argument: that when conventional means of resistance are hopeless or worn out, anything goes (anything that is "necessary" to win). Thus British Prime Minister Stanley Baldwin, writing in 1932 about the dangers of terror bombing:[1]

> Will any form of prohibition of bombing, whether by convention, treaty, agreement, or anything you like, be effective in war? Frankly, I doubt it, and in doubting it, I make no reflection on the good faith of either ourselves or any other country. If a man has a potential weapon and has his back to the wall and is going to be killed, he will use that weapon, whatever it is and whatever undertaking he has given about it.

The first thing that has to be said about this statement is that Baldwin does not mean his domestic analogy to be applied literally. Soldiers and statesmen commonly say that their backs are to the wall whenever military defeat seems imminent, and Baldwin is endorsing this view of extremity. The analogy is from survival at home to victory in the international sphere. Baldwin claims that people will necessarily (inevitably) adopt extreme measures if such measures are necessary (essential) either to escape death or to avoid military defeat. But the argument is wrong at both ends. It is simply not the case that individuals will always strike out at innocent men and women rather than accept risks for themselves. We even say, very often, that it is their duty to accept risks (and perhaps to die); and here as in moral life generally, "ought" implies "can." We make the demand knowing that it is possible for people to live up to it. Can we make the same demand on political leaders, acting not for themselves but for their countrymen? That will depend upon the dangers their countrymen face. What is it that defeat entails? Is it some minor territorial adjustment, a loss of face (for the leaders), the payment of heavy indemnities, political reconstruction of this or that sort, the surrender of national independence, the exile or murder of millions of people? In such cases, one's back is always to the wall, but the dangers one confronts take very different forms, and the different forms make a difference.

If we are to adopt or defend the adoption of extreme measures, the danger must be of an unusual and horrifying kind. Such descriptions, I suppose, are common enough in time of war. One's enemies are often thought to be—at least they are often said to be—unusual and horrifying.[2] Soldiers are encouraged to fight fiercely if they believe that they are fighting for the survival of their country and their families, that freedom, justice, civilization itself are at risk. But this sort of thing is only sometimes plausible to the detached observer, and one suspects that its propagandistic character is also understood by many of the participants. War is not always a struggle over ultimate values, where the victory of one side would be a human disaster for the other. It is necessary to be skeptical about such matters, to cultivate a wary disbelief of wartime rhetoric, and then to search for some touchstone against which arguments about extremity might be judged. We need to make a map of human crises and to mark off the regions of desperation and disaster. These and only these constitute the realm of necessity, truly understood. Once again, I am going to use the experience of World War II in Europe to suggest at least the rough contours of the map. For Nazism lies at the outer limits of exigency, at a point where we are likely to find ourselves united in fear and abhorrence.

That is what I am going to assume, at any rate, on behalf of all those people who believed at the time and still believe a third of a century later that Nazism was an ultimate threat to everything decent in our lives, an ideology and a practice of domination so murderous, so degrading even to those who might survive, that the consequences of its final victory were literally beyond calculation, immeasurably awful. We see it—and I don't use the phrase lightly—as evil objectified in the world, and in a form so potent and apparent that there could never have been anything to do but fight against it. I obviously cannot offer an account of Nazism in these pages. But such an account is hardly necessary. It is enough to point to the historical experience of Nazi rule. Here was a threat to human values so radical that its imminence would surely constitute a supreme emergency; and this example can help us understand why lesser threats might not do so.

In order to get the map right, however, we must imagine a Nazi-like danger somewhat different from the one the Nazis actually posed. When Churchill said that a German victory in World War II "would be fatal, not only to ourselves, but to the independent life of every small country in

Europe," he was speaking the exact truth. The danger was a general one. But suppose it had existed for Britain alone. Can a supreme emergency be constituted by a particular threat—by a threat of enslavement or extermination directed against a single nation? Can soldiers and statesmen override the rights of innocent people for the sake of their own political community? I am inclined to answer this question affirmatively, though not without hesitation and worry. What choice do they have? They might sacrifice themselves in order to uphold the moral law, but they cannot sacrifice their countrymen. Faced with some ultimate horror, their options exhausted, they will do what they must to save their own people. That is not to say that their decision is inevitable (I have no way of knowing that), but the sense of obligation and of moral urgency they are likely to feel at such a time is so overwhelming that a different outcome is hard to imagine.

Still, the question is difficult, as its domestic analogue suggests. Despite Baldwin, it is not usually said of individuals in domestic society that they necessarily will or that they morally can strike out at innocent people, even in the supreme emergency of self-defense.[3] They can only attack their attackers. But communities, in emergencies, seem to have different and larger prerogatives. I am not sure that I can account for the difference, without ascribing to communal life a kind of transcendence that I don't believe it to have. Perhaps it is only a matter of arithmetic: individuals cannot kill other individuals to save themselves, but to save a nation we can violate the rights of a determinate but smaller number of people. But then large nations and small ones would have different entitlements in such cases, and I doubt very much that this is true. We might better say that it is possible to live in a world where individuals are sometimes murdered, but a world where entire peoples are enslaved or massacred is literally unbearable. For the survival and freedom of political communities—whose members share a way of life, developed by their ancestors, to be passed on to their children—are the highest values of international society. Nazism challenged these values on a grand scale, but challenges more narrowly conceived, *if they are of the same kind*, have similar moral consequences. They bring us under the rule of necessity (and necessity knows no rules).

I want to stress again, however, that the mere recognition of such a threat is not itself coercive; it neither compels nor permits attacks on the innocent, so long as other means of fighting and winning are available. Danger makes only half the argument; imminence makes the other half.

Now let us consider a time when the two halves came together: the terrible two years that followed the defeat of France, from the summer of 1940 to the summer of 1942, when Hitler's armies were everywhere triumphant.

OVERRIDING THE RULES OF WAR

The Decision to Bomb German Cities

There have been few decisions more important than this one in the history of warfare. As a direct result of the adoption of a policy of terror bombing by the leaders of Britain, some 300,000 Germans, most of them civilians, were killed and another 780,000 seriously injured. No doubt, these figures are low when compared to the results of Nazi genocide; but they were, after all, the work of men and women at war with Nazism, who hated everything it stood for and who were not supposed to imitate its effects, even at lagging rates. And the British policy had further consequences: it was the crucial precedent for the fire-bombing of Tokyo and other Japanese cities and then for Harry Truman's decision to drop atomic bombs on Hiroshima and Nagasaki. The civilian death toll from Allied terrorism in World War II must have exceeded half a million men, women, and children. How could the initial choice of this ultimate weapon ever have been defended?

The history is a complex one, and it has already been the subject of several monographic analyses.[4] I can review it only briefly, attending especially to the arguments put forward at the time by Churchill and other British leaders, and always remembering what sort of a time it was. The decision to bomb cities was made late in 1940. A directive issued in June of that year had "specifically laid down that targets had to be identified and aimed at. Indiscriminate bombing was forbidden." In November, after the German raid on Coventry, "Bomber Command was instructed simply to aim at the center of a city." What had once been called indiscriminate bombing (and commonly condemned) was now required, and by early 1942, aiming at military or industrial targets was barred: "the aiming points are to be the built-up areas, not, for instance, the dockyards or aircraft factories."[5] The purpose of the raids was explicitly declared to be the destruction of civilian morale. Following the famous minute of Lord Cherwell in 1942, the means to this demoralization were specified: working-class residential areas were the prime targets. Cherwell thought it possible to render a third of the German population homeless by 1943.[6]

Before Cherwell provided his "scientific" rationale for the bombing, a number of reasons had already been offered for the British decision. From the beginning, the attacks were defended as reprisals for the German blitz. This is a very problematic defense, even if we leave aside the difficulties of the doctrine of reprisals (which I have already canvassed). First of all, it appears possible, as one scholar has recently argued, that Churchill deliberately provoked the German attacks on London—by bombing Berlin—in order to relieve pressure on R.A.F. installations, until then the major *Luftwaffe* target.[7] Nor was it Churchill's purpose, once the blitz began, to deter the German attacks or to establish a policy of mutual restraint.[8]

> We ask no favor of the enemy. We seek from them no compunction. On the contrary, if tonight the people of London were asked to cast their votes whether a convention should be entered into to stop the bombing of all cities, the overwhelming majority would cry, "No, we will mete out to the Germans the measure, and more than the measure, that they have meted out to us."

Needless to say, the people of London were not in fact asked to vote on such a convention. Churchill assumed that the bombing of German cities was necessary to their morale and that they wanted to hear (what he told them in a radio broadcast of 1941) that the British air force was making "the German people taste and gulp each month a sharper dose of the miseries they have showered upon mankind."[9] This argument has been accepted by many historians: there was "a popular clamor" for revenge, one of them writes, which Churchill had to satisfy if he was to maintain a fighting spirit among his own people. It is especially interesting to note, then, that a 1941 opinion poll showed that "the most determined demand for [reprisal raids] came from Cumberland, Westmoreland, and the North Riding of Yorkshire, rural areas barely touched by bombing, where some three-quarters of the population wanted them. In central London, conversely, the proportion was only 45 percent."[10] Men and women who had experienced terror bombing were less likely to support Churchill's policy than those who had not—a heartening statistic, and one which suggests that the morale of the British people (or perhaps better, their conventional morality) allowed for political leadership of a different sort than Churchill provided. The news that Germany was being bombed was certainly glad tidings in Britain; but as late as 1944, according to other opinion surveys, the overwhelming majority of Britishers still believed that the raids were directed solely against military targets. Presumably, that is what they wanted to believe; there was by then quite a bit of evidence to the contrary. But that says something, again, about the character of British morale. (It should also be said that the campaign against terror bombing, run largely by pacifists, attracted very little popular support.)

Reprisal was a bad argument; revenge was a worse one. We must concentrate now on the military justifications for terror bombing, which were presumably paramount in Churchill's mind, whatever he said on the radio. I can discuss these only in a general way. There was a great deal of dispute at the time, some of it technical, some of it moral in character. The calculations of the Cherwell minute, for example, were sharply attacked by a group of scientists whose opposition to terrorism may well have had moral grounds, but whose position, to the best of my knowledge, was never stated in moral terms.[11] Explicit moral disagreement developed most importantly among the professional soldiers involved in the decision-making process. These disagreements are described, in characteristic fashion, by a strategic analyst and historian who has studied the British escalation: "The . . . debate had been beclouded by emotion on one side of the argument, on the part of those who as a matter of moral principle objected to making war on civilians."[12] The focus of these objections seems to have been some version of the doctrine of double effect. (The arguments had, to the mind of the strategic analyst, "a curiously scholastic flavor.") At the height of the blitz, many British officers still felt strongly that their own air attacks should be aimed to minimize civilian casualties. They did not want to imitate Hitler, but to differentiate themselves from him. Even officers who accepted the desirability of killing civilians still sought to maintain their professional honor: such deaths, they insisted, were desirable "only insofar as [they] remained a by-product of the primary intention to hit a military target. . . ."[13] A tendentious argument, no doubt, yet one that would drastically have limited the British offensive against cities. But all such proposals ran up against the operational limits of the bomber technology then available.

Early in the war, it became clear that British bombers could fly effectively only at night and, given the navigational devices with which they were equipped, that they could reasonably aim at no target smaller than a fairly large city. A study made in 1941 indicated that of those planes that actually succeeded in attacking their target (about two-thirds of the attacking force), only one-third dropped their bombs within five miles of the point aimed at.[14] Once this was known, it would seem dishonest to claim that the intended target was, say, this aircraft factory and that the indiscriminate destruction around it was only an unintended, if foreseeable, consequence of the justified attempt to stop the production of planes. What was really unintended but foreseeable was that the factory itself would probably escape harm. If any sort of strategic bombing offensive was to be maintained, one would have to plan for the destruction that one could and did cause. Lord Cherwell's minute was an effort at such planning. In fact, of course, navigational devices were rapidly improved as the war went on, and the bombing of specific military targets was an important part of Britain's total air offensive, receiving top priority at times (before the June 1944 invasion of France, for example) and cutting into the resources allowed for attacks on cities. Today many experts believe that the war might have ended sooner had there been a greater concentration of air power against targets such as the German oil refineries.[15] But the decision to bomb cities was made at a time when victory was not in sight and the specter of defeat ever present. And it was made when no other decision seemed possible if there was to be any sort of military offensive against Nazi Germany.

Bomber Command was the only offensive weapon available to the British in those frightening years, and I expect there is some truth to the notion that it was used simply because it was there. "It was the only force in the West," writes Arthur Harris, chief of Bomber Command from early 1942 until the end of the war, "which could take offensive action . . . against Germany, our only means of getting at the enemy in a way that would hurt at all."[16] Offensive action could have been postponed until (or in hope of) some more favorable time. That is what the war convention would require, and there was also considerable military pressure for postponement. Harris was hard-pressed to keep his Command together in the face of repeated calls for tactical air support—which would have been coordinated with ground action largely defensive in character, since the German armies were still advancing everywhere. Sometimes, in his memoirs, he sounds like a bureaucrat defending his function and his office, but obviously he was also defending a certain conception of how the war might best be fought. He did not believe that the weapons he commanded should be used because he commanded them. He believed that the tactical use of bombers could not stop Hitler and that the destruction of cities could. Later in the war, he argued that only the destruction of cities could bring the fighting to a quick conclusion. The first of these arguments, at least, deserves a careful examination. It was apparently accepted by the Prime Minister. "The bombers alone," Churchill had said as early as September 1940, "provide the means of victory."[17]

The bombers alone—that poses the issue very starkly, and perhaps wrongly, given the disputes over strategy to which I have already referred. Churchill's statement suggested a certainty to which neither he nor anyone else had any right. But the issue can be put so as to accommodate a degree of skepticism and to permit even the most sophisticated among us to indulge in a common and a morally important fantasy: suppose that I sat in the seat of power and had to decide whether to use Bomber Command (in the only way that it could be used systematically and effectively) against cities. Suppose further that unless the bombers were used in this way, the probability that Germany would eventually be defeated would be radically reduced. It makes no sense at this point to quantify the probabilities; I have no clear notion what they actually were or even how they might be calculated given our present knowledge; nor am I sure how different figures, unless they were very different, would affect the moral argument. But it does seem to me that the more certain a German victory appeared to be in the absence of a bomber offensive, the more justifiable was the decision to launch the offensive. It is not just that such a victory was frightening, but also that it seemed in those years very close; it is not just that it was close, but also that it was so frightening. Here was a supreme emergency, where one might well be required to override the rights of innocent people and shatter the war convention.

Given the view of Nazism that I am assuming, the issue takes this form: should I wager this determinate crime (the killing of innocent people) against that immeasurable evil (a Nazi triumph)? Obviously, if there is some other way of avoiding the evil or even a reasonable chance of another way, I must wager differently or elsewhere. But I can never hope to be sure; a wager is not an experiment. Even if I wager and win, it is still possible that I was wrong, that my crime was unnecessary to victory. But I can argue that I studied the case as closely as I was able, took the best advice I could find, sought out available alternatives. And if all this is true, and my perception of evil and imminent danger not hysterical or self-serving, then surely I must wager. There is no option; the risk otherwise is too great. My own action is determinate, of course, only as to its direct consequences, while the rule that bars such acts is founded on a conception of rights that transcends all immediate considerations. It arises out of our common history; it holds the key to our common future. But I dare to say that our history will be nullified and our future condemned unless I accept the burdens of criminality here and now.

This is not an easy argument to make, and yet we must resist every effort to make it easier. Many people undoubtedly found some comfort in the fact that the cities being bombed were German and some of the victims Nazis. In effect, they applied the sliding scale and denied or diminished the rights of German civilians so as to deny or diminish the horror of their deaths. This is a tempting procedure, as we can see most clearly if we consider again the bombing of occupied France. Allied fliers killed many Frenchmen, but they did so while bombing what were (or were thought to be) military targets. They did not deliberately aim at the "built-up areas" of French cities. Suppose such a policy had been proposed. I am sure that we would all find the wager more difficult to undertake and defend if, through some strange combination of circumstances, it required the deliberate slaughter of Frenchmen. For we had special commitments to the French; we were fighting on their behalf (and sometimes the bombers were flown by French pilots). But the status of the civilians in the two cases is no different. The theory that distinguishes combatants from noncombatants does not distinguish Allied from enemy noncombatants, at least not with regard to the question of their murder. I suppose it makes sense to say that there were more people in German than in French cities who were responsible (in some fashion) for the evil of Nazism, and we may well be reluctant to extend to them the full range of civilian rights. But even if that reluctance is justified, there is no way for the bombers to search out the right people. And for all the others, terrorism only reiterates the tyranny that the Nazis had already established. It assimilates ordinary men and women to their government as if the two really made a totality, and it judges them in a totalitarian way. If one is forced to bomb cities, it seems to me, it is best to acknowledge that one has also been forced to kill the innocent.

Once again, however, I want to set radical limits to the notion of necessity even as I have myself been using it. For the truth is that the supreme emergency passed long before the British bombing reached its crescendo.

The greater number by far of the German civilians killed by terror bombing were killed without moral (and probably also without military) reason. The decisive point was made by Churchill in July of 1942:[18]

> In the days when we were fighting alone, we answered the question: "How are you going to win the war?" by saying: "We will shatter Germany by bombing." Since then the enormous injuries inflicted on the German Army and manpower by the Russians, and the accession of the manpower and munitions of the United States, have rendered other possibilities open.

Surely, then, it was time to stop the bombing of cities and to aim, tactically and strategically, only at legitimate military targets. But that was not Churchill's view: "All the same, it would be a mistake to cast aside our original thought . . . that the severe, ruthless bombing of Germany on an ever-increasing scale will not only cripple her war effort . . . but will create conditions intolerable to the mass of the German population." So the raids continued, culminating in the spring of 1945—when the war was virtually won—in a savage attack on the city of Dresden in which something like 100,000 people were killed.[19] Only then did Churchill have second thoughts. "It seems to me that the moment has come when the question of bombing German cities simply for the sake of increasing the terror, though under other pretexts, should be reviewed. . . . The destruction of Dresden remains a serious query against the conduct of Allied bombing."[20] Indeed it does, but so does the destruction of Hamburg and Berlin and all the other cities attacked simply for the sake of terror.

The argument used between 1942 and 1945 in defense of terror bombing was utilitarian in character, its emphasis not on victory itself but on the time and price of victory. The city raids, it was claimed by men such as Harris, would end the war sooner than it would otherwise end and, despite the large number of civilian casualties they inflicted, at a lower cost in human life. Assuming this claim to be true (I have already indicated that precisely opposite claims are made by some historians and strategists), it is nevertheless not sufficient to justify the bombing. It is not sufficient, I think, even if we do nothing more than calculate utilities. For such calculations need not be concerned only with the preservation of life. There is much else that we might plausibly want to preserve: the quality of our lives, for example, our civilization and morality, our collective abhorrence of murder, even when it seems, as it always does, to serve some purpose. Then the deliberate slaughter of innocent men and women cannot be justified simply because it saves the lives of other men and women. I suppose it is possible to imagine situations where that last assertion might prove problematic, from a utilitarian perspective, where the number of people involved is small, the proportions are right, the events hidden from the public eye, and so on. Philosophers delight in inventing such cases in order to test out our moral doctrines. But their inventions are somehow put out of our minds by the sheer scale of the calculations necessary in World War II. To kill 278,966 civilians (the number is made up) in order to avoid the deaths of an unknown but probably larger number of civilians and soldiers is surely a fantastic, godlike, frightening, and horrendous act.*

I have said that such acts can probably be ruled out on utilitarian grounds, but it is also true that utilitarianism as it is commonly understood, indeed, as Sidgwick himself understands it, encourages the bizarre accounting that makes them (morally) possible. We can recognize their horror only when we have acknowledged the personality and value of the men and women we destroy in committing them. It is the acknowledgment of rights that puts a stop to such calculations and forces us to realize that the destruction of the innocent, whatever its purposes, is a kind of blasphemy against our deepest moral commitments. (This is true even in a supreme emergency, when we cannot do anything else.) But I want to look at one more case before concluding my argument—a case where the utilitarian accounting, however bizarre, seemed so radically clear-cut to the decision-makers as to leave them, they thought, no choice but to attack the innocent.

---

*George Orwell has suggested an alternative utilitarian rationale for the bombing of German cities. In a column written for the leftist journal *Tribune* in 1944, he argued that the bombing brought the true character of contemporary combat home to all those people who supported the war, even enjoyed it, only because they never felt its effects. It shattered "the immunity of civilians, one of the things that have made war possible," and so it made war less likely in the future. See *The Collected Essays, Journalism and Letters of George Orwell*, ed. Sonia Orwell and Ian Angus, New York, 1968, Vol. 3, pp. 151–152. Orwell assumes that civilians had really been immune in the past, which is false. In any case, I doubt that his argument would lead anyone to begin bombing cities. It is an apology after the fact, and not a convincing one.

The Limits of Calculation

Hiroshima

"They all accepted the 'assignment' and produced The Bomb," Dwight Macdonald wrote in August 1945 of the atomic scientists. "Why?" It is an important question, but Macdonald poses it badly and then gives the wrong answer. "Because they thought of themselves as specialists, technicians, and not as complete men."[21] In fact, they did not accept the assignment; they sought it out, taking the initiative, urging upon President Roosevelt the critical importance of an American effort to match the work being done in Nazi Germany. And they did this precisely because they were "complete men," many of them European refugees, with an acute sense of what a Nazi victory would mean for their native lands and for all mankind. They were driven by a deep moral anxiety, not (or not most crucially) by any kind of scientific fascination; they were certainly not servile technicians. On the other hand, they were men and women without political power or following, and once their own work was done, they could not control its use. The discovery in November 1944 that German scientists had made little progress ended their own supreme emergency, but it did not end the program they had helped to launch. "If I had known that the Germans would not succeed in constructing the atom bomb," Albert Einstein said, "I would never have lifted a finger."[22] By the time he found that out, however, the scientists had largely finished their work; now indeed technicians were in charge, and the politicians in charge of them. And in the event, the bomb was not used against Germany (or to deter its use by Hitler, which is what men like Einstein had in mind), but against the Japanese, who had never posed such a threat to peace and freedom as the Nazis had.*

Still, it was an important feature of the American decision that the President and his advisors believed the Japanese to be fighting an

---

*In his novel *The New Men*, C. P. Snow describes the discussions among atomic scientists as to whether or not the bomb should be used. Some of them, his narrator says, answered that question with "an absolute no," feeling that if the weapon were used to kill hundreds of thousands of innocent people, "neither science nor the civilization of which science is bone and fibre, would be free from guilt again." But the more common view was the one I have been defending: "Many, probably the majority, gave a conditional no with much the same feeling behind it; but if there were *no other way* of saving the war against Hitler, they would be prepared to drop the bomb." *The New Men*, New York, 1954, p. 177 (Snow's emphasis).

aggressive war and, moreover, to be fighting it unjustly. Thus Truman's address to the American people on August 12, 1945:

> We have used [the bomb] against those who attacked us without warning at Pearl Harbor, against those who have starved and beaten and executed American prisoners of war, against those who have abandoned all pretense of obeying international laws of warfare. We have used it in order to shorten the agony of war . . .

Here again, the sliding scale is being used to open the way for utilitarian calculations. The Japanese have forfeited (some of) their rights, and so they cannot complain about Hiroshima so long as the destruction of the city actually does, or could reasonably be expected to, shorten the agony of war. But had the Japanese exploded an atomic bomb over an American city, killing tens of thousands of civilians and thereby shortening the agony of war, the action would clearly have been a crime, one more for Truman's list. This distinction is only plausible, however, if one renders a judgment not only against the leaders of Japan but also against the ordinary people of Hiroshima and insists at the same time that no similar judgment is possible against the people of San Francisco, say, or Denver. I can find, as I have said before, no way of defending such a procedure. How did the people of Hiroshima forfeit their rights? Perhaps their taxes paid for some of the ships and planes used in the attack on Pearl Harbor; perhaps they sent their sons into the navy and air force with prayers for their success; perhaps they celebrated the actual event, after being told that their country had won a great victory in the face of an imminent American threat. Surely there is nothing here that makes these people liable to direct attack. (It is worth noting, though the fact is not relevant in judging the Hiroshima decision, that the raid on Pearl Harbor was directed entirely against naval and army installations: only a few stray bombs fell on the city of Honolulu.)[23]

But if Truman's argument on August 12 was weak, there was a worse one underlying it. He did not intend to apply the sliding scale with any precision, for he seems to have believed that, given Japanese aggression, the Americans could do anything at all to win (and shorten the agony of war). Along with most of his advisors, he accepted the "war is hell" doctrine; it is a constant allusion in defenses of the Hiroshima decision. Thus Henry Stimson:[24]

As I look back over the five years of my service as Secretary of War, I see too many stern and heartrending decisions to be willing to pretend that war is anything else but what it is. The face of war is the face of death; death is an inevitable part of every order that a wartime leader gives.

And James Byrnes, Truman's friend and his Secretary of State:[25]

... war remains what General Sherman said it was.

And Arthur Compton, chief scientific advisor to the government:[26]

When one thinks of the mounted archers of Ghengiz Khan ... the Thirty Years War ... the millions of Chinese who died during the Japanese invasion ... the mass destruction of western Russia ... one realizes that in whatever manner it is fought, war is precisely what General Sherman called it.

And Truman himself:[27]

Let us not become so preoccupied with weapons that we lose sight of the fact that war itself is the real villain.

War itself is to blame, but also the men who begin it ... while those who fight justly merely participate in the hell of war, choicelessly, and there are no moral decisions for which they can be called to account. This is not, or not necessarily, an immoral doctrine, but it is radically one-sided; it evades the tension between *jus ad bellum* and *jus in bello*; it undercuts the need for hard judgments; it relaxes our sense of moral restraint. When he was choosing a target for the first bomb, Truman reports, he asked Stimson which Japanese cities were "devoted exclusively to war production."[28] The question was reflexive; Truman did not want to violate the "laws of war." But it wasn't serious. Which American cities were devoted exclusively to war production? It is possible to ask such questions only when the answer doesn't matter. If war is hell however it is fought, then what difference can it make how we fight it? And if war itself is the villain, then what risks do we run (aside from the strategic risks) when we make decisions? The Japanese, who began the war, can also end it; only they can end it, and all we can do is fight it, enduring what Truman called "the daily tragedy of bitter war." I don't doubt that that was really Truman's view; it was not a matter of convenience but of conviction. But it is a distorted view. It mistakes the actual hellishness of war, which is particular in character and open to precise definition, for the limitless pains of religious mythology. The pains of war are limitless only if we make them so—only if we move, as Truman did, beyond the limits that we and others have established. Sometimes, I think, we have to do that, but not all the time. Now we must ask whether it was necessary to do it in 1945.

The only possible defense of the Hiroshima attack is a utilitarian calculation made without the sliding scale, a calculation made, then, where there was no room for it, a claim to override the rules of war and the rights of Japanese civilians. I want to state this argument as strongly as I can. In 1945, American policy was fixed on the demand for the unconditional surrender of Japan. The Japanese had by that time lost the war, but they were by no means ready to accept this demand. The leaders of their armed forces expected an invasion of the Japanese main islands and were preparing for a last-ditch resistance. They had over two million soldiers available for the fighting, and they believed that they could make the invasion so costly that the Americans would agree to a negotiated peace. Truman's military advisors also believed that the costs would be high, though the public record does not show that they ever recommended negotiations. They thought that the war might continue late into 1946 and that there would be as many as a million additional American casualties. Japanese losses would be much higher. The capture of Okinawa in a battle lasting from April to June of 1945 had cost almost 80,000 American casualties, while virtually the entire Japanese garrison of 120,000 men had been killed (only 10,600 prisoners were taken).[29] If the main islands were defended with a similar ferocity, hundreds of thousands, perhaps millions, of Japanese soldiers would die. Meanwhile, the fighting would continue in China and in Manchuria, where a Russian attack was soon due. And the bombing of Japan would also continue, and perhaps intensify, with casualty rates no different from those anticipated from the atomic attack. For the Americans had adopted in Japan the British policy of terrorism: a massive incendiary raid on Tokyo early in March 1945 had set off a firestorm and killed an estimated 100,000 people. Against all this was set, in the minds of American decision-makers, the impact of the atomic bomb—not materially more damaging but psychologically more frightening, and holding out the promise, perhaps, of a quick end to the war. "To

avert a vast, indefinite butchery . . . at the cost of a few explosions," wrote
Churchill in support of Truman's decision, "seemed, after all our toils and
perils, a miracle of deliverance."[30]

"A vast indefinite butchery" involving quite probably the deaths of
several million people: surely this is a great evil, and if it was imminent,
one could reasonably argue that extreme measures might be warranted
to avert it. Secretary of War Stimson thought it was the sort of case I have
already described, where one had to wager; there was no option. "No man,
in our position and subject to our responsibilities, holding in his hand a
weapon of such possibilities for . . . saving those lives, could have failed
to use it."[31] This is by no means an incomprehensible or, on the surface
at least, an outrageous argument. But it is not the same as the argument
I suggested in the case of Britain in 1940. It does not have the form: if we
don't do *x* (bomb cities), they will do *y* (win the war, establish tyrannical
rule, slaughter their opponents). What Stimson argued is very different.
Given the actual policy of the U.S. government, it amounts to this: if we
don't do *x*, *we* will do *y*. The two atomic bombs caused "many casualties,"
James Byrnes admitted, "but not nearly so many as there would have been
had our air force continued to drop incendiary bombs on Japan's cities."[32]
Our purpose, then, was not to avert a "butchery" that someone else was
threatening, but one that we were threatening, and had already begun to
carry out. Now, what great evil, what supreme emergency, justified the
incendiary attacks on Japanese cities?

Even if we had been fighting in strict accordance with the war convention, the continuation of the struggle was not something forced upon us. It
had to do with our war aims. The military estimate of casualties was based
not only on the belief that the Japanese would fight almost to the last man,
but also on the assumption that the Americans would accept nothing less
than unconditional surrender. The war aims of the American government
required either an invasion of the main islands, with enormous losses of
American and Japanese soldiers and of Japanese civilians trapped in the
war zones, or the use of the atomic bomb. Given that choice, one might
well reconsider those aims. Even if we assume that unconditional surrender was morally desirable because of the character of Japanese militarism,
it might still be morally undesirable because of the human costs it entailed.
But I would suggest a stronger argument than this. The Japanese case
is sufficiently different from the German so that unconditional surrender should never have been asked. Japan's rulers were engaged in a more

ordinary sort of military expansion, and all that was morally required was that they be defeated, not that they be conquered and totally overthrown. Some restraint upon their war-making power might be justified, but their domestic authority was a matter of concern only to the Japanese people. In any case, if killing millions (or many thousands) of men and women was militarily necessary for their conquest and overthrow, then it was morally necessary—in order not to kill those people—to settle for something less. I have made this argument before (in chapter 7); here is a further example of its practical application. If people have a right not to be forced to fight, they also have a right not to be forced to continue fighting beyond the point when the war might justly be concluded. Beyond that point, there can be no supreme emergencies, no arguments about military necessity, no cost-accounting in human lives. To press the war further than that is to re-commit the crime of aggression. In the summer of 1945, the victorious Americans owed the Japanese people an experiment in negotiation. To use the atomic bomb, to kill and terrorize civilians, without even attempting such an experiment, was a double crime.[33]

These, then, are the limits of the realm of necessity. Utilitarian calculation can force us to violate the rules of war only when we are face-to-face not merely with defeat but with a defeat likely to bring disaster to a political community. But these calculations have no similar effects when what is at stake is only the speed or the scope of victory. They are relevant only to the conflict between winning and fighting well, not to the internal problems of combat itself. Whenever that conflict is absent, calculation is stopped short by the rules of war and the rights they are designed to protect. Confronted by those rights, we are not to calculate consequences, or figure relative risks, or compute probable casualties, but simply to stop short and turn aside.

17

NUCLEAR DETERRENCE

THE PROBLEM OF IMMORAL THREATS

Truman used the atomic bomb to end a war that seemed to him limitless in its horrors. And then, for a few minutes or hours in August 1945, the people of Hiroshima endured a war that actually was limitless in its horrors. "In this last great action of the Second War War," wrote Stimson, "we were given final proof that war is death."[1] *Final proof* is exactly the wrong phrase, for war had never been like that before. A new kind of war was born at Hiroshima, and what we were given was a first glimpse of its deadliness. Though fewer people were killed than in the fire-bombing of Tokyo, they were killed with monstrous ease. One plane, one bomb: with such a weapon the 350 planes that raided Tokyo would virtually have wiped out human life on the Japanese islands. Atomic war was death indeed, indiscriminate and total, and after Hiroshima, the first task of political leaders everywhere was to prevent its recurrence.

The means they adopted is the promise of reprisal in kind. Against the threat of an immoral attack, they have put the threat of an immoral response. This is the basic form of nuclear deterrence. In international as in domestic society, deterrence works by calling up dramatic images of human pain. "In the groves of *their* academy," wrote Edmund Burke of the liberal theorists of crime and punishment, "at the end of every vista, you see nothing but the gallows."[2] The description is uncomplimentary, for Burke believed that domestic peace must rest upon some other foundation. But there is this much to be said for the gallows: in principle, at least, only guilty men need fear the death it brings. About the theorists of deterrence, however, it must be said, "In the groves of *their* academy, at the end of every vista, you see nothing but the mushroom cloud"—and the cloud symbolizes indiscriminate slaughter, the killing of the innocent (as in Hiroshima) on a massive scale. No doubt, the threat of such slaughter, if it is believed, makes nuclear attack a radically undesirable policy. Doubled by a potential enemy, the threat produces a "balance of terror." Both sides are so terrified that no further terrorism is necessary. But is the threat itself morally permissible?

The question is a difficult one. It has generated in the years since Hiroshima a significant body of literature exploring the relation between nuclear deterrence and just war.[3] This has been the work mostly of theologians and philosophers, but some of the strategists of deterrence have also been involved; they worry about the act of terrorizing much as conventional soldiers worry about the act of killing. I cannot review this literature here, though I shall draw upon it freely. The argument against deterrence is familiar enough. Anyone committed to the distinction between combatants and noncombatants is bound to be appalled by the specter of destruction evoked, and purposely evoked, in deterrence theory. "How can a nation live with its conscience," John Bennett has asked, "and know that it is preparing to kill twenty million children in another nation if the worst should come to the worst?"[4] And yet, we have lived with that knowledge, and with our consciences too, for several decades now. How have we managed? The reason for our acceptance of deterrent strategy, most people would say, is that preparing to kill, even threatening to kill, is not at all the same thing as killing. Indeed it is not, but it is frighteningly close—else deterrence wouldn't "work"—and it is in the nature of that closeness that the moral problem lies.

The problem is often misdescribed—as in the following analogy for nuclear deterrence first suggested by Paul Ramsey and frequently repeated since:[5]

> Suppose that one Labor Day weekend no one was killed or maimed on the highways; and that the reason for the remarkable restraint placed on the recklessness of automobile drivers was that suddenly everyone of them discovered he was driving with a baby tied to his

front bumper! That would be no way to regulate traffic *even if it succeeds* in regulating it perfectly, since such a system makes innocent human lives the *direct object* of attack and uses them as a mere means for restraining the drivers of automobiles.

No one, of course, has ever proposed regulating traffic in this ingenious way, while the strategy of deterrence was adopted with virtually no opposition at all. That contrast should alert us to what is wrong with Ramsey's analogy. Though deterrence turns American and Russian civilians into mere means for the prevention of war, it does so without restraining any of us in any way. Ramsey reproduces the strategy of the German officers during the Franco-Prussian War who forced civilians to ride on military trains in order to deter saboteurs. By contrast with those civilians, however, we are hostages who lead normal lives. It is in the nature of the new technology that we can be threatened without being held captive. That is why deterrence, while in principle so frightening, is so easy to live with. It cannot be condemned for anything it does to its hostages. It is so far from killing them that it does not even injure or confine them; it involves no direct or physical violation of their rights. Those critics of deterrence who are also committed consequentialists have had to imagine psychic injuries. Thus Eric Fromm, writing in 1960: "To live for any length of time under the constant threat of destruction creates certain psychological effects in most human beings—fright, hostility, callousness . . . and a resulting indifference to all the values we cherish. Such conditions will transform us into barbarians. . . ."[6] But I don't know of any evidence that bears out either the assertion or the prediction; surely we are no more barbarians now than we were in 1945. In fact, for most people, the threat of destruction, though constant, is invisible and unnoticed. We have come to live with it casually—as Ramsey's babies, traumatized for life in all probability, could never do, and as hostages in conventional wars have never done.

If deterrence were more painful, we might have found other means of avoiding nuclear war—or we might not have avoided it. If we had to keep millions of people under restraint in order to maintain the balance of terror, or if we had to kill millions of people (periodically) in order to convince our adversaries of our credibility, deterrence would not be accepted for long.[7] The strategy works because it is easy. Indeed, it is easy in a double sense: not only don't we do anything to other people, we also don't believe that we will ever have to do anything. The secret of nuclear deterrence is that it is a kind of bluff. Perhaps we are only bluffing ourselves, refusing to acknowledge the real terrors of a precarious and temporary balance. But no account of our experience is accurate which fails to recognize that, for all its ghastly potential, deterrence has so far been a bloodless strategy.

So far as consequences go, then, deterrence and mass murder are very far apart. Their closeness is a matter of moral posture and intention. Once again, Ramsey's analogy misses the point. His babies are not really the "direct object of attack," for whatever happens on that Labor Day weekend, no one will deliberately set out to kill them. But deterrence depends upon a readiness to do exactly that. It is as if the state should seek to prevent murder by threatening to kill the family and friends of every murderer—a domestic version of the policy of "massive retaliation." Surely that would be a repugnant policy. We would not admire the police officials who designed it or those pledged to carry it out, even if they never actually killed anybody. I don't want to say that such people would necessarily be transformed into barbarians; they might well have a heightened sense of how awful murder is and a heightened desire to avoid it; they might loathe the work they were pledged to do and fervently hope that they never had to do it. Nevertheless, the enterprise is immoral. The immorality lies in the threat itself, not in its present or even its likely consequences. Similarly with nuclear deterrence: it is our own intentions that we have to worry about and the potential (since there are no actual) victims of those intensions. Here Ramsey has put the case very well: "Whatever is wrong to do is wrong to threaten, if the latter means 'mean to do.' . . . If counter-population warfare is murder, then counter-population deterrent threats are murderous."[8] No doubt, killing millions of innocent people is worse than threatening to kill them. It is also true that no one wants to kill them, and it may well be true that no one expects to do so. Nevertheless, we intend the killings under certain circumstances. That is the stated policy of our government; and thousands of men, trained in the techniques of mass destruction and drilled in instant obedience, stand ready to carry it out. And from the perspective of morality, the readiness is all. We can translate it into degrees of danger, high and low, and worry about the risks we are imposing on innocent people, but the risks depend on the readiness. What we condemn in our own government, as in the police in my domestic analogy, is the commitment to murder.*

But this analogy, too, can be questioned. We don't prevent murder any more than we control traffic in these bizarre and inhuman ways. But we do deter or seek to deter our nuclear adversaries. Perhaps deterrence is different because of the danger its advocates claim to avoid. Traffic deaths and occasional murders, however much we deplore them, do not threaten our common liberties or our collective survival. Deterrence, so we have been told, guards us against a double danger: first, of atomic blackmail and foreign domination; and second, of nuclear destruction. The two go together, since if we did not fear the blackmail, we might adopt a policy of appeasement or surrender and so avoid the destruction. Deterrence theory was worked out at the height of the cold war between the United States and the Soviet Union, and those who worked it out were concerned above all with the political uses of violence—which are not relevant in either the traffic or police analogies. Underlying the American doctrine, there seemed to lurk some version of the slogan "Better dead than Red" (I don't know the Russian parallel). Now that is not really a believable slogan; it is hard to imagine that a nuclear holocaust was really thought preferable to the expansion of Soviet power. What made deterrence attractive was that it seemed capable of avoiding both.

We need not dwell on the nature of the Soviet regime in order to understand the virtues of this argument. Deterrence theory doesn't depend upon a view of Stalinism as a great evil (though that is a highly plausible view) in the same way that my argument about terror bombing depended upon an assertion about the evils of Nazism. It requires only that we see appeasement or surrender to involve a loss of values central

---

* Would it make any difference if this commitment were mechanically fixed? Suppose we set up a computer which would automatically respond to any enemy attack by releasing our missiles. Then we informed our potential enemies that if they attacked our cities, theirs would be attacked. And they would be responsible for both attacks, we might say, since in the interval between the two, no political decision, no act of the will, would be possible on our side. I don't want to comment on the possible effectiveness (or the dangers) of such an arrangement. But it is worth insisting that it would not solve the moral problem. The men and women who designed the computer program or the political leaders who ordered them to do so would be responsible for the second attack, for they would have planned it and organized it and intended that it should occur (under certain conditions).

to our existence as an independent nation-state. For it is not tolerable that advances in technology should put our nation, or any nation, at the mercy of a great power willing to menace the world or to press its authority outwards in the shadow of an implicit threat. The case here is very different from that which arises commonly in war, where *our* adherence to the war convention puts us, or would put us, at a disadvantage vis-à-vis *them*. For disadvantages of that sort are partial and relative; various countermeasures and compensating steps are always available. But in the nuclear case, the disadvantage is absolute. Against an enemy actually willing to use the bomb, self-defense is impossible, and it makes sense to say that the only compensating step is the (immoral) threat to respond in kind. No country capable of making such a threat is likely to refuse to make it. What is not tolerable won't be tolerated. Hence any state confronted by a nuclear adversary (it makes little difference what the adversary relationship is like or what ideological forms it assumes), and capable of developing its own bomb, is likely to do so, seeking safety in a balance of terror.* Mutual disarmament would clearly be a preferable alternative, but it is an alternative available only to the two countries working closely together, whereas deterrence is the likely choice of either one of them alone. They will worry about one another's readiness to attack; they will each assume their own commitment to resist; and they will realize that the greatest danger of such a confrontation would not be the defeat of one side or the other but the total destruction of both—and possibly of everyone else too. This in fact is the danger that has faced mankind since 1945, and our understanding of nuclear deterrence must be worked out with reference to its scope and imminence. Supreme emergency has become a permanent condition. Deterrence is a way of coping with that condition, and though it is a bad way, there may well be no other that is practical in a world of sovereign and suspicious states. We threaten evil in order not to do it, and the doing of it would be so terrible that the threat seems in comparison to be morally defensible.

---

*This is obviously the grim logic of nuclear proliferation. So far as the moral question goes, each new balance of terror created by proliferation is exactly like the first one, justified (or not) in the same way. But the creation of regional balances may well have general effects upon the stability of the great power equilibrium, thereby introducing new moral considerations that I cannot take up here.

LIMITED NUCLEAR WAR

If the bomb were ever used, deterrence would have failed. It is a feature of massive retaliation that while there is or may be some rational purpose in threatening it, there could be none in carrying it out. Were our "bluff" ever to be called and our population centers suddenly attacked, the resulting war could not (in any usual sense of the word) be *won*. We could only drag our enemies after us into the abyss. The use of our deterrent capacity would be an act of pure destructiveness. For this reason, massive retaliation, if not literally unthinkable, has always seemed undo-able, and this is a source of considerable anxiety for military strategists. Deterrence only works, they argue, if each side believes that the other might actually carry out its threat. But would we carry it out? George Kennan has recently given what must be the moral response:[9]

> Let us suppose there were to be a nuclear attack of some sort on this country and millions of people were killed and injured. Let us further suppose that we had the ability to retaliate against the urban centers of the country that had attacked us. Would you want to do that? I wouldn't . . . I have no sympathy with the man who demands an eye for an eye in a nuclear attack.

A humane position—though one that should probably be whispered, rather than published, if the balance of terror is to be sustained. But the argument might look very different if the original attack or the planned response avoided cities and people. If a limited nuclear war were possible, wouldn't it also be do-able? And might not the balance of terror then be re-established on the basis of threats that were neither immoral nor unconvincing?

Over a brief timespan, in the late 1950s and the early 1960s, these questions were answered with an extraordinary outpouring of strategic arguments and speculations, overlapping in important ways with the moralizing literature I described earlier.[10] For the debate among the strategists focused on the attempt (though this was rarely made explicit) to fit nuclear war into the structure of the war convention, to apply the argument for justice as if this sort of conflict were like any other sort. The attempt involved, first, a defense of the use of tactical nuclear weapons in deterring and, if that failed, in resisting conventional or small-scale nuclear attacks; and it involved, secondly, the development of a "counter-force" strategy directed at the enemy's military installations and also at major economic targets (but not at entire cities). These two had a similar purpose. By holding out the promise of a limited nuclear war, they made it possible to imagine actually fighting such a war—they made it possible to imagine *winning* it—and so they strengthened the intention that lay behind the deterrent threat. They transformed the "bluff" into a plausible option.

Until the late 1950s, the tendency of most people was to regard the atomic bomb and its thermonuclear successors as forbidden weapons. They were treated on analogy with poison gas, though the prohibition on their use was never legally established. "Ban the bomb" was everyone's policy, and deterrence was simply a practical way of enforcing the ban. But now the strategists suggested (rightly) that the crucial distinction in the theory and practice of war was not between prohibited and acceptable weapons but between prohibited and acceptable targets. Massive retaliation was painful and difficult to contemplate because it was modeled on Hiroshima; the people we were planning to kill were innocent, militarily uninvolved, as removed from and ignorant of the weapons with which their leaders threatened us as we were of the weapons with which our leaders threatened them. But this objection would disappear if we could deter our adversaries by threatening a limited and morally acceptable destruction. Indeed, it might disappear so entirely that we would be tempted to give up deterrence and initiate the destruction ourselves whenever it seemed to our advantage to do so. This was certainly the tendency of much strategic argument, and several writers painted rather attractive pictures of limited nuclear war. Henry Kissinger likened it to war at sea—the very best kind of war, since no one lives in the sea. "The proper analogy . . . is not traditional land warfare, but naval strategy, in which self-contained, [highly mobile] units with great fire power gradually gain the upper hand by destroying their enemy counterparts without physically occupying territory or establishing a front line."[11] The only difficulty is that Kissinger imagined fighting a war like that in Europe.*

---

* Kissinger later moved away from these views, and they have pretty much dropped out of the strategic debates. But this picture of limited nuclear war is worked out in graphic detail in a novel by Joe Haldeman (*The Forever War*, New York, 1974), where the fighting goes on not at sea but in outer space. Many of the strategic speculations of the 1950s and 1960s have ended up as science fiction. Does this mean that the strategists had too much imagination or that the authors of science fiction have too little?

Tactical and counter-force warfare meets the formal requirements of *jus in bello*, and it was seized upon eagerly by certain moral theorists. That is not to say, however, that it makes moral sense. There remains the possibility that the new technology of war simply doesn't fit and cannot be made to fit within the old limits. This proposition can be defended in two different ways. The first is to argue that the collateral damage likely to be caused even by a "legitimate" use of nuclear weapons is so great that it would violate both of the proportionality limits fixed by the theory of war: the number of people killed in the war as a whole would not be warranted by the goals of the war—particularly since the dead would include many if not most of the people for whose defense the war was being fought; and the number of people killed in individual actions would be disproportionate (under the doctrine of double effect) to the value of the military targets directly attacked. "The disproportion between the cost of such hostilities and the results they could achieve," wrote Raymond Aron, thinking of a limited nuclear war in Europe, "would be colossal."[12] It would be colossal even if the formal limits on targeting were in fact observed. But the second argument against limited nuclear war is that these limits would almost certainly not be observed.

At this point, of course, one can only guess at the possible shape and course of the battles; there is no history to study. Neither moralists nor strategists can refer to cases; instead they design scenarios. The scene is empty; one can fill it in very different ways, and it is not impossible to imagine that limits might be maintained even after nuclear weapons had been used in battle. The prospect that they would be maintained and the war extended over time is so frightening to those countries on whose soil such wars are likely to be fought that they have generally opposed the new strategies and insisted upon the threat of massive retaliation. Thus, as André Beaufre has written, "Europeans would prefer to risk general war in an attempt to avoid war altogether rather than have Europe become the theater of operations for limited war."[13] In fact, however, the risks of escalation will be great whatever limits are adopted, simply because of the immense destructive power of the weapons involved. Or rather, there are two possibilities: either nuclear weapons will be held at such low levels that they won't be significantly different from or of greater military utility than conventional explosives, in which case there is no reason to use them at all; or their very use will obliterate the distinction between targets. Once a bomb has been aimed at a military target but has, as a side effect, destroyed a city, the logic of deterrence will require the other side to aim at a city (for the sake of its seriousness and credibility). It is not necessarily the case that every war would become a total war, but the danger of escalation is so great as to preclude the first use of nuclear weapons—except by someone willing to face their final use. "Who would even launch such hostilities," Aron has asked, "unless he was determined to persist to the bitter end?"[14] But such a determination is not imaginable in a sane human being, let alone in a political leader responsible for the safety of his own people; it would involve nothing less than national suicide.

These two factors, the extent even of limited destruction and the dangers of escalation, seem to rule out any sort of nuclear war between the great powers. They probably rule out large-scale conventional war, too, including the particular conventional war about which the strategists of the 1950s and 1960s were most concerned: a Russian invasion of western Europe. "The spectacle of a large Soviet field army crashing across the line into western Europe in the hope *and expectation* that nuclear weapons would not be used against it—thereby putting itself and the USSR totally at risk while leaving the choice of weapons to us—would seem to be hardly worth a second thought. . . ."[15] It is important to stress that the bar lies in the totality of the risk: not in the possibility of what the strategists called a "flexible response," finely adjusted to the scope of the attack, but in the stark reality of ultimate horror should the adjustments fail. It may well be that "flexible response" enhanced the value of a counter-population deterrent by making it possible to reach that final point in "easy" stages, but it is also and more importantly true that we have never begun the staged escalation and are never likely to begin it, because of what lies at the end. Hence the persistence of counter-population deterrence, and hence also the virtual end of the strategic debate, which petered out in the middle 1960s. At that point, I think, it became clear that given the existence of large numbers of nuclear weapons and their relative invulnerability, and barring major technological breakthroughs, *any imaginable strategy* is likely to deter a "central war" between the great powers. The strategists helped us to understand this, but once it was understood it became unnecessary to adopt any of their strategies—or at least, any particular one of them. We continue to live, then, with the paradox that pre-existed the debate: nuclear weapons are politically and militarily unusable only because and insofar as we can plausibly threaten to use them in some ultimate way. And it is immoral to make threats of that kind.

The Argument of Paul Ramsey

Before deciding (or refusing) to live with this paradox, I want to consider in some detail the work of the Protestant theologian Paul Ramsey, who has over a period of years argued that there exists a justifiable deterrent strategy. From the beginning of the moral and strategic debates, Ramsey has been a sharp opponent of the advocates of counter-city deterrence and also of those of its critics who think that it is the only form of deterrence and therefore opt for nuclear disarmament. He has condemned both these groups for the all-or-nothing character of their thinking: either total and immoral destruction or a kind of "pacifistic" inertia. He argues that these twin perspectives conform to the traditional American view of war as an all-out conflict, which must therefore be avoided whenever possible. Ramsey himself, I think, is a Protestant soldier in a different tradition; he would have Americans gird themselves for a long, continuous struggle with the forces of evil.[16]

Now if there is to be a justified deterrent strategy, there must be a justified form of nuclear war, and Ramsey has conscientiously argued "the case for making just war possible" in the modern age. He takes a lively and well-informed interest in the strategic debates and has at various times defended the use of tactical nuclear weapons against invading armies and of strategic weapons against nuclear installations, conventional military bases, and isolated economic objectives. Even these targets are only "conditionally" permissible, since the proportionality rule would have to be applied in each case, and Ramsey does not believe that its standards will always be met. Like everyone (or almost everyone) who writes about these matters, he has no zest for nuclear combat; his main interest is in deterrence. But he needs at least the possibility of legitimate warfare if he is to maintain a deterrent posture without making immoral threats. That is his central purpose, and the effort to achieve it involves him in a highly sophisticated application of just war theory to the problems of nuclear strategy. In the best sense of the word, Ramsey is engaged with the realities of his world. But the realities in this case are intractable, and his way around them is finally too complex and too devious to provide a plausible account of our moral judgments. He multiplies distinctions like a Ptolemaic astronomer with his epicycles and comes very close at the end to what G. E. M. Anscombe has called "double-think about double effect."[17]

But his work is important; it suggests the outer limits of the just war and the dangers of trying to extend those limits.

Ramsey's central claim is that it is possible to prevent nuclear attack without threatening to bomb cities in response. He believes that "the collateral civilian damage that would result from counter-force warfare in its maximum form" would be sufficient to deter potential aggressors.[18] Since the civilians likely to die in such a war would be the incidental victims of legitimate military strikes, the threat of counter-force warfare plus collateral damage is also morally superior to deterrence in its present form. These are not hostages whom we intend to murder (under certain circumstances). Nor are we planning their deaths; we are only pointing out to our possible enemies the unavoidable consequences even of a war justly fought—which is, we could honestly say were we to adopt Ramsey's proposal, the only sort of war we were preparing to fight. Collateral damage is simply a fortunate feature of nuclear warfare; it serves no military purpose, and we would avoid it if we could, though it is clearly a good thing that we cannot. And since the damage is justifiable in prospect, it is also justifiable here and now to call that prospect to mind for the sake of its deterrent effects.

But there are two problems with this argument. First, the danger of collateral damage is unlikely to work as a deterrent unless the damage expected is radically disproportionate to the ends of the war or the value of this or that military target. Hence Ramsey is driven to argue that "the threat of something disproportionate is not always a disproportionate threat."[19] What that means is this: proportionality in combat is measured, let's say, against the value of a particular missile base, while proportionality in deterrence is measured against the value of world peace. So the damage may not be justifiable in prospect (under the doctrine of double effect), and yet the threat of such damage may still be morally permitted. Perhaps that argument is right, but I should stress that its result is to void the proportionality rule. Now there is no limit on the number of people whose deaths we can threaten, so long as those deaths are to be caused "collaterally" and not by taking direct aim. As we have seen before, the idea of proportionality, once it is worked on a bit, tends to fade away. And then the entire burden of Ramsey's argument falls on the idea of death by indirection. That is indeed an important idea, central to the permissions and restraints of conventional war. But its standing is undermined here by the fact that Ramsey relies so heavily on the deaths he supposedly doesn't intend. He wants, like other deterrent theorists, to prevent nuclear attack by threatening to kill very large numbers of innocent civilians, but unlike other deterrent theorists, he expects to kill these people without aiming at them. That may be a matter of some moral significance, but it does not seem significant enough to serve as the cornerstone of a justified deterrent. If counter-force warfare had no collateral effects, or had minor and controllable effects, then it could play no part in Ramsey's strategy. Given the effects it does have and the central part it is assigned, the word "collateral" seems to have lost much of its meaning. Surely anyone designing such a strategy must accept moral responsibility for the effects on which he is so radically dependent.

But we have not yet seen the whole of Ramsey's design, for he doesn't pull back from the hardest questions. What if the likely collateral damage of a just nuclear war isn't great enough to deter a would-be aggressor? What if the aggressor threatens a counter-city strike? Surrender would be intolerable, and yet we cannot ourselves threaten mass murder in response. Fortunately (again), we don't have to. "We do not need . . . to threaten that we will use [nuclear weapons] in case of attack," Bernard Brodie has written. "We do not need to threaten anything. Their being there is quite enough."[20] So it is, too, according to Ramsey, with counter-city strikes: the mere possession of nuclear weapons constitutes an implicit threat which no one actually has to make. If the immorality lies in uttering the threat, then it may in practice be avoided—though one may wonder at the ease of this solution. Nuclear weapons, Ramsey writes, have a certain inherent ambiguity: "they may be used either against strategic forces or against centers of population," and that means that "*apart from intention*, their capacity to deter cannot be removed from them. . . . No matter how often we declare, and quite sincerely declare, that our targets are an enemy's forces, he can never be quite *certain* that in the fury or the fog of war his cities may not be destroyed."[21] Now, the possession of conventional weapons is both innocent and ambiguous in exactly the way Ramsey suggests. The fact that I am holding a sword or a rifle doesn't mean that I am going to use it against innocent people, though it is quite effective against them; it has the same "dual use" that Ramsey has discovered in nuclear weapons. But the bomb is different. In a sense, as Beaufre has said, it isn't designed for war at all.[22] It is designed to kill whole populations, and its deterrent value depends upon that fact (whether the killing is direct or indirect). It serves the purpose of preventing war only by virtue of the implicit threat it poses, and we possess it for the sake of that purpose. And men and women are responsible for the threats they live by, even if they don't speak them out loud.

Ramsey presses on. Perhaps the mere possession of nuclear weapons won't be enough to deter some reckless aggressor. Then, he suggests, we must distinguish "between the appearance and the actuality of being . . . committed to go to city exchanges. . . . In that case, only the appearance should be cultivated."[23] I am not sure exactly what that means, and Ramsey (for once) seems reluctant to say, but presumably it would allow us to hint at the possibility of massive retaliation without actually planning for it or intending to carry it out. Thus we are offered a continuum of increasing moral danger along which four points are marked out: the articulated prospect of collateral (and disproportionate) civilian deaths; the implicit threat of counter-city strikes; the "cultivated" appearance of a commitment to counter-city strikes; and the actual commitment. These may well be distinct points, in the sense that one can imagine policies focused around each of them, and these would be different policies. But I am inclined to doubt that the differences make a difference. To rule out the last for moral reasons, while permitting the first three, can only make people cynical about one's moral reasons. Ramsey aims to clear our intentions without prohibiting those policies that he believes necessary (and that probably are necessary under present conditions) for the dual prevention of war and conquest. But the unavoidable truth is that all these policies rest ultimately on immoral threats. Unless we give up nuclear deterrence, we cannot give up such threats, and it is best if we straightforwardly acknowledge what it is we are doing.

The real ambiguity of nuclear deterrence lies in the fact that no one, including ourselves, can be sure that we will ever carry out the threats we make. In a sense, all we ever do is "cultivate the appearance." We strain for credibility, but what we are putatively planning and intending remains incredible. As I have already suggested, that helps make deterrence psychologically bearable, and perhaps also it makes a deterrent posture marginally better from a moral standpoint. But at the same time, the reason for our hesitancy and self-doubt is the monstrous immorality that our policy contemplates, an immorality we can never hope to square with our understanding of justice in war. Nuclear weapons explode the theory of just war. They are the first of mankind's technological innovations that are simply not encompassable within the familiar moral world. Or rather, our familiar notions about *jus in bello* require us to condemn even the threat to use them. And yet there are other notions, also familiar, having to do with aggression and the right of self-defense, that seem to require exactly that threat. So we move uneasily beyond the limits of justice for the sake of justice (and of peace).

According to Ramsey, this is a dangerous move. For if we "become convinced," he writes, "that in the matter of deterrence a number of things are wicked which are not," then, seeing no way of avoiding wickedness, we will "set no limits on it."[24] Once again, this argument is precisely right with reference to conventional warfare; it catches the central error of what I have called the "war is hell" doctrine. But it is persuasive in the case of nuclear warfare only if one can describe plausible and morally significant limits, and that Ramsey has not done; nor have the strategists of "flexible response" been able to do it. All their arguments depend upon the ultimate wickedness of counter-city strikes. The pretense that this is not so carries with it dangers of its own. To draw insignificant lines, to maintain the formal categories of double effect, collateral damage, noncombatant immunity, and so on, when so little moral content remains is to corrupt the argument for justice as a whole and to render it suspect even in those areas of military life to which it properly pertains. And those areas are wide. Nuclear deterrence marks their outer limits, forcing us to contemplate wars that can never be fought. Within those limits there are wars that can and will and perhaps even should be fought, and to which the old rules apply with all their force. The specter of a nuclear holocaust does not invite us to act wickedly in conventional wars. Indeed, it probably is a deterrent there, too; it is hard to imagine a repetition of Dresden or Tokyo in a conventional war between nuclear powers. For destruction on such a scale would invite a nuclear response and a drastic and unacceptable escalation of the struggle.

Nuclear war is and will remain morally unacceptable, and there is no case for its rehabilitation. Because it is unacceptable, we must seek out ways to prevent it, and because deterrence is a bad way, we must seek out others. It is not my purpose here to suggest what the alternatives might look like. I have been more concerned to acknowledge that deterrence itself, for all its criminality, falls or may fall for the moment under the standard of necessity. But as with terror bombing, so here with the threat of terrorism: supreme emergency is never a stable position. The realm of necessity is subject to historical change. And, what is more important, we are under an obligation to seize upon opportunities of escape, even to take risks for the sake of such opportunities. So the readiness to murder is balanced, or should be, by the readiness not to murder, not to threaten murder, as soon as alternative ways to peace can be found.

PART FIVE

THE QUESTION OF RESPONSIBILITY

18

The Crime of Aggression: Political Leaders and Citizens

THE ASSIGNMENT OF RESPONSIBILITY IS THE CRITICAL TEST OF THE ARGU-ment for justice. For if war is fought not under the aegis of necessity but, most often, of freedom, then soldiers and statesmen have to make choices that are sometimes moral choices. And if they do that, it must be possible to single them out for praise and blame. If there are recognizable war crimes, there must be recognizable criminals. If there is such a thing as aggression, there must be aggressors. It is not the case that for every violation of human rights in wartime we can name a guilty person or group of persons. The conditions of war supply a plethora of excuses: fear, coercion, ignorance, even madness. But the theory of justice should point us to the men and women from whom we can rightly demand an accounting, and it should shape and control the judgments we make of the excuses they offer (or that are offered on their behalf). It does not point to people by their proper names, of course, but by their offices and circumstances. We learn the names (sometimes) only as we work our way through cases, attending to the details of moral and military action. Insofar as we name the right names, or at least insofar as our assignments and judgments are in accordance with the actual experience of war, sensitive to all its painfulness, the argument for justice is greatly strengthened. There can be no justice in war if there are not, ultimately, responsible men and women.

The question here is of moral responsibility; we are concerned with the blameworthiness of individuals, not their legal guilt or innocence. Much of the debate about aggression and war crimes, however, has focused on the latter issue, not the former. And as we read through these arguments, or listen to them, it often seems that what is being said is this: that if an individual is not legally liable for some particular act or omission but, as it were, merely immoral, not much can usefully be said about his guilt. For legal liability is a matter of definite rules, well-known procedures, and authoritative judges, while morality is nothing more than endless talk, where every talker has an equal right to his opinions. Consider, for example, the view of a contemporary law professor who believes that the "essentials" of "the question of war crimes" can be set forth "with tolerable clarity and brevity," so long as one caveat is accepted: "I shall make no attempt to say what is immoral—not because I believe morality unimportant, but because my views on it are entitled to no more weight than Jane Fonda's or Richard M. Nixon's, or yours."[1] Of course, morality *is* unimportant if all opinions are equal, because then no particular opinion has any force. Moral authority is no doubt different from legal authority; it is earned in different ways; but Professor Bishop is wrong to think that it doesn't exist. It has to do with the capacity to evoke commonly accepted principles in persuasive ways and to apply them to particular cases. No one can argue about justice and war, as I have been doing, without striving for an authoritative voice and laying claim to a certain "weightiness."

Moral argument is especially important in wartime because—as I have said before, and as Bishop's "brevity" makes clear—the laws of war are radically incomplete. Authoritative judges are rarely called to the business of judging. Indeed, there are often prudential reasons for not calling them, for even well-wrought judicial decisions are likely at certain moments in the history of international society to be understood only as acts of cruelty and vengeance. Trials like those that took place at Nuremberg after World War II seem to me both defensible and necessary; the law must provide some recourse when our deepest moral values are savagely attacked. But such trials by no means exhaust the field of judgment. We have more to do in these matters, and it is my purpose to do it here: to point at criminals and possible criminals across the whole range of wartime activity, though not to suggest, except tangentially, how we should deal with such people.[2] What is crucial is that they can be pointed at; we know where to look for them, if we are ready to look.

THE WORLD OF OFFICIALS

I will begin with the assignments and judgments that are required by the crime of war itself. That is to begin with politics rather than combat, civilians rather than soldiers, for aggression is first of all the work of political leaders. We must (naively) imagine them sitting around the elegant table of an old-fashioned chancellery or in the electronic fastness of a modern command room plotting illegitimate attacks, conquests, interventions. No doubt it is not always like that, though recent history provides ample evidence of direct and open criminal planning. "Statesmen" are more devious, aiming at war only indirectly, like Bismarck in 1870, and taking a very complicated view of their own efforts. Then it is not easy, perhaps, to mark out aggressors, though I think we should start with the assumption that it is always possible. The men and women who lead their people into war owe them and us an accounting. For every person who is killed, every drop of blood that falls is

> . . . . *a sore complaint*
> *Gainst him whose wrongs gives edge unto the swords.*

Listening to the excuses and lies, and also to the true accounts, of political leaders, we search for the "wrongs" that lie behind the fighting and are its moral cause.

The lawyers have not always encouraged this search. Until 1945, at least, they have held that "acts of state" cannot be the crimes of individual persons. The legal reasons for this denial lie in the theory of sovereignty, as it was once understood. Sovereign states by definition know no superiors, it was argued, and accept no external judgments: hence there is no way to prove the criminality of acts imputed to the state, that is, carried out by recognized authorities in the course of their official duties (unless domestic law provides procedures for bringing such proof to bear).[3] This argument is without moral effect, however, for in this regard states were never morally but only legally sovereign. All of us are capable of judging the acts of political leaders, and we commonly do so. Nor does legal sovereignty any longer provide protection against external judgments. Here Nuremberg is the decisive precedent.

But there is another, more informal version of the "act of state" doctrine, which refers not to the sovereignty of the political community but to the representativeness of its leaders. We are often urged not to condemn the acts of statesmen, or not to be too quick to condemn them, since, after all, these people are not acting selfishly or for private reasons. They are, as Townsend Hoopes wrote of America's leaders during the Vietnam War, "struggling in good conscience . . . to serve the broad national interest according to their lights."[4] They are acting for the sake of other people and in their name. The same assertion can be made on behalf of military officers, except when the crimes they commit are passionate or selfish. It might be made, too, on behalf of revolutionary militants who kill innocent people for the sake of the cause (not because of any personal grudge), even though the cause has no official but only a putative connection to the national interest. These are leaders, too; they may have risen to their "offices" by means not all that different from those adopted by more conventional officials, and they can sometimes say that acts of the movement or the revolution are as representative as acts of state. If this argument is acceptable in the case of statesmen and officers, I can see no reason to reject it in the case of revolutionaries. But it is a bad argument in all these cases, for it is false to suggest that representative functions are morally risk-free. They are instead peculiarly risky, precisely because statesmen, officers, and revolutionaries act for other people and with wide-ranging effects. They act sometimes so as to endanger the people they represent, sometimes so as to endanger the rest of us; they can hardly complain if we hold them subject to moral judgment.

Political power is a good that people seek. They aspire to office, connive at control and leadership, compete for positions from which they can do evil as well as good. If they hope to be praised for the good they do, they cannot escape blame for the evil. Still, blame is always resented, even when we may think it well-deserved, and it is important to try to say why this is so. Moral criticism goes very deep; it calls into question a leader's good faith and his personal rectitude. Since political leaders are rarely cynical about their work, and can never afford to appear to be cynical, they take such criticism seriously and dislike it intensely. Disagreement they can accept (if they are democratic leaders), but not accusations of criminality. Indeed, they are likely to treat all moral criticism as an illegitimate displacement of political controversy. I suppose they are right to recognize that morality is often a mask for politics. The case is the same with the law. Legal accusation can be a very powerful form of political attack, but though it is often used in that way, and often degraded in the use, it remains true nevertheless that political leaders are bound by the legal code and can rightly be charged and punished for criminal acts. Similarly with the moral code: though the terms of praise and blame are universally available and often misused, the code is still binding, and praise and blame are at least sometimes appropriate. The misuse of law and morality is common in wartime, and so we have to be careful not only in punishing political leaders for the wars they wage but also in stigmatizing them. They have no *a priori* claim to escape the stigma of aggression, however, when they violate the rights of another people and force its soldiers to fight.

Acts of state are also acts of particular persons, and when they take the form of aggressive war, particular persons are criminally responsible. Just who those persons are, and how many they are, is not always apparent. But it makes sense to begin with the head of state (or the effective head) and the men and women immediately around him, who actually control the government and make key decisions. Their accountability is clear, like that of the commanders of a military campaign for the strategy and tactics they adopt, for they are the source rather than the recipients of superior orders. When they defend themselves, they don't look up the political hierarchy, but across the battleline: they blame their opponents for forcing *them* to fight. They point to the intricate complexity of the pre-war maneuvering and to the extravagant demands and harassing actions of their adversaries. They have long stories to tell:[5]

> Who first attacked? Who turned the other cheek?
> Aggression perpetrated is as soon
> Denied, and insult rubbed into the injury
> By cunning agents trained in these affairs,
> With whom it's touch-and-go, don't tread-on-me,
> I-dare-you-to, keep-off, and kiss-my-hand.
> Tempers could sharpen knives, and do; we live
> In states provocative.

In order to work our way through the claims and counter-claims, we need a theory such as I have attempted to set forth in Part Two of this book. Often enough, despite the cunning agents, the theory is readily applied. It is worth setting down some of the cases about which we have, I think, no doubts: the German attack on Belgium in 1914, the Italian conquest of Ethiopia, the Japanese attack on China, the German and Italian interventions in Spain, the Russian invasion of Finland, the Nazi conquests of

Czechoslovakia, Poland, Denmark, Belgium, and Holland, the Russian invasions of Hungary and Czechoslovakia, the Egyptian challenge to Israel in 1967, and so on—the twentieth century makes for easy listing. I have argued that the American war in Vietnam belongs to the same series. Sometimes, no doubt, the going is more muddy; political leaders are not always in control of their own provocations, and wars do break out without anyone planning or intending to violate anyone else's rights. But insofar as we can recognize aggression, there should be little difficulty in blaming heads of state. The hard and interesting problems arise when we ask how responsibility for aggression is diffused through a political system.

At Nuremberg, the crime of aggression ("crime against peace") was said to involve "the planning, preparation, initiation, and waging of [aggressive] war." These four activities were distinguished from the planning and preparation of particular military campaigns and from the actual fighting of the war, which were (rightly) held to be noncriminal in character. Now, "planning, preparation, initiation, and waging" would appear to be the work of a fairly large number of people. But in fact the courts restricted the range of accountability so that convictions were obtained only against those officials who were part of "Hitler's inner circle of advisors" or who played such a major role in the making or execution of policy that their protests and refusals would have had a significant impact.[6] Persons lower down the bureaucratic hierarchy, though their contribution was cumulatively significant, were not held individually responsible. It is not at all clear, however, just where we should draw that line; nor is it clear that we ought to assign blame in the same way as we assign legal culpability. The best way to deal with these issues is to turn immediately to a critical case.

Nuremberg: "The Ministries Case"

In an important article on responsibility for crimes of war, Sanford Levinson has analyzed the Nuremberg verdicts, focusing especially on the trial of Ernst von Weizsaecker, who was State Secretary of the German Foreign Ministry from 1938 to 1943, second only to von Ribbentrop (one of the "inner circle") in the foreign policy hierarchy. I want to follow Levinson's account, and then draw some conclusions from it. Von Weizsaecker was charged with crimes against the peace and initially convicted, but the conviction was reversed upon review. His defense emphasized two points: first, that he took no part in actual policy planning, and secondly, that within the Foreign Ministry he opposed Nazi aggression; he was also involved, at least marginally, in underground opposition to Hitler's regime. The review court accepted this defense, emphasizing its second part: von Weizsaecker's diplomatic activity, which "aided and abetted" German war plans, was so important that it would have been held against him had he not criticized Hitler's policies within his ministry and passed information to more active opponents outside. Thus the line of criminal responsibility was drawn so as to include officials like von Weizsaecker, while he himself was acquitted because, though he clearly played a part in "preparing" an aggressive war, he also "opposed and objected to" that war.

The prosecution argued the insufficiency of this opposition: since he knew of plans for aggression, it was said, he had a positive duty to reveal those plans to the potential victims. But the court rejected this argument because of the risks such action would have entailed and also because it might have led to greater German losses on the battlefield.[7]

> One may quarrel with, and oppose to the point of violence and assassination, a tyrant whose programs mean the ruin of one's country. But the time has not yet arrived when any man would view with satisfaction the ruin of his own people and the loss of its young manhood. To apply any other standard of conduct is to set up a test that has never yet been suggested as proper and which, assuredly, we are not prepared to accept as either wise or good.

This is too strong, I think, for it is obviously not a question of "viewing with satisfaction" the battle losses of one's own side. One might be greatly saddened by them and still feel it morally right to protect the innocent people of the victim state. And surely we would think it both wise and good, indeed heroic, had some German opponent of Hitler warned the Danes or the Belgians or the Russians of the coming attacks. But there is probably no legal or moral obligation to act in this way. Not only the risk but also the inner pain that a man might feel at such a time is more than we require. On the other hand, von Weizsaecker's alternative actions, though they satisfied the judges, may have amounted to less than we require. For he continued to serve the regime whose policies he disapproved; he did not resign.

The issue of resignation came up more directly in connection with charges that von Weizsaecker was guilty of war crimes and crimes against humanity, the latter relating to the extermination of the Jews. Here, too, he argued "that minimal participation should be negated by the fact that he opposed what was being done." But in this case, intra-office opposition was not deemed sufficient. The SS had formally requested the Foreign Ministry's opinions in regard to its policy on the Jewish question. And von Weizsaecker, though he knew what that policy was, had voiced no objections. Apparently he thought his silence the price of his office, and he wanted to retain his office so that he "might be in a position to initiate or aid in attempts to negotiate peace" and so that he might continue to pass on information to Hitler's underground opponents. But the court held that "One cannot give consent to . . . the commission of murder because by so doing he hopes eventually to be able to rid society of the chief murderer. The first is a crime of imminent actuality while the second is but a future hope." The court did not believe that failure to resign was itself a matter of criminal liability. While it might be true that no "decent man could continue to hold office under a regime which carried out . . . wholesale barbarities of this kind," indecency is not a crime. But to hold office and keep silent was a punishable offense, and von Weizsaecker was sentenced to seven years in prison.[8]

Now, the criteria of "significant contribution" or the possibility of "significant protest" seem entirely appropriate in deciding upon trial and punishment. The standards of blame, however, are much more strict: we need to say more about indecency. If von Weizsaecker was bound to resign in protest, I don't see why lesser officials with similar knowledge were not similarly bound. In the United States during the Vietnam years, only a very small number of foreign policy officials resigned, most of them holding low-level positions, but those resignations were morally heartening (to those of us, at least, who knew their reasons) in a way which suggests that they should have been imitated.[9] The courage required to resign in Germany in the late 1930s or early 1940s was far greater than that required in the U.S. three decades later, where opposition to the war was public and vociferous. But it was not a death-defying courage that was necessary even in Germany, but something less, well within the reach of ordinary people. Many officials who failed to resign offered excuses for not doing so, which suggests that they recognized the imperative, however dimly. These excuses were mostly like von Weizsaecker's, focused on distant goods. But there were also men who remained in office in order to engage, often at great personal risk, in concrete and immediate acts of benevolence or sabotage. The most extraordinary of these was the SS lieutenant Kurt Gerstein, whose case has been carefully documented by Saul Friedlander.[10]

> Gerstein represented the type of man who, by virtue of his deepest convictions, disavowed the Nazi regime, even hated it inwardly, but collaborated with it in order to combat it from within and to prevent worse things from happening.

I cannot retell Gerstein's story here; it is enough to say that it demonstrates that it was possible to live a moral life even in the SS, though at a cost in personal agony (Gerstein eventually committed suicide) which we can expect few people to pay. Resignation is much easier, and sometimes, I think, we must take it as the minimal sign of moral decency.

Von Weizsaecker's case invites us to reflect on one further problem. The State Secretary was a diplomat who carried out negotiations with foreign countries under instructions from his superiors. But he was also an advisor to those superiors; his own views were frequently requested. Now advisors are in a curious position with regard to both legal and moral judgment. Their most important advice is often given orally, whispered in the ruler's ear. What is written down may be incomplete, tailored to the requirements of bureaucratic correspondence. We miss the nuances and qualifications, the subtle signs of doubt, the private emphases and hesitations. If sufficient documentation is available, we may go ahead and make judgments anyway. It's certainly not the case that only "line" and never "staff" officials can be held responsible for decisions made. But whispering in the ruler's ear is problematic; it is easier to suggest what should be said than what we should do if we suspect that it hasn't been said.

What von Weizsaecker said was probably insufficient, for according to his own account he urged nothing more than the likelihood of German defeat; his opposition to Hitler's policies were always expressed in expediential terms.[11] Perhaps those were the only terms likely to be effective in Germany during those years. That is probably true in other cases, too, even with governments less openly committed to a program of conquest. But it is often important to use the language of morality, if only to break through the forms of euphemism and silence with which officials conceal even from themselves the extent and nature of the crimes they are committing. Sometimes the best way for an advisor to say no is simply to give an accurate name to the policy he is being asked to approve. This point is beautifully made in a speech in Shakespeare's *King John*. With hints and indirection, John had ordered the murder of his nephew Arthur, Duke of Brittany. Later he came to regret the murder and turned on his courtier, Hubert de Burgh, who had carried it out.[12]

> Hadst thou but shook thy head or made a pause
> When I spoke darkly what I purposed,
> Or turned an eye of doubt upon my face,
> As bid me tell my tale in express words,
> Deep shame had struck me dumb, made me break off . . .
> But thou dist understand me by my signs,
> And didst in signs again parley with sin;
> Yea, without stop, didst let thy heart consent,
> And consequently thy rude hand to act,
> The deed which both our tongues held vile to name.

The speech is hypocritical, but it captures the common quality of bureaucratic acquiescence, and it suggests very forcefully that advisors and agents, when they have the opportunity, must speak out "in express words," using the moral language that we all know. They may be judged insufficiently tough or hard-headed if they talk that way. But to be "tough" enough to carry out policies that are literally unmentionable is either to be very cowardly or very wicked.

DEMOCRATIC RESPONSIBILITIES

What about the rest of us—citizens, let's say, of a state engaged in an aggressive war? Collective responsibility is a hard notion, though it is worth stressing at once that we have fewer problems with collective punishment. Resistance to aggression is itself "punishing" to the aggressor state and is often described in those terms. With reference to the actual fighting, as I have already argued, civilians on both sides are innocent, equally innocent, and never legitimate military targets. They are, however, political and economic targets once the war is over; that is, they are the victims of military occupation, political reconstruction, and the exaction of reparative payments. We may take the last of these as the clearest and simplest case of collective punishment. Reparations are surely due the victims of aggressive war, and they can hardly be collected only from those members of the defeated state who were active supporters of the aggression. Instead, the costs are distributed through the tax system, and through the economic system generally, among all the citizens, often over a period of time extending to generations that had nothing to do with the war at all.[13] In this sense, citizenship is a common destiny, and no one, not even its opponents (unless they become political refugees, which has its costs, too) can escape the effects of a bad regime, an ambitious or fanatic leadership, or an overreaching nationalism. But if men and women must accept this destiny, they can sometimes do so with a good conscience, for the acceptance says nothing about their individual responsibility. The distribution of costs is not the distribution of guilt.

At least one writer has tried to argue that political destiny is a kind of guilt: existential, unavoidable, frightening. For the soldier or citizen of a state at war, writes J. Glenn Gray in his philosophical memoir of World War II, is the member of a "coarse, vulgar, heedless, and violent" community and, willy-nilly, a participant in an enterprise "whose spirit is to win at any cost." He cannot cut himself loose.[14]

> He is bound to reflect that his nation has given him refuge and sustenance, provided him with whatever education and property he calls his own. He belongs and will always belong to it in some sense no matter where he goes or how hard he seeks to alter his inheritance. The crimes, therefore, that his nation or one of its units commits cannot be indifferent to him. He shares the guilt as he shares the satisfaction in the generous deeds and worthy products of nation or army. Even if he did not consciously will them and was unable to prevent them, he cannot wholly escape responsibility for collective deeds.

Maybe; but it is not an easy move from "the ache of guilt," which Gray almost lovingly describes, to hard talk about responsibility. It might be better to say of loyal citizens who watch their government or army (or their comrades in battle) doing terrible things that they feel or should feel ashamed rather than responsible—unless they actually are responsible by virtue of their particular participation or acquiescence. Shame is the tribute we pay to the inheritance that Gray describes. "A burning sense of shame at the deeds of his government and the acts of horror committed by German soldiers and police was the mark of a conscientious German at the close of the war." That is exactly right, but we won't ourselves blame that conscientious German or call him responsible; nor need he blame himself unless there was something he should have done, and could do, in the face of the horror.

Perhaps it can always be said of such a person that he could have done more than he did do. Certainly conscientious men and women are likely to believe that of themselves; it is a sign of their conscientiousness.[15]

> On this or that occasion he has been silent when he should have spoken out. In his own smaller or larger circle of influence he has not made his whole weight felt. Had he brought forth the civil courage to protest in time, some particular act of injustice might have been avoided.

Such reflections are endless and endlessly dispiriting; they lead Gray to argue that behind collective responsibility there lies "meta-physical guilt," which derives from "our failure as human beings to live in accordance with our potentialities and our vision of the good." But some of us, surely, fail more dismally than others; and it is necessary, with all due caution and humility, to mark out standards by which we can measure the respective failures. Gray suggests the right standard, though he goes on very quickly to insist that we can never apply it to anyone but ourselves. But that kind of self-regard is not possible in politics and morality. Judging ourselves, we necessarily judge other people, with whom we share a common life. And how is it possible to criticize and blame our leaders, as we sometimes must do, without involving their enthusiastic followers (our fellow citizens)? Though responsibility is always personal and particular, moral life is always collective in character.

This is Gray's principle, which I mean to adopt and expound: "*The greater the possibility of free action in the communal sphere, the greater the degree of guilt for evil deeds done in the name of everyone.*"[16] The principle invites us to focus our attention on democratic rather than authoritarian regimes. Not that free action is impossible even in the worst of authoritarian regimes; at the very least, people can resign, withdraw, flee. But in democracies there are opportunities for positive response, and we need to ask to what extent these opportunities fix our obligations, when evil deeds are committed in our name.

The American People and the War in Vietnam

If the argument in chapters 6 and 11 is right, the American war in Vietnam was, first of all, an unjustified intervention, and it was, secondly, carried on in so brutal a manner that even had it initially been defensible, it would have to be condemned, not in this or that aspect but generally. I am not going to re-argue that description, but assume it, so that we can look closely at the responsibility of democratic citizens—and at a particular set of democratic citizens, namely, ourselves.[17]

Democracy is a way of distributing responsibility (just as monarchy is a way of refusing to distribute it). But that doesn't mean that all adult citizens share equally in the blame we assign for aggressive war. Our actual assignments will vary a great deal, depending on the precise nature of the democratic order, the place of a particular person in that order, and the pattern of his own political activities. Even in a perfect democracy, it cannot be said that every citizen is the author of every state policy, though every one of them can rightly be called to account. Imagine, for example, a small community where all the citizens are fully and accurately informed about public business, where all of them participate, argue, vote on matters of communal interest, and where they all take turns holding public office. Now this community, let us say, initiates and wages an unjust war against its neighbors—for the sake of some economic advantage, perhaps, or out of zeal to spread its (admirable) political system. There is no question of self-defense; no one has attacked it or is planning to do so. Who is responsible for this war? Surely all those men and women who voted for it and who cooperated in planning, initiating, and waging it. The soldiers who do the actual fighting are not responsible as soldiers; but as citizens, they are, assuming that they were old enough to have shared in the decision to fight.* All of them are guilty of the crime of aggressive war and of no

---

*Why aren't they responsible as soldiers? If they are morally bound to vote against the war, why aren't they also bound to refuse to fight? The answer is that they vote as individuals, each one deciding for himself, but they fight as members of the political community, the collective decision having already been made, subject to all the moral and material pressures that I described in chapter 3. They act very well if they refuse to fight, and we should honor those—they are likely to be few—who have the self-certainty and courage to stand against their fellows. I have argued elsewhere that democracies ought to respect such people and ought

lesser charge, and we would not hesitate in such a case to blame them publicly. Nor would it make any difference whether their motive was economic selfishness or a political zeal that appeared to them entirely disinterested. Either way, the blood of their victims would complain against them.

Those who voted against the war or who refused to cooperate in the waging of it could not be blamed. But what would we think of a group of citizens that didn't vote? Had they voted, let's say, the war might have been avoided, but they were lazy, didn't care, or were afraid to come down on one side or the other of a hotly disputed issue. The day of the crucial decision was a day off from work; they spent it in their gardens. I am inclined to say that they are blameworthy, though they are not guilty of aggressive war. Surely those of their fellow citizens who went to the assembly and opposed the war can blame them for their indifference and inaction. This seems a clear counter-example to Gray's assertion that "No citizen of a free land can justly accuse his neighbor . . . of not having done as much as he should to prevent the state of war or the commission of this or that state crime. But each can . . . accuse himself. . . ."[18] In a perfect democracy, we would know a great deal about one another's duties, and just accusations would not be impossible.

Imagine now that the minority of citizens that was defeated could have won (and prevented the war) if instead of merely voting, they had held meetings outside the assembly, marched and demonstrated, organized for a second vote. Let's assume that none of this would have been terribly dangerous to them, but they chose not to take these measures because their opposition to the war wasn't all that strong; they thought it unjust but were not horrified by the prospect; they hoped for a quick victory; and so on. Then they are blameworthy, too, though to a lesser degree than those slothful citizens who did not even bother to go to the assembly.

These last two examples resemble the good samaritan cases in domestic society, where we commonly say that if it is possible to do good, without risk or great cost, one ought to do good. But when the issue is war, the obligation is stronger, for it is not a question of doing good, but of preventing

---

certainly to tolerate their refusals. (See the essay on "Conscientious Objection" in *Obligations*.) That doesn't mean, however, that the others can be called criminals. Patriotism may be the last refuge of scoundrels, but it is also the ordinary refuge of ordinary men and women, and it requires of us another sort of toleration. But we should expect opponents of the war to refuse to become officers or officials, even if they feel bound to share combat risks with their countrymen.

serious harm, and harm that will be done in the name of my own political community—hence, in some sense, in my own name. Here, assuming still that the community is a perfect democracy, it looks as if a citizen is blameless only if he takes back his name. I don't think this means that he must become a revolutionary or an exile, actually renouncing his citizenship or loyalty. But he must do all he can, short of accepting frightening risks, to prevent or stop the war. He must withdraw his name from this act (the war policy) though not necessarily from every communal action, for he may still value, as he probably should, the democracy he and his fellow citizens have achieved. This, then, is the meaning of Gray's maxim: the more one can do, the more one has to do.

We can now drop the myth of perfection and paint a more realistic picture. The state that goes to war is, like our own, an enormous state, governed at a great distance from its ordinary citizens by powerful and often arrogant officials. These officials, or at least the leading among them, are chosen through democratic elections, but at the time of the choice very little is known about their programs and commitments. Political participation is occasional, intermittent, limited in its effects, and it is mediated by a system for the distribution of news which is partially controlled by those distant officials and which in any case allows for considerable distortions. It may be that a politics of this sort is the best we can hope for (though I don't believe that) once the political community reaches a certain size. Anyway, it is no longer as easy to impose responsibility as it is in a perfect democracy. One doesn't want to regard those distant officials as if they were kings, but for certain sorts of state action, secretly prepared or suddenly launched, they bear a kind of regal responsibility.

When a state like this commits itself to a campaign of aggression, its citizens (or many of them) are likely to go along, as Americans did during the Vietnam War, arguing that the way may after all be just; that it is not possible for them to be sure whether it is just or not; that their leaders know best and tell them this or that, which sounds plausible enough; and that nothing they can do will make much difference anyway. These are not immoral arguments, though they reflect badly on the society within which they are made. And they can, no doubt, be made too quickly by citizens seeking to avoid the difficulties that might follow if they thought about the war for themselves. These people are or may be blameworthy, not for aggressive war, but for bad faith as citizens. But that is a hard charge to make, for citizenship plays such a small part in their everyday lives. "Free action in the communal sphere" is a possibility for men and women in such a state only in the formal sense that serious governmental restraint, actual repression, doesn't exist. Perhaps it should also be said that the "communal sphere" doesn't exist, for it is only the day-by-day assumption of responsibility that creates that sphere and gives it meaning. Even patriotic excitement, war fever, among such people is probably best understood as a reflex of distance, a desperate identification, stimulated, it may be, by a false account of what is going on. One might say of them what one says of soldiers in combat, that they are not to blame for the war, since it is not their war.*

But as an account of all the citizens, even in such a state, this is certainly exaggerated. For there exists a group of more knowledgeable men and women, members of what political scientists call the foreign policy elites, who are not so radically distanced from the national leadership; and some subset of these people, together with others in touch with them, is likely to form an "opposition" or perhaps even a movement of opposition to the war. It would seem possible to regard the entire group of knowledgeable people as at least potentially blameworthy if that war is aggressive and unless they join the opposition.[19] To say that is to presume upon the knowledge they have and their private sense of political possibility. But if we turn to an actual case of imperfect democracy, like the United States in the late 1960s and early 1970s, the presumption doesn't seem unwarranted. Surely there was knowledge and opportunity enough among the country's elites, the national and local leaders of its political parties, its religious establishments, its corporate hierarchies, and perhaps above all its intellectual teachers and spokesmen—the men and women whom Noam Chomsky has named, in tribute to the role they play in contemporary government, "the new mandarins."[20] Surely many of these people were morally complicitous in our Vietnam aggression. I suppose one can also say of them what many of them have said of themselves: that they were simply mistaken in their judgments of the war, failed to realize this or that, thought that was true when it was not, or hoped for this result

---

* But see the note in Anne Frank's *Diary*: "I don't believe that only governments and capitalists are guilty of aggression. Oh no, the little man is just as keen on it, for otherwise the people of the world would have risen in revolt long ago." I'm sure she is right about the keenness, and I don't want to excuse it. But we don't, for all that, call the little men war criminals, and I am trying to explain why we don't. (*The Diary of a Young Girl*, trans. B. M. Mooyaart-Doubleday, New York, 1953, p. 201.)

which never came about. In moral life generally, one makes allowances for false beliefs, misinformation, and honest mistakes. But there comes a time in any tale of aggression and atrocity when such allowances can no longer be made. I cannot mark out that time here; nor am I interested in pointing at particular people or certain that I can do so. I only want to insist that there are responsible people even when, under the conditions of imperfect democracy, moral accounting is difficult and imprecise.

The real moral burden of the American war fell on that subset of men and women whose knowledge and sense of possibility were made manifest by their oppositional activity. They were the ones most likely to reproach themselves and one another, continually asking whether they were doing enough to stop the fighting, devoting enough time and energy, working hard enough, working as effectively as they could. For most of their fellow citizens, anxious, apathetic, and alienated, the war was merely an ugly or an exciting spectacle (until they were forced to join it). For the dissidents, it was a kind of moral torture—self-torture, as Gray describes it, though they also tortured one another, wastefully, in savage internecine conflicts over what was to be done. And this self-torture bred a kind of self-righteousness *vis-à-vis* the others, an endemic failing on the Left, though understandable enough under conditions of aggressive war and mass acquiescence. The expression of that self-righteousness, however, is not a useful way to get one's fellow citizens to think seriously about the war or to join the opposition: nor was it useful in this case. It is not easy to know what course of action might serve these purposes. Politics is difficult at such a time. But there is intellectual work to do that is less difficult: one must describe as graphically as one can the moral reality of war, talk about what it means to force people to fight, analyze the nature of democratic responsibilities. These, at least, are encompassable tasks, and they are morally required of the men and women who are trained to perform them. Nor is it dangerous to perform them, in a democratic state, waging war in a distant country. And the citizens of such a state have time to listen and reflect; they, too, are in no immediate danger. War imposes harsher burdens than any these people have to bear—as we shall see when we consider, finally, the moral life of men at arms.

19

WAR CRIMES:
SOLDIERS AND THEIR OFFICERS

WE ARE CONCERNED NOW WITH THE CONDUCT OF WAR AND NOT ITS overall justice. For soldiers, as I have already argued, are not responsible for the overall justice of the wars they fight; their responsibility is limited by the range of their own activity and authority. Within that range, however, it is real enough, and it frequently comes into question. "There wasn't a single soldier," says an Israeli officer who fought in the Six Day War, "who didn't at some stage have to decide, to choose, to make a moral decision . . . quick and modern though [the war] was, the soldier was not turned into a mere technician. He had to make decisions that were of real significance."[1] And when faced with decisions of that sort, soldiers have clear obligations. They are bound to apply the criteria of usefulness and proportionality until they come up against the basic rights of the people they are threatening to kill or injure, and then they are bound not to kill or injure them. But judgments about usefulness and proportionality are very difficult for soldiers in the field. It is the doctrine of rights that makes the most effective limit on military activity, and it does so precisely because it rules out calculation and establishes hard and fast standards. Hence in my initial cases I will focus on specific violations of rights and on the defenses that soldiers commonly offer for these violations. The defenses are basically of two sorts. The first refers to the heatedness of battle and the passion or frenzy it engenders. The second refers to the disciplinary system of the army and the obedience it requires. These are serious defenses; they suggest the loss of self that is involved in warfare, and they remind us that most soldiers most of the time have not chosen the combat and discipline they endure. Where is their freedom and responsibility?

But there is a related issue that I must consider before trying to mark out the realm of freedom from the coercions and hysteria of war. The war convention requires soldiers to accept personal risks rather than kill innocent people. This requirement takes different forms in different combat situations, and I have already discussed these in considerable detail; my concern now is with the requirement itself. The rule is absolute: self-preservation in the face of the enemy is not an excuse for violations of the rules of war. Soldiers, it might be said, stand to civilians like the crew of a liner to its passengers. They must risk their own lives for the sake of the others. No doubt this is easy to say, less easy to do. But if the rule is absolute, the risks are not; it is a question of degree; the crucial point is that soldiers cannot enhance their own security at the expense of innocent men and women.* This might be called an obligation of soldiering as an office,

---

*Telford Taylor suggests a possible exception to this rule, citing a hypothetical case which has often been discussed in the legal literature. A small detachment of troops on a special mission or cut off from its main force takes prisoners "under such circumstances that men cannot be spared to guard them . . . and that to take them along would greatly endanger the success of the mission or the safety of the unit." The prisoners are likely to be killed, Taylor says, in accordance with the principle of military necessity. (*Nuremberg and Vietnam*, New York, 1970, p. 36.) But if it is only the safety of the unit that is in question (its mission may already have been accomplished), the proper appeal would be to self-preservation. The argument from necessity has not, despite Taylor, been accepted by legal writers; the argument from self-preservation has won greater support. In his military code for the Union Army, for example, Francis Lieber writes that "a commander is permitted to direct his troops to give no quarter . . . when his own salvation makes it impossible to cumber himself with prisoners." (Taylor, p. 36n.) But surely in such a case the prisoners should be disarmed and then released. Even if it is "impossible" to take them along, it is not impossible to set them free. There may be risks in doing that, but these are exactly the sorts of risks soldiers must accept. The risks involved in leaving wounded men behind are of the same sort, but that is not a satisfactory reason for killing them. For a useful discussion of these issues, see Marshall Cohen, "Morality and the Laws of War," in Held, Morgenbesser, and Nagel, eds., *Philosophy, Morality, and International Affairs*, New York, 1974, pp. 76–78.

but it is a hard question whether one can rightly be said to assume such obligations when one comes into the office as unwillingly as most soldiers do. Imagine a liner manned by kidnapped sailors: would the members of such a crew be bound, as the ship was sinking, to see to the safety of the passengers before seeing to their own?

I am not sure how to answer that question, but there is a crucial difference between the work of coerced crew members and that of military conscripts: the first group is not in the business of sinking ships, the second is. Conscripts impose risks on innocent people; they are themselves the immediate source of the danger and they are its effective cause. And so it is not a question of saving themselves, letting others die, but of killing others in order to improve their own odds. Now that they cannot do, because that no man can do. Their obligation isn't in practice mediated by the office of soldiering. It arises directly from the activity in which they are engaged, whether that activity is voluntary or not, or at least it arises so long as we regard soldiers as moral agents and even if we regard them as coerced moral agents.[2] They are not mere instruments; they do not stand to the army as their weapons do to them. It is precisely because they do (sometimes) choose to kill or not, to impose risks or accept them, that we require them to choose in a certain way. That requirement shapes the whole pattern of their rights and duties in combat. And when they break out of that pattern, it is a matter of some significance that they don't by and large deny the requirement. They claim, instead, that they literally were not able to fulfill it; that they were not at the moment of their "crime," moral agents at all.

IN THE HEAT OF BATTLE

Two Accounts of Killing Prisoners

In his fine memoir of World War I, Guy Chapman tells the following story. After a minor but bloody advance from one line of trenches to the next, he encountered one of his fellow officers, his face "slack and haggard, but not from weariness." Chapman asked him what was wrong.[3]

> "Oh, I don't know. Nothing. . . . At least. . . . Look here, we took a lot
> of prisoners in those trenches yesterday morning. Just as we got into
> their line, an officer came out of a dugout. He'd got one hand above

his head, and a pair of fieldglasses in the other. He held the glasses out to S_____, . . . and said, 'Here you are, sergeant, I surrender.' S_____ said, 'Thank you, sir,' and took the glasses with his left hand. At the same moment, he tucked the butt of his rifle under his arm and shot the officer straight through his head. What the hell ought I to do?"

"I don't see that you can do anything," I answered slowly. "What can you do? Besides I don't see that S_____'s really to blame. He must have been half mad with excitement by the time he got into that trench. I don't suppose he ever thought what he was doing. If you start a man killing, you can't turn him off like an engine. After all, he is a good man. He was probably half off his head."

"It wasn't only him. Another did exactly the same thing."

"Anyhow, it's too late to do anything now. I suppose you ought to have shot both on the spot. The best thing now is to forget it."

That sort of thing happens often in war, and it is commonly excused. Chapman's argument makes some sense: it is, in effect, a plea of temporary insanity. It suggests a kind of killing frenzy that begins in combat and ends in murder, the line between the two being lost to the mind of the individual soldier. Or it suggests a frenzy of fear such that the soldier cannot recognize the moment when he is no longer in danger. He is not, indeed, a machine that can just be turned off, and it would be inhumanly righteous not to look with sympathy on his plight. And yet, if it is true that enemy soldiers are often killed trying to surrender, it is also true that a relatively small number of men do the "extra" killing. The rest seem ready enough to stop as soon as they can, whatever the state of mind they had worked themselves into during the battle itself. This fact is morally decisive, for it suggests a common acknowledgment of the right to quarter, and it proves that the right can in fact be recognized, since it often is, even in the chaos of combat. It is simply not true of soldiers, as one philosopher has recently written, that "war . . . in some important ways makes psychopaths of them all."[4] The argument has to be more particular than that. When we make allowances for what individual soldiers do "in the heat of battle," it must be because of some knowledge we have that distinguishes these soldiers from the others or their circumstances from the usual ones. Perhaps they have encountered enemy troops who feigned surrender in order to kill their captors: then the war rights of other troops are made problematic in a new way, for one cannot be sure when killing is "extra." Or perhaps they have been under some special strain or have been fighting too long and are near to nervous exhaustion. But there is no general rule that requires us to make allowances, and sometimes, at least, soldiers should be censured or punished for killings that take place after the battle is over (though summary execution is probably not the best form of punishment). They should certainly never be encouraged to believe that a total lack of restraint can be excused merely by reference to the passions that cause it.

There are officers, however, who encourage exactly that belief, not out of compassion but calculation, not because of the heat of the battle but in order to raise the temperature of men in combat. In his novel *The Thin Red Line*, one of the best accounts of jungle fighting in World War II, James Jones tells of another incident of "extra" killing.[5] He describes a new army unit, its members un-blooded and without confidence in their ability to fight. After a hard march through the jungle, they come upon a Japanese position from the rear. There is a brief and savage fight. At a certain point, Japanese soldiers start trying to surrender, but some of the Americans cannot or will not stop the killing.[6] Even after the firefight is definitely over, those Japanese who have succeeded in surrendering are brutally treated—by men, so Jones wants to suggest, who are caught up in a kind of intoxication, their inhibitions suddenly gone. The commanding officer watches all this and does nothing. "He did not want to jeopardize the new toughness of spirit that had come over the men after achieving success here. That spirit was more important than whether or not a few Jap soldiers got kicked around or killed."

I suppose that soldiers must be "men of spirit," like Plato's guardians, but Jones' colonel has mistaken the nature of their spiritedness. It is almost certainly true that they fight best when they are most disciplined, when they are most in control of themselves and committed to the restraints appropriate to their trade. "Extra" killing is less a sign of toughness than of hysteria, and hysteria is the wrong kind of spiritedness. But even if the colonel's calculations were correct, he would still be bound to stop the killing if he could, for he cannot train and toughen his men at the expense of Japanese prisoners. He is also bound to act so as to prevent such killings in the future. This is a crucial aspect of what is called "command responsibility," and I will take it up in detail later on. It is important to stress now that it is a large responsibility; for the general policy of the army, expressed through its officers, the climate they create by their day-to-day actions, has far more to do with the incidence of "extra" killing than does the intensity of the actual fighting. But this doesn't mean that individual soldiers must be excused; indeed, it suggests once again that heatedness isn't the issue, but murderousness; and for their own murderousness individuals are always responsible, even when under the conditions of military discipline they are not exclusively so.

It is a feature of criminal responsibility that it can be distributed without being divided. We can, that is, blame more than one person for a particular act without splitting up the blame we assign.[7] When soldiers are shot trying to surrender, the men who do the actual shooting are fully responsible for what they do, unless we recognize particular extenuating circumstances; at the same time, the officer who tolerates and encourages the murders is also fully responsible, if it lay within his power to prevent them. Perhaps we blame the officer more, for his coolness, but I have tried to suggest that combat soldiers, too, should be held to high standards in such matters (and they will surely want their enemies held to high standards). The case looks very different, however, when combatants are actually ordered to take no prisoners or to kill the ones they take or to turn their guns on enemy civilians. Then it is not their own murderousness that is at issue but that of their officers; they can act morally only by disobeying their orders. In such a case, we are likely to divide as well as distribute responsibility: we regard soldiers under orders as men whose acts are not entirely their own and whose liability for what they do is somehow diminished.

SUPERIOR ORDERS

The My Lai Massacre

The incident is infamous and hardly needs retelling. A company of American soldiers entered a Vietnamese village where they expected to encounter enemy combatants, found only civilians, old men, women, and children, and began to kill them, shooting them singly or collecting them in groups, ignoring their obvious helplessness and their pleas for mercy, not stopping until they had murdered between four and five hundred people. Now, it has been argued on behalf of these soldiers that they acted, not in the heat of battle (since there was no battle) but in the context of a brutal and brutalizing war which was in fact, if only unofficially, a war against the Vietnamese people as a whole. In this war, the argument goes on, they had been encouraged to kill without making careful discriminations—encouraged to do so by their own officers and driven to do so by their enemies, who fought and hid among the civilian population.[8] These statements are true, or partly true; and yet massacre is radically different from guerrilla war, even from a guerrilla war brutally fought, and there is considerable evidence that the soldiers at My Lai knew the difference. For while some of them joined in the murders readily enough, as if eager to kill without risk, there were a few who refused to fire their guns and others who had to be ordered to fire two or three times before they could bring themselves to do so. Others simply ran away; one man shot himself in the foot so as to escape the scene; a junior officer tried heroically to stop the massacre, standing between the Vietnamese villagers and his fellow Americans. Many of his fellows, we know, were sick and guilt-ridden in the days that followed. This was not a fearful and frenzied extension of combat, but "free" and systematic slaughter, and those men that participated in it can hardly say that they were caught in the grip of war. They can say, however, that they were following orders, caught in the grip of the United States Army.

The orders of Captain Medina, the company commander, had in fact been ambiguous; at least, the men who heard them could not agree afterwards as to whether or not they had been told to "waste" the inhabitants of My Lai. He is quoted as having told his company to leave nothing living behind them and to take no prisoners: "They're all V.C.'s, now go and get them." But he is also said to have ordered only the killing of "enemies," and when asked, "Who is the enemy?" to have offered the following definition (in the words of one of the soldiers): "anybody that was running from us, hiding from us, or who appeared to us to be the enemy. If a man was running, shoot him; sometimes even if a woman with a rifle was running, shoot her."[9] That is a very bad definition, but it isn't morally insane; barring a loose interpretation of the "appearance" of enmity, it would have excluded most of the people killed at My Lai. Lieutenant Calley, who actually led the unit that entered the village, gave far more specific orders, commanding his men to kill helpless civilians who were neither running nor hiding, let alone carrying rifles, and repeating the command again and again when they hesitated to obey.* The army's judicial system singled him out for blame and punishment, though he claimed he was only doing what Medina had ordered him to do. The enlisted men who did what Calley ordered them to do were never charged.

It must be a great relief to follow orders. "Becoming a soldier," writes J. Glenn Gray, "was like escaping from one's own shadow." The world of war is frightening; decisions are difficult; and it is comforting to slough off responsibility and simply do what one is told. Gray reports soldiers insisting on this special kind of freedom: "When I raised my right hand and took the [army oath], I freed myself of the consequences for what I do. I'll do what they tell me and nobody can blame me."[10] Army training encourages this view, even though soldiers are also informed that they must refuse "unlawful" orders. No military force can function effectively without routine obedience, and it is the routine that is stressed. Soldiers are taught to obey even petty and foolish commands. The teaching process has the form of an endless drill, aimed at breaking down their individual thoughtfulness, resistance, hostility, and waywardness. But there is some ultimate humanity that cannot be broken down, the disappearance of which we will not accept. In his play *The Measures Taken*, Bertolt Brecht describes militant communists as "blank pages on which the Revolution writes its instructions."[11] I suppose there are many drill sergeants who dream of a similar blankness. But the description is a false one and the dream a fantasy. It is not that soldiers don't sometimes obey as if they were morally blank. What is crucial is that the rest of us hold them responsible for what they do. Despite their oath, we blame them for the crimes that follow from "unlawful" or immoral obedience.

Soldiers can never be transformed into mere instruments of war. The trigger is always part of the gun, not part of the man. If they are not machines that can just be turned off, they are also not machines that can

---

*It may be useful to suggest the sorts of commands that should be issued at such a time. Here is an account of an Israeli unit entering Nablus during the Six Day War: "The battalion CO got on the field telephone to my company and said, 'Don't touch the civilians . . . don't fire until you're fired at and don't touch the civilians. Look, you've been warned. Their blood be on your heads.' In just those words. The boys in the company kept talking about it afterwards. . . . They kept repeating the words. . . . 'Their blood be on your heads.'" *The Seventh Day: Soldiers Talk About the Six Day War*, London, 1970, p. 132.

just be turned on. Trained to obey "without hesitation," they remain nevertheless capable of hesitating. I have already cited examples of refusal, delay, doubt, and anguish at My Lai. These are internal confirmations of our external judgments. No doubt we can make these judgments too quickly, without hesitations and doubts of our own, paying too little attention to the harshness of battle and the discipline of the army. But it is a mistake to treat soldiers as if they were automatons who make no judgments at all. Instead, we must look closely at the particular features of their situation and try to understand what it might mean, in *these* circumstances, at *this* moment, to accept or defy a military command.

The defense of superior orders breaks down into two more specific arguments: the claim of ignorance and the claim of duress. These two are standard legal and moral claims, and they seem to function in war very much as they do in domestic society.[12] It is not the case, then, as has often been argued, that when we judge soldiers we must balance the necessities of military discipline (that obedience be quick and unquestioning) against the requirements of humanity (that innocent people be protected).[13] Rather, we view discipline as one of the conditions of wartime activity, and we take its particular features into account in determining individual responsibility. We do not excuse individuals in order to maintain or strengthen the disciplinary system. The army may cover up the crimes of soldiers or seek to limit liability for them with that end (or that pretended end) in view, but such efforts do not represent the delicate working out of a conception of justice. What justice requires is, first of all, that we commit ourselves to the defense of rights and, second, that we attend carefully to the particular defenses of men who are charged with violating rights.

Ignorance is the common lot of the common soldier, and it makes an easy defense, especially when calculations of usefulness and proportionality are called for. The soldier can plausibly say that he does not know and cannot know whether the campaign in which he is engaged is really required for the sake of victory, or whether it has been designed so as to hold unintended civilian deaths within acceptable limits. From his narrow and confined vantage point, even direct violations of human rights—as in the conduct of a siege, for example, or in the strategy of an anti-guerrilla campaign—may be unseen and unseeable. Nor is he bound to seek out information; the moral life of a combat soldier is not a research assignment. We might say that he stands to his campaigns as to his wars: he is not responsible for their overall justice. When war is fought at a distance, he may not be responsible even for the innocent people he himself kills. Artillery men and pilots are often kept in ignorance of the targets at which their fire is directed. If they ask questions, they are routinely assured that the targets are "legitimate military objectives." Perhaps they should always be skeptical, but I don't think we blame them if they accept the assurances of their commanders. We blame instead the far-seeing commanders. As the example of My Lai suggests, however, the ignorance of common soldiers has its limits. The soldiers in the Vietnamese village could hardly have doubted the innocence of the people they were ordered to kill. It is in such a situation that we want them to disobey: when they receive orders which, as the army judge said at the Calley trial, "a man of ordinary sense and understanding would, under the circumstances, know to be unlawful."[14]

Now, this implies an understanding not only of the circumstances but also of the law, and it was argued at Nuremberg and has been argued since that the laws of war are so vague, uncertain, and incoherent that they can never require disobedience.[15] Indeed, the state of the positive law is not very good, especially where it relates to the exigencies of combat. But the prohibition against massacre is plain enough, and I think it is fair to say that common soldiers have been charged and convicted only for the knowing murder of innocent people: shipwrecked survivors struggling in the water, for example, or prisoners of war, or helpless civilians. Nor is it a question here only of the law, for these are acts that not only "violate unchallenged rules of warfare," as the British field manual of 1944 states, but that also "outrage the general sentiments of humanity."[16] Ordinary *moral* sense and understanding rule out killings like those at My Lai. One of the soldiers there remembers thinking to himself that the slaughter was "just like a Nazi-type thing." That judgment is precisely right, and there is nothing in our conventional morality that renders it doubtful.

But the excuse of duress may hold even in a case like this, if the order to kill is backed up by a threat of execution. I have argued that soldiers in combat cannot plead self-preservation when they violate the rules of war. For the dangers of enemy fire are simply the risks of the activity in which they are engaged, and they have no right to reduce those risks at the expense of other people who are not engaged. But a threat of death directed not at soldiers in general but at a particular soldier—a threat, as the lawyers say, "imminent, real, and inevitable"—alters the case, lifting it out of the context of combat and war risk. Now it becomes like those domestic crimes in which one man forces another, under threat of immediate death, to kill a third. The act is clearly murder, but we are likely to think that the man in the middle is not the murderer. Or, if we do think him a murderer, we are likely to accept the excuse of duress. Surely someone who refuses to kill at such a time, and dies instead, is not just doing his duty; he is acting heroically. Gray provides a paradigmatic example:[17]

> In the Netherlands, the Dutch tell of a German soldier who was a member of an execution squad ordered to shoot innocent hostages. Suddenly he stepped out of rank and refused to participate in the execution. On the spot he was charged with treason by the officer in charge and was placed with the hostages, where he was promptly executed by his comrades.

Here is a man of extraordinary nobility, but what are we to say of his (former) comrades? That they are committing murder when they fire their guns, and that they are not responsible for the murder they commit. The officer in charge is responsible, and those among his superiors who decided on the policy of killing hostages. Responsibility passes over the heads of the members of the firing squad, not because of their oaths, not because of their orders, but because of the direct threat that drives them to act as they do.

War is a world of duress, of threat and counter-threat, so we must be clear about those cases in which duress does, and those in which it does not count as an excuse for conduct we would otherwise condemn. Soldiers are conscripted and forced to fight, but conscription by itself does not force them to kill innocent people. Soldiers are attacked and forced to fight, but neither aggression nor enemy onslaught forces them to kill innocent people. Conscription and attack bring them up against serious risks and hard choices. But constricted and frightening as their situation is, we still say that they choose freely and are responsible for what they do. Only a man with a gun at his head is not responsible.

But superior orders are not always enforced at the point of a gun. Army discipline in the actual context of war is often a great deal more haphazard than the firing squad example suggests. "It is a great boon of frontline positions," writes Gray, "that . . . disobedience is frequently possible, since supervision is not very exact where danger of death is present."[18] And in rear areas as well as at the front, there are ways of responding to an order short of obeying it: postponement, evasion, deliberate misunderstanding, loose construction, overly literal construction, and so on. One can ignore an immoral command or answer it with questions or protests; and sometimes even an overt refusal only invites reprimand, demotion, or detention; there is no risk of death. Whenever these possibilities are open, moral men will seize upon them. The law seems to require a similar readiness, for it is a legal principle that duress excuses only if the harm the individual soldier inflicts is not disproportionate to the harm with which he is threatened.[19] He is not excused for the murder of innocent people by the threat of demotion.

It has to be said, however, that officers are far more capable than enlisted men of weighing the dangers they face. Telford Taylor has described the case of Colonel William Peters, an officer in the Confederate Army during the American Civil War, who refused a direct order to burn the town of Chambersburg, Pennsylvania.[20] Peters was relieved of his command and placed under arrest, but he was never brought before a court martial. We may admire his courage, but if he anticipated that his superiors would ("prudently," as another Confederate officer said) avoid a trial, his decision was relatively easy. The decision of an ordinary soldier, who may well be subject to summary justice and who knows little of the temper of his more distant superiors, is much harder. At My Lai, those men who refused to fire never suffered for their refusal and apparently did not expect to suffer; and that suggests that we must blame the others for their obedience. In more ambiguous cases, the duress of superior orders, though it is not "imminent, real, and inevitable" and cannot count as a defense, is commonly regarded as an extenuating factor. That seems the right attitude to take, but I want to stress once again that when we take it we are not making concessions to the need for discipline, but simply recognizing the plight of the common soldier.

There is another reason for extenuation, unmentioned in the legal literature, but prominent in moral accounts of disobedience. The path that I have marked out as the right one is often a very lonely path. Here, too, the case of the German soldier who broke ranks with his fellow executioners and was promptly executed by them is unusual and extreme. But even when a soldier's doubts and anxieties are widely shared, they are still the subject of private brooding, not of public discussion. And when he acts, he acts alone, with no assurance that his comrades will support him. Civil protest and disobedience usually arise out of a community of values. But the army is an organization, not a community, and the communion of ordinary soldiers is shaped by the character and purposes of the organization, not by their private commitments. Theirs is the rough solidarity of men who face a common enemy and endure a common discipline. On both sides of a war, unity is reflexive, not intentional or premeditated. To disobey is to breach that elemental accord, to claim a moral separateness (or a moral superiority), to challenge one's fellows, perhaps even to intensify the dangers they face. "This is what is most difficult," wrote a French soldier who went to Algeria and then refused to fight, "being cut off from the fraternity, being locked up in a monologue, being incomprehensible."[21]

Now, *incomprehensible* is perhaps too strong a word, for a man appeals at such a time to common moral standards. But in the context of a military organization, that appeal will often go unheard, and so it involves a risk that may well be greater than that of punishment: the risk of a profound and morally disturbing isolation. This is not to say that one can join in a massacre for the sake of togetherness. But it suggests that moral life is rooted in a kind of association that military discipline precludes or temporarily cuts off, and that fact, too, must be taken into account in the judgments we make. It must be taken into account especially in the case of common soldiers, for officers are more free in their associations and more involved in discussions about policy and strategy. They have a say in the shape and character of the organization over which they preside. Hence, again, the critical importance of command responsibility.

COMMAND RESPONSIBILITY

Being an officer is not at all like being a common soldier. Rank is something men compete for, aspire to, glory in, and so even when officers were initially conscripted, we need not worry about holding them rigidly to the duties of their office. For rank can be avoided even when service cannot. Junior officers are killed at a high rate in combat, but still there are soldiers who want to be officers. It is a question of the pleasures of command; there is nothing quite like it (so I am told) in civilian life. The other side of pleasure, however, is responsibility. Officers take on immense responsibilities, again unlike anything in civilian life, for they have in their control the means of death and destruction. The higher their rank, the greater the reach of their command, the larger their responsibilities. They plan and organize campaigns; they decide on strategy and tactics; they choose to fight here rather than there; they order men into battle. Always, they must aim at victory and attend to the needs of their own soldiers. But they have at the same time a higher duty: "The soldier, be he friend or foe," wrote Douglas MacArthur when he confirmed the death sentence of General Yamashita, "is charged with the protection of the weak and unarmed. It is the very essence and reason of his being . . . [a] sacred trust."[22] Precisely because he himself, gun in hand, artillery and bombers at his call, poses a threat to the weak and unarmed, he must take steps to shield them. He must fight with restraint, accepting risks, mindful of the rights of the innocent.

That obviously means that he cannot order massacres; nor can he terrorize civilians with bombardment or bombing, or uproot whole populations in order to create "free-fire zones," or take reprisals against prisoners, or threaten to kill hostages. But it means more than that. Military commanders have two further and morally crucial responsibilities. First, in planning their campaigns, they must take positive steps to limit even unintended civilian deaths (and they must make sure that the numbers killed are not disproportionate to the military benefits they expect). Here the laws of war are of little help; no officer is going to be criminally charged for killing too many people if he does not actually massacre them. But the moral responsibility is clear, and it cannot be located anywhere else than in the office of commander. The campaign belongs to the commander as it does not belong to the ordinary combatants; he has access to all available information and also to the means of generating more information; he has (or ought to have) an overview of the sum of actions and effects that he is ordering and hoping for. If, then, the conditions set by the doctrine of double effect are not met, we should not hesitate to hold him accountable for the failure. Second, military commanders, in organizing their forces, must take positive steps to enforce the war convention and hold the men under their command to its standards. They must see to their training in this regard, issue clear orders, establish inspection procedures, and assure the punishment of individual soldiers and subordinate officers who kill or injure innocent people. If a great deal of such killing and injuring takes place, they are presumptively responsible, for we assume that it lay within their power to prevent it. Given what actually happens in war, military commanders have a great deal to answer for.

General Bradley and the Bombing of St. Lô

In July 1944, Omar Bradley, in command of American forces in Normandy, was engaged in planning a breakout from the invasion beachheads established the month before. The plan that he worked out, code-named COBRA and approved by Generals Montgomery and Eisenhower, called for the carpet bombing of an area three and a half miles wide, one and a half deep, along the Périers road outside the town of St. Lô. "Air bombing, we calculated, would either destroy or stun the enemy in the carpet" and so permit a quick advance. But it also posed a moral problem, which Bradley discusses in his autobiography. On July 20, he described the coming attack to some American newsmen:[23]

> The correspondents listened quietly to the outline of our plan, craned their necks as I pointed to the carpet and . . . tallied the air strength that had been assigned to us. At the close of the briefing, one of the newsmen asked if we would forewarn the French living within bounds of the carpet. I shook my head as if to escape the necessity for saying no. If we were to tip our hand to the French, we would also show it to the Germans. . . . The success of COBRA hung upon surprise; it was essential we have surprise even if it meant the slaughter of innocents as well.

Bombing of this sort, along the line of battle and in close support of combat troops, is permitted by positive international law. Even indiscriminate fire is permitted within the actual combat zone.[24] Civilians are thought to be forewarned by the proximity of the fighting. But as the correspondent's question suggests, this does not resolve the moral issue. We still want to know what positive measures might have been taken to avoid "the slaughter of innocents" or reduce the damage done. It is important to insist on such measures because, as this example clearly shows, the proportionality rule often has no inhibitory effects at all. Even if a large number of civilians lived in those five square miles near St. Lô, and even if all of them were likely to die, it would seem a small price to pay for a breakout that might well signal the end of the war. To say that, however, is not to say that those innocent lives are forfeit, for there may be ways of saving them short of calling off the attack. Perhaps civilians all along the battlefront could have been warned (without giving up surprise in a particular sector). Perhaps the attack could have been redirected through some less populated area (even at greater risk to the soldiers involved). Perhaps the planes, flying low, could have aimed at specific enemy targets, or artillery have been used instead (since shells could then be aimed more precisely than bombs), or paratroops dropped or patrols sent forward to seize important positions in advance of the main attack. I am in no position to recommend any of these courses of action, although, in the event, any of the last of them might have been preferable, even from a military point of view. For the bombs missed the carpet and killed or wounded several hundred American soldiers. How many French civilians were killed or wounded Bradley does not say.

However many civilians died, it cannot be said that their deaths were intentional. On the other hand, unless Bradley worked his way through the sorts of possibilities I have listed, it also cannot be said that he *intended not to kill them*. I have already explained why that negative intention ought to be required from soldiers; it is the domestic equivalent of what the lawyers call "due care" in domestic society. With reference to specific and small-scale military actions (like the bombing of cellars described by Frank Richards), the people required to take care are common soldiers and their immediate superiors. In cases such as the COBRA campaign, the relevant individuals stand higher in the hierarchy; it is on General Bradley that we rightly focus our attention, and on his superiors. Once again, I have to say that I cannot specify the precise point at which the requirements of "due care" have been met. How much attention is required? How much risk must be accepted? The line isn't clear.[25] But it is clear enough that most campaigns are planned and carried out well below the line; and one can blame commanders who don't make minimal efforts, even if one doesn't know exactly what a maximum effort would entail.

The Case of General Yamashita

The same problem of specifying standards comes up when one considers the responsibility of commanders for the actions of their subordinates. They are bound, as I have said, to enforce the war convention. But even the best possible system of enforcement doesn't preclude particular violations. It proves itself the best possible system by seizing upon these in a systematic way and by punishing the individuals who commit them so as to deter the others. It is only if there is a massive breakdown of this disciplinary system that we demand an accounting from the officers who preside over it. This, in effect, is the demand formally made upon General Yamashita by an American military commission in the aftermath of the Philippine campaign in 1945.[26] It was said of Yamashita that he was responsible for a large number of specified acts of violence and murder inflicted upon unarmed civilians and prisoners of war. That these acts had in fact been committed by Japanese soldiers no one denied. On the other hand, no evidence was presented to show that Yamashita had ordered the violence and murder nor even that he had known about any of the specified acts. His responsibility lay in his failure "to discharge his duty as commander to control the operations of the members of his command, permitting them to commit brutal atrocities. . . ." Defending himself, Yamashita claimed that he had been entirely unable to exercise control over his troops: the successful American invasion had disrupted his communication and command structure, leaving him in effective charge only of the troops whom he personally led, in retreat, into the mountains of northern Luzon; and these troops had committed no atrocities. The commission refused to accept this defense and sentenced Yamashita to death. His appeal was carried to the U.S. Supreme Court, which declined to review the case, despite memorable dissents by Justices Murphy and Rutledge. Yamashita was executed on February 22, 1946.

There are two ways of describing the standard to which Yamashita was held by the commission and the Court majority. The defense lawyers argued that the standard was one of strict liability, radically inappropriate in cases of criminal justice. That is to say, Yamashita was convicted without reference to any acts he committed or even to any omissions that he might have avoided. He was convicted of having held an office, because of the duties said to inhere in that office, even though the duties were in fact undo-able under the conditions in which he found himself. Justice Murphy went further: the duties were undo-able because of the conditions that the American army had created.[27]

> . . . read against the background of military events in the Philippines subsequent to October 9, 1944, these charges amount to this: "We, the victorious American forces, have done everything possible to destroy and disorganize your lines of communication, your effective control of your personnel, your ability to wage war. In these respects we have succeeded. . . . And now we charge and condemn you for having been

inefficient in maintaining control of your troops during the period when we were so effectively besieging and eliminating your forces and blocking your ability to maintain effective command."

This is probably an accurate description of the facts of the case. Not only was Yamashita unable to do the things that commanders should do, but if we push the argument back, he was in no sense the author of the conditions which made those things impossible. I should add, however, that the other judges did not believe, or did not admit, that they were enforcing the principle of strict liability. According to Chief Justice Stone, the question was "whether the law of war imposes on an army commander a duty to take such appropriate measures *as are within his power* to control the troops under his command. . . ." It is easy to answer that question affirmatively, but not at all easy to say what measures are "appropriate" under the adverse conditions of combat, disorganization, and defeat.

One wants to set the standards very high, and the argument for strict liability is utilitarian in character: holding officers automatically responsible for massive violations of the rules of war forces them to do everything they can to avoid such violations, without forcing us to specify what they ought to do.[28] But there are two problems with this. First of all, we don't really want commanders to do everything they can, for that requirement, taken literally, would leave them little time to do anything else. This point is never as telling in their case as it is in the case of political leaders and domestic crime: we don't require our leaders to do everything they can (but only to take "appropriate measures") to prevent robbery and murder, for they have other things to do. But they, presumably, have not armed and trained the people who commit robbery and murder, and these people are not directly in their charge. The case of military commanders is different; hence we must expect them to devote a great deal of time and attention to the discipline and control of the men with guns they have turned loose in the world. But still, not all their time and attention, not all the resources at their command.

The second argument against strict liability in criminal cases is a more familiar one. Even doing "everything" is not the same as doing it successfully. All we can require is serious efforts of specific sorts; we cannot require success, since the conditions of warfare are such that success isn't always possible. And the impossibility of success is necessarily an excuse—given serious effort, an entirely satisfactory excuse—for failure. To refuse to accept the excuse is to refuse to regard the defendant as a moral agent: for it is in the nature of moral agents (of human beings) that their best efforts sometimes fail. The refusal disregards the defendant's humanity, makes him into an example, *pour encourager les autres*; and that we have no right to do to anyone.

These two arguments seem to me right, and they exonerate General Yamashita, but they also leave us with no clear standards at all. In fact, there is no philosophical or theoretical way of fixing such standards. That is also true with regard to the planning and organization of military campaigns. There is no sure rule against which to measure the conduct of General Bradley. The discussion of double effect in chapters 9 and 10 pointed only in a fairly crude way toward the sorts of considerations that are relevant when we make judgments about such matters. The appropriate standards can emerge only through a long process of casuistic reasoning, that is, by attending to one case after another, morally or legally. The chief failure of the military commission and the Supreme Court in 1945, aside from the fact that they failed to do justice to General Yamashita, is that they made no contribution to this process. They did not specify the measures that Yamashita might have taken; they did not suggest what degree of disorganization might serve as a limit on command responsibility. Only by making such specifications, again and again, can we draw the lines that the war convention requires.

We can say more than this, I think, if we turn back briefly to the My Lai case. The evidence brought forward at the trial of Lieutenant Calley and the materials collected by newsmen carrying on their own investigations of the massacre clearly suggest the responsibility of officers superior to both Calley and Medina. The strategy of the American war in Vietnam, as I have already argued, tended to put civilians at risk in unacceptable ways, and ordinary soldiers could hardly ignore the implications of that strategy. My Lai was itself in a free-fire zone, routinely shelled and bombed. "If you can shoot artillery . . . in there every night," one soldier asked, "how can the people in there be worth so much?"[29] In effect, soldiers were taught that civilian lives were not worth much, and there seems to have been little effort to counteract that teaching except by the most formal and perfunctory instruction in the rules of war. If we are fully to assign blame for the massacre, then, there are a large number of officers whom we would have to condemn. I cannot put together a list here, and I doubt that all of them could have been or ought to have been legally charged and tried—though this might have been a useful occasion to apply, and improve upon, the

Yamashita precedent. But that many officers are morally chargeable seems certain, and their blameworthiness is not less than that of the men who did the actual killing. Indeed, there is this difference between them: in the case of the ordinary soldiers, the burden of proof lies with us. As in any murder case, we must prove their knowing and willful participation. But the officers are presumptively guilty; the burden of proof, if they would demonstrate their innocence, lies with them. And until we find some way of imposing that burden, we shall not have done all that we can do in defense of the "weak and unarmed," the innocent victims of war.

THE NATURE OF NECESSITY (4)

I have left the hardest question for last. What are we to say about those military commanders (or political leaders) who override the rules of war and kill innocent people in a "supreme emergency"? Surely we want to be led at such a time by men and women ready to do what has to be done—what is *necessary*; for it is only here that necessity, in its true sense, comes into the theory of war. On the other hand, we cannot ignore or forget what it is they do. The deliberate killing of the innocent is murder. Sometimes, in conditions of extremity (which I have tried to define and delimit), commanders must commit murder or they must order others to commit it. And then they are murderers, though in a good cause. In domestic society, and particularly in the context of revolutionary politics, we say of such people that they have dirty hands. I have argued elsewhere that men and women with dirty hands, though it may be the case that they had acted well and done what their office required, must nonetheless bear a burden of responsibility and guilt.[30] They have killed unjustly, let us say, for the sake of justice itself, but justice itself requires that unjust killing be condemned. There is obviously no question here of legal punishment, but of some other way of assigning and enforcing blame. What way, however, is radically unclear. The available answers are all likely to make us uneasy. The nature of that uneasiness will be apparent if we turn again to the case of British terror bombing in World War II.

The Dishonoring of Arthur Harris

"He will perhaps go down in history as a giant among the leaders of men. He gave Bomber Command the courage to surmount its ordeals. . . ." So

writes the historian Noble Frankland about Arthur Harris, who directed
the strategic bombing of Germany from February 1942 until the end of the
war.[31] Harris was, as we have seen, the determined advocate of terrorism,
resisting every attempt to use his planes for other purposes. Now, terror
bombing is a criminal activity, and after the immediate threat posed by
Hitler's early victories had passed, it was an entirely indefensible activity.
Hence Harris' case isn't really an example of the dirty hands problem. He
and Churchill, who was ultimately responsible for military policy, faced
no moral dilemma: they should simply have stopped the bombing campaign. But we can take it as an example, nonetheless, for it apparently had
that form in the minds of British leaders, even of Churchill himself at the
end. That is why Harris, though of course criminal charges were never
brought against him, was not treated after the war as a giant among the
leaders of men.

He had done what his government thought necessary, but what he
had done was ugly, and there seems to have been a conscious decision
not to celebrate the exploits of Bomber Command or to honor its leader.
"From this work," writes Angus Calder, "Churchill and his colleagues
at last recoiled. After the strategic air offensive officially ended in mid-
April [1945], Bomber Command was slighted and snubbed; and Harris,
unlike other well-known commanders, was not rewarded with a peerage."
In such circumstances, not to honor was to dishonor, and that is exactly
how Harris regarded the government's action (or omission).[32] He waited
a while for his reward and then, resentfully, left England for his native
Rhodesia. The men he led were similarly treated, though the snub was not
so personal. In Westminster Abbey, there is a plaque honoring those pilots
of Fighter Command who died during the war, listing them all by name.
But the bomber pilots, though they suffered far heavier casualties, have
no plaque; their names are unrecorded. It is as if the British had taken to
heart Rolf Hochhuth's question:[33]

> Is a pilot who bombs
> population centers under orders
> still to be called a *soldier*?

All this makes a point, though it does so indirectly and in so equivo-
cal a fashion that we cannot but notice its moral awkwardness. Harris and
his men have a legitimate complaint: they did what they were told to do

and what their leaders thought was necessary and right, but they are dishonored for doing it, and it is suddenly suggested (what else can the dishonor mean?) that what was necessary and right was also wrong. Harris felt that he was being made a scapegoat, and it is surely true that if blame is to be distributed for the bombing, Churchill deserves a full share. But Churchill's success in dissociating himself from the policy of terrorism is not of great importance; there is always a remedy for that in retrospective criticism. What is important is that his dissociation was part of a national dissociation—a deliberate policy that has moral significance and value.

And yet, the policy seems cruel. Stated in general terms, it amounts to this: that a nation fighting a just war, when it is desperate and survival itself is at risk, must use unscrupulous or morally ignorant soldiers; and as soon as their usefulness is past, it must disown them. I would rather say something else: that decent men and women, hard-pressed in war, must sometimes do terrible things, and then they themselves have to look for some way to reaffirm the values they have overthrown. But the first statement is probably the more realistic one. For it is very rare, as Machiavelli wrote in his *Discourses*, "that a good man should be found willing to employ wicked means," even when such means are morally required.[34] And then we must look for people who are not good, and use them, and dishonor them. Perhaps there is some better way of doing that than the way Churchill chose. It would have been better if he had explained to his countrymen the moral costs of their survival and if he had praised the courage and endurance of the fliers of Bomber Command even while insisting that it was not possible to take pride in what they had done (an impossibility that many of them must have felt). But Churchill did not do that; he never admitted that the bombing constituted a wrong. In the absence of such an admission, the refusal to honor Harris at least went some small distance toward re-establishing a commitment to the rules of war and the rights they protect. And that, I think, is the deepest meaning of all assignments of responsibility.

CONCLUSION

The world of necessity is generated by a conflict between collective survival and human rights. We find ourselves in that world less often than we think, certainly less often than we say; but whenever we are there, we experience the ultimate tyranny of war—and also, it might be argued, the ultimate incoherence of the theory of war. In a troubling essay entitled "War and Massacre," Thomas Nagel has described our situation at such a time in terms of a conflict between utilitarian and absolutist modes of thought: we know that there are some outcomes that must be avoided at all costs, and we know that there are some costs that can never rightly be paid. We must face the possibility, Nagel argues, "that these two forms of moral intuition are not capable of being brought together into a single, coherent moral system, and that the world can present us with situations in which there is no honorable or moral course for a man to take, no course free of guilt and responsibility for evil."[35] I have tried to avoid the stark indeterminacy of that description by suggesting that political leaders can hardly help but choose the utilitarian side of the dilemma. That is what they are there for. They must opt for collective survival and override those rights that have suddenly loomed as obstacles to survival. But I don't want to say, any more than Nagel does, that they are free of guilt when they do that. Were there no guilt involved, the decisions they make would be less agonizing than they are. And they can only prove their honor by accepting responsibility for those decisions and by living out the agony. A moral theory that made their life easier, or that concealed their dilemma from the rest of us, might achieve greater coherence, but it would miss or it would repress the reality of war.

It is sometimes said that the dilemma ought to be concealed, that we should draw the veil (as Churchill tried to do) over the crimes that soldiers and statesmen cannot avoid. Or, we should avert our eyes—for the sake of our innocence, I suppose, and the moral certainties. But that is a dangerous business; having looked away, how will we know when to look back? Soon we will avert our eyes from everything that happens in wars and battles, condemning nothing, like the second monkey in the Japanese statue, who sees no evil. And yet there is plenty to see. Soldiers and statesmen live mostly on this side of the ultimate crises of collective survival; the greater number by far of the crimes they commit can neither be defended nor excused. They are simply crimes. Someone must try to see them clearly and describe them "in express words." Even the murders called necessary must be similarly described; it doubles the crime to look away, for then we are not able to fix the limits of necessity, or remember the victims, or make our own (awkward) judgments of the people who kill in our name.

Mostly morality is tested only by the ordinary pressures of military conflict. Mostly it is possible, even when it isn't easy, to live by the requirements of justice. And mostly the judgments we make of what soldiers and statesmen do are singular and clearcut; with whatever hesitations, we say yes or no, we say right or wrong. But in supreme emergencies our judgments are doubled, reflecting the dualist character of the theory of war and the deeper complexity of our moral realism; we say yes *and* no, right *and* wrong. That dualism makes us uneasy; the world of war is not a fully comprehensible, let alone a morally satisfactory place. And yet it cannot be escaped, short of a universal order in which the existence of nations and peoples could never be threatened. There is every reason to work for such an order. The difficulty is that we sometimes have no choice but to fight for it.

Afterword: Nonviolence and the Theory of War

THE DREAM OF A WAR TO END WAR, THE MYTH OF ARMAGEDDON (THE last battle), the vision of the lion lying down with the lamb—all these point toward an age definitively peaceful, a distant age that lies across some unknown time-break, without armed struggle and systematic killing. It will not come, so we have been told, until the forces of evil have been decisively defeated and mankind freed forever from the lust for conquest and domination. In our myths and visions, the end of war is also the end of secular history. Those of us trapped within that history, who see no end to it, have no choice but to fight on, defending the values to which we are committed, unless or until some alternative means of defense can be found. The only alternative is nonviolent defense, "war without weapons," as it has been called by its advocates, who seek to adjust our dreams to our realities. They claim that we can uphold the values of communal life and liberty without fighting and killing, and this claim raises important questions (secular and practical questions) about the theory of war and the argument for justice. To treat them as they deserve would require another book; I can offer only a brief essay, a partial and tentative analysis of the ways in which nonviolence relates, first, to the doctrine of aggression, and then to the rules of war.

Nonviolent defense differs from conventional strategies in that it concedes the overrunning of the country that is being defended. It establishes no obstacles capable of stopping a military advance or preventing a military occupation. "Although minor delaying actions against the incursions of foreign troops and functionaries may be possible," writes Gene Sharp, "civilian defense . . . does not attempt to halt such entry, and cannot successfully do so."[1] That is a radical concession, and I don't think that any government has ever made it willingly. Nonviolence has been practiced (in the face of an invasion) only after violence, or the threat of violence, has failed. Then its protagonists aim to deny the victorious army the fruits of its victory through a systematic policy of civilian resistance and noncooperation: they call upon the conquered people to make themselves ungovernable. I want to stress that it is not war but civilian resistance that has usually been regarded as a last resort, because war holds out at least the possibility of avoiding the occupation that evokes or requires the resistance. But we might reverse this ordering were we to decide that resistance is as likely to end the occupation as military action is to prevent it, and at a much lower cost in human lives. There is as yet no evidence that that proposition is true, "no cases in which . . . civilian defense has caused an invader to withdraw."[2] But no nonviolent struggle has ever been undertaken by a people trained in advance in its methods and prepared (as soldiers are in the case of war) to accept its costs. So it might be true; and if it is, we should have to regard aggression very differently from the way we do at present.

It might be said that nonviolence abolishes aggressive war simply by virtue of the refusal to engage the aggressor militarily. Invasion is not morally coercive in the ways I described in chapter 4, men and women cannot be forced to fight, if they have come to believe that they can defend their country in some other way, without killing and being killed. And if there really is some other way, at least potentially effective, then the aggressor cannot be charged with forcing them to fight. Nonviolence de-escalates the conflict and diminishes its criminality. By adopting the methods of disobedience, noncooperation, boycott, and general strike, the citizens of the invaded country transform aggressive war into a political struggle. They treat the aggressor in effect as a domestic tyrant or usurper, and they turn his soldiers into policemen. If the invader accepts this role, and if he responds to the resistance he encounters with curfews, fines, jail sentences, and nothing more, the prospect is opened up of a long-term struggle, not without its difficulties and painfulness for civilians, but far less destructive than even a short war, and winnable (we are assuming) by those same civilians. Allied states would have no reason to intervene militarily in such a struggle; which is a good thing, since if they too were committed to nonviolent defense, they would have no means of intervening.

But they could bring moral and perhaps also economic pressure to bear against the invaders.

This, then, would be the position of the invaders: they would hold the country they had "attacked," could establish military bases wherever they pleased, and enjoy whatever strategic benefits these yielded them (vis-à-vis other countries, presumably). But their logistics problems would be severe, for unless they brought along their own personnel, they could not depend upon the local transportation or communication systems. And since they could hardly bring along an entire workforce, they would have great difficulty exploiting the natural resources and the industrial productivity of the invaded country. Hence the economic costs of the occupation would be high. The political costs might well be higher. Everywhere their soldiers would encounter sullen, resentful, withdrawn, and noncooperative civilians. Though these civilians would never take up arms, they would rally, demonstrate, and strike; and the soldiers would have to respond, coercively, like the hated instruments of a tyrannical regime. Their military élan might well fade, their morale erode, under the strains of civilian hostility and of an on-going struggle in which they never experienced the release of an open fight. Eventually, perhaps, the occupation would become untenable, and the invaders would simply leave; they would have won and then lost a "war without weapons."

This is an attractive, even though it is not a millennial, picture. Indeed, it is attractive precisely because it is not millennial, but conceivable in the world we know. It is only just conceivable, however; for the success I have described is possible only if the invaders are committed to the war convention—and they won't always be committed. While nonviolence by itself replaces aggressive war with political struggle, it cannot by itself determine the means of struggle. The invading army can always adopt the common methods of domestic tyrants, which go well beyond curfews, fines, and jail sentences; and its leaders, though they are soldiers, may well be tempted to do that for the sake of a quick "victory." Tyrants will not, of course, lay siege to their own cities or bomb or bombard them; nor will invaders who encounter no armed opposition.[3] But there are other, probably more efficient, ways of terrorizing a people whose country one controls, and of breaking their resistance. In his "Reflections on Gandhi," George Orwell points out the importance of exemplary leadership and wide publicity in a nonviolent campaign and wonders whether such a campaign would even be possible in a totalitarian state. "It is difficult to see how Gandhi's methods could be applied in a country where opponents of the regime disappear in the middle of the night and are never heard from again."[4] Nor would civilian resistance work well against invaders who sent out squads of soldiers to kill civilian leaders, who arrested and tortured suspects, established concentration camps, and exiled large numbers of people from areas where the resistance was strong to distant and desolate parts of the country. Nonviolent defense is no defense at all against tyrants or conquerors ready to adopt such measures. Gandhi demonstrated this truth, I think by the perverse advice he gave to the Jews of Germany: that they should commit suicide rather than fight back against Nazi tyranny.[5] Here nonviolence, under extreme conditions, collapses into violence directed at oneself rather than at one's murderers, though why it should take that direction I cannot understand.

If one faces an enemy like the Nazis, and if armed resistance is impossible, it is virtually certain that the men and women of the occupied country—those who have been marked out for survival, at any rate, and perhaps even those who have been marked out for death—will yield to their new masters and obey their decrees. The country will grow silent. Resistance will be a matter of individual heroism or of the heroism of small groups, but not of collective struggle.

The success of nonviolent resistance requires that soldiers (or their officers or political leaders) refuse at some early point, before civilian endurance is exhausted, to carry out or support a terrorist policy. As in guerrilla war, the strategy is to force the invading army to bear the onus of civilian deaths. But here the onus is to be made especially clear (especially unbearable) by the dramatic absence of any armed struggle in which civilians might be collusive. They will be hostile, certainly, but no soldiers will die at their hands or at the hands of partisans who have their secret support. And yet, if their resistance is to be broken decisively and quickly, the soldiers will have to be prepared to kill them. Since they are not always prepared to do that, or since their officers are not always sure that they will do it again and again, as might be necessary, civilian defense has had a certain limited effectiveness—not in expelling an invading army, but in preventing the attainment of particular goals set by its leaders. As Liddell Hart has argued, however, these effects have only been possible[6]

> against opponents whose code of morality was fundamentally similar [to that of the civilian defenders], and whose ruthlessness was thereby restrained. It is very doubtful whether non-violent resistance would

have availed against a Tartar conqueror in the past, or against a Stalin in more recent times. The only impression it seems to have made on Hitler was to excite his impulse to trample on what, to his mind, was contemptible weakness—although there is evidence that it did embarrass many of his generals, brought up in a better code . . .

If one could count on that "better code" and look forward to a nonviolent test of wills—civilian solidarity against military discipline—there would, I think, be no reason to fight: political struggle is better than fighting, even when victory is uncertain. For victory in war is also uncertain; and here it might be said, as it cannot easily be said in the case of war, that the citizens of the occupied country will win if they deserve to win. As in the domestic struggle against tyranny (so long as the struggle doesn't degenerate into massacre), we judge them by their capacity for self-help, that is, by their collective determination to defend their liberty.

When one cannot count on the moral code, nonviolence is either a disguised form of surrender or a minimalist way of upholding communal values after a military defeat. I don't want to underestimate the importance of the second of these. Though civilian resistance evokes no moral recognition among the invading soldiers, it can still be important for its practitioners. It expresses the communal will to survive; and though the expression is brief, as in Czechoslovakia in 1968, it is likely to be long remembered.[7] The heroism of civilians is even more heartening than that of soldiers. On the other hand, one should not expect much more from civilians confronted with a terrorist or potentially terrorist army than brief or sporadic resistance. It is easy to say that "Non-violent action is not a course for cowards. It requires the ability and determination to sustain the battle whatever the price in suffering. . . ."[8] But this sort of exhortation is no more attractive than that of a general telling his soldiers to fight to the last man. Indeed, I prefer the exhortation of the general, since he at least addresses himself to a limited number of men, not to an entire population. The case is similar with guerrilla war, which has this advantage over civilian resistance: it recapitulates the military situation where only a relatively few people are asked "to sustain the battle"—though the others will suffer too, as we have seen, unless the opposing army fights in accordance with the war convention.

The comparison with guerrilla war is worth pursuing further. In an armed insurrection, the coercing and killing of civilians by enemy soldiers has the effect of mobilizing other civilians and bringing them into the insurgent camp. The indiscriminate violence of their opponents is one of the major sources of guerrilla recruitment. Nonviolent resistance, on the other hand, is possible on a significant scale only if civilians are already mobilized and prepared to act together. The resistance is simply the physical expression of that mobilization, directly, in the streets, or indirectly, through economic slowdowns and political passivity. Now the coercion and killing of civilians is likely to break the solidarity of the resistance, spreading terror through the country and eventually producing a dulled acquiescence. At the same time, it may demoralize the soldiers who are called upon to do what appears to them—if it appears to them—indecent work, and it may undercut support for the occupation among the friends and relatives of those soldiers. Guerrilla war can produce a similar demoralization, but the effect is compounded by the fear soldiers must feel in the face of the hostile men and women among whom they are forced to fight (and die). In the case of nonviolent defense, there will be no fear; there will only be disgust and shame. The success of the defense is entirely dependent upon the moral convictions and sensibilities of the enemy soldiers.

Nonviolent defense depends upon noncombatant immunity. For this reason, it is no service to the cause to ridicule the rules of war or to insist (as Tolstoy did) that violence is always and necessarily unrestrained. When one wages a "war without weapons," one appeals for restraint from men with weapons. It is not likely that these men, soldiers subject to military discipline, are going to be converted to the creed of nonviolence. Nor is it critical to the success of the "war" that they be converted, but only that they be held to their own putative standards. The appeal that is made to them takes this form: "You cannot shoot at me, because I am not shooting at you; nor am I going to shoot at you. I am your enemy and will remain so as long as you occupy my country. But I am a noncombatant enemy, and you must coerce and control me, if you can, without violence." The appeal simply restates the argument about civilian rights and soldierly duties that underlies the war convention and provides its substance. And this suggests that the transformation of war into a political struggle has as its prior condition the restraint of war as a military struggle. If we are to aim at the transformation, as we should, we must begin by insisting upon the rules of war and by holding soldiers rigidly to the norms they set. The restraint of war is the beginning of peace.

POSTSCRIPT:
A DEFENSE OF JUST WAR THEORY

IN THE YEARS SINCE THIS BOOK WAS FIRST PUBLISHED, JUST WAR THEORY has become a minor academic industry; it has proved particularly engaging for contemporary philosophers, though political theorists and legal scholars are also working on the difficult issues of morality and war. The literature seems vast, given what writing on this subject was like in the middle years of the last century. Vietnam is the major reason for the surge of interest, but interest has been sustained by America's subsequent wars, which have been greater in number and longer in duration than anyone expected.

Many recent books and articles are critical of what is called standard (or even orthodox) just war theory, which this book is often taken to represent. I have read some of this literature, but mostly I have listened to the critical arguments at lectures and academic conferences in the United States and abroad—and sometimes I have responded to them. I want to respond here, not to particular philosophers but to the cohort of recent academic writers about war who believe that the distinctiveness of just war theory is unnecessary; war's dilemmas are in no way exceptional; they do not differ from the moral dilemmas of everyday life, and they can be dealt with by the familiar methods of analytic philosophy. What is at issue, in part, is the very subject of the theory. What is just war theory about?

There are at least two answers to this question, one of which I want to defend as strongly as I can. The first answer is that just war theory is about war, and the second answer is that just war theory is about moral philosophy. The difference is most simply a matter of focus. Toward what issues, what hard questions, what specific circumstances, is the theorist's attention directed? But we might also think of it in a backward looking way. What was the theorist reading before she began writing? And since I bear some small responsibility for the academic industry, I will begin autobiographically, with my own reading matter.

Before I wrote *Just and Unjust Wars*, I read some key texts in Catholic moral theology and early international law—Augustine, Aquinas, and Vitoria; Grotius and Puffendorf, and a few others. I read a handful of nineteenth- and twentieth-century legal textbooks and a couple of contemporary theorists, like Paul Ramsey, the most important Protestant writer on war in the 1950s and 1960s. But the greater part by far of my reading was not in theory at all but in military history, both academic and popular, and then in the memoir literature produced by soldiers of different ranks (preferably the lower ranks: junior officers and foot soldiers, who make the toughest moral decisions on the battlefield); and then in wartime journalism and commentary (especially about Vietnam, the immediate occasion of my own writing). Finally I read many of the novels and poems that deal with the experience of fighting and the company of soldiers. The nontheoretical genres, and the books and articles they include, seemed to me the critically necessary material for my project—partly because I had never been a soldier myself and I needed to learn as much as I could about the experience of war. But I also focused on histories, memoirs, essays, novels, and poems because I wanted the moral arguments of my book to ring true to their authors— and to the men and women about whom they were writing.

Looking over the recent flood of books and articles about justice and injustice in war, I sense that many authors are not reading the way I did. They are preoccupied with the academic literature about moral philosophy and just war theory. They are reading the journals, not the journalists; they are reading each other. This is a common academic practice, but it has always seemed to me problematic—especially when the subject is politics and war.

After reading each other, these theorists argue with each other (and sometimes with the rest of us), disagreeing about significant theoretical points and about fine points, too. Some of the disagreements are about ethical issues like self-defense and responsibility—issues that arise not only in wartime but also in civil society in time of peace and in many ordinary domestic contexts. Many of these theorists take the view that issues of this sort can be delineated most clearly and addressed most conclusively in contexts far removed from war and even in hypothetical and elaborately constructed cases that have no historical or practical reference at all. So they have no need to read, say, military history; the debate is focused elsewhere, and all that is necessary is to read the works of the other participants in the debate.

I don't want to deny the possible usefulness of this sort of philosophical labor. Issues that arise in war, but also in other real and imagined contexts, can certainly be addressed, illuminated, and perhaps even resolved, in the other contexts. But I worry that the illuminations and resolutions won't ring true to the people I have always tried to address, for whom war is a primary subject and a personal experience. But how can that be? Surely if we have figured out what personal responsibility (for example) means—in the way that many contemporary philosophers figure things out, by abstracting from particular cases, by inventing examples that test every possible definition, by calling each other to account with increasingly refined examples—then we also know what personal responsibility means in war. There is no point in reading historical analyses of military decisions, or subjective accounts of decision making in the field, or fictional narratives about combat, since none of these are designed for philosophical purposes. What counts is the cleverness of the design and the questions that it highlights and helps us answer.

For these theorists wars and battles are like street crimes and marital disputes in civil society; they involve the same kind of moral dilemmas. They are "cases" to which theorists need to apply the rules of everyday morality. In order to figure out the rules, they may start from the cases, playing with them, changing their details, even inventing possible and impossible variations that test our understanding of the rules as they are, or as they might be, or should be. But these theorists have no commitment to the actual cases until they know the applicable rules, and hypothetical cases will do just as well in figuring things out—perhaps better, since they impose no reality constraints on their designers. Still, all the cases, real and hypothetical, are in some sense familiar, that is, they can be imagined to arise, however improbable they are, in everyday life.

I want to argue, against this view, that wars and battles are not "cases" to which the law and morality of everyday life can be applied; by definition, they don't take place in civil society. War is a long-standing human practice (however uncomfortable we are with it), which represents a radical break with our ordinary social activities. The practice of war has been argued about and reflected on over many centuries, and it has its own law and even its own morality—which have been produced through the adaptation of ordinary law and morality to the peculiar circumstances of war. If we want to understand why that adaptation was necessary and what it has produced, we need to turn first to war itself. We need to understand what wars and battles are, how they have been experienced over the years, and how their moral and legal rules have been worked out. That's the point of reading military history and soldiers' memoirs. Only then can we turn to particular wars, particular battles, and particular incidents in battles; only then do we have cases to which we can apply the rules and come to grips with the peculiar tensions to which these applications are subject. And then, finally, we will be in a position to argue for or against revisions of the rules. We can learn a lot about the rules and the tensions and the possibly necessary revisions by reading what earlier international lawyers and just war theorists have written, but some of their key arguments will seem strange or incomprehensible unless we begin with the literature of war itself.

It is especially strange that just war theory, in its standard form, requires us to judge the conduct of a war independently of our judgment of its character, so that what soldiers are permitted to do or barred from doing in battle doesn't depend on whether their war is just or not. I am going to focus here on this strange requirement, which lies at the center of contemporary philosophical debates. What the required independence of the two judgments means is that we grant soldiers on both sides, whether their cause is just or unjust, an equal right to fire their guns, so long as they aim only at each other and not at innocent civilians. We treat soldiers on the battlefield as moral equals. Many (it may be most) of the philosophers working on these issues today are highly critical of this equality, and of the separation of *ad bellum* justice from *in bello* justice. They think it is obviously wrong to judge soldiers by how well they fight, without reference to the rightness or wrongness of the war they are fighting. They want soldiers fighting a just war to be able to do things, like firing their guns, that soldiers fighting an unjust war are barred from doing. And their argument makes a lot of sense if, as I wrote about one of them, we imagine war to be a peacetime activity. Indeed, standard just war theory is untenable if we take wars and battles to be like street crimes and marital disputes.

We need an example here, not hypothetical, so let's compare aggressive war to a bank robbery in, say, Philadelphia, the city of brotherly love. Let Philadelphia represent a peaceful civil society. We would certainly not judge the conduct of the robbery independently of the wrongfulness of robbing banks, as if the wrong didn't make a difference. It does make a difference. If there is a shoot-out between the bank robber and a bank guard, it can't be the case that the two of them have an equal right to shoot so long as neither of them aims at innocent bystanders. Though they are both subject to moral constraints, the guard has rights that the robber obviously doesn't have. So, by analogy, shouldn't we say that the just warrior, defending his country, has rights that the unjust warrior, invading the country, doesn't have?

This is the central challenge (though there are others, related to this one) posed by many contemporary moral philosophers to the standard or orthodox theory of just war—the theory that I have tried to develop and defend. According to the standard theory, aggressive war is indeed a crime, but it isn't the crime of the ordinary soldiers who fight it. The criminals are the men and women, mostly men, the political and military leaders, who consult together and decide, let's say, to attack a neighboring country. The Nuremberg tribunal got it right, then, when it indicted the heads of the Nazi party, state, and army, and allowed ordinary German soldiers to go home. But how can these soldiers be guiltless, who marched into Poland, Russia, Belgium, France, and so many other countries? To answer that question (which I have now put in the strongest possible way), we must focus on what actually happens in the world of war. For this is a world where life is radically unlike life in Philadelphia or in any peaceful civil society, even one beset by armed and possibly violent bank robbers.

What is special, what is peculiar, about war? I have a short list of features that moral and political theorists, philosophers too, should attend to—a list that could be expanded. It is designed only to serve the immediate purposes of my argument here.

First, the circumstances of war are intensely coercive, and they are coercive in ways that are probably not equaled anywhere else. Slavery and imprisonment are highly coercive institutions, and conscription for military service is sometimes compared to them (by its opponents). The comparison can be useful in political debates, though it is greatly exaggerated. But it is hard to exaggerate the coerciveness of the battlefield, where life is always at risk and soldiers are compelled to act in ways that have no precedent in their own, or in any, civilian experience. Command decisions are also subject to the coerciveness of war—hence the claim of "military necessity." Moral theorists who try to set limits to that claim, as I tried to do in *Just and Unjust Wars*, must acknowledge its possible force. In the heat of battle, officers are driven to do cruel things, which they would never imagine doing in domestic society, by the belief that they have no alternative or, rather, that the only alternative is defeat—which they take to mean subjection and possibly death, not so much for themselves as for their country and their fellow citizens. If we want, sometimes, to challenge that belief, we must understand the circumstances that produce it.

Some of the legal and moral institutions of war acknowledge and even legitimize its coerciveness. Consider the prisoner of war convention (I will repeat here an argument I make in chapter 3), which makes the practice of individual or group surrender on the battlefield possible. Surrender is an implicit agreement: the surrendering soldier, threatened with death, agrees to give up fighting, and his captors agree, whether they think his war just or unjust, to provide him with what lawyers call "benevolent quarantine for the duration of the war." But this is an agreement that the captive has made under extreme duress, and according to the ordinary law and morality of domestic life, it cannot have any binding force. And yet we recognize and accept its binding force, so that soldiers who try to escape from a prisoner of war camp are treated as if they have broken their word and thereby acted contrary to the law and morality of·war; they are subject to punishment, even to capital punishment. I suppose one could argue that in the "original position," as it is described by John Rawls, all potential soldiers would agree to the prisoner of war convention and that this hypothetical consent gives it binding force. But then we would have to explain why many prisoners try to escape and rejoin the fighting and why we celebrate their efforts—why they are commonly described as heroes in books and films when they might plausibly be described as men who have broken their (hypothetical or tacit) promise and put a useful and humane convention at risk.

The coerciveness of war explains the prisoner of war convention, for there is no other way to allow soldiers to stop fighting without being killed. But there is a second feature of war that explains why some soldiers violate the convention and why we call them heroes.

Second, war is an intensely collective and collectivizing experience. When political or moral theorists talk about war, and especially about just war, they commonly begin with the right of individual self-defense. But this is only a bare beginning, and as an introduction to the understanding of warfare, it is somewhat misleading. Wars are fought by individuals, indeed, but not by individuals who are principally engaged in defending themselves. They are members of a collective, to which they attach value, often great value, and they are engaged in a project that is not merely their own. Most often the collective is a state, but it can also be a militant organization that functions like a state: it recruits fighters for a cause, trains and organizes them, and sends them into battle. The cause of many militant organizations is to establish a state; the cause for which states organize armies is to defend their own existence and the common life and individual lives of their citizens.

It is a fact of our moral history that many individuals are willing to risk their lives for these causes. This is not easy to understand. If states exist primarily to defend life, then how can life be sacrificed to defend the state? That is the question posed most clearly in the political theory of Thomas Hobbes, to which he offered no satisfactory answer. And in fact the defense of the state (and the pursuit of the cause of any militant organization) not only requires the defenders to put their own lives at risk but also requires them to put the lives of many other people at risk—the fighters they oppose, most obviously, but also the civilians they and their opponents claim to be defending. Some philosophers, working upward, so to speak, from individual self-defense, doubt that any of this can be justified. The value of my life, or yours, may justify violent self-defense, but it is hard for these philosophers to understand how any collective could have that kind of value.

They have not, however, succeeded in convincing the rest of us. Patriotism and loyalty are, no doubt, often misguided, but they shouldn't be incomprehensible. Collectives like the state (or the army of the state) are indeed instrumental; they have no intrinsic value. But they make possible, and then they defend, another collective, a community whose existence is of centrally important value to (most of) its members. This value has many sources: history and memory, traditions of belief and practice, a culture of political engagement, the continuity of families, the sense of place, the immediacy of a way of life. When these seem to be in danger, many of us will risk our lives in their defense. Even in ordinary times, we are, all of us, collectivists of some sort—on behalf of our families, or religious communities, or nations, or nation-states. But this is a fairly weak collectivism, which only sometimes wins out over individual self-interest. The acceptance of martyrdom in a time of religious persecution is the chief example of this kind of victory. Persecution creates conditions something like those experienced in a nation under attack, when the sense of danger intensifies our collectivist sensibilities, our patriotism and loyalty. And then the defense of the common life—and of the necessary agencies of that defense, like states and armies—regularly trumps the defense of the self. That is why captured soldiers will sometimes try to escape from the prisoner of war camp: they want to resume the fighting (and they are willing to accept the risks of doing that) because they think that the victory of their nation or the success of their cause is critically important.

The intensified collectivism of war also intensifies the coerciveness of war. In some wars, soldiers fight because they have been impressed or conscripted. But when the common life is in danger or when people think it is in danger, citizens will rush to enlist in the army. We call them volunteers, but they are probably acting under very strong social pressure and also under the pressure of their own consciences—where conscience means what the word suggests: the knowledge they share with God, in the original religious formulation, or the knowledge they share with other members of their community, in secular understandings. In wartime, and commonly in both the religious and secular versions, what young men and women know is that they ought to volunteer (conscientious objection is exceptional even when it is permitted). This is collectivized knowledge, and it provides a powerful push toward what is only in a highly qualified sense a "voluntary" enlistment.

Once you are in the army, you are a member of a very strong collective of combatants, and all the people you leave behind are members of another strong collective, the civilian population. These memberships are matters of life and death—hence they are "strong" in ways that no other memberships, no peacetime memberships, can ever be. I may be a committed professional, a lawyer, doctor, or teacher; I may be a devout member of a religious community, or a political party activist, or a class-conscious worker, but none of these affiliations, though they are undoubtedly very important, is collectivized in as radical a way as combatants and noncombatants are, where being a member determines whether you can, or cannot, be targeted and killed. Perhaps there are soldiers who, given the morality of everyday life, don't deserve to be targeted (they are against the war; they shoot their guns in the air), perhaps there are civilians who do deserve to be targeted (they are fierce and uncompromising hawks). In the circumstances of war, we cannot make these distinctions.

The moral equality of soldiers finds its parallel in the moral equality of civilians. Individuals are incorporated into both these collectives without regard to their personal moral standing. By contrast, in peacetime civil society, life and death decisions are made, in hospitals and court-rooms, for example, with careful attention to individual cases. Soldiers may receive that kind of attention after the war, if they are tried for war crimes. But when the two armies are engaged, and civilians are radically at risk, individual attentiveness isn't possible. We fight with soldiers; we don't fight with civilians.

The collectivism of war extends, so to speak, all the way down. It would be wrong to think of a battle as a series of encounters between individual soldiers. War is often chaotic, and soldiers are sometimes cut off from their units, forced to fight on their own, thinking at that moment only of their own survival. But battles commonly are collective engagements, shaped by a strategic plan and then by the tactical decisions of field commanders, which are enforced by rigorous military discipline. Soldiers fight together, helping each other, hoping to survive but aiming at a local victory: a target destroyed, a hill captured, a road opened, an enemy battalion outflanked or surrounded. The local victory has value only as a part of some larger scheme, but if that value is real to the soldiers involved, it justifies the risks they take, and it may justify (as self-defense would not) the risks they impose on nearby civilians. Soldiers make individual decisions about the risks they take and the risks they impose, but they make these decisions in the context of the collectivism (and the coerciveness) of war.

No one reading the literature of war can miss the sense of its strange-ness—and its awfulness. To be forced to risk your life, again and again, for collective purposes: this is not what anyone wants for himself or for the people he cares about. He may think that it is important to fight (it some-times is); he may even think that the cause is worth dying for (it sometimes is), but he would rather be doing something else. The sense that many sol-diers have of being radically committed and of wishing so strongly that they weren't—that too probably finds no easy equivalent in ordinary life. And this internally contradictory but emotionally powerful sense is com-mon to soldiers on both sides of the battle. Indeed, soldiers on both sides recognize, if only intermittently, the feelings they share; they see them-selves in the others.

Perhaps one can construct hypothetical cases that reproduce this fea-ture, or other features, of wartime experience, though I doubt that cases taken from civil society (the bank robber and the bank guard, for exam-ple) or any of the hypothetical and constructed cases (variations on the famous trolley car story, say) actually get close enough. And I worry that theorists who focus on these kinds of cases aren't thinking about war at all. They are not interested, or not sufficiently interested, in what actually happens on the battlefield and what it feels like to be there.

Third, war is a world of radical and pervasive uncertainty. The outcome of skirmishes and battles is hard to predict; the life chances of any particular soldier change from minute to minute; the knowledge available to officers making decisions is painfully limited. These physical and factual uncertainties probably can't be matched in ordinary civilian life, and they exist alongside moral uncertainties that almost certainly can't be matched. Most often in civilian life we have a fairly good idea about what ought to be done or about who can tell us what ought to be done. Moral practice has a certain habitual quality, and moral and legal authority is routinized. But in the anarchic society of states, which is also the world of war, both morality and authority are radically contested.

This doesn't mean that individual soldiers and groups of soldiers won't be convinced of the justice of their cause; they will be convinced, or most of them will, with whatever lingering anxieties. The soldiers of country A will follow the lead of their parents and peers, of their teachers and preachers, and of their prime ministers and presidents (this is another example of the collectivizing tendency of warfare). The difficulty is that all these people, from parents to presidents, exist in two entirely separate sets. And the soldiers from country B, opponents of country A, will be equally convinced, and some of them similarly anxious; they will be following the same leads. And there is no one in the world, literally no one, to whom these two groups of soldiers can turn for impartial and authoritative guidance. Uncertainty exists, so to speak, at the highest level. In international society, there are virtually no cases where warring states, and the neutral states watching them, agree on a single moral, political, or military description of the war; nor is there any routine way of appealing from this or that description to some ultimate judge. Wars end, one way or another, but disagreement doesn't. The moral contests outlast the battles—as we can see if we compare the history books produced for state schools in the victorious and in the defeated country.

But what if a particular soldier knows that the war his country is fighting is unjust? Or what if the rest of us know that and think he should know it too? How can he fight in such a war? How can anyone fighting unjustly claim a right to kill his opponents, who are fighting justly? These are rhetorical questions; they are commonly asked by philosophers who insist that *jus ad bellum* determines *jus in bello*—or, at least, that the two can't be independent of each other—and who further insist that they know which of the warring states has *ad bellum* justice on its side. Reflecting on the certainty that, it seems to me, underlies these questions, I am reminded of Oliver Cromwell's response to similar certainties among Puritan ministers during the English Revolution: "Think ye in the bowels of Christ, that ye may be wrong!" That's not where I think, but I take the point. Given the circumstances of war, soldiers have a right to be wrong, and they have a right to think that they may be wrong and to defer to the decisions of (let's say) their democratically elected leaders. They also have a right to think that though they should oppose the war as citizens, they are bound to fight it as soldiers—because there are many states that would not survive for long in the world of war, in international society as it exists today, without a disciplined army. And, finally, soldiers have a right to refuse to fight in a war they believe to be unjust; in cases like the Nazi war effort with which I began this argument, refusal is certainly the best response. But it is an act of heroism, and it can't be morally required; unheroic conduct isn't criminal conduct.

But mostly soldiers sincerely believe that their war is just, for reasons that seem sufficient to them, and this belief gives a certain shape to their battles, which are fought between soldiers certain of their cause in a world where all causes are uncertain. I am not making a relativist argument here; I have argued over many years that (most) wars, on one side or the other, are objectively just or unjust. But this objectivity has no political or judicial embodiment. There is no agent of objectivity. And that is one reason for the deep principle of (standard, orthodox) just war theory: that soldiers have an equal right to fight, whether their cause is, or isn't, objectively just. Soldiers on both sides have exactly the same rights and obligations. If they are captured, they must be treated similarly and equally, that is, in accordance with the (morally strange) prisoner of war convention. And after the war, they should be encouraged and helped in exactly the same way to go home and resume their civilian existence.

In fact, all the special features of the world of war conspire to produce this principle of warrior equality, which obviously has no domestic equivalent (again: bank robbers and bank guards are not equals, even if the bank turns into a battlefield). The different forms of wartime coerciveness—social pressure, conscription, army discipline, military necessity—impact the soldiers on both sides in roughly the same way. The heightened sense of collective belonging and commitment is felt in similar ways by all of them. And they all live with the same uncertainties.

If we want to constrain the conduct of soldiers on the battlefield, we must recognize these similarities. We must insist that all soldiers, whether they think their cause is just or unjust, and whether we think their cause is just or unjust, have the same rights and, what is even more important, the same obligations. No group of soldiers, claiming to be just warriors, can arrogate to themselves rights they deny to others or claim exemption from everyone else's obligations—for if that is allowed and justified, there will soon be no constraints at all.

The moral equality of soldiers is perhaps the strangest rule of war. But philosophers who deny its morality seem to me to miss the force of that preposition: "rule *of* war." To understand the rule, you have to take an interest not only in moral theory, which accounts for the strangeness of the rule, but in war itself, which accounts for the existence of the rule.

NOTES

PREFACE TO THE FIRST EDITION

1. The most concise and forceful exposition of these reasons is Stanley Hoffmann, "International Law and the Control of Force," in *The Relevance of International Law*, ed. Karl Deutsch and Stanley Hoffmann (New York, 1971), pp. 34–66. Given the present state of the law, I have most often cited positivists of an earlier age, especially W. E. Hall, John Westlake, and J. M. Spaight.

2. The pioneering work of this sort is Myres S. McDougal and Florentino P. Feliciano, *Law and Minimum World Public Order* (New Haven, 1961).

3. For a useful study of these writers, see James Turner Johnson, *Ideology, Reason, and the Limitation of War: Religious and Secular Concepts, 1200–1740* (Princeton, 1975).

1 AGAINST "REALISM"

1. This and subsequent quotations are from *Hobbes' Thucydides*, ed. Richard Schlatter (New Brunswick, N.J., 1975), pp. 377–85 (*The History of the Peloponnesian War*, 5: 84–116).

2. Dionysius of Halicarnassus, *On Thucydides*, trans. W. Kendrick Pritchett (Berkeley, 1975), pp. 31–33.

3. See F. M. Cornford, *Thucydides Mythistoricus* (London, 1907), esp. ch. XIII.

4. *The Trojan Women*, trans. Gilbert Murray (London, 1905), p. 16.

5. Werner Jaeger, *Paideia: The Ideals of Greek Culture*, trans. Gilbert Highet (New York, 1939), I, 402.

6. H. W. Fowler, *A Dictionary of Modern English Usage*, second ed., rev. Sir Ernest Gowers (New York, 1965), p. 168; cf. Jaeger, I, 397.

7. *Plutarch's Lives*, trans. John Dryden, rev. Arthur Hugh Clough (London, 1910), I, 303. Alcibiades also "selected for himself one of the captive Melian women. . . . "

8. *Hobbes' Thucydides*, pp. 194–204 (*The History of the Peloponnesian War*, 3:36–49).

9. Thomas Hobbes, *Leviathan*, ch. IV.

10. *The Charterhouse of Parma*, I, chs. 3 and 4; J. F. C. Fuller, *A Military History of the Western World* (n.p., 1955), II, ch. 15.

11. C. W. C. Oman, *The Art of War in the Middle Ages* (Ithaca, N.Y., 1968), p. 137.

12. Raphael Holinshed, *Chronicles of England, Scotland, and Ireland*, excerpted in William Shakespeare, *The Life of Henry V* (Signet Classics, New York, 1965), p. 197.

13. *Henry V*, 4:7, ll. 1–11.

14. David Hume, *The History of England* (Boston, 1854), II, 358.

15. René de Belleval, *Azincourt* (Paris, 1865), pp. 105–06.

16. See the summary of opinions in J. H. Wylie, *The Reign of Henry the Fifth* (Cambridge, England, 1919), II, 171ff.

17. For an excellent and detailed account, which suggests that Henry's action cannot be defended, see John Keegan, *The Face of Battle* (New York, 1976), pp. 107–12.

2 THE CRIME OF WAR

1. Clausewitz should now be read in the new translation by Michael Howard and Peter Paret, *On War* (Princeton, 1976). But this book appeared after my own work was finished; I have quoted Clausewitz from a graceful, though abridged version by Edward M. Collins, *War, Politics, and Power* (Chicago, 1962), p. 65. Cf. Howard and Paret, p. 76.

2. Press conference, January 12, 1955.

3. Clausewitz, p. 64. Cf. Howard and Paret, pp. 75–76.

4. Clausewitz, pp. 72, 204. Cf. Howard and Paret, pp. 81, 581.

5. John Ruskin, *The Crown of Wild Olive: Four Lectures on Industry and War* (New York, 1874), pp. 90–91.

6. Wilfred Owen, "Anthem for Doomed Youth," in *Collected Poems*, ed. C. Day Lewis (New York, 1965), p. 44.

7. Thomas Hobbes, *Leviathan*, ch. XXI. For a description of primitive warfare of this sort, see Robert Gardner and Karl G. Heider, *Gardens of War: Life and Death in the New Guinea Stone Age* (New York, 1968), ch. 6.

8. Quoted in J. F. C. Fuller, *The Conduct of War, 1789–1961* (n.p., 1968), p. 16.

9. Machiavelli, *History of Florence* (New York, 1960), Bk. IV, ch. I, p. 164.

10. Ruskin, p. 92.

11. *War and Peace*, trans. Constance Garnett (New York, n.d.), Part Two, III, p. 111.

12. "A Terre," *Collected Poems*, p. 64.

13. Fuller, *Conduct of War*, p. 35.

14. Thomas Sackville, Earl of Dorset, "The Induction," *Works*, ed. R. W. Sackville-West (London, 1859), p. 115.

15. This and the following quotations are from William Tecumseh Sherman, *Memoirs* (New York, 1875), pp. 119–20.

3 THE RULES OF WAR

1. Louis Simpson, "The Ash and the Oak," *Good News of Death and Other Poems*, in *Poets of Today* II (New York, 1955), p. 162.

2. See for example, Fuller, *Conduct of War*, ch. II ("The Rebirth of Total War").

3. Edward Rickenbacker's *Fighting the Flying Circus* (New York, 1919) is a lively (and typical) account of the chivalry of the air. In 1918, Rickenbacker wrote in his flight diary: "Resolved today that . . . I will never shoot at a Hun who is at a disadvantage . . ." (p. 338). For a general account, see Frederick Oughton, *The Aces* (New York, 1960).

4. Quoted in Desmond Young, *Rommel: The Desert Fox* (New York, 1958), p. 137.

5. Eisenhower, *Crusade in Europe* (New York, 1948), pp. 156–57.

6. Ronald Lewin, *Rommel as Military Commander* (New York, 1970), pp. 294, 311. See also Young, pp. 130–32.

7. Quoted in Robert W. Tucker, *The Law of War and Neutrality at Sea* (Washington, D.C. 1957), p. 6n. Tucker's discussion of the legal issues is very useful; see also H. Lauterpacht, "The Limits of the Operation of the Law of War," in 30 *British Yearbook of International Law* (1953).

8. *Henry V*, 4:1, ll. 132–35.

9. Francisco de Vitoria, *De Indis et De Iure Belli Relationes*, ed. Ernest Nys (Washington, D.C., 1917): *On the Law of War*, trans. John Pawley Bate, p. 176.

10. Randall Jarrell, "The Death of the Ball Turret Gunner," in *The Complete Poems* (New York, 1969), p. 144.

11. See below, ch. 18. For a historical account of these issues, see C. A. Pompe, *Aggressive War: An International Crime* (The Hague, 1953).

12. Quincy Wright, *A Study of War* (Chicago, 1942), I, 8.

13. Gardner and Heider, *Gardens of War*, p. 139.

14. *First Samuel*, 17:32.

15. Johan Huizinga, *Homo Ludens* (Boston, 1955), p. 92.

16. *War and Peace*, Part Ten, XXV, p. 725.

17. For a discussion of this agreement, see my essay "Prisoners of War: Does the Fight Continue After the Battle?" in *Obligations: Essays on Disobedience, War and Citizenship* (Cambridge, Mass., 1970).

18. *Moltke in Seinen Briefen* (Berlin, 1902), p. 253. The letter is addressed to J. C. Bluntschli, a noted scholar of international law.

4 LAW AND ORDER IN INTERNATIONAL SOCIETY

1. *Henry V*, 1:2, ll. 24–28.

2. The judges distinguished "aggressive acts" from "aggressive wars," but then used the first of these as the generic term: see *Nazi Conspiracy and Aggression: Opinion and Judgment* (Washington, D.C., 1947), p. 16.

3. Quoted in Michael Howard, "War as an Instrument of Policy," in Herbert Butterfield and Martin Wight, eds., *Diplomatic Investigations* (Cambridge, Mass., 1966), p. 199. Cf. *On War*, trans. Howard and Paret, p. 370.

4. John Westlake, *Collected Papers*, ed. L. Oppenheim (Cambridge, England, 1914), p. 78.

5. See Ruth Putnam, *Alsace and Lorraine from Caesar to Kaiser: 58 B.C.–1871 A.D.* (New York, 1915).

6. Henry Sidgwick, *The Elements of Politics* (London, 1891), pp. 268, 287.

7. *Leviathan*, ch. 30.

8. *Leviathan*, ch. 15.

9. For a critique of this analogy, see the two essays by Hedley Bull, "Society and Anarchy in International Relations," and "The Grotian Conception of International Society," in *Diplomatic Investigations*, chs. 2 and 3.

10. See Vitoria, *On the Law of War*, p. 177.

11. Lenin, *Socialism and War* (London, 1940), pp. 10–11.

12. Edmund Wilson, *Patriotic Gore* (New York, 1966), p. xi.

13. It is worth noting that the United Nations' recently adopted definition of aggression closely follows the paradigm: see the *Report of the Special Committee on the Question of Defining Aggression* (1974), General Assembly Official Records, 29th session, supplement no. 19 (A/9619), pp. 10–13. The definition is reprinted and analyzed in Yehuda Melzer, *Concepts of Just War* (Leyden, 1975), pp. 26ff.

14. *On the Law of War*, p. 170.

15. See L. Oppenheim, *International Law*, vol. II, *War and Neutrality* (London, 1906), pp. 55ff.

16. C. A. Pompe, *Aggressive War*, p. 152.

17. Quoted in Pompe, p. 152.

18. Quoted in Franz Mehring, *Karl Marx*, trans. Edward Fitzgerald (Ann Arbor, 1962), p. 438.

19. *Minutes of the General Council of the First International: 1870–1871* (Moscow, n.d.), p. 57.

20. Roger Morgan, *The German Social-Democrats and the First International: 1864–1872* (Cambridge, England, 1965), p. 206.

21. "First Address of the General Council of the International Working Men's Association on the Franco-Prussian War," in Marx and Engels, *Selected Works* (Moscow, 1951), I, 443.

22. "Second Address . . . ," *Selected Works*, I, 449 (Marx's italics).

23. *Selected Works*, I, 441.

24. See the arguments made by Churchill at the time: *The Gathering Storm* (New York, 1961), chs. 17 and 18; also Martin Gilbert and Richard Gott, *The Appeasers* (London, 1963). For a recent scholarly reappraisal somewhat more sympathetic to Chamberlain, see Keith Robbins, *Munich: 1938* (London, 1968).

25. Gerald Vann, *Morality and War* (London, 1939).

26. Max Jakobson, *The Diplomacy of the Winter War* (Cambridge, Mass., 1961), p. 117.

27. Jacobson reports an admission by the Swedish prime minister that had Sweden been publicly committed to assist Finland in the autumn of 1939, the Soviet Union would probably not have attacked (p. 237).

5 ANTICIPATIONS

1. D. W. Bowett, *Self-Defense in International Law* (New York, 1958), p. 59. My own position has been influenced by Julius Stone's critique of the legalist argument: *Aggression and World Order* (Berkeley, 1968).

2. Quoted from the *Annual Register*, in H. Butterfield, "The Balance of Power," *Diplomatic Investigations*, pp. 144–45.

3. Francis Bacon, *Essays* ("Of Empire"); see also his treatise *Considerations Touching a War with Spain* (1624), in *The Works of Francis Bacon*, ed. James Spedding *et al.* (London, 1874), XIV, pp. 469–505.

4. *Oxford English Dictionary*, "threaten."

5. M. D. Vattel, *The Law of Nations* (Northampton, Mass., 1805), Bk. III, ch. III, paras. 42–44, pp. 357–78. Cf. John Westlake, *Chapters on the Principles of International Law* (Cambridge, England, 1894), p. 120.

6. Jonathan Swift, *The Conduct of the Allies and of the Late Ministry in Beginning and Carrying on the Present War* (1711), in *Prose Works*, ed. Temple Scott (London, 1901), V, 116.

7. As late as the eighteenth century, Vattel still argued that a prince "has a right to demand, even by force of arms, the reparation of an insult." *Law of Nations*, Bk. II, ch. IV, para. 48, p. 216.

8. Compare the argument of Hugo Grotius: "The danger . . . must be immediate and imminent in point of time. I admit, to be sure, that if the assailant seizes weapons in such a way that his intent to kill is manifest, the crime can be forestalled; for in morals as in material things a point is not to be found which does not have a certain breadth." *The Law of War and Peace*, trans. Francis W. Kelsey (Indianapolis, n.d.), Bk. II, ch. I, section V, p. 173.

9. Walter Laquer, *The Road to War: The Origin and Aftermath of the Arab-Israeli Conflict, 1967-8* (Baltimore, 1969), p. 110.

10. Edward Luttwak and Dan Horowitz, *The Israeli Army* (New York, 1975), p. 212.

11. Luttwak and Horowitz, p. 224.

6 INTERVENTIONS

1. "A Few Words on Non-Intervention" in J. S. Mill, *Dissertations and Discussions* (New York, 1873), III, 238–63.

2. See Irving Howe, ed., *The Basic Writings of Trotsky* (New York, 1963), p. 397.

3. John Norton Moore, "International Law and the United States' Role in Vietnam: A Reply," in R. Falk, ed., *The Vietnam War and International Law* (Princeton,

1968), p. 431. Moore addresses himself specifically to the argument of W. E. Hall, *International Law* (5th ed., Oxford, 1994), pp. 289–90, but Hall follows Mill closely.

4. For a brief survey, see Jean Sigmann, *1848: The Romantic and Democratic Revolutions in Europe*, trans. L. F. Edwards (New York, 1973), ch. 10.

5. Charles Sproxton, *Palmerston and the Hungarian Revolution* (Cambridge, 1919), p. 48.

6. "Non-Intervention," pp. 261–62.

7. See S. French and A. Gutman, "The Principle of National Self-determination," in Held, Morgenbesser, and Nagel, eds., *Philosophy, Morality, and International Affairs* (New York, 1974), pp. 138–53.

8. This is the general position of R. J. Vincent, *Nonintervention and World Order* (Princeton, 1974), esp. ch. 9.

9. Sproxton, p. 109.

10. See, for example, Hall, *International Law*, p. 293.

11. "On the Principle of Non-Intervention" (Oxford, 1860), p. 21.

12. See Hugh Thomas, *The Spanish Civil War* (New York, 1961), chs. 31, 40, 48, 58; Norman J. Padelford, *International Law and Diplomacy in the Spanish Civil Strife* (New York, 1939) is an incredibly naïve defense of the nonintervention agreements.

13. A useful statement of this position can be found in the essay by John Norton Moore already cited; see note 3 above. For an example of the official view, see Leonard Meeker, "Vietnam and the International Law of Self-Defense" in the same volume, pp. 318–32.

14. I shall follow the account of G. M. Kahin and John W. Lewis, *The United States in Vietnam* (New York, 1967).

15. "On the Principle of Non-Intervention," p. 16.

16. See Gregory Henderson, *Korea: The Politics of the Vortex* (Cambridge, Mass., 1968), ch. 6.

17. Kahin and Lewis, p. 146.

18. Ellery C. Stowell suggests some possible examples in *Intervention in International Law* (Washington, D.C., 1921), ch. II. For contemporary legal views (and newer examples), see Richard Lillich, ed., *Humanitarian Intervention and the United Nations* (Charlottesville, Va., 1973).

19. Quoted in Philip S. Foner, *The Spanish-Cuban-American War and the Birth of American Imperialism* (New York, 1972), I, 111.

20. Quoted in Stowell, p. 122n.

21. See, for example, Julius W. Pratt, *Expansionists of 1898* (Baltimore, 1936) and Walter La Feber, *The New Empire: An Interpretation of American Expansion* (Ithaca, 1963); also Foner, I, ch. XIV.

22. Foner, I, ch. XIII.

23. F. E. Chadwick, *The Relations of the United States and Spain: Diplomacy* (New York, 1909), pp. 586–87. These lines are the epigraph to Walter Millis' account of the war: *The Martial Spirit* (n.p., 1931).

24. Millis, p. 404; it should be noted that Millis also writes of the American decision to go to war: "Seldom can history have recorded a plainer case of military aggression . . ." (p. 160).

25. For a contemporary account by a British journalist, see David Loshak, *Pakistan Crisis* (London, 1971).

26. John Westlake, *International Law*, vol. I, *Peace* (2nd ed., Cambridge 1910), pp. 319–20.

27. Thomas M. Franck and Nigel S. Rodley, "After Bangladesh: The Law of Humanitarian Intervention by Military Force," 67 *American Journal of International Law* 304 (1973).

28. Julius Stone, *Aggression and World Order*, pp. 99.

7 WAR'S ENDS, AND THE IMPORTANCE OF WINNING

1. "The Range in the Desert," *The Complete Poems*, p. 176.

2. B. H. Liddell Hart, *Strategy* (2nd rev. ed., New York, 1974), p. 339: Liddell Hart himself holds a different, and a much more sophisticated, position.

3. *War, Politics and Power*, p. 233; cf. the new translation of Howard and Paret, p. 595.

4. The work of Reinhold Niebuhr was the major inspiration of this group, Hans Morganthau its most systematic theorist. For works more immediately relevant to my purposes in this chapter, see George Kennan, *American Diplomacy: 1900–1950* (Chicago, 1951); John W. Spanier, *The Truman-MacArthur Controversy and the Korean War* (Cambridge, Mass., 1959); Paul Kecskemeti, *Strategic Surrender: The Politics of Victory and Defeat* (New York, 1964). For a useful critique of the "realists," see Charles Frankel, *Morality and U.S. Foreign Policy*, Foreign Policy Association Headline Series, no. 224 (1975).

5. Spanier, p. 5.

6. Kecskemeti, pp. 25–26.

7. On the connection between Wilson's "world view" and his desire for a compromise peace, see N. Gordon Levin, Jr., *Woodrow Wilson and World Politics: America's Response to War and Revolution* (New York, 1970), pp. 43, 52ff.

8. *The Hinge of Fate* (New York, 1962), p. 600.

9. Kecskemeti, pp. 217, 241.

10. *Hinge of Fate*, p. 600; see also Churchill's cabinet memorandum of January 14, 1944, p. 599.

11. *American Diplomacy*, pp. 87–88.

12. Robert Phillimore, *Commentaries upon International Law* (Philadelphia, 1854), I, 315.

13. Kecskemeti, p. 219.

14. See Raymond G. O'Connor, *Diplomacy for Victory: FDR and Unconditional Surrender* (New York, 1971).

15. Kecskemeti, p. 240.

16. For a general view of punishment as public condemnation, see "The Expressive Function of Punishment," in Joel Feinberg, *Doing and Deserving* (Princeton, 1970), ch. 5.

17. Glen D. Paige, *The Korean Decision* (New York, 1968), pp. 218–19.

18. *Strategy*, p. 355.

19. Quoted in Spanier, p. 88.

20. Quoted in David Rees, *Korea: The Limited War* (Baltimore, 1970), p. 101.

21. *Concepts of Just War*, pp. 170–71.

22. Liddell Hart, *Strategy*, p. 338.

23. Hume, *Theory of Politics*, ed. Frederick Watkins (Edinburgh, 1951), pp. 190–91.

8 WAR'S MEANS AND THE IMPORTANCE OF FIGHTING WELL

1. *Elements of Politics*, pp. 253–54.

2. *Elements of Politics*, p. 254; for a contemporary statement from a roughly similar point of view, see R. B. Brandt, "Utilitarianism and the Rules of War," 1 *Philosophy and Public Affairs* 145–65 (1972).

3. Byron Farwell, *The Great Anglo-Boer War* (New York, 1976), p. 209.

4. *The Law of Land Welfare*, U.S. Department of the Army Field Manual FM 27-10 (1956), para. 3. See the discussion of this provision in Telford Taylor, *Nuremberg and Vietnam* (Chicago, 1970), pp. 34–36, and Marshall Cohen, "Morality and the Laws of War," *Philosophy, Morality, and International Affairs*, pp. 72ff.

5. *Elements of Politics*, p. 264.

6. For an example of the "morality" of the feud, see Margaret Hasluck, "The Albanian Blood Feud," in Paul Bohannan, *Law and Warfare: Studies in the Anthropology of Conflict* (New York, 1967), pp. 381–408.

7. The story is told in Ignazio Silone, "Reflections on the Welfare State," 8 *Dissent* 189 (1961); De Sica's film *Two Women* is based on an incident from this period in Italian history.

8. *On the Law of War*, pp. 184–85.

9. Deuteronomy 21:10–14. This passage is ignored in Susan Brownmiller's analysis of the "true Hebraic concept . . . of rape" in *Against Our Will: Men, Women, and Rape* (New York, 1975), pp. 19–23.

10. See, for example, McDougal and Feliciano, *Law and Minimum World Public Order*, p. 42 and *passim*.

9 NONCOMBATANT IMMUNITY AND MILITARY NECESSITY

1. S. L. A. Marshall, *Men Against Fire* (New York, 1966), chs. 5 and 6.

2. Wilfred Owen, *Collected Letters*, ed. Harold Owen and John Bell (London, 1967), p. 458 (14 May 1917).

3. *Good-bye to All That* (rev. ed., New York, 1957), p. 132.

4. *The Collected Essays, Journalism and Letters of George Orwell*, ed. Sonia Orwell and Ian Angus (New York, 1968), II, 254.

5. *The Fortress: A Diary of Anzio and After* (Hammondsworth, 1958), p. 21.

6. *Sardinian Brigade: A Memoir of World War I*, trans. Marion Rawson (New York, 1970), pp. 166–71.

7. Archibald Forbes, quoted in J. M. Spaight, *War Rights on Land* (London, 1911), p. 104.

8. *Instructions for the Government of Armies of the United States in the Field*, General Orders 100, April, 1863 (Washington, 1898), Article 69.

9. M. Greenspan, *The Modern Law of Land Warfare* (Berkeley, 1959), pp. 313–14.

10. G. E. M. Anscombe, *Mr. Truman's Degree* (privately printed, 1958), p. 7; see also "War and Murder" in *Nuclear Weapons and Christian Conscience*, ed. Walter Stein (London, 1963).

11. See Sir Frederick Smith, *The Destruction of Merchant Ships under International Law* (London, 1917) and Tucker, *Law of War and Neutrality at Sea*.

12. H. A. Smith, *Law and Custom of the Sea* (London, 1950), p. 123.

13. Tucker, p. 72.

14. Tucker, p. 67.

15. Doenitz, *Memoirs: Ten Years and Twenty Days*, trans. K. H. Stevens (London, 1959), p. 261.

16. *The Destruction of Convoy PQ 17* (New York, n.d.), p. 157; for other examples, see pp. 145, 192–93.

17. *Nazi Conspiracy and Aggression: Opinion and Judgment*, p. 140.

18. Doenitz, *Memoirs*, p. 259.

19. *Old Soldiers Never Die* (New York, 1966), p. 198.

20. Kenneth Dougherty, *General Ethics: An Introduction to the Basic Principles of the Moral Life According to St. Thomas Aquinas* (Peekskill, N.Y., 1959), p. 64.

21. Dougherty, pp. 65–66; cf. John C. Ford, S. J. "The Morality of Obliteration Bombing," in *War and Morality*, ed. Richard Wasserstrom (Belmont, Calif., 1970). I cannot make any effort here to review the philosophical controversies over double effect. Dougherty provides a (very simple) text book description, Ford a careful (and courageous) application.

22. For a philosophical version of the argument that it cannot make a difference whether the killing of innocent people is direct or indirect, see Jonathan Bennett, "Whatever the Consequences," *Ethics*, ed. Judith Jarvis Thomson and Gerald Dworkin (New York, 1968).

23. Reginald Thompson, *Cry Korea* (London, 1951), pp. 54, 142–43.

24. I have been helped in thinking about these questions by Charles Fried's discussion of "Imposing Risks on Others," *An Anatomy of Values: Problems of Personal and Social Choice* (Cambridge, Mass., 1970), ch. XI.

25. Quoted from the published text of Marcel Ophuls' documentary film, *The Sorrow and the Pity* (New York, 1972), p. 131.

26. Thomas Gallagher, *Assault in Norway* (New York, 1975), pp. 19–20, 50.

10 WAR AGAINST CIVILIANS: SIEGES AND BLOCKADES

1. *The Works of Josephus*, trans. Tho. Lodge (London, 1620): *The Wars of the Jews*, Bk. VI, ch. XIV, p. 721.

2. See, for example, Elena Skrjabina's remarkable memoir, *Siege and Survival: The Odyssey of a Leningrader* (Carbonville, Ill., 1971).

3. Charles Chaney Hyde, *International Law* (2nd rev. ed., Boston, 1945), III, 1802.

4. *The Works*, p. 722.

5. M. H. Keen, *The Laws of War in the Late Middle Ages* (London, 1965), p. 128, for an account of aristocratic obligations in such cases.

6. *The Art of War*, trans. Ellis Fameworth, rev. with an intro. by Neal Wood (Indianapolis, 1965), p. 193.

7. Spaight's discussion is the best: *War Rights*, pp. 174ff.

8. *The Works*, p. 718.

9. I shall follow the account of León Goure, *The Siege of Leningrad* (Stanford, 1962).

10. Goure, p. 141; *Trials of War Criminals before the Nuremberg Military Tribunals* (Washington, D.C., 1950), XI, 563.

11. The citation is from Hyde, *International Law*, III, 1802–03.

12. Spaight, pp. 174ff.

13. Spaight, pp. 177–78.

14. Hall, *International Law*, p. 398.

15. *The Code of Maimonides: Book Fourteen: The Book of Judges*, trans. Abraham M. Hershman (New Haven, 1949), p. 222; Grotius, *Law of War and Peace*, Bk. III, ch. XI, section xiv, pp. 739–40.

16. See Skrjabina, *Siege and Survival*, "Leningrad."

17. Deuteronomy 20:20.

18. *Hobbes' Thucydides*, pp. 123–24 (2:19–20); *War Commentaries of Caesar*, trans. Rex Warner (New York, 1960), pp. 70, 96 (*Gallic Wars* 3:3, 5:1).

19. A. C. Bell, *A History of the Blockade of Germany* (London, 1937), pp. 213–14.

20. Spaight, p. 138.

21. Hall, *International Law*, p. 656.

22. B. H. Liddell Hart, *The Real War: 1914–1918* (Boston, 1964), p. 473.

23. The studies were carried out by German statisticians, but the results are accepted by Bell. He is a little reluctant, however, to regard these results as a sign of the "success" of the British blockade: see p. 673.

24. Bell, p. 117. Cf. the same argument made by a French historian, Louis Guichard, *The Naval Blockade: 1914–1918*, trans. Christopher R. Turner (New York, 1930), p. 304.

11 GUERRILLA WAR

1. *The Sorrow and the Pity*, pp. 113–14.

2. For a useful survey of the legal situation, see Gerhard von Glahn, *The Occupation of Enemy Territory* (Minneapolis, 1957).

3. See, for example, W. F. Ford, "Resistance Movements and International Law," 7–8 *International Review of the Red Cross* (1967–68) and G. I. A. D. Draper, "The Status of Combatants and the Question of Guerrilla War," 45 *British Yearbook of International Law* (1971).

4. Quoted in Draper, p. 188.

5. Quoted in Douglas Pike, *Viet Cong* (Cambridge, Mass., 1968), p. 242.

6. Mao Tse-tung, *Selected Military Writings* (Peking, 1966), p. 343.

7. Dickey Chapelle, "How Castro Won," in *The Guerrilla—And How to Fight Him: Selections from the Marine Corps Gazette*, ed. T. N. Greene (New York, 1965), p. 223.

8. Draper, p. 203.

9. See Michael Calvert, *Chindits: Long Range Penetration* (New York, 1973).

10. Draper, pp. 202–04.

11. *Guerrilla Parties Considered with Reference to the Laws and Usages of War* (New York, 1862). Lieber wrote this pamphlet at the request of General Halleck.

12. Jeffrey Race, *War Comes to Long An* (Berkeley, 1972), pp. 196–97.

13. See *The Guerrilla—And How to Fight Him*; John McCuen, *The Art of Counter-Revolutionary War* (London, 1966); Frank Kitson, *Low Intensity Operations: Subversion, Insurgency, and Peacekeeping* (Harrisburg, 1971).

14. *Seven Pillars of Wisdom* (New York, 1936), Bk. III, ch. 33, p. 196.

15. For a graphic description of soldiers going beyond these limits, see Victor Kolpacoff's novel of the Vietnam War, *The Prisoners of Quai Dong* (New York, 1967).

16. Race, p. 233.

17. Jonathan Schell, *The Military Half* (New York, 1968), pp. 14ff.

18. For an account of forcible deportation, see Jonathan Schell, *The Village of Ben Suc* (New York, 1967).

19. *The Military Half*, p. 151.

20. Orville and Jonathan Schell, letter to *The New York Times*, Nov. 26, 1969; quoted in Noam Chomsky, *At War with Asia* (New York, 1970), pp. 292–93.

21. See the description of the camps that the British set up for Boer farmers: Farwell, *Anglo-Boer War*, chs. 40, 41.

22. Sir Robert Thompson, *Defeating Communist Insurgency* (New York, 1966), p. 125.

23. Don Oberdorfer, *Tet* (New York, 1972), p. 202.

24. Schell, *The Military Half*, pp. 96, 159.

25. Kitson, p. 138.

26. *Street Without Joy* (New York, 1972), ch. 7.

27. See the account of Regis Debray, *Che's Guerrilla War*, trans. Rosemary Sheed (Hammondsworth, 1975).

12 TERRORISM

1. But Liddell Hart, the foremost strategist of the "indirect approach," has consistently opposed terrorist tactics: see, for example, *Strategy*, pp. 349–50 (on terror bombing).

2. Rear Admiral L. H. K. Hamilton, quoted in Irving, *Destruction of Convoy PQ 17*, p. 44.

3. *Politics*, trans. Ernest Barker (Oxford, 1948), p. 288 (1314a).

4. *The Just Assassins*, in *Caligula and Three Other Plays*, trans. Stuart Gilbert (New York, 1958), p. 258. The actual historical incident is described in Roland Gaucher, *The Terrorists: From Tsarist Russia to the OAS* (London, 1965), pp. 49, 50n.

5. J. Bowyer Bell, *The Secret Army: A History of the IRA* (Cambridge, Mass., 1974), pp. 161–62.

6. Gerold Frank, *The Deed* (New York, 1963), pp. 248–49.

7. James E. Bond, *The Rules of Riot: Internal Conflict and the Law of War* (Princeton, 1974), pp. 89–90.

8. Pike, *Viet Cong*, p. 248.

9. Race, *War Comes to Long An*, p. 83, which suggests that it was precisely the *best* public health officers, teachers, and so on who were attacked—because they constituted a possible anti-communist leadership.

10. Pike, p. 250.

11. Pike, p. 251.

12. The argument, I suppose, goes back to Machiavelli, though most of his descriptions of the necessary violence of founders and reformers have to do with the killing of particular people, members of the old ruling class: see *The Prince*, ch. VIII and *Discourses*, I:9 for examples.

13. *The Wretched of the Earth*, trans. Constance Farrington (New York, n.d.), pp. 18–19.

14. *Gillo Pontecorvo's The Battle of Algiers*, ed. Piernico Solinas (New York, 1973), pp. 79–80.

13 REPRISALS

1. G. Lowes Dickinson, *War: Its Nature, Cause, and Cure* (London, 1923), p. 15.

2. H. Brocher, "Les principes naturels du droit de la guerre," 5 *Revue de droit international et de legislation comparée* 349 (1873).

3. Robert B. Asprey, *War in the Shadows: The Guerrilla in History* (New York, 1975), I, 478.

4. Frits Kalshoven, *Belligerent Reprisals* (Leyden, 1971), pp. 193–200.

5. Kalshoven, pp. 78ff.

6. See, for example, the essays of H. J. McCloskey and T. L. S. Sprigge in *Contemporary Utilitarianism*, ed. Michael D. Bayles (Garden City, N.Y., 1968).

7. Spaight, *War Rights*, p. 120.

8. Spaight, p. 462.

9. McDougal and Feliciano, *Law and Minimum World Public Order*, p. 682.

10. See Robert Katz, *Death in Rome* (New York, 1967) for an account of one of the most brutal Nazi reprisals.

11. Spaight, p. 463n.

12. Greenspan is typical: "Only in exceedingly grave cases should there be resort to reprisals." *Modern Law of Land Warfare*, p. 411.

13. Lieber, *Instructions*, Article 27 (emphasis added).

14. Kalshoven, pp. 263ff.

15. McDougal and Feliciano, p. 684.

16. Churchill, *The Grand Alliance* (New York, 1962), p. 359. A distinction similar to the one I am defending here is suggested by Westlake: ". . . the laws of war are too deeply rooted in humanity and morality to be discussed on the footing of contract alone, except it may be some parts of no great importance which convention might have settled otherwise than it has." *International Law*, II, 126.

17. See Kalshoven on "non-belligerent reprisals," pp. 287ff.

18. Luttwak and Horowitz, *The Israeli Army*, p. 110.

19. For accounts and evaluations of the raid, see Richard Falk, "The Beirut Raid and the International Law of Reprisal," 63 *American Journal of International Law* (1969) and Yehuda Blum, "The Beirut Raid and the International Double Standard: A Reply to Professor Falk," 64 *A.J.I.L.* (1970).

20. See the general condemnation voted by the Security Council on April 9, 1964, cited in Sydney D. Bailey, *Prohibitions and Restraints in War* (London, 1972), p. 55.

21. Hans Kelson, *Principles of International Law*, 2nd ed., rev. Robert W. Tucker (New York, 1967), p. 87.

14 WINNING AND FIGHTING WELL

1. *The Chinese Classics*, trans. and ed. James Legge, vol. V: *The Ch'un Ts'ew with The Tso Chuen* (Oxford, 1893), p. 183.

2. *Military Writings*, p. 240.

3. Quoted in Arthur Waley, *Three Ways of Thought in Ancient China* (Garden City, New York, n.d.), p. 131.

4. *Military Writings*, pp. 81, 223–24.

5. *Basic Tactics* (New York, 1966), p. 98.

6. *The Chinese Classics*, V, 183.

7. *The Need for Roots*, trans. Arthur Wills (Boston, 1955), p. 159.

8. *A Theory of Justice* (Cambridge, Mass., 1971), p. 379. Compare Vitoria: ". . . whatever is done in right of war receives the construction most favorable to the claims of those engaged in a just war." *On the Law of War*, p. 180.

9. This seems to be G. E. M. Anscombe's position in the two essays already cited: *Mr. Truman's Degree* and "War and Murder."

10. For a discussion of what it means to "override" a moral principle, see Robert Nozick, "Moral Complications and Moral Structures," 13 *Natural Law Forum* 34–35 and notes (1968).

15 AGGRESSION AND NEUTRALITY

1. Philip C. Jessup, *Neutrality: Its History, Economics, and Law* (New York, 1936), IV, 80 (emphasis added).

2. W. E. Hall, *The Rights and Duties of Neutrals* (London, 1874) is the best account of the laws of neutrality.

3. Westlake, *International Law*, II, 162.

4. The speech is reprinted in *The Theory and Practice of Neutrality in the Twentieth Century*, ed. Roderick Ogley (New York, 1970), p. 83.

5. *Theory and Practice of Neutrality*, p. 74.

6. Liddell Hart, *The Real War*, pp. 46–47.

7. For an example of the American response, see James M. Beck, *The Evidence in the Case: A Discussion of the Moral Responsibility for the War of 1914* (New York, 1915), esp. ch. IX.

8. *Socialism and War*, p. 15.

9. Nils Oervik, *The Decline of Neutrality: 1914–1941* (Oslo, 1953), p. 241.

10. Oervik, p. 223.

11. Churchill, *The Gathering Storm* (New York, 1961), Bk. II, ch. 9.

12. *Assignment to Catastrophe* (New York, 1954), I, 71–72.

13. *Time Unguarded: The Ironside Diaries 1937–1940*, ed. Roderick Macleod and Denis Kelly (New York, 1962), p. 211.

14. *Ironside Diaries*, p. 185.

15. *Ironside Diaries*, p. 216.

16. *History of the Second World War* (New York, 1971), p. 53.

17. *Ironside Diaries*, p. 238.

18. *The Gathering Storm*, p. 488.

19. Oervik, p. 237.

20. For an account of the campaign, see J. L. Moulton, *A Study of Warfare in Three Dimensions: The Norwegian Campaign of 1940* (Athens, Ohio, 1967).

21. *History of the Second World War*, p. 59. Cf. General Ironside's entry for February 14, 1940: "Winston is now pressing for his laying of mines in neutral Norwegian waters as the only means of forcing the Germans to violate Scandinavia and so give us a chance of getting into Narvik." *The Ironside Diaries*, p. 222.

16 SUPREME EMERGENCY

1. Quoted in George Quester, *Deterrence Before Hiroshima* (New York, 1966), p. 67.

2. See J. Glenn Gray, *The Warriors: Reflections on Men in Battle* (New York, 1967), ch. 5: "Images of the Enemy."

3. But the claim that one can never kill an innocent person abstracts from questions of coercion and consent: see the examples cited in chapter 10.

4. See Quester, *Deterrence* and F. M. Sallagar, *The Road to Total War: Escalation in World War II* (Rand Corporation Report, 1969); also the official history by Sir Charles Webster and Noble Frankland, *The Strategic Air Offensive Against Germany* (London, 1961).

5. Noble Frankland, *Bomber Offensive: The Devastation of Europe* (New York, 1970), p. 41.

6. The Story of the Cherwell minute is told, most unsympathetically, in C. P. Snow, *Science and Government* (New York, 1962).

7. Quester, pp. 117–18.

8. Quoted in Quester, p. 141.

9. Quoted in Angus Calder, *The People's War: 1939–1945* (New York, 1969), p. 491.

10. Calder, p. 229; the same poll is cited by Vera Brittain, a courageous opponent of British bombing policy: *Humiliation with Honor* (New York, 1943), p. 91.

11. ". . . it was not [Cherwell's] ruthlessness that worried us most, it was his calculations." Snow, *Science and Government*, p. 48. Cf. P. M. S. Blackett's post-war critique of the bombing, worked out in narrowly strategic terms: *Fear, War, and the Bomb* (New York, 1949), ch. 2.

12. Sallagar, p. 127.

13. Sallagar, p. 128.

14. Frankland, *Bomber Offensive*, pp. 38–39.

15. Frankland, *Bomber Offensive*, p. 134.

16. Sir Arthur Harris, *Bomber Offensive* (London, 1947), p. 74.

17. Calder, p. 229.

18. *The Hinge of Fate*, p. 770.

19. For a detailed account of this attack, see David Irving, *The Destruction of Dresden* (New York, 1963).

20. Quoted in Quester, p. 156.

21. *Memoirs of a Revolutionist* (New York, 1957), p. 178.

22. Robert C. Batchelder, *The Irreversible Decision: 1939–1950* (New York, 1965), p. 38. Batchelder's is the best historical account of the decision to drop the bomb, and the only one that treats the moral issues in a systematic way.

23. A. Russell Buchanan, *The United States and World War II* (New York, 1964), I, 75.

24. "The Decision to Use the Atomic Bomb," *Harper's Magazine* (February 1947), repr. in *The Atomic Bomb: The Great Decision*, ed. Paul R. Baker (New York, 1968), p. 21.

25. *Speaking Frankly* (New York, 1947), p. 261.

26. *Atomic Quest* (New York, 1956), p. 247.

27. *Mr. Citizen* (New York, 1960), p. 267. I owe this group of quotations to Gerald McElroy.

28. Batchelder, p. 159.

29. Batchelder, p. 149.

30. *Triumph and Tragedy* (New York, 1962), p. 639.

31. "The Decision to Use the Bomb," p. 21.

32. *Speaking Frankly*, p. 264.

33. The case would be even worse if the bomb were used for political rather than military reasons (with the Russians rather than the Japanese in mind): on this point, see the careful analysis of Martin J. Sherwin, *A World Destroyed: The Atomic Bomb and the Grand Alliance* (New York, 1975).

17 NUCLEAR DETERRENCE

1. "The Decision to Use the Bomb," in *The Atomic Bomb*, ed. Baker, p. 21.

2. *Reflections on the Revolution in France* (Everyman's Library, London, 1910), p. 75.

3. See, for example, *Nuclear Weapons and Christian Conscience*, ed. Stein; *Nuclear Weapons and the Conflict of Conscience*, ed. John C. Bennett (New York, 1962); *The Moral Dilemma of Nuclear Weapons*, ed. William Clancy (New York, 1961); *Morality and Modern Warfare*, ed. William J. Nagle (Baltimore, 1960).

4. "Moral Urgencies in the Nuclear Context," in *Nuclear Weapons and the Conflict of Conscience*, p. 101.

5. *The Just War: Force and Political Responsibility* (New York, 1968), p. 171.

6. "Explorations into the Unilateral Disarmament Position," in *Nuclear Weapons and the Conflict of Conscience*, p. 130.

7. See the novel *Fail-Safe* by Eugene Burdick and Harvey Wheeler (New York, 1962) for a possible scenario.

8. Paul Ramsey, "A Political Ethics Context for Strategic Thinking," in *Strategic Thinking and Its Moral Implications*, ed. Morton A. Kaplan (Chicago, 1973), pp. 134–35.

9. George Urban, "A Conversation with George F. Kennan," 47 *Encounter* 3:37 (September 1976).

10. For a review and critique of this literature, see Philip Green, *Deadly Logic: The Theory of Nuclear Deterrence* (Columbus, Ohio, 1966).

11. *Nuclear Weapons and Foreign Policy* (New York, 1957), p. 180.

12. *On War*, trans. Terence Kilmartin (New York, 1968), p. 138.

13. See the article "Warfare, Conduct of" in the *Encyclopaedia Britannica* (15th ed., Chicago, 1975), *Macropaedia*, Vol. 19, p. 509.

14. *On War*, p. 138.

15. Bernard Brodie, *War and Politics* (New York, 1973), p. 404 (author's emphasis).

16. The bulk of Ramsey's articles, papers, and pamphlets are collected in his book *The Just War*; see also his earlier work *War and the Christian Conscience: How Shall Modern War Be Justly Conducted?* (Durham, 1961).

17. "War and Murder," p. 57.

18. *The Just War*, p. 252; see also p. 320.

19. *The Just War*, p. 303.

20. *War and Politics*, p. 404.

21. *The Just War*, p. 253 (author's emphasis); see also p. 328.

22. "Warfare," p. 568.

23. *The Just War*, p. 254; see also pp. 333ff.

24. *The Just War*, p. 364. Ramsey is paraphrasing Anscombe's critique of pacifism: see "War and Murder," p. 56.

18 THE CRIME OF AGGRESSION: POLITICAL LEADERS AND CITIZENS

1. Joseph W. Bishop, Jr., "The Question of War Crimes," 54 *Commentary* 6:85 (December 1972).

2. See the suggestion of Sanford Levinson, "Responsibility for Crimes of War," 2 *Philosophy and Public Affairs* 270ff. (1973).

3. For a useful account of this doctrine, tracing it back to the jurisprudence of John Austin, see Stanley Paulson, "Classical Legal Positivism at Nuremberg," 4 *Philosophy and Public Affairs* 132–58 (1975).

4. Quoted in Noam Chomsky, *At War with Asia*, p. 310.

5. Stanley Kunitz, "Foreign Affairs," in *Selected Poems: 1928–1959* (Boston, 1958), p. 23.

6. *Trials of War Criminals Before the Nuremberg Military Tribunals*, vol. 11 (1950), pp. 488–89; see the discussion in Levinson, pp. 253ff., and in Greenspan, *Modern Law of Land Warfare*, pp. 449–50.

7. *Trials of War Criminals*, vol. 14 (n.d.), p. 383; see Levinson, p. 263.

8. *Trials of War Criminals*, vol. 14, p. 472; see Levinson, p. 264.

9. For a discussion of the Vietnam cases, see Edward Weisband and Thomas M. Franck, *Resignation in Protest* (New York, 1976).

10. *Kurt Gerstein: The Ambiguity of Good*, trans. Charles Fullman (New York, 1969).

11. *Trials of War Criminals*, vol. 14, p. 346.

12. *King John* 4:2, ll. 231–41.

13. For the contemporary law of reparations, see Greenspan, pp. 309–10, 592–93.

14. *The Warriors*, pp. 196–97.

15. *The Warriors*, p. 198.

16. *The Warriors*, p. 199.

17. In thinking about these issues, I have been greatly helped by the essays in Joel Feinberg's *Doing and Deserving*.

18. *The Warriors*, p. 199.

19. See Richard A. Falk, "The Circle of Responsibility," in *Crimes of War*, ed. Falk, G. Kolko, and R. J. Lifton (New York, 1971), p. 230: "The circle of responsibility is drawn around all who have or should have knowledge of the illegal and immoral character of the war."

20. *American Power and the New Mandarins* (New York, 1969).

19 WAR CRIMES: SOLDIERS AND THEIR OFFICERS

1. *The Seventh Day: Soldiers Talk About the Six Day War* (London, 1970), p. 126.

2. I owe this point to Dan Little.

3. Guy Chapman, *A Passionate Prodigality* (New York, 1966), pp. 99–100.

4. Richard Wasserstrom, "The Responsibility of the Individual for War Crimes," in *Philosophy, Morality, and International Affairs*, p. 62.

5. *The Thin Red Line* (New York, 1964), pp. 271–78.

6. On the difficulties of surrender in the midst of a modern battle, see John Keegan, *The Face of Battle*, p. 322.

7. See the discussion of this point by Samuel David Resnick, *Moral Responsibility and Democratic Theory*, unpublished Ph.D. dissertation (Harvard University, 1972).

8. Seymour Hersh, *My Lai 4: A Report on the Massacre and its Aftermath* (New York, 1970); see also David Cooper, "Responsibility and the 'System,'" in *Individual and Collective Responsibility: The Massacre at My Lai*, ed. Peter French (Cambridge, Mass., 1972), pp. 83–100.

9. Hersh, p. 42.

10. *The Warriors*, p. 181.

11. *The Measures Taken*, in *The Jewish Wife and Other Short Plays*, trans. Eric Bentley (New York, 1965), p. 82.

12. The best account of the present legal situation is Yoram Dinstein, *The Defense of Obedience to Superior Orders in International Law* (Leiden, 1965).

13. McDougal and Feliciano, *Law and Minimum World Public Order*, p. 690.

14. Quoted in Kurt Baier's analysis of the Calley trial, "Guilt and Responsibility," *Individual and Collective Responsibility*, p. 42.

15. See Wasserstrom, "The Responsibility of the Individual."

16. Quoted in Telford Taylor, *Nuremberg and Vietnam*, p. 49.

17. *The Warriors*, pp. 185–86.

18. *The Warriors*, p. 189.

19. McDougal and Feliciano, pp. 693–94 and notes.

20. *Nuremberg and Vietnam*, p. 55n.

21. Jean Le Meur, "The Story of a Responsible Act," in *Political Man and Social Man*, ed. Robert Paul Wolff (New York, 1964), p. 204.

22. Quoted in A. J. Barker, *Yamashita* (New York, 1973), pp. 157–58.

23. Omar N. Bradley, *A Soldier's Story* (New York, 1964), pp. 343–44.

24. For the relevant law, see Greenspan, *Modern Law of Land Warfare*, pp. 332ff.

25. See Fried, *Anatomy of Values*, pp. 194–99.

26. I shall follow the account of A. Frank Reel, *The Case of General Yamashita* (Chicago, 1949).

27. Reel, p. 280: the appendix of this book reprints the Supreme Court decision.

28. On strict liability, see Feinberg, *Doing and Deserving*, pp. 223ff.

29. Hersh, p. 11.

30. "Political Action: The Problem of Dirty Hands," 2 *Philosophy and Public Affairs* (1973), pp. 160–80.

31. Frankland, *Bomber Offensive*, p. 159.

32. Calder, *The People's War*, p. 565; Irving, *Destruction of Dresden*, pp. 250–57.

33. *Soldiers: An Obituary for Geneva*, trans. Robert David MacDonald (New York, 1968), p. 192.

34. *The Discourses*, Bk. I, ch. XVIII.

35. 1 *Philosophy and Public Affairs* (1972), p. 143.

AFTERWORD: NONVIOLENCE AND THE THEORY OF WAR

1. *Exploring Nonviolent Alternatives* (Boston, 1971), p. 93; cf. Anders Boserup and Andrew Mack, *War Without Weapons: Non-Violence in National Defense* (New York, 1975), p. 135.

2. Sharp, p. 52.

3. But an enemy state might threaten to bomb rather than invade; on this possibility, see Adam Roberts, "Civilian Defense Strategy," in *Civilian Resistance as a National Defense*, ed. Roberts (Hammondsworth, 1969), pp. 268–72.

4. *Collected Essays, Journalism, and Letters*, vol. 4, p. 469.

5. Louis Fischer, *Gandhi and Stalin*, quoted in Orwell's "Reflections," p. 468.

6. "Lessons from Resistance Movements—Guerrilla and Non-Violent," in *Civilian Resistance*, p. 240.

7. For a brief account of Czech resistance, see Boserup and Mack, pp. 102–16.

8. Sharp, p. 66; but he believes that the degree and extent of suffering will be "vastly smaller" than in regular warfare (p. 65).

INDEX

Young Bill and Benny play in a New Jersey alleyway while staying with relatives during Helen and Arthur's nuptials in England. A network of aunts and grandparents took loving care of the young brothers, despite the apparent paucity of playthings, Bill's safety-pinned coat, and their general dishevelment.

Bill, in acolyte robes, poses for a photo in 1925 with young Barton and Rosemary on the side lawn of Lilac Hedges. Helen and Arthur indulged Barton and Rosemary, who had a less disciplined upbringing than Bill and Benny.

3

4

Left: Arthur and teenage Barton on the Atlantic City boardwalk. Helen and Arthur enjoyed dressing Barton and Rosemary in fine clothes and taking them on indulgent family outings. *Right:* Bill and Benny in Annapolis, 1929, before the brigade of midshipmen marched from Bancroft Hall to the football stadium, a tradition that continues to precede every navy home game. Bill and FDR shared a passion for navy football, which they discussed often. When Congress threatened to cancel the 1942 game to conserve rubber and fuel for the war, the Roosevelt White House would not hear of it.

5

St. Joseph's Chapel, Christ School for Boys, Arden, North Carolina. Daily homilies here helped shape adolescent Barton's character. These lessons would later guide him as a prisoner of war. An alumni war memorial stands near the entrance of the chapel.

Bill and Benny pose with Barton after his graduation from Christ School in June of 1934. The older brothers took an active interest in Barton's academic performance, as they wanted him to follow them to the US Naval Academy.

Barton poses at Lilac Hedges with proud Helen and Arthur following his graduation from US Naval Supply Corps School at Harvard University and US Navy induction ceremony. Barton would be wounded and taken prisoner barely three months after this photo was taken. *September 1941.*

Barton at Allenhurst, the Jersey Shore locale where he learned to swim in the Atlantic surf. His strong skills and confidence in the water are credited with his assistance to several prisoners struggling in the water at Subic Bay after their prison ship was bombed.

Barton raises a glass in toast at a bar in New York City prior to his departure for the Philippines. He was always at the center of social activities, at both after-work parties in New York City and as a prisoner of war. *November 1941.*

Nurses walk the grounds of the lovely and spacious Sternberg Hospital before the war. Barton, Charles, and a number of other navy patients were ferried across Manila Bay to Sternberg after Cavite Naval Base was bombed on December 10, 1941, but when Manila fell, General MacArthur only ordered that the facility's army patients be moved to safety.

11

Bill and Romie on their wedding day. Benny (right of groom) was Bill's best man and only attendant, the custom of the day. Rosemary Cross, standing to the left of the bride, was one of Romie's attendants. The marriage suffered from Bill's long hours at the White House after war was declared and subsequent orders to the Pacific. *Chevy Chase, Maryland, September 10, 1938.*

12

A naval intelligence officer re-plots battle lines in an exhibit in Churchill's subterranean map room, the heart of his secret complex hidden beneath Westminster between Parliament and #10 Downing Street. Churchill's map room served as the model for the White House Map Room, which was established in the White House basement in 1942 by Bill Mott. That map room was also a closely guarded, twenty-four-hour center, run by rotating shifts of carefully selected watch officers, fielding incoming cables from intelligence sources, war officials, and Allied leaders.

13

A rendering of the White House Map Room, where Bill spent sixteen months keeping Allied leaders informed and protecting the war's secrets. The furniture was moved to the room's center so Roosevelt could observe the updated war activity from his wheelchair. Bill Mott is seated at a teletype table to the far right of Roosevelt. This rendering was created in 1994 based on former watch officer George Elsey's recollections, as told to artist William Gemmell, head of White House Calligraphy and Graphics. The illustration hangs in the Map Room today.

14

SEES EVERYTHING *Something*   HEARS EVERYTHING *a little*   TELLS NOTHING *less*

This three monkeys cartoon was taped to the back of the Map Room door, which was guarded around the clock. The penciled edits were added by Secretary of War Stimson. Bill Mott used the cartoon as a visual aid to train new watch officers on the need for absolute secrecy concerning the room's activities.

15

Photo of FDR, a gift to Bill Mott at his departure from the White House. The inscription reads: *For Bill Mott from his friend, Franklin Roosevelt.* Bill Mott often described his close relationship with the president and FDR's and Eleanor's frequent inquiries about his brothers, Benny and Barton.

Benny Mott on the platform outside Sky Control, USS *Enterprise*, 1942.

Benny's genial nature, valuable understanding of carrier battle maneuvers, and the vantage point of his Sky Control post attracted the company of war correspondents. *Enterprise* narrowly escaped the Pearl Harbor sneak attack and was one of the few carriers available to conduct early 1942 hit-and-run raids on Japanese-held islands. Here he is sharing a sandwich with Keith Wheeler, *Chicago Sun-Times*, and Joe Custer, UPI, while they wait to hear the results of one of the raids.

Benny in civilian clothes visiting with his toddler daughter Jeanne Marie (Mara, later) before the war. Jeanne Marie was always uppermost in Benny's mind during *Enterprise* battles; he fought to protect her future liberties and to keep her safe from a scurrilous enemy.

Benny Mott (left) and two unidentified officers try to relax aboard *Enterprise* at the end of the Marcus Island raid, March 4, 1942.

Bilibid Prison was such a desolate, crumbling facility that the Filipinos had closed it before the war. The Japanese reopened Bilibid to serve as a way station for processing prisoners of war being shipped to Japan. Barton, Charles, and their ensign fraternity were held at Bilibid a number of times during their imprisonment and passed through its forbidding gates one last time on December 13, 1944, to board the *Oryoko Maru*, the last ship out of Manila Bay before it was sealed off to enemy shipping.

21

Before U. S. invasion of Philippines this copy of LIFE was read by hundreds of Americans and guerrillas in the Mindanao jungles.

"I KNOW OF NOTHING OUT HERE THAT HAS DONE MORE GOOD."
Lieutenant Rosenquist

When MIS-X operative Harold Rosenquist was finally allowed to board USS *Narwhal* to initiate his belated rescue of the prisoners at Davao Penal Colony, he carried with him several copies of the *Life* magazine article about the electrifying stateside effect of the atrocity stories told by the ten Davao escapees. The story spread rapidly through Mindanao's "jungle telegraph." It was their first confirmation that the home front understood their struggles and successes, and passionately supported them.

22

Admiral Chester Nimitz signs the Japanese surrender agreement on USS *Missouri*, September 2, 1945. The inscription reads: *To Captain William C. Mott, with best wishes, warm regards, and great appreciation of your contribution to the war effort, which made possible the above scene. C.W. Nimitz, Fleet Admiral, USN.*

23

First group of jubilant ex-POW's pose for navy photographers as they depart the Pacific for their home countries. Helen Cross scrutinized this photo when it appeared in the *New York Times* in early September 1945.

After three years of reading about her brilliant exploits in the Pacific, crowds gather as victorious *Enterprise* returns stateside after the war. More than a quarter million visitors toured the Big E during Navy Day festivities in New York City the week of her return.

Shusuke Wada listens to charges against him at the Japanese War Crimes Tribunal in Tokyo. The despised interpreter's life sentence for inhumane treatment of war prisoners was commuted after the end of Allied occupation of Japan. His boss, Davao Commandant Lieutenant Toshino, was convicted and executed for ordering the killing of war prisoners in his charge.

Conference delegate Bill Mott at the 1947 International Red Cross Convention in Stockholm. Here he helped draft the Geneva Convention's new Article III, which put in place the strongest ever protections for prisoners of war. The measures were adopted by the Swiss Federal Council in 1949. To date, 196 countries, including Japan, are signatories.

The author's parents before a White House dinner in the early 1950s.

Three Mott siblings (author far left) with cousin Barton Cross-Tierney and a new generation of Lilac Hedges dogs on the property's south lawn. The photo was taken during a visit that ended abruptly after an emotional adult argument on the porch.

Author-bride with her father in the Bishop's Garden of Washington National Cathedral before her marriage to John Freeman in 1996. Bill Mott passed away on All Saints' Day in 1997 at the age of eighty-six.

The sick continuous ache, the shaking fear the Japs will kill their prisoners as help approaches, and now—this! It is the final horror. Dear God, dear God, grant that this not be true! After three years, must American lads be sunk by their own country? I stumble around in a fog, talking to Barton's picture and crying until I am weak. I got out all his baby pictures, his Christ School pictures, my son—my dear lad! Come soon!

Benny did everything he could to calm his mother. Too little was known for her to draw the worst conclusion, he reasoned. He pointed out the unreliable and often strident nature of the Bataan Relief Organizations' reports—particularly since, in this case, the enemy was its source of information. But privately, he too was troubled, making it harder to muster reassuring arguments in which he didn't fully believe.

The Pacific Fleet—including *Enterprise*—was closing in on the Philippines, and its carrier planes and submarines routinely fanned out ahead of the fleet to soften enemy resistance—in this case to prepare for MacArthur's imminent landings. The cruising formation of the now-gigantic fleet was forty miles long and nine miles wide. With a fleet that size, communications in the heat of battle were challenging under a single, unified command; under an unrehearsed command divided between the army and the navy, such tragic incidents would not surprise Benny.

Tacking away from the topic, Benny tried a different approach. Why didn't she come with him to Elizabethtown? It would be an interesting excursion with the added benefit of taking her mind off the news. Helen was reluctant, but Benny prevailed on her to fix her hair, put on some nice clothes, and go hear him speak on behalf of the navy she was coming to despise.

At Elizabethtown, wearing a black dress with little adornment, Helen took her seat among the thousands of war-industry workers. Benny's mission was to present a special award to the plant's workforce for its phenomenal output: a coveted fourth star on its hard-earned army-navy E flag. The *E* on the pennant stood for Excellence. As a way of acknowledging the importance of home front workers to the war effort, the E flag was awarded to individual plants rather than to parent companies for exceptional yield and product quality; additional merit stars could be earned, as was the case on this occasion. The hard-earned E flags flew over war materiel facilities all over the country, and lapel pins reflecting the honor were worn proudly by every plant employee.

Benny received an introduction that would have made any mother proud. "Please welcome USS *Enterprise* gunnery and antiaircraft officer, Commander E. Bertram Mott—New Jersey's own!" Benny was hailed at length for his role on the storied *Enterprise* in the formidably difficult early months of the war, where he had "seen action at Pearl Harbor, Tokyo, Midway, Guadalcanal, and other points in the Southwest Pacific, fighting against overwhelming odds."

There was full, respectful applause as Benny approached the lectern and held up his hand to acknowledge the accolades. When he cleared his throat and looked out at the sea of faces, the room quieted in anticipation. Despite her darkened mood, Helen allowed a sense of pride in her firstborn son as Benny began to speak:

"Because of your faithful efforts toward victory, the Armed Forces today are *again* conferring upon you the highest civilian honor on the production front. The depth-charge pistols and booster extenders you make here are playing a dramatic part in our antisubmarine warfare in the Pacific.

"We normally think of depth charges as only being carried by destroyers and escort vessels, but not any longer—this critical antisubmarine ordnance is on *all* aircraft carriers. I know that our flyers on the *Enterprise* spotted many Jap submarines from the air, and we successfully depth-charged them more than once—thanks to you!" Benny smiled and gestured to the crowd with both hands.

At this, the thousand-strong audience clapped and cheered. Already fierce patriots, enthusiasm for their work had reached and remained at a new high after the Dyess story detailing the Japanese atrocities toward American prisoners broke. They were as fired up now as they had been in the immediate aftermath of Pearl Harbor. Benny then took them back to those first days of the war, recalling the desperate position of the country following the Pearl Harbor attack:

"The expansion of our military and naval establishments to their present formidable proportions would have been impossible without the complete mobilization of our war industries to provide these vital tools. If we have emerged from the shadows of unpreparedness and initial defeat, the credit belongs in enormous part to the skill, labor, and cooperation of the production front. The credit belongs to you."

He paused again, smiling at the wild, self-congratulatory applause and more than a few whistles.

"At the time," he continued, "the job of the US Fleet—or what was left of it—was to hold the line. We faced battle every time we left port. We knew we were overmatched, yet did not dare lose a single action. We were at sea constantly, under great nervous strain. Without a doubt, every single officer and crew member realized his enormous personal responsibility—to the nation."

The applause was building in enthusiasm, if that was even possible. Benny responded with a controlled nod, despite a surge of emotion welling up inside. It had been exactly as he'd said just now, hadn't it? That was the very feeling, every hour of every day aboard the *Enterprise*—no exaggeration.

He would never forget KGMB's Webley Edwards's somber farewell to him at Pearl Harbor in the early-morning hours of December 9, 1941. They had been standing amid the ruins in the predawn darkness, their faces lit only by the burning USS *Arizona*.

"It's up to you carrier boys now," Edwards had said, slapping Benny on the back. "You're all we've got left." Prescient words.

Benny was home now, which had been his fondest wish. But all he could think of right now, right here in the middle of giving this speech, was that ship. *His* ship. He yearned for her explicit rules and creeds and clarity of purpose. It was a hard life, but orderly, honorable, and worthy. He ached for the simplicity of a sailor's order of priorities, drilled into him from plebe year forward: Ship. Shipmate. Self.

In fact, the very hardships from which Benny had sought relief, from the inconsequential to the significant—hard bunks; earsplitting shelling; lack of privacy; a constantly vibrating deck; navy chow; the uncertain sequence of anticipation, fear, relief, and euphoria; and the monotonous, ticking meter of the sea when the bombs weren't dropping—were what he missed now. All those things, as well as the ready companionship of thousands of shipmates struggling under identical pressures. He was so lonely now, and so alone. Benny had to work to suppress the sudden, indescribable longing to be back aboard his beloved *Enterprise*.

After clearing his throat, he returned to the task at hand. "Planes from the *Enterprise* reached Pearl Harbor at the height of the sneak attack on December seventh. The task force to which *Enterprise* was assigned reached the blasted harbor the following day to see the saddest sight any of us had ever seen: battleships, cruisers, installations, blasted beyond recognition."

He paused an overlong moment at the memory of it. The audience grew quiet. Hundreds of heads nodded somberly; many began to cry. Virtually everyone in the audience had someone dear off fighting the war, and a considerable number had already lost loved ones.

"For the next year, the *Enterprise* was in one action after another—Gilbert and Marshall Islands, then Wake and Marcus Islands, in quick succession. Then came our raid on Tokyo in which *Enterprise* joined *Hornet* and her task force—"

He couldn't finish the next sentence. The audience had snapped out of its momentary mourning as though a switch had been flipped. Every last person was out of his or her seat, cheering and stamping their feet. Benny smiled and nodded, smiled and nodded.

"We fought against overwhelming odds, endured great hardship, living for the day when our great new fleet would be ready. That fleet—thanks to millions of American men and women in shipyards, mines, and factories such as yours—is near completion. If we have come out of the shadows of initial defeat, again, the credit belongs to the skills and labor and cooperation of the production front. And because of that, at long last, the initiative is ours. We have the ball, and we are going places."

Helen smiled and lifted her leaden hands from her lap to join in the next ovation. With time and a measure of luck, perhaps these fiery, patriotic words would again have meaning for her, she hoped, half listening as Benny wound down with highlights from the battles of Midway, Guadalcanal, and Santa Cruz.

"And now," Benny said after the room quieted, "here is your flag. Fly it proudly above your plant until the Stars and Stripes wave in triumph over the ruins of Berlin and the ashes of Tokyo."

AFTER SEEING BENNY OFF on the train back to Washington, Helen returned directly home and sat down at her desk with a full draft of ink in her fountain pen and a clean sheet of powder-blue Lilac Hedges stationery. Benny had done a fine job, but it seems her mind had been elsewhere during most of his speech. She had a letter to write, and by the time she got home, she knew what it had to say.

October 5, 1944

Dear Mr. President,

Word has come to me of the sinking of Japanese transports loaded with American prisoners off the coast of Mindanao on September 7.
I do not yet know if my youngest son Barton was among them— like those doomed men, he too was imprisoned at Davao Penal Colony.

However the horror and stupidity remain the same. To endure nearly three years of Japanese treatment—then to be sunk like a rat in a trap by one of your own American submarines!

Why sink transports in the first place? Why sink transports going north in any event? What about the colossal stupidity of the Joint Chiefs of Staff, not to foresee such movement of those abandoned American men and forbid the shelling of any northbound transport in waters off Mindanao?

If your son, a classmate of Barton's, had been imprisoned on Mindanao, you would have seen to it, wouldn't you, that such stupidity of the Joint Chiefs were corrected by orders from you?

Mr. President, you will probably never see these lines from any other agonized mother. To think, Americans, trapped in a hold being sunk by an American submarine!

> *Yours very sadly,*
> *Helen C. Cross*

The next day, she unburdened to her diary:

No sleep, no food. Rosemary called from New York—it seems Arthur has known it for two weeks and carried the awful news alone. Whether Barton was on that ship or not, the horror of it sickens me. But I must keep up, somehow. Arthur and I try to keep on, but we are so lonely for our lad.

32

★ ★ ★

HOPES DASHED

BY EARLY JUNE, TENSION at GHQ in Brisbane had risen to a fever pitch. Had Harold Rosenquist made contact with the prisoners at Davao without arousing Japanese suspicion? Were the friends Steve Mellnik had left behind, Doc Cain and Johnny King, still alive and able to help? Without word from Rosenquist, the agonizing days passed slowly. Mellnik made repeated visits to the GHQ's radio receiving room to check for incoming messages. For weeks, nothing.

Finally, the news arrived via Signal Corps radiogram in mid-June. Signed by Rosenquist, it said, "Walked around Penal Colony. Found no, repeat, no POWs . . . Convicts say they were evacuated ten days ago, probably to Manila."

Momentarily unsteady, Steve Mellnik lowered himself into his chair and reread the cryptic message, maddening in its dearth of detail. He then covered his face and sobbed.

★ ★ ★

SUBSEQUENT MISSIVES FROM ROSENQUIST contained better news: all was not lost, it turned out. There were still several hundred Dapecol prisoners on Mindanao. Two separate work details had been detained to complete airfields on the island, including one called Lincayan. Rosenquist was racing the clock, he intimated, to rescue those remaining prisoners. With American planes flying frequent reconnaissance missions overhead, the nervous Japanese were expected to ship them out, and soon.

This time Wendell Fertig did not interfere with Rosenquist's rescue planning, likely due to guilt over the fate of the more than 1,200 prisoners removed after his first meeting with Rosenquist. With the aid of Claro Lauretta's guerrillas and Jim McClure and Jim Haburne, two escapees from a Dapecol fence detail, the scheme began to crystallize. "We are working to locate the garrison where [the prisoners] are quartered, the guard strength, and the [potential for] their release," Rosenquist radioed Mellnik.

With mounting resentment toward Courtney Whitney, whom Rosenquist privately blamed for his failure to reach the other prisoners in time, Rosenquist asked escapees McClure and Haburne to pen statements on the potential success of a Dapecol rescue had Rosenquist been allowed to depart Australia earlier, as planned originally.

Haburne wrote:

```
"After staying in this particular prison camp for nineteen
months, going to and from Davao City on work details, see-
ing the communication system of the Japanese, the number of
guards in the prison, how they were armed, and after stay-
ing with various units in Davao Province for months after
I escaped, I am sure that those prisoners of war could have
been saved if Major Rosenquist had gotten to Davao Province
before he did."
```

McClure was more specific:

Major Harold Rosenquist told me he was here to release the
prisoners at Davao Penal Colony . . . and should have arrived on the east coast of Mindanao by a submarine [no
later than] May 28, 1944, but that the submarine commander
was off course and decided to proceed to the west coast . . .
I gave all the information I could to Major Rosenquist
about the conditions . . . when I left the prison camp--
number of guards, how they were armed, location of Japanese outposts, communications from the Colony to Davao City
and . . . the best possible way to attack the Colony . . . I
believe that [had] Lieutenant Rosenquist arrived in Davao
Province not later than May 1944, all of the American prisoners of war could have been released . . . [T]he job could
have been completed with minimal loss of troops.

Rosenquist refocused his efforts to rescue the men laboring at Lincayan
Airfield. First, he dispatched a letter via Filipino courier to smuggle into the
prisoner barracks at the airfield. It was addressed to Colonel Rufus H. Rogers, a trusted friend of Colonel John McGee, one of the two *Yashu Maru*
passengers who had jumped over the rail and survived. McGee had made it
back to Mindanao and joined the guerrillas, and he felt certain that Rogers
was alive and on the Lincayan detail.

August 11, 1944

TO: Lt. Col Rogers USA

Prisoner of War.

    This message is written with a prayer to God that it may
be safely delivered to you, that you and all the remaining

POWs at Lincayan may know that you have not been forgotten
all these months, that you can be encouraged that freedom
from the Japs is near. It has taken some time and the
hurtling of some obstacles to get here . . . but whatever
may happen, it is the result of the untiring effort of Col.
Steve Mellnik to bring you a message, and perhaps help to
the boys who were at the Penal Colony.

You will be glad to hear that the entire story of
the atrocities of the Japs on the "Death" March, their
treatment of Americans at Cabanatuan and Davao Penal
Colony were given by Mellnik and McCoy to <u>Life Magazine</u>
which published the whole story . . . in the February 7,
1944 issue. I have a battered copy, shown to hundreds of
Filipinos who have befriended our party as well as many
Americans now fighting with the guerrilla units here.
Remember Lt. Jim McClure? He is now with me, escaped with
Wohlfield, Watson, Campbell, and Haburne. We heard that
the others were recaptured and killed. Is that so? And were
there any reprisals?

Col. John McGee escaped from the boat taking the 1,220
[<u>sic</u>] to Manila, jumping off at Zamboanga, now safe at
"A" corps Hq . . . McGee gave me your name as a reliable
contact . . . so here's hoping fervently that you get this
message, and that you believe it!

Accomplishing that first step, we have to rely on you
for some facts to effect your release and that of others.

1. What hours of the day do you work, where, under what
    guards?
2. Help us to help you by giving us all the information
    possible. We have at least 100 men with arms, ammo and

grenades. The risk should not be too great for the
protection of you and your comrades.

Most any day now, maybe before you receive this message,
Lincayan Airfield will be bombed. SWPA and General
MacArthur know you are there and have been informed of
your barrack location. The advantage of the bombing and
resulting confusion may offer you the best opportunity for
escape. If that comes true, make for the guerrilla units
north of you; they are not far. I am writing this letter
within 25 kms of the Airfield.

The war progress is given on the back of this letter.
Is it any wonder you can be encouraged . . . It has been
so long but read the news and judge for yourself. May God
grant the delivery of this message and your reply safely
here.

HAR

It is not known whether Rosenquist's missive reached Colonel Rogers,
the senior officer of the Lincayan detail, before US Navy planes swooped
down and began dropping bombs on the airfield in mid-August. The prisoners cheered as the bombs blasted large craters into the runway they had
just built, rendering it unusable. Their incensed guards slapped and kicked
the men nearly insensate before marching them back to the barracks, which
were, in fact, untouched during the raid.

From that point forward, the prisoners were put on reduced rations
and confined to the heavily guarded barracks. Then, on September 3, they
were marched barefoot to the local dock, where they joined the hundred-
man prisoner detail that had been rebuilding the airfield east of Davao City.
Together the 750 men crammed into the hold of the *Erie Maru*, the same

unmarked Japanese freighter that had taken them from Manila to Davao in October 1942. The ship departed immediately in a Manila-bound convoy; it would make one Mindanao stop en route—at Moro Bay in Zamboanga Province.

When the news of the sudden departure of the final DAPECOL draft reached him at Claro Lauretta's guerrilla headquarters, Rosenquist was devastated. "Guess I won't get the chance to do what I really came here for," he wrote mournfully. Ex-prisoners McClure, Haburne, and the guerrillas of Lauretta's regiment were equally distraught. They had been so close.

THE MINUTE THE LOCAL coastwatcher saw American prisoners being loaded onto *Erie Maru*, he sent a radio dispatch to Mindanao's guerrilla headquarters. With American carrier planes and submarines now patrolling Mindanao waters in force, *Erie Maru*—lacking explicit markings as carrying prisoners of war—had little chance of making it past the patrols.

When guerrilla headquarters received the dispatch, it promptly radioed MacArthur's headquarters in Brisbane, which in turn notified the navy. Thus alerted, the submarine patrol allowed *Erie Maru* to pass. When her convoy stopped overnight at Zamboanga, another coastwatcher, Don LeCouvre, sent another dispatch through the same channels, and *Erie Maru* was again allowed safe passage when it departed the following morning.

But late on the night LeCouvre sent the first dispatch, the prisoners were removed from *Erie Maru* and loaded onto another ship, *Shinyo Maru*. LeCouvre promptly tapped out a second message, marking it Priority. The prisoners had been moved, it said, and were now aboard a different transport named *Shinyo Maru*, also unmarked. He directed that patrols be advised and allow it to proceed unmolested.

LeCouvre's urgent bulletin was forwarded to Brisbane, as required by the Divided Command structure, with directions to transmit it immediately to navy submarines patrolling off Zamboanga. But this time, LeCouvre's flickering message languished at an empty switchboard at MacArthur's Brisbane headquarters (GHQ). By the time the message was transmitted from there to the navy, *Shinyo Maru* had already departed Zamboanga.

JOHN MORRETT WAS ONE of the lucky survivors of the torpedo attack by the USS *Paddle*. He remembered two massive blasts inside the hull of the *Shinyo Maru* where they were quartered. The first pulverized men all around him, and the second brought large ceiling beams crashing down on them. Prisoners were covered in blood and piled in mangled positions all over one another—arms, legs, and bodies broken.

Miraculously spared, Morrett climbed the ladder to find the deck strewn with dead Japanese soldiers. But others had grabbed their weapons and were firing through blast holes and hatch openings at the trapped prisoners below and at any that had escaped into the water.

Denver Rose was beyond relieved when he was plucked with several others from the sea by a circling Japanese patrol boat. But his reaction was short-lived. "They tied our hands behind our backs . . . [and] started to machine gun us, but then changed their minds . . . One by one they took us to the aft end of the ship and shot us with a rifle . . . I was the fourth man up." But Denver Rose escaped back into the water after severing his rope manacle with a wire cable.

Japanese executions of prisoners trying to escape the doomed *Shinyo Maru* were not just acts of Bushido-sanctioned rage. They were following explicit orders. An August 1944 War Ministry order, issued to all prison camp commanders, directed that all remaining POWs be killed. It also proposed methods for their final disposition. The order read, in part:

```
Whether they are destroyed individually or in groups, or
however it is done, with mass bombing, poisonous smoke, poi-
sons, drowning, decapitation, or what, dispose of them as the
situation dictates. In any case, it is the aim not to allow
```

the escape of a single one, to annihilate them all, and not
to leave any traces.

On September 12 a chilling radio dispatch from a coast-watcher station in northern Zamboanga lit the airwaves. Local guerrillas had picked up eighty-three survivors of a torpedoed ship, it said. They had floated with the tide to the shoreline and were being cared for by Filipino civilians in a local barrio. The rest of the prisoners aboard *Shinyo Maru* were presumed dead.

Colonel John McGee, now working with a guerrilla unit near Zamboanga, received a subsequent dispatch: the eighty-three survivors needed immediate medical attention and were being taken to Sindangan City. Before departing to assist his onetime fellow prisoners, McGee radioed GHQ in Brisbane. Could these injured men gain submarine passage to Australia?

In Australia, Courtney Whitney reviewed the dispatches concerning the *Shinyo Maru* sinking and its relatively few survivors. With casual detachment, he penciled a note on the radiogram regarding a submarine rescue of the surviving prisoners. "This is a headache," he wrote in his elegant script, "but can be worked out."

As Shakespeare penned in *Richard II*, "Such is the breath of kings."

33

★ ★ ★

SETBACKS

MEDICAL AIR EVACUATION FROM the mid-Pacific to Pearl Harbor was by far the fastest option, but it had its downsides. The shriek of the Douglas C-54 Skymaster transport's engines as it climbed ten thousand feet from Guam's reclaimed Northwest Field surely caused Bill Mott's head to ache as much as his ailing gut. The flat chill of the prone aluminum berths, hinged to the metal curve of the plane's interior, felt less like a bed than being splayed on New Jersey's frigid Mill Pond after an ice skating spill, minus the laughs. But Bill was in decent spirits.

The reason was none other than "Terrible" Turner himself. The boss had a hard, gruff exterior, Bill mused, but inside, the irascible admiral was as soft as a grape. With everything the commander of the Pacific Amphibious Forces had been through during Operation Forager—and with everything he still had to do—Kelly Turner had personally arranged for this junior officer's transportation and (relative) comfort, as a father might a son. Better yet, his parting words had been for Bill to get well and to return as his permanent aide and flag secretary!

He *would* get better, Bill thought—he would *will* it. His grandmother Lauretta had marveled over his determined boyhood recovery from a grievous bout of typhoid fever. Perhaps he imagined her voice above the engines' high whine, remembered her soft hands, with their gentle scent of Hinds hand cream, caressing his burning forehead. Thoughts of his kindly grandmother, who had cared for that small, sick boy when it seemed nobody else had the time or inclination, were always a source of strength.

Inside the plane, disfigurement and pain were everywhere. By their first hop at Kwajalein, two marines—barely visible under a tangle of tubes draining pus and administering morphine—had died. The flight nurse, in baggy GI shirt and pants, took their pulses one last time to be sure before recording the names and serial numbers and pulling the sheets over their ashen faces. Such scenes of misery and mercy characterized the entire flight from the Marianas.

Under the circumstances, Bill could not yet bring himself to engage in Turner's parting literary gift: Somerset Maugham's popular tale of a young man's search for meaning in a postwar world. He drifted in and out of fitful sleep through the time zones. When awake, he cradled Turner's pronouncement that his orders would be made permanent, but he worried about not being found fit to resume duty—yet another hurdle in his quest to reach Barton.

It was nearly dusk when the pilot lowered his blighted cargo through the mist onto the concrete strip at Hickam Field. After a final insult of precautionary vermin delousing, Bill and the handful of other "walking wounded" made their way into a waiting hospital bus. Stretcher cases would follow separately.

The patients gazed out the bus window at the passing sights: the dimming harbor, reconstructed hangars, and an acres-wide stretch of white crosses marking the graves of those killed on December 7, 1941. A baritone grind of gears and a sudden shift into low signaled the final approach to Pearl Harbor's base hospital. The reticent driver steered his last load of infirmities of the day up the steep macadam drive.

Made of fireproof steel and concrete, Aiea Heights Naval Hospital was a brand-new, four-floor beacon of modern architecture. Surrounding the main hospital was a veritable village of temporary structures—mostly trailers and corrugated iron Quonset huts—that had been erected hastily to meet the hospital's rapidly expanding patient load. The new structures were painted dark green to blend into the towering backdrop of primeval-looking Norfolk and Keiki pines. Rising sharply behind the evergreens was the darkening Pali Lookout, its peak shrouded in cloud. Aiea Heights seemed a world unto itself.

Bill grasped an outstretched hand at the foot of the bus steps. Nurses armed with clipboards and the sort of kindly warmth unknown aboard any navy ship greeted the walking wounded. *Maybe this won't be so bad after all.*

In January 1944, the year-old hospital had rostered only 1,709 patients—1,358 of them still recovering from wounds received at Tarawa the previous November. But patient intake at Aiea had exploded by midsummer when the last group of Operation Forager casualties arrived. In June and July an additional 6,256 casualties from Saipan were logged, followed by 1,848 from Tinian and Guam. When Bill Mott arrived at Aiea in August, he had 7,667 fellow patients—in a facility built to accommodate an imponderable 5,000 casualties at any one time.

Bill was placed under the joint care of Aiea's chief of medicine, Captain Manley Capron, and the deputy chief, Commander Edward Delbridge. The next few weeks were a blur of waking, sleeping, poking, prodding, and invasive gastrointestinal procedures. His days at Aiea blended one into the next, punctuated only by rotating call nurses and Somerset Maugham's needling reminder that this phase of his life would in time yield to some unknown other.

A bright spot was the weekly call from ever-loyal Benny, who happened to be well schooled in the byzantine process of reaching a patient in the back warrens of Aiea's mini-bureaucracy—a mission as challenging, they would joke, as getting past the enemy alive. What fine medicine to laugh with Benny again! And whether or not Benny expressed his relief in those calls, he had feared as much for Bill's life at Saipan as Bill had ever worried over him on the *Enterprise*.

They talked at length about their unwitting role reversal: Benny now getting his fill of hard-nosed, self-important admirals, generals, and bureaucrats, and Bill now all too familiar with cramped quarters, K rations, carnage, and ever-present death. But the switched roles gave them all the more in common. After each restorative conversation, Benny always dutifully promised to communicate Bill's improving health status to the rest of the family.

JUST BEYOND AIEA'S STEELY confines, the long-simmering Pacific command rivalry had resurfaced once again. In late July 1944, President Roosevelt himself finally entered the army-navy fray over the direction and overall command of the Pacific War. FDR had been frustrated by months of conflicting advice from his top advisors on how to resolve it. As commander in chief of the army and the navy, he decided to sidestep all the bias and go hear from his Pacific commanders himself. The seminal meeting took place a stone's throw from Aiea Heights Naval Hospital, which the president visited afterward.

More than two and a half years into the war, command of the Pacific War zone was still divided in half. General MacArthur was still the supreme allied commander of the Southwest Pacific Area (SWPA), and Admiral Nimitz, commander in chief, Pacific Ocean Areas (POA), in charge of the rest of the Pacific theater. Conflicts had burned between the two commands since the start of the war—over strategy, objectives, delegation of ships, and jealously guarded latitudes and longitudes. Each fracas had been handled on a case-by-case basis by the Joint Chiefs of Staff, with neither Admiral Nimitz nor General MacArthur ever having to answer to the other.

The two commanders had progressed across their respective Pacific battlegrounds, however, and were both now on the doorstep of enemy home territory. The time for the separate command axes to converge had come. Critical decisions were now at hand, including where and when that convergence should occur, and which commander would lead the combined final thrust against mainland Japan.

The core conflicts had not changed. By pay grade measurement, MacArthur was the more senior in rank of the two flag officers and would not report to someone junior to him, but the Pacific was a naval theater by its very nature, and placing an army officer in overall command of an ocean battlefield was still just as unacceptable to the navy.

Not inconsequential to the unique Pearl Harbor summit was that 1944 was an election year, and Roosevelt had just accepted the Democratic Party nomination for a fourth presidential term. At the same time, MacArthur was enjoying broad media speculation as a possible Republican presidential contender. Summoning MacArthur to Hawaii—over his strenuous objections to "leaving his command," especially for the Nimitz stronghold of Oahu—served the additional purpose of cementing FDR's credentials as MacArthur's boss.

MacArthur agreed to attend the conference only when directly ordered by General Marshall. He still managed to convey his displeasure by rolling up late to Admiral Nimitz's dockside ceremony greeting FDR's ship—in a flag-wielding, open-air touring car, flanked by a deafening escort of motorcycles and wearing a bomber jacket with his corncob pipe between his teeth. Reporters crowded around him nonetheless, their cameras flashing, as MacArthur knew they would.

Despite that inauspicious beginning, the July 27 summit proceeded amicably in a luxurious villa at the Pearl Harbor Officers Club. Inside a map-hung room with balconies offering sweeping views of Waikiki, the parties discussed the various topics and even agreed on some of them. There was consensus that Japan could not continue to aggressively wage war without continuing to draw food, oil, and raw materials from its southern supply sources in the Dutch East Indies and Malaysia. How best to accomplish the crucial goal of cutting Japan's access to those supplies was disputed vigorously.

In a plan known in senior navy circles as "Admiral King's baby," Admiral Nimitz proposed bypassing the Philippines entirely—inspiring clenched jaws in the MacArthur delegation—and seizing the more proximate Formosa (present-day Taiwan). Nimitz argued that, with Formosa in Allied hands, a fail-safe blockade could be imposed that would decisively sever Japan from its supply sources. Simple geography. Nimitz also favored Formosa over the Philippines as the logical forward base for subsequent attacks on mainland Japan. It was closer to China, from which Allied bombers could easily reach Japan's home islands, and was ideally suited as a rendezvous point from which to invade mainland Japan—if and when that time came.

By seizing Formosa, Nimitz added tactfully, the Allies could end the war more quickly and with significantly fewer *Filipino* casualties—certainly fewer than would occur during a complex and lengthy invasion of the seven-thousand-island atoll of the Philippines. Chafed by his exclusion from the meeting, Admiral King had vigorously urged Nimitz to make another point in his absence: that war progress should not be slowed, nor excessive blood shed, for the purpose of servicing MacArthur's sentimentality or restoring his reputation. The more genteel Admiral Nimitz declined to make that point.

General MacArthur countered with commanding eloquence for the retaking of the Philippines. He presented strongly and without notes, fully aware that his reputation and military legacy depended on it. He reminded the group that the Philippines was an American commonwealth, and the United States had a constitutional responsibility to liberate her people. Taking the Philippines first would also enable the Allies to sever Japan from its supply sources. He reiterated his "personal guarantee"—previously circulated in Hawaii and Washington by General Sutherland—that the

Philippines campaign could be accomplished in thirty days to six weeks, with "inconsequential" losses.

"The eyes of all Asia will be watching," he then admonished Roosevelt, warning that America's postwar image in that part of the world would be tarnished forever if the Philippines were bypassed. Nor did he miss the opportunity to salt the old wound of "America's failure" to send ships and reinforcements to beleaguered Bataan and Corregidor in their hour of need, abandoning not only an alleged promise to do so, but also loyal Filipinos and tens of thousands of Americans as well.

Any plan to bypass the Philippines, MacArthur declared, was "utterly unsound." With signature theatrics and sweeping hand gestures, he stood before the map and patiently explained his long-planned amphibian invasion—beginning at Mindanao and thrusting northward up the island chain to Leyte, and then Luzon. He emphasized the flow of intelligence from Filipino guerrillas since the enemy occupation, maintained at great risk to those involved. It was unconscionable, he concluded, that the United States even *consider* not honoring MacArthur's much-publicized promise to return.

"Give me an aspirin," ordered the president after enduring three hours of General MacArthur's oratory. "In fact, give me another aspirin to take in the morning. In all my life, nobody has ever talked to me the way MacArthur did."

Roosevelt would need that second aspirin. On the following day, MacArthur took advantage of a private moment with the president to press one last point. "I daresay [if the Philippines were bypassed], the American people would be so aroused that they would register the most complete resentment against you at the polls this fall." To Candidate Roosevelt, this was heard as a threat—exactly as MacArthur had intended it.

WHAT THE SUMMIT PARTICIPANTS did not yet know was that the US Submarine Service had already imposed a virtual supply blockade of Japan. From recently won bases at Saipan and Guam, bands of roving submarine "wolf packs," as they were known, were sending one merchant vessel after another—carrying hundreds of tons of oil, iron ore, coal, bauxite, rubber, aluminum, arms, ammunition, aircraft, and enemy troops—to the ocean floor. By the end of Operation Forager, few enemy merchant vessels entering or departing Japanese-controlled ports were spared by Allied submarines. In fact, what they had already accomplished would come to be known as the most effective undersea war in the history of human conflict.

The submarine force had grown in size, agility, and effectiveness since December 7, 1941, when the United States ordered unrestricted submarine warfare—that is, submarine attacks on merchant vessels without warning—voiding its international treaty to the contrary. Under the gutsy guidance of Vice Admiral Charles Lockwood—"Uncle Charlie" to his devoted men—these wolf packs swaggered along the Pacific's undersea lanes like vigilante posses: mission driven, armed to the teeth, and bristling for kills.

They went by such names as Ben's Busters, Ed's Eradicators, Clyde's Cannibals, and Whittaker's Wolves, and the enormity of destruction they conferred on the enemy vied with that of Allied surface fleets many times their size. Just like their warships and aircraft, Japanese merchant ships transporting military personnel and cargo (including food) had to be destroyed in order to prevent them from aiding Japan's war effort or inflicting future harm.

The submariners possessed another deadly weapon: code breakers. By 1944, their cryptanalysts were reading Japanese transmissions with relative ease, providing the undersea combatants with exact sailing dates and times and course, speed, and composition of formations and convoys—though much less precise data on their cargo. This made it possible to triangulate convoy positions, allowing the wolf packs to lie in wait and then fire torpedoes deep into the unsuspecting ships' hulls. The nimble subs would then dive hundreds of feet to evade depth charges dropped by the enemy ships. Barton Cross would have swelled with pride at the war performance of the submarines that had once been under his care. But he might also have been justifiably nervous, given the dramatic rise in 1944 of Allied prisoners traveling between enemy ports in unmarked Japanese merchant ships.

WHILE NO FINAL AGREEMENT was reached at the Pearl Harbor conference, it was clear that MacArthur's emotional arguments and political intimations made their mark on Roosevelt. MacArthur's enduring—if self-propagated—status as American Hero, his broad conservative newspaper following, and his "strongest nonconcurrence" for any plan that omitted the Philippines would ultimately force the hand of a campaign-minded president.

The final decision was handed down six weeks later, on September 8, 1944: the next military objective in the Pacific would be the Philippines. MacArthur would land at Mindanao in October and progress to Leyte Island by December 20, 1944. In the meantime, the Joint Chiefs directed Admiral Nimitz to prepare for the subsequent invasions of Iwo Jima and Okinawa. An invasion of Formosa was tabled, much to Admiral King's disappointment.

But just four days after these decisions were handed down, Admiral Halsey—whose aggressive Third Fleet had been clearing Japanese shipping in the southern Philippines—reported minimal enemy resistance around Mindanao. In fact, said Halsey, "there was no shipping left to sink."

He followed with a bold three-part suggestion to Admiral Nimitz: that (1) Mindanao be bypassed entirely, (2) the invasion of the Philippines instead begin at Leyte, and (3) the Leyte invasion date be set for October 20.

Nimitz and the Joint Chiefs agreed, believing that Halsey's proposal could shorten the Pacific War. The Philippines invasion plan was thus revised accordingly. But there was a crucial omission in this grand revisiting of Pacific strategy in the summer and autumn of 1944. Both President Roosevelt and his Joint Chiefs had dodged their last, best chance to put the Pacific theater under a single, unified command. Interservice rivalries and political considerations had teamed to prevent that logical course of action—even as the mammoth forces of the US Army and Navy were about to converge.

In the upcoming Philippine invasion, therefore, the navy's Seventh Fleet, with its home port in Australia and under MacArthur's purview, would continue to report to Brisbane GHQ. Admiral Halsey's Third Fleet would operate under navy command. These two fleets, consisting of many hundreds of ships of every description, were about to converge in enemy-infested waters without so much as a common radio frequency.

This flawed command structure was in stark contrast to the one in place throughout the island-by-island sweep across the Central Pacific. In that sequence of campaigns, Admiral Spruance oversaw all aspects of each invasion, from shore bombardment, to air cover, to fire support, to troop landings, to operations ashore. A unified command structure had made crucial split-second decision-making possible—especially at the Battle of Saipan.

At Saipan, Admiral Spruance directed Kelly Turner to land tens of thousands of troops under heavy enemy resistance while Navajo code talkers communicated minute-by-minute enemy positions to marines ashore and to ships offshore. Spruance simultaneously ordered his fast carrier task force to sortie from Saipan and attack the Japanese Fleet in the Philippine Sea and another contingent of ships to remain and protect the Saipan landings. The continuous and coordinated flow of intelligence and communications to and among these disparate units and attack forces—under rapidly shifting battle conditions—saved lives and ultimately determined the battle's positive outcome. Conversely, army and navy forces merging off the Philippines would answer to two separate maestros—each with vastly different training and each free to indulge his respective interpretation of risk and success. This arrangement would prove particularly detrimental to urgent communications in the heat of battle.

Thanks to MacArthur's insistence on complete control of communications within his command area, the Seventh and Third Fleets would not be permitted to communicate directly with each other. Astoundingly, they instead had to relay their messages through an intermediary army radio station. The messages would be rebroadcast to the intended recipients only after army receipt and evaluation. It was a prescription for mortal trouble, as already evidenced by the preventable sinking of the *Shinyo Maru*. It could take hours for a dispatch to get from one fleet to the other, and they could easily arrive out of sequence—or too late.

WHILE DELIBERATIONS OVER FUTURE Pacific strategy coursed their way to this imperfect solution, Bill Mott's condition improved. By early September, he was declared healed and itching to get back to Admiral Turner and the Iwo Jima and Okinawa invasion planning. Negotiating his way out of Aiea Heights, however, was proving difficult.

Orders for his release had stalled somewhere in the bureaucracy, with few explanations forthcoming. Finally, Bill discovered the problem, and it was serious: diligent Dr. Delbridge had recommended, due to the severity of Bill's initial diagnosis—bleeding, potentially perforated stomach ulcers, with possibility of relapse—that he not return to sea duty. Bill was stunned and furious in equal parts. To come this far and then be sidelined not by his eyes but his *stomach*?

From his hospital cot, Bill began working the navy's front and back channels, a skill long in the honing. And he wasn't above charming Aiea's nursing staff to his cause. But his real weapon was feisty Admiral Turner, who, on hearing Delbridge's recommendation, charged up Aiea Heights's macadam drive and asserted himself on Bill Mott's behalf.

"You listen to me, goddammit!" Turner growled at Dr. Delbridge, within an inch or two of his nose. "You show me Mott's most recent tests supporting your goddamn order. If you can find me a goddamn ulcer, you win. If you can't find me an ulcer, I want him released to my command. Period!"

Delbridge replied evenly that it wasn't a matter of the most recent tests, which did indeed indicate that Bill Mott was healed; the problem was with Bill's initial diagnosis, given shipboard before his air evacuation from the Marianas. That diagnosis had indicated a very serious condition, one with the potential—if not the likelihood—for relapse.

When Turner demanded verification, a baffled Dr. Delbridge came up empty-handed. It seemed the paperwork detailing the original diagnosis had gone missing—it couldn't be found anywhere in the hospital.

Bill Mott sat quietly and listened to the two men. Piping up might lead to questions he didn't wish to answer. Fortunately, it never came to that. Turner pressed his position and won the point, if not a friend in Dr. Delbridge. Bill Mott was thus cleared for discharge.

Just as he was preparing to return to *Rocky Mount*, however, another setback almost knocked him back to his hospital cot. The news came in a reluctant call from Benny. At Aiea, Bill had enjoyed weeks of barely concealed optimism about Rosenquist's rescue mission, in which he had placed soaring hope. That dream came to an abrupt end with Benny's call.

If that had been the worst news—that the prisoners had been removed from Davao before Rosenquist could act—it would have been bad enough; but Benny's additional revelation was beyond his imagining. A *US Navy submarine* had torpedoed the Japanese merchant ship carrying the Davao prisoners in its hull? Instead of being rescued by a navy submarine—an image that had animated the sweetest of Bill's dreams—Barton had possibly been *torpedoed* by one?

And their mother knew! Benny delivered this final blow with the greatest reluctance, knowing it would be a dagger to Bill's heart. "My God," was all he could manage. Of all the problems he had anticipated, this was not among them.

Benny assured Bill that he was working tirelessly in Washington to corner the details. He was already in contact with two different branches at the Pentagon to learn all he could. It was not clear that Barton had been among the approximately 680 prisoners killed—it wasn't even certain that he was on that ship. In any case, there were some survivors, he said, and eventually they would be sent to Washington for a thorough debriefing. Maybe he could learn more then.

Meanwhile, Benny had requested the fated ship's roster and a list of the dead from the Captured Personnel and Casualty Branches. He made inquiries with the judge advocate generals' and army provost marshal offices, the International Red Cross, and the State Department, all of which had a keen interest in the circumstances surrounding the *Shinyo Maru* sinking and its survivors. Benny had gone to great lengths to penetrate the bureaucracy and get the facts, but so far he had little to show for it. It was a situation Bill understood all too well.

Benny tried to offer hope, but for Bill there was no solace. The very term "surviving prisoners" brought on waves of nausea. But it was the thought of his mother receiving such news that laid him the lowest. Bill felt sure she would see only this: for all his efforts, he had failed her spectacularly. Again.

34

★ ★ ★

THROUGH A PRISM:
MACARTHUR'S RETURN

I.

THE PRISONERS AT CABANATUAN knew in their bones that the Americans were closing in. It was just a matter of time. But would that seminal moment come in time to save them? The men alternately rejoiced and lamented as reports of Allied gains vied with rumors of accelerating prisoner shipments to Japan. Camp morale swung from high to low with each version of "the news."

The Davao prisoners had dreaded returning to Cabanatuan, perhaps Charles Armour most of all. His invective-laced complaints filled the scalding boxcar on their train ride north. No doubt Barton shared in the grumbling, but he was emphatically not unhappy at this juncture, still buoyed by the single, cherished letter he received before leaving Davao and by the positive war news at Cebu. He returned to Cabanatuan's rice fields without complaint.

Unlike many of the prisoners, his mind, spirit—even his body, though reduced—were sound. Not only had his center held these three long years, but his trials had undraped a character of steel and an expansive soul. The ragged shrapnel wound from December 1941, which had marked the beginning of his journey to manhood, was now a pigment-free scar in the shape of a lightning bolt. Like a birthmark, it was a constant reminder of where it had all started. Barton's peers revered him for his optimism, selflessness, humor, and—no minor attribute among deprived and desperate men—an innate sense of fairness. If only he could make it home to live out these good lessons. By mid-1944, Barton's prayers had distilled to a single incantation: that they be rescued before it was too late.

"We're going home," he would say to his fellow ensigns, over and over. "We just keep our heads down, and we're all going home." Reflexively, Barton drew from this incorruptible reserve to nudge Charles to his way of thinking. Cabanatuan wasn't nearly as bad as when they left it in 1942, he pointed out. And, anyway, it wouldn't be long now. If he had anything to do with it, Ozark fried pie—Charles's avowed favorite—would be the 1944 Thanksgiving feature at Lilac Hedges. "Its first-ever appearance north of the Mason-Dixon Line, if its last!" Charles surrendered one foul mood after another with a playful swing at the best friend he'd ever had; Barton would raise his hands in mock defense and, as always, throw back his head and laugh.

Barton's optimism aside, Cabanatuan had improved markedly during their absence, if only by prison camp squalor standards. Its cruel former commandant, Lieutenant Colonel "Blood" Mori, had been replaced, an enormous relief to the returnees. While many more had died since their October 1942 departure for Mindanao—nearly three thousand men were interred in acres of shallow graves around the camp—prisoner work teams had made life-saving improvements. They'd built a septic system and irrigation ditches, and obtained permission from the Japanese to douse the latrines with chemicals to reduce contagion. The death toll from infectious disease, particularly dysentery, had dropped dramatically with these changes.

Vegetable gardens also now dotted the compound on every inch of tillable soil, their yields coaxed from tiny seeds pocketed on farming details and variously boasting eggplant, okra, corn, radishes, beans, carrots, peppers, and papaya. That the quantities were small mattered little to famished men desperate to supplement a rice-and-salt diet. In fact, another ritual had been established in the ensigns' absence: *quanning*. "Quan" could be a noun or a verb—even an event—but at its core, it was the repreparation of the miserly rice issue with the day's random harvest, which consisted of any other edibles the men could get their hands on. Garden pickings were prized, but so were ingestible grasses, meat from cats, snakes, and rats, and the occasional purloined egg or chicken.

One thing that had not changed at Cabanatuan was the wary, short-tempered contingent of guards, even with the departure of Commandant Mori. Allied war gains had not improved their disposition, nor had word of the multiple prisoner escapes from Davao, from which these men had just arrived. In fact, the returning draft was initially sequestered, but eventually moved into the main camp. That was a happy day for the ensigns: reuniting with friends not seen in almost two years.

Among such comrades were Barton's former barrack mates Ensigns Andrew Long and George Petritz, and new navy acquaintances too, including fellow Supply Corps officers Chuck Wilkins and Bob Granston. The gaggle of young naval officers found strength in their swelled ranks and for the next several months "stuck together in all things."

In the evenings, they quanned, sang, joked, played cards, and told and retold stories of home and family. The men also indulged in a curiously popular pastime: intense recipe-swapping sessions. While it might seem unusual for perpetually famished men, discussing recipes subliminally conferred the comforts of home-cooked food as well as the promise of someday returning to such pleasures. One evening over tiny servings of okra-dotted rice, the men hilariously debated Charles Armour's Brunswick stew ("sounds awful no matter how much of that shit you put in there"). On such nights, the rise and fall of laughter in the ensigns' barracks was comparable to any revelry floating out of a good New York bar.

The Davao returnees had been back at Cabanatuan about three months when the most restorative moment of their imprisonment occurred. Some would recall it as the most exhilarating moment of their lives. The date was September 21, 1944.

At 0900, the ensigns were already south of camp breaking a sweat in the rice fields. Only clanging caribao tack, trilling birds, and the occasional shrill order broke the Luzon countryside's pastoral quiet. Then, like a stand of alerted deer, one after another of the prisoners looked up from their labors and toward the mountain-rippled horizon. They stood stock-still, hearing something.

The faint hum became a low rumble which grew more insistent by the minute. Planes? The prisoners were familiar with the sound of Japanese planes, but these engines had a different timbre—more finely tuned, yet bolder. Also, the rising growl was coming from the north instead of the west where Japanese airfields were located. Then, suddenly, what started as a hum burst into a roaring crescendo.

The ensigns could only gasp as the guards ran for cover. Despite advances in aeronautic design since their incarceration, the ensigns knew American carrier planes when they saw them. The white stars inside a red-rimmed blue blaze under the wings confirmed the prisoners' fondest hopes. "My God!" blurted Ken Wheeler. "They're ours!"

Over the lush, green peaks of the Sierra Madre Mountains came a thundering series of carrier aircraft formations from Admiral Halsey's Third Fleet, including an air group from USS *Enterprise*. Eight-plane squadrons flew in proud Vs, each flanked by fighter escorts darting protectively in and out of the clouds above them. The versatile aircraft veered variously west toward the Japanese-held airfields and south toward Manila Bay. Minutes after the first flyover, the distant detonation of bombs at Clark Field could be heard.

The ensigns laughed and cried, waving ragged pieces of clothing over their heads and shouting out prayers of thanks. After nearly three years of isolation and brutality, the vaguest encouragement was held dear, but *this*! Pent-up emotions burst their locks as one of the formations passed right over the prisoners' heads. One prisoner pointed skyward, boldly shouting in the direction of the guards peeping from their foxhole, *"Ichibon American hikoki!"* (American plane number one!). Ignoring the risks, the other prisoners picked up the chant, like long-shot underdogs belting out the school cheer. *"Ichibon American! Ichibon! Ichibon!"* (Number one American! Number one! Number one!).

They had barely recovered from the initial euphoria when another wave of planes roared over, like an encore to a wildly appreciative audience. Two pilots dropped down, tipped their wings, and their rear gunners fired in salute to the ecstatic assembly below. Four more planes amused themselves by buzzing the guard towers, driving their occupants down from the nests and up against the inner fence.

Camp administration abruptly called off all work details, but not before the grand finale: a dogfight between one of the American fighters and a Japanese Zero, in plain view of Cabanatuan. Trailing smoke, the US Hellcat dove at its opponent, getting hot on his tail before making good on every round he fired. The Zero's wing blown off, it broke apart and twisted earthward, slamming into a distant hill. A steady plume of smoke rose from the crash site, entertaining the prisoners for hours afterward.

By this time, the guards had emerged from protective ditches and rounded up the field-workers. Bony and barely clothed, the men goosestepped and sang "God Bless America" all the way back to the stockade. One prisoner recorded the experience in his diary:

"We sat down in the mud and cried . . . just pounding the water . . . We turned to each other with unseeing tear-filled eyes . . . It was the most beautiful sight . . . the first actual proof that our side was winning."

"What a day!" another recalled, "It is impossible to describe the thrill and varied emotions we felt. Gladness, happiness, joy, pride, desire to laugh, cry and shout all at the same time."

Camp administration was badly flustered by the flyovers. In apparent reprisal, the prisoners received no meal that evening—which did nothing to repress their elation. In every barrack, scenes of the day were replayed again and again, bringing alternating tears and incredulous laughter. Better still, damage reports trickled in via clandestine radio: a number of Japanese aircraft and runways at Clark Field had been laid to ruin, and as many as a dozen enemy ships had been sunk in Manila Harbor.

To the last man at Cabanatuan, hopes hit a new high that day. With American airpower in such force over Luzon, they were confident that liberation was near. In any case, they certainly wouldn't be going to Japan now. Unopposed formations flew over the camp again the next day, bolstering that confidence all the more. But the sudden and aggressive show of American force over Luzon had the Japanese revising their own thinking.

The aerial displays had eliminated any lingering doubts that American landings in the Philippines were imminent. As a result, the Japanese decided to accelerate the shipping of their remaining war prisoners to Japan. Their rationales were multiple, but primary among them was that the thousands of American prisoners of war in the Philippines were symbols of their power in East Asia. To relinquish them to victorious American forces would constitute an unacceptable loss of face. Neither did the Imperial Army want liberated prisoners assisting the invading force, nor attesting to criminal mistreatment suffered at their hands. Worker-starved factories in Japan also needed more manpower for war production. For all these reasons, prisoner shipments to the home islands shifted from "as necessary" to "urgent" priority.

In the days and weeks that followed the September air raids, bullish optimism at Cabanatuan began to fade. There were no more flyovers, and the guards insisted that the men would soon be leaving for Japan. Why? *Why?* They tortured themselves with endless speculation. Freedom, which had seemed so tantalizingly close, now seemed to be slipping away.

II.

What the prisoners could not have known was that Central Luzon's guerrilla force—thousands strong and well armed—had been poised for months to break them out of Cabanatuan. One highly respected guerrilla leader, Major Robert Lapham, an unsurrendered American army officer from Davenport, Iowa, desperately wanted to liberate the camp where many of his friends were imprisoned. Lapham was a force majeure: one measure of his effectiveness at thwarting the enemy was the $1M bounty the Japanese had posted for his capture. His Luzon Guerrilla Armed Forces (LGAF), or "Lapham's Raiders," had expanded to more than thirteen thousand well-trained men; by 1944, LGAF controlled the entire northern half of Luzon's great central plain, an area of thousands of square miles.

Lapham had kept Cabanatuan under continuous surveillance since 1942, and had helped smuggle in food, medicine, and even weapons in anticipation of one day freeing the prisoners. But his requests to raid the camp had been rejected repeatedly by Courtney Whitney at SWPA headquarters in Brisbane. "Too risky," came the replies. Some suspected that Whitney kept Lapham's proposals from General MacArthur, whom, they believed, would have supported the plan wholeheartedly.

Lapham felt a renewed urgency to raid Cabanatuan in the fall of 1944. The Japanese had gruesomely executed a group of Filipinos recently caught supplying aid to the prisoners through an elaborate underground network run by two American widows of men who had died at the camp. Margaret

Utinsky and Claire Phillips had avoided detection through a variety of clever means for nearly three years, but their luck ran out that summer. They were captured and tortured within an inch of their lives. The Filipinos caught supporting their efforts were not so lucky.

Lapham was alarmed by the executions as well as obvious Japanese reinforcement of Luzon, but he was also encouraged by a report from the leader of the local guerrilla group that had been shadowing the camp. Captain Juan Pajota rode miles on horseback one night to inform Lapham that there were only about two thousand POWs now interned at Cabanatuan down from a high of some eight thousand after the fall of Corregidor.

To Lapham and Pajota, this presented their best opportunity to raid the camp and liberate those prisoners. The numbers were manageable, and the Japanese were preoccupied with preparations for the imminent American landings. The guerrilla leaders discussed "every imaginable aspect of the rescue operation" that night. A third Luzon guerrilla leader, Lieutenant Colonel Bernard Anderson, concurred enthusiastically that the timing was ideal for a prison break.

So once again, in late September 1944, Major Lapham radioed Brisbane for permission to rescue the prisoners at Cabanatuan. Once freed, Lapham assured, the men would be cared for within a vast network of guerrilla-protected Filipino villages and enclaves. Then they would be rotated to Chick Parsons's and the submarine *Narwhal*'s Luzon rendezvous point: secluded Dibut Bay, fifty miles to the east. On *Narwhal*'s last trip to Dibut Bay, it had not only surfaced, but docked, and openly unloaded supplies for the guerrillas. To Lapham, sending an empty *Narwhal* back to Australia was a crime. "If we wait much longer," he argued, "we'll be able to rescue what's left in one caribao cart."

But Courtney Whitney turned Lapham down yet again—this time with the slim assurance that prisoner liberation would be given priority once MacArthur's troops arrived on Luzon. And in any case, Whitney said, there were no submarines to spare for this purpose.

★ ★ ★

MORALE AT CABANATUAN FELL to a new low with the sudden October arrival of fifty British and Dutch prisoners. Lee Stiles confided to his diary: "These men are in very bad shape." US Marine lieutenant colonel Curtis Beecher, the camp's senior officer, recorded his own impression. "They were a pitiful sight to behold."

As the resident prisoners scrambled to find clothing and mess kits to share with the gaunt new arrivals—surviving laborers from the Thailand-Burma "Death Railway"—they heard their horrific tale.

In Singapore on July 4, 1,289 of them had been crammed in the hull of a Japan-bound merchant ship, the *Hofuku Maru*. Due to engine trouble, the ship had detoured to Manila, arriving on July 19. They remained in *Hofuku Maru*'s hull in Manila Harbor for *eight* weeks while the ship's engines were dismantled and taken ashore for repair. Stuffed in a dark, crowded hold, they watched in terror for weeks on end as men all around them died of heat prostration, disease, hunger, and thirst.

But that wasn't the worst of it. On September 21, when *Hofuku Maru* finally departed Manila Bay in a ten-ship convoy, it was bombed by the very carrier planes that had brought such jubilation flying over the prisoners at Cabanatuan that same day. More than a thousand Dutch and British prisoners died in the attack.

The dazed, oil-drenched survivors were taken to Bilibid for treatment. The seriously wounded remained at Bilibid, and the remaining fifty were sent to Cabanatuan. "British state that American bombers are too bloody accurate," wrote Lee Stiles after hearing their stories. The existing prisoners now had something new to worry about.

On October 7, with these hellish images in mind, the hopes of the men at Cabanatuan were officially dashed with an announcement by camp administration: except for those unable to travel, they were all going back to Bilibid, now little more than a transfer station for shipment to Japan. Leave the mosquito nets behind, the guards taunted; they would not be needed in the frigid Japanese winter.

Lieutenant Colonel Beecher was ordered to make a list of "able-bodied" prisoners for shipment to Japan. With little to distinguish the weak from the genuinely ill, any man able to walk was put on the list. Armour, Cross, Ferguson, Granston, Long, Petritz, Wheeler, Wilkins, Wuest—all the ensigns. When a dozen trucks pulled up to remove them from Cabanatuan, Juan Pajota's guerrilla scouts could only look on helplessly as more than 1,600 prisoners—including the travel-weary British and Dutch survivors—boarded the truck beds.

Unlike previous journeys, the men were not lashed together or blindfolded, allowing them to observe the frantic Japanese reinforcement of Luzon in anticipation of the American invasion. Truck convoys full of Japanese soldiers were observed all along the road, traveling in both directions. Numerous air transports also passed overhead, with troop-packed gliders in tow, a method of conveyance the long-isolated prisoners had never seen. Droves of *Manileros* clogged the route as well; family after family evacuating the city on foot, their personal belongings balanced on their heads and backs.

With bridges impassable thanks to the recent American bombings, the prisoner convoy had to take a lengthy detour and enter Manila from the northwest, extending the uncomfortable journey by several hours. When they passed through Bilibid's forbidding gates after midnight, they were offered roomier sleeping quarters than before; another draft of 1,800 prisoners had just departed for Japan. The name of their ship was *Arisan Maru*.

III.

Just after midnight on October 20, 1944, an American naval force of 738 ships converged in the Philippine Sea and began filing through the channel leading to Leyte Gulf. The ships carried 160,000 troops, ammunition, equipment, and enough supplies to last months. General MacArthur had spent the evening alternately pacing the bridge of the cruiser, USS *Nash-ville*, and in her wardroom putting final touches on a speech he would soon broadcast through a prepositioned Signal Corps microphone on Leyte's Red Beach.

Devastating preinvasion bombardment rained down death on Leyte the next morning. After watching the display and reminiscing about his young lieutenant days on Leyte as an army surveyor at Tacloban, MacArthur returned to his cabin for an early lunch. When the beachhead was declared secure, the general reappeared in a fresh khaki uniform, sunglasses, and signature corncob pipe. He then descended into an awaiting navy barge, followed by Courtney Whitney (soon to be promoted to general), General Sutherland, and the new Philippine president, Sergio Osmeña, successor to the late Manuel Quezon, who'd died of tuberculosis in August. A phalanx of eager photographers and correspondents followed.

The barge churned through Leyte's busy waters—until it was stopped short by a sandbar. With autonomous authority under such circumstances, the transport's beachmaster told his passengers that they must exit and wade the rest of the way in, interfering with MacArthur's vision of stepping ashore—immaculate and dry—and striding to an awaiting bouquet of microphones.

The skipper pulled the release lever, and the barge's ramp rattled into the shallow surf. After casting him a mordant glare, MacArthur began sloshing toward shore when a cameraman snapped the iconic shot of the wading general and his entourage. In a matter of hours, the famous photograph had flashed around the world. MacArthur's terse expression would settle into the American conscience as a reflection of his grit, determination, and restored honor, not his flash of rage toward an impertinent barge skipper and otherwise all things United States Navy.

On the beach, MacArthur made his way to the microphones. "People of the Philippines," he began, "I have returned!" In the next moment, the heavens opened up, releasing a torrential downpour. MacArthur raised his voice to compete with the pounding rain. "By the grace of Almighty God," he continued, "our forces stand again on Philippine soil—soil consecrated in the blood of our two peoples."

He delivered the rest of his speech against a dueling backdrop of heavy rain and raging combat in the hills behind him, to great dramatic effect and the thrill of an archipelago-wide radio audience. "The hour of your redemption is here . . . *Rally to me!*" he exhorted emotionally. "Let the indomitable spirit of Bataan and Corregidor lead on! As the lines of battle roll forward to bring you within the zone of operations, rise and strike! Strike at every favorable opportunity! For your homes and hearths, strike! For future generations of your sons and daughters, strike! In the name of your sacred dead, strike!"

As General MacArthur delivered his florid oratory, Colonel Whitney stood by wearing a self-satisfied smile. Delivering his prewar client Douglas MacArthur back to the Philippines—where the wealthy Whitney had left behind millions in gold and chromium mining assets—would ensure both men's places in history, and their lifetime financial security as well.

IV.

On October 10, shortly before MacArthur's vaunted Leyte landing, 1,803 prisoners, mostly American, were marched from Bilibid Prison to Manila's Pier 7. When the draft arrived at the docks, they were relieved that the awaiting transport, *Arisan Maru*, was far too small for all of them. They traded bets on who would get to return to Bilibid. But the Japanese were of a different mind, determined to squeeze every last prisoner aboard.

Shivers McCollum was in one of the early boarding groups. The farther into the ship's bowels he and that long line of prisoners were pressed, the more stifling it became. After 600 were loaded and the center hold was full, still more came, and more after them—until all 1,803 men were packed in, standing back to chest and fighting panic. The stygian enclosure was barely large enough for a quarter their number. No sooner were they loaded than the freighter promptly backed away from the pier. An unknown number of prisoners died of suffocation in the first forty-eight hours.

When *Arisan Maru*'s captain was alerted to American carrier pilots patrolling above, he steered into a cove at Palawan Island to wait out the threat. So many men died and were thrown overboard during the layover that some 800 prisoners could be moved to the forward hold, thus relieving severe crowding belowdecks. On October 20, the *Arisan Maru* returned briefly to Manila Bay to replenish supplies. Despite an incoming typhoon, she hastened back out in a twelve-ship northbound convoy the following morning. The prisoners were thrown about in the high seas, coating them in their own vomit and kicked-up coal dust from the hold's previous cargo. Under these conditions, about a third of them had contracted dysentery, resulting in a further coating of fecal filth and the additional torture of swarming flies.

AS THE CONVOY PLIED north, two submarine wolf packs, Banister's Beagles and Blakely's Behemoths, lurked in their path, anticipating attempts by the Japanese navy to foil Allied troop landings at Leyte.

Shortly before midnight on October 23, Commander George Henry Browne of USS *Snook* ordered, "Up periscope!" He cupped his eyes tight to the lens goggle to confirm a beeping surface-radar report. Sure enough, as Browne arced the periscope around, a convoy of Japanese ships hove into view. *Snook* wasted no time firing her first round of torpedoes, and then another and another. In seconds, the dark waters surrounding *Arisan Maru* became a shooting gallery.

After diving deep following the banner kills, the sea wolves climbed from the depths the next morning in search of more prey. They had sunk eight of the convoy's ships the night before, but four others were still afloat and in range. At four thirty in the afternoon USS *Shark* commander Ed Blakely sighted one of them through his periscope. It was barely making seven knots—piece of cake for *Shark*. Blakely radioed his fellow Behemoths: *Shark* was closing on *Arisan Maru*. Since the ship carried no markings or flag indicating its prisoner of war cargo, he could not have known the wholesale slaughter his next command would render.

Three torpedoes roared out of *Shark*'s forward compartments. Blakely lowered his periscope and waited for the explosions to reverberate against the submarine, confirming the kill. Instead, depth charges from two of the other Japanese ships in the convoy came laddering down toward *Shark*. Again and again they came, seventeen crashing explosions in all. Bubbles, oil, clothes, cork, and other debris surfaced shortly. Urgent, repeated calls to Blakely from *Seadragon* and *Blackfish*—"Come in Nan-Zebra-Foxtrot-Oboe!"—brought no response. USS *Shark* was never heard from again.

Aboard *Arisan Maru*, Japanese deck guards watched the bristling wake of the first torpedo race toward the bow of the ship. They made it to the rail just in time to witness a near miss, even as they spotted the rooster tails of a second torpedo hurtling toward the aft section. Spared again, by a hair. The panicked guards then drew their guns and fired at the handful of prisoners on the deck who had been cooking rice for the evening meal, sending the startled men back down into the hold double time.

It was at this moment that *Shark*'s third torpedo ripped into the hull of *Arisan Maru* and exploded amid the prisoners. Hundreds were instantly pulverized. Body parts, bones, and debris flew in every direction, and the hold was coated in blood. At its epicenter, the massive carnage yielded no remains "bigger than a dime," recalled prisoner Calvin Graef.

In the ensuing melee, the guards cut the ladder rope to the forward hold and pounded the rear hatch shut before rowing away in the doomed *Arisan Maru*'s rubber lifeboats. Despite the shock of this additional setback, surviving prisoners acted instinctively to escape. They stacked a pyramid of corpses high enough for them to reach and dislodge the hatch and climb out. Those who made it into the water swam toward the Japanese destroyer that their former guards had just boarded. But when the prisoners heard the splash of bullets and saw Japanese sailors pushing survivors away from the side with long poles, they realized the wisdom of going no closer.

It was nightfall on the South China Sea when the remaining ships in their original convoy disappeared over the horizon. *Arisan Maru* survivors rode the midsea swells on pieces of wreckage or abandoned rubber lifeboats, calling out to one another until only a handful of voices could still be heard. The closest land, Formosa, was 225 miles to the east.

After two days, nine of the original 1,803 draft were still alive. Four were recaptured, but fortune smiled on the other five, who were rescued by a Chinese fishing junk. The Cantonese family operating the boat knew too well what would happen if they were apprehended by the Japanese. They took careful steps to keep the five survivors covered and destroyed all remnants of their raft.

The junk and its surprising catch came ashore at Namyung, Canton. The fishermen fed, bathed, and clothed the grateful men, and then risked their lives to help them evade roving enemy patrols. The mayor of Namyung made contact with Chiang Kai-shek's military leaders and US Army Air Forces, who came to their rescue. The survivors of the *Arisan Maru* disaster were promptly evacuated to Washington for debriefing, even as the final draft of Bilibid prisoners waited in agony for word of their own shipment to Japan.

V.

On October 20, before Helen Cross extinguished her bed lamp for another night of fitful rest, she confided a final thought to her diary:

October 20, 1944

News of MacArthur's Philippine invasion came last night, but I am so
cold and numb with the horror of it all that I feel no elation. God be
with prisoners everywhere—their position caught between Japs and
Americans is of particular terror. I just have a sick feeling that cannot
be comforted.

Her only diary entry the following day was, "Sick terror over Barton
stops my pen."

35

★ ★ ★

WHAT BENNY KNEW

BEING A RELIGIOUS MAN, Johnny Morrett bent his head in prayer often during the long series of flights from the Pacific to Washington, DC. Two months earlier, his prison ship, the *Shinyo Maru*—carrying 750 prisoners of war—had been sunk off Mindanao by an American submarine. Morrett had been one of the lucky eighty-two survivors, and he just couldn't stop thanking God.

SHINYO MARU'S ALARM WHISTLE was still "screeching like a wounded child" when Morrett jumped into the water and grabbed a pair of floating timbers—two-by-fours, about six feet long. Miraculously, he managed to dodge the spray and splatter of rifle fire from Japanese guards manning the listing vessel's rails, as well as the wrath of enemy scout planes periodically buzzing down and dropping depth charges on the American submarine that had torpedoed the ship.

As Morrett quietly scissor-kicked away from the fast-sinking wreck, he heard another prisoner thrashing in the water nearby. "I can't swim!" the man cried. Paddling over to him, Morrett shouted, "Grab onto the boards!" But no sooner had the man grasped the makeshift raft than a Japanese bullet found its mark, cleaving the man's skull. He slumped forward onto Morrett, who, with a measure of self-loathing, pushed the dead man away with his foot while keeping a watchful eye on Lieutenant Hashimoto, among the cruelest of the Davao guards, directing rifle fire from the bridge.

Staying low in the water, Morrett spotted the head of another prisoner, Major Harry Fischer, drifting with the tide toward shore. Morrett called out to Fischer and urged him to grab onto his makeshift raft.

Together the two survivors kept their heads and bodies as submerged as possible, looking back only once in response to a loud crackling sound—like the crumpling of heavy tinfoil, Morrett would recall. It was the ship's final gasp before thrusting upward and slipping beneath the surface. Five hundred prisoners were still trapped in her hull.

In the evening twilight, Morrett and Fischer saw more bobbing heads scattered across the water's surface: other survivors were either drifting landward with the tide or actively swimming toward shore. Faceless voices called out to one another, and a loose consensus developed: once ashore, they should all make for the heavy foliage fringing the beach. When their feet touched the sandy bottom, Morrett and Fischer—fueled by freedom-induced adrenaline—raced toward the underbrush.

But once in the thicket, they heard a threatening sound. *"Pssst! Pssst!"* Hearts pounding, the two men dropped low before turning toward the source: three grinning, shirtless Filipinos less than five feet away, bolo knives hanging at their sides. Tapping their muscular chests with their thumbs, they called out, "Guerrillas! . . . *Guerrillas!*" Forgetting himself, Morrett sprang to his feet and hugged one of them.

The scenes that followed were the province of dreams. The guerrillas, who moved like cats—noiseless, quick, and efficient—gathered up the first group of survivors on the shoreline and spirited them along a maze of dirt paths to a clearing. There, another group of Filipinos holding candles covered the shivering, mostly naked men with blankets and fed them raw eggs, boiled *camotes*, and bananas. The Filipinos were as gratified to be helping these Americans as the survivors were grateful; this resistance group had been fighting the Japanese for nearly three years.

An armed contingent of guerrillas led the revived men inland along a trail. They walked by the light of the moon, single file, for hours. The shipwrecked prisoners held up admirably despite their injuries and the trauma of the day. While they'd been pressed into many difficult marches in the Philippines, this was their first toward freedom and there would be no slowing or stopping on *their* account.

Those with bullet wounds or fractures were placed on the backs of caribao or, in the case of one man with a broken jaw and several broken ribs, on a mattress carried by four boys. The procession continued through intermittent jungle, tribal areas, tiny villages, and across bodies of water in outrigger canoes, all the while in the guerrillas' protective custody.

On the fifth day, the survivors were met by their old Davao comrade Lieutenant Colonel John McGee, and learned of his daring leap from the prisoner transport that had departed Mindanao before they did. McGee was now working with guerrilla leader Robert Bowler—the same Robert Bowler who had intercepted Harold Rosenquist when he first landed on the wrong side of Mindanao the previous May.

After his escape from *Yashu Maru*, McGee had contacted Wendell Fertig and requested a role in his guerrilla command. Fertig dismissed the request, disparaging McGee as another crazed POW escapee who thought he knew exactly how to win the war. But Colonel Bowler—himself a seasoned army officer—knew better and immediately took McGee under his Mindanao guerrilla wing. Not only had Bowler grown wary of Fertig himself, but he was a prewar colleague of John McGee's, a fellow West Point graduate, and a combat-hardened veteran.

And so when Bowler learned of the *Shinyo Maru* sinking, he did not radio Wendell Fertig as he had on Rosenquist's arrival. Not this time. Here, finally, was Bowler's chance to help the prisoners that had been held on Mindanao. Instead, he summoned like-minded McGee. The two men quickly forged a plan to convey the former prisoners—many of whom needed significant medical attention—off the island.

In the meantime, natives with first aid kits did what they could. They cleaned deep lacerations and bullet wounds with Merthiolate, and then sewed and bandaged them. They applied salves to infected ulcerations and immobilized broken bones, easing them into slings made out of improbable patchworks of cloth. And while a dentist saw to broken teeth, Bowler and McGee divided the able-bodied into three platoons, gave them khakis, shoes, and ammunition, and trained them in the use of the new American carbine. All eighty-two survivors were then moved to a heavily secured guerrilla camp to await the arrival of the USS *Narwhal*—the navy submarine that would take them to Australia.

WHEN HIS FLIGHT FINALLY arrived at Washington's Bolling Field, Morrett and two other survivors traveling with him—USAAF captains Bert Schwarz and Gene Dale—were met by Major Ellis Gray, chief of the army's Captured Personnel Branch. Gray arranged a private car to take the trio to the swank new Statler Hotel at the corner of Sixteenth and K Streets NW, a short walk from the White House. Gray told the men to bill any expenses to the War Department and to get some sleep—Pentagon and other debriefings would be lengthy and tiring, he said, and would take at least a couple of weeks.

At the Statler, Morrett finalized his *Shinyo Maru* casualty list—including branches of service, ranks, and hometowns. These 667 men either had gone down with the ship or were shot flailing in the water following the fatal torpedo blast. Morrett, now the ad hoc adjutant of the survivor group, had readily agreed to prepare the list; these men had been his close friends, and he wanted their fates to be known. Nonetheless, the tabulation had been sad, grim, and slow.

Morrett and the other survivors then assisted the War Department with the heartrending task of notifying the next of kin. Next came the long debriefing sessions with numerous military and other government divisions concerning Philippine airfield conditions, disposition of Japanese troops, guerrilla operations, and many thousands of prisoners still listed as "missing in action."

One of the debriefings was at a location described only as "Box 1142." It was the top secret MIS-X headquarters in Virginia, from which Lieutenant Harold Rosenquist had been dispatched to rescue them nearly a year before. Among other epiphanies at that remarkable compound, the *Shinyo Maru* survivors witnessed a stark contrast between the treatment afforded German POWs being detained there and their own treatment as prisoners of the Japanese.

Japanese atrocities toward Allied prisoners in the Philippines had roiled Washington ever since the Dyess story's first electrifying airing eleven months earlier. Morrett and his fellow escapees were asked to provide actionable examples of Japanese mistreatment of prisoners of war. They proceeded to provide lengthy depositions at the State Department, the Pentagon, and the Offices of the Judge Advocate and Adjutant Generals.

In each case, there were also questions on how the *Shinyo Maru* came to be sunk, which the survivors answered in detail. But even in the context of a global war in which ships were being sunk daily, the escapees were surprised at the low priority given the possibility that this had been a case of Americans firing on Americans. The subject of friendly fire, it seemed, was not a friendly one at the Pentagon.

It was through the Navy Casualty Section that Benny Mott learned of the *Shinyo Maru* survivors' arrival in Washington. Commander Jacobs and his successor, Commander H. B. Atkinson, were complying dutifully with Bill's request to let Benny know of *any* developments that might shed light on Barton's fate. Benny's Ship Characteristics and Fleet Requirements

Office was two long corridors away from Casualty. But despite the Pentagon's size and byzantine layout, "hot dope" traveled fast.

With predictable apprehension, Benny leafed slowly through Johnny Morrett's casualty list. He turned each page carefully, running his index finger down column after column until he reached the last name on the last page.

Another reprieve! Barton was not a *Shinyo Maru* casualty. But where was he now? What could these men tell him about his brother? Benny finally left a note for Morrett at the Statler Hotel, requesting a call. Could they get together?

Days went by before Benny heard back. Between debriefings, Morrett had priority personal matters of his own to attend to, most importantly a reunion with his fiancée, Pat Taylor, who since his capture had joined the Waves. She was now working at the Navy Department in Washington! He had phoned her after landing in San Francisco when he first set foot on American soil. "Pat, darling, I'm home!" he'd said. "I've missed you so much!" While she'd sounded happy to hear his voice, he sensed restraint. Maybe it was just shock, he decided—after all, he'd been listed as missing for nearly three years.

Morrett could barely contain his excitement when Pat arrived for their reunion dinner at the Statler. Trim and athletic, dark haired and beautiful, she looked stunning in her Wave uniform. The engagement ring he'd given her before his deployment still sparkled on her left hand. And in the little spare time he'd had since his return, Morrett had bought her a strand of pearls. The wrapped box bulged from his uniform pocket while they waited to be seated.

But over dinner in the Statler's chandelier-bedecked dining room, Pat broke the bitterest of news. He'd been gone so long, she explained uncomfortably, that she had given him up for dead. She was dating someone else now. She was open to two suitors, she said, incredibly, but the engagement was off.

A devastated Morrett—pearls still in his pocket—returned to his fellow ex-prisoners in their Statler suite. When he opened the door, he got another surprise. In front of him were Calvin Graef and four other friends he hadn't seen since his group of 750 men departed the Davao Penal Colony to work on the Lasang Airfield. Johnny Morrett's merciful God seemed to be playing tricks on him now.

Already unmoored, Morrett was speechless at first. But over the course of the evening, and with the help of a few cold Ballantines, the others caught him up on what seemed incomprehensible to all of them. A month after the *Shinyo Maru* went down, Graef and 1,800 others had boarded another Japanese transport, the *Arisan Maru*, which met an identical fate—torpedoed by an American submarine.

After all their debriefings but before the two survivor groups left Washington—variously for hospital treatment, war bond drives, or home—they were escorted to the White House to meet with a warm and sympathetic President Roosevelt. Following that, they were taken to meet with Secretary of War Stimson and Army Chief of Staff General Marshall.

In his quiet, dignified way, Marshall apologized to the former prisoners for help not arriving before the fall of Bataan and Corregidor. He offered no excuses, just that American forces weren't in a position to rescue them at the time. The men thanked Marshall for his candor and expressed no bitterness. Realizing they were in the company of two historic figures at the crest of a historic war, they apparently only wished to remember the moment that way.

ONE OF THE SURVIVORS' other final meetings in Washington was with Benny Mott. It took place shortly before Christmas 1944, and while its precise location is unknown, most likely it was in the Statler's darkened, smoky bar, where the survivor group often congregated. Benny caught up with three of them—Johnny Morrett, Bert Schwarz, and Calvin Graef, all onetime fellow prisoners of Barton Cross.

Talking with stricken families since their return had taken a toll on the group. So many weeping responses had overwhelmed them. Not only did each conversation rekindle their survivor guilt, but also it extended their grief over hundreds of lost friends. But when meeting with Benny, Morrett, Schwarz, and Graef had relatively good news.

When Morrett's detail departed Davao for Lasang, he assured Benny, Barton was alive and well at the prison camp. And even though there was no *Arisan Maru* casualty list yet, Calvin Graef felt certain that Barton Cross was still at Cabanatuan in early October when he and the first draft of prisoners were trucked from Cabanatuan to Bilibid.

News that Barton was still alive when these men departed the Philippines was good reason for Benny to sponsor a round of drinks. But the news wasn't all good. This was the first that Benny had heard of the *Arisan Maru*—another ship loaded with American prisoners sunk by *another* American submarine. Unlike the *Shinyo Maru* incident, the *Arisan Maru* sinking—which would constitute the worst disaster in US naval history— was apparently a taboo topic in senior military circles.

Graef also told Benny about the arrival of British and Dutch prisoners at Cabanatuan after *their* prison ship had been bombed, this one in Manila Bay by US carrier planes. That had come right out of the Brits' mouths, he said. The grim sum of facts shared by these survivors had Benny reeling.

He could tell none of this to his family, he decided—at least not now. News of the *Shinyo Maru* alone had undone Helen Cross. Were she to learn of this apparent cascade of prison ship sinkings off the Philippines, he feared it would finish her.

In any case, Benny would have to get official corroboration of these terrible reports. Yes, that's what he would do: more research was needed before he could assume they were accurate. In the meantime, Benny was determined to rescue his family life.

He was focused on getting his modest new house in suburban Maryland ready for a very special holiday visit from his wife and daughter; they were coming all the way from California. Jeannette was accompanying young Jeanne Marie on a custodial visit to see him, but Benny's fondest wish was that maybe, just maybe, he and Jeannette could put their marriage back together. No better time to do it than Christmas, and lonely Benny had made special plans for the three of them.

When mother and child arrived, however, both were feverish and unwell, probably with the flu. After they opened the Christmas gifts that Benny had lovingly purchased and wrapped, he insisted they take to bed while he went to the store in search of juice, soup, and aspirin. His disappointment was acute, but there was nothing else to be done. After mother and daughter settled into their room, Benny threw the Christmas wrappings into the fireplace and left for the store.

His Packard taillights had barely disappeared around the corner when the discarded wrapping paper went up in a giant whoosh of flames, sending errant sparks onto the carpet. Within minutes, the carpet, drapes, and furniture were consumed in flames. When Benny turned back onto Sleaford Place, three fire trucks blocked the road and fat canvas hoses snaked across his front yard. Firemen trained high arcs of water onto the flames lapping at his roof, a scene that likely reminded him of the devastating fires that killed so many of his gunnery crew at the Battle of Santa Cruz.

Benny threw the car into park and raced toward the house, panicked that his wife and little girl were still inside. But then he saw poor little Jeanne Marie huddled in a blanket next to one of the firemen, shaking and crying. Jeannette was talking to the fire captain; when she spied Benny, she cast an icy glance his way. It was a look he knew too well.

WHILE THE MATTER OF his burned-down house—and divorce— was sorted out, Benny resumed his research on Barton's whereabouts. Bill had been exhorting Benny to check with this officer or that Pentagon branch for updated POW intelligence. MacArthur had claimed to be making great strides in liberating the Philippines. "What of the war prisoners?" Bill wrote Benny.

Benny's last letter to Bill had noted one promising development. Another prisoner, a navy ensign and, he suspected, a prison colleague of Barton's, had just escaped and was being flown from the Philippines to Washington. His name was George Petritz. He had escaped from *another* Japan-bound ship that was sunk, this one in Subic Bay. All Benny knew so far was that he was being evacuated to Washington from the Leyte beachhead. The man needed immediate medical care and would be going to Bethesda Naval Hospital upon his arrival. Benny promised Bill he would visit Petritz as soon as they would let him.

But when Benny finally had his visit with George Petritz, he was so disconsolate over the doomed scenario Petritz described, he could not bring himself to write Bill about it—or at all—for months. This must have been difficult for Benny, but given the choices, reticence seemed preferable to the truth.

36

★ ★ ★

THE *ORYOKO MARU*

FOR THE PRISONERS QUARTERED at Bilibid Prison after the Allies landed at Leyte, the final months of 1944 were an emotional seesaw. Days-long American air raids over Manila in late October seemed to signal imminent liberation; but when the raids paused, prison guards insisted they were going to be shipped to Japan at the next opportunity.

The agony was in knowing that even if they survived a voyage to Japan, it would be months or years before they might be freed, instead of possibly days or weeks. Optimists like Barton Cross believed they would be rescued. Pessimists like Charles Armour believed this was just another case of his being the "fuckee."

The men craned to watch navy carrier planes carry out their attacks on Manila through barred windows on Bilibid's second story. They hooted and cheered every time a plane swooped down at enemy targets all around them; even the weakest hospital cases rose from their cots to thrill at the sight. Another source of satisfaction was the sight of their guards dashing for freshly dug foxholes at the sound of air raid sirens. "The demoralizing effect of inadequate rations is balanced by US Navy bombings [over Manila and Manila Bay]," confided navy prisoner Lieutenant David Nash to his diary. "The raids are spectacular and we watch them regularly . . . They gradually assure us that the Japanese are going to be unable to evacuate us to Japan."

The reigning emotions at Bilibid at that time—hope and apprehension—were perhaps best expressed in a letter to his family written by Ensign Shields Goodman:

> We are presumably awaiting transportation to Japan . . .
> [If so] I shall leave this letter with one of the hospital
> patients because the prisoners here will undoubtedly be
> back in American hands before those sent north to Japan.
> I have great hopes that our forces will come in before the
> Nips can get us out. We hear that Americans have landed 350
> miles to the south of us . . . Our planes have been overhead
> nearly every day since we arrived here. They have bombed
> the airfields and the port area and we hear that there are
> no Nip freighters or any other ships in the harbor . . . We
> feel that our insurance against being sent north becomes
> more concrete with each air raid . . . Happy day it's going
> to be when we are all reunited again. These last . . . years
> will fall away from us like leaves from a tree in fall, and
> it will seem . . . that we have never been apart.

Bilibid was spared any harm thanks to the large "PW" markings on its roof and exterior walls; clearly, the Yanks knew where they were. The prisoners might not have known when their troops would storm the gates, but even the worst skeptics believed it would be soon. Excitement and tensions ran high as they listened to contraband radio broadcasts confirming MacArthur's landing at Leyte. And they knew that MacArthur's troops were going to press north and west toward Luzon, compounding their hopes.

What they did not know was that the Leyte campaign had gotten bogged down, a factor that would alter their fate in ways that could not have been comprehended at the time. Unexpected Japanese reinforcements landing on Leyte's west coast were delivering fierce resistance to the Sixth Army approaching from the east—giving MacArthur his first taste of a fanatical, suicidal defense.

Another factor that helped slow the Leyte campaign was deployment of the enemy's first organized kamikaze force. The term "kamikaze," meaning "divine wind," had evolved into an enduring symbol of Japanese homeland protection after a sudden sea storm thwarted Mongol Kublai Khan's twelfth-century invasion of Japan. In Leyte Gulf, divine wind took the form of squadrons of fuel-bloated, explosive-laden planes flown on one-way suicide missions into Allied ships.

A steady onslaught of kamikazes rained down death on Leyte Gulf. The speed of their descent so confounded antiaircraft defenses that thirty-four ships were sunk and 288 others suffered serious damage. Hundreds of sailors died hideous deaths. The airborne attacks also suspended troopship unloading, which further exacerbated delays ashore.

It would take sixty-seven days to secure Leyte Island, double what MacArthur had confidently predicted for the *entire* campaign to retake the Philippines. The November 20 invasion of his next objective, Mindoro Island—which would also seal off Manila Bay to all Japanese shipping—had to be pushed back. In fact, the Mindoro landings were postponed and postponed again until definitively rescheduled for December 15. Advance carrier air strikes to clear enemy ships of all kinds from local waters would begin at dawn, December 14.

★ ★ ★

ON NOVEMBER 25 A fierce wind blew over Bilibid Prison, and the skies grew dark and ominous. A seaborne typhoon then roared across Manila and southern Luzon, bringing whipping rain and low, heavy clouds— and an abrupt end to six weeks of almost continuous US air raids. After so many weeks of being buoyed by them, the prisoners were dismayed by their sudden halt. Worse, when the storm passed, the planes did not return.

The men fretted and cursed and debated endlessly the possible reasons, even as they strained their eyes and ears for renewed activity. More discouraging was fresh chatter among the guards about the possibility of getting a transport into Manila Bay to ship the prisoners north. "What has happened?" wrote Marine Lieutenant Colonel Curtis Beecher in his journal. "Are we to find out that some serious setback has occurred just when our prospects seem so bright?"

Unaware of the complex revision of the Philippine invasion timeline, the prisoners knew only that the long, reassuring buzz of American aircraft had stopped as abruptly as it had begun. The calendar turned to December under silent skies, and the men grappled with newfound despair. They filled the hours as best they could—trading yet more recipes even as their rations grew impossibly smaller.

One glacial day after another passed this way. To distract from the gathering gloom, detailed instruction in Italian, Greek, French, German, and Polish recipes was added to the usual American gourmandizing. Incipient sommeliers lectured on wine pairings. One memorable presentation was given by Warwick Potter Scott, a navy lieutenant whose pedigreed name and bearing conferred enhanced authority on the subject: the proper sequencing of wine service at a thirteen-course dinner party, such as might be thrown at his home on Philadelphia's Main Line. The room was filled with attentive note takers, and there were a number of earnest follow-up questions. There was little else to do but pace the prison yard, talk longingly of home, and speculate endlessly on what would happen to them next.

On December 12 the uncertainty came to an end in the form of a breathless runner from Manila's Japanese military headquarters. His urgent message was for Bilibid's commandant. Time was of the essence, he told Commandant Nogi Naraji. During the bombing break, a transport ship had made it into Manila Bay. He must prepare a prisoner draft for immediate departure for Japan. Nogi ordered the navy doctors to prepare a manifest of all prisoners capable of travel.

"Our worst fears," wrote Curtis Beecher, "are finally realized."

In a hastily drafted protest letter, a group of senior officers and navy doctors formally objected. The letter forcefully asserted that moving war prisoners through active combat zones was a violation of the Geneva Convention. It also cited recent prison-ship sinkings, indicating that the specific dangers they faced were well understood. But Lieutenant Nogi had the power only to carry out orders, not alter them.

The ensigns shook their heads in dismay as they walked in a circle while coerced medical officers nodded grimly that one after another of them was fit for travel. Charles Armour—who by this time was suffering from beriberi, a painful thiamine deficiency—observed that if you were fit enough to cast a shadow, you were well enough to go.

At *tenko* that evening, a final manifest of 1,619 men was announced—two-thirds of Bilibid's remaining population. The group was primarily composed of officers, chaplains, navy doctors, and corpsmen; they would depart for Japan the following morning. Lieutenant Nogi, a former Seattle physician who had been relatively kind to the prisoners, tried to reassure them in his remarks that evening. There had been no air raids for eighteen days, he said to the sullen assembly; the waters were again safe for travel. David Nash confided in disgust to his diary, "He knew as well as we did it meant suicide."

After nearly three years to the day of hoping and waiting, the indefatigable band of ensigns—Charles Armour, Barton Cross, Earl Ferguson, Bob Glatt, Shields Goodman, Bob Granston, Andrew Long, Ken Wheeler, Chuck Wilkins, Bob Wuest, and George Petritz—scanned the list and gave one another a somber, knowing nod. Every single one of them was on it. They listened numbly to their instructions. They would be mustered at 0400, divided into three boarding groups, and embark on the familiar march to the waterfront. Their destination, once again, was Pier 7, the one-time "Million Dollar Pier."

None of them slept that night. They talked, collected scant possessions, and ate whatever saved Red Cross rations they had set aside.

Some wrote wills and farewell letters to next of kin should they not make it home. These were buried in sealed jars or entrusted to the few hospital corpsmen or patients not designated to depart. Still, throughout the night, a chorus of silent prayer drifted heavenward: *Please, God, let an American air raid cancel the voyage.*

Despite the supplications, they were rousted by the clangorous guardhouse bell at 0400. After a final meal—a teacup of *lugao*—the men organized into their boarding groups. Serial roll calls ensued. Then, inexplicably, the prisoners were ordered back to their quarters, reigniting hope. "Well, we haven't gone yet," said one, bravely. For the next few hours, optimism made a comeback. Bets were placed that their luck would turn, the ever-popular collateral being a steak dinner in Frisco.

At noon, however, the draft was resummoned, recounted, and ordered to fall in. Long columns of four abreast moved out of Bilibid's forbidding gates one last time. Those left behind looked on mournfully, as if witnessing their departure for the guillotine. The pitiful, heavily guarded procession—to the last man, thin, weak, and barely clothed—stretched a quarter of a mile.

With the exception of George Petritz and Shields Goodman, the ensigns were placed under the command of Colonel Curtis Beecher. The forty-seven-year-old marine—a decorated Great War veteran, whose commendations included the Croix de Guerre, the Silver Star, and the Purple Heart—was universally respected, even by the Japanese. The ensigns placed every remaining ounce of faith in him.

But Beecher had his own misgivings. "It was hot in the noon-day sun," he wrote of the march from Bilibid to the docks. "Everyone had lost weight and was in much poorer physical condition since their arrival at Bilibid . . . Many were barely able to walk, and quite a number were picked up along the route after passing out . . . It was a poor start for what at best would be an arduous journey."

The column stumbled past the Metropolitan Theater, across the Pasig Bridge, past the Legislative Building and the Walled City, Intramuros, colonial Manila's historic core, and General MacArthur's prewar headquarters. In every direction, weeds, trash, and abandoned buildings lined cratered streets. Approaching the harbor, they passed the Manila Hotel and then the Army and Navy Club, the latter no doubt evoking bittersweet memories for Barton. The rising sun flew atop its flagpole, and the once-boisterous poolside bar was boarded up. The grounds, trim and verdant in 1941, were vacant and overgrown.

But at each turn, bands of street boys were silhouetted against the ruins, flashing their signature V signs. Inside houses along the route, radio volumes were turned up to blaring as the procession passed, another defiant signal of loyalty to the Americans.

HOT AND EXHAUSTED FROM the four-kilometer march, the ragged columns finally massed at Pier 7 around one thirty in the afternoon. With characteristic optimism, Barton was encouraged when he eyed the awaiting vessel at the dock. Handsome-looking cabins and parlors lined every level. It was large, attractive, and multidecked—more like a luxury travel liner than a troop transport, Barton observed, to a derisive Charles. *Oryoko Maru* was painted on her sides and stern.

Admittedly, the ship did appear considerably more comfortable than any other they had been hosted on so far; with just a little crowding, there might even be room to accommodate all of them in the topside cabins. Barton's initial reaction was shared by a number of the others: this might not be so bad after all.

But there was an ominous retrofit to the civilian liner: antiaircraft gun mounts on the bow, stern, and along the decks in between. The ship bore no flag or markings indicating that it would be carrying Allied prisoners. Nevertheless, some satisfying sights awaited them at the waterfront.

This was their first close-up of the tremendous damage that American naval aircraft had inflicted on the port facilities: sunlight poured through gaping holes in docks and sheds all around the pier. Out in the harbor, masts from dozens of sunken Japanese ships poked through the surface like scattered stubble in a winter cornfield.

When the prisoners arrived at Pier 7, it was already jammed with civilian Japanese carrying bundles of personal belongings. They, too, it seemed, were preparing to board *Oryoko Maru*. The prisoners took heart that this obvious exodus meant the Japanese knew they were about to lose the Philippines. The majority of the civilians were women in brightly colored kimonos, their babies and children in tow. In addition, a large contingent of Japanese troops were preparing to board and a sprinkling of merchant seamen as well, likely former crew of ships sunk in Manila Bay.

While these groups streamed up *Oryoko Maru*'s gangway, the prisoners were held for hours without food or water in a sweltering metal warehouse alongside the pier. They grew increasingly discouraged by the loading: the ship looked crowded already without a single one of the 1,619 of them yet aboard. There was further disappointment when the odious Mr. Wada and his heartless boss, Lieutenant Junsaboro Toshino from Davao Penal Colony, appeared at the dock. Toshino, they learned, would be in charge of the prisoner draft. But the Davao contingent knew all too well that Toshino vested wide-ranging authority in his malevolent interpreter.

Shusuke Wada was new to Colonel Beecher, as he had not left Cabanatuan with the Davao contingent. But the seasoned marine sized up the problem quickly. "Wada was a detestable, gnome-like man, with a screeching, high-pitched voice," Beecher wrote. "I went up to him on the dock to ask a question in connection with the loading and got a snarly, arrogant reply. It was then that I found out that he was going with us, and I felt we were going to have a hard time with him . . . [T]he very fact that all business had to be done through him gave him authority . . . [H]e could refuse to transmit requests and put his own interpretation on orders by his commander."

It was late afternoon by the time all the Japanese passengers were loaded. Then, clearly anxious to weigh anchor and depart while they still could, guards rousted the prisoners to their feet and issued boarding instructions. Three holds belowdeck were assigned to them. The aft hold would be loaded first, the forward hold second, the center last.

It took more than an hour for the first group of seven hundred men, including Petritz, Goodman, and Warwick Potter Scott, to disappear down the long ladder into the aft hold. Guards used various means to hasten the process. At the bottom of the narrow steps stood Sergeant Dau, another Davao guard loathed by the prisoners who knew him. Dau and three Formosan conscripts urged prisoners farther and farther back into the hold's dark reaches—Dau with the aid of a drawn sword, his privates with brooms. With no source of ventilation but the open hatch, those in the rear of the space began to faint well before the loading was complete.

Early cries for air and water from the aft hold were fully audible to the second group climbing the gangway. Barton, Charles, and approximately six hundred others fell in behind Colonel Beecher. They were herded across the hot deck toward the bow, where another hatch revealed a steep, narrow ladder lowering twenty feet into darkness. Their final destination was similar to the one at the rear of the ship: a black and airless space measuring approximately sixty by one-hundred feet, with a four-foot-high wooden shelf extending around the sides.

When the forward cargo space was filled to capacity, with barely room for the men to sit and still 150 to be loaded, Colonel Beecher asked Mr. Wada—standing at the top of the ladder—if the rest of the group could please be redirected to other quarters. The hold was full, Beecher said; men would suffocate if any more were added. But Wada brusquely declined. "*Ippai! Ippai!*" he snarled, which means "chock full."

The loading continued with the help of another familiar Davao sentry: Kazutane Aihara, whose fondness for swatting the men's legs with sharpened lengths of bamboo the Davao prisoners also remembered. Now Aihara used a shovel to press them so deep into the forward hold that men were wedged in the tiny corners of the bulkhead and against the hot side plates of the ship. They sat tight against one another, knees drawn to their chests. Without portholes or vents, their breathing quickly became labored.

On the dock, the temperature was approximately 90 degrees. On the metal-seamed deck, it was closer to 100. Halfway down the ladders, it was hotter still, and in the loaded holds, the temperature quickly reached 120 degrees or more. Having been given no water since their teacup of *lugao* that morning, men along the bulkheads tried to lick the beads of moisture from the rising cloud of perspiration forming on the boards.

The final group of about three hundred descended into the center hold. These were the fortunate ones on *Oryoko Maru*: the center hold had ventilation and, while crowded, it was far from *ippai*.

It was under these conditions that *Oryoko Maru* cast off at sunset. Buckets containing a mixture of seaweed, fish, and rice were lowered into the three holds, but in the dark, distribution was uneven and chaotic; most men managed to grab a handful, but many clawed two, and others got none. Water was lowered as well, but in quantities so small it ran out while being ladled near the hatch openings. The men in the rear got none at all. Panic began to rise.

Oryoko Maru's slow, cautious course through the harbor shipwrecks failed to generate the air circulation the prisoners had hoped for with the movement of the ship. She then halted at the breakwater to await the convoy of freighters and destroyers with which *Oryoko Maru* would travel north. As each hour passed, conditions in the baking, oxygen-deprived holds grew more desperate. In addition to the maddening thirst, overflowing latrine buckets spilled, and their dungeon floors became a shallow bath of human waste.

While the ship awaited the escort vessels, prisoners in the aft hold began begging for air and water. Mr. Wada shouted back, "There is no water for you! You are disturbing the Japanese women and children! If you do not remain quiet I will close the hatch!" This brought no end to their cries. Rising chants of "Air! Water! Air! Water!" continued. Similar pleas came from the forward hold.

Wada responded by slamming shut the aft-hold hatch, its only source of ventilation. This happened around ten o'clock, marking a sharp descent into the most terrifying night in the lives of those who survived it. Colonel Beecher stood watch in the forward hold throughout the night, attempting to keep order—but, as he wrote later, "I have seen death, starvation, brutality, and torture, but have never experienced anything like those 12–14 hours. Men [went] crazy, moaning, groaning, singing or just muttering to themselves . . . It was pitch black, the moaning of the crazed and dying and the shouts of men fighting and killing each other."

During their long imprisonment, all the prisoners had suffered periods of terrible thirst; but that night on *Oryoko Maru*, they experienced the converging mind-altering tortures of extreme thirst and acute oxygen deprivation. The lucky ones suffocated to death before sunrise. Others, increasingly weak and dehydrated, went out of their minds.

Some drank what urine they could drain from their own bodies or from the waste buckets. Others slit open their own veins, or those of their neighbor, with switchblades or broken glass in order to suck the blood. Still others became violent in the hellish dark, beating to death those near them with fists or empty canteens for real or imagined transgressions. Some—including Barton Cross with Earl Ferguson and Robert Granston with Chuck Wilkins—paired up for mutual support and protection. They hung back quietly in the rear recesses of the hold's shelving as madness reigned all around.

At 0300 *Oryoko Maru* again weighed anchor and got under way, this time in convoy. Turning north into the South China Sea, the convoy hugged the relative shelter of Bataan's jagged coastline. The date was now December 14.

At first light, a weary Colonel Beecher ascended the ladder and asked the sentry for a word with Mr. Wada. When the hunchback appeared, Beecher informed him that men below were dead and dying from suffocation and thirst. The burly marine, who towered over Wada, negotiated vigorously for water and requested that the prisoners be allowed to rotate onto the deck for air.

Wada relented on the water request, allowing a detail to come up and fill buckets from a cabin bathtub. The group worked quickly, managing to procure enough for one half a canteen cup per man; for men with swelling, paper-dry tongues, it was better than nothing.

After the water was distributed, Beecher reiterated his request to Wada that prisoners be allowed brief rotations to the deck, beginning with those who had lost consciousness. While Beecher waited for Wada to consult with Lieutenant Toshino on the matter, the lookout in the ship's crow's nest began calling excitedly, *"Hikoki! Hikoki! Takusan hikoki, American! Kaigoon hikoki, takusan!"* The ship's air raid alarm followed.

On the deck above, the prisoners heard the drumming of running feet mixed with deafening bursts of antiaircraft fire. Pleading for calm at regular intervals, Beecher angled himself onto the ladder, where he could see the action through the open hatch.

THE AIR SQUADRON BEARING down on the convoy was led by Commander Robert Riera, Annapolis class of 1935 and a former *Enterprise* colleague of Benny's. One of her rising star pilots, Riera was awarded the Navy Cross for his daring sorties from *Enterprise* in the battle at Leyte Gulf.

Now flying missions off *Enterprise*'s sister carrier *Hornet*, Riera's December 14 log noted the targeting of a northbound convoy creeping along the Bataan coast. At 0710, near the entrance to Subic Bay, Riera gave the signal, and one Helldiver after another dove down behind him with all they had: bombs, rockets, and relentless sprays of machine gun fire.

Beecher watched from the ladder in suspended disbelief as eight Helldivers peeled into steep dives toward them. Concussive explosions followed, each violently shaking the ship's bulkheads. Not lucky misses, Beecher knew; they were going after the destroyer and freighter escorts first. *Oryoko Maru*'s antiaircraft gunners fired furiously at the dive bombers, bringing fierce responses from the planes' rear and wing gunners.

The atmosphere in the hold turned quiet and expectant as guns hammered away and bombs dropped all around them. Over the cacophony, one of the chaplains, Father Duffy, raised his voice in prayer: "Forgive them, Father. They know not what they do."

Commander Frank Bridget, a navy flyer himself, sat atop the aft ladder and, in the words of one witness, "as cool as a tennis match referee, reported the action." Bridget: "Flight of American navy planes headed this way. Two peeling off to attack a freighter . . . another hitting a tanker . . . several burning ships in view. Here they come! Everybody duck!"

The trembling prisoners heeded Bridget's warning as they heard the plane engines accelerate into their dives. The prisoners heeded his every word, but David Nash recalled "hop[ing] to hell they would score and hop[ing] to hell they wouldn't." One by one, the bombs hit the water, each with a violent *thump* before exploding. The ship bounced like a bathtub toy, and the men below were soon covered with dust and rust chips shaken loose by the detonations.

Suddenly light and air poured into the hold; burning shrapnel had ripped a jagged hole in the side of the ship. Dozens were wounded, but the hole brought improved airflow and enabled a better view of the action.

Now they could see their own planes retreat, circle, and roar back for a strafing run. Riera's audacious bombers dropped their bombs from 1,200 feet but strafed at nearly mast height. Bright flashes preceded the rapid chatter of guns firing hundreds of burning rounds down *Oryoko Maru*'s throat.

Fifty-caliber machine gun bullets—forged by patriotic factory workers in places such as Elizabethtown, Tulsa, Texarkana, and Ypsilanti—peppered the ship and its human cargo. Scorching bullets and casings ricocheted into the holds. Between attacks, doctors and corpsmen crawled from man to man, dressing fresh wounds with scraps of cloth torn from clothing of the dead.

The worst carnage was above them. Japanese gun crews and their serial replacements had stood and died at their mounts. Pooling blood from the deck dripped down onto the calm, moustachioed Commander Bridget, who continued to interpret the action from his slatted perch. "Not going to Japan, boys. Still right off Subic. Not going to Japan . . ."

In one- and two-hour intervals, Riera's squadron returned to attack the convoy at least nine separate times that day. At nightfall, *Oryoko Maru* was the only ship in the doomed cortege still afloat, and barely at that. With a broken rudder and riddled with holes, she limped into Subic Bay. Doctors were ordered up from the holds to treat wounded Japanese. On return, they confirmed massive casualties throughout the upper decks, cabins, parlors, and dining areas. The topside first-class cabins had been particularly hard hit, they said; chintz window dressing offered no protection from bombs and bullets.

With so many dead and the ship's sides punctured, oxygen supply for the surviving prisoners had improved. But in all other respects, the second night in the hold was as bad or worse than the first. Screams of the insane competed with groans of the wounded, and fights between possessed men could not be stopped.

By dawn on December 15, an eerie quiet hung over the crippled *Oryoko Maru*. The ship was dead in the water about five hundred yards off Olongapo, the onetime US Navy base. Subic's gentle current rippled against her hull as morning light filtered into the hold. Able to see again, doctors began moving about, treating wounds as best they could and gathering up the dead. They worked with dispatch; the bombers were expected to return to resume their work.

When the dazed prisoners gradually came to, they realized that except for a few guards, the Japanese passengers had all been evacuated. Were they being kept aboard intentionally to be sunk by their own navy? The answer came at 0800; the distant grind of airplane engines confirmed the imminent return of Riera's squadron.

Within minutes, unopposed bombs came whistling down. A large explosion convulsed the ship, and she heeled sharply to port. The aft hold had taken the direct hit, instantly killing some 250 prisoners. More died when the guard Aihara emptied his pistol at blast survivors rushing the aft-hold ladder.

In the forward hold, just as listening prisoners began to expect the worst, Mr. Wada spat down new orders: "Abandon ship!" The men were to remove all clothes and shoes and swim ashore. At this, the surviving prisoners seemed to regain a modicum of sanity, even discipline, as they worked together to first hoist up the wounded. Wada ordered Colonel Beecher to depart for shore and organize the incoming prisoners. The imperturbable Commander Bridget took charge on deck.

Bridget reiterated Wada's orders: remove any remaining clothes and shoes, exit the ship from the port side (which faced Olongapo), and swim ashore. The Japanese Naval Landing Party had set up machine guns on the beach and seawall. Orders were to shoot anyone who swam off course. "They mean what they say," Bridget warned.

Ensigns Earl Ferguson and Barton Cross emerged slowly from beneath the wooden shelving in the rear of the hold, weak and shaken, but unharmed. Two other ensigns, Robert Granston and Bob Glatt, did the same. Chuck Wilkins, Granston's best friend and initial *Oryoko* companion, was dead. Like many who had wisely paired up in the hold, faithfully dividing whatever sustenance came their way and keeping watch while the other slept, they had survived the worst of it aboard *Oryoko Maru*.

Separated from Charles since the beginning of the voyage, Barton was no doubt grateful when he saw his tall, gaunt figure stumble across the eerie space. At the ladder, the ensigns tried to assess the losses to their once inseparable band. Word quickly reached them that Ensigns Shields Goodman and Warwick Potter Scott had died in the bomb blast of the aft hold. They could not locate George Petritz, and fretted that he, too, had met the same fate in the aft hold.

Topside, the men gulped the humid air as if it were forbidden fruit. By the time Barton cleared the hatch, the deck was crowded with prisoners, and several had already begun the swim toward shore. Suddenly they heard the drone of airplane engines on the southern horizon; seconds later, four dive bombers descended toward *Oryoko Maru*. Almost in unison, the unmistakably white, bare-assed prisoners, both on deck and in the water, started waving their arms and shouting.

The formation leveled off as if to commence a bombing run when suddenly a plane on the flank waggled its wings and passed low over the scene without dropping its load. The rest of the planes followed suit. They then circled and retreated to the south without firing a shot. Finally, it seemed, they knew.

Charles Armour had never learned to swim. He didn't believe he could make the quarter mile to the beach. Astonishingly, several other prisoners had the same problem. Though weakened, Barton was in relatively decent condition, and years of tackling the Jersey Shore's burly waves had made him a strong and confident swimmer. Once in the water, he beckoned to Charles—who, not surprisingly, had refused to shed his clothes or cap.

In the water, Barton secured Charles under one arm and paddled toward Olongapo with the other. When their feet touched sandy bottom, they waded toward Colonel Beecher, who was standing at the shoreline. Beecher's attention had been drawn to swimmers struggling against the tidal current. Could Barton help them? he asked. Without a word, Barton dove back in and swam toward his floundering fellow prisoners.

Oryoko Maru was nearly empty when David Nash went looking for life jackets for other nonswimmers still on deck. Revived by fresh air and some candy and raw cabbage he found, Nash scavenged further and came across a chest of medical supplies in an aft passageway. Knowing it would prove invaluable ashore, he tried with difficulty to drag it to where it could be lowered onto a raft. In searching for assistance, he saw someone—breathing but unconscious—lying on a high shelf in the aft hold. It was Ensign George Petritz.

Nash approached and shook his friend's foot. "If you're alive you better get the hell out of here," he told Petritz. "Everyone else is just about gone." Disoriented but unhurt, Petritz managed to get to his feet and follow Nash, who had asked him for help getting the medicine chest ashore. "I will help you load it onto the raft," Petritz said, "but I'll never be taken alive by the Japanese again."

After loading the supplies and shoving Nash off, Petritz did some scavenging of his own.

He found Japanese clothing, a life preserver, and a jar of brown sugar and Japanese celery. After gobbling all that he could stomach, he put on the clothes and life preserver and lowered himself over the starboard side. Once in the water, he slipped under a floating wooden crate and waited. When he estimated that the lowering sun's reflected glare on the water would impair the gunners' view from the beach, Petritz slipped off the life preserver— which made him too buoyant in the salt water—and began swimming toward the far shore.

He swam for nearly an hour before coming across a *banca* with two Filipinos aboard: a boy and his grandmother. Seeing that he was American, the boy pulled Petritz aboard, and they took him ashore. Giving him his first taste of freedom in nearly three years, local villagers and guerrillas fed and protected Petritz as they might a family member. In time, they arranged for his conveyance to the Leyte beachhead in a navy PT boat. From there, he was evacuated stateside and eventually to Bethesda Naval Hospital outside Washington, DC.

37

★　★　★

END GAME IN THE PACIFIC

PLANNING THE SEQUENTIAL AMPHIBIOUS invasions of Iwo Jima and Okinawa was a months-long undertaking and the most complicated of the Pacific War. Where invasion rehearsals were staged was a minor logistic in the epic context. But when Leyte Island in the Philippines was selected for the Okinawa rehearsals, the earth moved under Bill's feet. He hoped only that it wouldn't be too late.

His long-sought goal of reaching Barton finally seemed at hand, and Admiral Turner knew it. Late on the evening of the Okinawa rehearsals decision, a wound-up Turner telephoned his groggy flag secretary to discuss a matter to which he'd given considerable thought: Bill should take liberty on their arrival at Leyte, Turner told his startled aide.

The Philippines should be firmly in hand by their scheduled arrival in March, the admiral continued. He wanted Bill to take the earliest possible opportunity to search for his brother. With the sequential D-days for Iwo Jima and Okinawa—code-named Detachment and Iceberg, respectively—set sequentially for February 19 and April 1, the flagship might be conducting rehearsals in the Philippines for as long as three weeks between the two invasions. This would give Bill ample time to go ashore and investigate.

Bill listened quietly at first, too stunned to respond. But when Turner finally paused for breath, he gratefully accepted the admiral's offer; this was no time for forced selflessness.

Turner said he hoped to meet Barton after all the good things he'd heard—maybe even aboard the flagship, if it could be arranged. After a pause that gave them both a moment to savor the scenario, Turner returned to the mechanics of his proposal. First, he indicated that the planners' five-day estimate to secure Iwo Jima might be overly optimistic. But even a week's delay would still have them at Leyte by early March, he hoped. Either way, Bill would have time to go ashore. By that time, the Philippines would almost certainly be in Allied hands, and there would be some system in place for locating prisoners.

If his penchant for alcohol had been a factor in Turner's unusual late-night call, that concern was vacated when the energetic amphibian commander reiterated his overture the next morning, and even made recommendations on where Bill might make inquiries. As though to counterbalance his sanguine proposals, Turner also cautioned Bill to prepare for what he might or might not find.

His boss's interest struck a deep chord, especially since Bill's quest to find out about Barton had become an increasingly lonely and discouraging enterprise. Recent communications from his mother and Arthur devolved into diatribes against the president, the Joint Chiefs of Staff, and—not least—the United States Navy. Nothing less than Barton's safe return home would assuage them now.

More disturbing was that Bill's latest entreaties to Benny seemed to be falling on deaf ears. It had been weeks since his last letter inquiring about the latest dope from the Casualty Branch and escaped prisoners now in

Washington. Why had Benny not responded? In the meantime, Bill had done his own sleuthing, but it brought scant comfort.

Captain Mac McCollum, back in Australia with the Seventh Fleet, confirmed that prisoners had been aboard some of the recent enemy ships sunk off the Philippines. All had been quartered on Japanese merchant vessels traveling north toward Japan. None had been flagged as carrying prisoners of war. Maddeningly, no manifests were available, but Bill had faith that McCollum was motivated to get his hands on them; he was as anxious about his cousin Shivers as Bill was about Barton.

Next came the news of a prisoner massacre on the Philippine island of Palawan. Survivor affidavits stated that on December 14, upon hearing US planes approaching Palawan, Japanese guards at Puerto Princesa herded 150 prisoners into air raid shelters—wood-lined, subterranean enclosures recently constructed by the prisoners themselves on orders by their captors. When the prisoners were loaded, the guards poured gasoline through shelter air slats and tossed in flaming grenades. The pits exploded into raging infernos.

Engulfed in flames, screaming prisoners rushed the exits only to be met by guards with machine guns, bayonets, and clubs. Miraculously, eleven of the 150 prisoners escaped in the melee, though all badly burned. They survived thanks to their quick interception by Filipino civilians and transport to the Leyte beachhead by yet another guerrilla band. Palawan survivors were on their way to Washington, where they would be treated and debriefed. Such reports threatened to reulcerate Bill's stomach.

One encouraging rumor made its way to Bill just before he shoved off for Iwo Jima. Another prisoner rescue plan was in the works: this time from a prison camp on Luzon. The plan seemed to be gaining traction thanks to the advocacy of one particular American guerrilla on Luzon, Major Robert Lapham. Convinced that more prisoner slaughter was in store, Lapham had persisted in his call to liberate prisoners from a place called Cabanatuan before it was too late. Most of the camp's population had been removed in October, but apparently hundreds of prisoners were still there.

Bill's pulse shot up and down with every report, each one maddeningly devoid of details that might hint at how Barton fit into it all. Which prisoners had been massacred? Which had gone down with their ships? Which were candidates to be rescued? Did the escaped naval ensign, George Petritz, have any of these answers—or news of Barton? As the amphibians set sail for Iwo Jima in January 1945, Bill sent Benny one last letter, summarizing his findings.

Hinting at recently garnered intelligence, he listed unanswered questions and offered Benny guidance on where he might find answers. What, for example, was the status of the Palawan survivors and this Ensign Petritz—all, presumably, in Washington now? Why hadn't he heard back? Was Benny too beset by his own troubles? Or did he know something too dreadful to share?

NEW OBSTACLES LOOMED AHEAD of the amphibians' departure for Iwo Jima. It might have been Bill's obdurate navy perspective, but one way or another, they all seemed to lead back to Douglas MacArthur. The general's consecutive setbacks in retaking the Philippines had now seriously thrown off the schedules for Operations Detachment and Iceberg.

MacArthur had assured the Joint Chiefs—and President Roosevelt— that he would take Leyte with four divisions in thirty to forty-five days and begin air strikes on Luzon shortly thereafter. But with nine divisions and in twice that time, the job still wasn't done. Since six weeks' spacing between MacArthur's Philippine and Nimitz's Iwo Jima invasion was necessary—as they were using the same combatant ships for their respective operations— Detachment had to be postponed from January 20 to February 3, and then again to February 19.

The April 1 invasion date for Okinawa (Iceberg) could *not* be postponed, due to the predictable onset of the pernicious spring typhoon season. MacArthur's every delay in retaking the Philippines therefore shortened the amphibians' rehearsal hiatus in the Philippines—and Bill's window to search for Barton.

Admiral Turner and his planners had little time to grouse about MacArthur or his slipping timetable. They had more immediate problems. Amphibious warfare techniques were evolving so rapidly that fresh lessons from recent invasions had rendered many of their planning labors obsolete. From hydrography and underwater demolition to the loading and unloading of mammoth amounts of supplies to beachhead organization and gunfire support, amphibian invasion "best practices" were in a constant state of change. More than once, they had to scrap entire planning sections and start over.

Such were the challenges facing Admiral Turner and his strategists as they labored through eighteen-hour days over a four-month period, from October 1944 to January 1945, to choreograph the invasions of Iwo Jima and Okinawa. Comparable in size and scope to the amphibious landings at Normandy—itself years in the planning—the Iwo Jima and Okinawa campaigns would pull thousands of ships and nearly a million men from every branch of service.

A primary difference between these operations and their European counterpart was supply-line logistics: the supply line across the English Channel in support of the Normandy invasion was approximately ninety nautical miles. The supply line for Iwo Jima and Okinawa would stretch an incomprehensible four thousand miles.

ON JANUARY 10, 1945, staff and crew saluted as Admiral Turner's colors soared up the yardarm of his brand-new flagship, the USS *Eldorado*. Weeks of shakedown followed before she nosed out of the Pearl Harbor channel bound for Iwo Jima, but by all accounts, it wasn't much of a sight. Like her predecessor the USS *Rocky Mount*, *Eldorado* resembled a drab cargo vessel barely able to navigate an inland waterway—a crafty disguise for the electronic nerve center of the amphibian fleet and most powerful communications and operations center ever set afloat.

From her state-of-the-art CIC deep within the armor of the ship's hull, staff could monitor and direct shore and air battles as never before. The control room was outfitted with a dizzying alphabet soup of the latest in radar and sonar equipment: SP, SG, PPI, DRT, CASCU, CAP, TBS.

Together these various devices facilitated real-time communications among all sectors of the amphibious machine: from weather updates, to troop interaction ashore, to detection and defense against enemy threats, be they planes, ships, mines, or submarines. Updates on all the above were applied continuously to illuminated Lucite boards lining the CIC. Shipborne technology had traveled light-years since the morning of December 7, 1941, when the USS *Enterprise*'s Jack Baumeister had puzzled behind a black curtain over a radar report on his single, low-resolution screen.

When *Eldorado* hove into Iwo Jima's waters in mid-February, an assault force of some nine hundred ships came into view. Extending to every horizon was an anchorage of aircraft carriers, destroyers, transports, hospital ships, landing vessels, and scores of smaller vessels taxiing among them. Each was poised to play its specific role in the painstakingly choreographed invasion of Iwo Jima.

Also known as "Sulphur Island," the objective was a putrid, eight-square-mile heap of scrub, volcanic ash, and razor-sharp kunai grass, which crawled with biting, typhus-carrying insects. The terrain resembled a Hollywood moonscape. The island was a treeless, cratered, inhospitable piece of ground yielded from boiling magma vomited forth in prehistory through an errant crack in the earth's crust. Reeking gasses hissed from ubiquitous rock fissures, its beaches were black as death, and Mount Suribachi, Iwo's 550-foot volcanic high ground, menaced over its general wretchedness. But to war planners, Iwo Jima was solid gold.

Reverently labeled "the unsinkable aircraft carrier," it boasted a trio of airstrips half the flight distance to Japan from the current B-29 bases in the

Marianas. It was also valued for its powerful symbolism in Japan. As a Japanese infantry officer wrote in his diary in June 1944, long before the Iwo Jima assault was planned, "Iwo Jima is the doorkeeper to the Imperial capital."

On February 16, war correspondents crowded into Admiral Turner's wardroom for a final prebattle briefing. With his usual powder-keg intensity, Kelly Turner studied Bill's fresh supply of intelligence communiqués, memorizing which facts could be publicized ahead of battle and which could not. Press censorship had relaxed considerably since the war's dismal early going. The powers in Washington had learned—to their collective surprise following the seismic response to the Davao escapees' atrocity reports— that strong media coverage actually galvanized public support, which in turn boosted faltering war bond sales.

As a result, the gathering correspondents would be reporting more about the battle for Iwo Jima than would ever have been allowed three years earlier. And with *Eldorado*'s broadcast capacity rivaling that of Radio Honolulu, their stories of valor and heartbreak would be received stateside before any spilled blood had dried—rather than the days, via ship or floatplane, that it had taken to sound the horrors of Guadalcanal.

Readying their notepads and pencils that morning were some of the world's best-known journalists. A handful of them had covered the Pacific War since the first scrappy hit-and-run carrier raids, as well as Turner's own baptism by fire at Guadalcanal—the Battle of Savo Island.

Bob Sherrod of *Time* and *Life* and Keith Wheeler of the *Chicago Sun-Times* were there, along with Walter Davenport of *Collier's*, John Marquand of *Harper's*, Hamilton Freon and Clark Lee of the Associated Press, and John Lardner of the *New Yorker*. With heavy straps and loaded with equipment, photographers Lou Lowery of *Leatherneck* magazine and Joe Rosenthal of AP also jostled for position, along with a pool of radio broadcasters that included NBC's popular Bud Foster.

Bill greeted the correspondents as they filed into Admiral Turner's inner sanctum. As the ship's censor, he was already acquainted with a number of them from the long days and nights aboard *Rocky Mount* during the battles for Saipan, Tinian, and Guam. That was when he'd met Sherrod and Wheeler, who had regaled him with tales of riding along in *Enterprise* Sky Control with Benny Mott during the 1942 carrier raids. "You must be little Benny!" Wheeler had crowed at their first meeting.

Bemused to hear a nickname he hadn't heard since plebe year, Bill nodded in cautious assent. The warm and garrulous Wheeler moved on to a geyser of Benny stories, making Bill happy and sad at the same time. These were stories about Benny in Benny's World of the USS *Enterprise*. In two short years, it seemed this veteran correspondent had pocketed more priceless anecdotes about his older brother than Bill had accumulated in a lifetime.

Hearing such tales from these new acquaintances felt like watching his brother through a hidden camera with his *other* family, in his *other* home—constellations away from their proprietary, Garden State–rooted, three-decade fraternal past. It felt good having big-shot reporters like Wheeler and Sherrod laud Benny, but it made Bill homesick for his brother's companionship. Perhaps the reverse had been felt aboard *Enterprise* in those dark days of 1942. Otherwise Wheeler might never have heard of "Little Benny."

THE ROOM CAME TO a hush when Admiral Turner moved to the microphone. He assembled his papers and cleared his throat like a maestro tapping his music stand. The briefing had been his idea, and for good reason. Counteracting MacArthur's widely publicized criticism of the navy's amphibious campaigns as "unnecessary slaughter" had been a principal motivator. A 1944 *Time* cover story featuring "Terrible Turner" wearing his best sneer had also had its effect.

Turner had long put the demands of his job over tending to his public image. He had belatedly come to appreciate that this neglect had contributed to a distorted public perception of the navy's amphibious campaigns in the Pacific. MacArthur's anti-navy diatribes had gained him an edge in the interservice public relations war, and Turner considered it a point of honor to set the record straight.

Life magazine's Robert Sherrod recalled the February 16 press conference aboard *Eldorado* vividly: "[It] was a rather emotional affair—there was the sort of pit-of-the-stomach emotion one feels when he knows many men who love life are about to die. Kelly Turner, peering over his spectacles and looking like Grant Wood's *American Gothic* farmer, ran the conference."

"The primary objective," Turner began, "is to capture Iwo Jima for fighters which can accompany B-29 bombers in their raids on Japan . . . We expect losses, of ships, and of troops," he continued solemnly. Turner's entire demeanor—including the full back brace he wore daily—reflected the leaden weight of that burden.

"They will be considerable."

He paused and looked into the faces around the room, as though to allow a moment for that unavoidable reality to be absorbed.

"But we are taking steps to keep them as low as possible . . . Iwo Jima is as well defended as any other fixed position in the world today. *Gibraltar* would be a setup by comparison . . . We are going to have losses, but we expect to take the position."

He continued at length on the details of the upcoming operation, finishing his remarks by explaining that *Eldorado* would have to leave Iwo Jima "after a few days, to prepare for future operations."

"Everyone knew he was talking about Okinawa," Sherrod recalled, "but he did not name it."

The next to take the microphone was USMC General Holland "Howlin' Mad" Smith who would be in charge of the tens of thousands of US Marines fighting ashore. The gathered assembly needed no introduction to Smith; he had already led a number of hard-won Pacific campaigns in the Gilberts, Marshalls, and Marianas. The general's delivery was punctuated by deep, collecting breaths.

"There is very little I can add," he began haltingly. "The stage is set.

There has been a tremendous amount of preparation by a large number of officers and men. Everything that can be done has been done . . .

"This is not set up," Smith then said abruptly, wagging his finger as though he'd heard a rumor. "Anybody who indulges in such wild flights of fancy has had no experience against these Japs. Every cook and baker will be on the beach with some kind of weapon . . . Aerial photographs show that the number of pillboxes has increased since October and especially since December, and the Japs on Iwo have no barracks aboveground. We have got to dig them out . . . There is no maneuver ground. This is a frontal attack."

Smith paused.

"The proper way to do it is as quickly as possible," he resumed, stressing the One and Only Marine Way. "We are not accustomed to defensive positions. There is nothing more detrimental to [Marine] morale than to be stabilized. Almost every weapon the Japs have got can reach us on the beaches. We may have to take high casualties—maybe forty percent of the assault troops."

Here he paused again.

"In Admiral Turner we have full confidence—we would rather go to sea with him in command than any other admiral under whom we have served. The navy brought us out here, and we have never yet had to swim ashore . . . though sometimes it has been close."

He allowed a smirk at the jab, which referred to the abrupt pullback of navy ships during the first landings on Guadalcanal. There were reports that by the end of his remarks, the tough-as-nails, foul-mouthed, cigar-chomping "Howlin' Mad" Smith was misty-eyed. He concluded by saying, simply, "We have never failed, and I don't believe we shall fail here."

There was universal surprise when Admiral Turner introduced the next speaker: Secretary of the Navy James Forrestal. He had traveled all the way from Washington to observe firsthand the battle for Iwo Jima.

"It has just been said," Forrestal began, "that you are honored to have me here . . . Quite the reverse is true. It is a high privilege to see in action the quality of leadership America has produced. I have seen Admiral Turner before, in the summer of 1942. His job was to take Guadalcanal with the US Marines. It was a tough job—a very tough job. But that was his mission, and he did it. The American people still do not realize the narrow margin of that pivot point of the Pacific War.

"I am also impressed," he continued, "by the meticulous precision of these operations; the amount and extent of planning that is required. This is a different kind of war that must be fought out here. These assaults on limited land areas present a tough task . . . Iwo Jima, like Tarawa, leaves very little choice except to take it by force of arms, by character, and courage."

Secretary Forrestal ended by giving generous due credit. "My hat is off to the marines. I think my feeling about them is best expressed by a letter written by a major general to his wife after Tarawa. He said, 'I can never again see a United States Marine without experiencing a feeling of reverence.'"

THREE DAYS OF THE most intense naval bombardment of the Pacific War immediately got under way. The ships' pounding of Iwo Jima came after seventy-four straight days of *aerial* bombardment, the longest ever ahead of a Pacific invasion. In all, 7,500 tons of bombs were dropped, and 22,000 shells were lobbed at the tiny atoll, mostly—the marines would soon find out—for naught.

The Japanese had tunneled down seventy-five feet beneath Iwo's barren landscape and constructed a vast, impregnable bulwark, which the long cannonade barely scratched. Miles of tunnels linked subterranean command posts, living quarters, ammunition dumps, and hundreds of concealed pillboxes with forty-inch-thick walls. Mount Suribachi alone had seven levels of passageways connecting a thousand individual chambers. There were multiple entrances, exits, stairwells, and interconnecting corridors, all lined with an ultrahard concrete made from plentiful indigenous volcanic ash.

Iwo Jima's D-day—February 19—began at 0830 with Admiral Turner's customary bellow through the ships' speakers, "Land the landing force!" Waves of marine-loaded landing craft and amtracs cranked away from the anchorage toward the beaches at the signal.

At the shoreline, however, they were stopped in their tracks by soft, black volcanic ash, exposing men and machines to torrents of fire coming from concealed subterranean hideouts. By the end of Day One, two thousand casualties littered the beaches and barely beyond.

CINCPAC's After Action Report detailed the unfolding horror:

> With each wave, boats would be picked up and thrown broadside onto the beach, where succeeding waves swamped and wrecked them and dug them deeply into the sand, beyond hope of salvage . . . [They] . . . could not be dragged up even when assisted by caterpillars. The coarse volcanic sand had no cohesive consistency . . . Troops debouched from the landing crafts struggled up the slopes under heavy fire, ankle deep in it. Wheeled vehicles bogged to their frames, tanks stalled in the surf, and the 40% grade of the cinder slope brought amphibious tractors to a halt. As vehicles left the LST ramps, they immediately sank down, their spinning treads banking the sand back under the ramps, making it harder for each succeeding vehicle.

In his first Iwo dispatch from *Eldorado*, Robert Sherrod summarized the early landings with astounding understatement: "The Jap plan of defense was plain. Only a few men would defend the beaches. The mortars and machine guns from the hillside caves . . . would stop the landing."

Up on deck, Turner, Smith, Forrestal, and rotating flag staff watched through binoculars with jaws clenched. Rising smoke and ash obscured their view, but beachhead reports confirmed quickly what their collective gut already had: the landings had emphatically not gone according to plan.

Little ground had been gained, and bullet-riddled bodies were strewn along miles of beach.

Bill barely saw his bunk in the grim early going of Iwo Jima. He spent most of that time shuttling between Admiral Turner's quarters and the CIC. He also monitored relays among the Navajo code talkers; the admiral demanded every decoded transmission as soon as it was available. Tensions ran high as Navajo receivers in *Eldorado*'s CIC transcribed each gruesome transmission ("Catching all hell from the quarry"; "Taking heavy casualties and can't move. Mortars killing us"), and Bill delivered them dutifully to Admiral Turner.

By February 21—D-day Plus 2—Holland Smith's dreaded estimates had already become reality: casualties on the beach were running 40 percent. "[The beach] is a two-mile stretch of death . . . all of it ours," reported Staff Sergeant David Dempsey. "An officer in charge of a tank landing boat received a direct shell hit while trying to free his boat from the sand. He was blown in half. A life preserver supports the trunk of his body in the water."

That evening brought another rude surprise. The hundreds of warships at anchor themselves came under siege. Fifty planes, thirty-two of them kamikazes, dropped from a low cloud ceiling just before nightfall— the witching hour for such raids, nerve-frayed crews would learn—and thrust themselves with savage ferocity at ships in the anchorage. The carrier *Bismarck Sea* was hit by two planes and sank in ninety minutes. Attempts to rescue the hundreds of sailors left foundering in dark and heavy seas continued through the night, but more than three hundred were lost. Several other ships were damaged; a mere foretaste of what was to come.

To protect the ship's battle command center, not to mention the secretary of the navy, *Eldorado* briefly withdrew to a protected position that night. From that point forward, a raw fear hung over the seven-mile-wide flotilla. Kamikazes seemed to select targets at random and were nearly impossible to defend against.

There was much discussion of this terrifying new threat in the 0400

CIC briefing on D-day Plus 3. Among the decisions made was that the press would not be allowed to report on this disturbing new enemy tactic. Recently returned from the beachhead, a shaken Robert Sherrod handed Bill his draft copy for review. Its opening line was: "Iwo Jima can only be described as a nightmare in hell."

Sherrod then dropped a bomb of his own. "Wheeler's been hit. He got it right through the neck when he stood up in the shell hole." Bill's dismay at the loss registered before Sherrod could add that his foxhole companion at Attu, Tarawa, Kwajalein, Saipan, and Tinian "was lucky, actually—he fell into the arms of two doctors and less than ten feet from a box of plasma. On his way to Aiea Heights by now."

Otherwise the day began much as the previous two had: with high casualty reports and gained ground measured in yards. On the other side of the command center, a glum Secretary Forrestal studied aerial photographs of the thoroughly pocked objective. "The planes just can't do it on an island like this," he said. Forrestal had hoped to go ashore to observe the operation, but Holland Smith would not allow it.

D-day Plus 4 began rainy and gray, reflecting the mood inside the smoky nerve center. Clacking teletype and the pinging, buzzing, and beeping of electronics were interrupted less by conversation than by the percussive snap of metal cigarette lighters. Next to the Navajo transmission operators—perhaps the busiest of all—were the men directing evacuation of the wounded to hospital ships already overflowing with casualties.

Around midmorning, the somber din was broken by an unusually excited transmission over the Navajo radio net. It was from code talker Teddy Draper to Holland Smith's command post on the beach. Bill stood impatiently over the translator as he methodically transcribed this message: "Asdla-ma-as-tso-si tse-nihl gah tkin nesh-chee dzeh Ashihi, Tkin Ts-a Ma-e A-Kha: Belasana Be Moasi. Bi-tsan-dehnah-jad-ah n-kih tseebii Dzeh Nakia, taa has-clish-nih Besh-legai-a-lah-ih Lin Klizzie . . . nihl neeznaa n-kih nos-bas."

When he finished, the translator handed Bill the piece of paper. Bill blinked his bloodshot eyes and studied the document:

```
To: 5th Marine Division Info: ADC
From: LT 28 E Company, 3rd Platoon:


Sergeant Ernest Thomas [USMCR] platoon raised US flag and
secured Mt. Suribachi at 1020.
```

A tremendous chorus of cheers and ships' horns reverberated throughout the anchorage as Bill clutched the message and loped in the direction of Admiral Turner. He found his boss standing on the flag bridge in the mist, already training his field glasses to Iwo Jima's highest elevation where Old Glory was rippling in the breeze.

ON MARCH 9 *ELDORADO* hastened out of Iwo Jima waters, even though the battle would rage on for two more weeks. The five-day estimate to secure the island had been weeks short of the mark; their delayed departure further shrank the flagship's planned rehearsal hiatus in the Philippines. That delay was exacerbated by a seven-hundred-mile detour to Guam to collect a surprise addition to the Okinawa leadership team.

In a dispatch straight from Washington, US Army Lieutenant General Simon Bolivar Buckner had been ordered to replace USMC General Holland Smith as commander of all landed forces at Okinawa. Grounded in spite, the decision was a direct result of Holland Smith's controversial demand for the replacement of Army General Ralph Smith at Saipan in the heat of battle.

Senior army brass all the way up to General Marshall had seethed over the incident ever since, and this would be their revenge. The revered Holland Smith thus became the highest-ranking victim of an interservice power struggle that had plagued the Pacific War from its inception. Not only would he not lead the invasion at Okinawa, the ground force charged with taking the next objective would be army infantry this time, not marines; a first for Admiral Turner and the amphibians. Moreover, neither Buckner nor his infantry had any previous amphibious assault experience.

It was an inauspicious beginning. Admiral Turner and General Buckner had only one thing in common: neither had ever landed a field army—another immense bait-and-switch for the planners. Moreover, this newlywed amphibian team now had less than half the allotted time to rehearse landing an untested force on a land mass fifty-six times the size of Iwo Jima and maniacally defended by 120,000 Japanese. Despite these escalating pressures, Admiral Turner insisted that Bill go ashore at Leyte as planned.

On the evening of March 15, *Eldorado* finally led the amphibian task force into Leyte Gulf and Bill took the launch to the beachhead the next morning. He hurried from Quonset hut to Quonset hut making inquiries to harried staff at each stop. It took half that first day to learn he was on the wrong island. Evacuating prisoners were being processed at a place called San Fernando la Union, and the central repository for prisoner records was Bilibid Prison in Manila. Both places were on Luzon.

The next morning, March 17, Bill's Irish luck was with him. He caught a transport to Luzon's Poro Point on Lingayen Gulf, also now a bustling Allied beachhead. Bill hitched a ride into San Fernando la Union with an army sergeant. They chatted amiably as the jeep lurched along a sandy road lined with mango groves and into the ruins of San Fernando. Bill walked toward a shrapnel-pocked train station, next to which stood a temporary structure with a "Replacement Center" sign over the door. This was where he'd been told that ex-prisoners were being processed. Was his search for Barton about to come to an abrupt end?

He found the enclosure mostly empty. One hundred twenty-five US Navy prisoners had just been put on a ship in Lingayen Gulf and evacuated to the States, a sympathetic army nurse told him; would he like to see the list? The manifest was of prisoners recently liberated from Bilibid. In his initial split-second review, Bill's heart made the wildest of leaps. He thought he'd caught the prize: "Cross, USNR, Cavite Navy Yard." Could it be? He had to steady himself before tracing his finger back to the spot, for a careful rereading. "Cross, Cornelius, USNR, Cavite Navy Yard." The crush of disappointment lengthened with the discovery that there were no other Crosses on either the "liberated" or subsequent "rescued" lists supplied by the nurse.

That didn't mean Barton hadn't survived, she assured an obviously disappointed Bill. Too little was known at this point. And yes, she added, he *should* go to Manila. Thousands of prisoner records were at Bilibid; tens of thousands, actually.

Back at Poro Point, Bill boarded one of the many PT boats traveling back and forth between Lingayen Gulf and Manila Bay. A call at Manila during his midshipman cruise had dimmed in Bill's memory, but he remembered the general layout of the city. Given the reported condition of Manila's roads and likely difficulty finding transportation, he might have to make his way to Bilibid on foot. The Lingayen nurse had warned that GIs working at the prison had only just started to make sense of the jumble of records, grave registrations, and other documents left in total disarray by the fleeing Japanese.

Reports of Manila's final ravaging had prepared Bill for a city radically altered from what he remembered. But what came into focus during the slow putter toward Pier 7 was beyond his bleakest imaginings. The sheer volume of floating wreckage—bodies drifting past scores of overturned hulks, masts poking up like dead trees from a swamp. The bay was nearly unnavigable. The stench of rotting flesh in the tropical heat forced Bill to pick his way up the bomb-pocked pier with his nose covered with a handkerchief.

US troops had stormed Manila in early February, but there had been another month of vicious street-by-street, building-by-building, and floor-by-floor combat before the city was declared secure. MacArthur himself had only entered Manila's smoldering remains on March 4, and not along a cheering parade route feting his sixty-fifth birthday as he had once envisioned. Between the rubble from blasted buildings and the bomb-cratered, body-strewn pavement, the streets were barely passable—even for General MacArthur. An estimated hundred thousand civilians had died in the final struggle, many first brutally raped or mutilated. The bodies of countless *Manileros*—men, women, and children—were covered with pieces of corrugated tin or other debris to preserve some tiny measure of dignity.

Bill walked north past the wreckage, his destination the intersection of Azcarraga and Quezon. The prison was circled on a map that the kindly Replacement Center nurse had given him—though most of the places and streets it marked had long since been destroyed. Homeless dogs roamed, sniffing mounds of trash and other leavings of a citizenry caught between warring armies: a child's shoe, a broken doll, a cane, a smashed baby stroller.

Along the way, Bill checked himself against unrealistic hopes and girded for bad news. Who could possibly have survived this devastation? With little time left, he hoped to find critical clues on Barton's whereabouts—before all the information was shipped out and dispersed among the Pentagon's harried bureaus.

When he finally arrived at Bilibid, he found a letter appended to the heavy entrance gate. It had been posted by fleeing Japanese guards:

> The Bilibid Hospital
> Manila P.I.
>
>
> February 4, 1945
> 11:30 A.M. (Tokyo)
>
>
> 1. The Japanese Army is now going to release all the
>   prisoners of war and internees here on its own accord.

2. We are assigned to another duty and will be here no
   more;
3. You are at liberty to act and live as free persons;
4. We shall leave here foodstuffs, medicines and other
   necessities of which you may avail yourselves for the
   time being.

Another sign read simply:

Lawfully released prisoners of war and internees are quartered here. Please do not molest them unless they make positive resistance.

                                    Imperial Japanese Army

At the prison office, Bill described his quest to the GI on duty. He responded, as the nurse on Lingayen had, that army officials had only just
begun to sift through the thousands of records and grave registrations the
Japanese had left behind. And more were arriving, daily, from several other
prison compounds. He would do what he could to help, but recommended
that Bill first review the batch of grave-registration lists. It might save them
both a lot of time.

Even with the clerk's assistance, this task alone took Bill the better part
of the day; the thousands of names were neither alphabetized nor divided
by service. At the start of each list, Bill braced himself for what he might
find. But when he came to the last page of the last one, he allowed a measure of relief. While he knew these lists were hardly an exhaustive accounting of prisoner dead, A. Barton Cross Jr., USNR, was not on any of them.

He then turned to the dozens of other rosters stuffed in various files,
few of which had been reviewed—or even translated. "Bilibid—1942,
1943, 1944, 1945." "Cabanatuan—Camp 1, Camp 2, and Camp 3."

"DAPECOL; O'Donnell." "Puerto Princesa." And on and on. There were also dozens of recovered jars that prisoners had buried containing messages, sketches, letters, and diaries. It was overwhelming, and Bill came to the rueful conclusion that he'd arrived too late to rescue Barton but too early to grasp what had happened to him.

As he pored over prison camp rosters, the clerk pulled another stack of lists from a box on the floor. These were prisoner transport manifests, he explained; maybe Bill should go through these next. This was when Bill began to fully comprehend the extent of the massive prisoner transfers from the Philippines to Japan—aboard ships named *Shinyo Maru, Hofuku Maru, Yashu Maru, Rakuyo Maru,* and *Oryoko Maru.* It was here he learned that Mac McCollum's cousin Shivers had been aboard the fated *Arisan Maru.*

The final manifest was of the last prison ship to depart Manila Bay before the Allies sealed it off to enemy traffic. The ship had departed December 13, almost exactly twelve weeks earlier. Bill was momentarily stunned. After all this time, *Oryoko Maru* manifest in hand, here it was, finally: Cross, Arthur Barton Jr., Ensign, USNR. He peppered the clerk with questions on what was known of this ship and its destination, then rose wearily and thanked him. He would be back, he said, but it might be awhile; he was shoving off for Okinawa shortly.

While the PT commander negotiated his way out of the shipwreck-ridden Manila Bay, Bill was quiet. But when it came time for them to turn south toward *Eldorado's* Leyte anchorage, he made an impulsive request. Might they detour briefly north—to Subic Bay?

The sympathetic helmsman, who by now knew the story, pushed up the throttle and made a graceful northward arc into the South China Sea. But no clues of past disasters awaited Bill at Subic Bay—it had been under refurbishment by army engineers for weeks.

"The ones that could swim made out better than the ones that couldn't, that much I can tell you," the Bilibid clerk had said. He didn't have much more information than that, just that the survivors that did make it ashore needed clothing and other supplies. And he knew that only because the navy doctors who were being evacuated from Bilibid when he arrived told him that they had been ordered to assemble supplies for the prisoners who had just shipped out on *Oryoko Maru*. The ship had been bombed not long after exiting Manila Bay, they were told. But there *had* been a large number of survivors.

"Where did it go down?" Bill had asked, with out-of-body composure.

"Subic Bay, off Olongapo. Survivors came ashore by the old navy base. I mean, damn, the last ship the Japs got out, and it gets sunk."

It was nightfall before the PT boat pulled into Leyte Gulf. After expressing heartfelt thanks to the PT commander and the promise of a steak dinner after the war, Bill boarded *Eldorado*, saluted the officer of the deck, and went straight to his cabin. He wanted to write Benny about the day's events while they were fresh in his mind. He hadn't found Barton, but he hadn't found him dead, either.

With *Eldorado*'s imminent departure, there was no more time to run down the details of Barton's doomed ship—or the survivors. It would have to wait until their return to Manila, after Okinawa.

38

★ ★ ★

A SAILOR'S NIGHTMARE

APRIL 13, 1945, EAST longitude time, dawned sunny and warm off Okinawa, but it would soon become the blackest Friday the thirteenth Bill Mott would ever remember. At 0700 he was in *Eldorado*'s CIC poring over two final drafts on the same critical subject. One was the first-ever press communiqué on the Kamikaze Corps. The other, stamped "S-E-C-R-E-T," was a directive from Admiral Turner to all hands. Entitled "Information and Means for Combating Suicide Plane Attacks—Revision 1," the memo had been hastily drafted the previous evening at the conclusion of another massive kamikaze raid on the ships standing off Okinawa—the second since the invasion of the island began.

Just 340 miles from Kyushu, Japan's southernmost island, Okinawa was prized by the Allies for its proximate air base potential for a final assault on mainland Japan. For this same reason, preventing Okinawa's fall was crucial to the Japanese. A fight to the finish had been expected.

The Easter Sunday landings of tens of thousands of army troops had gone eerily unopposed—unlike the furious and bloody start at Iwo Jima. Kelly Turner was so amazed, he radioed Admiral Nimitz at his CINCPAC headquarters on Guam: "I may be crazy," Turner said, "but it looks like the Japs have quit the war." Having seen intercepts indicating the enemy was lying in wait farther inland, Admiral Nimitz flashed back, "Delete all after 'crazy.' " By the end of Okinawa's first week, that intelligence proved brutally correct. Only after Allied troops moved inland did the enemy bare itself— both on the island and over the 1,418-ship anchorage.

Despite ongoing pleas by Robert Sherrod, war correspondents had been forbidden to report on the intensifying kamikaze menace since its debut at Leyte Gulf the previous October. The months-long news embargo had been intended to protect soldier and sailor morale, among other reasons. But the carnage from these last two attacks—by rapid, sequential waves of kamikaze bands called *kikusui*—changed all that.

Hundreds of planes at a time had screamed over the horizon at random intervals and hurled themselves at the anchorage. The first of these airborne banzai charges began at dusk on April 6. Like swarms of angry bees, hundreds of aircraft at a time dropped through the low cloud ceiling, fanned out, and roared toward target ships. Of all the scenarios anticipated in the thousands of pages of Iceberg planning documents, this one had not even been dreamed of.

Stunned fleet defenses were quickly overwhelmed in the first attack. Three destroyers, two ammunition ships, and one landing vessel were sunk. Ten other ships were damaged so severely that they were forced to withdraw. But *kikusui* number one was far from over. At dusk the next day, hundreds more planes lit up radar screens across the fleet.

Flyers from Admiral Mitscher's fast carrier group shot down a number of them, but 116 hell-bent suiciders punched through the protective air perimeter. The next line of defense was Combat Air Patrol (CAP)—made up of Hellcats and "whistling death" Corsairs—which splashed 55 more. But

61 kamikazes still managed to pierce both air defense rings and strike at the fleet's 1,200 ships. The rest was up to the ships' antiaircraft batteries.

Literally shooting in the dark, gunners sent up thousands of tracer shells, leaving a mad scribble of red lines through the Southern Cross. They shot down 39 of the attackers, but 22 were able to complete their deadly missions. A cacophony of distress signals erupted, jamming circuits. Fire and rescue triage began immediately—in rolling seas, billowing smoke, and stygian darkness.

The second twenty-four-hour *kikusui* had ended the previous evening, April 12. Eighteen more ships, including *Enterprise*, were crippled in the onslaught. A five-hundred-kilogram bomb exploded at the turn of her bilge, causing severe shock damage. An hour later, a second "Yokosuka Judy" just missed *Enterprise*'s starboard bow, but its bomb detonated, puncturing the carrier below the waterline.

Frantic control parties miraculously sealed the breach, even as water gushed through with the force of a colossal fire hose. Their heroics prevented *Enterprise*'s capsize, but the mighty carrier was also forced to withdraw for major repairs. It was one action by that gallant crew that Bill was grateful Benny had missed.

By the morning of the thirteenth, the number of navy casualties in the waters off Okinawa competed with those ashore, and the injuries weren't just physical. The suggestive crackling of ships' loudspeakers alone had become cause for emotional breakdowns among crews. Across the flotilla, officers and men were inching toward nervous exhaustion from the perennial state of high alert.

For the antiaircraft gunners, the worst part was a *kamikaze* pilot's deep maniacal stare as he bore down—even if hit and aflame—through a barrage of bullets. For others, it was the sight of fellow crewmen ejected high into the air and blown apart. Back down they inevitably came, like so many broken pieces of a toy soldier: a helmeted head, a booted foot, a flaming torso. Such images wedged deeply into survivors' psyches, and nervous breakdowns had become as numerous as the climbing fatalities.

And the previous night, as if in celebratory finale to *kikusui* number two, the Japanese also launched their first *oka*: a rocket-boosted suicide glider that could dive at speeds of five hundred miles per hour. The debut *oka* hit destroyer USS *Mannert L. Abele* with such force that she broke apart and sank in five minutes.

Admiral Nimitz had thus far resisted making the kamikaze threat public, partly for morale reasons but also to deny the Japanese confirmation of their successes. He finally relented the previous evening. The American people, he decided, needed to know about these "witches on broomsticks" and the increasingly diabolical mental state of the enemy. Bill proofed the final release before transmitting:

CINCPOA PRESS RELEASE #72, APRIL 13, 1945

The Commander in Chief, U.S. Pacific Fleet and Pacific Ocean Areas, has authorized the following statement:

For some months the Japanese have been employing aircraft on a gradually increasing scale in suicidal attacks upon our forces in the Western Pacific. These aircraft were initially piloted by a group of pilots who were known as the "Kamikaze Corps" by the Japanese. The enemy has made much in his propaganda of this "sure-death-sure-hit" suicide technique which is simply an attempt to crash planes on the decks of our ships.

The "suicide attack" and the so called "Kamikaze Corps" are the products of an enemy trapped in an increasingly desperate situation. Pushed back upon their own inner defenses the Japanese have resorted to fanatical methods which, from a purely military viewpoint, are of doubtful value.

The "Kamikaze Corps" is apparently being used not only to attempt to damage our ships but also to stir the lagging spirits of the Japanese people. Although these "sure-death-sure-hit" pilots are reported to be volunteers, many have very

willingly become survivors of "suicide" missions and are now
[our] prisoners of war.

The "suicide" technique is continuing at the present time.
Although it is always considered and prepared for as a factor in estimating the enemy's capabilities, it cannot prevent
our continuing success in the war in the Pacific.

The press release was directed as much at the Japanese as it was at the
American public.

THE SECOND DOCUMENT WAS Admiral Turner's amended guide-
lines for combating the suicide attacks. Reflecting very recent intelligence
from the previous evening, this latest All Hands Tips-for-Survival primer
had updated guidelines on radar, CAP vectoring and tactics, communications among ships, and revised directives on radical maneuvering, antiaircraft defense, damage control, rescue, repair, and salvage. It began with a
simple restatement of the problem:

The principal difference between suicide plane attacks by
the Japanese on a large scale and conventional airplane attacks are as follows:

(a) The range of enemy attack is greater because no return
    trip is necessary;
(b) Percentage of hits is higher because the missile is
    aimable right up to the point of impact;
(c) Suicide pilots are more determined and daring and are
    not deterred by actual or psychological obstacles;
(d) The suicide plane, with or without a bomb, is an extremely
    effective incendiary agent because of the gasoline car-
    ried;

(e) No standard pattern of attack is apparent and to date no
     cure-all solution has been found.

Bill understood the primal fear a kamikaze attack inspired. On Easter Saturday—twenty-four hours ahead of the paschal invasion of Okinawa— he had just left USS *Indianapolis*'s mess, where he'd thought to catch a quick breakfast following the final pre-invasion briefing on Admiral Spruance's flagship. But a recalcitrant stomach shortened his meal, and he quickly exited the mess to catch the launch back to *Eldorado*. The time was 0710.

On his way up to the quarterdeck, he paused at the shrill report of the boson's whistle. Before he could comprehend its meaning, Bill was knocked off his feet by a rocking explosion from below. Sure as hell, the ship had been struck by a torpedo, he thought, scrambling to his feet.

Only after fire and rescue teams emerged from the *Indianapolis* mess carrying the charred remains of his fellow breakfasters did Bill learn it had been the work of a kamikaze. One fast-acting gunner had deflected the aim of the suicider, whose plane sank off the fantail. But its bomb had released just before crashing, penetrating the port quarter's deck armor and tearing through the mess, a berthing compartment, and fuel tanks before exploding under the hull.

The wounded *Indianapolis* was forced to withdraw to a California shipyard for repairs—the start of a tragic odyssey for the famed cruiser. Admiral Spruance reluctantly shifted his flag to the USS *New Mexico*.

Bill's timely departure from the mess left him shaken. It was the first of many deeply unsettling blows off miserable Okinawa. Another took place a few minutes later as he labored over the twin kamikaze missives.

The duty radioman alerted him to an urgent message that was starting to click through: "To All Hands: From Secnav to All Nav." Navy Secretary Forrestal was not one to send routine messages in the heat of battle. Bill hovered over the teletype, as was his habit, reading each new line as it hammered out Secnav's message. The first sentence stunned him no less than had it reported a death in his own family. Forrestal wrote:

I have the sad duty of announcing to the naval service the death of Franklin Delano Roosevelt, the President of the United States, which occurred on twelve April.

The world has lost a champion of democracy who can ill be spared by our country and the Allied cause. The Navy which he so dearly loved can pay no better tribute to his memory than to carry on in the tradition of which he was so proud.

Colors shall be displayed at half mast for thirty days beginning 0800 thirteen April West Longitude Date insofar as war operations permit. Memorial services shall be held on the day of the funeral to be announced later at all yards and stations and on board all vessels of the navy, war operations permitting.

Wearing of mourning badges and firing of salutes will be dispensed within view of war conditions.

The president had died suddenly of a cerebral hemorrhage at "the little White House" in Warm Springs, Georgia, near the healing mineral waters that had long soothed his polio-withered legs. Vice President Harry S. Truman had taken the Oath of Office within hours of FDR's death. A new president! Choked with sadness and deeply preoccupied, Bill made for Admiral Turner's cabin just as ships' loudspeakers sounded the report across the fleet. The announcers' voices were thick with emotion:

"Attention! Attention! All hands! President Roosevelt is dead! Repeat, our supreme commander, President Roosevelt, is dead."

A typhoon roaring over the horizon could not have struck with greater impact an audience with scant memory of any other sitting president. Roosevelt had led the country for twelve turbulent years—a majority of the sailors' young lives. They mourned all the more because Roosevelt had been the navy's president, a sailor at heart.

As Bill carried Forrestal's memo to Admiral Turner's cabin, he replayed his last Oval Office conversation with Roosevelt. *"Mr. President, I hate to leave, but you may be sure I'll be back for the peace conference."* Roosevelt had met his gaze and then looked away. *"Well, son, I'm not sure there will ever be one."*

He pondered anew what the late president had meant. Had Roosevelt sensed his imminent death? Or had he hinted at some other terrible meaning beyond Bill's comprehension? Bill paused at the forecastle rail and watched with an aching heart as hundreds of national ensigns fluttered to half-mast.

A memorial service on *Eldorado*'s fantail was scheduled for the following morning, April 14. Rites would begin at 1000 hours to coincide with the late president's state funeral in Washington, DC. They had learned by radio that Mrs. Roosevelt wanted Dewitt Moore—a popular American soloist and, coincidentally, *Eldorado*'s radar intelligence officer—to sing two of the Anglophile president's favorite hymns at the ship's service, both by British composers. One was "Faith of Our Fathers"; the other, not surprisingly, was "Eternal Father Strong to Save," or simply the "Navy Hymn," known and cherished for a century by sailors of the American and British navies.

The next morning, a throng of war correspondents looked on as Chaplain Valentine Junker, Admiral Turner, and hundreds of officers and sailors in their crisp dress whites lined up in arrow-straight rows on the *Eldorado*'s aft deck. But Chaplain Junker barely got off his opening line of prayer when the familiar wail of sirens and nerve-shattering general quarters signaled the approach of another horde of kamikazes.

Kikusui number three had begun.

The tidy assembly burst apart like so much spilled milk, and the fantail emptied in seconds. Every crew member dashed to battle stations—above, below, fore, and aft—to defend against the onslaught. They all knew that triangulation of *Eldorado*'s steady radio beacon made her a prime and constant target.

Admiral Turner himself—onetime fleet gunnery officer—took over the ship's voice command circuit and began directing fire. He took this unusual step increasingly at Okinawa, to provide an extra measure of reassurance to a thoroughly rattled crew.

Officers and crew made a determined trek back to the fantail after the wave of assailants was repelled. The enemy would not cancel *Eldorado's* tribute to their beloved late president. Waiting on the aft deck were radio correspondents who had lashed together a bouquet of microphones so that all Americans might hear Moore's sonorous rendering of the "Navy Hymn"—from the heart of the fleet in the heat of battle—sung in dirge for their president:

> *Eternal Father, strong to save*
> *Whose arm hath bound the restless wave,*
> *Oh hear us when we cry to thee,*
> *For those in peril on the sea.*

Admiral Turner seemed in a trance during the service, likely reflecting on his own experiences with his late commander in chief. His most memorable had been in the tension-laden spring of 1939. Roosevelt had personally requested that Turner lead a goodwill mission to Tokyo, ostensibly to escort the late Japanese ambassador Saito's ashes to home soil.

Not one to be tapped for diplomatic anything, a flattered Turner executed the ceremonial mission flawlessly. In Tokyo Bay, throngs of Japanese had toured his ship, the USS *Astoria*, and Imperial poets and musicians dedicated verses and lyrics to the vessel that had brought Saito's ashes home. A special Japanese "Welcome Astoria March" was composed and formally performed before the ship's company. Turner's mission helped measurably in thawing diplomatic relations with Japan at the time, but the sentiments were short-lived—demonstrated not least by *Astoria's* sinking at Guadalcanal three years later.

Returned from his musings, Admiral Turner spoke briefly before Chaplain Junker's benediction:

"The president's death is a great loss to our country, and especially it is a loss to the war effort of which he was our firm and unquestioned leader. Undoubtedly, the fact that President Roosevelt personally spent himself so freely in this struggle was the underlying cause of his death. Thus he is a battle casualty in exactly the same sense as those who give their lives in battle out here."

BY MID-MAY 1945, PRESIDENT Truman's burdens had shifted, if not lightened. Nazi Germany had surrendered, but in the Pacific, the US Army's struggle to claim Okinawa had ground to a halt. Lines had barely advanced in the face of savage Japanese resistance on ambush-ridden terrain, all the more treacherous from eleven inches of rainfall. Unabating kamikaze attacks continued to pummel the sentinel Fifth Fleet; casualties both on and off shore were running sky high.

Navy losses at Okinawa had already surpassed all records for a single campaign. "I doubt if the army's slow, methodical [approach to] fighting really saves lives in the long run," Spruance grumbled to his chief of staff. In late April, Admiral Nimitz told General Buckner that the stalemate was losing him "a ship and a half a day." Nimitz proposed that the marines make an amphibious landing behind enemy lines to break the impasse. Buckner objected vigorously: this was a ground battle under US Army command, and the navy should not interfere.

Nimitz was also concerned about the toll that the vicious, protracted engagement was taking on his three top Okinawa commanders, Admirals Spruance, Mitscher, and Turner. To Bill and the rest of *Eldorado*'s flag staff, Kelly Turner seemed to be suffering the most. The continuous high alert and murderous destruction of his amphibious vessels and crews afforded Turner little rest and exacerbated his chronic back pain.

At Okinawa, Terrible Turner was as irascible and foulmouthed as any of them had ever seen him, itself a milestone. Things got worse in May with the introduction of kamikaze speedboats, or *kaiten*, which took aim at ships' hulls in the dark of night. At each *kaiten* alert, Bill reluctantly awoke Turner to make the call on whether a "smoke" order should be issued to enshroud the ships for protection. The procedure had become a critical defense tool by spoiling the aim and navigation of these seaborne assailants.

On May 17, well after Turner had retired to his quarters, the alert came once again: *kaiten* were on the prowl. Reluctantly, Bill knocked on his exhausted boss's cabin door. Getting no response after several tries, he turned the handle and peeked inside. Admiral Turner was in a deep slumber—*very* deep. The scent rising from a nearby glass told the story.

A mix of pineapple juice and grain alcohol—the latter procured from Sick Bay—was the suspected somnolent. Unable to arouse Turner, Bill quietly closed the admiral's door and made for the deck. He first advised Commander Paul S. Theiss, Turner's chief of staff, to evaluate the need for a smoke order. Then he visited the ship's doctor, who needed no introduction to Turner's condition. The doctor, an unsmiling New Hampshire reservist, got defensive.

"He said it was for a sore on his foot, and, to be honest, I didn't follow that story," the doctor said without a trace of empathy. "I just want you to know that I can't be taking this responsibility," he continued. "I'm going to have to put something in it that will make him throw it up. It won't kill him, of course, but it will make him violently ill."

Of all the crises Bill had come to anticipate at Okinawa, this was one he hadn't seen coming. He quietly asked the doctor to forbear until he took the matter under advisement. He then called a meeting of the *Eldorado* flag staff. After much deliberation, the higher-ups made a decision: Bill should make his way over to Spruance's flagship *New Mexico* and report the problem to the Fifth Fleet's head surgeon.

Incredulous, Bill reminded them of his relatively junior status on the flag staff and recommended that someone more senior be elected to ferry their collective concerns over to the *New Mexico*. But Bill was the only *reserve* officer among them, they reasoned. The rest of them were on a promising career trajectory in the regular navy. In their view, he could afford the certain career disembowelment that would result from reporting one's commanding officer for drinking on the job in the middle of the largest amphibious campaign of the Pacific War.

As the specter of Bill's cancelled naval career played out in his head, he proceeded to Admiral Spruance's flagship with the same enthusiasm he might feel for being a *kaiten*'s next victim. He paced *New Mexico*'s quarter-deck for an hour, discussing the problem with the fleet surgeon and Admiral Spruance's own flag secretary, Chuck Barber. When they finished, the fleet surgeon indicated he would take the matter from there. Not at all sure what that meant, Bill returned to *Eldorado* with a heavy heart.

The following morning, Admiral Turner was advised that Admiral Harry Hill, his second in command, was taking over for him at Okinawa. Turner was to report to Admiral Nimitz at his forward headquarters on Guam. A contagious glumness spread across *Eldorado* en route to Guam. It affected everyone except, curiously, Admiral Turner. For the duration of the trip, he rested, read, and sipped orange juice without additives from the granite-faced ship's doctor.

At Guam, Turner received a desultory flag staff salute as he debarked *Eldorado*. Smartly returning the salute, Kelly Turner appeared fully restored—confident, self-possessed, and impatient as ever. He charged up Guam's Fonte Plateau, nicknamed "Nimitz Hill." It was the eve of his sixtieth birthday.

Chester Nimitz greeted Turner with a broad smile. In fact, he had decided to order a respite from battle for all three of his Okinawa commanders—Admirals Spruance, Mitscher, *and* Turner—out of a growing concern that the prolonged, high-stress nature of that campaign would diminish their effectiveness, not to mention their mental and physical health. All three men had been in continuous combat since the start of pre-bombardment at Iwo Jima, a record three months straight.

When Admiral Halsey and his new flagship the USS *Missouri* arrived at Okinawa to take over command from Admiral Spruance, the Japanese were confused anew. Once again, it seemed, the Third Fleet had overnight "replaced" the Fifth Fleet.

KELLY TURNER EMERGED FROM his meeting in Guam with a promotion to full admiral. Nimitz had chosen to mark the occasion by giving credit where it was due, pineapple-juice additives notwithstanding. Turner had brilliantly conceived, executed, and prevailed in every Pacific campaign he had undertaken. Nimitz would say later that he knew of no other navy admiral who could have performed that feat.

Along with his prized fourth star, Turner carried new orders back to *Eldorado*. They were to make sail for Manila immediately. Their mission was to coordinate Operation Olympic—the Allies' long-anticipated assault on Japan's home islands—with General MacArthur. The objective was to seize the island of Kyushu and secure its airfields and ports for Operation Coronet, the subsequent invasion of the island of Honshu and its capital, Tokyo. The sequential operations were code-named Downfall.

Of all *Eldorado*'s celebrants, Bill Mott was perhaps the most electrified by Admiral Turner's reversal of fortune. Not only did it seem that both their once-careening naval aspirations were back on course, but also they were returning to Manila! Bill's best and last chance to reach Barton had just fallen into his lap.

Spirits were well restored aboard *Eldorado* en route to Manila. Admiral Turner, too, was pleased by the turn of events, particularly over the other options, but he was deeply skeptical about Olympic and Coronet. With the stratospheric losses at Okinawa top of mind, he knew the death toll from a mainland Japan invasion would be exponentially higher.

Turner's naval superiors agreed. They believed that a greatly weakened Japan could be finished off (with far fewer casualties) by adopting a dual strategy of aerial bombing and imposition of a naval blockade. Admirals Nimitz, Spruance, and King had all made this case. But the Joint Chiefs of

Staff had proceeded instead with MacArthur's preference: a heroic, decisive, and dramatic ground invasion of Japan.

With the war in Europe concluded, Americans—including President Truman—had turned their full attention to the shocking slaughter at Okinawa. Its soaring cost in human life was attracting greater and greater public scrutiny. Hundreds of thousands—including Americans, Japanese, civilians, and Okinawan conscripts—had already died, and the battle continued to rage.

Okinawa headlines coincided with those announcing the doubling of mandatory Selective Service call-ups and mass troop redeployments from Europe to the Pacific. The impact of these sobering reports was exacerbated by the belated and brutal physical evidence of the Pacific War pouring into mainland US hospitals. Aiea Heights Naval Hospital had long since filled to overcapacity. The Pacific wounded were now overwhelming stateside medical facilities. It was against this grim backdrop that President Truman became increasingly uncomfortable with the potential for calamitous casualties from an amphibious invasion of mainland Japan.

Truman made clear to a war-weary public and his Joint Chiefs that he intended to end the Pacific War with as few additional American casualties as possible. In his two short months as president, preventing "another Okinawa from one end of Japan to the other" had become a paramount objective. In mid-June 1945 he decided to give Olympic and Coronet another hard look.

Meanwhile, with Admiral Turner's repeated blessing, Bill debarked *Eldorado* as soon as she made anchor in Manila Bay. Olympic's scheduled invasion date was at least four months away, allowing him enough of a reprieve to complete his investigation into Barton's whereabouts. Finding prisoner files at Bilibid much better organized, he was able to get right to work. He was only a few hours into poring over manifests and prison population lists when he came across an electrifying new document. It was a tally of the dead and missing from the fated *Oryoko Maru*.

During his March visit to Bilibid, Bill learned that Barton had boarded *Oryoko Maru* on December 13. He also learned that that ship was sunk in Subic Bay two days later. This newly discovered document confirmed both those findings, and now that Barton had survived the *Oryoko Maru*, his name was not on the official casualty list.

With renewed optimism, Bill peppered Bilibid office staff with questions on what else was known about the prisoners who swam from the wreck and made it ashore. At the end of the day, he thanked them and made his way back to *Eldorado*. These new discoveries—and the range of possible scenarios for survival that they offered—left room for hope. Back in his quarters, he wrote of the day's findings to his sister Rosemary instead of Benny, despairing of his brother's continued noncommunication.

```
                            Office of the Commander
                            Amphibious Forces,
                            US Pacific Fleet
                            Lieutenant Rosemary Cross
                            Office of the Commandant
                            Brooklyn Navy Yard
                            Brooklyn, New York


                            July 3, 1945


                  CONFIDENTIAL


Dear Muff,


    I have delayed writing you or any of the family as I
wanted to first investigate further into Barton's status.
Every time I started a letter, he was always uppermost in my
mind, and I found it difficult to speak of anything else.
```

Before departing for Okinawa, I spent some time in the
Philippines and naturally did everything humanly possible
to run down concrete news of Barton. At that time, I wrote
rather completely of my findings to Benny and asked him to
investigate further in Washington. I enclose copies of those
two letters, to which, incidentally, I have not yet received
an answer.

Perhaps, there was no answer. At any rate, I can now
take up where I left off in my letter of March 24th. Most
of the information is negative, but is of the most reliable
kind. I have pursued an exhaustive investigation of the
rumor in the attached letter that the ship Barton boarded
was sunk. I am now able to report the following with fair
assurance of accuracy:

(a) Barton survived the sinking of December 13 in Subic
    Bay. I learned this from a list of the dead and missing
    from this sinking that the Japanese left behind at
    Bilibid Prison.

(b) He was evacuated to Japan or Korea on a ship which left
    the Philippines on December 27th.

(c) It is not known whether this ship ever reached port
    nor is it known, on the other hand, that it did not. The
    presumption is that it did.

(d) People out here are expecting that Japan will notify
    Washington through Geneva of the prisoners which were
    taken to Japan or Korea in that ship.

Of course I shall continue to do everything I can from
this end. I am trying desperately, with every available
minute, to turn every stone where there might be a clue.

I am going to visit in the near future several of the places where Barton was held, in hopes that someone will remember him, for whatever small comfort that may be. In this I am somewhat handicapped by not having with me a picture of him. Could you forward a snapshot by return mail?

Much of the information which I have given you is confidential and its disclosure in the wrong places could get me in very serious trouble; therefore I beg of you to see to it that it stays within the family. My request is that you talk it over with Arthur and, above all, keep it away from crack pot [POW] organizations like that one in North Dakota or Texas. Please ask Arthur--and whatever you decide to tell Mother--not to disclose any of the information I have given.

What if anything, Benny has done to contact Ensign Petritz (see enclosed letters), I do not know. It seems to me that a talk with him might be fruitful, especially since [Petritz] knew Barton. You can find out where [Petritz] is by going to, or calling, Washington and asking George Elsey at the White House to get the information on his present whereabouts from the Bureau for you. If George is not there, Lt. Marian Enright in the Navy Bureau of Personnel, or her boss who is a classmate of mine named MacDonald, will help you I'm sure.

There is also in the Bureau a section which deals exclusively with prisoner of war problems. It used to be headed by a Commander Jacobs (now a Captain and still there), but I am sure he has been superseded by now. All of these places should be visited, but I can't be both places at once. Please don't disclose to them the source of your information and I implore you to keep Mother from writing

letters to Senators and the Navy Department. They will do
no good and would very probably handicap me in further
investigation. Also, don't jump down Benny's throat till you
know what he's accomplished. He may have done everything
possible. I have some hope of being in Washington later this
month, and there is much more I will be able to tell you
then. In the meantime, please let me know what you find
out, if anything. I feel as though my other two letters on
this matter were dropped down the drain. I know Benny has
his troubles and is terribly busy, but the uncertainty of
not knowing what he was doing and not hearing from him
prompted me to put the facts in your hands. Please handle
them circumspectly.

I have been working terribly hard for the last six
months with very little respite. I am looking forward to the
day when I arrive in New York and my big little sister can
take me out and pour civilization all over me.

Devotedly,

Bill

He reread the letter before sending it off, making minor edits here and there. He'd done the best he could and hoped at least that providing this update, such as it was, would bring relief from the anxiety of knowing *nothing*.

His disappointment that Barton was no longer in the Philippines was acute, and now the Allied plan to invade mainland Japan brought new anxiety. The Palawan massacre of 150 prisoners was ordered by a camp commander who'd believed the island was under imminent Allied attack. In the Gilbert Islands, a group of prisoners was beheaded, another group at Ballale bayoneted to death, and another on Wake Island executed by machine gun—all following Allied bombing raids. Given this pattern of retributive intent, the incipient Japanese home-island invasions would place the 168,000 Allied prisoners still in Japanese hands in their gravest danger yet.

Yet Bill still found reason for hope, both because Barton's name was not on the *Oryoko Maru*'s casualty list and because of the relatively high number of fellow survivors of the sinking: 1,300 out of 1,619. With luck—if one could call it that—Barton might have been shipped to Korea instead of to Japan. In any case, Barton had, by all available accounts, survived three years of bestial enemy treatment. Bill prayed this meant his brother had developed both resilience and survival skills, just as he had at the Citadel and Annapolis. If only those instincts might serve him a few more months.

39

★ ★ ★

IN THE END, A QUESTION OF CASUALTIES—AND SEA POWER

PRESIDENT TRUMAN WAS STILL on a steep learning curve in the summer of 1945. It seemed that Roosevelt had shared relatively little with his last vice president, including the very existence of the White House Map Room and the fact that the world war was being run out of it. Nor had Truman been told that enemy codes had been cracked and were supplying crucial intelligence to the Allies.

To the surprise of his top military advisors, however, the new president, a onetime respected army colonel, took quick grasp of strategic options in the Pacific and their relative stakes in American blood and treasure. Daily "gloves off" Map Room briefings expedited the process, and it wasn't long before Harry Truman had two seminal concerns.

The first was Okinawa, by far the bloodiest battle of the Pacific War, which was still not won. The second was a looming shortage of combat-ready troops for a final assault on Japan—this despite a hundred thousand men a month being called up, double the rate twelve months earlier. Truman's twin dilemmas weren't Map Room secrets; they were front-page news across the war-weary country. By mid-June, these concerns—compounded by a growing fear of unprecedented casualties from an invasion of Japan proper—prompted him to make new inquiries. He started with his chief of staff, Admiral William Leahy.

Fleet Admiral Leahy's opinion mattered. He was a senior military strategist who had served in the Roosevelt White House since the dark days of 1942. He knew every aspect of this world conflict, and he was no advocate of a ground invasion of Japan. Admiral Leahy also favored the "bomb and blockade" option; to him the statistics seemed to prove the point.

The air campaign was causing withering destruction: six hundred thousand tons of enemy shipping had been sunk in June alone. The strategic naval blockade was not only limiting the ability of resource-dependent Japan to wage war but also severely curtailing its ability to feed seventy-two million citizens. In a desperate act, Japan had begun to organize schoolchildren to gather a million tons of acorns to be ground for flour due to drastically declined stocks of rice and wheat.

To Leahy, the collective evidence weighed heavily in favor of continuing this strategy. He believed it would force Japan's capitulation and save countless American lives. This was the strategy preferred by most navy brass, and it was a hard-won point of view.

After increasingly deadly amphibious campaigns to capture enemy-held islands across the Pacific, the navy had become well acquainted with Japan's fighting spirit. Surrender was unthinkable, and in every Pacific campaign, they had fought nearly to the last man. The relative few still standing had shown a strong preference for *hara-kiri* over the shame of being taken prisoner.

The navy knew that Japan would defend her home soil even more fanatically—to the last woman and child. Ever-rising casualties on Okinawa, with the largest toll among civilians, reinforced that view. And Admiral Leahy—in whose experience, honesty, and intellect President Truman placed great faith—firmly agreed.

★   ★   ★

AT THE ABRUPT START of his presidency, Truman had vowed to carry on "the legacies of [his] illustrious predecessor." One such legacy was a decision made in September 1944 at Octagon, the second Allied conference held in Quebec. At that meeting, Roosevelt and Churchill agreed that an invasion of mainland Japan must follow Germany's capitulation.

By June 1945, however, Truman's misgivings about this preordained course were too powerful to ignore. On June 17 he confided to his diary, "I have to decide Japanese strategy—shall we invade Japan proper or shall we bomb and blockade? This is my hardest decision to date . . . I'll make it when I have all the facts."

The next day, he asked Admiral Leahy to call a meeting of the Joint Chiefs of Staff. The topic would be the singular matter of casualties that might result from a ground invasion of Japan versus alternative solutions for ending the Pacific War. Leahy promptly dispatched a top secret memorandum:

```
The White House
Washington


                          14, June 1945


              URGENT--IMMEDIATE ACTION
        MEMORANDUM FOR THE JOINT CHIEFS OF STAFF:


The President today directed me to inform the Joint Chiefs
of Staff that he wishes to meet . . . in the afternoon
of [June] 18th, in his office, to discuss details of our
campaign against Japan.

    He expects at this meeting to be thoroughly informed
of our intentions and prospects in preparation for his
discussions with Churchill and Stalin.
```

He will want information as to the number of men of the army
and ships of the navy that will be necessary to defeat Japan.

He wants an estimate of the time required and an
estimate of the losses in killed and wounded that will
result from an invasion of Japan proper.

He wants an estimate of the time and the losses required
and the losses that will result from an effort to defeat
Japan by isolation, blockade, and bombardment by sea and
air forces . . .

It is his intention to make his decision on the campaign
with the purpose of economizing to the maximum extent
possible the loss of American lives.

Economy in the use of time and money is comparatively
unimportant.

I suggest that a memorandum discussion of the above
noted points be prepared in advance for delivery to the
president at the time of the meeting.

                         William D. Leahy

The memorandum took the JCS and their war-planning staffs by surprise. The memo's phrase, "it is his intention to make his decision on the campaign," was especially unwelcome to army planners. As General George Lincoln put it, the army viewed Operation Olympic as "a matter of fact."

Olympic was to be the army's—and Douglas MacArthur's—glorious and climactic hour in the Pacific War. It would be the largest military assault in history: MacArthur was to lead as many as fourteen divisions against the Japanese, as opposed to Eisenhower's nine at Normandy. Moreover, the invasion had *already* been approved by one commander in chief (and Churchill, too) and was deep into the planning phase.

And regarding Leahy's specific request on behalf of the president for prospective casualty estimates, there was a unity of reluctance. Quantifying casualty estimates to a sitting president ahead of an invasion? This would set a dangerous precedent, they feared, even though the army had already developed those numbers.

Army planners had obtained casualty estimates from their surgeon general in order to assess invasion requirements for battlefield medical needs: corpsmen, morphine, plasma, bandages, scalpels, body bags. But army brass feared that disclosing even that relatively low casualty projection (135,000) might persuade Truman to alter or cancel Olympic—not to mention their recent order of an additional 500,000 Purple Heart medals.

In the end, the army declined to comply with the request by their commander in chief. When the Joint Chiefs gathered in the Oval Office four days after receiving Leahy's directive, they instead presented the president with more palatable ratios of Allied versus Japanese losses from *previous* campaigns. General Marshall presented the chart. It indicated that the Leyte campaign had resulted in the lowest Allied versus enemy losses (1:4.6) and the final days at Iwo Jima the highest (1:1.25). Okinawa, which was still going on, was a close second, 1:2.

Taking exception, Admiral Leahy reminded the group that the president had asked for *actual* loss *projections*, and suggested US casualties resulting from an invasion of Kyushu (Olympic) would most likely resemble losses at Okinawa, currently running at 35 percent of total forces. Since the upcoming Olympic assault force size was known to meeting attendees—766,700—simple arithmetic would have yielded Olympic's potential for loss of life. That number, 268,345 casualties—equal roughly to total American losses over the entire three and a half years on the European Front—would certainly have raised eyebrows. Curiously, however, that percentage was not converted into a casualty estimate at the June 18 JCS meeting.

Truman asked instead whether *more* Japanese defenders at Kyushu than currently projected for Olympic—which Marshall estimated at 350,000—might be transported from other Japanese islands, thereby pushing the ratio of American casualties even higher. General Marshall confidently replied in the negative; daily air raids were preventing the Japanese from reinforcing the area. Marshall then read aloud from a telegram he had just received from General MacArthur:

"I believe the [Olympic] operation presents less [*sic*] hazards of excessive loss than any other that has been suggested . . . and its *decisive effect* will eventually save lives." General Marshall said he agreed with MacArthur's stated position and a unanimous JCS vote to proceed with Olympic followed.

After the vote, President Truman reluctantly assented to Olympic despite the fact he had been denied the requested casualty projections by his most senior military advisors. But he withheld approval of Coronet, the follow-on invasion of Honshu, saying he would revisit that decision at a later date.

Admiral King voted with the majority at the Joint Chiefs meeting that day, but not because his position had changed on the wisdom of a mainland invasion. He simply understood the need to proceed with its *planning*. The chief of naval operations was as shrewd as he was cantankerous. He was merely postponing withdrawal of his support for Olympic until later in the summer. He knew his defection would result in a titanic army-navy clash over final Pacific strategy—and, denied unanimity among his military chiefs, would likely void Truman's support for the invasion.

Admiral King did, however, fire off a complaint-riddled memo to his fellow chiefs after the June 18 meeting. His first objection was that the army's antiseptic casualty ratio presentation had omitted all of the navy's casualty projections provided by Admiral Nimitz. Given the real-time horrors taking place on Okinawa, this was a particular irritant to King. He further stated that the overall casualty data presented to Truman was "not satisfactory." "[I]t appears to me the Chiefs of Staff will [eventually] have to give an estimate of casualties expected in the operation," King admonished.

In response, General Marshall assured King that naval losses should and would be included in a revised casualty brief for the president. But there is no archival evidence that a revised brief was ever submitted to Truman—the man on whose shoulders the fate of those lives ultimately rested.

On July 6, three weeks after the Oval Office casualty estimate meeting, President Truman, Admiral Leahy, and a contingent of White House staff boarded the USS *Augusta* for a transatlantic sail to Germany. Their final destination was Potsdam, for the thirteenth Allied war conference. During the twenty-two days it took for *Augusta* to reach its first port at Plymouth, England, Truman's June 18 query regarding Japan's potential to bolster its Kyushu defenses had become a reality. The developing scenario of massive new enemy reinforcements now mooted earlier troop strength estimates.

But it was the arrival of a different piece of highly classified news that commanded the greater of President Truman's attention: an urgent report confirming the success of an atomic bomb test in New Mexico's Alamogordo desert. An astoundingly powerful new weapon, the president learned, had just been added to the US arsenal. It was, to borrow from MacArthur, a weapon of *decisive effect*—minus the potential for stratospheric American casualties.

IRONICALLY, THE JAPANESE INTERCEPTS confirming skyrocketing enemy troop buildup on Kyushu had come from MacArthur's own G-2 at Manila. Specifically, they had been provided by Central Bureau, his persistently autonomous intelligence operation, which had grown from dozens of cryptanalysts to thousands since its humble 1942 beginnings in Melbourne, Australia.

Despite serial efforts by the War Department to bring Central Bureau under its control, MacArthur had resisted all attempts to tether it to Washington intelligence gathering. While similar intercepts suggesting the buildup on Kyushu may have been netted at the War Department's listening posts, those analysts were not the ones to sound the alarm; it was MacArthur's own intelligence chief, General Willoughby.

In his July 29 analysis summarizing decrypted intercepts of the previous two weeks—distributed "locally" to senior Olympic planners in Manila—Willoughby made his dismay official: a full twelve weeks ahead of X-day (Olympic's November 1 invasion date), enemy garrisons on Kyushu had *already* reached previously predicted invasion maximums—"with," Willoughby wrote, "no end in sight."

Also confirmed was a vast arsenal of suicide weapons under development at Kyushu, as well as the training of a "Patriotic Citizens Fighting Corps," a millions-strong civilian combatant force. In addition, all schools would be closed in order to mobilize thousands of children for the defense. "There are no civilians in Japan," read one decrypted message. In all, the Japanese were preparing for a "no withdrawal" water's-edge defense—a marked shift from Okinawa, where defenders had lain in wait for Allied troops to move inland before pouncing.

As July progressed, intercepts revealed more and more alarming data. The breadth and size of the suicide arsenal was as troubling as the massing of additional enemy troops. Admiral Turner's landing craft, charged with ferrying hundreds of troops at a time to Kyushu's beaches, were named as primary kamikaze targets. Also targeted would be Turner's 1,500-ship amphibian-support force, expected to be anchored just beyond Kyushu's breakers.

At least ten thousand kamikaze planes were hidden across the island—in mines, under viaducts and railway tunnels, even department store basements. A large number of them were of such balsa-light construction that they would not be detectable by ships' radar, rendering useless the crucial kamikaze detection and defense tactics developed at Okinawa. Thousands of suicide pilots were said to be in training, with emphasis on night operations.

An assortment of other suicide weapons were also verified. There would be thousands of flying bombs (*oka*), human-manned torpedoes and suicide attack boats (*kaiten* and *koryo*), midget suicide submarines (*kairyu*), and navy swimmers transformed into human mines (*fukuryu*). These, too, would be capable of evading radar detection. The size and strength of the incipient suicide force at Kyushu already exceeded what had been hurled at the Fifth Fleet over three months at Okinawa. And X-day was still twelve weeks away.

When the intelligence summaries on metastasizing troop and kamikaze strength landed on Admiral Turner's desk, they hit Olympic's amphibian commander like a one-two punch. Much the wiser following his three years of planning and executing ever-larger amphibious campaigns, Turner had developed a powerful acumen for applying raw intelligence to invasion realities.

To Kelly Turner, the revised intelligence boiled down to this: a recipe for American slaughter on an epic scale. He quickly calculated casualty estimates based on the new intelligence. The math was grim; he estimated at least 600,000 American casualties—more than quadruple the army estimate of one month earlier (which had not included potential navy losses). And with Leyte, Luzon, Saipan, Iwo Jima, and Okinawa all as guides, Japanese casualties would run much higher, undoubtedly into seven figures.

Turner sent for Bill Mott and got right to the point. Manila intelligence summaries were not routinely forwarded to Washington, and President Truman needed to see these numbers. As a former White House naval aide, could Bill get this new intelligence to the attention of the president? Turner believed that with these new battle ratios and casualty projections in hand, Truman would cancel Olympic in favor of options less costly in American blood and treasure.

Bill replied that he was confident he could get the materials to the attention of the president. Turner told him to pack. Bill's first stop would be Guam, where he would provide Admirals Spruance and Nimitz's aides with the data; from there he would proceed to Washington.

"Temporary Additional Orders, as orally assigned" were promptly drawn up:

```
Upon receipt of these orders you will proceed aboard first
available government transportation to the port in which
the Commander of the Fifth Fleet may be [Guam]. Upon ar-
rival at this port, report to the Commander Fifth Fleet for
```

such temporary additional duty as has been orally assigned
to you . . . Upon completion of this temporary duty you will
further proceed and report to the following named places for
such temporary additional duty as has been orally assigned
to you in Washington, DC . . . Upon completion thereof, you
will return to your present station.

At Guam, Bill was greeted by his old friend Chuck Barber, Admiral Spruance's flag secretary. The two men had not seen each other since their late-night meeting with the Fifth Fleet's chief surgeon aboard the USS *New Mexico*. After discussing Bill's classified delivery, he was off to Washington, DC.

THE OPPORTUNITY TO RETURN to Washington should have provided a happy, if brief, family reunion for Bill and his wife and children. But Romie and the children were in Nova Scotia, and Benny was away on a multiplant inspection tour. Pressing questions regarding Barton that Bill had hoped to resolve would have to wait.

His family's absence may have felt like a reprieve, if an uncomfortable one. Bill had changed since going to sea, and not just in terms of new gray hairs, the doubling of his Lucky Strike habit, or even the new lines creeping across his forehead from a constantly furrowed brow. Between ill health, a frustrating struggle to find Barton, and sequential, increasingly violent amphibious campaigns, Bill's time-honored optimism was flagging. Perhaps he wasn't ready for that to be detected by those who knew him best. Like Larry Darrell in Maugham's *The Razor's Edge*, Bill had been altered by war in ways he was only beginning to understand himself.

"Sixteen hundred Pennsylvania Avenue," Bill instructed the driver as they pulled away from hot, dusty Bolling Field.

Returning here for the first time in two years, Bill indulged a deferred moment of grief. The absence of President Roosevelt struck first, but also missing was Mrs. Roosevelt's warm greeting and concerned inquiries about his family. As he turned corner after corner in the familiar manse, he absorbed the absence of one White House colleague after another—all departed following FDR's death in April and the abrupt arrival of the Truman administration.

Gone were the old reliables who had taught him his White House knots—Grace Tully, Steve Early, Admiral Brown—along with so many other ghosts of Roosevelt's tight-knit White House staff. Despite the warm hero's welcome Bill received from butler Alonzo Fields and switchboard operator Hacky Hackmeister, there were few other familiar faces. As his footsteps echoed along the black-and-white harlequin hallways, he belatedly mourned the passing era.

Bill understood his delivery had to travel via the most secure of conduits, an important consideration when Admiral Turner assigned him the task. The materials he carried had a higher classification than "Most Secret." The term "Ultra" was rarely spoken aloud, and documents carrying that designation were usually destroyed following eyes-only reviews by select officials. His rigorous White House training in the absolute primacy of their security made him the ideal delivery boy.

But what were President Truman's habits for receiving classified enemy intercepts? Admiral Leahy's method for getting these to President Roosevelt was to have Map Room naval aides personally present them twice a day. On many a morning, Bill had been the presenter while Roosevelt shaved in his bathroom. He would simply close the toilet seat, sit down, and read the secret digests aloud.

The afternoon briefings had been held either in the Map Room or down the hall in Admiral McIntire's office. There Roosevelt either read or was read the material while McIntire massaged his withered legs or packed his chronically congested sinuses with a cocaine-based antihistamine. Regardless of where he was, Roosevelt was always keenly interested in these briefings, sometimes even asking to read the individual decryptions on which they were based.

The intelligence value of these intercepts was so high that Bill had no reason to suspect Admiral Leahy had discontinued sharing them with President Truman. But with Leahy and Truman both now at Potsdam, there were only two secure methods for getting them the sensitive materials. The first was via the White House Map Room encoding machine (ECM), which transmitted to a receiving unit in the traveling map room that accompanied the president. The second was via a locked, specially keyed mail pouch, in which pressing documents were assembled daily at the White House and dispatched by air to President Truman and Admiral Leahy.

Using the Map Room ECM presented at least two drawbacks: not only were the documents of the most sensitive nature, but also they were likely too lengthy to be encoded verbatim. Map Room watch-officer procedure for conveying the import of long documents was to distill them to a page or less, which in this case Bill feared might result in critical omissions. That concern was exacerbated by the fact that a very new trainee was currently manning the Map Room: Bill's former watch officers, the seasoned George Elsey and Frank Graham, and Truman's new naval aide, James Vardaman Jr., had all gone to Potsdam.

Vardaman, a Missouri banker and political operative with a brief wartime reserve commission, inspired little confidence as an intelligence officer. Moreover, just before departing for Potsdam, he had hastily recruited a St. Louis confidant, an attorney named Clark Clifford, to cover the Map Room in his absence. While Bill had no specific objections to the initiate Clifford, this was a far cry from the exacting recruitment protocols of 1942 that he had painstakingly put in place. In any case, this was not a mission to risk entrusting to a novice trainee with scant military background.

So he decided on the air dispatch option and addressed it to Admiral Leahy's attention. It would be in his hands at Potsdam by the next morning. Regardless of who logged the pouch at the other end, Bill knew that Admiral Leahy would find this intelligence of seminal interest and that he had the final say on what—and in what order—was placed before the president.

Bill then delivered his final copy to the Pentagon, presumably to Admiral King's attention, and headed back to the airfield.

WHILE BILL NODDED ON and off on his long return journey to Manila, confirmation of the altered Kyushu defense picture was already shaking things up on the ground. At the Pentagon, a memorandum was prepared by the Joint War Planning Committee—the staff arm of the Joint Chiefs—suggesting alternative recommendations:

> [T]he possible effect upon the Olympic operations of this build-up and concentration is such that . . . commanders in the field should review their estimates of the situation, reexamine objectives in Japan as possible alternates to Olympic, and prepare plans for operations against such alternate objectives.

MacArthur was furious, particularly given the source of the information: his *own* intelligence operation. In an attempt to discredit his intelligence chief General Willoughby, MacArthur replied:

> I am certain . . . that the Japanese potential reported to you . . . is greatly exaggerated . . . I do not, repeat do not, credit the heavy strengths reported to you in southern Kyushu. There should not, repeat not, be the slightest thought of changing the Olympic operation. The plan is sound and will succeed. Throughout the Southwest Pacific, intelligence has pointed to greatly increased enemy forces. Without exception this buildup has been found to be erroneous.

With all evidence so irrefutably to the contrary, MacArthur's emphatic statement gave even his supporters pause, some already aware of

MacArthur's potential for mendacity. General Marshall had recently confided to War Secretary Stimson that MacArthur "is so prone to exaggerate and so influenced by his own desires, that it is difficult to trust his judgment." But none ever said so publicly, so enormous was MacArthur's popularity and perceived importance to American morale in wartime.

Bill's first return leg concluded at an Oakland airfield on Monday evening, August 6. His next flight wasn't scheduled to depart until August 8. Before making for the officers' quarters on the Presidio, he telephoned a few friends in the area, hoping to avoid spending the next two days alone. With luck, he reached a law school classmate who invited him to lunch in downtown San Francisco the next day. Bill would be very impressed by their fellow diner, the friend said, and gave him directions to the Bohemian Club at the northeast corner of Post and Taylor Streets. They certainly had plenty to discuss, didn't they?

The reference was lost on Bill, who had been in the air during the White House's climactic announcement on the Pacific War's climactic event. And due to the three-hour time difference, the report was in none of that day's West Coast papers. But by the time Bill reached the assigned San Francisco street corner for lunch on August 7, he was up to speed on the biggest war news since Pearl Harbor.

President Truman himself had issued the statement: that on August 6 the United States had exploded an atomic bomb over a city named Hiroshima, "a major quartermaster depot and port of embarkation for the Japanese. In addition to large military supply depots, it manufactured ordnance, mainly large guns and tanks, and machine tools, and aircraft-ordnance parts."

Like the rest of the country, Bill was surprised. He could only make educated guesses as to this bomb's impact on the war or its relationship to his very recent mission to the White House. At first reading, it was hard to imagine a weapon of exponentially greater power than those he witnessed in the withering bombardment of Saipan, Iwo Jima, and Okinawa. But one of the West Coast accounts claimed that this single bomb was "equal to the load of 2,000 B-29s and more than 2,000 times the blast power of what previously was the world's most devastating bomb."

He also learned that President Roosevelt had appointed a commission back in 1939 to investigate use of atomic energy for military purposes. Suddenly Bill wondered anew: Could *this* have been the meaning behind Roosevelt's parting comment to him regarding a peace conference? *"Well, son, I'm not sure there will ever be one."*

Bill combed the morning newspapers for details ahead of his luncheon. The August 7, 1945, *San Francisco Chronicle* could only speculate on its impact:

```
JAPAN HIT BY ATOM BOMB--MIGHTIEST WEAPON
IN HISTORY! TOKYO ADMITS HEAVY DAMAGE

Associated Press WASHINGTON, August 6--
The most terrible destructive force ever harnessed by
man--atomic energy--is now being used against Japan
by the United States. The Japanese face a threat
of utter destruction and their capitulation may be
greatly speeded up . . . The existence of this great
new weapon was announced personally in a statement
by President Truman, released by the White House at
11:15 Eastern Standard Time.
```

With newspapers tucked under his arm, Bill entered the Bohemian Club beneath its Shakespeare-inspired motto, "Weaving Spiders Come Not Here"—intended to discourage business or political conversation. He located his luncheon party in a wood-paneled dining room adorned with blinking mahogany owls. It turned out Bill recognized both men; the surprise addition was former president Herbert Hoover—an apparent fellow Bohemian. Here, finally, was a bit of news he could share with his mother that would meet unequivocal approval.

Given the august company and the day's headlines, the diners' conversation was lively from the start, if strictly out of compliance with the club's motto. Prognostications on the bomb's power and impact on Hiroshima led the way, followed by guesses as to its impact on the war. Could an invasion of Japan now be avoided? Hoover surprised the table with his remarkably detailed understanding of homeland invasion logistics as well as its potential casualty yield. How this one-term, extremely unpopular Republican president was so thoroughly well informed on the topic was a mystery to his luncheon companions.

Conversation then turned to conjecture on the new weapon's chemical properties. Hoover, who had something of a science background, pulled out his engraved gold pen and began scratching out periodic table configurations and isotopic ratios for uranium on a "BC" engraved napkin. He also hazarded a few guesses on the chain of reactions necessary for nuclear fission. The busy calculations ran over onto the linen tablecloth, which visibly irritated their waiter. In any case, by the arrival of coffee, the diners agreed on one thing: if this terrible new weapon could expedite the end of the war, it would be well worth the reported devastation.

ON THE AFTERNOON OF August 8, another uncomfortable air transport lumbered off an Oakland runway bearing Bill on the next-to-last leg of his five-day odyssey; a distance of 5,800 miles. The mid-Pacific dot that was Guam was growing fatter and greener as they lowered toward the island's airfield—when something unusual caught Bill's attention. Against Apra Harbor's deep blue waters, otherwise stocked with gunmetal-gray warships, a zinc-white vessel drew the eye like a splash of paint on dress blacks. A hospital ship was making anchor.

A phalanx of nurses and hundreds of sailors hovered near the mooring, and a long queue of stocky ambulances with red crosses on their roofs stretched beyond the bend in the road. Bill looked on with a sense of dread as the USS *Tranquility*'s crew secured her lines. With no Pacific battles raging at the moment, what could this spectacle mean?

He was soon to learn that the line of stretchers being handed down *Tranquility*'s gangway carried surviving *Indianapolis* crew members. Out of a crew of 1,199, these were the 316 lucky survivors of four days in shark-infested waters.

After its top secret delivery of the first atomic bomb to awaiting pilots on Tinian Island, *Indianapolis* had sailed south, stopped briefly at Guam, then set out for Leyte, another 1,350 miles. Traveling without escorts or shipboard sonar, the storied cruiser was defenseless against a Japanese submarine lurking halfway between the Philippines and Guam. In the dead of night, it had fired two torpedoes into *Indianapolis*, cutting the ship in half. She sank almost immediately. CINCPAC's forward headquarters at Guam was in a collective state of shock that the one-time Fifth Fleet flagship could have gone missing, unreported, for so long. Bill drew no closer to the scene after he landed. His threshold for absorbing the death of friends had long since been reached.

By the time he completed his seventeen-thousand-mile odyssey and reported back to Admiral Turner in Manila, alternatives to Olympic were already under consideration, despite General MacArthur's vigorous objections. Bill's delivery to Washington had, he believed, helped bring about the desired result.

Yet next steps in the Pacific were anything but clear. Despite the dropping of a second atomic bomb on August 9—on Mitsubishi Steel and Arms Works at Nagasaki on the island of Kyushu—Allied firebombing of mainland Japan had continued apace. And reluctantly redeployed troops from the European theater were still arriving by the thousands in Manila for retraining against a very different enemy.

Even after the stunning devastation conferred by two atomic bombs, Japan had not communicated any intention to surrender. It was the Japanese military, not her emperor or diplomats, who were running the war, and they had shown no inclination for retreat. Accordingly, General Marshall made no change to his imminent vacation plans, evidence alone that Japan's capitulation was not expected.

But before the second week of August 1945 was out—a week that included Russia's declaration of war against Japan and the Red Army's entry into Manchuria—Japanese military leaders were finally brought to their knees by their own emperor. On August 14, Prime Minister Kantaro Suzuki notified the Allies of Emperor Hirohito's issuance of an Imperial rescript accepting the unconditional surrender terms laid out in the Potsdam Declaration. The next day, Hirohito made a rare radio address to a weeping nation, announcing his decision.

Developments proceeded at a sprint after that. Truman named General MacArthur supreme commander for Allied Powers (SCAP), in which capacity he would lead postwar occupation of a vanquished Japan. Not surprisingly, MacArthur's crowning rankled navy feathers. But when Admiral Nimitz learned that MacArthur was also chosen to accept Japan's surrender, he displayed a rare flash of anger. He growled that this appeared to give the army credit for winning the Pacific War and resolved not to attend the ceremony. Only when Navy Secretary Forrestal stepped in was the day saved for both Admiral Nimitz and navy posterity.

Forrestal suggested that the surrender ceremony be held aboard a US Navy battleship, USS *Missouri*, in Tokyo Bay. Secretary Forrestal also ensured that the Pacific Fleet commander would cosign the surrender document with MacArthur. Thus assuaged, Nimitz flew to Tokyo Bay, arriving a day ahead of MacArthur. In this, deservedly, the commander in chief of the Pacific Fleet was the first to witness the most formidable display of naval power ever assembled in a single anchorage.

Admiral Nimitz settled into temporary quarters aboard the USS *South Dakota* and promptly convened a large group of war correspondents. He had a few things to say for—and on—the record. On the evening of August 29, Nimitz reminded the press of the pivotal role the US Navy had played throughout the Pacific conflict. Japan's surrender came before any invasion was necessary, he said, because of "sea power, spearheaded by carrier-borne aircraft and an excellent . . . submarine force."

Nimitz said that US naval sea power had made the use of the atomic bomb possible by its seizing of mid-Pacific atolls from which planes could carry it to Japan. "Without sea power," said Nimitz, "we could not have advanced at all."

AS THE WAR'S CLOSING events swirled around Manila, one in particular stood out for Bill Mott: the order to immediately free all prisoners of war. Better yet, Operation Swift Mercy decreed that prisoners being held in Japan must be transported to and processed in Manila before their repatriation to the United States. After enduring weeks of wildly fluctuating assumptions, Bill felt a shiver of expectation.

Admiral Halsey promptly dispatched hospital ships and a special task force to Japan to retrieve Allied prisoners from camps previously located by aerial reconnaissance. Most were suffering from severe malnutrition and other illnesses, ranging from serious to critical. In late August, navy photos of the first ecstatic group of liberated prisoners—from Omori, a camp near Tokyo—appeared on the front page of nearly every major American newspaper.

Preparations were under way in Manila to receive the tens of thousands of emaciated ex-POWs, with first arrivals expected by the third or fourth of September. Offices were set up to evaluate hospital and troopship rosters against uncorroborated grave-registration lists and lists of the missing. Infirmaries, dispensaries, and reception centers—and thousands of cots—were requisitioned and set up all over Manila.

On September 1, just as the first prisoner-loaded hospital ships prepared to depart Japan, Admiral Turner and his flag staff departed Manila for a particular battleship in Tokyo Bay. The formal Japanese surrender would be held at 0900 the next day on the USS *Missouri*, which was still Admiral Halsey's flagship.

After the ceremony, while a grand display of a thousand naval aircraft roared over Tokyo Bay, Admiral Turner asked Admiral Hall, freshly minted commander of the Tokyo Naval Force, if a sedan might be made available to take him and his staff into Tokyo. Hall referred the request to General Robert Eichelberger, the army area commander. Eichelberger hedged, saying that the army had not yet established patrols in Tokyo and could not ensure Turner's safety. But he did not say no, and in a manner unknown, a sedan was procured.

Admiral Turner and his entourage thus drove off, stopping first at a police station to get directions to the shrine of Admiral Tōgō, victor of the Tsushima Strait Battle in the 1904–05 Russo-Japanese War. Turner had been greatly impressed by the Tōgō shrine during his 1939 diplomatic mission to Japan aboard *Astoria*.

"We went into the police station to get a road map," recalled one staffer. "The police were very polite to us, and we were very polite to them. When we came out of the police station, Admiral Turner said, 'When they surrendered, they really surrendered.'"

Standing before the Tōgō shrine, Admiral Turner made this prescient observation: "If we play our cards well, the Japanese will become our best and most worthwhile friends. They have certain fundamental virtues in their character, which in time, I hope, will be appreciated by all worthwhile Americans. We should be most careful to respect their Gods and their traditions, and I hope they will come in time to respect ours."

Here again Turner was his usual thoughtful and brilliant, and the moment left an indelible print on his flag staff. But Bill was still privately roiled by persistent rumors of post-surrender reprisals against Allied war prisoners. As stunning and memorable as the day's events had been, he could think only of getting back to Manila. Once there, he would dissect every single roster of ships returning prisoners from Japan and search the faces of debarking men for Barton.

40

★ ★ ★

NO PEACE AT LILAC HEDGES

SEPTEMBER 1945 BEGAN AT Lilac Hedges as it had for decades. Despite the ecstasy of Japan's surrender and the subsequent agony of waiting to hear from or about Barton, Helen had her autumn gardening schedule to keep. Without a conventional job, she battled corrosive anxiety by working her seeds and soil as hard as any man labored at the office. Arthur had his textile business to keep him from going mad with the waiting.

They had relished the joyful news of Japan's unexpected surrender, toasting each other with highballs. "To Barton!" Then came the ongoing news of Allied prisoner liberations from such alien place names as Omori, Sian, Kyuryu, Sham Shui Po, Kanchanaburi, Mukden, Karenko, Nong Pla-duck, Konan; after which came gleeful media reports of POWs reuniting with their jubilant families. Their nerves frayed as the days grew shorter and the list of liberated places longer, with no news of their son.

As the month wore on, Bill's regular but increasingly anxious assurances from Manila had yielded little. So preoccupied was Helen that she barely sniffed at Bill's own good news: that the Pacific admirals had formally recommended his transfer from the reserves to the regular navy, a long-sought goal.

With little else to distract her each morning after seeing Arthur off for the train, Helen took to the garden before the sun cleared the oak canopy on the east lawn. She would first drag a heavy brick across the porch to wedge open the door so as not to miss the much-awaited telephone call. Then, after fastening her bandana and donning her dirt-smudged apron, she gathered up her tulip, tiger, and rockery trowels, a mattock, hoe, and shrub rake, and went to work.

There were endless spent blooms to pinch, rosebushes to corset, and arbors to tie up. And with so much of her landscaping ripped away in last year's hurricane, there was the planting of new hemlocks, dogwoods, and Japanese maples to oversee. And then she must turn to the rigors of mulching, using the rich nutrient yield of fallen leaves already flecking her lawn. Ticking off tasks on these to-do lists became Helen's units of measure for marking time in September 1945.

As each day progressed, she kept a vigilant ear above autumn birdsong and honking geese for the mailman's footsteps and the particular pace of passing cars. Any day now, the mailman might bring joyful, if belated, tidings—and if no car slowed to a stop in front of her house, no uniformed officer could emerge with news she could not bear to hear.

How she missed Sable! For years, he had accompanied her morning garden rounds, courting her moods and patiently listening to her musings. But the graying spaniel had suddenly passed away in late January. Helen was convinced Barton's beloved dog finally died of a broken heart.

So she forged ahead alone that September, mapping out a gardening regimen that would take her through October, she calculated, what with putting in the young saplings, tulip and crocus bulb planting and transplanting, raking, composting, and mulching. Soon enough would come the job of spreading that black gold over her sleeping beauties in carefully delineated quadrants. This alone would take days.

But Helen did not follow her scripted plan to the letter that autumn. Early in the month, she declined to pull up the summer annuals on schedule—why void the lovely mounds of white impatiens lighting up the lilacs' understory before Barton's return? The same occurred the day she had scheduled cutting back her hydrangea. They still had good color, she reasoned, some deepened to a purplish garnet, others a sun-kissed bronze. Wouldn't he love to drive up after so long and see her garden "just so"?

She had loved it more than she ever let on when Barton would say, "Everything looks swell, Ma!" He had always complimented her horticultural flair. While she rarely spoke of it, his gift of noticing even the most mundane garden adjustment made her feel uniquely appreciated.

That September, it seemed that every one of Helen's gardening decisions had a Barton counterpart. She coaxed Lilac Hedges's summer glory to hang on so that Barton could see it before the garden faded to browns and grays.

THE FIRST FREED WAR prisoners in Japan had been from a camp called Omori. The September 7 article said they were actually liberated at the end of August, before the surrender was formally signed. Helen was trembling by the time she finished reading the front-page piece in the *New York Times*. With the help of a magnifying glass, she scrutinized the accompanying photo: a dirty band of gaunt, shirtless, exhilarated men. It caught them in a state of sheer exuberance, midshout, midlaugh, some with fingers fixed in Vs, others waving British and American flags.

"What of Barton?" she groaned. She asked this again and again, to her diary and out loud, but no longer to Sable, whose reliable attention and empathy she particularly missed now.

Besides her various trowels, Helen's only other weapons for taming anxiety were her fountain pen and typewriter. Since Japan's mid-August surrender announcement, she had repeatedly written both the army and navy. The war was over! Prisoners were being released all over Asia! Where was her son? September dragged into the double digits, and the gardening and letters continued apace, but replies from Washington never varied: "At last report to this Department, Ensign Cross was interned as a prisoner of war in the Philippines."

News of a darker nature had also begun to agitate Helen. Following each camp's liberation came a fresh round of press accounts—no longer subject to a war censor's pen—on Japanese treatment of their onetime captives. Front pages were crammed with one chilling ex-prisoner interview after another. The stock tales were of starvation, beatings, and beheadings, but another, more troubling, theme was also emerging.

The men told repeatedly of being shipped to Japan from conquered territories, shoved deep in the bowels of unmarked Japanese transports. So frequent were these stories that the press dubbed these vessels "hell ships." Drastic conditions and stunning cruelty aboard these ships spilled out daily in black and white. Worse, went the stories, as many as a dozen of these vessels had been attacked en route by the United States Navy.

If these accumulating newspaper reports were accurate, prisoner transports exiting the Philippines received particular attention by the US Navy. According to one survivor account, hundreds died from a single air squadron strike on his prison ship in Subic Bay at the end of 1944. Subsequent air strikes killed hundreds more prisoners before their voyage was done.

Carrier pilots' orders had been to "eliminate" all enemy shipping except hospital ships or those transporting prisoners of war, but none of the latter were marked as such. This was a flagrant violation of the Geneva Convention, but Japan had not been a signatory to those global rules of conduct. Helen simmered. *Hadn't the navy learned by that point that the Japanese were not marking their prisoner transports? She had written Roosevelt on this subject over a year earlier!*

The fall equinox came and went at Lilac Hedges with still no word from Ensign Cross. Helen was certain she knew the name of every Japanese prison camp in Asia by this time. They sounded unbidden in her head, in sync with the mourning meter of autumn crickets or to the rhythm of her shoes sloshing through wet grass, like a bad tune that cannot be banished: Saitami, Hokkaido, Shikoku, Ofuna, Shinagawa, Kawasaki . . . She spat out the names on the ever-lengthening list of liberated prison camps.

With each report, Arthur's forced optimism grew less convincing, even as he assured his fretting wife that there were still camps in Korea yet to be liberated. She just needed to be patient.

And so September dragged on, day in and day out.

On Tuesday, September 25, various morning headlines held little interest for Helen or Arthur. That the 1945 World Series would pit the Detroit Tigers against the Chicago Cubs was a disappointment to any self-respecting baseball fan. One sportswriter dubbed it the "World's Worst Series." Another quipped that he didn't think either team could win. Though they could have used the distraction, Helen and Arthur couldn't muster their usual enthusiasm for America's final baseball contest of the season.

Then there was the bit about Secretary of War Henry Stimson and his "deserving" retirement from public service. As far as Helen and Arthur were concerned, Stimson had neither protected their son at the start of the war nor done anything to bring him home at the end of it.

Arthur made for the train a little after eight, and Helen set out for the garden. When dark skies and wind gusts threatened rain in late morning, she headed back toward the house. But as she started up the porch steps, the mailman's distinctive gait stopped her in her tracks. Having sent off so many inquiries, she could only hope that today he brought a glimmer of news.

After placing her clippers and cuttings on the step and pulling off her garden gloves, she gratefully accepted the short stack of mail. With the dexterity of a card shark, she leafed through the mix of bills and letters. She stopped at the prize card—finally, a letter from the navy! With a mix of anticipation and nervousness, she sat down on the step and ripped open the envelope. Inside was a one-page letter, folded in thirds and neatly typed.

Dear Mr. and Mrs. Cross:

It is with deep regret that this Bureau informs you that it is in receipt of a cablegram from the International Red Cross in Tokyo, dated 19, September, 1945, stating that your son died of acute enteritis on 30 January 1945 while aboard a Japanese transport ship apparently en route to a prisoner of war camp in Japan.

The delay in the arrival of this information is a result of the slowness with which the Japanese Government has cooperated in the handling of the information concerning prisoners of war.

The Bureau deeply regrets its inability to supply further information at this time. The cablegram from the International Red Cross was brief and did not state the place of burial, type of ceremony, or medical attention administered. Now that the Japanese have surrendered, additional information is becoming available daily. Should further details be received concerning your son, they will be forwarded to you from the Navy Department.

The various agencies of the government having jurisdiction over settlement of death benefits in cases involving deceased naval personnel have been informed. These agencies will forward to you the necessary forms to be used in order to file a claim for any benefits to which you may be entitled.

The Navy Department extends sincere sympathy to you in

```
your great sorrow and hopes that you may find comfort in
the knowledge that your son gave his life in the service of
his country.

                         By direction of the Chief of
                         Naval Personnel.
                         Sincerely Yours,
                         H. B. Atkinson
                         Commander, USNR
                         Officer in Charge
                         Casualty Section
```

How long did it take for this news to sink in—that her son had been dead already *eight months*? How long for Helen to begin sobbing and rocking back and forth on that porch stair, for her bandana to slide off, for the strands of gray mingled with defiant red to mat her face, the tear-soaked letter still in hand? Had she already known on some unconscious level—felt that ominous, marrow-deep inkling that only a mother can decrypt?

At some point, Helen must have managed her way back into the house, past her War Mother's Flag still boasting a proud quartet of blue stars. It had adorned the front window for nearly four years now. Soon enough, a fellow War Mother would arrive, discreetly, and sew gold thread over the third one down to announce the incomprehensible loss of a dear child to a distant war.

There were no uniformed officers at her door to thank for their kindness in her moment of great anguish, no body to weep over, no forehead to stroke one last time, and, without a body, no funeral to plan. All conventional palliatives for a mother's grief were denied her. Helen had only this letter from the Navy Department to respond to—and respond she would. Her heart would bleed with purpose, she determined, through the nib of her pen.

That they had declined to notify her in person was perhaps the greatest insult. Her four children all naval officers and the navy too busy to come to her home, even with the war concluded? And her dear one's death due to "acute enteritis"? After everything she had read in the previous three weeks, she rejected this with every fiber of her being. Years of incompetence, and now lies!

Arthur mourned as any well-trained son of the British Empire might— silently and stoically. He reeled from the death of his namesake, but spoke little of it and cried less. While Helen announced her grief with vehemence, Arthur's only solace was work, to which he returned in too few days following the terrible news.

Helen abandoned her gardening for the rest of 1945—anguish and rage had snuffed out the joy it had once brought her. But she did not sit idle. As autumn leaves fell unanswered on tufting grass and spiking weeds and chill winds blew them about neglected beds, stacks of letters weighed down the mailman in his daily retreat from Lilac Hedges.

Her first round of salvos—to the army, the navy, and President Truman— demanded the names and addresses of surviving prisoners who had known her son. If Pentagon and White House powers couldn't or wouldn't help her learn the truth, she resolved to get the answers elsewhere. Once she received the contact information, she would solicit Barton's prison comrades for answers.

In the meantime, she gathered as much information as she could on the much-publicized hellships, easily confirming that her son had died after seven weeks of incarceration in the rusted, boiling-then-freezing hulls of three such vessels. The first two, *Oryoko Maru* in Subic Bay and *Enoura Maru* at Takao Harbor, Formosa, had been laid to waste by exploding bombs dropped by navy carrier planes, each time killing and wounding hundreds more American prisoners.

Surviving prisoners of the second prison ship bombing at Takao Harbor, including Barton, were transferred to the hull of a third ship, *Brazil Maru*. This last crumbling, stinking hulk then set course for Japan—into the teeth of its coldest winter in decades. All were starving, ill, and emaciated, and many had untreated shrapnel wounds from the previous bombings.

Prisoners in the horse manure–laden hull of the *Brazil Maru* died by the hour. The death rate on this final, bitter leg to the enemy's homeland reached forty men a day, their purpling corpses stacked like cordwood together with the men in the hull.

With every new revelation, Helen absorbed fresh shock and grief. Then she gathered herself up and fired off a fresh barrage of accusations and questions to Washington. As postwar press scrutiny of these doomed prisoner voyages intensified, Helen became increasingly convinced that Barton was a victim of friendly fire. Official replies never satisfied.

Even as the navy resisted her building rationale that Barton was killed by one of his own, Helen reasserted her mounting evidence against them. Article after article, all drawn from survivor accounts, continued for months after the war. Without wartime censorship, the military was powerless to stem the rising tide of damning information.

One brutally candid fourteen-part series, based on some of the first press interviews after surrender, left Helen shattered. Barton had been on every one of the ships described in the cruel forty-nine-day odyssey.

In the syndicated "Cruise of Death," Pulitzer Prize–winning correspondent George Weller of the *Chicago Daily News* spared no detail. The series ran in December 1945 and was carried by major newspapers across the country:

```
          SEVEN WEEKS IN JAP-MADE HELL
       Story of Cruise of Death of 1600 American
          Prisoners Told by the 300 Who Lived


       George Weller Pieces Together the Record
             of Bombs, Suffocation, Starvation,
                Murder on Voyage from Manila.


    This is the story of a cruise of death. It is the
    story of 49 days of savagery and tragedy unequaled
```

in the war in the Pacific, of a Jap-made hell from
which approximately 300 Americans from more than
1600 emerged, alive . . .

Survivors were interviewed in prison and rest
camps in the Pacific.

It is the story of a twisting, tortuous journey
on prison ships from Manila to southern Japan during which men died from Japanese bullets, American
bombs, suffocation, starvation and murder. Some went
insane . . . Its accuracy is unquestionable.

The story begins in Manila. December 13, 1944 . . .

DOWN AT THE NAVY Department's Casualty Section, a perspiring
Commander Atkinson doggedly responded to each of Helen Cross's salvos,
but he never wavered from the navy's original claim of Barton's cause of death:

Dear Mrs. Cross:

Receipt is acknowledged of your letters addressed to
President Truman and referred to this Bureau for reply
concerning your son, the late Ensign Arthur Barton Cross, Jr.

Although you state your son died as a result of
Allied bombing attacks on a Japanese prison ship, the
records available to this Bureau indicate he died of acute
enteritis. There is no evidence available in the Navy
Department to substantiate your belief that your son died
as a result of Allied bombings.

After the war was over with Japan in August, 1945,
the captured enemy records were carefully translated

and scrutinized for clues as to the fate of Army and Navy
personnel who had fallen into the hands of the enemy.

In some instances, it was learned that naval personnel
who had survived Japanese attacks had subsequently been
taken into custody and killed by the Japanese. Other
prisoners died of disease due to malnutrition, among whom
was listed your son.

Your anxiety to learn the details of your son's death
is appreciated and it is regretted there are no additional
facts known in his case.

Sincere sympathy is again extended to you in the loss
of your son.

> By direction of the Chief of
> Naval Personnel.
> Sincerely Yours,
> Commander H. B. Atkinson
> Officer in Charge
> Casualty Section
> Bureau of Naval Personnel
> Washington 25, DC

Yet Atkinson had a mother, too, and he did what he could to assuage the
aggrieved Helen Cross. He sent a warm personal note with Barton's Purple
Heart medal, awarded posthumously for wounds he received in the December 1941 bombings at Cavite. He thought she might also like to know that
Barton had been promoted to Lieutenant (jg) while a prisoner, something
he expected would make her very proud. But Atkinson's efforts were unre-
quited. She replied to his every missive (with courtesy copies to members
of Congress and President Truman) with withering scorn:

Dear Sir:

    Answering your last letter I was for a moment confused—it had been so long since I had addressed the President and then only when the Navy seemed quite unconcerned.

    As to your Purple Heart, its late arrival was not mentioned to me by my family who intercepted it in fear of further anguish being brought me. However since the story of [sic] a Major General receiving one for a broken leg received when he fell drunk from a second story—this medal leaves me quite indifferent.

    If that is all the Navy has to offer those poor devils whom it bombed and killed after three years of horrible imprisonment by the Japs, you may have your Purple Heart back.

    As to my son's death, he was bombed by Navy fliers in Subic Bay and again by Navy hands off of Formosa, and after such sufferings reportedly died of exhaustion and pneumonia which might be blamed on the Japs.

    This was not the work of Army fliers, mind you—thank God that their branch was not guilty of so terrible a mistake!

    And then, what does the Navy do? Does it send one ranking surviving officer who might have been with our dear one in his last hours? No, you killed our son, not even in fair battle either, and never has there been such callous disregard of heart-broken relatives as the Navy has shown in this instance.

    Furthermore, though my son has been gone from this earth for approaching a year, and the Red Cross has notified me of his insurance and back pay, not any of this has reached me. Not that ten times the amount would atone for one of my son's fingers, it just further confirms dilatory Navy procedure.

    Don't take this personally. It is the Navy we despise, "Bull" Halsey who gave orders to those fliers and the brass hats in safe places who

*didn't care. Only Congressional investigations will cure Navy arrogance
and stupidity.*

*The public is awake to it—witness how few officers of the Reserve
care to remain in such an organization.*

*Very sincerely,
Helen C. Cross*

*cc: President Harry S. Truman
Senator Albert Hawkes (R-NJ)*

More-satisfying responses to Helen's missives were trickling in from
Barton's comrades who had survived the ordeal. Most were written from
beds at military hospitals across the country and arrived over a period of
several weeks. Helen hungrily read and reread each moving fellow-prisoner
testimonial. They were her sole consolation, providing a montage of Barton's world over the past three years and filling dozens of blanks she had
long agonized over.

The letters were also full of anecdotes and unabashed declarations
of respect and affection for their lost friend. She and Arthur both were
amazed—and taken aback—by the picture that emerged of their son, who
had been transformed in his bondage. The letters attested to the courage,
strength, honor, and persistent optimism Barton had to the last—none easy
traits to retain under such conditions. They described at length the difference "Bart" had made in their respective lives, which, they attested variously, had been critical to their own survival.

Who was this person these fellow prisoners described? Could her son
really have left home such a boy and in captivity become such a *man*?

"In all those three years, under humiliating and weakening conditions, Bart
was ever the gentleman, a true inspiration to all who knew him!" wrote one.

Another said: "I was with Bart under all kinds of conditions, and I can truthfully say he was one of the finest men I have ever known. He never complained. He was cheerful and courageous until the end." And another: "He organized a Sunday choir, concerts, a glee club, and baseball games— and even a baseball team that played against the Jap guards. His courage was unbelievable, and his morale building efforts were continuous among officers and men in both the prison camps and aboard the prison ships."

Each treasured account added its own texture, depth, and color to a portrait of the man this grieving mother's boy had become beyond her care. The correspondence was mostly from naval ensigns and young lieutenants. Some had been quartered with Barton since the Philippines fell; others had known him only at one camp or another. One man said he didn't really get to know Barton until they were thrust together on the last of the three hellships, but under such conditions, he wrote, they formed a sure and fast bond.

Their precise recounting of Barton's final moments varied to a degree, doubtless due to their own drastically diminished conditions. One fellow prisoner claimed Barton had succumbed to wounds incurred when a navy bomb struck their ship at Takao, Formosa. Another said Barton had died from starvation and exposure. One said dysentery had claimed him; another said it was pneumonia, of which so many had died on that final, frigid voyage. Try though she did, Helen was unable to reconcile these accounts. Perhaps, she mused, he had fallen victim to all of them.

Barton's fellow prisoners all stressed that by the end of the forty-nine-day trip, those still alive were barely so. They unanimously declared it a miracle that any of them had survived. The final numbers were grim. Of the 1,619 prisoners that departed Manila on December 13, 1944, 450 arrived alive in Japan on January 30, 1945. Of those, 161 died in Japanese labor camps shortly thereafter.

Describing the details of Barton's last days and hours was painful for Barton's fellow prisoners, but tell they did, perhaps believing that the only possible salve for his family was the truth.

41

★ ★ ★

FINAL HOURS

Dear Mrs. Cross,

I have been in the hospital for several weeks and just received your letter. I am very sorry that I have not written you sooner--but then too, I didn't want to merely write a letter and let it go at that . . .

Bart and I were captured in Manila on January 1, 1942. He and I were together all the time until his death. We were in camps on Luzon, moved to Davao, Mindanao, and then back to Cabanatuan on Luzon in the summer of 1944. We were returned to Bilibid Prison in Manila that October and left there on December 13, 1944, on a Japanese ship bound for Japan. This ship was sunk . . .

> Charles W. Armour to Helen Cross, dated November 2, 1945, from a naval hospital in Memphis, Tennessee

My Dear Mrs. Cross,

    I am so glad that you have written me. I do appreciate
the many unanswered questions that must be in the minds of
Bart's family. I know he would wish that I be as truthful
and frank as possible with his family. With that in mind,
I shall do my very best to accurately recall the important
things.

    I met Bart at Bilibid Prison after the fall of Bataan.
From that time on, we were in the same camps and became
close friends . . .

               Kenneth R. Wheeler, dated November 3, 1945, from
                      a naval hospital at Oak Knoll, California

Dear Mrs. Cross,

    Yes, I did know your son. I only wish I could talk with
you about him in person rather than set the facts down
in an impersonal letter, but I will do the best I can. I'm
awfully sorry I didn't know how close I was to you when
I traveled to Philadelphia to see Captain and Mrs. Wuest.
Their son Bob was also a close friend of ours, and I wanted
to give them his U. of Penn ring I managed to bring back. He
died on the trip from Manila to Moji, Kyushu, and, like you,
they had little or no information about his death . . .

    Bart and I met after the surrender [at Corregidor]
and were sent to Cabanatuan, where we ensigns all lived in
one barrack. In the fall of 1942, Bart and quite a number
of other naval personnel were sent to Davao on Mindanao.
About July 1944, I believe, the Davao detail returned to

Cabanatuan, and we were all together again. We ensigns had quite a bit of fun at Cabanatuan. We stuck together in all things and that in itself made life a lot easier. That October, we were all sent down to Bilibid to await transportation to Japan.

Because of American raids on Manila, we were kept at Bilibid until December 13th. Then a typhoon gave the Nips the break they were waiting for. We were loaded onto the "Oryoko Maru" that same afternoon and sailed within several hours. American planes began bombing the ship on the 14th and sank her on the 15th. Bart and most of the other ensigns made it ashore. We were kept there at Subic for 5 days . . .

> Andrew Long Jr., dated November 6, 1945, from a
> military hospital in Springfield, Missouri

DECEMBER 15, 1944

IT WAS LATE AFTERNOON by the time surviving *Oryoko Maru* prisoners were herded together on the beach and marched to an improbable new enclosure: a tennis court on the former US Naval Base at Olongapo. It was only about five hundred yards away, but the men staggered the distance from the combined trauma of shock, exhaustion, hunger, and thirst. They also struggled to carry their two hundred wounded, some at the point of death.

A scowling Mr. Wada greeted Colonel Beecher—still damp and attired only in socks and boxer shorts—at the tennis court gate. Waving the ship's manifest, the interpreter demanded a survivor count. Beecher agreed, but insisted wisely that he be allowed a confirming second count before certifying it. A miscount in the chaos could falsely indicate escape, triggering a fresh round of Japanese reprisals; this he wished to avoid at all costs.

Beecher's method was to send a hundred prisoners through the court gate at a time, but so many passed back and forth carrying in the wounded that he quickly lost track. The process took hours, with no certain count at the end of it.

The following morning, Beecher began a second count after mustering a burial detail to inter the three men who died in the night. He then dragged the tall referee's chair to the court's center and began calling roll. It went badly from the start. Beecher recalled,

[W]hen a man didn't answer to his name, it had to be repeated
several times in order to be sure the man who . . . was actually missing. The doctors and corpsmen had to nudge patients
to respond, as many were in such condition as to be unable
to recognize their names when called . . . When there was no
answer, I asked, "Well, does anyone know what happened to
him?" A voice might say "I think he passed out last night" or
"I believe I saw him with the dead on the deck of the ship."
Then there would be contradictions. "The hell you did! He
was in the bay next to me. A bomb fragment got him." Another
might respond, "How could a bomb have got him when I saw him
swimming away from the ship?"

The sun was low on the horizon on December 16 by the time a survivor count of 1,320 prisoners was submitted. Beecher calculated that some 50 of the 300 casualties had occurred during the two horrific nights aboard *Oryoko Maru*; the rest died during the aerial attacks or at the hands of guards gunning from the seawall. They had shot any prisoner deemed to be swimming off course.

By dusk the second day, an order of sorts had emerged on the Olongapo tennis court. So, too, had the prisoners' realization that they had survived the *Oryoko Maru* only to endure a bizarre new phase of suffering. On the ship, they had endured suffocating heat, maddening thirst, random acts of murder, and a vicious—if unwitting—attack by their own navy. Those fortunate enough to make it ashore now questioned how lucky they really were.

The tennis court measured sixty feet by eighty feet, barely larger than the ship's hold. To fit, they were packed into eleven lines of a hundred men each, their legs either drawn knees to chest or scissored around the man in front of them.

The wounded were housed in the court "hospital," a sand-and-gravel width behind the faded baseline shaded by a piece of torn sheeting. Surviving doctors, themselves depleted and barely clothed, did what they could to dress wounds while calculating which men's hours were numbered and beyond care.

There was a water source at the court—a significant relief. But accessing the single, trickling spigot was no small effort. The men queued up at all hours, and guards were posted by the spigot around the clock. A lucky few still had a cup or canteen to fill for their effort, but most had to hold their mouths to the water for as long a draught as the guards would allow.

Despite their unpleasant new circumstances, the prisoners were relieved to no longer be heading to Japan. Every hour they remained in the Philippines, went the thinking, their chances for rescue by the fast-approaching Allies improved.

BARTON AND CHARLES CONDUCTED a survivor count of their own on the tennis court. Two members of their tight ensign fraternity—George Petritz and Shields Goodman—had not been seen since the order to abandon ship. Nor had Ensigns Chuck Wilkins and Warwick Potter Scott. They mourned quietly, remembering their late comrades with anecdotes drawn from three years of shared misery and privation.

Small sacrifices had made big differences. Charles reluctantly shared his old navy cap for an hour or so at a time so that the others could get temporary relief from the head-scorching sun. Before doing so, he removed a tiny address book from the inside flap in which he'd painstakingly recorded dozens of recipes over the years. The significance of the miserly Charles's hat loan was not lost on the others. His accumulated recipes had become almost as important to him as food itself. That hat had safeguarded them as much as it did his head.

Somehow Barton had hung on to his strapped canteen, despite the lengthy amount of time he'd spent in the water. He traveled back and forth to the spigot line at all hours, each time returning to pass the canteen around to the ensigns. When it was empty, he got back in the water queue. Barton engaged in his usual self-deprecating banter to deflect their gratitude, but his colleagues knew the man better by now.

In this manner, water was plentiful on the tennis court, but food was not. Their first food was finally tossed through the court gate on the second day, but in the form of two seventy-pound sacks of uncooked rice. Without cooking facilities, two level tablespoons of hard rice kernels were meted out to each prisoner. To supplement the meal, several reached through small openings in the fence perimeter and pulled up grass. A forearm's width of bare ground soon surrounded the enclosure.

As the prisoners chewed their stony rations, Admiral Halsey's planes returned in full view of the tennis court. Against a brilliant azure sky, one bomb load after another found their marks on the listing *Oryoko Maru*. Prisoner cheers went up with each direct hit, with the biggest whoop reserved for when the hated vessel burst into flames and slipped beneath the surface.

An apprehensive silence followed when Commander Riera and his air group made a circle and flew directly toward them. The planes circled and dove, circled and dove, striking fuel depots and other targets all around the prisoners. They seemed to be taking pains to avoid the court itself, igniting fresh hope among the prisoners. This must mean the flyers knew that these were the abandoned soldiers and sailors of Bataan, Cavite, and Corregidor. Surely they would hasten to send help. But yet another cruel spike in optimism ended in disappointment. There was no rescue, and no planes returned after December 16.

As the calendar pages turned, misery on the tennis court compounded. By noon each day, tropical heat pushed the concrete slab to over 100 degrees. The barely clad men baked and blistered on the black, unshaded surface. When afternoon mercifully faded to dusk, the relief was brief. Chill evening breezes transformed the court into a cold, hard torture rack. At night, protruding hips and ribs were marked by purpling welts and bruises. The men huddled together for warmth.

The evening winds also brought clouds of biting flies and mosquitoes. The insects feasted on open wounds, and sunburned skin turned to gooseflesh. Of those long nights on the tennis court, Manny Lawton recalled that the prisoners were "cold, hurting, and hungry. Few slept." By the third day, cases of gangrene had set in.

Removal of a gangrenous arm with a mess kit knife was the first surgical procedure in the court hospital. The patient was Marine Corporal Eugene L. Specht. The arm had taken a bullet that guards fired into the ship's hold on December 15. After hearing his options, Specht agreed with the medics: his only chance at survival was removal of the arm.

Poor Specht screamed in agony and had to be held down for the procedure. Afterward, the surgeon wrapped the bloody stump in a dirty towel, and, mercifully, the patient fell asleep. The next day, Specht was buried by the seawall alongside the accumulating prisoner dead.

On the fifth day, a convoy drew up to the tennis courts
and we were ordered to load.

Kenneth Wheeler to Helen Cross

★   ★   ★

THE NINETEEN TRUCKS THAT lumbered up on December 20 felt like a celestial vision. The prisoners had begun to wonder how much longer they could endure brutal exposure and a diet of 55 calories a day. After Lieutenant Toshino loaded the trucks to overcapacity, the convoy snaked out of sight. The six hundred prisoners that remained on the tennis court—Barton and Charles among them—were left to mull their fates.

There were benefits for those left behind, however. That night, they received a triple ration of rice from their unpredictable captors—six level spoonfuls of dry grain instead of two, plus a spoonful each of salt and dried fish. There was also more room to spread out on the court. With that and the extra food in their bellies, they slept a little better that night.

They were nonetheless relieved when told to prepare for their own move. Following a generous breakfast of *ten* spoonfuls of raw rice and more dried fish, Mr. Wada ordered the ensigns to clean the tennis court. Barton's mordant quips over the absurdity of this task elicited laughter—good and ancient medicine—even as the men labored to comply. Humor was their sole remaining antidote for misery, and it could not be taken away.

While the ensigns swabbed the blood- and feces-splattered tennis court, guards drew their swords and cut large tree branches to camouflage the trucks. A familiar mix of dread and anticipation returned when the prisoners learned why. The truck drivers reported that American pilots were actively patrolling above the main roads.

The truck ride was an uncomfortable zigzag over roadbeds rutted by weather, neglect, and war. At the intermittent buzz of approaching planes, the convoy lurched into ravines or under roadside tree canopies for cover. But when the trucks pressed northeast across the Zambales Mountains and away from the sea, the prisoners found cause for encouragement.

Could there be no more enemy ships to remove them from Luzon? With every hairpin turn, morale rose again with the prospect they might be liberated. But ominous signs mixed with positive ones. A steady stream of Japanese soldiers passed their convoy, variously hauling weapons, food, large guns, and ammunition. Recalled Colonel Beecher, "We felt . . . that the Japs were moving into position somewhere . . . We hoped . . . we would still be in the Philippines when [the final battle] took place."

The thirty-seven-mile truck ride ended at San Fernando, Pampanga, a town deep in Luzon's central plains. The last tennis court draft was marched along the town's vacant main street to a deserted cinema. After entering under the bullet-ridden marquee, the men groped in the dark. When their eyes finally adjusted, they saw that the theater's seats had been pulled up and tossed into an orchestra pit. Its singular water source was a spigot outside a barbed wire fence surrounding the theater. That spigot, and the latrines— slit trenches dug behind the rear of the building—could be accessed only by climbing through a small window. Still, the abandoned cinema was protected from the sun by day and from biting wind and insects by night.

They felt a spark of jealousy, however, when they learned that the earlier prisoner draft was being held at the town jail, which had plumbing and cooking facilities—even cots. But when their first cooked meal in a week appeared shortly after their arrival, all was forgiven. It had been prepared— unbidden—by their colleagues at the jail. The meal of steaming rice, seaweed, and *camotes* arrived on a sheet of corrugated roofing, and the men gratefully wolfed it down.

On the second evening in San Fernando, Mr. Wada called Colonel Beecher to the entrance of the cinema. Eventually they would resume their trip to Japan, Wada told a disappointed Beecher. He then directed the colonel to select fifteen sick and wounded—those least able to make a sea journey—so they could be sent to a hospital. Beecher was elated but also conflicted, for hundreds of prisoners easily met the criteria.

Fifteen men were finally culled from among the most extreme cases at the jail and theater. When the patients were loaded onto the two truck beds, Beecher recalled thinking, *Well, there go at least fifteen prisoners who in spite of their wounds are pretty lucky. They'll get back to Bilibid and probably pull through; certainly better off than us left behind.*

But Beecher was tragically mistaken, unaware that Lieutenant Urabe at Manila POW headquarters had ordered Toshino to exterminate any POWs unable to withstand further movement. A shallow grave had been prepared before the trucks arrived at a cemetery south of town. When Lieutenant Toshino and Sergeant Tanoue Suketoshi reached the darkened site, the patients were bound and dragged to the grave's long border. Sergeant Tanoue then drew his sword and decapitated the first seven men. When their heads and bodies failed to fall cleanly into the grave, an irritated Toshino ordered the guard detail to bayonet the remaining patients.

ON THE FOLLOWING DAY, Christmas Eve, the prisoners' stooped and thinning frames converged on San Fernando's vacant main street for a dubious yuletide march. Their destination was the San Fernando train station. The men were upbeat, buoyed by rumors that they were heading back to Bilibid. But at the bomb-cratered train platform, a short line of hot, windowless boxcars awaited. The prisoners grew quiet with dread when Mr. Wada announced that 185 men must board each car.

Even the sadistic Wada could not overcome simple physics: there was not enough space on the train for all the prisoners, crammed in or not. Only when air raid sirens signaled the approach of American bombers did Wada order the remaining prisoners on the platform to mount the cars' rickety ladders and take seats on the rooftops. Two guards were posted with each group of roof riders; they numbered twenty and thirty a car. Bandaged prisoners were instructed to wave their arms and shout if the planes zeroed in on the train.

Despite obvious danger and discomfort, Charles, Barton, and Jack Ferguson felt nothing but gratitude to have won spots on top. Engine smoke and soot blew on them throughout, and it was a cold, hazardous ride, but that was far preferable to another long trip inside the suffocating boxcars.

There were other upsides, too. One was the excellent view of dogfights between American and Japanese planes as the train pulled out of San Fernando, and of the bombing of Clark Field against a magnificent sunset. Smoke plumes from downed Japanese planes wafted skyward in the distance.

The train chugged deep into the night, passing through one darkened barrio after another. Despite the advancing hour on Christmas Eve, local Filipinos gathered and called to them from each train platform: "Merry Chrees-mass, Joe!" As the train rolled through, they tossed bananas, eggs, sugarcane, and mangoes up to the ragged roof riders, and groups of children broke into spontaneous caroling. The prisoners waved and wept, grateful beyond words for the moral support and life-saving offerings.

His body was cold, dirty, and depleted, but his fellow prisoners all recalled that Barton's spirits soared on this particular night. He felt free as air, and his mass of curly, unkempt hair whipped in the wind just as it had when he stuck his head out the Packard window on family drives to the Jersey Shore. His quick, glancing green eyes took in every detail. My God, he said to Charles and Jack, what stories they would have to tell when they got home! This Christmas train, their long camaraderie, the big-hearted Filipinos—still defiant, loyal, and generous to the Americans despite their own privations and long struggle—would make for grand tales in their old age. Tales of faith, sacrifice, generosity, and persistence in the face of seemingly hopeless odds.

This night threw the qualities of a transformed Barton Cross into high relief. His eager fellowship and routine sacrifices had earned him deep respect among his prisoner peers. But Barton believed he had survived the long ordeal only *because* of those sacrifices, not in spite of them—and that's if he ever admitted to sacrificing at all.

His strongest conviction had been the most infectious: that their iron-clad fellowship was their best defense against the worst the Japanese could throw at them. It fortified them all, mentally, physically, and emotionally.

The strength of this indivisible bond had become religion for Barton the prisoner. On this Christmas Eve, the shallow vanities of Barton's former self—that insulated youth of 1941—had long since faded away.

THE ENGINE LURCHED NORTH at the first track switch, away from Manila. If not to Bilibid, then where? They were desperate enough to pray for the despised Cabanatuan, as the train approached the last possible switch that could take them there.

But when the conductor did not oblige at that final split, a new apprehension seized the prisoners. They all knew their Luzon geography by now. Lingayen Gulf, the last remaining Luzon port still in enemy hands, had suddenly become the only possible terminus, which almost certainly meant shipment to Japan.

After seventeen hours and a final belch of choking smoke, the wood-burning engine jerked to a halt at 0400 Christmas morning. For the men on top, the platform sign confirmed their arrival at another town named San Fernando, this one a small coastal village in the La Union Province. The salty report of sea air filled Barton's nostrils—and his memory. For countless summers, detecting that first briny scent through that open Packard window had stirred anticipation of the Jersey Shore's many delights. This morning it brought a dread so great it threatened nausea.

Barton followed his comrades down the boxcar ladder to join gasping prisoners pouring out of the interiors. Discouraged, famished, and chilled to the bone, the reassembled ensigns said little. There was no need to parry over the meaning of this destination. Instead, they reflexively huddled together when ordered to lie down on the cold and crowded platform. A prescient few first snapped up scraps of dried coconut littering the landing and crammed them into their mouths. It was a Christmas morning none who survived would ever forget.

They were rousted at dawn and marched a few kilometers to the perimeter grounds of an abandoned trade school outside the town. Memories of savage thirst always present, the search for water began immediately. All they could locate was a muddy, hand-dug well by the latrine pit. One after another prisoner gorged from the fouled supply after "purifying" it with iodine drops. Potable or not, fear of water deprivation overwhelmed even the most cautious by this point. Without pots or a heat source to boil the water, the revised wisdom was that one might just as well die from typhoid or dysentery as thirst.

One rice ball per man was meted out for Christmas dinner, after which the prisoners surrendered to sleep on the trade school grounds. But no sooner had they dozed off than a Japanese sentry appeared with new orders. They must rise and march to the shore of Lingayen Gulf and await their ship. The sudden, unhappy news was met in turns with shock and angry objections, followed by a flash of violence near the rice supplies. A small but determined group of prisoners overpowered their own colleagues guarding the food and clawed what they could, spilling precious supplies before being brought under control. Military discipline within the prisoner ranks had disintegrated once again. It was no match for the primal powers of hunger and fear.

After the melee, the overweary prisoners formed up in customary columns of four and stumbled onto the shore road. It was a breezy, pastoral hike, in stark contrast to their demoralized state. As they walked past moonlit hedges of flowering hibiscus and mango trees, they snatched what they could, gobbling down fruit, flowers, and leaves alike.

Evidence of the looming peril grew with every step.

"The march was about two miles," Major John Wright recalled, "over a rough road with bare feet . . . Oil storage tanks had been blasted to bits, buildings knocked down, and there were many bomb craters . . . Japanese . . . beach defenses—pillboxes, barbed wire, foxholes—all indicated they expected an invasion any hour. We wondered anew whether it would come soon enough to save us."

★   ★   ★

THE PRISONERS WERE HALTED at a windblown spit of sand and ordered to sit. A menacing Lingayen Gulf churned before them. It was just past midnight, and the moon over the water illuminated as many anchored Japanese vessels as it did ruined masts and sunken ship stacks breaking the surface. The men burrowed into the sand to protect from the stiff gulf winds as trucks, horses, ammunition carts, and troops hurried past on the road behind them.

Manny Lawton wrote: "With our bony frames molded into the soft sand . . . it was more comfortable than . . . the cement tennis court. Still, we shivered and shook . . . Two men died that night . . . By midmorning [the heat] was intense. Nothing stood up to the sun but a thin growth of stunted brown grass."

As on the tennis court, no sooner did the night's cold give way to daybreak than they were tormented by tropical sun beating down from every angle. There was the added agony of their bare skin on blistering-hot sand, and thirst again reached crisis proportions. Colonel Beecher implored Mr. Wada for water, to no avail.

However, Wada did relent to Beecher's suggestion that the prisoners be allowed to rotate into the gulf to bathe blisters and allow the salt water to absorb into thirsty pores. The system worked until one water-crazed officer dashed in and began gulping seawater. Just as the guards lifted their rifles and took aim, the man's fellow POWs dragged him back onto the beach.

When the equatorial sun slipped behind a pink-and-purple reef of clouds on the horizon, its majesty was no doubt lost on the prisoners. To them, sunset meant only one thing: the imminent arrival of the night winds. In this manner—searing by day and freezing by night—the prisoners spent forty-eight hours on the sands of Lingayen Gulf.

On December 27 the moon and Orion were high in the night sky when the prisoners were rousted and led across a narrow strip of land to a wooden pier. The transition went relatively smoothly until Mr. Wada ordered the men to board two barges alongside the pier, knocking hard against the pilings. Both vessels were fifteen feet below, and there were no ladders. The prisoners hung back in fear.

"*Speedo! Speedo!*" exhorted Lieutenant Toshino. At this, Wada ordered the guards to employ their rifle butts and push the prisoners off the dock. The result was a fresh round of sprains, broken bones, and bruises. Several missed the barges entirely. One officer was pulled lifeless from the tossing waters. The guards laughed.

At first light, the packed barges finally inched out into Lingayen Gulf toward two Japanese freighters. *Enoura Maru* was lettered on one, *Brazil Maru* on the other. The ships' captains seemed as anxious as Lieutenant Toshino to join the departing convoy before the inevitable return of American planes. "*Speedo! Speedo! Speedo!*" The guards waved clubs and rifles to expedite boarding. Neither ship bore Red Cross or other protective markings.

Colonel Beecher led the larger draft of 1,070 prisoners—including most of the ensigns—onto *Enoura Maru*. Barton and Charles were grateful that Beecher had remained in charge of their group and not diverted to the other freighter. If the Japanese respected any of them, they respected Curtis Beecher.

They filed past hundreds of wounded Japanese soldiers on *Enoura Maru*'s upper decks before the long prisoner queue began another cautious descent into a deep cargo hold. This time a pungent wave of ammonia fumes stopped them in their tracks. The hold was covered in fresh horse manure.

Major John Wright wrote: "[T]he filth was disgusting. The ship had brought cavalry [horses] to Luzon and we loaded into the hold [right after] . . . Scattered in with the manure was millet and oats . . . This was picked out grain by grain and eaten."

Some men shoveled the manure aside, others, beyond such a task, simply lay down in the dung. Large flies covered their mouths, faces, and eyes. But soon the prisoners were distracted from the present misery by a bigger problem: explosions rocked the ship's starboard side. *One. Two. Three.*

"Navy submarine torpedoes," said Lieutenant David Nash. The seasoned naval officer recognized the tenor of the blasts, which narrowly missed them. The convoy quickly hastened out of harbor and pointed north, hugging the Philippine coastline for protection for as long as possible.

On *Enoura Maru*, the prisoners slipped further into degradation. "We were dirty, bearded, and full of diarrhea," Carl Engelhart wrote. "We ate from our hats, from pieces of cloth, from our hands . . . A handful of rice clutched against a sweaty naked chest, so the flies could not get it, eating like an animal with befouled hands."

"Starving men forget discipline, forget honor, and forget self-respect," wrote John Wright.

Manny Lawton put it more bluntly: "Only survival mattered."

On New Year's Eve—day five of the voyage—a riot broke out in the hold. Servers were suddenly punched and thrown aside while distributing food in the semidarkness. The mob of hunger-crazed prisoners bit and slapped their way to the buckets, and then clawed at their contents. Tubs of precious soup and tea—the most sustenance offered since departing Leyte—were spilled in the melee. The raiders got their fill, while others got nothing. By the time *Enoura Maru* made anchor at Takao, Formosa, later that night, twenty-one more prisoners had died.

WITHOUT EXPLANATION, THE PAIR of prison ships lay at anchor for several days in Takao Harbor. Fervent hopes that their arrival at Formosa would mean fresh sustenance from imagined shore supplies faded quickly. Mr. Wada repeatedly denied prisoner pleas for additional food and water. "American submarines sink Japanese supply ships. No food for you," he replied.

The prisoners wallowed and despaired in the fetid hold; four or five more men died each day. They barely stirred at the intermittent buzz of planes overhead. Would American planes strike this ship, too? More than a few prayed they would. The men's growing desperation for food and water mattered far more than the rat-a-tat of antiaircraft fire from the deck.

Not only had swearing, fighting, and incredible filth become the norm, but disease was now sharply on the rise. Dysentery patients were moved in increasing numbers to "the hospital area," a planked platform directly above the hold. The helpless patients' uncontrollable diarrhea dripped through the floorboards onto the prisoners in "the pit" below. On January 5 John Wright wrote: "Two more deaths last night, two more today. Just waiting, wondering, and praying."

In the second week of January, it finally seemed the ship was being readied for departure. The number of deaths on both ships allowed for consolidation, and the *Brazil Maru* prisoners were moved to *Enoura Maru*. The Japanese also laid in new supplies, including several burlap sacks of sugar. A large tanker was brought alongside them as well, signaling the assembly of a convoy. But the new arrangements brought new troubles.

Stored sugar within feet of starving men was too great a temptation for Charles Armour and others. Despite stern Japanese warnings, Charles broke open one of the bags and gobbled down handful after handful. A stubble of sugar crystals covered the lower half of his face. Emboldened, other prisoners followed suit. Either too honorable or too fearful of reprisal, Barton withdrew from the scene.

After spying loose sugar at the foot of the hold's ladder, a passing guard called out to his superiors in urgent staccato. Seconds later, an angry Mr. Wada appeared at the top of the ladder. "You will surrender the thieves!" he demanded. No food or water until this was done, he warned. The silence that ensued surprised no one. Experience had taught them that deliverance of anyone under such circumstances meant certain torture and likely execution.

Colonel Beecher made a plea for volunteers to step forward on behalf of the whole, promising extra rations. After a weighted silence, a tired but resolute voice called out. "I'll go." A sea of bodies parted with deference as a man named Hannenkrant, an army medic, headed for the ladder. Then another voice rang out. All eyes settled on a young British sergeant named

Trapp. A pall of shame hung over the rest of them as the two brave men disappeared up the ladder.

Miraculously, the pair returned within an hour after only being cuffed and slapped. The prisoners speculated that their captors had spared them out of respect for their raw, and by now rare, courage.

At 0930 on January 9, a relative calm prevailed in the hold as breakfast was distributed. The prisoners were settling into their meal just as a loud whine of diving aircraft shattered the quiet. There was a burst of running and shouting above them, then the rapid *ack-ack* from the antiaircraft guns.

ON THIS SAME MORNING, General MacArthur's ground troops came ashore in full force at Luzon's Lingayen Gulf. As with MacArthur's mid-December Mindoro landings, Admiral Halsey's Task Force 38 was summoned for air support and the beachhead was secured before the day was through. Halsey's carrier pilots began their sorties early that morning, targeting multiple sites from which the enemy might attack Allied ships unloading in Lingayen Gulf. Airfields in southern Formosa were their primary objectives, but the airmen also prized any shipping in Formosan harbors, particularly tankers.

At 0915 on January 9, target coordinator Commander Robert Riera— and his same Air Group Eleven that had decimated *Oryoko Maru* in December—sortied from the USS *Hornet* in a tidy line. Carrying 250- and 500-pound bombs, the twelve fighter planes rounded the tip of southern Formosa in as many minutes. After climbing through tier after tier of scattered clouds, they broke into the clear at 6,500 feet. Takao Harbor spread out like an aerial photograph beneath them. It was "the only spot so favored on the coast," Riera noted in his after-action report. "Twenty-five ships were counted in Takao's inner harbor, more in its outer perimeter, a bomber's dream. Some [ships] were moored in pairs, presenting unusually attractive targets."

One after another, each plane went into a 5,000-foot dive and dropped its load onto the oil tanker and the *Enoura Maru* next to it. "Four good hits were observed, with others probable . . . antiaircraft [fire] moderate. The most successful antishipping strike flown by this squadron to date," Riera boasted.

THE FORWARD HOLD AND engine room received direct hits. The bomb intended for the second hold—where most of the prisoners were eating breakfast—exploded alongside the ship, shredding the starboard hull. Beams and hatch covers crashed down, and torrents of steel splinters and shrapnel sprayed into the hold.

The result was a smoke-filled hell pit of ripped flesh, severed limbs, and crushed skulls. David Nash recalled the horror: "Before it could register in our minds, we were being jarred by falling bombs . . . All around us were killed and wounded . . . A near miss had made a sieve of the side of the ship. One sight haunted me for days. That was a man whose skull was laid wide open and yet he breathed for hours. About that time, I discovered that my leg was bleeding from a deep gouge. I don't know when I received it."

Ken Wheeler also recounted the scene: "When the dust and fire cleared away, I was stunned [by] the carnage . . . Over 300 in our group were killed outright. Almost everyone was wounded . . . The hatches, hatch covers, and massive plank . . . had been blown into the hold on top of us."

Those not crushed to death were pinned beneath the fallen beams.

There was a stunned silence in the hold after the attack, as dazed survivors took stock. After the initial trauma, those able to move started toward their wounded comrades. Barton was in shock following the blast, and his head ached, but his injuries were nothing compared with those around him. The macabre scene unfolded like a soundless nightmare. Ensigns Bob Wuest and Jack Ferguson were both mortally wounded and covered in blood. Without immediate assistance from the Japanese, they—and hundreds of other wounded—would surely die. Barton joined the other able-bodied who were crafting crude tourniquets and splints while they waited for medics.

Nothing was heard from the Japanese for hours after the blast, and the situation rapidly deteriorated. Finally, Colonel Olson, with his forearm blown off and a rag tied above the elbow, mounted the ladder and called out for Mr. Wada. He appeared after several long minutes and glared down at Olson like an angry chimera. "I ask nothing for myself," Olson began boldly, "but these men are dying. In . . . the name of the Gods that you believe in, can't you do something for them? They will die without bandages or medicine or food and water."

Mr. Wada curled his lips, baring a mouthful of yellow, protruding teeth. "They were your planes that bombed ship," he sneered. "They were your planes, and they have killed our men too. We don't care if you die." With that, he disappeared.

At Wada's departure, the only sound below was the weeping and moaning of grown men who had lost every last hope. But then another voice called out—urgent, steady, and clear. Every man recognized the speaker. "Listen to me, men! You must listen to me!" It was the deep, resonant voice of Father Cummings, the Catholic chaplain who had earned universal authority the hard way: by going through every inch of the agony with them. Some had been with "Father Bill" since Bataan; others gratefully remembered his prayers and counsel at various prison camps, and all of them during the *Oryoko Maru* ordeal. The hold went silent as men of all faiths strained to listen.

The beloved priest who at Bataan had declared, "There are no atheists in foxholes," did not follow with a plea for faith. Instead, Father Cummings simply began praying aloud in his comfortingly familiar tone: "Our Father, who art in Heaven, hallowed be thy name . . ." Some men murmured the Lord's Prayer along with him; others followed with closed eyes and clasped hands. They listened as never before.

"Father Cummings's prayer," wrote Sidney Stewart, "floated like a benediction . . . caressing every one of us."

"It penetrated our very souls," wrote David Nash.

As if by celestial intervention, Japanese guards shortly thereafter began lowering bandages, bottles of iodine, mercurochrome, and buckets of water into the hold. Encouraged, survivors started to reorganize and function; some dressed wounds with the new supplies, while others cleared away debris and began the grisly task of stacking bodies by the hatch.

Two more days would pass before the Japanese sent down working parties to remove the dead; an excruciating process that itself took another two days. Thirty bodies at a time were loaded onto cargo nets attached to a cable, and then winched out of the hold and deposited onto an awaiting barge. The bodies jumped grotesquely as the crane operator jerked the cable for amusement, laughing as bloody pieces of flesh and body parts splattered and slid on the barge's cambered surface.

"So passed an additional four hundred," Beecher lamented. "For the eight hundred or so men [remaining], though more dead than alive, the ordeal was far from over."

IT WAS DURING THIS postbombing grimness at Takao, Formosa, that Barton Cross—separated from his closest comrades either by death, incapacitation, or unknown shipboard circumstances—teamed up with another ensign, one he only came to know after returning to Cabanatuan from Davao Penal Colony. Like Barton, "Bob" Granston was reeling from loss. Chuck Wilkins had died aboard *Oryoko Maru*. The two Washington natives had been best friends at the University of Washington at Seattle and signed up for the Navy Supply Corps together. Barton and Bob forged a bond through a paradoxical combination of need, shared grief, inborn optimism, and the will to survive.

Granston wrote Helen Cross of their survival pact aboard *Enoura Maru*: "It was from this point forward that Bart and I joined forces and shared our fortunes. And we did, in every respect. We slept when we could sleep together to keep one another warm, we evenly divided every morsel of our food and every drop of our water. I am sure you can see why Bart meant so much to me."

All prisoners knew that "buddying" greatly improved survival odds. It had become protocol by this point. Prisoners who withdrew from others, whether due to exhaustion, delirium, or irreversible misery, did not last long.

Over the next twenty days, there would be no secrets between Bart Cross and Bob Granston. The two men came to know as much about each other as any of their respective friends, lovers, or family members had ever known. Indulging in the continuum of stories that had shaped their young lives up to those frigid, dark hours was the only remaining salve that could not be wrested away. With their tacit pact sealed, they moved together to the final ship that would carry them to Japan.

> Barton was a very close friend of mine, and I shall
> always cherish that friendship born in a common struggle.
>
> Robert Granston to Helen Cross

ON JANUARY 14, THE shrunken prisoner band—shivering, filthy, bandaged, and emaciated—moved from the crippled *Enoura Maru* back to the *Brazil Maru*, which had not been damaged in the American air attack. Those who died in the difficult transfer were thrown overboard. The *Brazil Maru* then weighed anchor and pressed north in a twelve-ship convoy. Inconceivably, on this voyage, the men suffered their greatest hardship since departing Manila.

> During this last trip, food and water were almost non-
> existent. We all became weaker every day. Many went to sleep
> at night and never woke up the next morning. They were
> just simply too weak from cold and lack of food and water to
> carry on.
>
> Charles Armour to Helen Cross

* ★ ★

THE SHIP SAILED INTO the coldest Asian winter in forty years. Icy drafts whooshed through the hold as they reached cruising speed—a cruel harbinger of what lay ahead. On the first night out of Takao, twenty men died. *Brazil Maru*'s daily death rate rose unabated after that.

Through a winter scrum each morning, just enough light slanted belowdecks to permit a body count of those who had passed away overnight. The dead were first stripped of desperately needed clothing and then piled in a passageway. After each morning count, they were removed to the deck and buried at sea. Only in this manner was initial overcrowding on the third ship relieved. Day and night, chaplains murmured last rites to the point of monotony.

Barton's resilience slowly ebbed aboard the *Brazil Maru*. Less than a day after Bob Wuest's wounded, wasted corpse was cinched and spiraled out of the hold, Jack Ferguson followed in the same manner. One after another, the haunting remains of the dearest friends Barton had ever known—the men he'd bolstered and who had bolstered him—twisted naked and lifeless out of sight.

Until Father Cummings himself died, the good chaplain asked for a moment of silence every evening so that he might offer a brief prayer. His voice grew progressively fainter and weaker until he could no longer speak his comforting refrain: "Eternal rest grant unto them, O Lord, and let perpetual light shine upon them. May the souls of the faithful departed, through the mercy of God, rest in peace. Amen."

Despite the increasingly nightmarish environs, "Bart" and "Bob" always retreated to the transformative refuge of conversation. They moved through the annals of their respective lives—stories large and small, successes and failures, love interests, and their families and homes. Even as hollowed-out men all around scrambled like rodents for the tiniest edible or spoonful of water, even as the ship dodged submarine fire and pitched in the high seas, even as they wallowed in a hold slick with filth and disease and shivered in subfreezing temperatures, the two men indulged in the simple joy of story-telling, sourced entirely from their pasts.

> I came to know all of you, intimately, for Bart introduced each of you to me. We swapped endless yarns and family stories. Bart described you all in detail and never once gave up hope he would see you again . . . In turn, I paraded my family life before his eyes. He was fascinated by my family, certainly less prominent than the Crosses, but it is a warm, close family. There were so many stories he wanted to hear over and over again . . . By so doing we passed many long hours and forgot for long stretches of time the hopelessness of our situation.
>
> Robert Granston to Helen Cross

THERE WAS A CADENCE to their yarn swappings. One would start with a story about a time, a place, or a life episode. A corresponding chronicle from the other would follow, related in some way to the initial story. Characters from their respective pasts burst out of dusty sterling frames and old leather albums they'd long since left behind. One elaborately rendered scene after another hovered above them like guardian spirits.

Granston's childhood vignettes were in stark relief to Barton's. His renderings were of an alluring world of rural western life on a small farm outside Seattle, Washington. Barton was mesmerized. With all its formalities and unvoiced tensions, Lilac Hedges was galaxies away from the open and affectionate traditions of the Granston family farm. His heart swelled with vicarious pleasure over freedoms he had never even dreamed of.

The simple abundance of a boisterous Granston dinner was a Barton favorite. With each sentence, Bob filled out the dreamscape of an unadorned farm kitchen full of heavenly smells and happy faces, a weathered, wide-board table groaning with freshly harvested delights—all enjoyed amid lively conversation, pea-shooting, and frequent laughter. Barton sat rapt, knees to chest, like a child. He salivated over the menu, but also the textured riches of a raucous, informal, and intensely loving home.

Barton's stories centered on growing up in New Jersey, but also described ventures into New York City, the stuff of dreamy escapes for Bob Granston. Barton waxed on his early taste of independence at Christ School, and his surprising and enduring epiphanies there.

He also told, with a weakening smile, of his truncated baseball and singing careers, both of which reached their zenith in prison camp. Then there was the almost–love of his life, a girl named Eve that he'd met at Pearl Harbor before setting sail for Manila.

Bob Granston was a keen observer, even in his own fragile state. He saw that all Barton's childhood and teen recollections had a similar subtext: of being prodded to become something he was not. Nor did it take Granston long to figure out that the Cross clan hailed from a higher social order than his own, or to grasp that material wealth was no guarantee of happiness.

But despite their differences, or perhaps because of them, the two men bonded like alloyed steel. They talked to exhaustion each evening. The power of such unburdening was surely a comfort to Barton. The simple exercise of seeing his brief life through the compassionate eyes of another both resolved its disappointments and affirmed its value. Only when the final half-light withdrew from the hold each evening and their wasting brethren grew indistinct did Bart and Bob draw close for warmth and doze off.

IN THE LAST FRIGID week of January, Barton reached the limits of human endurance. Snow swirling into the hold could neither revive him nor cool his burning forehead. Granston urged him on by the hour, but a triple assault of dysentery, pneumonia, and infection springing from a hidden head wound—likely obscured by a wild mat of filthy hair—joined forces with exposure, starvation, and thirst to immobilize him.

Barton now depended upon Granston like an infant, and Granston did not disappoint. He divided whatever sustenance came his way—every sip of water and infinitesimal issue of rice was split and shared. He would raise Barton's head, open his mouth, and spoon it in, dose by tiny dose. But by the time they arrived at Moji Port in Japan on January 28, Barton was drifting in and out of consciousness.

I know I have not spared you much--I have gone into great detail that might well have been kept from the Cross family. But your letter was a plea for information (good or bad) about Bart. It is in answer to that plea and my own love for Bart that I have written of all the conditioning circumstances that led directly and indirectly to his death.

Robert Granston to Helen Cross

WHEN *BRAZIL MARU* DOCKED at Moji on January 29, a contingent of Japanese military personnel boarded the ship and peered into the hold. At the sight of the five-foot-high corpse pile, they turned and departed in shock. Hours later, the prisoners were instructed to organize in alphabetical order to receive an issue of clothing.

At the call of their name, each prisoner went up to the deck to receive an issue of green flannel Japanese military uniforms, shoes, and woolen overcoats. With Barton unable to sit up, much less stand or talk, Bob Granston made for the ladder when "Cross" was called. He returned to the hold with the chilly garb, damp to the touch and smelling vaguely of mildew and cigarette smoke. He proceeded to dress his friend, still clinging to life but in a feverish stupor.

In due course, Bob's own name was called and he again scaled the ladder to the deck. But when he reached for his clothing issue, Mr. Wada squinted hard at him, then whipped into a fury. Believing he had caught Granston attempting to hoard clothing, Wada barked an unintelligible order, prompting the nearby guard to pummel and punch Bob until he stumbled backward into the hold, where he lay stunned and bleeding as the clothing muster droned on.

On January 30, 500 survivors of the original 1,619 prisoner draft that had departed Manila forty-nine days earlier queued up to debark onto Japanese soil. After the final indignities of head-to-toe disinfectant dousing and the insertion of glass rods up their rectums to test for dysentery, they exited the ship.

Scores of incapacitated were carried off first and laid on the dock. It will never be known if Barton was aware that, in his case, the task was performed by Charles Armour. Stooped and grunting under the weight, a determined Charles gently placed Barton on the dock and then crumbled to a seated position next to him.

Japanese medical examiners, visibly shocked by the group's condition, began their assessments, moving with their clipboards quietly among the men on the cold wooden platform. Their superiors, meanwhile, deliberated over what to do with these diseased and emaciated prisoners of war.

Charles sat glum and silent next to his incognizant friend, waiting his turn to be examined. He had aged dramatically over his imprisonment. The distinctive lope had turned to a halting gait, thanks to beriberi and other assaults on Charles's body. A receding veil of thin blond strands bared a pate dark with freckles, and his once-strong Saxonesque face was hollow, lined, and expressionless. All fierceness and resistance were gone. Back when there was energy and cause for laughter, Charles would joke that for every hair he lost, Barton seemed to gain ten; even now, Barton's resting head was an unruly mass of brown waves.

Remorse rolled over Charles, or perhaps it was regret that he had taken this good and true friend too much for granted for too long. He watched his friend's chest rise and fall, rise and fall, grateful now for every breath Barton drew. He closed the top button on the Japanese overcoat that Bob Granston had put on him, and pulled the collar up around Barton's ears.

How Barton would have laughed at the sight of himself wearing a Japanese uniform, Charles thought. "Over my dead body!" He would have laughed that big, ironic, endearing laugh and thrown his head back the way he always did. As if in response to Charles's musings, Barton inhaled deeply and released an encouraging sigh. But following that exhale, there were no more.

Charles looked on in disbelief, choking back tears. Here was Charles Armour—so willing to take his own life three years earlier, placing others' lives at risk in the process—still alive. And here lay Barton Cross, who had protected him at every turn—not only from the Japanese, but also from himself—dead.

With a spark of the old Charles, he gritted his teeth at the approaching Japanese medical technician. But he did not resist when the gloved examiner crouched down to feel for Barton's pulse, first on his wrist, then on his neck. Detecting none, the examiner unbuttoned the overcoat and turned Barton's body over for a closer look, showing particular interest in the back of his head. After scrawling a few notes on a pad, he moved on to the next case.

It would be sixty-four years before that Japanese medical examiner's findings—slipped untranslated into Barton Cross's long-archived naval personnel file—would be discovered, translated, and the dual causes of his demise revealed.

Beside the date January 30, 1945, was written: "Acute enteritis and death from bomb wound to the head."

EPILOGUE

IN 2009 I REOPENED the long-closed inquiry into my Uncle Barton's death. I requested all documents bearing his name from the International Committee of the Red Cross in Geneva—still the reigning global authority on *prisonniers de guerre*. A year later and after a payment of 100 Swiss francs, the documents arrived. I also procured Barton's naval personnel file from the military records archive in St. Louis.

Both sets of records contained an official copy of Barton's death certificate. It was dated September 14, 1945, curiously, nearly two weeks after the formal Japanese surrender and more than seven months after his passing. The given cause of death was "acute enteritis" (dysentery). But this same ailment, I discovered, was cited as the killer of hundreds of other expired prisoners pulled from *Brazil Maru* on its January 30, 1945, arrival at Moji, Japan. How did they know how these men died so long after the fact? Virtually all their death certificates were created that September, seven months later, and most by the same bilingual Japanese scribe. His name was

"Huryojohokyoku," a very recent hire at General MacArthur's occupation headquarters in Tokyo.

It was impossible to discern on what medical basis this postmortem diagnosis was made. But after reviewing volumes of archives, it appears to have been generic shorthand for a presumptive mix of dysentery, starvation, dehydration, exposure, and unimaginable cruelty. Barton's personnel file, however, contained an additional clue; there was one Japanese document that, unlike every other in his file, had no companion translation. Locating a bilingual Japanese national willing to translate that wartime document was challenging. But I succeeded thanks to the assistance of a family member who works with a team of young Japanese professionals at Patagonia.

The document was a routine prisoner tracking record maintained by Barton's captors. Its first entry was the date Barton was seized from Sternberg Hospital in Manila. The last entry was dated January 30, 1945; the place, Moji, Japan. Between the two, every ailment, medical treatment, and prison camp relocation had been dated and entered with chilling Japanese efficiency. So startling was the translation's final entry, however, that I sought a second translation from an independent source: this time by linguists at the Tokyo office of a prominent US law firm.

The second translation corroborated the first. Entitled "Other Information," the ailment acute enteritis was indeed cited, presumably by the Japanese medic examining prisoners on the Moji dock—both dead and alive. But it was written in a sequence that altered its import entirely: "Acute enteritis, and death from bomb wound to head." Helen Cross had been right all along.

Was this significant omission simply a military snafu, or was it a case of intentional deception intended to hide a friendly fire incident? How is it that this never-translated prisoner record had not been discovered until now? Why hadn't my father, who had pursued the case for four years after the war, found it?

First of all, postwar mishandling of prisoner records and other wartime documents, both by the Japanese in the weeks before their surrender and by Allied occupiers in the months and years afterward, has been uniformly described as deplorable. Thousands of records were destroyed, misfiled, or lost by one party or the other. Secondly, it was not until after 1952, which marked the end of the Allied occupation of Japan, that thousands of war-record-stuffed file cabinets began to be repatriated to the United States. My own conclusion is that Bill Mott's search, which lasted until 1949, ended before the document surfaced in Barton's long-archived personnel file—which probably occurred sometime in the 1950s.

That scenario notwithstanding, the following statistic has never been formally acknowledged by the US government: of the 21,039 POW deaths that occurred aboard Japanese transports during World War II, most were the result of unwitting attacks by either Allied submarines or war planes.

FOR MORE THAN THREE years after the war ended, my grandmother Helen continued to fire off inquiries to political and military powers in Washington, demanding more information about Barton's death. Over time, however, responses to her letters ebbed. Just as fighter aircraft were dumped into the sea, tanks were left to rust on distant Pacific islands, and warships were cut up for scrap, Helen's fierce salvos were quietly filed away.

While waiting for answers that never came, she traveled to Barton's alma mater, Christ School in Arden, North Carolina, to establish the Barton Cross Memorial Scholarship. Deprived of her son's adult years, she chose to memorialize Barton's adolescence by honoring individuals who "best exemplified his qualities of character, citizenship, and leadership." Barton had developed these attributes during his time at Christ School, and it helped him—and helped him help others—endure a long and harsh imprisonment.

Every spring thereafter, until her passing in 1967, Helen made the 750-mile drive to Arden to announce the scholarship winner at the commencement-eve banquet. The recipient was always a member of the junior class whose senior year tuition was to be paid with the award. Helen was known to approach the lectern quietly and make eye contact with each boy as she recalled her son before the hushed assembly.

"Shortly before leaving for the Philippines," she would begin, "Barton spoke lovingly of Christ School, saying that his most cherished ideals were forged through his training and associations there. He also asked that, if he did not return, a cross bearing his name be placed in the school's chapel yard." While that final request has not been fulfilled, a granite memorial was erected in 2011 near the campus chapel bearing his name, along with other alumni killed in foreign wars.

BENNY—OR UNCLE BERT, our own affectionate name for him— met and married Helen Lacey after the war. Over five decades of marital bliss followed. But Benny had another postwar love: preservation of the USS *Enterprise*, both the ship itself and its historic and heroic naval legacy. While most soldiers and sailors who fought in World War II wanted nothing more than to bury those memories and get on with their lives, Benny wanted just the opposite.

He published numerous postwar essays on Pacific naval warfare and firsthand accounts of iconic *Enterprise* battles, both critical sources for this book. He was also instrumental in setting up the USS *Enterprise* (CV-6) Association and helped lead the effort to establish the carrier as a floating museum. It was to be located on the Potomac River near the Washington Monument.

The vision had an auspicious beginning. The most decorated warship in American naval history received a celebrity homecoming in October 1945. One hundred and one fighter planes kicked off the biggest Navy Day celebration on record as they escorted *Enterprise* up the Hudson River at sunrise and into New York Harbor. The thundering flyover had awakened an entire city by the time she tied up at Pier 26.

New York headlines competed to memorialize the occasion: "The

Pride of the Navy Comes Home in Dawn's Early Light"; "The Unsinkable *Enterprise* Enters Harbor as Bands Play"; "Hunter, Home from the Kill"; and "The Big E, Fightin-est Carrier—In!"

Fireboats sprayed gushers, bands played, military units marched down the avenues, and huge crowds of navy Waves and Red Cross girls gathered to cheer the *Enterprise* crew—who obligingly lined the rails and cheered back. Long queues of patriots and their children snaked up her gangplank in good and bad weather, all wanting to board the famous carrier they had been reading about since 1941. They climbed into her turrets, ran their hands along her gun barrels, and toured her cavernous hangars, messes, and wardrooms. Before exiting the ship, they invariably crouched down to touch the grooved Douglas fir planking of her revered flight deck.

On Navy Day proper, the crew traded grateful salutes with President Harry Truman. I can only imagine Benny's pride when *Enterprise*'s night fighter group growled up the Hudson at dusk and put on a show for some four to six million spectators, including an estimated 1.5 million from New Jersey, who lined the opposite banks for miles. The planes roared over the anchored ships in salute formation and then circled back with lights blazing in a V-for-victory formation. Their finale was greeted with deafening cheers—a third and final flyover was in a glorious "E" formation in honor of their mother ship.

Following Navy Day festivities, Truman promptly approved Navy Secretary James Forrestal's request that the *Enterprise* be "permanently enshrined in an appropriate location as a visible symbol of American valor and tenacity in war, and of our will to fight all enemies who assail us."

The president's approval seemed to ensure the carrier's preservation, but over time, budget concerns grew and private fundraising foundered. In 1958, after languishing twelve years at a Bayonne, New Jersey, shipyard, the *Enterprise* was slated for the scrap heap. Benny was devastated.

Several symbolic features of the ship, however, were preserved for posterity. The *Enterprise* bell rests at the entrance to the Naval Academy's

Bancroft Hall and is rung only after midshipmen victories over West Point. The battle flag flown from her tripod mast during the harrowing Battle of Santa Cruz is on permanent display at the Aviation Museum in Pensacola, Florida. Her sixteen-foot-long stern plate, a massive steel work bearing the ship's name in raised letters, greets visitors to Veterans' Memorial Park in River Vale, New Jersey, and her two-story-high anchor marks the entrance to the Washington Navy Yard.

Unfortunately, the plan to crown the new Annapolis football stadium with *Enterprise*'s Sky Control tower was cancelled due to maintenance estimates on its outdated steel construction. But happily, the promised honor was upheld. A cement replica, named *Enterprise* Tower, was erected there instead.

IN 2012, I TRAVELED to England to meet Benny's daughter, Jeanne Marie. I had never met my cousin (who had taken on the nickname Mara) because she moved to England when I was very young. Over scones and a pot of Earl Grey tea, Mara shared difficult wartime memories that still pained, even in her late seventies. She remembered Benny's long absences, and then his homecoming, shortly after which their home in Bethesda burned down. "Sleaford Place," she shuddered. "Terrible."

An accomplished equestrian, Mara said she left home in her late teens and made a living exercising horses owned by a series of wealthy patrons. One of these, a British doctor, became her husband. Dr. and Mrs. Hodgson had no children, but instead dedicated their lives to British dressage and their beloved thoroughbreds. Benny visited Mara and Dr. Hodgson often at their home in Surrey, renewing their bond and healing old scars. Their visits were long, warm, and conversation filled. This, of course, was the joyful and hoped-for outcome that had populated Benny's dreams aboard the wartime *Enterprise*.

Last Christmas, I received a package bearing a British postmark. Inside was a small wrapped gift: Benny's 1930 Annapolis class ring. Mara's enclosed note thanked me again for my visit, saying it had been an important catharsis. Now widowed, she had sold her home in Surrey, she said, and was planning to travel abroad for an indefinite period. She asked that the ring remain in our family forever.

MY FATHER WAS IN Manila in September 1945 when he learned that Barton would not be returning. He contacted the Navy Casualty Branch at the Pentagon to notify them that he would travel immediately to Lilac Hedges to break the difficult news himself—per his 1942 instructions to that office. When he learned that the Casualty Branch had already notified the family by letter, he cancelled his travel plan. Instead of returning home to crushing sadness and certain anger, Bill stayed put and began the long and complicated investigation into Barton's death and the search for his remains.

Four years later, the search yielded results. An army recovery team had discovered a mass grave near Moji Harbor in 1946. These unknowns had been removed to another site, and then to a third location in 1949, at which point they were positively identified. The long-awaited news reached Bill via a cryptic memorandum from the US Army quartermaster at Tokyo after a lengthy stopover at the Bureau of Naval Personnel in Washington.

```
Subject: Cross, Arthur B., Jr., Ens., Identification of
remains


The remains of Unknowns X-385 through X-444, cremated
in a communal urn, British Commonwealth War Cemetery,
Yokohama, Japan, formerly interred at the USAF Mausoleum
#1, Honshu, Japan, have been identified as the recoverable
remains of 302 Allied personnel, one of whom is the subject
named decedent.
```

It is unclear how X-385 through X-444—which would seem to denote 59 Unknowns—came to equal 302 individuals, but at least after four years of searching, Barton's final resting place had been confirmed. Helen and Arthur declined to travel to Japan to view the site; this was left to my father, who promised to take photographs, in what must have been an awkward exchange. In May 1949, he boarded a military transport for the long trans-Pacific flight.

There were a number of familiar stops along the way, likely in connection with his official duties at the time. The itinerary included Midway, Guam, Saipan, Okinawa, and Manila, all postwar American military bases. I frequently imagine him on this somber mission—reflecting back on the amphibians' tear across the Pacific—as his plane lowered through the clouds toward those once hotly contested atolls.

In Tokyo, MacArthur's SCAP headquarters provided a car and driver that took him the twenty-five miles to Yokohama, a journey replete with scenes of a rebuilding country and a populace bent on erasing its belligerent war personality from national memory. When he arrived at the cherry-blossom-adorned British Commonwealth Cemetery of the Allied War Dead, Bill retrieved his camera and looped the brown leather strap around his neck.

The dreaded destination was visible from hundreds of yards away: a large, square, marble columbarium flanked by fields of graves on three sides and topped with a towering white cross. He walked past saluting sentries and line after line of headstones bearing familiar American, English, and Australian surnames. Inside the shrine, he faced a single interior adornment: a polished metal urn anchored in a rectangular marble pedestal.

Above it was etched:

In the urn below rest the ashes of 333 sailors, soldiers and airmen of the British Commonwealth, the United States of America and the Kingdom of the Netherlands who died as prisoners of war in Japan. The names of 232 are inscribed on these walls. The identity of their 51 comrades is unknown. There be of them that have left their name behind that their praises might

be reported, and some there be which have no memorial. But their righ-
teousness hath not been forgotten and their glory shall not be blotted out.

Long rows of names were engraved on the facing walls—some very recently. Since the listings were organized by service and country rather than
alphabetically, Bill had to first locate the US Navy insignia, beneath which
he read through lengthy columns of surnames. Peterson, Church, Good-
paster, Conover, Weeks, Magnusan, Murchison, Austin, Gardner, Butler,
McGee, Baker . . . And then, finally, there it was: Arthur Barton Cross Jr.,
Ensign, USN, age 25.

Did he reach up and run his fingers along the sharply etched letters before surrendering to overwhelming guilt and sorrow? Whatever the answer
to that question, my father took advantage of several opportunities in his
life to redeem that loss. In many respects, both his professional and personal postwar lives were parallel progressions toward honoring his brother's sacrifice and ensuring that he had not died in vain.

IN 1946, COMMANDER BILL Mott became chief of the navy's International Law Branch and Foreign Claims Office. In this capacity, he served
as a delegate to the International Red Cross Conference in Stockholm. I
cannot imagine any more productive an outlet for a grieving brother of a
perished prisoner of war. In Bill's work as a conference delegate, he played a
direct hand in reforming the 1929 Geneva Convention regarding the treatment of war prisoners. Working to ensure that future POWs would not suffer as Barton and his colleagues had—and would live to come home—was
both redemptive and a powerful palliative.

Any signatory to the revised and greatly expanded Articles would be
bound by their strengthened protections, including proscriptions against
torture, acts of violence, and other inhumane treatment. It also required
that prisoners be provided adequate housing, food, and clothing, and that
medical care be provided. And just as important, it required that any ships

carrying sick or wounded prisoners be explicitly marked. The Convention's new Article III—which put in place the strongest protections in history for prisoners of war—was adopted by the Swiss Federal Council in 1949. To date, 196 countries have committed to obey them, including Japan.

CAPTAIN BILL MOTT'S ORDERS to Pearl Harbor had been to serve as legal advisor to the new commander in chief of the Pacific Fleet, Admiral Arthur Radford, a rising star in the constellation of navy admirals. Admiral Radford's and my father's worldviews were identical, especially regarding their postwar commitment to "peace through strength." A veteran of both world wars, Admiral Radford was an ardent and controversial advocate of expanded investment in ship strength and carrier aviation in an era of shrinking military budgets and a civilian-minded Congress. But it was also an era of rising global instability, Radford argued relentlessly, and my father became a lifelong disciple of his fierce opposition to any policy or budget designed to contract American naval strength or readiness, both with respect to ships and personnel. A strong navy, he believed, was also the best protection for crews posted to dangerous places. It would keep future Bartons out of harm's way.

In October 1950, President Truman made a stopover at Oahu en route to his Wake Island meeting on the expanding Korean crisis with General MacArthur. One of my father's most pleasant duties was to accompany the president on his early-morning walks. As the two made their way around the Makalapa Crater one of those mornings, the president and my father got into a conversation on the complicated geopolitics resulting from America's use of the atomic bomb. At some point, Truman shook his cane and said, "Aren't you the young man who brought back the estimates of six hundred thousand American casualties if we invaded mainland Japan?" Bill was prompt with his reply. "Yes, sir, I am."

That, the president said, is why it was the right thing to do.

"As commander in chief, I would never approve an operation where there was an estimate of six hundred thousand American casualties. I had no credible evidence that Emperor Hirohito or the Japanese military had any intention of suing for peace. And that is why I authorized the dropping of the atomic bomb."

This oft-repeated story brought my father both pride and solace. It affirmed his part, however large or small, in preventing a ground invasion of Japan, which saved hundreds of thousands of lives, including his own, if not his brother's. And it had spared their families as well—from a grief he knew too well.

Admiral Mott's last set of active duty orders came at the start of John F. Kennedy's presidency. The 1960 appointment was to serve as the navy's twenty-first judge advocate general. He had in that position another opportunity to keep young men out of harm's way—and also to help bring an end to a tense and dangerous nuclear standoff with Russia.

In the fall of 1962, my father proposed an alternative to mounting Pentagon support for a military strike against Russian-backed, nuclear-armed Cuba. The alternative was for the US Navy to repel approaching arms-laden Russian vessels by establishing a perimeter of American warships around the island nation, cordoning off its seaborne approaches. He had first proposed the idea of a naval "quarantine" (also called a shipping interdiction or defensive maritime zone), to President Eisenhower in 1955. That Oval Office meeting had been convened to evaluate nonbelligerent options for protecting Formosa (now Taiwan) from incursions by Communist-controlled mainland China via the Formosa Strait.

The Cuban Missile Crisis had intensified by the day in October 1962. Finally, after reviewing all his options, President Kennedy, himself a former naval officer and PT boat commander, chose the naval quarantine over the others. After announcing his decision, the president turned to CNO admiral George Anderson and said, "Well, Admiral, it looks as though this is up to the navy." Anderson replied, "Mr. President, the navy will not let you down."

And it didn't. The quarantine was put in place immediately and was an unqualified success. One after another Russian vessel reversed course at the five-hundred-mile arc of American warships arrayed off the coast of Cuba. The standoff ended without a single shot being fired.

This historic action is frequently referred to as a naval blockade, but blockades can be imposed only in times of war, which is why such terminology was carefully avoided, at least at the time. War was precisely what the quarantine sought to prevent. Having been through one war and lost so much, my father saw high value in the tactic of brandishing American naval strength without having to use it. The role he played in helping to end the Cuban Missile Crisis was one of his proudest accomplishments.

It was as a parent, however, that he faced perhaps his best opportunity to compensate for Barton's death. During the Vietnam War, my brother Adam was a US Air Force officer flying intelligence missions over combat zones in the North. From his post in Saigon, he contacted our father at his office in Washington, DC.

Adam had a favor to ask: Could Dad arrange for his temporary detail to the USS *Forrestal*, out in the Gulf of Tonkin? In Adam's mind, "that was where the action was." Our father replied that he could easily arrange it; his good friend and Annapolis classmate Admiral James Reedy was commander of the Seventh Fleet and as such had oversight of the carriers in the Tonkin Gulf. But his response to Adam was an unequivocal "No." Years ago, he told Adam, he had, with the best of intentions, used his influence to arrange another family member's military orders: his brother Barton's.

"That," he said, "is why I no longer play God with orders." It was after my father denied Adam's request that a freak Zuni rocket exploded on the flight deck of the USS *Forrestal*, still in the Gulf of Tonkin, and set off a chain of explosions that sparked a devastating fire; 134 of her crew were killed and another 161 severely injured.

MY SIBLINGS AND I all remember another particular story, just the way my father told it. He gave many speeches throughout his career, as a high-ranking officer in the navy and later as an executive in the private sector, as head of two legal nonprofits he founded, and on behalf of the American Bar Association. After one of these speeches, the story went, a man approached him and introduced himself as a fellow prisoner of Barton's. The man was reportedly near tears and spoke haltingly. "I escaped from that camp where we were imprisoned together," the man told Dad. "But it wasn't supposed to be me—it was Barton they wanted with them. I was the alternate. Only your brother refused to go for fear the Japanese would make good on their threat to execute ten prisoners for every escapee. So I was selected to take his place."

The man said his guilt over this matter had worsened over the years, and when he heard that Dad would be speaking locally, he decided to come and confess to him what had happened. I do not remember what my father replied, only that he thanked the man for his courage and candor, and told him that he, for his own reasons, also struggled with the memory of Barton.

My father told this story infrequently, but often enough and so emotionally that it is etched in my memory and that of my siblings. Before I typed this just now, I called and asked them to tell me again what they remembered of it, and it had not changed. Perhaps we remember this story so well, and other similar ones, because they all seemed to awaken a rarely exposed emotional side of Bill Mott.

We could not get enough of these stories—in part because of how animated he became when he told them. But we also loved them because of their personalized historical content. We heard about Churchill's Map Room code name ("Former Naval Person"), his jumpsuit and drinking habits after midnight, the rakish angle of FDR's cigarette holder, and Madame Chiang's soft southern contralto yet unpopularity with White House domestic staff for the way she clapped her hands when she wanted something. They riveted, always.

Madame Chiang was one of my father's favorite White House visitors, in part, perhaps, because of Helen's Wellesley connection. But he spoke of her often, and when he visited Taiwan during his JAG tenure (1960), he saw her again, and wrote about it in a letter home. "Our visit to the presidential palace was the highlight of the trip. Suffice it to say ... I felt Madame Chiang stole the show. She is as I remember her from my White House days—a gracious, charming woman. She doesn't look a day older, in fact she has grown more beautiful with age." Madame Chiang apparently remembered him warmly as well; he brought home a sleeve of her paintings she had given him, and also two beautiful painted vases. The letter from which I just quoted lives inside one of them.

The stories were especially seductive because they unmasked a rarely seen side to a deeply emotional man, one that we knew more for his exhortations on parsimony, ladylike behavior, and school performance, and his own mental discipline. They were the one window we had on what lay beneath that tough exterior.

BILL AND ROMIE'S MARRIAGE disintegrated soon after his return from the Pacific. Many factors led to the divorce, not least of which was the corrosive mix of Bill's postwar grief and Romie's own emotional struggles, which had worsened over the lonely two years her husband had been half a world away with Admiral Turner and the amphibians. But even out of this personal defeat, an opportunity for love and family emerged.

A year after the divorce, Bill met Edith Grace, a Boston native and wartime analyst for the Manhattan Project at the Massachusetts Institute of Technology. Shortly after their nuptials in 1947, the newlyweds moved to Pearl Harbor, where the first of four more Mott children was born. Not only did my father find love, but he built the large, boisterous, and loving family that had eluded him in his own childhood. We all went on to have families of our own, and restored that cousin joy interrupted one summer evening, decades earlier, by the argument on our grandmother's porch.

PART OF MY QUEST to repair that broken day was not just to learn our Uncle Barton's story but also to track down the men who had witnessed it.

I wanted to know how his fellow POWs had gotten on with their lives, and whether part of Barton had remained with them. Some were simply lost after coming home, but others had moved on just as I had imagined Barton would have.

Charles Armour's mother also received a letter from the navy in September 1945, but hers relayed that Charles was alive and would be returning stateside—to a naval hospital in Memphis, 125 miles from their home in Little Rock. Charles would need time to recuperate, the letter said, and discouraged the family from visiting him in the hospital. Finally, one day in October 1945, a taxi pulled up to the curb at 501 Holly Street, and Charles Armour stepped out. His sister Jane had an indelible memory of that moment.

Jubilant when she looked out the window and saw her brother emerge from the taxi, she raced out the front door to greet him. But Charles was oddly quiet and standoffish. "On the surface he was home, but he . . . looked at me like I was a stranger," she recalled. Charles later told the family about his beriberi, which had damaged his heart. He was also being treated for dysentery and scurvy, and the scars on his face and hands were from multiple skin cancer surgeries he'd undergone at the Memphis hospital.

Charles's ailments were not all physical. He frequently sat at home by himself, staring at nothing in particular. "I guess he was just remembering things," Jane said. In the afternoons, he would dress in his naval uniform and go to the town movie theater to watch newsreels and movies about the war. Sometimes he would sit through the same show two or three times. "He didn't know anything about what had gone on, what happened in the war, what it all looked like," Jane said.

Charles married a nurse that he'd met at the Memphis Naval Hospital. Following a simple ceremony, Charles and Millie had a celebratory dinner at the Peabody Hotel and danced to Al Jolson. Charles died of a heart attack in 1953.

Widow Millie recalled years later that Charles never could seem to get enough to eat, especially rice. Ironically, he had insisted she cook it the way the Japanese did, steamed and served in balls. He told her that the prisoners whittled away the hours trading favorite home recipes. They had sustained themselves on the memory of the tastes and smells of home-cooked food. They would get into fights over whose mother was the best cook, he'd told her, and showed her his faded navy cap where he had stored the recipes away. "Sad," Millie recalled.

When he talked about his time as a prisoner, which was infrequent, it was usually late at night while they were lying in bed. He talked a lot about that tennis court, she remembered, and the long voyage to Japan. But he got uncomfortable talking about the latter because he said it reflected badly on our own. "If someone died on the prison ship," he said, "others would scratch at them and drink their blood." Asked if Charles had done that, Millie replied she didn't know, he never said, but that he frequently woke up at night screaming and sitting bolt upright. At one point, he warned her: "If I start fighting you, if I start touching you and screaming, don't fight back."

In an interview shortly after his 1945 release, one unidentified officer who survived the forty-nine-day journey from Manila to Moji told a newsman, "Yes, the Japs are as bad as you say. But we, the three hundred or so [that survived], we are devils, too. If we had not been devils, we could not have survived. When you speak of the good and the heroic, don't talk about us. The generous men, the unselfish men, are the men we left behind."

WITH ONLY A LETTER to Helen Cross postmarked November 1945 and a long-defunct return address to go on, I searched endlessly for Robert Granston, the other man who was with Barton at the end. Finding no obituary, I looked in every veteran database, directory, and archive. After two years of searching, my persistence finally paid off. I came across a transcript of an "oral history" interview he had given in 2002—at a tiny public library in Palm Coast, Florida. With that, I went to the electronic White Pages for Palm Coast and located a telephone number. When I dialed it, Bob Granston answered on the second ring.

His first reaction to my stumbling introduction was shock—then tears. Bob said he had just been thinking about Barton the other day, remembering their final hours together. He was eighty-nine years old. I flew to Florida to see him the following week. When I pulled my rental car up to his house and saw a pair of matching Japanese-made Lexuses in the driveway, I suspected this was a man who had forgiven his former enemies and gotten on with his life.

Unlike Charles Armour, Bob Granston had survived the war with body, mind, heart, and soul intact. He told me he weighed 102 pounds at his release, but once returned to a hearty diet of Granston farm food, he was up to 190 pounds in no time. He credited his survival of tropical diseases and harsh treatment to the powerful immunities he gained from a childhood full of farm dirt, germs, and love.

One month and a day after his release, Bob married his high school sweetheart, Norma, the girl he had described in detail to Barton in those final dark and frigid hours aboard the *Brazil Maru*. Two children, Jeff and Sharon, soon followed. After earning a Stanford MBA, he moved his family to Washington, DC, where Bob continued his navy career for thirty more years. After retiring as a captain, he moved to Florida.

PERHAPS THE MOST REWARDING connection I made in my commemorative search for Uncle Barton was with his namesake, my cousin Barton Cross-Tierney, Aunt Rosemary's son. This was the young cousin with whom we had been playing badminton when loud voices on the porch broke the peace at Lilac Hedges back in the 1960s.

The announcement that her brother would not be returning began Aunt Rosemary's long descent from life of the party to angry, depressed, and increasingly alcohol dependent. She married briefly after the war, but reportedly only to sire a son to "replace" her brother. She succeeded in this—and named that one son Barton Cross-Tierney—and then promptly divorced the father. It would not be her last divorce.

As children, we were always cautious around Aunt Rosemary. She had a penchant for sudden and terrifying outbursts—at the navy, at my father, at young Barton, and even at our grandmother Helen, whom we called Kiki. Rosemary's impaired ability to parent, however, provided Kiki a special opportunity: she played a dominant role raising our Cousin Barton, who bears a striking resemblance to his namesake.

Careers, family, and Cousin Barton's move to the West Coast in his twenties resulted in our losing touch for decades. But after another determined search, and with the help of my sister Diane Mott Davidson, I located him. He had moved back to New Jersey and lived within minutes of where this story began. I made that eerily familiar drive from Washington, DC up to Monmouth County a week later. It was a long-deferred and happy reunion.

On some level, we all knew that Rosemary had started the row on the porch, but we knew nothing of the unresolved sadness at the heart of it. The impact that confusing and painful experience had on me did not diminish with time. I couldn't solve it as an eight-year-old, but in researching and writing this account as an adult—and connecting with the characters who had shaped it—I found a measure of peace and a way to honor my uncle's surprising legacy. His was the big heart that had bestowed on fellow prisoners a will to get to the next day, a love born in the twilight games of three Jersey brothers. From Barton came the brotherhood that, even after his death, helped forge our family and its deeds.

On that unforgettable return to New Jersey, my cousin produced a dust-covered cardboard box with no markings on the outside. We sat cross-legged on the floor and opened it together. Inside were the numerous letters from fellow prisoners, Uncle Barton's posthumously awarded Purple Heart, and a cache of old family photographs, letters, and other archives crucial to this story. Cousin Barton had stored that box for nearly twenty years before my visit. He had never opened it.

Afterword

I thought it would take a year or two to excavate and reconstruct this story. It took me ten years. I started by sorting through documents at my dining room table, which back then fit into a single box. I now rent an office, and my archival cache has expanded to fill two file cabinets and the surfaces of two large tables. They are crammed and stacked with timelines, maps, documents, letters, and unpublished and privately published recollections, memoirs, and letters from men imprisoned with Barton in the Philippines; men who served on the USS *Enterprise*, the USS *Rocky Mount*, and the USS *Eldorado*; and men who served in the White House Map Room from 1942 to 1945. I have two ceiling-height bookcases as well, filled with volumes on the above subjects, many long-out-of-print primary sources procured from antique booksellers after lengthy waits.

My inquiry took me from the National Prisoner of War Museum and Archives on the grounds of the notorious Confederate prison camp in Andersonville, Georgia, to navy bases, hospitals, and former prison camps in the Philippines, to the homes of onetime war prisoners and colleagues of Barton Cross and to that of my father's first White House Map Room hire, the late George Elsey. Interlibrary loans allowed me access to reels of microfiched articles from long-defunct New Jersey newspapers. I interviewed dozens of individuals who collectively knew the three brothers, both in peace and in war.

My interviews with these old colleagues, as well as Helen's diary entries, penned recollections, and letters to the Cross family, helped me flesh out their actions and comprehend the depth of their relationships, particularly those formed among the ensigns and other prisoners. I was surprised at the number of human details—the gestures, the mannerisms, the dialogue and expressions— that these men recalled, and how vivid the moments remained. For my immediate family members, I also drew from my own memories of their habits—Benny pinching his nose constantly, and my father always clearing his throat before speaking, or raising his finger to make a point.

Other key resources were the Roosevelt Presidential Library in Hyde Park, New York; the MacArthur Memorial Archives in Norfolk, Virginia; the Truman Presidential Library in Independence, Missouri; the Naval Historical Center at the Washington Navy Yard; the National Personnel Records Center in St. Louis; the National Archives; the International Red Cross in Geneva; Ateneo University in Manila; the US Naval Institute in Annapolis, Maryland; and student archives at the US Naval Academy, Wellesley College, Christ School for Boys, the Citadel, and the University of North Carolina at Chapel Hill.

In the digitized Japanese war crime tribunal records located online, I discovered that Charles Armour's nearly lifelong home was the house of his parents, built at 501 Holly Street, Little Rock, Arkansas. I learned that long after the Armour clan departed, it was purchased by nonfiction author and editor James Morgan, who wrote a fascinating book about the unique home and all its prior occupants. Jim provided incredibly valuable insight on Charles Armour, and later, excellent input on this entire story. I am proud to call him my friend.

I wrote hundreds of letters over the course of my research, and to my delight and surprise, I received a number of long and informative replies, many of which led to unforgettable meetings and telephone calls.

In January 2005 I traveled to the Philippines with a group of former veterans and prisoners who had fought there, and their families. Our group was feted by Filipino dignitaries throughout Manila—all the way up to Malacanang Palace— in celebration of the sixtieth anniversary of that city's liberation from the Japanese. We stayed at the Manila Hotel, across from the Army and Navy Club of Manila, and from there traveled to every prison camp on Luzon.

The trip to the Philippines took place very early in my quest. At the time, I understood that Barton had been wounded and was treated at Sternberg

Hospital, but I still did not know where he was taken after January 1, 1942. He was not rostered at Cabanatuan until late spring of that year. While the Philippines trip filled critical blanks, it did not solve that mystery. Where were the hospital patients in that intervening period? While inquiries wended their way to one possible source after another, I delved into other parts of the story.

Fortunately, my father gave several interviews about his time at Naval Intelligence, in the White House, and with Admiral Turner, and his accounts are also found in a number of history books. I found his Naval Intelligence and White House correspondence files, ordered chronologically from 1940 to 1943, after he passed away in 1997. These were a fascinating and potent primary source for this book.

Benny's first-person perspective is reflected throughout this story. Fortunately, he wrote eyewitness accounts of many of his *Enterprise* experiences—including the Wake Island bomber delivery in November 1941, the attack on Pearl Harbor, the carrier's early hit-and-run raids, the Doolittle Raid, and the seminal sea battles at Midway and Santa Cruz. Some were published in USNA's *Shipmate* magazine, but my father also had a complete file of his brother's letters and war essays, virtually all written from "the perspective of the antiaircraft officer." Benny's camaraderie with war correspondents resulted in personal anecdotes recalled in the books they wrote about their experiences on the *Enterprise*, especially their early coverage of the Pacific Front.

All the while, I continued to search for clues on what happened to the Sternberg navy patients after the fall of Manila. I regularly checked for new entries in the Veterans History Project database of interviews being conducted around the country. It was here, in 2007, that I got my first big break. In one such interview, a nurse who had served at Sternberg Hospital early in the war described the chaotic New Year's Eve when the army patients were removed to the Manila docks for evacuation. The interviewer asked, "What happened to the navy patients?" She replied, "I don't know, I was sent to Corregidor after that. They just stayed there, I guess."

That interview had been conducted under the auspices of the navy's medical branch, the Bureau of Medicine and Surgery (BUMED). I promptly contacted BUMED, and after several referrals around a very large bureaucracy, I was connected to its historian in Washington, DC. The gentleman gave me some useful leads, and almost as an afterthought added an astounding additional piece of information: the Philippines had closed most of its American military facilities (airfields, bases, hospitals) in the mid-1990s, and had been boxing and returning American files to the respective military units stateside over a period of years. It seemed that a large number of medical files from the 1940s had been discovered in a storage area at the former Cavite Naval Station, since renamed Sangley Point Naval Station. Apparently they had been overlooked in the file repatriation process and were very recently shipped to BUMED, he told me. They were in storage right there, on-site.

At the time of this discovery, BUMED was headquartered on "Navy Hill," a historic campus of buildings, including the old naval observatory, located across the street from the State Department in Washington, DC—a thirty-minute drive from my home. When I arrived, the gentleman on the phone led me to an unheated storage area filled with brown file boxes. They were not labeled, much less alphabetized, so I just sat down on the floor and went through each and every one.

Box after box contained daily records kept by the navy doctors, pharmacist's mates, and corpsmen of the men they treated after the Japanese bombing of the Cavite Navy Yard. This medical staff moved with and continued to care for these patients at Sternberg Hospital and beyond—until they and their patients together became prisoners of the Japanese. Not only did I now know where Barton Cross had been during that missing period and what his condition was, in astounding detail, I had actually toured these intervening prison holds—Santa Scholastica Women's College and Pasay School—during my trip to the Philippines, so I knew exactly where they were and what they looked like.

When my *cousin* Barton came to my mother's funeral at Arlington National Cemetery in January 2008, he brought with him our grandmother Helen's diaries from the 1940s, which had been in another box he saved from Lilac Hedges after the house was sold. Helen's entries were so powerful, unique, and relevant, I knew I had to incorporate her diarist voice. In this same time frame, I arranged for the translation of an all-important Japanese document in Barton's personnel file, the only one lacking a companion English translation.

Slowly, from this accumulating trove, I assembled the story of *The Jersey Brothers*. It took longer than I had planned, but it was worth the wait.

—SALLY MOTT FREEMAN

Acknowledgments

When I stumbled upon my father's White House correspondence files shortly after his death, I was shocked and thrilled in equal measure. How long, I wondered, had this historic cache—found stacked behind a cabinet in the rear of my parents' attic—been up there? That discovery, along with a curled black-and-white photograph of the three brothers with "Christ School" written on the back, marked the beginning of this long journey. But this effort was emphatically not a solo quest; scores of people helped me along the way.

For their love, patience, and faith in this project, I am deeply grateful to the following people: my husband, John Freeman, who provided insightful commentary on more drafts than he may care to recall; my two sons, Christopher and Bobby Lawrence, for their early reads and unwavering support, and also my stepson Alexander Freeman for his uncanny ability to produce file cabinets out of thin air; to my siblings, Janie Mott Fritz, Adam Sutherland Mott, Diane Mott Davidson, Lucy Mott Faison, and Bill Mott Jr., and my cousins, Barton Cross-Tierney and Mara Mott Hodgson, for sharing their own memories and family archives; to my late brother-in-law, beloved Captain Tom Fritz, for his early feedback and accumulated trove of stories told him by my father and, as a former chief of staff at the Office of Naval Intelligence, his expert ability to interpret their high relevance; and to Bremen Schmeltz of Patagonia, Inc., attorneys Bob Lawrence and Mark Weeks, and translators Kayoko Morimitsu and Jennifer Connelly of the Tokyo office of Orrick, Herrington & Sutcliff LLP, for their invaluable assistance in translating Japanese documents.

Thanks also to my many-decade friend and Sweet Briar classmate, Megan Morgan, for her persistent faith, insightful comments, reliable wit and humor, and technical expertise in readying this manuscript for submission; to Major General Matthew Caulfield, USMC (Ret.), I offer a smart salute for his generous military review of an early draft, which greatly improved key sections on the US Marines and the amphibious campaign, and to both he and his wife, Patricia, for all those delightful and encouraging dinners at the Army Navy Club on Farragut Square. I am also indebted to the late Heno Hutson, Citadel graduate, US Marine, Christ School graduate and, later, its headmaster, for opening Christ School's door to me and making key introductions—to Denis Stokes, director of Christ School's External Affairs, and Paul Krieger, headmaster. These gentlemen, together with Mary Pope Maybank Hutson and Claire Dennison Griffith, provided valuable insight into Christ School's history and culture.

Thanks, too, to the following individuals, who gave of their knowledge, resources, moral support, and time in so many different ways: Ron Parsons, USMC (Ret.), Grace Lourence Brunner, Ted and Diane Cadwallader, Elsie Zamora, Mike Rawl, Kathleen Kernisan, Ann Brinsmead, Leigh and Rick Leverrier, Liz Haile Hayes, Barbara Kafka, Al Leonard, Betty Jo Dominick, John Duff, Tad Tharp, Lynn O'Rourke Hayes, Anita McBride, former Chief of Staff to First Lady Laura Bush and board member, White House Historical Association, and to family friend Kevin Kinsella, at whose San Diego home I typed "The End" in front of a window overlooking the mighty Pacific.

My deep respect and gratitude are also due to PhD historians and Mott family history experts Cousin Margaret "Peg" Steneck and her husband, Nicholas Steneck; Judith and the late Duane Heisinger for sharing their painstaking research regarding the movement of navy prisoners of war in the Philippines; to Robert Granston, for filling in so many blanks, and to both he and his wife, Iris, for their gracious hospitality; to John Lukacs, for his superb research and book, *Escape from Davao*, and for introducing me to the late Colonel Jack Hawkins, USMC, a Davao escapee; to Dee Grashio, widow of another escapee, Sam Grashio; to the late Roger Mansell, preeminent archivist of Pacific POW databases; to archivist James Zobel, MacArthur Memorial Archives, as well as the archivists at the Citadel, Wellesley College, USNA, UNC Chapel Hill, the *Asbury Park Press*, and Bernadine at the Morris County Clerk's Office; to Washington Navy Yard historian Jack Green, archivists Randy Sowell, Truman Presidential Library, and Bob Parks, FDR Presidential Library, and Don Pettijohn, Andersonville, GA, National Prisoner of War Museum; to Sandra Rosenquist, daughter of Harold Rosenquist, for sharing her recollections and a copy of her father's wartime diary; to author Barrett Tillman, for his canon of excellent books and articles on the USS *Enterprise*, and for sharing his early interviews with Benny Mott. I am also grateful to the heroes who make up the USS *Enterprise* Association, and Benny's *Enterprise* shipmates, Barney Barnhill and Bernard Peterson.

On the craft of writing a book of this nature, there is another group of friends and mentors to whom I am deeply grateful: the marvelous instructors, my fellow board members, and the strong literary community at the Writer's Center, with particular thanks to Barbara Esstman, Jim Mathews, Tom Young, Catherine Mayo, and Ken Ackerman; and the professors and classmates at the Iowa Summer Writing Festival, where during a transformative few weeks the structure for telling this story emerged. And last but not least, I am endlessly grateful to my all-star ICM literary agent, Binky Urban, and her colleague Molly Atlas, for their enthusiastic embrace of this life project, as well as to my all-star team at Simon & Schuster: Executive Editor extraordinaire Priscilla Painton, president and publisher Jon Karp, assistant editors Megan Hogan and Sophia Jimenez; just the best!

Notes

1: APRIL 1942, LUZON, THE PHILIPPINES

6–7 At approximately 1100 hours: Details of December 8–10 Japanese attacks on Cavite Naval Base and Manila: Clay Blair Jr., *Silent Victory: The U.S. Submarine War Against Japan* (Annapolis, MD: Naval Institute Press, 1975), 129–35.

9 Barton missing from USS *Otus*, December 10, 1941: *Otus* Ship's Log, December 10, 1941, National Archives (NARA), College Park, MD.

10 US Navy patients left behind at Sternberg Hospital:

- Recollections of Captain Ann Bernatitus, USN (nurse): Oral history dated January 25, 1994. Bernatitus recalled the shock of navy nurse Bertha Evans: "The Army got their patients down [to the docks] and put them on a hospital ship. Bertha said, 'What about the Navy patients? What's supposed to happen to them?' Nothing. They just sat there." Historian, Bureau of Medicine and Surgery (BUMED), Washington, DC.

- *Pass in Review* (newsletter of the Idaho Military Historical Society and Museum) interview with Dorothy Danner, nurse, USN: "On December 31, they were really jolted when the army patients were rushed down to the port area to be taken aboard an inter-island ship bearing a huge red cross. They wondered, why not our navy patients? They thought they would be evacuated any minute."

11 Charles Armour's fragile mental state and attempted suicide prior to the outbreak of war was disclosed in a letter written to Canacao Hospital personnel by the USS *Louisville* ship's doctor. Armour's file, National Personnel Records Center, St. Louis.

11 "A total of 224 officers and enlisted men:" George Korson, *At His Side: The Story of the American Red Cross Overseas in World War II* (New York, Coward-McCann Inc., 1945), 22.

12 Over the next several months: Re Prisoner movement from Canacao to Sternberg, Santa Scholastica, Pasay, and Cabanatuan:

- Captain L. B. Sartin (Medical Corps, USN) kept a journal of the movements of all medical personnel and patients (later prisoners) that had been on the original Canacao hospital patient roster (BUMED).
- Pharmacist's Mate Robert Kentner recorded medical personnel and patient movement from outbreak of hostilities until February 5, 1945. Entries included descriptions of the patient marches and boxcar ordeals. "Kentner's Journal" was recovered from Sangley Point, Philippines, in September 1960. Source: BUMED, Washington, DC.
- Letters to Cross family from surviving prisoners, and UNC/Chapel Hill alumni newsletter obituary on A. Barton Cross.
- Chi Phi *Chuckett* article on Cross, November 1945 issue.

13 The Kempeitai eyed the navy patients and:

- "We were the only American unit left behind in Manila": Captain Robert G. Davis (Medical Corps, USN), Journal, 1941–1945.
- "Dr. Kentner's Journal" also confirms the capture of USN medical personnel and their navy patients from Sternberg Hospital on January 1–2, 1942.

15 He didn't want his family to know: Barton Cross "Happy Christmas" telegram sent from Army and Navy Club, and MacArthur radiogram (original, printed on heavy card stock) re wounded patient evacuation from Manila to Australia aboard SS *Mactan*: William C. Mott, official correspondence file, 1940–1943.

2: BENNY

30 "Battle Order Number One": Captain E. Bertram Mott (USN, ret.), *Shipmate*, May 1985.

32 *Enterprise* return to Pearl Harbor following Japanese attack: Edward P. Stafford, *The Big E: The Story of the USS* Enterprise (New York: Ballantine Books, 1962), 14–60.

38 "Hundreds of thousands of pounds": Ibid., *Big E*, 33.

38 "It's up to you carrier boys now": Eugene Burns, *Then There Was One: The USS Enterprise and the First Year of War* (New York: Harcourt Brace & Co., 1944), 18.

3: HELEN

47 Barton Cross was born prematurely (Fall River, MA), while Helen and Arthur were touring textile plants for Arthur's company. Fall River was a strong northeastern textile center at the time.

49 "One eleven-year-old neighbor": Interview with Bill and Benny's childhood friend Al Leonard, March, 2006.

4: BILL

52 Merchant ship sinkings by U-boats along US East Coast: David Kennedy, *Freedom from Fear: The American People in Depression and War, 1925–1945* (New York: Oxford University Press, 1999), 488.

52 District of Columbia's transition to wartime footing: David Brinkley, *Washington Goes to War* (Thorndike, ME: Thorndike Press, 1988), 215–20.

54 "I have my eye on a chap named Mott": Joel McCrea, Oral History, *Setting Up Map Room in White House and Other Incidents in Connection with Service There*, March 1973, FDR Presidential Library, Hyde Park, New York, 4.

54 "Fix up a room for me like Churchill's": George Elsey, *An Unplanned Life: A Memoir* (Columbia: University of Missouri Press, 2005), 18.

55 USNA induction protocols in the 1930s: Kendall Banning, *Annapolis Today* (New York: Funk & Wagnalls Company, 1938), 65–79.

56 Snellen vision tester used at USNA: Ibid., 7–12.

61 "Dear Benny, My new job is quite interesting": WCM official correspondence file, April 1942.

61 WCM Republican background, working for a Democratic president: from the John Toland interviews:

The first time the President came into the Map Room when I was there—I hadn't been there very long—the Secret Service announced, "The President of the United States." The Secret Service was not allowed to remain in the room, so I took over the president's wheelchair. Now, we had a lot of equipment in there, and we put ramp-coverings over all the wires so you could wheel his chair over them. First I took him around and showed him the disposition of the fleet. We had a file cabinet in the corner and somehow I got the wheelchair stuck in the corner between the map of North Africa and the file cabinet. And the damn thing wouldn't come out. You know how the little wheel in the back goes cross wise? The sweat began to pour down my back, and I thought of all the places they sent naval officers who got presidents stuck in corners. Like Iceland. And the President looked up at me and said, "Young man, are you trying to file me?" Well, this kind of broke the ice and I had sense enough to straighten the wheel and got him out of there.

Well, my grandfather was chairman of the New Jersey State Republican Committee. So was my uncle, after him. The President eventually found me out and kidded me about it. But anyway my grandfather considered the family disgraced because I went to work for "that man." I tried to explain to him, you know, naval officers follow orders. These were my orders. When I finally got leave to visit Rockaway [NJ] my grandfather was still upset about this—he wouldn't even listen to the fireside chats—and my grandmother said, "Why don't you go in and tell Grandfather that story. It's a good story." So I went into his study, and he was sitting at his roll top desk. He listened very quietly while I told the story, kind of rapidly. When I repeated the punch line, "Young man, are you trying to file me?" in a heartbeat, my grandfather said, "Young man, you have just missed the opportunity of the century."

62 "Every task force, every convoy": War Secretary Stimson's diary entry, April 12, 1942.

63 Map Room procedures and personnel memoranda: Boxes 194 and 195, Roosevelt Presidential Library, Hyde Park, NY.

63 Map Room cables: Robert Sherwood, *Roosevelt and Hopkins: An Intimate History* (New York: Harper & Brothers, 1948), 498–510.

64 Map Room initiate process and annotated "Three Monkeys" cartoon vignette: George Elsey, *An Unplanned Life*, 20–48.

65 In penning Mott's promotion, Captain McCrea wrote:

"The Situation Room at the White House, which is now administered by Lieutenant Mott, is a receiving room for all military matters of interest to President Roosevelt. It is the function of Lieutenant Mott to collect and organize all military intelligence of interest to the President.

Mott must have many contacts with high ranking officers of our own military as well as officers of the British Chiefs of Staff. [H]e is entrusted with specific directives dealing with most secret matters by the President, Mr. Harry Hopkins, Admiral Leahy, myself and others. Also, in my frequent absence, Lieutenant Mott is the Senior Naval officer present in the White House to carry out naval matters.

In view of these responsibilities as well as his outstanding performance of his duties and furtherance of the prestige of the navy, his promotion to the rank of Lieutenant Commander is recommended."

5: CABANATUAN, SPRING 1942

72 Prisoner work details, rising incidence of disease and death, and other insights and observations on life at Cabanatuan: Lieutenant Colonel William E. Dyess, *The Dyess Story* (New York: G.P. Putnam's Sons, 1944), 120–37; Duane Heisinger, *Father Found: Life and Death as a Prisoner of the Japanese in World War II* (Maitland, FL: Xulon Press, 2003), 237–64; Kenneth Wheeler, "Friends," in . . . *For My Children* (unpublished memoir); Donald Wills, *The Sea Was My Last Chance* (London: McFarland and Co., 1992), 26–35; Bob Wodnik, *Captured Honor: POW Survival in the Philippines and Japan* (Washington State University Press, 2003), 59–68.

6: WHITE HOUSE MAP ROOM, APRIL 1942

74 WCM routine in Map Room, examining incoming cables, adjusting grease pencil markings on maps: Elsey, *Unplanned Life*, 19–25.

76 MacArthur press releases from Philippines: Richard Connaughton, *MacArthur and Defeat in the Philippines* (New York: Overlook Press, 2001), 223–28.

77 Personnel losses at Pearl Harbor: National Park Service Historical Statistics, USS *Arizona* Memorial, Hawaii.

80 Note: the navy's Bureau of Navigation was responsible for all naval personnel issues in early 1942. It was renamed Bureau of Personnel (BUPERS) later that year.

7: "THIS FORCE IS BOUND FOR TOKYO"

83 Re Admiral Halsey: "perfect willingness" to divide the Pacific Ocean with the Japanese. We'll take the top half, they can have the bottom": James Hornfischer, *Neptune's Inferno: The US Navy at Guadalcanal* (New York: Bantam Books, 2011), 210.

85 Re Task Force 16 and Doolittle Raid mission recollections: Bertram Mott, "Memories of the Tokyo Raid," *Shipmate*, 1961; Bernard Peterson, telephone interview with author (November 2007); *Briney to the Blue*, Petersen's self-published battle recollections, 48–49; James Barnhill, telephone interview with author (November 2007); Barnhill's privately published battle recollections, *My Enterprise Battles*.

89 "The Dauntless pilot had spotted an enemy patrol vessel fifty miles ahead": Stafford, *Big E*, 78.

89–90 Additional details on Task Force 16 formation and Doolittle Raid: Ibid., 74–79.

8: BARTON, 1930–1941

97 Hazing that Barton endured at the Citadel is detailed in letter from Helen Cross to USNA commandant.

97 A detailed description of plebe hazing at the Citadel: Pat Conroy, *My Losing Season* (New York: Bantam Books, 2002), 100–107.

99–107 Details of Barton's abbreviated tenure at USNA: Midshipman A. B. Cross Jr. USNA student file, Nimitz Library, USNA Archives, Annapolis, MD.

9: THE PERILS OF ESCAPE—AND A LITTLE BASEBALL

116 Ten-and-one squads and execution of Staunton Ross Betts: Tarleton E. Woods, *March of Death: An American Soldier's 1,216 Days as a POW of the Japanese* (Spartanburg, SC: Honoribis Press, 2006), 37–38.

117–118 William Wordsworth, "Lines Composed a Few Miles Above Tintern Abbey on Revisiting the Banks of the Wye During a Tour," July 13, 1798.

119–20 Description of Charles Armour's house in Little Rock, AR, perspectives on his childhood and family relationships: James Morgan, *If These Walls Had Ears: The Biography of a House* (New York: Warner Books, 1996), 43–90.

121–22 Barton Cross formed a prisoner baseball team and arranged a game with the Japanese guards: "In Memoriam on Brother Cross," Chi Phi *Chuckett*, November 1945; included stories about his imprisonment, informed by interviews with fellow prisoners.

10: A BROTHER'S BURDEN: THE SEARCH

124–25 Newspaper article and photograph of Ensign A. B. Cross noting his status as missing in action: *Red Bank (NJ) Register*, March 12, 1942, Rutgers University Archives, microfiche obtained via interlibrary loan with Montgomery County Library, Rockville, MD.

133–34 Captain Newsom's letter from Darwin, Australia, to Bill Mott: WCM correspondence file. Same letter also found in Barton Cross's USN personnel file.

11: MIDWAY

142 Admiral King's perspective, judgment, and personality: Andrew Roberts, *Masters and Commanders: How Four Titans Won the War in the West, 1941–1945* (New York: HarperCollins, 2009), 195, 404–8.

145–49 Eyewitness recollections of Midway battle: Benny Mott essay and letters to Bill Mott; Peterson, Midway chap., *Briney to the Blue*, and author interview; Barnhill, *My Enterprise Battles*, and telephone interview with author; Stafford, *Big E*, 82–106.

146 "a wiry, energetic man": Ibid., 91.

146 "From stem to stern": Ibid., 93.

146 "On the flank of the enemy's anticipated thrust": Arnold Olsen, Midway, USS *Enterprise* CV-6 Association Public Affairs Issue.

147 B. Barnhill filming battle: James "Barney" Barnhill, self-published battle recollections, *Galloping Ghost.*

150 "On the way back to Pearl the radio was busy": Stafford, *Big E,* 117.

12: UNDER SIEGE: JN-25

152 "Dear Bill, I haven't had much time to write, as you might imagine": WCM official correspondence file, June 1942.

155–58 *Chicago Tribune* leak that US had broken Japanese naval code (JN-25) and WCM White House meeting with Captain Larry Safford: transcript of WCM interview with John Toland obtained from Franklin D. Roosevelt Presidential Library, Hyde Park, NY; and Clay Blair Jr., *Silent Victory: The U.S. Submarine War against Japan* (Annapolis MD: Naval Institute Press, 1975), "The Midway Security Leak," 256–60.

13: TO DAVAO: *EN AVANT!*

160 "There was one overriding thought on every prisoner's mind: would [Davao] be better than Cabanatuan?" *Life* magazine interview with Mellnik and McCoy, published February 7, 1944, following their escape, return to the United States, and lifting of gag order.

163–65 Journey from Cabanatuan to Davao Penal Colony: Kenneth R. Wheeler, "For My Children" chapter: "Davao Penal Colony"; Heisinger, *Father Found,* 329–39; Davao references in letters to Mott/Cross family from Barton Cross's fellow prisoners.

14: AND THEN THERE WAS ONE: USS *ENTERPRISE* VERSUS JAPAN

169 "Dear Benny, The suspense I have gone through since hearing from you last": WCM correspondence file, October 1942.

173–75 MacArthur claimed Nimitz had violated the divided command structure: James P. Drew, LCDR, USN, "Tarnished Victory: Divided Command in the Pacific and Its Consequences, et al." (Thesis, Fort Leavenworth, KS, 2009).

173–75 Dispute between MacArthur and Nimitz regarding Guadalcanal and for scarce military resources in Pacific: Blair, *Silent Victory*, 295; Winston Groom, *1942: The Year That Tried Men's Souls* (New York: Atlantic Monthly Press, 2005), 260–61.

173–75   Harm caused by divided military command structure at Guadalcanal and beyond: James P. Drew, LCDR, USN, "Tarnished Victory: Divided Command in the Pacific and Its Consequences, et al." (Thesis, Fort Leavenworth, KS, 2009).

176–83   Benny's viewpoint: Captain E. Bertram Mott, undated Santa Cruz battle retrospective essay, "The Battle of Santa Cruz and Guadalcanal from the Anti-Aircraft Viewpoint."

178–81   Battle sequence, Santa Cruz: Stafford, *Big E*, 192–211.

179   Reporters' observations during and after Battle of Santa Cruz: Richard Tregaskis, *Guadalcanal Diary* (New York: Random House, 1943), 62–70.

15: THE OTHER WAR: ARMY-NAVY FOOTBALL

184–85   Condition of USS *Enterprise* at Nouméa following Santa Cruz battle: Stafford, *Big E*, 241–43.

190   "Parsons was only sworn in to the United States Navy when a fellow Philippine reserve officer awakened him in the middle of the night on December 8, informing him that the entire personnel and equipment of the Luzon Stevedoring Company had been taken into the United States Navy. He was then sworn in by Admiral Hart as a lieutenant, senior grade." Travis Ingham, *Rendezvous by Submarine* (New York: Doubleday Doran, 1945), 23–24.

190–92   Background and lead-up to 1942 army-navy football game and game statistics: http://forwhattheygave.com/category/army-navy-football; Gene Schoor, *100 Years of Army Navy Football: A Pictorial History of America's Most Colorful and Competitive Sports Rivalry* (New York: Henry Holt, 1989), 112–14.

16: HAPPY DAYS AT THE PENAL COLONY

193–200   Details of prisoner life at Davao as observed by local Filipinos who worked at or near the colony: Mari Virginia Yap Morales, *Diary of the War: WW II Memoirs of Anastacio Campo* (Quezon City, PI: Ateneo University Press, 2006), 51–131.

193–200   The following diaries and memoirs also contributed to author insight into the prisoner experience at Davao: David Nash, Nash Diary; Hugh McGee, *Rice and Salt* (San Antonio: Naylor, 1962); Stephen Mellnik, *Philippine Diary 1939–1945* (New York: Van Nostrand Rheinhold, 1969); Carl S. Nordin, *We Were Next to Nothing: An American POW's Account of Japanese Prison Camps and Deliverance in World War II* (Jefferson, NC: McFarland & Company, 2004), 73–82.

197–200   Davao Christmas celebration: Morales, *Diary of the War*, 51–131; Kenneth Wheeler, "Christmas at DAPECOL" chapter, in "For My Children"; Red Cross packages to prisoners: Wheeler, "For My Children"; John M. Wright Jr., *Captured on Corregidor: Diary of an American P.O.W. in World War II* (Jefferson, NC: McFarland & Co., 2009), 66–69; Heisinger, *Father Found*, 327–28.

18: ESCAPE: CRIME AND PUNISHMENT

211–14   Primary and secondary sources consulted on Davao prisoner escape and aftermath: John D. Lukacs, *Escape from Davao: The Forgotten Story of the Most Daring Prison Break of the Pacific War* (New York: Simon & Schuster, 2010); Mellnik, *Philippine Diary*; Melvin McCoy, *Ten Escape from Tojo*; Dyess, *Dyess Story*; Samuel Grashio and Bernard Norling, *Return to Freedom* (Spokane, WA: University Press, 1982); 2010 author interview with the late Jack Hawkins at his home near Quantico, VA (arranged thanks to the kind assistance of John Lukacs).

212–14   The morning of April 4, 1943: The escape from Davao Penal Colony and effect on prisoners left behind: Heisinger, Father Found, 333–39; Wheeler, "No Escape," in "For My Children."

212–14   After the escape from Davao Penal Colony, effect on prisoners left behind: Heisinger, *Father Found*, 333–39; Wheeler, "No Escape," in "For My Children."

213–14   Punishment of prisoners in Barracks 5 to 8: Wheeler, "No Escape," in "For My Children"; Nash, Nash Diary; McGee, *Rice and Salt*, 103–8.

19: FAREWELL TO THE WHITE HOUSE

219   "You know I have been trying for some time to get some kind of sea duty": Excerpt of letter from Bill to Benny, WCM correspondence file, May 1943.

225 William C. Mott new orders: personal correspondence file, 1940–1943; WCM's USN personnel file; WCM Navy Orders file.

20: A TALE OF ATROCITIES

232–38 Debriefing of Dyess, Mellnik, and McCoy in Australia: Colonel Allison W. Ind, *Allied Intelligence Bureau: Our Secret Weapon in the War Against Japan* (New York: David McKay, 1958), 180–82; Mellnik, *Philippine Diary*, 279–316.

233 The guerillas fed and clothed them: William Wise, *Secret Mission to the Philippines: The Story of "Spyron" & the American-Filipino Guerrillas of World War II* (New York: E. P. Dutton, 1968), 112.

233 Improving state of guerrilla resistance movement in the Philippines: Ibid.

234 Guerrilla radiograms sent from PI to MacArthur HQ in Brisbane regarding prisoners in Philippines: Paul P. Rogers, *The Bitter Years: MacArthur and Sutherland* (New York: Praeger Publishers, 1990), 4.

236 "This is superb": A very good index of Whitney's habitual dealings with MacArthur: Paul P. Rogers, *The Good Years: MacArthur and Sutherland* (New York: Praeger, 1990), 296.

237–38 The GHQ audience showed intensified interest: William Wise, *Secret Mission to the Philippines: The Story of "Spyron" & the American-Filipino Guerrillas of World War II* (New York: E. P. Dutton, 1968), 112.

237 Training of guerrillas in the Philippines during World War II: Larry Schmidt, USMC, "American Involvement in the Filipino Resistance Movement on Mindanao During the Japanese Occupation, 1942–1945" (academic paper, Fort Leavenworth, KS, 1982). Excellent background on training protocols and intelligence transmission between Australia and guerrillas.

21: AUGUST 1943: ALLIED WAR
SUMMIT, QUEBEC, CANADA

239–40 Preparation for and references to Quadrant conference: Elsey, *Unplanned Life*, 36–40.

239–44 Quebec Conference attendees, vignettes, and general tenor of conference: Doris Kearns Goodwin, *No Ordinary Time: Franklin & Eleanor Roosevelt: The Home Front in World War II* (New York: Simon & Schuster, 1994),

459–62; John Costello, *The Pacific War 1941–1945* (New York: Harper-Collins, 1981), 416–17.

240–42   Admiral King and Quadrant: Roberts, *Masters and Commanders*, 195, 407; John Byrne Cooke, *Reporting the War: Freedom of the Press from the American Revolution to the War on Terrorism* (New York: St. Martin's Press, 2007).

241   Quadrant Conference outcomes: Robert H. Ferrell, ed., *The Eisenhower Diaries* (New York: Norton, 1981), 48, 50.

243   Reading of Dyess affidavit excerpts at Quadrant: Monday, August 23, 1943, Minutes of Combined Chiefs of Staff meeting, Château Frontenac, Quebec. Source: Franklin D. Roosevelt Presidential Library, Hyde Park, NY.

244–45   FDR's ritual before dictation: Grace Tully, *Franklin Delano Roosevelt: My Boss* (Chicago: Peoples Book Club, 1949), 80–82.

245   FDR and Helen Cross correspondence: Cover memo to FDR on Helen Cross's incoming from Miss Grace Tully: "Letter from Mrs. A Barton Cross Lilac Hedges, Oceanport, New Jersey. Her son is Lt. Com. Mott. Source: Roosevelt Presidential Library, Hyde Park, NY.

245   Excerpt of 1943 MacArthur letter to FDR: Lukacs, *Escape From Davao*, 284.

22: REVENGE ON THE INNOCENT AND A COVERT PLAN

249–50   After crouching for thirty days in feces-strewn wire hutches: Heisinger, *Father Found*, 333–39; Wheeler, "No Escape," in "For My Children."

252–57   Secret MIS-X plan to spring Davao prisoners and description of Claro Lauretta's guerrilla resources: Mellnik, *Philippine Diary*, 280–86.

253–57   Mellnik's recall of his first conversation with Harold Rosenquist and later General Sutherland in Washington is entered here nearly verbatim: Ibid., 299–305.

255–56   Captain Lauretta's reference to doctors and hospitals operating in the hills of Mindanao: Ingham, *Rendezvous by Submarine*, 153.

255   A note on MacArthur's political and financial aspirations and their effect on policy and war theater decisions: In 1943, General Sutherland traveled to Washington for war planning conferences and also to promote General MacArthur's candidacy for the presidency. Himself the son of a senator and

wise to the ways of Washington, Sutherland worked with Senator Arthur Vandenberg of Michigan to get the War Department to rescind the order preventing MacArthur from seeking or accepting political office. Source: http://www.arlingtoncemetery.net/rksuther.htm.

Roosevelt felt pressured to keep MacArthur happy because he was a Republican, a household name, and potential future presidential candidate, depending on the course of the war. He did not interfere when, in February 1942, MacArthur accepted a payment of $500,000 ($7.5 million in current value) from Philippine president Manuel Quezon. MacArthur's staff members also received payments: $75,000 for Sutherland, $45,000 for Richard Marshall, and $20,000 for another low-level aide, Sidney Huff. Eisenhower, after being appointed Supreme Commander Allied Expeditionary Force, was also offered money by Quezon, but Eisenhower declined the offer. These revelations were made public by historian Carol Petillo in 1979 after she uncovered correspondence and archived bank deposits and later by Rogers, *MacArthur and Sutherland: The Good Years* and *The Bitter Years* (2 vols.), 1990, 1991.

23: SECRETS INSIDE THE OXYGEN TENT

259 Oxygen tent operation: Margeurite Klein, "Nursing Care in Pneumonia," *American Journal of Nursing* (October 1941).

260–61 Standard procedures for evacuating Americans caught behind enemy lines in the PI: Americans were routinely evacuated from prearranged rendezvous points after USS *Narwhal* and USS *Nautilus* had delivered their cargo to the guerrillas. Four hundred seventy-two Americans boarded the emptied submarines in the Philippines between 1943 and 1945 in this manner: Wise, *Secret Mission to the Philippines*, 141–43; Edward Dissette and H. C. Adamson, *Guerrilla Submarines* (New York: Ballantine Books, 1972), 236; Mellnik, *Philippine Diary*, 288.

261 "[T]hey had been working intensely on a plan to extract the prisoners at Davao Penal Colony—well ahead of Rosenquist's departure for Brisbane. Stories of MIS-X success facilitating escape and evasion in Europe, well behind enemy lines—in areas crawling with Germans—were legion. Let this be the answer to a thousand prayers. And now Rosenquist, MIS-X plan in

hand—approved by Sutherland—was in Australia." Willoughby, *Guerrilla Resistance Movement in the Philippines*, 175–77.

261   Captain McCollum's concern for his cousin Shivers: "I was trying very hard to get these people saved. I had a personal interest in it because my favorite first cousin was a prisoner there. He was an army officer, Shivers McCollum." Rear Admiral Arthur McCollum's Oral History, Source: USNI, Annapolis, MD.

262   General Sutherland and decision-making at GHQ: Rogers, *Good Years: MacArthur and Sutherland*, 230–35.

262   Courtney Whitney biographical background: RG-16 "Biographical Sketch," Papers of Major General Courtney Whitney, 1942–1947, MacArthur Memorial Archives, Norfolk, VA.

262   Courtney Whitney's long-standing mercantile interests in the Philippines: Peggy Seagrave, *Gold Warriors* (London: Verso Press, 2002), 93–94.

262   Whitney was more MacArthur loyalist than military professional: RG-16 "Biographical Sketch," Papers of Major General Courtney Whitney, 1942–1947, MacArthur Memorial Archives, Norfolk, VA.

263   Eleanor Roosevelt's telephone call to Newport hospital per WCM interview with John Toland:

WCM: "I came down with double pneumonia and nearly died, they later told me. They didn't have penicillin readily available in those days, and I was in the infirmary, then the hospital in Newport, Rhode Island. This was while I was at the Naval War College. I was in an oxygen tent, and Mrs. Roosevelt found out about it, and she called the hospital and got the night nurse and said, 'This is Mrs. Roosevelt, and I'd like to inquire about Billy Mott.' And she only got that far when the nurse snapped, 'Yes? Well, this is your Aunt Fanny,' and hung up. She reported it the next morning and there was an investigation.

"But that's the way she was, a very warm person. Here's another interesting example of how they cared about the White House staff. We burned coal to heat our home in those days, and we had an automatic device—I forget what you call them—that fed coal into the firebox. A part broke on it, and consequently we had no heat. We had a small child, and my wife was pregnant at the time, as I recall. I was wondering how I was going to keep my family from freezing when the telephone rang. They said, 'We understand you have a problem; that you need some heating. Mrs. Roosevelt has some electric heaters in the White House attic, and you can borrow them.' Then the Secret Service arranged to fly the coal feeder part in from Cleveland. By the way, I also realized that this meant that the home telephones of those of us that worked in the Map Room were tapped. I had told nobody at the White House about this problem."

24: HERO OF BATAAN VERSUS THE WAR DEPARTMENT

264–67   A censored William Dyess's frustrated attempts to publicize details of Japanese treatment of its prisoners in the Philippines: Lukacs, *Escape from Davao*, 277–336, and Dyess, *Dyess Story*.

25: BAD TIDINGS

270   "The exterior was bare and boxy": Christopher Gray, "Streetscapes: The Henry Hudson Hotel, 353 West 57th Street; From Women's Clubhouse to WNET to $75 a Night," *New York Times*, January 4, 1998.

276   Japanese atrocities revealed to an outraged American public: *New York Times*, January 28, 1944, A1, and other newspapers, e.g., *Los Angeles Examiner*, "Yanks Starved, Beheaded, Buried Alive By Captors"; and in following days, *NYT* headline, "Ruin Japan! Is Cry of Aroused Nation."

26: POLITICS IN BRISBANE

278–81   Courtney Whitney's role in the fate of prisoners at Davao Penal Colony: A lengthy description of the Rosenquist mission and its failure provides strong support of the view that Courtney Whitney and, to a slightly lesser degree, R. J. Marshall (deputy chief of staff) were responsible for the intentional detainment of Rosenquist at Brisbane for the purpose of dooming the rescue plan: Major General Charles A. Willoughby, *The Guerrilla Resistance Movement in the Philippines* (New York: Vantage Press, 1972), 56–63.

280–81   Mellnik and Rosenquist run into difficulties with Courtney Whitney at Brisbane GHQ: Mellnik, *Philippine Diary*, 386–92.

280–81   But from the moment Courtney Whitney got word: Courtney

Whitney's role in the fate of prisoners at Davao Penal Colony; Major General Charles A. Willoughby, *The Guerrilla Resistance Movement in the Philippines* (New York: Vantage Press, 1972), 56–63.

281 "I'm staying out of this G-2 brawl": Memorandum from Acting Chief of Staff General Richard Marshall, February 1944, MacArthur Memorial Museum and Archives, Norfolk, VA.

281 Original documents, radiograms, and memoranda between staff at MacArthur's GHQ and between GHQ and guerrillas in the Philippines: MacArthur Memorial Museum and Archives, Norfolk, VA.

27: "PROCEED TO KWAJALEIN"

282–83　Bill Mott Orders to Pacific: WCM interviews with John Toland, September, October, and December 1979; WCM Navy Orders file.

282–83　Kelly Turner biographical data: Fifth Amphibious Fleet database, NARA, College Park, MD.

286 Size of Joint Expeditionary Force: T. D. Stamps and V. J. Esposito, *A Military History of World War II: Operations in the Mediterranean and Pacific Theaters* (West Point, NY: United States Military Academy, 1953), 382.

28: THE BEST-LAID PLANS

291–92　Colonel Whitney's improvement of nascent guerrilla operations in the Philippines and training of new recruits: Mellnik, *Philippine Diary*, 279–86.

291–93　Courtney Whitney's block of rescue plan: Mellnik's and Willoughby's memoranda and, later, their books, all finger Whitney in crafting the serial delays of the Rosenquist rescue mission.

292 "Whitney's influence too strong." Harold Rosenquist diary entry. Sandra Rosenquist Kahn.

293 Sutherland influence at GHQ: Rogers, *Good Years: MacArthur and Sutherland*, 230–35.

296–302　Interaction between Rosenquist and Fertig on Mindanao: In his ghostwritten memoir, Fertig admits to disobeying GHQ prisoner rescue order Rosenquist handed him. Wendell Fertig, *They Fought Alone* (New York: Lippincott Company, 1963), 383–89.

In "A Critical Review of *They Fought Alone*," Captain Clyde Childress criticizes Fertig's military disobedience. Childress, who reported to Fertig, stated that Fertig was vain and self-absorbed—and routinely disdainful of General MacArthur and GHQ's oversight of the guerrillas. "Had Fertig . . . engaged in better communication with his superiors in Australia and his guerrilla commanders on Mindanao, this fiasco could have been avoided . . . There were guerrillas already in place that were perfectly capable of performing the task that Rosenquist was sent in to do. Had the guerrillas been directed to keep the Penal Colony under surveillance, this failed mission and the loss of the POWs might have been prevented."

29: INITIATION AT SAIPAN

310 "By mid-1944, the United States Navy was about to surpass all the world's navies combined": History International Documentary: *Imperial Sunset at Saipan*.

311 "Peace at War" poem, WCM, 1944, WCM poetry file.

315 Coastwatcher Chapman's sighting of the Japanese fleet in San Bernardino Strait and Stahl's assistance in relaying his message to Fifth Fleet: Robert Stahl, "The Turkey Shoot," chap. 9 in *You're No Good to Me Dead: Behind Japanese Lines in the Philippines* (Naval Institute Press Special Warfare Series, Annapolis, MD: Naval Institute Press, 1995), 100–102.

321–23 Smith vs. Smith: From WCM interview with John Toland: "I was right in the middle of that one . . . It was just the difference in the way the marines and the army operated. The army believes in artillery barrages, etc. . . . and the Marines say, 'Oh Christ. Go in and take your losses.' The same thing happened on Okinawa. The marines had their part of the island cleaned up in no time. Of course, the army will say they didn't have the same kind of opposition, but this was the marine way. Wherever you put a marine division alongside an army division, you're going to have trouble!"

323–24 Source for Manila casualties in final Japanese rampage: Daws, *Prisoners of the Japanese*, 534.

30: DECAMPMENT

328–32   First-person accounts of the DAPECOL prisoners' journey from
Mindanao to Bilibid, a three-week ordeal: In addition to surviving prisoner
letters sent to the Cross family, accounts by the following were excellent
resources: Manny Lawton, *Some Survived* (Chapel Hill, NC: Algonquin
Books of Chapel Hill, 2004), 138–48; McGee, *Rice and Salt*, 126–45;
Alan McCracken, *Very Soon Now, Joe* (New York: The Hobson Book Press,
1947), 130–64.

331   "His morale was sky high": Postwar letter from Ensign Andrew Long Jr. to
Helen Cross regarding Barton Cross's outlook in late 1944.

31: SEPTEMBER 1944, LILAC HEDGES

337   Under an unrehearsed divided command between the army and the navy,
such incidents: James P. Drew, LCDR, USN, "Tarnished Victory: Divided
Command in the Pacific and Its Consequences, et al." (Thesis, Fort Leavenworth, KS, 2009).

338–31   Benny's munitions factory speech: Source: *Rockaway (NJ) Record*,
October 6, 1944. Benny delivered similar awards and stateside speeches to
numerous converted munitions plants around the country. These factories
variously made bomb sites, pistols, rifle receivers, and torpedoes.

341–42   Helen Cross letter to President Roosevelt regarding the *Shinyo Maru*
POW transport sinking: A. Barton Cross Jr. Naval Personnel File, National
Personnel Records Center, St. Louis.

32: HOPES DASHED

344   Major Harold Rosenquist told me he was here to: Sworn statement by
escapee Jim McClure, MacArthur Memorial Museum and Archives, Norfolk, VA.

344–45   Several sworn testimonials from both guerrillas and escaped prisoners working with the Mindanao guerrillas averred that Rosenquist's plan to
rescue the prisoners from the Davao Penal Colony would have succeeded
if Rosenquist had been allowed to depart Australia even one month earlier
than he did. MacArthur Memorial Archives, Norfolk, VA.

344–45 With mounting resentment toward Courtney Whitney: A lengthy description of the Rosenquist mission and its failure provides strong support of the view that Courtney Whitney and, to a slightly lesser degree, R. J. Marshall (deputy chief of staff) were responsible for the intentional detainment of Rosenquist at Brisbane for the purpose of dooming the rescue plan: Major General Charles A. Willoughby, *The Guerrilla Resistance Movement in the Philippines* (New York: Vantage Press, 1972), 56–63.

345 This message is written with a prayer to God that it: Letter from Harold Rosenquist to Lieutenant Colonel Rogers, POW, MacArthur Memorial Museum and Archives, Norfolk, VA.

345–46 Letter from Harold Rosenquist to Colonel Rogers at Lincayan Airfield (Lasang): Source: MacArthur Memorial Archives, Norfolk, VA.

348 Re Coastwatcher LeCouvre's urgent POW ship change message to army GHQ at Brisbane and its failure to forward it to US Navy submarines monitoring enemy shipping in the area: Virginia Hansen Holmes, *Guerrilla Daughter* (Kent, Ohio: Kent State University Press, 2009), 149.

348 As required by the divided command structure: James P. Drew, LCDR, USN, "Tarnished Victory: Divided Command in the Pacific and Its Consequences, et al." (Thesis, Fort Leavenworth, KS, 2009).

349 Official Japanese order to kill all POWs: Doc 2701, Exhibit "O" Source: NARA, War Crimes, Japan, RG 24, Box 2015.

349–50 Re *Shinyo Maru* survivor accounts: Heisinger, *Father Found*, 394–95; John Morrett, *Soldier Priest* (Roswell, GA: Old Rugged Cross Press, 1993), 110–14.

350 This is a headache: Penciled a note on the radiogram regarding a submarine rescue of the surviving *Shinyo Maru* prisoners, MacArthur Memorial Museum and Archives, Norfolk, VA.

33: SETBACKS

352–53 Medical air transport insight, description: Keith Wheeler, *The Pacific Is My Beat* (New York: E. P. Dutton, 1943).

355–57 Background and details regarding 1944 Pearl Harbor summit, July 27, 1944: Costello, *Pacific War*, 491–96.

356–57   Re MacArthur guarantee that Luzon campaign would be completed in thirty days to six weeks: George Dyer, *The Amphibians Came to Conquer: The Story of Admiral Richmond Kelly Turner* (US Marine Corps, 1991), 975.

357   "Give me an aspirin . . . In fact, give me another aspirin to take in the morning": William Manchester, *American Caesar: Douglas MacArthur 1880–1964* (Boston: Little, Brown and Company, 1978), 369.

357–59   Submarine warfare effectiveness: Blair, *Silent Victory: True*, 17–20 and 87–88; Larry Bond, *Crash Dive: Stories of Submarine Combat* (New York: Tom Doherty, 2010), 234–37.

359   Re Halsey's orders under divided command scenario: E. B. Potter, *Nimitz* (Annapolis, MD: Naval Institute Press, 2008), 325.

359–61   Divided command insight: "MacArthur's Navy—Admiral Kinkaid and the Seventh Fleet and Admiral Halsey and the Third Fleet . . . a divided command creating a very dangerous situation indeed in the face of a brave and determined enemy." Edwin P. Hoyt, *How They Won the War in the Pacific: Nimitz and His Admirals* (New York: Lyons Press, 2000), 422.

360–61   Additional divided command insight: Lieutenant Commander Thomas J. Cutler, "MacArthur, FDR, and the Politics of Leyte Gulf," *Naval History* 23 No. 5 (October 2009).

360–61   Re MacArthur's tight control over communications between the Seventh Fleet and Halsey's Third Fleet attack forces: "MacArthur was so damned insistent on having his own fleet and his own people that he wouldn't let, would not have, any direct channel of communication between Halsey [Third Fleet] and the Seventh Fleet. There were no radio channels set up. Halsey was working for Nimitz, and so MacArthur would not include him in any of the operations plans. They had this long, complicated communications plan for the Seventh Fleet . . . There was no setup for that outfit to communicate directly with Halsey. It was part of MacArthur's hatred of the navy or craving for power or something—I don't know which, but he insisted on it being that way." From oral history of Admiral George Van Deurs: USNI, 487.

34: THROUGH A PRISM: MACARTHUR'S RETURN

367–70   First-person accounts of USN flyers over Luzon, September 21, 1944:
Wheeler, "For My Children," 78–80; Heisinger, *Father Found*, 407–9 (including diary entries by Manny Lawton and Lee Stiles); Lawton, *Some Survived*, 108–110; Thomas Hayes, "Bilibid Journal," 149–53.

367–68   After *Enterprise's* Air Group 20 (led by Commander Robert Riera) supported the September 1944 Peleliu invasion, they struck Japanese airfields and shipping in and around the Philippines: http://www.cv6 .org/1944/1944.htm.

367–68   Admiral King's Second Report to the Secretary of the Navy, Combat Operations March 1944–March 1945.

370–71   Major Robert Lapham overtures to Courtney Whitney at GHQ for permission to conduct a Cabanatuan rescue mission: William Breuer, *The Great Raid*, 141–42; Charles W. Sasser, *Raider*, 119; Ray Hunt and Bernard Norling, *Behind Japanese Lines: An American Guerrilla in the Philippines*, 196–98; Robert Lapham and Bernard Norling, *Lapham's Raiders: Guerrilla Raiders in the Philippines, 1942–1945*, 177–78.

372   Sinking of *Hofuku Maru*: "British state the American bombers are too bloody accurate": Heisinger, *Father Found*, 410 (quoting from Lee Stiles's diary); "They were a pitiful sight to behold": Recollection of Curtis Beecher when he first saw *Hofuku Maru* survivors arriving at Bilibid. Unpublished recollection entitled "A Survivor's Account of Americans Who Were Prisoners of the Japanese in the Philippine Islands April, May 1942–December 1944," Brigadier General Curtis Beecher, USMC, Douglas County Museum, Roseburg, OR; *Hofuku Maru* survivors taken to either Bilibid or Cabanatuan: Sources: Cecil Peart, Peart's Journal; Heisinger, *Father Found*; and McCracken, *Very Soon Now, Joe*.

375   Delivering his prewar client Douglas MacArthur back to the Philippines: RG-16 "Biographical Sketch," Papers of Major General Courtney Whitney, 1942–1947, MacArthur Memorial Archives, Norfolk, VA., Peggy Seagrave, *Gold Warriors* (London: Verso Press, 2002), 93–94.

375   Courtney Whitney's prewar activities and investments in the Philippines: Whitney worked for the top Manila law firm, Dewitt, Perkins & Enrile (as did the father of MacArthur's G-2 assistant chief, Joseph McMicking).

The firm handled all MacArthur's investments and financial affairs in the Philippines. Another major client was Benguet Consolidated Mines, the country's largest gold mining operation, in which MacArthur had a considerable investment. In 1936 Courtney Whitney was president of Benguet Consolidated Mines, either concurrent with his law partnership or immediately prior to it. Source—July 1936 American Chamber of Commerce of Manila—quoted below:

[Benguet] Consolidated Mines recently reported good results from its development work . . . of the vast chromite mine in Masinloc, Zambales. Courtney Whitney, Benguet's President, is in the United States working on the sale of this ore. [Benguet's] gold production has also improved steadily; gold output for the period under discussion is much higher than in 1935.

Total gold production in the five years preceding WWII was 37 tons per year, the Philippines' most lucrative export.

375   MacArthur's Philippine-derived wealth: General MacArthur sold his shares in Benguet after the war for more than $1 million.

377   Re *Arisan Maru* sinking: Calvin Graef, Official Statement to the War Department, December 5, 1944, www.rockawaymemories.com/JosephAngelone01.htm; William Bowen, *The Arisan Maru Tragedy*; Gavan Daws, *Prisoners of the Japanese: POWs of World War II in the Pacific* (New York: William Morrow, 1994); "no bigger than a dime": Calvin Graef and Melissa Masterson, *Ride the Waves to Freedom* (Kearney, NE: Morris, 1999), 73, telling of Graef's imprisonment and survival following the sinking of the *Arisan Maru*.

36: THE *ORYOKO MARU*

391   Shields Goodman's letter: "A letter from Bilibid Prison," *Shipmate*, November 1989, 13–14.

393–94   Curtis Beecher observations: Curtis T. Beecher memoir, unpublished.

394–95   Bilibid Prison, December 1944: Pharmacist's Mate Robert W. Kentner, diary entries on rostered patients and naval medical personnel.

398–404   Recollections of *Oryoko Maru*: Lawton, *Some Survived*, 145–54.

398–406   Prisoner experiences described in this chapter: family letters, diaries, unpublished memoir, as well as author interviews with survivors.

401 "Hikoki! Hikoki!": Wheeler, "For My Children," 83.

401 Robert Riera log entries: USS *Hornet* log and USS *Enterprise* ship's muster, November, December 1944, and January 1945, www.cv6.org/company/muster/display_ag.asp?page=VB-20 and usshornet.org.

402 Description of Commander Frank Bridget's announcements of American planes attacking the prison ship: "as cool as a tennis match referee, called the action": Lawton, some survived, 160.

402 The men "hoped to hell they would score and hoped to hell they wouldn't," according to David Nash: Heisinger, *Father Found*, 456.

37: END GAME IN THE PACIFIC

415–17 Iwo Jima press conference: Robert Sherrod, *On to Westward: The Battles of Saipan and Iwo Jima* (New York: Duell Sloan and Pearce, 1945), 154–61.

417–18 Iwo Jima statistics: Ronald H. Spector, *Eagle Against the Sun: The American War with Japan* (New York: Macmillan, 1985), 495, and Sherrod, *On to Westward*, 163.

417–20 D-Day and D-Days Plus 1, 2, 3 at Iwo Jima: CINPAC Monthly Operations Report, February 1945, noted in Dyer, *Amphibians Came to Conquer*, vol. 2, 1027.

420 Text of Navajo message on Iwo Jima flag raising: *"Ashdla-ma ... nos-bas ...":* Sally McClain, *Navajo Weapon: The Navajo Code Talkers* (Tucson, AZ: Rio Nuevo, 1944), 179–81.

38: A SAILOR'S NIGHTMARE

429 *Kikusui:* Literal translation is "floating chrysanthemums," the longtime symbol of Imperial Japan. Operation Kikusui at Okinawa consisted of more than 1,500 army and navy suicide-bent aircraft. Operation Kikusui was launched in ten waves between April and June 1945: http://ww2db.com/battle_spec.php?battle_id=15.

429 Correspondent Robert Sherrod's recollection of early censorship of kamikaze attacks: Sherrod, *On to Westward*, 292–93.

429–30 Note on kamikazes at Okinawa: The rate of early ship losses to the kamikaze threat was stemmed by the establishment of an outer defense perimeter of radar picket ships. These vessels bore the greatest burden. Of the 206 ships that served on radar picket duty, nearly 30 percent were sunk or damaged by kamikazes, making theirs the most hazardous naval surface duty in World War II. Toward the end of the battle, the radar picket ships became the prime kamikaze targets as Japanese pilots despaired of getting through the "big blue blanket"—the constant presence of the blue-painted Hellcats and Corsairs over the fleet at all hours—to reach larger prey.

431–433   Admiral Turner All Hands memo re Kamikaze Corps and April 13, 1945, and RKT Statement on Roosevelt's death: RKT general file, Navy Yard, Washington, DC.

433   USS *Indianapolis* kamikaze attack, March 31, 1945: Thomas B. Buell, *The Quiet Warrior: A Biography of Admiral Raymond A. Spruance* (Annapolis, MD: USNI Press, 1987), 378; William C. Mott oral history; www.ussindianapolis .org.

434–40   The ships of the Third Fleet also formed the basis of the Fifth Fleet. When the Pacific Fleet sailed under Admiral Halsey's flag, the force was named the Third Fleet. The ships were redesignated as the Fifth Fleet when sailing under the command of Admiral Spruance. Halsey and Spruance would alternate command of the fleet for major operations, allowing the other admiral and his executive staff time to prepare for the subsequent campaign. A secondary benefit was that this system (due to the flag changes) confused the Japanese into thinking that they were actually two separate fleets—and that our naval capacity was twice its actual size.

436   Refrain of hymn, "Eternal Father Strong to Save," Rev. William Whiting (1825–1878).

437   "I doubt if the slow, methodical Army approach": Spruance letter to Carl Moore: Buell, *Quiet Warrior*, 387.

437   Exchange between Nimitz and Buckner on bringing in marines behind enemy lines: Costello, *Pacific War*, 565.

438–40   Admiral Turner drinking incident: Transcript and tapes of WCM interviews with John Toland, November 30, 1979; December 6, 1967, and WCM letters to VADM George Dyer during his research for *Amphibians Came to Conquer*. These letters and memoranda, other personal stories re amphibians, are part of a research cache in papers of VADM

Dyer, located in Manuscript and Division, Library of Congress, Washington, DC.

440–41 Admiral Spruance on Turner's drinking habits: "I always felt I could handle Kelly and his drinking . . . I never saw him tight during working hours, except once on Guam after he had finished up at Okinawa. His breath would knock you down at fifteen feet. His head was clear as a bell." Dyer, *Amphibians Came to Conquer*, vol. 2, 1161; Admiral Turner's statement on FDR's death, Ibid., p. 965.

441 June–July 1945 casualties pouring into US hospitals from all theaters of war: McKitterick Clarence Smith, *U.S Army Medical Department: Hospitalization and Evacuation in World War II* (Office of the Chief of Military History, USA, 1956), 200–213.

441 Truman hoped "that there was a possibility of preventing an Okinawa from one end of Japan to another": D. M. Giangreco, *Hell to Pay: Operation Downfall and the Invasion of Japan* (Annapolis, MD: United States Naval Institute Press, 2009), 60, and footnote, 303.

445–46 Likelihood of retributive action against prisoners in Japan: Frank, *Downfall*, 161.

451 Okinawa battle and nonbattle casualty estimates: There are a range of Okinawa casualty estimates in military literature. Historian and author Richard Frank's statistics are widely acknowledged as the most reliable: Richard Frank, "The Pacific War's Biggest Battle," *USNI Naval History* 24, no. 2 (April 2010):

US Army and Marine casualties (killed and wounded) at Okinawa numbered 82,229. For the navy, 1,465 kamikaze sorties sank 36 ships and damaged 368. The carnage among naval personnel was the highest ever suffered in a single naval campaign, mostly from kamikazes. 4,907 sailors died, with a nearly equal number wounded—a ship casualty rate of one in four. Japanese casualties at Okinawa were far greater: 107,539 soldiers were killed—23,764 of them presumed to have died sealed in caves. The highest death toll of all was among Okinawans: 142,058, more than a third of the island's civilian population.

451 If Operation Olympic had been launched and carried to completion it would have dwarfed "into insignificance" any other amphibious assault

attempted in history. USN (Ret) Vice Admiral Daniel E. Barbey, *MacArthur's Amphibious Navy: Seventh Amphibious Force Operations 1943–1945* (Annapolis, MD: United States Naval Institute Press, 1969), 321.

39: IN THE END, A QUESTION OF
CASUALTIES—AND SEA POWER

449–50   Admiral Leahy's June 1945 memo to Joint Chiefs regarding Operation Olympic: Memo SM-2141, US Department of Defense.

451   Army Surgeon General's casualty estimates: Richard B. Frank, *Downfall: The End of the Imperial Japanese Empire* (New York: Random House, 1999), 135–36.

451   Olympic casualty estimates as of June 18, 1945: General HQs, US Army Forces in the Pacific (USAFPAC) Staff Study: Operation Olympic, 32.

451   Re Truman denied the casualty data he requested: Frank, *Downfall*, 144–45.

452   General Marshall's estimates of MacArthur's overall battle ratio of 22.6:1 was later revised to 5:1.

453–55   Excerpts from Willoughby memos on Kyushu buildup stressed gravity of new intelligence, per his Amendment 1 to G-2 Estimate of the Enemy Situation with Respect to Kyushu:

> "The rate and probable continuity of Japanese reinforcements into the Kyushu area are changing that tactical and strategic situation sharply . . . [T]here is a strong likelihood that additional major units will enter the area before target date; we are engaged in a race against time by which the ratio of attack effort vis-à-vis defense capacity is [now] perilously balanced . . . If this deployment is not checked, it may grow to a point where we attack on a ratio of one (1) to one (1), which is not the recipe for victory."

453–54   Autonomy of SWPA's Central Bureau, MacArthur's intelligence gathering operation: Edward J. Drea, *MacArthur's ULTRA: Codebreaking and the War Against Japan, 1942–1945* (Lawrence: University Press of Kansas, 1992), 28–29.

453–55   Additional sources on chronology of Japanese buildup on Kyushu: Douglas A. MacAeachin, Joint Report by CIA's Center for the Study of Intelligence and the Harvard University program for Studies of Intelligence and Policy: "The Final Months of the War with Japan: Signals Intelligence,

US Invasion Planning, and the A-Bomb Decision"; Giangreco, *Hell to Pay*; Frank, *Downfall*.

454 "suicide weapons being developed on Kyushu": Ibid., 212.

454 Ten thousand planes hidden in "mines, railway tunnels": James Martin Davis, "Operation Olympic: An Invasion Not Found in History Books," *Quan*, September 2003.

455–63 WCM to Washington, Summer 1945: WCM's Naval Orders show RKT dispatched him to Washington with latest report on spiking enemy troop strength on Kyushu. Story retold in lengthy WCM interview in *Daily Progress*, Charlottesville, Virginia's, main newspaper, on August 6, 1995 (fiftieth anniversary of Hiroshima).

A second source is an undated "joint letter of criticism" from both my parents sent to the *Daily Progress* editor, responding to a previously published editorial dated April 25, 1995, which had suggested the US apologize to Japan for dropping the atomic bombs. The letter was joint because my mother had worked as a data analyst on Project Manhattan at MIT in Boston (though its employees did not know the precise objective of their work until after the fact). The letter objected to "factual misstatements" in a previous LTE in the *Daily Progress*. After a brief discussion of my mother's role came the relevant passage from my father:

> I, the other half of our household, had been through three costly amphibious assaults on the Marianas, Iwo Jima, and Okinawa, where casualties grew with each invasion and the coming of the kamikazes. In the final weeks before the bomb was dropped, I was in Manila Bay helping to coordinate the planning for our amphibious invasion of mainland Japan. At that time, the estimate was that we would suffer 600,000 casualties in the invasion.
>
> When that estimate reached the invasion commander, Admiral R. K. Turner, he sent for me and asked whether as a former White House aide to President Roosevelt I might be able to bring this intelligence to the attention of President Truman. When I responded in the affirmative, I was ordered back to Washington on the next plane, and I did get the estimate to the attention of the President.

457–58　Bill orally summarized important enemy intercepts to Roosevelt, frequently in his bathroom while (the president) shaved: David Kahn, "Roosevelt Magic and Ultra," *Cryptologia* 16, no. 4 (1992).

458　Communications traffic and Leahy and Truman receipt of documents from Washington at Potsdam: Elsey, *Unplanned Life*, 86–87.

458　Official Log of the president's trip to "Berlin Conference," July 6–August 7, 1945, www.trumanlibrary.org.

458　Clark Clifford: James Vardaman hired Clifford for Map Room duty shortly before the conference at Potsdam as a "stand-in" watch officer so that Vardaman could travel to the conference. Matthew Connelly and William Rigdon Oral Histories, Harry S. Truman Library, Independence, MO.

460　Mott further disclosed in the August 6, 1995, *Daily Progress* article: "I was having lunch at that exclusive men's club in San Francisco with former president of the United States Herbert Hoover. A mutual friend had invited both of us to lunch. The bomb had been dropped, and Hoover was drawing formulas on napkins and the tablecloth, which was annoying the hell out of our waiter. Hoover had a scientific background and was trying to figure out the formula for the bomb. At the time, he said he thought that dropping the bomb was a good idea."

460　MacArthur was "so prone to exaggerate": From War Secretary Henry Stimson's diary, December 27, 1944, per footnote on page 419 in Frank's *Downfall*. Frank also noted a March 30, 1945, diary entry by Stimson along similar lines, when MacArthur's fitness to command the final invasion of Japan was being debated in Washington.

462　President Hoover had provided the Roosevelt Administration with casualty estimates for a final assault on Japan: D. M. Giangreco, "Casualty Projections for the US Invasions of Japan, 1945–1946; Planning and Policy," *Journal of Military History* 61 (July 1997): 521–82.

464–65　Admiral Nimitz opinion on importance of sea power to Pacific victory: Walter R. Borneman, *The Admirals: Nimitz, Halsey, Leahy, and King—The Five-Star Admirals Who Won the War at Sea* (New York: Little, Brown, 2012), 453–54.

465　Processing freed prisoners via Manila: Reports of General MacArthur:

MacArthur in Japan: The Occupation Military Phase, vol. 1, supp., 1966, Library of Congress Catalog Card Number: 66-60006.

465–66 Admiral Turner and flag staff at Tojo Shrine, Tokyo, September 2, 1945: Dyer, *Amphibians Came to Conquer*, 1114–15.

40: NO PEACE AT LILAC HEDGES

475 Excerpt from "Cruise of Death," by George Weller, *Chicago Daily News*, December 8, 1945.

41: FINAL HOURS

493 "The march was about two miles": Wright, *Captured on Corregidor*, 111.

494 "With our bony frames": Lawton, *Some Survived*, 180.

495–96 Torpedo explosions that missed *Enoura Maru* at Lingayen Gulf: David Nash later confirmed that the torpedoes that missed their ship were fired by the USS *Blenny*, commanded by Lieutenant Commander William Hazzard, who—along with Air Group Commander Robert Riera—was a 1935 Annapolis classmate of Nash's.

496 "We were dirty, bearded": Unpublished memoir, E. Carl Engelhart, 162.

496 "Only survival mattered": Lawton, *Some Survived*, 186.

497–98 Sugar theft incident: Wheeler, "For My Children," 93–94.

498–501 Bombing of *Enoura Maru* and removal of the dead: Wright, *Captured on Corregidor*, 122–24.

499–500 Colonel Olson's bravery and Father Cummings's prayers aboard *Enoura Maru*: Sidney Stewart, *Give Us This Day* (New York: W. W. Norton, 1956), 211–13.

501–07 Barton Cross and Robert Granston aboard *Brazil Maru*: Two-day SMF interview with Granston in Palm Coast, Florida, and Granston's November 1945 letter to Helen Cross.

511 More than 126,000 Allied prisoners were transported in 156 voyages on 134 Japanese merchant ships. More than 21,000 Americans were killed or injured from "friendly fire from American submarines or planes": Gregory F. Michno, *Death on the Hellships: Prisoners at Sea in the Pacific War* (Annapolis, MD: United States Naval Institute Press, 2001), Appendix, 317.

Select Bibliography

MAJOR INTERVIEWS BY AUTHOR

Barney Barnhill (USS *Enterprise*), by telephone, January 2006.

Warren Elder, former POW, Luzon, Philippines, January 2005.

George Elsey, Irvine, CA, March 2007.

Robert Granston, Palm Coast, FL, February 2006 and several later interviews by phone.

Dee Grashio, widow of Davao escapee Samuel Grashio, by telephone, Spring 2005.

Jack Hawkins (USMC, retired), Quantico, VA, 2010.

Judith Heisinger, widow of Duane Heisinger (son of former POW Samuel Laurence Heisinger, USN and author of *Father Found*), Northern VA, 2008 and 2010.

Al Leonard, childhood friend of Bill and Benny Mott, by telephone, March 2006.

Roger Mansell, Center for Japanese Prisoner of War Research, Palo Alto, CA, January 2005.

Senator John McCain, US Senate, Washington, DC, 2006.

Bernard Peterson (USS *Enterprise*), by telephone, January 2006.

Sandra Kahn Rosenquist, daughter of Harold A. Rosenquist, by telephone, May 2007 and October 2008.

Mac Showers (Naval Intelligence), by telephone, June 2007.

Robert Wolfensky, former POW, Luzon, Philippines, January 2005.

RESEARCH VENUES

Ateneo University, Manila, Philippines.

Cabanatuan, Bilibid, O'Donnell, and Pasay prison camps, Santa Scholastica Womens College, Philippines.

Center for Research, POWs Under the Japanese, Palo Alto, CA.

Churchill Map and War Rooms, London, England.

Citadel, Charleston, SC.

Citadel, Le Château Frontenac, Quebec, Canada.

Embassy of the Philippines, Washington, DC.

Library of Congress Manuscript Div., Washington, DC.

MacArthur Memorial Archives, Norfolk, VA.

National Archives (NARA), College Park, MD, and Washington, DC.

National Personnel Records Center, St. Louis, MO.

Naval Historical Library, Navy Yard, Washington, DC.

Prisoner of War Museum and Library, Andersonville, GA.

Roosevelt Presidential Library and Archives, Hyde Park, NY.

Rutgers University Library and Archives, New Brunswick, NJ.

US Naval Academy (USNA) Archives and Library, Annapolis, MD.

US Naval Institute (USNI), Annapolis, MD.

US Navy (USN) Bureau of Medicine and Surgery (BUMED), Washington, DC.

USS *Hornet*, San Francisco, CA.

USS *Yorktown*, Charleston, SC.

PARTIAL LIST OF REFERENCES

Andrew, Christopher. *For the President's Eyes Only.* New York: Harper Perennial, 1996.

Andrews, Robert. *Masters and Commanders: How Four Titans Won the War in the West, 1941–1945.* New York: HarperCollins, 2009.

Arnold-Forester, Mark. *The World at War.* New York: Stein and Day, 1973.

Banning, Kendall. *Annapolis Today.* New York: Funk and Wagnalls, 1938.

Barbey, Daniel E. *MacArthur's Amphibious Navy, Seventh Amphibious Force*

Operations 1943–1945. Annapolis, MD: United States Naval Institute Press, 1969.

Barnhill, James C. *The Galloping Ghost.* Self-published, March 1987.

Bartsch, William H. *December 8, 1941: MacArthur's Pearl Harbor.* College Station: Texas A&M University Press, 2003.

Bishop, Gordon. *Gems of New Jersey, Written for the Star-Ledger.* Englewood Cliffs, NJ: Prentice-Hall, 1985.

Bliven, Bruce, Jr. *From Pearl Harbor to Okinawa: The War in the Pacific, 1941–1945.* New York: Random House, 1960.

Bocksel, Arnold A. *Rice, Men and Barbed Wire: A True Epic of Americans as Japanese POWs.* Hempstead, NY: Michael B. Glass, 1991.

Bond, Larry. *Crash Dive: True Stories of Submarine Combat.* New York: Tom Doherty, 2010.

Borneman, Walter R. *The Admirals: Nimitz, Halsey, Leahy, and King—The Five-Star Admirals Who Won the War at Sea.* New York: Little, Brown, 2012.

Brands, H. W. *Traitor to His Class: The Privileged Life and Radical Presidency of Franklin Delano Roosevelt.* New York: Anchor Books, 2008.

Breuer, William B. *MacArthur's Undercover War: Spies, Saboteurs, Guerrillas, and Secret Missions.* New York: John Wiley and Sons, 1995.

Brinkley, David. *Washington Goes to War.* Thorndike, ME: Thorndike Press, 1988.

Buell, Thomas B. *The Quiet Warrior: A Biography of Admiral Raymond A. Spruance.* Annapolis, MD: USNI Press, 1987.

Bureau of Naval Personnel. *The Gunnery Officer.* Navpers, 1955.

Camus, José S. *Rice in the Philippines.* Manila: Bureau of Printing, 1921.

Caraccilo, Dominic J., ed. *Surviving Bataan and Beyond: Colonel Irvin Alexander's Odyssey as a Japanese Prisoner of War.* Mechanicsburg, PA: Stackpole Books, 1999.

Childress, Clyde (USA, retired). A Critical Review of *They Fought Alone.*" *Bulletin of the American Historical Collection* 31, no. 1 (January 2003). AHC consists of some thousands of books, articles, and photographs related to the American experience in the Philippines and to the relationship of the two countries.

Churchill, Winston S. *The Grand Alliance: The Second World War.* Boston: Houghton Mifflin, 1950.

Connaughton, Richard. *MacArthur and Defeat in the Philippines*. New York: Overlook Press, 2001.

Costello, John. *The Pacific War: 1941–1945*. New York: HarperCollins, 1981.

Cross, Helen Chamberlain. Wartime diaries and letters, 1940–1946.

Davis, R. G., Captain, MC, USN, MOIC. *Canacao Journal: A Report and a Journal, 1941–1945*, PI (Hospital Corps Archives, Bureau of Medicine and Surgery, June 1946.

Daws, Gavan. *Prisoners of the Japanese: POWs of World War II in the Pacific*. New York: William Morrow, 1994.

Difford, Floramund Fellmeth. *An Angel's Illustrated Journal: It Has Taken Sixty Years to Explain Why She Was on the Mactan and Not a Prisoner*. Toledo, WA: Chapters of Life, 2005.

Dissette, Edward, and H. C. Adamson. *Guerrilla Submarines*. New York: Ballantine Books, 1972.

Dower, John W. *War Without Mercy: Race and Power in the Pacific War*. New York: Pantheon Books, 1986.

Dyer, George C. *The Amphibians Came to Conquer: The Story of Admiral Richmond Kelly Turner*. 2 vols. Washington, DC: Department of the Navy, 1991.

Dyess, William E. *The Dyess Story*. New York: G. P. Putnam's Sons, 1944.

Elsey, George M. *An Unplanned Life: A Memoir*. Columbia: University of Missouri Press, 2005.

Erickson, Commander George E., Jr., JAGC, USNR. *Transcript of Oral History Interview of Rear Admiral William C. Mott, USN, retired*. Charlottesville, VA, 1991.

Frank, Richard B. *Downfall: The End of the Japanese Imperial Empire*. New York: Penguin, 1999.

Giangreco, D. M. *Hell to Pay: Operation Downfall and the Invasion of Japan*. Annapolis, MD: United States Naval Institute Press, 2009.

Glines, Carroll V. *Doolittle's Tokyo Raiders*. New York: Van Nostrand Reinhold, 1981.

Goodwin, Doris Kearns. *No Ordinary Time: Franklin & Eleanor Roosevelt: The Home Front in World War II*. New York: Simon & Schuster, 1994.

Gordon, John Steele. *An Empire of Wealth: The Epic History of American Economic Power*. New York: HarperCollins, 2004.

Gordon, Richard M., and Benjamin S. Llamzon, PhD. *Horyo: Memoirs of an American POW.* St. Paul, MN: Paragon House, 1991.

Grashio, Samuel, and Bernard Norling. *Return to Freedom.* Spokane, WA: University Press, 1982.

Groom, Winston. *1942: The Year That Tried Men's Souls.* New York: Atlantic Monthly Press, 2005.

Grove, Martin, and Martin Stephen. *Sea Battles in Close-Up: World War 2.* Annapolis, MD: United States Naval Institute Press, 1998.

Heisinger, Duane. *Father Found: Life and Death as a Prisoner of the Japanese in World War II.* Maitland, FL: Xulon Press, 2003.

Hoyt, Edwin P. *How They Won the War in the Pacific: Nimitz and His Admirals.* New York: Lyons Press, 2000.

Ind, Colonel Allison W. *Allied Intelligence Bureau: Our Secret Weapon in the War Against Japan.* New York: David McKay, 1958.

Irwin, Richard T. *A History of Randolph Township, Morris County, New Jersey.* Hicksville, NY: Exposition Press, 1976.

Kennedy, David. *Freedom from Fear: The American People in Depression and War, 1925–1945.* New York: Oxford University Press, 1999.

Kennedy, Robert S., Pedro C. Gonzales, Edward C. Dickinson, Hector C. Miranda Jr., and Timothy H. Fisher. *A Guide to the Birds of the Philippines.* New York: Oxford University Press, 2000.

Kentner, Robert W. *War Diary: Canacao Naval Hospital.* Unpublished, located at Bureau of Medicine and Surgery, Washington, DC.

Kuykendall, Ralph S., and A. Grove Day. *Hawaii: A History, from Polynesian Kingdom to American Commonwealth.* New York: Prentice-Hall, 1948.

Levie, H. *Documents on Prisoners of War.* Newport, RI: Naval War College Press, 1979.

Levie, H. *Prisoners of War in International Armed Conflict.* Newport, RI: Naval War College Press, 1979.

Life. December 23, 1940.

Life. March 31, 1941.

The Lucky Bag. Naval Academy Yearbooks, Years 1930, 1933.

MacArthur, Douglas. *Reminiscences: General of the Army.* New York: McGraw-Hill, 1964.

Map Room Letters, Background Reading Files, Watch Officer Instructions, Memos, Telegrams (Boxes 13, 14, 15, 194, 195). Roosevelt Presidential Library, Hyde Park, NY, Map Room Files.

Masterson, Melissa. *Ride the Waves to Freedom: Calvin Graef's Survival Story.* Kearney, NE: Morris, 1999.

McClain, Sally. *Navajo Weapon: The Navajo Code Talkers.* Tucson, AZ: Rio Nuevo, 1994.

McCullough, David W. *Three Score and Ten: A History of Christ School, Arden, North Carolina, 1900–1970.* Alexander, NC: WorldComm, 1996.

McGee, John Hugh. *Rice and Salt.* San Antonio: Naylor, 1962.

Meacham, Jon. *Franklin and Winston: An Intimate Portrait of an Epic Friendship.* New York: Random House, 2003.

Mellnik, Stephen M. *Philippine Diary, 1939–1945.* New York: Van Nostrand Reinhold, 1969.

Meredith, Lee. *Grey Ghost: The Story of the Aircraft Carrier Hornet.* Sunnyvale, CA: Rocklin Press, 2001.

Michno, Gregory F. *Death on the Hellships: Prisoners at Sea in the Pacific War.* Annapolis, MD: United States Naval Institute Press, 2001.

Miller, Donald L. *The Story of World War II.* New York: Simon & Schuster, 2001.

Miller, Francis Trevelyan. *History of World War II.* Philadelphia: John C. Winston, 1945.

Monohan, Evelyn M., and Rosemary Neidel-Greenlee. *All This Hell: U.S. Nurses Imprisoned by the Japanese.* Lexington: University Press of Kentucky, 2003.

Morgan, James. *If These Walls Had Ears: The Biography of a House.* New York: Warner Books, 1996.

Morton, Louis. *The Fall of the Philippines.* U.S. Army in World War II: The War in the Pacific. Washington, DC: Office of the Chief of Military History, Department of the Army, 1953.

Mott, Captain Bertram E. *Memoirs of World War II Sea Engagements.* Orange County, CA.

Mott, Lieutenant Commander William C. Personal Correspondence, White House Files, 1940–1943.

National Park Service Historical Statistics, USS *Arizona* Memorial, Hawaii.

Navy Department, *Ordnance and Gunnery Instructions for Naval Armed Guards on*

Merchant Ships, 1944. 4th ed. Washington, DC: United States Government Printing Office, 1944.

Official Gazette. Manila, the Philippines, January 1942–1944, vols. 1–44.

Olson, Colonel John E. *O'Donnell: Andersonville of the Pacific, Extermination Camp of American Hostages in the Philippines.* Lake Quivra, KS: J. E. Olson, 1985.

Oral history dated January 25, 1994, provided courtesy of the Historian, Bureau of Medicine and Surgery: Recollections of Captain Ann Bernatitus, USN. Washington, DC: Naval Historic Center, Washington Navy Yard.

Paul, Doris A. *The Navajo Code Talkers.* Pittsburgh: Dorrance, 1973.

Pearson, Judith L. *Belly of the Beast: A POW's Inspiring True Story of Faith, Courage, and Survival Aboard the Infamous WWII Japanese Hell Ship* Oryoku Maru. New York: New American Library, 2001.

Peart, Cecil Jesse. Pharmacist's Mate, USN, *Daily Journal 1944–1945.* Unpublished, located at Bureau of Medicine and Surgery, Washington, DC.

Peterson, Bernard. *Briney to the Blue: Memoirs of WWII.* Self-published, 1992.

Pictet, J. *Commentary on the Geneva Convention Relative to the Treatment of Prisoners of War.* Geneva: International Committee of the Red Cross, 1960.

Potter, E. B. *Bull Halsey.* Annapolis, MD: United States Naval Institute Press, 1985.

Potter, E. B., and Chester W. Nimitz. *The Great Sea War: The Story of Naval Action in World War II.* Englewood Cliffs, NJ: Prentice Hall, 1960.

POW. *The Fight Continues After the Battle.* Washington, DC: United States Government Printing Office, 1955.

Prange, Gordon W. *At Dawn We Slept: The Untold Story of Pearl Harbor.* New York: McGraw-Hill, 1981.

Prisoners of War Bulletins. Washington, DC: American National Red Cross. Issues dating from June 1942 to May 1945.

Red Bank Register. Red Bank, New Jersey, Princeton, NJ: New Jersey State Archive, Microfiche Division 1941–1945.

Redmond, Lieutenant Juanita. *I Served on Bataan.* New York: J. B. Lippincott, 1943.

Report on American Prisoners of War Interned by the Japanese in the Philippines. Office of the Provost Marshall, Washington, DC: November 1945.

RG-16 Biographical Sketch. Papers of Major General Courtney Whitney, 1942–1947. MacArthur Memorial Archives, Norfolk, VA.

Rhea, Milton A. *War Is Hell.* Victoria, Can.: Trafford, 2003.

Rockaway (NJ) Record. Princeton, NJ: New Jersey State Archive, Microfiche Division, 1941–1945.

Rogers, Paul P. *The Good Years: MacArthur and Sutherland; The Bitter Years: MacArthur and Sutherland.* 2 vols. New York: Praeger, 1990, 1991.

Romulo, Brigadier General Carlos P. *My Brother Americans.* Garden City, NY: Doubleday, Doran, 1945.

Roscoe, Theodore. *United States Submarine Operations in World War II.* Annapolis, MD: United States Naval Institute Press, 1949.

Rothberg, Abraham. *Eyewitness History of World War II.* Vol. 4, *Victory.* New York: Bantam Books, 1962.

Sartin, L. B. (Captain), Med Corps USN, Journal, PI, 1941–1945.

Schmidt, Larry, USMC. "American Involvement in the Filipino Resistance Movement on Mindanao During the Japanese Occupation, 1942–1945." Academic paper, Fort Leavenworth, KS, 1982. (General background on birth of aid and intelligence between guerrillas and Australia.)

Seagrave, Peggy. *Gold Warriors.* London: Verso Press, 2002. (Background on Courtney Whitney.)

Sears, David. *At War with the Wind: The Epic Struggle with Japan's World War II Suicide Bombers.* New York: Citadel Press, 2008.

Sherrod, Robert. *On to Westward: The Battles of Saipan and Iwo Jima.* New York: Duell Sloan and Pearce, 1945.

Sherwood, Robert E. *Roosevelt and Hopkins: An Intimate History.* New York: Harper & Brothers, 1948.

Shoemaker, Lloyd R. *The Escape Factory: The Story of MIS-X, America's Ultra Secret Masterminds of World War II's Greatest Escapes.* New York: St. Martin's Press, 1990.

Shofner, Austin Conner, USMC. Diary, 1941–1943. Tennessee State Library, Microfilm.

Sperber, A. M. *Murrow: His Life and Times.* New York: Fordham University Press, 1998.

Stafford, Commander Edward P., USN. *The Big E: The Story of the USS Enter-prise*. New York: Ballantine Books, 1962.

Stahl, Robert. *You're No Good to Me Dead: Behind Japanese Lines in the Philip-pines*. Annapolis MD: United States Naval Institute Press, 1995.

Stevenson, William. *A Man Called Intrepid*. Guilford, CT: Lyons Press, 1976.

Stewart, Sidney. *Give Us This Day*. New York: W. W. Norton, 1956.

Sulzberger, C. L. *World War II*. New York: American Heritage Press, 1985.

Sun Tzu. *The Art of War*. Translated by Samuel B. Griffith. New York: Oxford University Press, 1963.

Tenney, Lester I. *My Hitch in Hell: The Bataan Death March*. Washington, DC: Brassey's, 1995.

Tillman, Barrett. *Clash of the Carriers: The True Story of the Marianas Turkey Shoot*. New York: Penguin Group, 2005.

Tillman, Barrett. *Enterprise: America's Fightingest Ship and the Men Who Helped Win World War II*. New York: Simon & Schuster, 2012.

Toland, John. *Infamy: Pearl Harbor and Its Aftermath*. New York: Berkley Books, 1982.

——. *The Last 100 Days*. New York: Random House, 1966.

Toland, John. Transcript of Toland's 1982 series of interviews with William C. Mott regarding Naval Intelligence operations leading up to Pearl Harbor and Mott's subsequent service in the White House Map Room. Acquired from Roosevelt Presidential Library, Hyde Park, NY.

Tregaskis, Richard. *Guadalcanal Diary*. New York: Random House, 1943.

Truman, Harry S. *Memoirs*. Vol. 1, *Year of Decisions*. Garden City, NY: Doubleday, 1955.

Tunny, Noel. *Winning from Down Under*. Brisbane: Boolarong Press, 2010.

US Army. *The Fall of the Philippines*. U.S. Army in World War II: The War in the Pacific. Washington, DC: Center of Military History, United States Army, 1989.

U.S. Division of Naval History. *History of Ships Named Enterprise*.

United States Navy. *The Bluejackets' Manual*. Annapolis, MD: United States Naval Institute, 1943.

USNI Oral Histories: Chick Parsons, Admiral Joel McCrea, Admiral A. H.

McCollum, Admiral Stuart Murray, Admiral George Dyer, Admiral Van Deurs, Captain Joseph Rochefort, Admiral Arthur S. Carpender, Admiral Ernest Eller, Captain Slade Cutter, Admiral Gerald Bogan, Admiral Raymond D. Tarbuck, and Admiral Bernard Bieri.

USS *Otus* Ship's Log. Obtained from National Archives, College Park, MD.

van der Vat, Dan. *The Pacific Campaign: World War II—The U.S.-Japanese Naval War 1941–1945.* New York: Simon & Schuster, 1991.

Veronico, Nicholas A., and Armand H. Veronico. *Battlestations! American Warships of WWII.* St. Paul, MN: MBI, 2001.

Waggener, Nelson. *Memories of World War II While in the Southwest Pacific.* Self-published, 1979.

Wheeler, Keith. *The Pacific Is My Beat.* New York: E. P. Dutton, 1943.

Wheeler, Kenneth R. *For My Children.* Unpublished manuscript, no date.

Wiest, Andrew, and Gregory Louis Mattson. *The Pacific War: The Campaigns of World War II.* St. Paul, MN: MBI, 2001.

Willoughby, Major General Charles A. *The Guerrilla Resistance Movement in the Philippines.* New York: Vantage Press, 1972.

Wills, Donald. *The Sea Was My Last Chance.* London: McFarland, 1992.

Willson, Captain Russell. *Watch Officer's Guide: United States Navy.* Annapolis, MD: United States Naval Institute, 1941.

Wodnik, Bob. *Captured Honor: POW Survival in the Philippines and Japan.* Pullman: Washington State University Press, 2003.

Woods, Tarleton E. *March of Death: An American Soldier's 1,216 Days as a POW of the Japanese.* Spartanburg, SC: Honoribis Press, 2006.

Wordsworth, William. "Lines Composed a Few Miles Above Tintern Abbey on Revisiting the Banks of the Wye During a Tour, July 13, 1798."

Zich, Arthur. *The Rising Sun.* Alexandria, VA: Time-Life Books, 1977. (Japan's policies in conquered territories, 148–49.)

Image Credits

Index

About the Author

SALLY MOTT FREEMAN is serving her fourth term as board chair of the Writer's Center (TWC) in Bethesda, MD. The Writer's Center hosts hundreds of writing workshops annually and over seventy literary events a year, featuring authors of local, national, and international renown. Freeman previously served as a media and public relations executive in both the public and private sectors.

She was a speechwriter at the Federal Communications Commission and later the agency's News Media Division Chief, as well as Director of Legislative and Public Affairs for FmHA, the finance arm of USDA. In the private sector, she was a vice president in the telecom practice at Fleishman Hillard, Inc., and later ran corporate communications for two technology trade associations.

Freeman graduated with a degree in English literature from Sweet Briar College, which awarded her its 2016 Distinguished Alumna award, and spent a year studying Renaissance literature at the University of Exeter, England. She and her husband, John Freeman, have four adult children and live in Bethesda, Maryland.

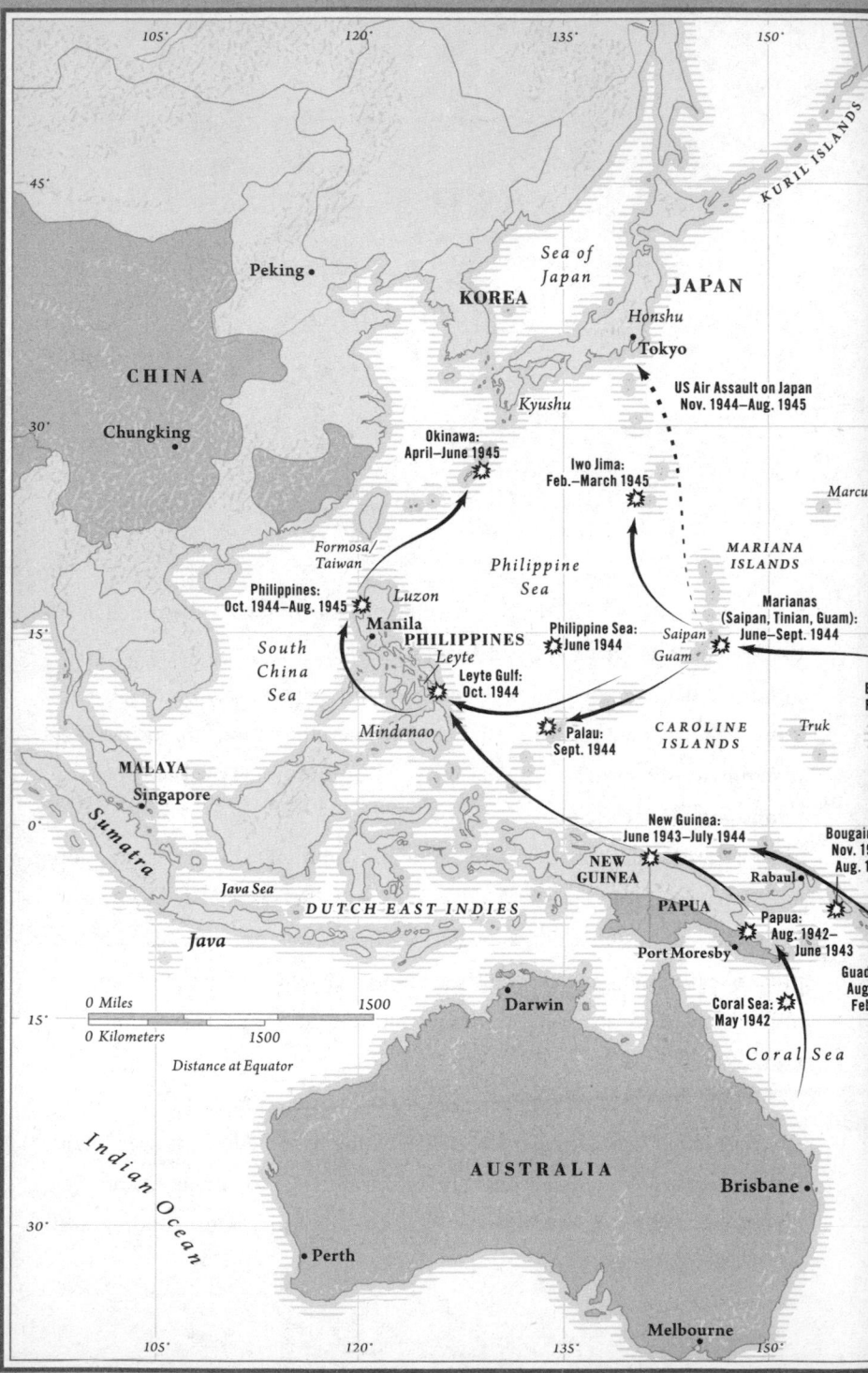

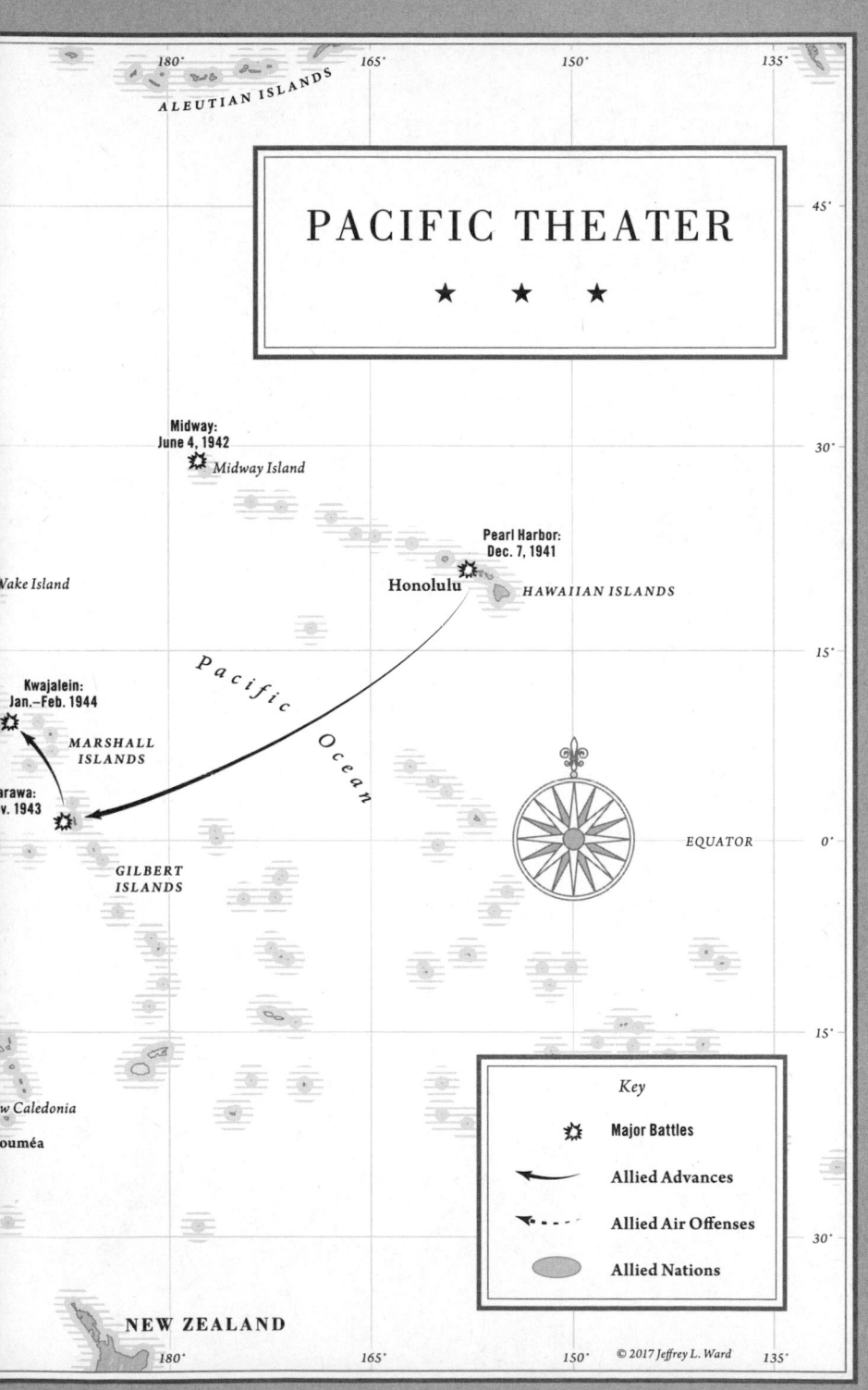